Linux NFS and Automounter Administration

Craig Hunt
Linux Library

Erez Zadok

San Francisco Paris Düsseldorf Soest London

SYBEX

Associate Publisher: Dick Staron
Contracts and Licensing Manager: Kristine O'Callaghan
Acquisitions Editor: Maureen Adams
Developmental Editor: Tom Cirtin
Editors: Susan Berge, Rebecca Rider
Production Editor: Mae Lum
Technical Editor: Sean J. Schluntz
Book Designer: Bill Gibson
Graphic Illustrator: Tony Jonick
Electronic Publishing Specialist: Nila Nichols
Proofreaders: Nelson Kim, Mae Lum, Laurie O'Connell, Nancy Riddiough
Indexer: Ted Laux
Cover Designer: Ingalls & Associates
Cover Illustrator: Ingalls & Associates

Library of Congress Card Number: 2001086972

ISBN: 0-7821-2739-8

Manufactured in the United States of America

10 9 8 7 6 5 4 3 2 1

Summary of Common NFS Export and Mount Options *(continued)*

Option	Export/Mount	Meaning
exec	Mount	Allow execution of binaries.
fg	Mount	Try mount in the foreground.
hard	Mount	Wait for the NFS server indefinitely, regardless of timeouts.
hide	Export	Do not expose subsidiary mounted file systems below this mount point.
insecure_locks	Export	Do not authenticate NLM protocol requests.
insecure	Export	Originating ports are greater than 1024.
intr	Mount	Allow users to interrupt hung processes.
lock	Mount	Enable NFS locking.
mounthost=*ARG*	Mount	Contact rpc.mountd on host *ARG*.
mountport=*N*	Mount	Contact rpc.mountd on an alternate port.
mountprog=*N*	Mount	Contact rpc.mountd using an alternate RPC program number.
mountvers=*N*	Mount	Contact rpc.mountd using an alternate protocol version number.
namlen=*N*	Mount	Maximum length of supported file names on server.
nfsprog=*N*	Mount	Contact NFS server using an alternate RPC program number.
nfsvers=*N*	Mount	Contact NFS server using an alternate protocol version number.
no_all_squash	Export	Do not map all UIDs and GIDs.
no_auth_nlm	Export	Synonymous with insecure_locks.
no_root_squash	Export	Do not map UID 0 requests.

continued in back →

To Martha and Michal, who missed many nights with אבא .

Foreword

Considering the importance of file sharing, the dearth of books about the Network File System (NFS) should be surprising, yet isn't. The great mass of Windows-based clients has warped space and time to such an extent that even Linux servers have been caught in the gravity well. Administrators catering to the needs of Windows clients begin to think of network services in terms of Windows services, and file-sharing software becomes synonymous with Samba. Of course, mastering Samba is essential, which is why the Craig Hunt Linux Library includes the book *Linux Samba Server Administration*, but mastering Samba alone is not enough.

Linux servers share files with other Linux clients. They also share files with Unix servers and Unix clients. All of these systems depend on NFS to share files over the network. As the number of Linux desktop clients increases, the administrator's need for accurate, complete NFS information also grows. *Linux NFS and Automounter Administration* provides detailed NFS information that is up to date, not out of date.

Of equal importance for Linux users is the Berkeley Automounter daemon (Amd). This powerful tool mounts devices and file systems when they are needed. For the desktop user, this means there is no need to manually mount a device, such as a CD-ROM, to read it. For the network administrator, Amd provides unified naming that can be centrally managed. This means that Amd can be configured so that a user's home directory follows the user to any desktop in the office. Amd can do these things and much more, assuming it is properly configured.

Given the importance of Amd as well as the power and complexity of this tool, I was amazed that this is the first book on the subject. Erez Zadok addresses this oversight by creating a book that will help you understand and master Amd. Erez is the man to do it. He maintains Amd and the Amd mailing list and gives talks about Amd. He even incorporated Amd into his research work. I personally found the Amd material in *Linux NFS and Automounter Administration* fascinating and informative. I hope you enjoy reading this book as much as I did.

Craig Hunt

April 2001

Acknowledgments

This book, as with any other large document, is the result of the team effort of many people. After noticing my Usenix LISA tutorial on Amd, Craig Hunt contacted me and offered me the opportunity to write this book. Knowing the topics of Amd and NFS rather well, I thought to myself, "How hard could it be?" Little did I know. Writing this book was a complex and tedious task. Craig has been my guiding light throughout this effort, answering my many technical and presentation questions, and always finding the best way to present complex material.

The team at Sybex is truly amazing—a well-oiled machine. For the first time in my professional career, I had many people ready to help me with a large document. Because of their constant guidance and dedication to improving the prose, it was a pleasure to know that nothing would have escaped their eagle eyes.

Maureen Adams, the acquisitions editor, guided the business side during the development of this book. Tom Cirtin served as the development editor during the initial phases of this book and had to answer many of my newbie questions. Mae Lum was my production editor; her guidance helped me deliver portions of text by their deadlines. Mae was always available to answer my many questions. Susan Berge was my main editor; I found remarkable her skill in understanding the intricacies of English and her concern for the accuracy of the prose.

Additional thanks go to the technical editor, Sean J. Schluntz, whom Sybex recruited out of a call I posted on my Web site for technical reviewers; the electronic publishing specialist, Nila Nichols; the proofreaders, Nancy Riddiough, Laurie O'Connell, Nelson Kim, and Mae Lum; another editor who worked on a couple of chapters, Rebecca Rider; the illustrator, Tony Jonick; the indexer, Ted Laux; the cover copywriter, Carl Montgomery; the contracts and licensing manager, Kristine O'Callaghan, who helped me with the legal side of things; and the editing manager, Brianne Agatep, who survived my constant nitpicking by helping me make the most of Sybex's author templates.

I would like to thank the many people who helped to maintain Amd in the past. Many of them contributed hundreds of fixes, greatly easing my job of maintaining Amd. These contributors are listed in www.am-utils.org/AUTHORS.txt. Special thanks to the following three co-maintainers of am-utils: Ion Badulescu, who contributed most of the support for Autofs in Amd and constantly maintains Amd to ensure it runs properly despite the constant changes to Linux kernels; Nick Williams, who is the most familiar with Amd's inner guts and especially the asynchronous RPC and background NFS operations; and Rainer Orth, who has contributed quite a lot in a span of three to four years, including advanced support for Amd on Solaris systems.

Additional thanks go to the maintainers of the NFS software and documentation, Autofs, and the Linux kernel. You have produced remarkable software, without which this book would not have much to discuss.

I would like to thank Jan-Simon Pendry and Ion Badulescu for agreeing to do a peer review of this book. I hope this book meets Jan-Simon's expectations as the original author of Amd. Ion's immense expertise with Linux and NFS guaranteed quality discussion of those two topics. Many times I had asked Ion questions that needed quick answers, and he would answer them no matter what time of the day or night it was.

Finally, special thanks go to Martha. Not only did she hold a full-time job, but she also took care of our daughter, Michal, to allow me the time to focus on this book. And all of this while I was finishing a doctorate degree at Columbia University and starting a faculty job at SUNY at Stony Brook. Martha's understanding and patience are quite remarkable. I feel particularly privileged to have such an understanding partner in life.

Contents at a Glance

Contents

Code Listings

Tables

Introduction

Linux is rapidly gaining popularity. Several vendors, including Compaq and Silicon Graphics, are shipping hardware with preinstalled Linux. Linux is the number one choice for server administrators to run WWW, FTP, and news servers (see `www.leb.net/hzo/ ioscount`). Many companies sell third-party software for Linux, prepackaged Linux distributions, and hardware platforms specially suited for running Linux. The large selection of software available for Linux makes it a top choice for servers. With office productivity software such as WordPerfect from Corel and StarOffice from the Star Division of Sun Microsystems, and with desktop environments such as Gnome and KDE, Linux is quickly becoming a viable alternative to Windows for desktops and laptops.

Sites are deploying Linux because it provides excellent performance and reliability, is simple to set up and maintain, and integrates easily into heterogeneous Unix/Windows environments. Another of Linux's strengths is its support for a plethora of file systems. In addition to some file systems that are only available on Linux, Linux can access file systems written on Windows, Solaris, BSD systems, and many more, making it an excellent platform for integrating various types of clients. Linux, in fact, is a perfect operating system to integrate Unix and Windows systems on a network.

The importance of distributed file systems can hardly be exaggerated. The true purpose of a network is to share information. Distributed file systems play an essential role in meeting this purpose. The most popular distributed file system for Unix and Linux hosts is the Network File System (NFS), originally designed by Sun Microsystems.

NFS is perfect for exchanging files between any Unix and Linux systems. With NFS, users do not notice whether a file is located on the server or on the desktop client. NFS allows you to share information in a transparent and seamless manner.

NFS, however, requires configuration and maintenance on each client and server that uses it. When sites grow large enough, and especially when they become heterogeneous, administrators look for ways to automate or centralize the administration of their NFS clients and servers. That is what an automounter does.

The Berkeley Automounter (Amd) is an essential part of a large or heterogeneous site using NFS. Amd automatically mounts remote servers and local resources on an as-needed basis and provides a unified naming scheme that is maintained at a central location. In addition, Amd improves the reliability and scalability of NFS by unmounting volumes that have not been used recently and providing support for replicated and fail-over volumes: when one server is down, Amd can pick another. Finally, Amd runs identically on dozens of Unix platforms and includes many powerful features to satisfy even the most demanding or complex site needs.

Why a Linux Book on NFS and Amd

Why do we need a book on NFS and Amd? First, a new book on NFS was needed. Few books exist on the subject and those that do exist are dated because so much has changed on the Internet, in the field of distributed file systems, and in operating systems since those books were published. Today's operating systems, including Solaris, Irix, AIX, HPUX, Digital Unix, Tru64, and of course, Linux, support NFSv3. NFSv3 changes the NFS protocol and supports a different transport protocol for communicating between clients and servers. As such, many new options are available to site administrators when configuring NFS access. A book that adequately covers NFSv3 is an important part of any system administrator's bookshelf. Furthermore, the newest protocol, NFSv4, is under development by the Internet community. Soon, several vendors including Linux vendors will offer working prototypes of NFSv4 clients and servers. A book that prepares administrators to manage NFSv4 clients and servers was needed.

Second, a book on the Amd automounter was needed. No book covers Amd, an automounter that is a critical component of many large sites. (The Amd tutorial I gave at LISA '99 was the first and only time in years that new material was presented on this subject.) Older NFS books cover the original SunOS automounter, which is no longer in use. Amd is very popular and is used at many sites. Its greatest advantage is that it works the same way on many different platforms, which makes it the best automounter for heterogeneous or large sites. An alternative to Amd is Autofs, an automounter similar to the one used on modern Solaris and Irix systems. This book provides coverage of Autofs, and shows when and how it is used with Amd.

Third, a book on NFS *and* Amd was needed, because the two topics share much in common. Amd cannot work without NFS. Amd is a special-purpose user-level NFS server, and many of its mounting options are similar to those used to mount NFS volumes. Amd's most common use is to automate the mounting and unmounting of remote NFS volumes. For administrators who maintain hosts that use NFS, running Amd is the next logical step. An administrator who uses and manages NFS is likely to use and manage Amd as well. Furthermore, Amd has many useful features that go beyond just managing NFS mounts: Amd can automate mounts of any other file system that a host supports.

In addition, a book providing adequate coverage of NFS security and performance issues was needed. Security concerns are an integral part of any computing system and nowadays must be considered from the outset, not as an afterthought. Since NFS is a network-based file system, performance optimization is important. Ironically, performance needs and security concerns often clash with each other. Therefore, any book on a topic concerning distributed computing systems must discuss the security and performance implications of every choice made.

Finally, a book covering NFS and Amd *on Linux* was needed. Linux is very popular and is becoming even more so. Using NFS and Amd on Linux installations is becoming an increasingly common part of site configurations. This book covers all of the specifics required by Linux systems without losing sight of the requirements of heterogeneous installations. One of the major mistakes vendors have made in past years is ignoring interoperability for fear of losing business to competitors. This hurt the computer industry as a whole and resulted in antagonism among users and administrators in heterogeneous environments. Linux, on the other hand, takes the approach of interoperating with any other operating system. This is one of Linux's greatest strengths but is also a source of configuration complexity: for Linux to interoperate with so many other systems, it must support many more features than those systems. This book takes advantage of the high degree of portability and interoperability of NFS and Amd to present these subjects in a manner that is friendly to sites running multiple operating systems.

The Ongoing Development of Amd

In the same way that NFS is evolving to NFSv3 and NFSv4, Amd is undergoing major changes. In the case of Amd, I have been intimately involved with these changes.

The Amd package has been without an official maintainer since 1992. Several people have stepped in to maintain it unofficially. The most notable distributions were the "upl" (Unofficial Patch Level) releases of Amd that I created. The last such unofficial release was upl102. Because of constant patching and aging, Amd became more difficult to maintain: the code was messy and hard to follow, new patches were getting increasingly difficult to apply, and many features and new ports were missing.

I met the original author of Amd, Jan-Simon Pendry, in the summer of 1993 at a Usenix conference in Cincinnati. At that time I was maintaining Amd unofficially. Jan-Simon and I discussed the status of Amd. He told me then that I could do whatever I wanted with Amd. I took it upon myself to clean up the code, making it easier to port to new platforms, add new features, keep up with the many new feature requests, and deal with the never-ending stream of bug reports.

I have been working on an official release of Amd on and off since January of 1996. The new suite of tools was named am-utils (Auto-Mounter Utilities), in line with GNU naming conventions, befitting the contents of the package. In October of 1996, I had received enough offers to help me with this task that I decided to create a mailing list for this group of people. Around the same time, Amd had become an important part of my early Ph.D. thesis work, resulting in my performing more work on am-utils.

Am-utils version 6.0 was numbered with a new major release number to distinguish it from the last official release of Amd (*5.x*). Many new features were added, such as the use of a GNU configure system, NFS version 3 support, a runtime configuration file (`amd.conf`), many ports to new systems, more scripts and programs, as well as numerous bug fixes. Another reason for the new major release number was to alert old-time users of Amd that user-visible interfaces may have changed. To ensure that Amd would work well for the next 10 years and be easier to maintain, it was necessary to remove old or unused features and change various syntax files. However, great care was taken to ensure the maximum possible backward compatibility.

In 2000, I solicited help with maintaining am-utils from several long-time contributors to the package. I recruited Ion Badulescu, who helped with the Autofs port; Nick Williams, who originally helped Jan-Simon Pendry write Amd; and Rainer Orth, who contributed many fixes during the past three years. Together, this team maintains am-utils as well as developing it for the future. Am-utils version 6.1 is in development now.

Who Should Buy This Book

Who is this book for? Anyone with two or more systems. The moment you have more than one system, you want to share information between them. NFS enables sharing that information by giving each host access to the other hosts' file systems. With Amd, NFS access can be centrally managed. Amd improves the scalability of NFS mounts by unmounting unused volumes and mounting on demand only those that are needed. Amd also provides a uniform naming access for all file systems around a given site, regardless of the individual file servers' local mounts. Therefore, Amd allows users to administer their own boxes locally, while still maintaining an overall uniform mount strategy centrally—truly the best of both worlds.

This book is not a beginner's introductory book on NFS or Amd, since both of those have been in use for years. In addition, this book expects readers to have a basic familiarity with Unix and networking principles, especially TCP/IP. While enough introductory material is provided, this book focuses on material concerning NFS that is not available elsewhere:

- NFS versions 3 and 4
- NFS using TCP
- Advanced configuration and usage examples
- Specialized Linux security features that can be used with NFS
- Detailed debugging using protocol traces
- Performance tuning based on the specifics of the site's LAN and WAN configuration
- Interoperability with other systems

Numerous sites around the world use Amd. This is the first and only book to cover the Amd automounter and thus is the only source of information on this complex, feature-loaded, popular automounter. This point alone is reason enough to buy this book.

While this book is targeted at the Linux community, it also has appeal for the greater Unix community. NFS is available on every Unix system, and Amd is a highly portable software that compiles and runs on over 70 different Unix platform combinations. Most of what this book discusses is applicable to other Unix systems. Therefore, this book should be useful to every Linux or Unix system administrator.

If you are responsible for administering a network, you are responsible for managing the sharing of information across that network. NFS and Amd are two of the tools you will use to accomplish this task. If you are a systems administrator, you need to master NFS and Amd. This book provides the perfect marriage of these two topics and can help you manage your site.

How This Book Is Organized

This book is divided into three parts: "The Network File System," "The Amd Automounter," and "Appendices." The three parts compose fourteen chapters and four appendices.

The first two parts progress in a similar fashion: after an introductory chapter that includes a quick example, the subsequent chapters cover typical setups. There is a chapter on testing and debugging configurations, a chapter on performance tuning, and a chapter on advanced topics.

The book is full of practical examples, each of which was tested and verified in a real setup. This provides many canned solutions to common problems that administrators need to solve. Studying examples of solutions to real problems is one of the best ways to learn about or teach a subject.

Each of the two main parts of the book—NFS and Amd—is designed so the chapters in each part could be read in order. A novice or mid-level administrator, for example, should read all chapters in a part. An advanced administrator who might be familiar with NFS or Amd, however, can skip the introductory material and jump right into the chapters covering the more advanced topics, such as performance tuning, security concerns, and configuration testing.

The many examples in this book focus on specific systems: Red Hat Linux 7 and am-utils 6.0 or 6.1. Shell script examples use the bash/ksh syntax. Examples based on specific systems help illustrate many functions. However, if you use any other Linux or am-utils software, you need not worry; most of the examples and the accompanying discussions are applicable to all Linux systems and will work for years to come. Furthermore, whenever possible, we discuss NFS and Amd differences between Linux and non-Linux systems. This helps increase the appeal of the book to a larger community and provides more complete coverage of the topics.

Finally, Amd is a user-level NFS server that automounts other file systems, most often those that other NFS servers export. Whereas much common behavior and features exist between NFS and Amd, each of their respective parts stands alone. Readers need not read chapters in one part to understand another.

Next we briefly discuss the contents of each of this book's elements.

Part 1: The Network File System

The first part of the book covers the Network File System (NFS). Although each chapter covers Linux-specific material, wherever possible, a section near the end of that chapter covers information regarding other operating systems.

Chapter 1: NFS Basics and Protocols   This chapter covers the fundamentals: how NFS works, the NFS protocols, and what transports NFS works with. Chapter 1 provides information essential for understanding how to distribute file systems using NFS. It describes why NFS was designed the way it was; for example, its statelessness and initial use of UDP, and what improvements NFSv3/TCP offers. The chapter also covers other protocols used in conjunction with NFS: the portmapper, mount daemon, lock daemon, status daemon, and more.

Chapter 2: Configuring NFS   This chapter shows how to configure NFS servers and clients. It covers the RPC services that run on each side, the networking protocols needed, and an assortment of configuration files. This chapter also describes advanced NFS configurations and uses. These include, for example, UID mappings, mounting NFS over a wide-area network, partial file-system exports, and restricting NFS exports to subsets of a site based on DNS domains or NIS netgroups.

Chapter 3: NFS Performance   This chapter covers how to measure and improve the performance of your NFS service. It discusses tools used to test performance of the network and of NFS in particular. It shows how the various mount options used by NFS can affect its performance, and how to decide what version of the NFS protocol and transport to use.

Chapter 4: Securing NFS   File service security is important in any networked environment. This chapter describes how to secure your files on the server side and how to export the minimal access required for clients. The chapter continues to discuss the use of client-side host-based security to ensure that an authorized client is not subverted into gaining additional access. It also briefly describes how to secure other related services that may affect NFS: TCP/IP protocols, NIS/DNS, and RPC services such as the `portmapper`, `mountd`, `lockd`, `statd`, and more.

Chapter 5: NFS Diagnostics and Debugging This chapter shows users how to use network tools to diagnose NFS access problems such as denied mount permissions, data corruption, hung servers, and stale file handles. It describes configuration problems that may be related to NFS, software bugs, and hardware failures, and includes a long list of potential NFS problems on Linux (and non-Linux) systems and their resolution.

Chapter 6: NFS Version 4 This chapter covers the latest NFS protocol, version 4. It describes the motivation for this complex protocol's design and the goals set by its designers. Additionally, it discusses details of the many protocol procedures and operations, callbacks, and error messages. The chapter also shows how to configure and use NFSv4 on Linux.

Chapter 7: Building and Installing the Linux Kernel and NFS Software This chapter shows how to configure, compile, and install the Linux kernel—either from original sources or from already-packaged binaries. It provides information on choosing the right set of kernel options that are useful for running NFS servers on Linux systems, and options that are practical for using Linux systems as NFS clients. This chapter also shows how to configure the Linux kernel for the many add-on features that Amd can use, such as new file systems like SGI's XFS or BSD's FFS.

Part 2: The Amd Automounter

The second part of the book covers the Amd automounter, also known as the Berkeley Automounter (to distinguish it from Sun Microsystems' original automounter). As in Part 1, each chapter covers Linux-specific material, but wherever possible, a section near the end of that chapter covers information regarding other operating systems.

Chapter 8: Overview of the Amd Automounter This chapter covers the basics: how an automounter works, how Amd works, its relationship to NFS, and why automounting is useful. The chapter includes a couple introductory examples of simple Amd configurations.

Chapter 9: The Amd Configuration File This chapter covers the syntax and many options of an Amd configuration file, typically /etc/amd.conf. This configuration file controls the overall runtime behavior of Amd. Each configuration file option comes with an example or two showing its use. Also discussed are Amd command-line options, all of which are covered by an amd.conf file.

Chapter 10: Automounter Maps Understanding mount maps is the key to managing Amd configurations. Mount maps describe the servers, file systems, and volumes under Amd's control. The maps determine which path names, when accessed, will result in the automatic mounting of servers and file systems. Each entry in a mount map can compose many selectors, variables, and options that determine its dynamic behavior. Each map entry can use any number of other native file systems recognized by Amd.

Chapter 11: Runtime Automounter Administration This chapter shows how to run Amd, how to check its status, and how to change its status using Amq, the auto-mounter query tool. This chapter covers tracing Amd configuration problems using Amq, the logs, and various debugging options, as well as how to recover from hung or dead software. The chapter also discusses how to use Amd with various information services that can provide maps for it: NIS, NIS+, Hesiod, LDAP, and more.

Chapter 12: Advanced Amd Uses This chapter presents and explains in detail several advanced examples using Amd. These examples are designed to show the upper limits of what Amd can do. We describe at least two solutions to each problem depicted in the examples and explore their pros and cons. This chapter also covers advanced optimization techniques for Amd maps and how to configure replicated and fail-over volumes using Amd.

Chapter 13: Autofs This chapter shows how to use Linux's Autofs, an advanced kernel-based automounter. It covers configuration and Autofs mount maps. Since Amd can work both with and without Autofs, the main focus of this chapter is to show how to use Amd to achieve the same functionality that other Autofs-based automounters provide and how to convert from using Autofs on one host to using Amd across an entire site.

Chapter 14: Building and Installing the Automounter Software This chapter shows how to configure, compile, and install the am-utils package—either from original sources or from already packaged binaries. It also shows how to configure some of the new services that Amd can use, such as LDAP and Hesiod.

Part 3: Appendices

The third and last part of this book concludes with four appendices.

Appendix A: Sources in the am-utils Package This appendix lists the full sources in a recent version of the am-utils package, and what each source file is used for.

Appendix B: Online Resources This appendix lists online resources, URLs for retrieving more information, sources, and software discussed in this book. These resources are listed in several generic ways to ensure they are valid even years after listing.

Appendix C: Amd Log and Debug Messages This appendix lists the many logging and debugging messages that Amd can display during its run, and what each message means.

Appendix D: Amd Configuration-File Parameters and Command-Line Flags This appendix tabulates all the Amd configuration-file (`amd.conf`) parameters, alongside any Amd command-line flags that are functionally equivalent to those parameters.

Conventions Used in This Book

This book uses certain typographic styles to help you quickly identify important information and avoid confusion over the meaning of words such as on-screen prompts. In particular,

- A normal, proportionally spaced font is used for the bulk of the text in the book.

- *Italicized text* indicates technical terms that are introduced for the first time in a chapter. Italics are also used for emphasis.

- A `monospaced font` is used to indicate the contents of configuration files, messages displayed at a text-mode Linux shell prompt, file and program names, and Internet URLs.

- *`Italicized monospaced text`* indicates a variable—information that differs from one system or command run to another, such as the name of a client computer or a process ID number.

- **`Bold monospaced text`** is information that you should type into the computer, usually at a Linux shell prompt. This text can also be italicized to indicate that you should substitute an appropriate value for your system.

In addition to these text conventions, which can apply to individual words or entire paragraphs, a few conventions are used to highlight segments of text:

> ***NOTE***   A Note indicates information that is useful or interesting, but is somewhat peripheral to the main discussion. A Note might be relevant to a small number of networks, for instance, or refer to an outdated feature.

> ***TIP***   A Tip provides information that can save you time or frustration, and that may not be entirely obvious. A Tip might describe how to get around a limitation, or how to use a feature to perform an unusual task.

> ***WARNING***   Warnings describe potential pitfalls or dangers. If you fail to heed a Warning, you may end up spending a lot of time recovering from a bug or even restoring your entire system from scratch, or you may have to reboot your system.

Sidebars

A Sidebar is like a Note, but longer. Notes are no more than one paragraph long, while Sidebars are typically several paragraphs long. The information in a Sidebar is useful but does not fit into the main flow of the discussion.

Help Us Help You

Computer systems and especially software change all the time. Users of computer systems and software are constantly frustrated by the continuous need to keep up to date. This book was written to provide the most accurate and updated information available. Great care was taken to ensure that the information herein would still be valid years from now. Nevertheless, any large book with many details is likely to contain a few typographical errors. Furthermore, as time goes by, the software described in this book will continue to evolve and change. If you have any corrections, comments, or suggestions for improvements, please send them to us at support@sybex.com. To find out the latest information about this book and Amd, go to www.am-utils.org/book. To contact the author for information about Amd, as well as general information, go to www.cs.sunysb.edu/~ezk or e-mail the author directly at ezk@cs.sunysb.edu. Also, if you find the material in this book interesting and you would like to pursue a graduate degree in this area or conduct research on similar topics, contact the author.

Part 1

The Network File System

Featuring:

- An introduction to the Network File System, NFS

- Components of NFS clients and NFS servers

- Discussion of the XDR and RPC networking

- Description of current NFS protocols

- Configuring NFS clients and servers

- Improving the performance of NFS

- Securing NFS

- Diagnosing and fixing NFS problems

- The future: NFS version 4 protocol

- Building and configuring the Linux kernel and NFS software

NFS Basics and Protocols

1

Files are the basic storage unit of most computers. Easy access to one's files is an assumed part of day-to-day operations. In the Internet age, a user's files may reside on one machine but be accessed from another machine. Remote access to files is absolutely essential. Unfortunately, new complications arise with remote access:

- How to ensure seamless access to remote files as if they were local
- How to secure file data over public networks
- How to access files when networks or servers misbehave or are down
- How fast can you access your files over a network
- And more...

Over the past two decades, several file systems have been developed to allow remote access to files. The *Server Message Block* (SMB) protocol, used by Windows machines, allows machines to share access to remote folders and printers. The *Andrew File System* (AFS), invented at Carnegie-Mellon University, is a complex, high-performance file system that makes extensive use of caching to perform well. The *Coda* file system was invented for use in environments with a highly variable quality of network connectivity. In particular, the Coda file system can handle disconnected operations—computers that disconnect from the network for an arbitrary length of time and then reconnect again. Coda synchronizes files between disconnected clients and servers after reconnection.

The *Network File System* (NFS) is the most widely used network-based file system. NFS's initial simple design and Sun Microsystems' willingness to publicize the protocol and code samples to the community contributed to making NFS the most successful remote access file system. NFS implementations are available for numerous Unix systems, several Windows-based systems, and others. While not perfectly interoperable, heterogeneous NFS systems can exchange data together homogeneously with little user notice. For the most part, users are rarely aware that their files are being served over the network; they do not have to change their behavior or any programs they used before.

In this chapter, we introduce NFS. We begin by describing the basic operating principles; then we describe the many components that make up this complex system. We follow this with the details of the NFS protocols and how they evolved. We end with an example illustrating how to configure and use NFS.

NFS Versions

There are several revisions—or protocols—of NFS. Version 3 of NFS (NFSv3) is rapidly becoming the default version on most Linux systems. This version is available in the latest Linux 2.2 and 2.4 kernels. For the purposes of this book, we are assuming that readers are using one of these kernels and therefore they are using NFSv3; we will not be discussing NFSv2 at great length. To use the latest versions of NFS with Linux, a special user-level set of utilities is needed; these can be found in the nfs-utils package, version 0.2.0 or newer. To find out how to retrieve and install these new versions on Linux, see Chapter 7, "Building and Installing the Linux Kernel and NFS Software."

The specification for the latest version of NFS, version 4, is finalized but relatively new. At least one prototype implementation of this protocol version exists for Linux, but it is far from stable. It will be a long while before it becomes the default version of NFS for Linux. NFSv3 became stable on Linux more than six years after its original debut, and this was for a moderately complex improvement over the NFSv2 protocol. Compared to NFSv3, NFSv4 is significantly more complex. Therefore, we do not assume that users will be using NFSv4 soon, and we only describe NFSv4 briefly in Chapter 6, "NFS Version 4."

The first implementation of NFS on Linux was in a user-level daemon called unfsd. Since then, NFS implementations under Linux have moved into the kernel, where they perform faster and more reliably. To distinguish these kernel-based implementations from user-based implementations, the former were prefixed with k—so it would be knfsd instead of unfsd, or just nfsd. Other parts of NFS have also been moved into the kernel, as we see later in this chapter. However, to simplify our discussions, we have assumed that NFS is implemented in the kernel, and we have dropped the k prefix from those services.

NOTE   We do not discuss or use the older user-level NFS daemon (unfsd). We strongly recommend that administrators move away from that older, slower, and unreliable NFS server.

Overview of NFS

In this section, we overview the primary ideas that make up NFS. There are several such ideas:

- Remote procedure calls
- Retransmissions of messages
- Idempotent operations
- A stateless server
- File handles to identify files
- Caching on the client
- Maintaining Unix file system semantics

Remote Procedure Calls

Remote Procedure Calls (RPCs) are a programming paradigm that allows a local process to call a function that is implemented by a remote process as if the local process were calling its own function. RPCs allow the NFS system to be split into two parts: a component that runs on the client (or calling) host and a component that runs on the server (or called) host. An NFS client can call file system functions—implemented as RPCs—on the server as if the functions, and hence the files, were local.

Retransmissions and Idempotent Operations

In a network-based communication, software systems must handle lost packets and messages. The RPC system was designed to resend RPC messages automatically, at a given configurable interval, for up to a configurable number of retries. Since NFS is based on RPC, it supports *retransmissions* of protocol messages automatically. If the network is unreachable (because it got disconnected for a period of time or because the NFS server crashed and is rebooting), an NFS client will resend its messages several times before giving up. This ensures that NFS continues to function even when transient problems occur.

The flip side of the retransmission ability is the danger of duplicate messages. In any network, especially one that uses the *User Datagram Protocol* (UDP), duplicate packets could occur. If a duplicate RPC message is sent to an NFS server, the NFS server will try to process that message again, possibly performing the same operation repeatedly. Therefore, it is important that the NFS protocol and its operations all be *idempotent*—executing them again does not change the outcome. The decision to make sure all NFS operations are idempotent figured heavily into the protocol design and into the key design feature of the NFS server, its statelessness, which is discussed next.

A Stateless Server

One important aspect of a distributed file system design is its handling of network failures and how well it recovers from host crashes. This point is crucial for the consistency and reliability of data. In local file systems, such as EXT2, a user has a strong guarantee that the data just saved in a `write` system call is actually saved to disk. Should the machine crash, the data will remain on disk.

Consider the case of a client-server statefull distributed file system. A client writes some data using the `write` system call. The data goes over the wire from the client to the server. To improve performance, a statefull server might cache that data in memory and return a successful return code to the client. The server can schedule to save the data onto physical media at a later time. Since the client received a successful return code, it believes that the data must have been saved to stable media—a usual assumption when the `write` system call returns successfully. However, if the server crashes after signaling the client that `write` succeeded but before the server had a chance to synchronize the data to stable media, that data would be lost. When that happens, the client's assumption of a successful write becomes incorrect.

There are several ways to improve the reliability of statefull servers while maintaining high performance. However, a much easier way to ensure reliable crash recovery is to make the server *stateless*; such a server keeps no state, therefore avoiding any loss of data during crashes. With a stateless server, the client can be assured that when a remote NFS operation succeeds, the remote file system is guaranteed to be consistent, even if the remote server crashes.

The assumption that NFS servers are stateless simplifies the NFS server code and the NFS protocol significantly. To ensure data consistency, the NFS client host just waits for a previously available remote server that has crashed to reboot. This wait state often locks all the processes that were performing operations on the remote server, which results in the infamous but necessary error message "NFS server not responding—still trying." Once the server comes back up, the NFS client that was waiting for the server to come back up can resume its operation.

One of the unfortunate results of the statelessness of the NFS server is poor performance. The server must write to disk all data it receives from clients before it returns successfully to the client. This synchronous writing operation is one of the largest drawbacks of NFS, and it impacts its performance significantly. Below we discuss several solutions that were invented to improve performance through client-side caching.

Note that the NFS client is not stateless and it does keep cached data in order to improve performance. If the client crashes, some data may be lost, but that is no different from a client host crashing in the middle of a write operation to a local disk. This is very different from when a server crashes; when this happens, many clients' data could be lost all at once, and those clients are now left in an inconsistent state of making wrong assumptions about the validity of their data.

File Handles

NFS clients and servers handle many files at once. Often, a client may issue many system calls on a single file, each call turning into one or more NFS operations over the wire. The client and server must agree about which files both should apply a series of operations to. For that reason, NFS servers issue *file handles* to clients. File handles are unique identifiers that the server generates for each file that a client uses.

These identifiers are anywhere from 32 to 64 bytes of data in length. File handles are opaque to the client—it does not know what the individual bytes in each handle are for. Only the server understands file handles. NFS servers generally encode enough information on the local disks to allow the servers to find out the exact file name that a remote client wishes to access. Servers usually encode the following pieces of information in each file handle:

- A file system identifier, an index number of a mounted local file system
- The inode number of the file within the file system
- An inode generation number, described below, under "Maintaining Unix Semantics"
- Other information as they see fit, usually listed in the C header file `/usr/include/linux/nfsd/nfsfh.h`

Recall that the server is stateless; therefore, it cannot keep an association (state) that maps file handles to actual files on the server's disks. The server generates its own file handles and encodes in them everything that it needs to find out the exact file that any given file handle was generated for. Clients receive these file handles from the NFS server, and they must not modify them. Instead, the clients must send back the same file handles the server provided when these same clients wish to access the same files. When NFS servers get the returned file handles, even (and especially) after a server crash, they can decode the file handle and tell exactly which file the client wishes to apply the particular operation to. This is possible because the file handle encodes information that uniquely identifies the exact file within a given file system that resides on the server.

If an NFS client passes a file handle to an NFS server that the server is unable to decode, the server will refuse to use that file handle; the NFS server will return an error code back to the client telling it that the file handle is *stale*. Stale file handles happen most often when a file system on a remote file server is moved, the file system is reformatted or restored, or the mount point for the file system changed. See Chapter 5, "NFS Diagnostics and Debugging," for how to handle stale file handles.

Client-Side Caching

As we just mentioned above, servers are stateless but clients are not. To improve performance, clients cache file data and file attributes.

NFS clients and servers employ a special I/O daemon (rpciod) in order to cluster multiple write operations from the client. When several consecutive write buffers accumulate, rpciod will issue a single large write request to the NFS server. This can improve performance manyfold, especially when a client process performs many small writes or appends to the same file. Note that client-side caching and buffering via rpciod does not violate the statelessness of the server, but it does increase the chance of greater data loss should the client crash.

NFS clients also cache attributes. This is intended to speed up operations that look up file attributes (such as the lstat system call) and operations that change file attributes (such as chmod or chgrp). This behavior also has annoying side effects since changed file modes do not propagate immediately from one client to a server, and certainly, they do not propagate immediately from a server to another client.

This behavior also has security implications. Consider two clients, A and B, that read the same file, possibly at the same time. Though client A might change the mode of the file so it is more restrictive and should no longer be readable by client B, client B might still cache the previous more permissive modes. This allows client B to continue to access a file that it is no longer supposed to.

Maintaining Unix Semantics

Several complications arise from Unix's particular file system semantics. These semantics must be maintained accurately so that user processes could mix access to local and remote files without any noticeable difference.

Inode Generation Numbers

The first such semantic issue has to do with inode numbers, the file index numbers that help locate the data of the file on disk. When a file is removed, its inode is also removed. That inode number, however, can be reused at a later date to create a new file. Inode numbers can be recycled shortly after becoming available, or much later, depending on the system usage and the operating system.

NFS servers encode the inode number of a file in the file handle so that they can identify the exact file that a client wants to access. Consider what happens if that file was removed, possibly on the server itself or by another client, and then another file was created that had the same inode number. If the NFS client host retained its file handle and tried to use it, the NFS server would find the new file with the same (old) inode number and would incorrectly think that it was the file that the client wanted to use. This scenario can result in serious data corruption.

For that reason, NFS servers add another piece of information into the mix that makes up the NFS file handle: an *inode generation number*. This number is usually an integer that gets incremented each time the same inode number is reused, or it is a time stamp of the file's creation time. Either way, it is an additional piece of information that helps the stateless server correctly identify the exact file that is being used.

Hidden *.nfs* Files

Another quirky piece of Unix file system semantics is the ability to open a file, unlink (delete) it, and still be able to access the file's data as long as the file remains open. This particular behavior was originally intended to allow programs to access temporary unnamed files in a way that guaranteed that the physical storage for those files was reclaimed as soon as the process using them closed the files' descriptors. Unfortunately, this behavior was used more often by attackers of Unix systems determined to hide their intentions by using unnamed files.

Since the NFS server is stateless, it is not allowed to keep any state on the current status of files. In particular, the server cannot tell when a file is opened or closed (these two operations are not even part of the v2 and v3 NFS protocols). Therefore, the NFS client-side code has to handle this case specially. The client side can do so because it does know when a file has been unlinked while being opened. When the client sees this unlink operation, it issues an NFS call to *rename* the file to a hidden file whose name starts with `.nfs` and ends with a sequence of characters and digits that guarantee the uniqueness of that special dot file.

The NFS client code remembers the renamed file name. When the client sees the close operation, it then issues an NFS call to actually delete the .nfs file, therefore removing its physical storage.

This behavior preserves this odd Unix semantics as closely as possible. Occasionally, clients can crash and leave behind .nfs files that the client no longer knows about. These stale files must be cleaned. For that reason, most systems add a daily cron job to look for and delete old .nfs files.

File and Record Locking

Modern Unix systems provide several system calls that allow a process to lock a whole file or a smaller region of a file while accessing it. This is most often used to guarantee that only one process at a time can be modifying a shared file. Unfortunately, proper support for locking requires that the operating system maintain a state about the locked files. Since the actual files reside on the server, locking information (state) must be maintained on the server. This state must be maintained on the server to guarantee that clients from different hosts do not all try to write to the same file at the same time.

So, it appears that NFS server hosts have to keep some state, but the NFS server itself (nfsd) was designed to be stateless. To reconcile these two opposing needs, the original designers of NFS opted to create a separate locking daemon (lockd) that NFS clients must communicate with to guarantee consistent locking behavior.

Components of the Network File System

The NFS system is complex and contains many components that interact with each other over special protocols. The different components use various configuration and state files. Figure 1.1 shows the main components of NFS and the primary configuration files. On the upper part of the figure we see an NFS server, and on the lower part an NFS client host. Each host has its own kernel-level services: *eXternal Data Representation* (XDR), *Remote Procedure Call* (RPC), NFS client or server, I/O daemon, and locking daemon. Each host also has its own user-level services. Both kernel-level and user-level services depend on the function that the host has: an NFS client or an NFS server. In addition, there are special configuration files (usually in /etc) that are used on each host based on its function. Note that if a host is both an NFS server and an NFS client, it will have to run the services on both parts of Figure 1.1.

Figure 1.1   The components of an NFS system

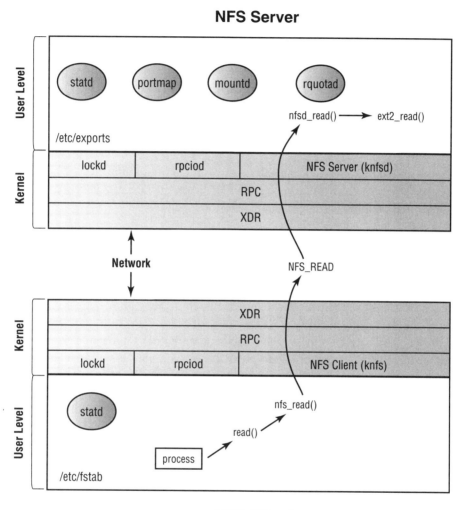

Figure 1.1 also shows the flow of data for a simple read operation, when an NFS client wants to read a file from an NFS server. We describe that data flow at the end of this chapter.

In the next sections, we begin by describing each component of an NFS system. We discuss them in dependency order, describing a component first before other components that use it. Once we have described each component's function, we can put them all in context and show you how the overall NFS system works.

XDR: eXternal Data Representation

The basic need of a distributed file system such as NFS is to exchange data across a network between heterogeneous machines. Most CPUs use one of two ways to represent data in memory:

Big-endian   A *big-endian* machine stores the most-significant byte of a machine word on the left side of a register. For example, the integer 2 as represented in hexadecimal on a big-endian machine would be 0x00000002.

Little-endian   A *little-endian* machine stores the least-significant byte of a machine word on the left side of a register. On such a machine, the integer 2 (in hexadecimal) would be represented as 0x02000000.

Since there are two such representations for data, it is imperative that when a big-endian machine exchanges data with a little-endian machine, they both agree on the representation of the data being exchanged. If they did not agree on a common format, these machines could corrupt data. For this reason, the Internet standard for exchanging data over the network is in *network order*, which is big-endian. This means that little-endian machines, such as Intel-based ones, must convert data to big-endian format before sending it over the wire, and they must convert it back to little-endian (which is their own *host order*) when they read data from the network. This process must be done very carefully and consistently.

The *eXternal Data Representation* (XDR) system was designed to simplify data exchange among networked hosts. XDR can encode any arbitrary data in a uniform manner and prepare it to be sent over the network. XDR can also take an arbitrary data stream off the network and decode it into its original data units.

XDR comes with libraries and functions that can encode and decode many primitive types: integers, longs, floating-point numbers, strings, bytes, and more. Programmers using XDR can build more and more complex encoding functions using basic ones. For example, they can create an XDR encoding function for a complex data structure that contains simpler native types, and then they can create an even more complex XDR function that builds on top of that.

XDR offers a powerful method to encode arbitrarily complex data structures in a uniform network order and ensures that when the data arrives on the other end, it can be decoded into the exact data structure that the sender encoded. The ability to transfer data structures across a network is the first necessary component of sharing files over a network.

RPC: Remote Procedure Call

XDRs provide a mechanism to exchange data uniformly across a network. *Remote Procedure Calls* (RPCs) provide a method for calling functions on another host. Most programming languages allow you to call functions in your own program or in libraries that the program links with; these languages also allow you to pass data to the function and to return data back from the function. Together, XDR and RPC allow you to do the same—only on remote hosts.

RPCs allow programmers to provide shared services in a single location designated as the server. Many clients can access those services as easily as they would if they were calling a function in their local C library. With RPCs, code and services can be shared more easily between hosts.

The RPC system also allows for implementation versioning. A server can provide multiple implementations of a given service, and clients making RPC calls can choose the implementation they want to use. This allows network-wide services to evolve naturally over time (even in an incompatible manner), while maintaining backward compatibility; therefore, newer RPC clients can use the latest versions of the RPC service, while older ones can use older (yet compatible) versions of the RPC service. This versioning ability will prove to be very useful to the evolution of the NFS protocol.

Refer back to Figure 1.1. Here we see that in order for two machines to exchange information, they must go through the RPC layer, which in turn uses the XDR layer to encode the data. When an RPC client calls an RPC server, the client has to provide the server with at least this basic information:

- The name of the remote host
- The program number of the remote service, uniquely identifying the RPC service
- The version of the service (a number)
- The number of the exact remote procedure to execute on the remote service
- The arguments and data to pass to the remote service
- Placeholders for the arguments and data to get back from the remote service

The Portmapper

Now that we have the ability to create many RPC services, all versioned, and each with their own set of procedures, we have to decide how they should be advertised to clients. Traditionally in Unix, each service gets assigned a port number on which to listen: Telnet on port 23, FTP on port 21, SSH on port 22, SMTP on port 25, and so on. This agreement on the port number is important; without it, clients would not know how to contact the service. Unfortunately, a limited number of port numbers is available (generally only 65535), and even fewer are available to privileged (root) services—the first 1024 ports. Therefore, if we are to support many possible RPC services, we cannot dedicate a port number to each such service; if we did, we would quickly run out of available ports.

The *portmapper* solves this problem. Each RPC service has its own program number, a large number that is either assigned to the service or can be designated by the programmer of the service. The portmapper maps the RPC program number to the actual port the service runs on.

The portmapper, however, can do more than that. When an RPC program wishes to make its services available to clients to contact, it registers its service with the portmapper. It provides the portmapper with the following information:

- The program number that it uses for the service
- The version of the service that it supports
- The transports that it supports: UDP, TCP, or both

RPC servers can register multiple services, versions, and transports to use by registering each tuple (*<service, version, transport>*) individually with the portmapper. The portmapper records this information so that when an RPC client contacts it to call an RPC service, the portmapper can tell it what port the service listens on. Then the RPC client can contact that service directly. The only requirement for RPC clients to contact the portmapper is that the portmapper itself must have a preassigned port number: 111.

Getting RPC Information

The portmapper may be the mother of all RPC services, but it is also an RPC service itself. As such, it has an implementation version and transports that it supports. To find out this information about any RPC service, including the portmapper, use the rpcinfo program. Listing 1.1 shows the five forms of typical use for the rpcinfo command.

Listing 1.1   Usage of the rpcinfo program

```
Usage: rpcinfo [ -n portnum ] -u host prognum [ versnum ]
       rpcinfo [ -n portnum ] -t host prognum [ versnum ]
```

```
rpcinfo -p [ host ]
rpcinfo -b prognum versnum
rpcinfo -d prognum versnum
```

The first two forms contact a remote *host* and query the NULL (first) procedure of *prognum*. This form is intended to test if a remote service is up and responding using UDP (-u); the second form tests using TCP (-t). You can optionally specify the version number (*versnum*) of the service you wish to verify.

Normally, rpcinfo will contact the remote portmapper to find out which port number the service listens on. If you know that port number, you can specify it using the -n option. For example, to test if a remote NFS server (RPC program number 100003) named aladdin supports protocol version 3 using UDP, run the command as seen in Listing 1.2.

Listing 1.2   Testing the availability of an RPC service

```
[ezk]$ rpcinfo -u aladdin 100003 3
program 100003 version 3 ready and waiting
```

The second form of usage for rpcinfo is the most often used one—listing the RPC services that run on a given host. To list the RPC services on a host, run rpcinfo -p as seen in Listing 1.3.

Listing 1.3   Listing the RPC services running on a host

```
[ezk]$ rpcinfo -p
   program vers proto   port
    100000    2   tcp    111  portmapper
    100000    2   udp    111  portmapper
    100004    2   udp    981  ypserv
    100004    1   udp    981  ypserv
    100004    2   tcp    984  ypserv
    100004    1   tcp    984  ypserv
    100007    2   udp    995  ypbind
    100007    2   tcp    997  ypbind
    100024    1   udp    964  status
    100024    1   tcp    966  status
    100011    1   udp    896  rquotad
    100011    2   udp    896  rquotad
    100005    1   udp   1037  mountd
    100005    1   tcp   1024  mountd
    100005    2   udp   1037  mountd
    100005    2   tcp   1024  mountd
```

```
100005   3   udp   1037   mountd
100005   3   tcp   1024   mountd
100003   2   udp   2049   nfs
100003   3   udp   2049   nfs
100021   1   udp   1038   nlockmgr
100021   3   udp   1038   nlockmgr
100021   4   udp   1038   nlockmgr
100021   1   tcp   1025   nlockmgr
100021   3   tcp   1025   nlockmgr
100021   4   tcp   1025   nlockmgr
100001   3   udp    941   rstatd
100001   2   udp    941   rstatd
100001   1   udp    941   rstatd
100008   1   udp   1040   walld
300019   1   tcp    975   amd
300019   1   udp    976   amd
```

Listing 1.3 shows the RPC services on this host, many of which are related to NFS and will be described in the sections that follow.

The third form of usage for `rpcinfo` sends an RPC broadcast command for a given service and version of that service. It returns the IP address and name of every host that responds. For example, to find out which hosts support the `nlockmgr` service version 4, run the command as seen in Listing 1.4.

Listing 1.4 Querying for all hosts that support an RPC service

```
[ezk]$ rpcinfo -b 100021 4
172.29.1.65 lorien.dev.example.com
172.29.1.66 jigglypuff.dev.example.com
172.29.1.67 kendo.dev.example.com
172.29.1.57 toreador.dev.example.com
172.29.1.3 aladdin.dev.example.com
172.29.1.126 corvair.dev.example.com
172.29.1.87 atlast.dev.example.com
172.29.1.61 rewind.dev.example.com
```

The fourth and last form of usage for `rpcinfo` removes an association of program number (RPC service) and version number from the portmapper. Only the superuser can execute this command because once the association is removed, that service can no longer be used!

> **NOTE** Many RPC programs use a different service name from the actual program name. Most often, a program such as /usr/sbin/rpc.mountd is represented by the RPC portmapper as mountd. Throughout this chapter, we will refer to the service name of the program using the short form, and to the actual program name using the longer form that begins with the rpc. prefix.

The Portmapper RPC Protocol

For a given version, each RPC service can support any number of procedures. These procedures are individual functions that RPC clients can call. Being an RPC service itself, the portmapper is no different. The following procedures are defined for the (latest) portmapper protocol, version number 4:

PMAPPROC_NULL   Every RPC program has this NULL procedure (also called *procedure 0)* because its number is zero, which is sometimes known as the *ping* procedure. This procedure does not take or return arguments. Its purpose is for RPC clients to call and find out if a service exists and is running for a given version of a protocol.

PMAPPROC_SET   The SET procedure registers an RPC program number, version number, and protocol transport type with the portmapper.

PMAPPROC_UNSET   This procedure deregisters an RPC service from the portmapper.

PMAPPROC_GETPORT   The GETPORT procedure returns the port number for a given RPC program number and version.

PMAPPROC_DUMP   The DUMP procedure returns the list of all services registered with the portmapper. It is used with rpcinfo -p.

PMAPPROC_CALLIT   This procedure is used to make the portmapper call a procedure of *another* RPC service on the same host. Normally, you would not need to use this procedure; you would call the RPC service directly. On Linux, the CALLIT procedure is limited to UDP only, it performs no authentication, and it does not return any error information. It is therefore of limited use, and not very secure.

The Mount Daemon

XDR, RPC, and the portmapper are generic parts of the RPC system on which NFS is based. The *mount daemon* (mountd) is the first RPC service we cover that is specific to

NFS. This server implements the MOUNT protocol. It retrieves a list of *exported* directories from a configuration file called /etc/exports. This configuration file describes which directories this NFS server allows remote NFS clients to access. NFS clients contact mountd to request initial access to an NFS volume. The mountd daemon checks the list of currently exported volumes against the credentials of the NFS client and responds, either allowing or denying access.

If the daemon grants access, it returns a *root file handle* to the NFS client. This file handle is the NFS system identifier for the top-level directory of the exported volume. This piece of information is important to the NFS client. Using the root file handle, an NFS client can, for example, request listing of the entries in that directory, read or write files within that directory, or get handles for additional files or subdirectories. In other words, without the root file handle, an NFS client cannot begin to access any files that are in that volume.

The *rpc.mountd* Program

The rpc.mountd program is the user-level RPC daemon that processes MOUNT requests from clients. Administrators list volumes to export in the file /etc/exports. A special tool, exportfs, maintains a current list of exported volumes in the file /var/lib/nfs/xtab. The rpc.mountd server reads the current export list from that file. We show an example using these files later in this chapter, and we detail their format and options in Chapter 2, "Configuring NFS."

The rpc.mountd daemon supports the command-line options seen in Listing 1.5.

Listing 1.5   Usage of the rpc.mountd program

```
Usage: rpc.mountd [-Fhnv] [-d kind] [-f exports-file] [-V version]
        [-N version] [--debug kind] [-p|--port port] [--help]
        [--version] [--exports-file=file]
        [--nfs-version version] [--no-nfs-version version]
```

-d or **--debug**   Turn on debugging. All debugging messages are logged via syslog to the LOG_DAEMON service.

-F or **--foreground**   Do not daemonize rpc.mountd. Instead, the server remains running in the foreground. This is useful if you wish to debug it using a debugger such as gdb.

-f *ARG* or **--exports-file** *ARG*   By default, rpc.mountd reads export information from /etc/exports when the daemon starts up. With this option, it reads the export information from a file specified by *ARG*. Note that rpc.mountd also reads export information from `/var/lib/nfs/xtab`; we describe these files in greater detail in Chapter 2.

-h or **--help**   Prints the help message shown in Listing 1.5.

-N *ARG* or **--no-nfs-version** *ARG*   The daemon is capable of returning NFS root file handles for multiple versions of NFS. If, however, you do not wish the daemon to support a certain version of NFS, you can specify it with this option, as *ARG*. This is most often useful when you do not wish to use a buggy or unstable implementation of the NFSv3 protocol:

```
[root]# rpc.mountd --no-nfs-version 3
```

-V *ARG* or **--nfs-version** *ARG*   This option is the opposite of the -N option: it forces `rpc.mountd` to offer the version as specified in *ARG*.

-p *ARG* or **--port** *ARG*   Usually, `rpc.mount` will bind to a port that is randomly assigned to it by the portmapper. If you wish to force `rpc.mountd` to use another port, specify it in *ARG*.

-v or **--version**   Print the version of the daemon and exit.

The MOUNT Protocol

The latest version (3) of the MOUNT protocol implemented by `rpc.mountd` supports the following RPC procedures:

MOUNTPROC_NULL   This is the ping procedure for testing the `rpc.mountd`'s responsiveness.

MOUNTPROC_MNT   An NFS client passes the name of a directory it wishes to mount. If the client is authorized to access that directory, this procedure returns the root NFS file handle for that directory to the NFS client. Also, `rpc.mountd` updates the remote mount table file `/var/lib/nfs/rmtab`.

MOUNTPROC_DUMP   Return the full list of remotely mounted file systems, as listed in the `/var/lib/nfs/rmtab` file. This list includes the names of remote hosts that mount this NFS server's file systems, and the names of the directories that they mount.

MOUNTPROC_UMNT   Delete an entry from `/var/lib/nfs/rmtab`, which is a pair of hostname and directory name that the remote host mounts.

MOUNTPROC_UMNTALL   Delete all entries for `/var/lib/nfs/rmtab` for the NFS client host that calls this procedure.

MOUNTPROC_EXPORT and MOUNTPROC_EXPORTALL   Return the full list of all exported file systems and the names of the machines that are allowed to mount these file systems.

MOUNTPROC_PATHCONF   Return the POSIX *pathconf* information to the client. This information includes file system parameters about the server, such as the maximum allowed length for a path name, the maximum length for a file name, etc.

The NFS Locking Daemon

Unix supports locking files or portions of files (such as record locks) to ensure that no two people can attempt to write the same part of the file. This guarantees data consistency. On a single host, the kernel maintains information about user processes that acquired file locks and ensures the appropriate handling of lock requests and file access while files are locked. The key part in ensuring consistent locking is that there is a central authority—the kernel—that must arbitrate lock and write requests.

In a distributed file system such as NFS, many clients may wish to lock the same remote file. The most logical choice for the central lock arbitration authority is the NFS server itself because only it has access to the actual locked file. To maintain this locking information, however, the NFS server would have to track which client locked which file or a portion of a file. However, the NFS server was designed to be stateless, and thus it cannot maintain any state. For this situation, the solution Sun came up with was to add another RPC protocol to handle locking operations.

The RPC *Locking Daemon*, rpc.lockd, implements the *NFS Lock Manager* (NLM) protocol. The NLM protocol was designed to support multiple clients wishing to lock files consistently through NFS. NFS clients make RPC calls to the local rpc.lockd, which communicates with the remote rpc.lockd to ensure consistent locking of files. The rpc.lockd server uses another daemon, rpc.statd, which implements a status monitoring service; we describe rpc.statd below.

NOTE   At this stage, astute readers might begin to wonder why there are so many components of the NFS system; for instance, why is this locking protocol not integrated together with the NFS server nfsd? If you are asking this question, you would be right, but it took more than 15 years to do just that: integrate all of these extra protocols into the NFS protocol. See Chapter 6, "NFS Version 4." You will not be disappointed.

The *rpc.lockd* Program

In older Linux systems, rpc.lockd was not implemented at all. In later kernels, such as those distributed with Red Hat 7, a kernel-level thread implementation of this service is included;

it is sometimes called klockd. In Linux 2.2.18 and 2.4 kernels, the klockd thread is spawned from the knfsd thread on demand.

The rpc.lockd program takes no arguments or switches. It starts the NLM RPC service, if the kernel had not already started it. There are several ways to find out if your kernel supports the NLM service in the kernel. First, you can run modprobe lockd and then check to see if a lockd module is listed in the output of lsmod. Second, you can run ps axf and look for an output such as seen in Listing 1.6.

Listing 1.6   Process listing output for in-kernel NFS services

```
737 ?        SW      22:22 [nfsd]
745 ?        SW       0:00 \_ [lockd]
746 ?        SW       0:09      \_ [rpciod]
```

Whenever you see processes listed in square brackets, it usually (but not always) indicates that these are kernel threads (*kthreads*). *Kernel threads* are independent programs that run in the kernel: they are fast since they are in the kernel, and they are independent so they can execute actions on their own, separately from the main kernel itself. Listing 1.6 shows three such kthreads. The main one is nfsd, which automatically spawns lockd as needed, which automatically spawns rpciod (described below).

The NFS Lock Manager Protocol

The latest version (4) of the NLM protocol implemented by rpc.lockd supports the following RPC procedures:

NLMPROC_NULL   This is the ping procedure for testing the rpc.lockd's responsiveness.

NLMPROC_TEST   This procedure tests to see if a lock is available to the NFS client that wants to lock a file.

NLMPROC_LOCK   This procedure creates a lock for a range of bytes within a file (which could subsume the entire file if desired). If the server is unable to provide the lock because another client may hold it, then the client can wait for the lock. The client can then CANCEL the request or wait until it gets the GRANTED response; both of these choices are described next.

NLMPROC_CANCEL   When a client asks to lock a file and the file is locked by another client, the requesting client must block waiting for that lock to be released. Sometimes, the waiting client may opt to cancel that request and do something else instead. This procedure cancels a pending request for a lock.

NLMPROC_UNLOCK   This procedure removes a lock that was previously given for a range of bytes within a file.

NLMPROC_GRANTED   This procedure is initiated by the server and sent back to the client (via a callback) to tell the client that a request for a lock has been granted.

NLMPROC_SHARE   The remaining four procedures are used primarily by MS-DOS clients utilizing PC-NFSD. This procedure creates a share reservation for a file on an MS-DOS system, essentially locking an entire file while it is in use by MS-DOS.

NLMPROC_UNSHARE   This procedure releases a share reservation for a file on an MS-DOS system.

NLMPROC_NM_LOCK   This procedure establishes a non-monitored lock on a file. It is used primarily on single-threaded systems, such as MS-DOS, that cannot utilize the Network Status Monitor protocol. Clients using this procedure are responsible for clearing out server locks.

NLMPROC_FREE   If a client that used a non-monitored lock crashes, it may leave locks on the server that must be cleaned up. This procedure instructs a server to remove all locks for the calling client.

The NFS Status Daemon

As we described above, the `rpc.lockd` daemon coordinates locks between NFS clients and an NFS server. We explained how `rpc.lockd` maintains state about who holds locks, on which files, and for what byte ranges in the file. The problem is what happens when the host that maintains lock state, the NFS server running `rpc.lockd`, reboots and loses that state information. If it lost information about locks, NFS clients that acquired those locks could no longer use them. The solution Sun came up with was to add yet another RPC protocol to handle the recovery of locking information.

The *Network Status Monitor* (NSM) protocol was originally designed as a general-purpose active state sharing service for RPC systems. In practice, however, only `rpc.lockd` makes use of this service—for maintaining state about NFS locks. Furthermore, over time, the protocol had actually devolved to include passive state sharing messages.

To ensure that this state information is not lost upon server reboot, `rpc.statd` saves its state information on disk, in files under the directory /var/lib/nfs/sm. Each file in that directory is named after the client that holds any locks.

If an NFS server crashes and reboots, when it comes back up, `rpc.lockd` asks `rpc.statd` for any known locks. If there were any locks recorded in /var/lib/nfs/sm, then the NFS server's `rpc.statd` and `rpc.lockd` daemons provide that information to their counterparts on each NFS client that held any locks. This is done before the NFS server is fully ready to serve file access requests in order to ensure that all NFS clients are back in sync with any NFS servers that granted them locks.

The *rpc.statd* Program

The rpc.statd program supports only one startup option. By default, this program daemonizes (backgrounds) itself. If you specify the -F option, rpc.statd will remain running in the background. This is most useful when you are debugging the daemon using tools such as gdb.

The Network Status Monitor Protocol

The latest version (1) of the NSM protocol implemented by rpc.statd supports the following RPC procedures:

SM_NULL   This is the ping procedure for testing the rpc.statd's responsiveness.

SM_STAT   This procedure tests if a given host is being monitored. This procedure is part of the original active monitoring design and may not be fully implemented in rpc.statd.

SM_MON   This procedure tells rpc.statd to begin monitoring a given host. The procedure is used by rpc.lockd before granting the very first lock to the host. That way, if the NFS server host crashes, rpc.statd will be able to inform the client about these locks when the server comes back up.

A process using this procedure must supply a callback routine to invoke when the status of the monitored host has changed. This way a client that has asked to monitor a host can be informed by a remote RPC client when any change in status had taken place. This is used with the SM_NOTIFY procedure described below.

SM_UNMON   This procedure tells rpc.statd to stop monitoring a given host. It is usually used by rpc.lockd after releasing the last lock of that client host.

SM_UNMON_ALL   This procedure tells rpc.statd to stop monitoring all hosts. It is usually not used by rpc.lockd.

SM_SIMU_CRASH   If rpc.lockd crashes on the client, all lock information on the client is lost. When rpc.lockd is restarted, it sends a message to the local client's rpc.statd to inform the status daemon that the host had crashed and is now back up. This message simulates a crash from the client's point of view: rpc.statd informs all NFS servers that the lock state had been lost by sending them the NLM_UNLOCK RPC message. This procedure is an artifact of poor past designs and implementations of this service: this message had to be sent when some services of the NFS system failed.

The Network File System

PART 1

This procedure is not too practical on recent Linux systems since their `rpc.lockd` service is implemented in the kernel, and it is thus not that likely to crash as often as user-level daemons might. If the kernel module for `rpc.lockd` crashes, a more severe situation requiring a complete host reboot may occur—no need to simulate that.

SM_NOTIFY   When `rpc.statd` crashes on a host and then comes back up, it must inspect the state of monitored hosts it recorded in `/var/lib/nfs/sm`. For each host listed there that has asked for status monitoring, this client sends this NOTIFY message to the remote host. When a remote `rpc.statd` receives such a notification, it invokes the callback procedure registered with the original SM_MON request prior to this client's crash. This series of notifications and callbacks is intended to restore the state of all status monitoring to its original condition before the crash.

The NFS Remote Quota Daemon

The `rpc.rquotad` daemon implements the RQUOTA protocol. It is currently used by only one program: `quota`. This program displays quota information about one or more users. With NFS in place, the `quota` program can also contact remote `rpc.rquotad` servers to retrieve quota information for users of remote file systems.

NOTE   The `rpc.rquotad` daemon does not enforce quotas nor is it used to provide quota information for the parts of NFS that do enforce quotas: the NFS server itself. On Linux, the NFS server always enforces quotas whether `rpc.rquotad` runs or not.

The `rpc.rquotad` program itself is very simple. It takes no arguments and is usually started at boot time from the `/etc/rc.d/init.d/nfs` startup script.

Similarly, the RQUOTAD protocol is very simple. The latest version (2) of the RQUOTAD protocol implemented by `rpc.rquotad` supports the following two RPC procedures:

RQUOTAPROC_GETQUOTA   This procedure returns the list of all available quotas from the remote server, including those that are not activated (in use at the time).

RQUOTAPROC_GETACTIVEQUOTA   This procedure returns only the list of active in-use quotas.

The NFS I/O Daemon

Since the NFS server is stateless, it may not keep any information that could be lost if the server crashed. This means that when an NFS client writes data to the server, the server must write it to stable storage immediately. Unfortunately, that synchronous write is slow. Furthermore, the server may have to update additional metadata, which causes further synchronous writes of disk blocks. This problem seriously affected performance of early NFS servers. The solution to this problem was to add yet another statefull server to the NFS system that improved the performance of writes over NFS.

Traditionally, the `rpciod` server runs on the NFS client. It interfaces with the rest of the kernel and collects write requests to remote NFS servers. Instead of sending each write request to the remote NFS server, the `rpciod` server collects them and sends writes in larger, but less frequent batches. In particular, `rpciod` looks for consecutive writes to a file that can be combined into a larger sequential write. When `rpciod` has gathered enough writes, it sends them as one large NFS write request. This saves lots of network bandwidth and extra work for the NFS server.

With `rpciod`, local NFS users can perform writes and those writes will return immediately with a successful return code. However, note that the data has now been buffered on the local host and will be lost if the local host crashes. The assumption with the design of `rpciod` was that if the local host crashed, much more data could be lost anyway, and that the loss of buffered data was a reasonable compromise that yielded in greatly improved performance. Surely it is better than an NFS server crashing and losing lots more data that many clients believe to have been written to stable storage.

In the latest versions of Linux, the `rpciod` service is implemented as a kernel thread and is invoked automatically by the in-kernel NFS server or client as needed.

The NFS Client Side

Now that we have described all other components of NFS, we begin discussing the actual NFS components. We start with the NFS client-side code. In the next section, we cover the NFS server-side code and the NFS protocols.

The NFS *client-side* code had always resided in the kernel in Linux. More recent versions of Linux also support newer NFS protocols as well as TCP transports. Your Linux system must support client-side NFS to be able to mount remote NFS servers. To find out if your system supports the client-side NFS, see if `nfs` is listed in `/proc/filesystems`. If it is not, run `modprobe nfs` to check to see if NFS support is available as a loadable kernel module, and then check `/proc/filesystems` again. If you cannot find `nfs` listed in

`/proc/filesystems`, your client host does not support NFS. Go to Chapter 7, "Building and Installing the Linux Kernel and NFS Software," for details on how to add the right NFS support to your Linux system.

The main function of the NFS component on the client side is to translate system call requests into their NFS protocol RPC messages and send these messages over to the remote NFS server. The NFS client side also coordinates with the local I/O daemon (`rpciod`), the locking daemon (`rpc.lockd`), and the status-monitoring daemon (`rpc.statd`).

The NFS Server

The *NFS server*, `nfsd`, is at the heart of the NFS system. It listens for RPC requests from remote hosts and interprets them according to the NFS protocol. It sends responses back to clients using RPCs. It also communicates with other components that run on the NFS server host: the locking daemon `rpc.lockd`, the status daemon `rpc.statd`, and the I/O daemon `rpciod`.

NOTE   The term *NFS server* can have multiple meanings. Some consider it to mean the whole host that serves files over the NFS protocol. Some will use the term to refer to the whole NFS system: client hosts and server hosts sharing files. Others will assume that the NFS server is only the actual component or program that implements the NFS protocol: `rpc.nfsd` if in user-level, and `nfsd` or `knfsd` if running in the kernel. In this book, we endeavor to use terms that clearly distinguish these cases.

The *rpc.nfsd* Program

The *rpc.nfsd* supports only one option and also takes one argument. By default, `nfsd` listens on the reserved port 2049. If you want it to listen on a different port (for testing or security reasons), say 2050, run it as `rpc.nfsd -p 2050`.

When a client contacts `nfsd`, the server processes that client's request until completion. While the server processes that client request, other clients cannot contact the server. To solve this problem, multiple instances of the NFS server are usually started. For Linux, these instances are kernel threads. That way, the NFS server can process several requests at once. By default, Red Hat starts eight `nfsd` threads. If you have a particularly busy NFS server, and you wish to start 30 threads, you can run `rpc.nfsd 30` on that server.

NFS Version 1

Why did the first NFS protocol start at 2? Was there ever an NFS protocol version 1? Yes, there was one. It was a prototype NFS server used internally by Sun Microsystems at their labs. It was never released to the public. Most traces of any documentation or sources it had appear to have been lost over the past two decades. It was the same time that the RPC system was being developed as well. As Sun engineers were developing NFS, their first prototype changed enough that they decided to give it a new number. The main use of having two NFS protocol versions at that time was to make sure the RPC system and the NFS server were capable of handling multiple versions of the same RPC service, and that they could fall back to older versions if newer ones did not exist.

NFS Version 2

The first NFS protocol ever released publicly (in the early 80s) was version 2. Many of the procedures of this protocol have corresponding system calls. Recall that the key unit that describes a file is the NFS file handle. In the descriptions of the 18 protocol procedures below (including the NULL procedure) in this version, we will emphasize the purpose of the file handle where appropriate:

NFS_NULL   This is the ping procedure for testing to see if the nfsd is up and responding for a given protocol version.

NFS_GETATTR   This procedure gets the attributes of a file, such as the owner, group, and mode bits.

NFS_SETATTR   This procedure sets the attributes of a file, similar to what chmod, chgrp, and chown can do.

NFS_ROOT   This procedure is obsolete—it was never used or implemented. Its original intent was to return the root file handle of a file system, but this functionality was moved to the MOUNT protocol's MOUNTPROC_MNT function.

NFS_LOOKUP   This is one of the key procedures and it is invoked more often than other procedures. You give this procedure two key pieces of information: a file handle for a directory, and the name of a file you wish to find in that directory. The LOOKUP procedure checks to see if the file exists in that directory. If it does not, you get back an error code. If it does exist, this procedure returns a new file handle for the file just looked up. You can use this new file handle, for example, as an argument to the READ procedure in order to read data from that file.

NFS_READLINK   This procedure returns the value of a symbolic link, or what it points to. The returned value is usually an arbitrary string that the NFS client has to process one component at a time—an action also called *traversing a symlink*.

NFS_READ   This procedure reads a number of bytes from a file, given the file's handle, a start offset to read, and the number of bytes to read. You will notice that nowhere in the NFS protocol are there explicit procedures for opening, seeking into, or closing a file; this is due to the server's statelessness and the need for each procedure to be idempotent. A normal Unix kernel keeps state after you open a file; this state is captured by a file descriptor data structure that includes a pointer to the current read head within a file. That way, a read() system call can find the point where it left off on the last read and just read the next few bytes. But with NFS, we cannot keep state. That is why each NFS_READ call must specify the exact offset to begin reading from.

NFS_WRITECACHE   This is the second and last obsolete procedure in NFSv2. Its original intent was to improve the performance of the NFS server by allowing the server to cache data without writing it to disk (at a risk of data loss should the server crash). The idea was that the NFS server could cache data, and that the NFS client would know about it, and because of this, it would not assume that the data was written to stable storage. Then, the client would issue a WRITECACHE procedure to ensure that the data got written to disk. That way, the server could cache data and the client could force a bulk write of the data to disk.

This procedure was not implemented in NFSv2 for several reasons. First, it would have made the NFS server statefull. Second, the I/O daemon provided an alternate method for improving performance by clustering writes on the client's side. Third, it was thought that the NFSv2 protocol would evolve and this procedure could be implemented in the next version of the protocol. As it turned out, this procedure was not really implemented in NFSv3 either, and it was not until NFSv4 that serious performance issues were addressed at the protocol level.

NFS_WRITE   This procedure is very similar to the READ procedure above: it writes a number of bytes to a file from a given offset. Again, this procedure is idempotent for the same reasons that the READ procedure is.

NFS_CREATE   This procedure is akin to an open or creat system call. It creates a new file in a directory specified by the directory's file handle and returns the new file handle for the new file.

NFS_REMOVE   This procedure deletes a file from a directory, just as the unlink system call does.

NFS_RENAME   This procedure renames a file just as the rename system call does.

NFS_LINK   This procedure creates a hard-link to an existing file, just as the `link` system call does.

NFS_SYMLINK   This procedure creates a symbolic link, just as the `symlink` system call does.

NFS_MKDIR   This procedure creates a new directory, just as the `mkdir` system call does.

NFS_RMDIR   This procedure deletes an existing directory, just as the `rmdir` system call does.

NFS_READDIR   This procedure reads a number of entries in a directory, just as the `readdir` system call does. Note that the procedure does not necessarily return all of the entries in a directory. It may only return a subset of those and an indicator to the client that the client must pass back to the server. That opaque indicator helps the NFS server find where to resume reading directory entries (again, because the server must not keep any state).

NFS_STATFS   This procedure provides statistics on a remote file system, such as its size, how much of it is used, and how much remains. This is similar to the `statfs` system call and is used by programs such as `df`.

For the most part, the NFSv2 protocol returns to clients error codes that resemble normal system call return codes. A zero indicates success. Other error codes include NFSERR_ PERM (permission denied), NFSERR_NOENT (no such entry), and so on. The most popular error code that was newly added specifically for NFS was NFSERR_STALE. This one is returned when the NFS server is unable to decode the file handle that the client passed to it, a condition known as a *stale file handle*. A stale file handle occurs most often when an NFS server's file system is reformatted or mounted differently, but it could also occur as a result of network corruption or even a security break-in.

Like any protocol designed for the first time, NFSv2 was not without its own ambiguities and problems. One of the most serious ambiguities was in the precise meaning of the file handle—the file identifier that NFS servers create and pass to clients. Clients must not try to interpret the file handle's internal meaning (byte by byte). However, the protocol did not address the relationship between identical file handles and identical files. Specifically, it was not made clear if two identical file handles from the same server represent the same file, a hard-linked file by another name, or otherwise. It was also not made clear if two different file handles must represent different files. These and other concerns were addressed in future revisions of the NFS protocol.

NFS Version 3

More than a decade after the initial release of the NFS protocol, the next version was released by Sun. During that decade, NFS has gained immense popularity and was deployed on numerous systems. Experienced users and vendors alike were demanding a new protocol that would address serious problems with the NFSv2 protocol. With NFSv3, Sun made a good effort in addressing some of the most serious performance and security deficiencies in the protocol. The major changes in the protocol and its implementation included the following:

- Support for TCP transports as well as UDP. NFSv2 used only UDP because TCP was deemed too slow and costly at the time. Since TCP is a reliable transport and UDP is not, however, the NFSv2 protocol had to build its own reliability mechanism on top of UDP, which complicated its implementation. With TCP, much of that complication was removed.

- Support for 64-bit file systems. NFSv2 only handled 32-bit file systems, which limited the maximum file size to 2GB. NFSv3 greatly increases the maximum file size that can be used over NFS, more than eight billion gigabytes!

- Longer file handles. NFSv3 doubled the size of the file handle to 64 bytes. This was primarily done to make it more difficult for attackers to guess or fake file handles.

- Since NFSv2 used UDP, it limited the maximum number of bytes that could be transferred at once to 8KB. NFSv3 extends this range to 64KB. Ironically, the UDP specification allows up to 64KB bytes in a packet, but the original RPC implementation used by NFSv2 limited packet sizes to 8KB.

- To improve security, NFSv3 supports Kerberos authentication.

- To improve performance, new operations were created and file attributes are automatically returned on most calls, greatly reducing the number of times that some of the more popular procedures had to be invoked.

- To further improve performance, the NFSv3 server is allowed to cache data. This requires that NFSv3 clients know of this and are able to ask the server to commit cached data to stable storage.

The NFSv3 protocol has 22 procedures (including the NULL procedure), which we have listed below. Most of the procedures did not change. When a procedure remained basically the same, we did not describe it at length. Two unused procedures in NFSv2 were removed: ROOT and WRITECACHE.

NFSPROC3_NULL   Test if the `nfsd` for version 3 is up and running.

NFSPROC3_GETATTR   Get the attributes of a file.

NFSPROC3_SETATTR   Set the attributes of a file, such as owner and mode bits.

NFSPROC3_LOOKUP   Find a file in a directory. This procedure was improved by returning the mode of the directory in which it looked up the file. That way a client could tell if the mode bits of the directory had changed remotely, especially if they had changed so that the user is no longer allowed access.

NFSPROC3_ACCESS (new to NFSv3)   Test for access to a file, even if the file resides on a server that does not use traditional Unix mode bits, such as ACLs. Version 2 of the NFS protocol was very Unix centric, and assumed that all access to files was controlled by traditional Unix mode bits.

In addition, this procedure avoids problems with root users accessing files over NFSv2; in NFSv2, those root users could have their UID (0) mapped to nobody (for security reasons). But in NFSv2 this UID mapping was not handled consistently and could result in partial failures to access files by root. The new ACCESS procedure took care of that because NFS clients can test explicitly if access is granted before trying to read or write files.

NFSPROC3_READLINK   Return the value of a symbolic link.

NFSPROC3_READ   Read bytes from a file. This procedure was improved to better handle reading near the end of the file, where a read request may return fewer bytes than it was asked for.

NFSPROC3_WRITE   Write bytes from a file. This procedure was changed in two ways. First, it can indicate to clients that fewer bytes were written than were requested. Second, the write could be performed asynchronously, meaning that the data may remain cached in the server and a success status code is returned to the NFSv3 client.

NFSPROC3_CREATE   Create a new file. This procedure was improved to allow the creation to fail if the file already existed, a condition that could happen if multiple NFS clients try to create the same file at the same time.

NFSPROC3_MKDIR   Create a new directory.

NFSPROC3_SYMLINK   Create a symbolic link to a file.

NFSPROC3_MKNOD (new to NFSv3)   Create special files such as block and character devices. In NFSv2, creation of these files was done as special cases of the CREATE procedure.

NFSPROC3_REMOVE   Delete a file.

NFSPROC3_RMDIR   Delete a directory.

NFSPROC3_RENAME   Rename a file.

NFSPROC3_LINK   Create a hard-link to a file.

NFSPROC3_READDIR   Read a number of entries for a directory. This procedure was improved in NFSv3 to extend the number of bits used to describe the offsets of directory entries in a directory, thus allowing for better interoperability with other systems.

NFSPROC3_READDIRPLUS (new to NFSv3)   Improve the performance for some of the most popular operations. Often, when users list the contents of a directory, they run ls -l. To accomplish this in NFSv2, first the contents of the directory had to be retrieved (READDIR) and then the attributes of each entry had to be found (GETATTR). Most READDIR operations in NFSv2 were followed by a flurry of GETATTR requests.

The READDIRPLUS improves the performance of this common operation. In one message, it returns a list of entries in a directory as well as the attributes for each. This greatly reduces server and network load.

NFSPROC3_FSSTAT (renamed in NFSv3)   Provides the same statistics on a remote file system as the older STATFS procedure performed in NFSv2, such as its current and maximum size, total and current number of available inodes (which was not always available in NFSv2), etc.

NFSPROC3_FSINFO (new to NFSv3)   Helps interoperability between different systems. It returns to the caller information about the remote file system, such as whether the file system supports symlinks and hard links, what the preferred and maximum read and write sizes are, and more.

NFSPROC3_PATHCONF (new to NFSv3)   Returns file system parameters about the server, such as the maximum allowed length for a path name, the maximum length for a file name, etc. (added to comply with POSIX standards and especially the pathconf system call).

NFSPROC3_COMMIT (new to NFSv3)   Instructs an NFS server to flush all cached data onto stable storage. Since the WRITE procedure in NFSv3 allows asynchronous writes, this COMMIT procedure became necessary so that NFS clients could ensure that the data they sent was written reliably. Together, the asynchronous WRITE and COMMIT procedures help to improve the performance of NFS in version 3.

On a quiet local area network with little stress on NFS servers, NFSv2 may work just as well as NFSv3. But you will most likely prefer NFSv3 if one or more of these conditions exist:

- You want your Linux system to interoperate with many other systems.
- You want to increase the reliability of your NFS service, through the use of a better-defined protocol.

- You want better performance for busy servers.
- Your networks exhibit high latency or performance that varies constantly.

The next version of the NFS protocol, NFSv4, greatly improves over NFSv3 and changes it significantly. For one, the server is no longer stateless and other RPC protocols (MOUNT, RQUOTA, locking and status) are now integrated into the protocol. The NFSv4 standard is now complete, but it is still new. A few prototype implementations exist, including one for Linux. We discuss NFSv4 in more detail in Chapter 6, "NFS Version 4." Next, we show a full example of the operation of NFS with existing protocols.

An Example

Now that we have discussed all of the various components of the NFS system individually, as well as the protocols used, we are ready to examine how the system works in practice. We show this through a simple example: a client named moon that wishes to access a file system named /home from a server named earth.

Start by setting up the NFS server. First, make sure that all the right programs are running. The steps to start the various NFS services on the server are in Listing 1.7.

Listing 1.7   Enabling and starting NFS server services

```
[root]# chkconfig nfslock on
[root]# chkconfig nfs on
[root]# /etc/rc.d/init.d/nfslock restart
[root]# /etc/rc.d/init.d/nfs restart
```

Next, we have to allow the client host to mount the NFS server's file system. Do this by configuring a file named /etc/exports, as seen in Listing 1.8.

Listing 1.8   An example NFS server /etc/exports file

```
/home       moon(rw)
```

The /etc/exports entry from Listing 1.8 tells the NFS server to allow access to the /home file system to a host named moon. Right after the hostname, in parentheses, we list the permission options for host moon. The rw indicates that client host will be allowed to write to that file system.

Finally, ensure that the various NFS programs are aware of the changes to the /etc/exports file by running the exportfs program, as seen in Listing 1.9.

Listing 1.9   Exporting file systems to an NFS client

```
[root]# exportfs -rv
```

The exportfs program informs rpc.mountd of any changes in the list of allowed file systems to export. Verify that the NFS server is running by checking with rpcinfo, as seen in Listing 1.10.

Listing 1.10   Checking that all NFS server services are running

```
[ezk]$ rpcinfo -p
   program vers proto   port
    100000    2  tcp     111  portmapper
    100000    2  udp     111  portmapper
    100024    1  udp     957  status
    100024    1  tcp     959  status
    100011    1  udp     728  rquotad
    100011    2  udp     728  rquotad
    100003    2  udp    2049  nfs
    100003    3  udp    2049  nfs
    100021    1  udp    1026  nlockmgr
    100021    3  udp    1026  nlockmgr
    100021    4  udp    1026  nlockmgr
    100005    1  udp    1027  mountd
    100005    1  tcp    1024  mountd
    100005    2  udp    1027  mountd
    100005    2  tcp    1024  mountd
    100005    3  udp    1027  mountd
    100005    3  tcp    1024  mountd
```

At this stage the NFS server is set up. Now configure the NFS client. First, ensure that the client-side NFS software is available. Assuming that support for the NFS file system is either compiled into the kernel or available as a loadable module, then run the commands seen in Listing 1.11 to ensure that nfs appears in the listing of /proc/filesystems.

Listing 1.11   Checking for NFS client-side support

```
[root]# modprobe nfs
[root]# grep nfs /proc/filesystems
nodev   nfs
```

The next stage is to configure the local client's configuration files so that the remote file system is mounted at boot time. Add an entry to /etc/fstab to do this, as seen in Listing 1.12.

Listing 1.12 An example NFS client-side /etc/fstab file

```
# device      mountpoint  fs-type  options  dump  fsckorder
earth:/home   /home       nfs      rw       0     0
```

Use the /etc/fstab entry in Listing 1.12 to configure the NFS client to mount the /home partition from server earth onto the /home directory (mount point) of the local host, and then use the mount options that allow the client to read and write the remote file system. To test that the entry worked, you can either reboot your client or simply run the mount command as seen in Listing 1.13.

Listing 1.13 Mount all NFS entries in /etc/fstab

```
[root]# mount -a -t nfs
```

Note that you could also mount the remote file system by hand, as seen in Listing 1.14, without the need to specify it in /etc/fstab.

Listing 1.14 One-time mounting an NFS server by hand

```
[root]# mount -t nfs earth:/home /home
```

After running the mount command, you can run df to see that the entry is indeed mounted, and then you could inspect the /home directory on the host moon to see what contents it has:

```
[ezk]$ df
Filesystem            1k-blocks     Used Available Use% Mounted on
/dev/sda1                879078   820825     12840  98% /
earth:/home             6224742  5352649    554811  91% /home
[ezk]$ ls -F /home
ezk/    martha/   lost+found/
```

At this point, you can access files in /home as if they were local. If you wish to unmount the file system, run the command as seen in Listing 1.15.

Listing 1.15 Unmounting an NFS file system

```
[root]# umount /home
```

You will notice that unmounting an NFS file system is no different from unmounting any other file system. That is because NFS integrates so seamlessly with the rest of the system. Despite this seamlessness, NFS performs many actions in the background.

The Network File System

PART 1

We now describe what happens when you try to access a file from a remote NFS server, say, by reading the contents of /home/ezk/.profile. Refer back to Figure 1.1, which shows the flow of data and operations for a read operation like the one below:

1. A user process calls the read system call.

2. The system call is translated in the kernel into an nfs_read function and the NFS client-side code is invoked.

3. The NFS client encodes the information and calls the RPC procedure NFS_READ.

4. The RPC information is encoded via XDR and transmitted over the network to the NFS server.

5. The server host receives the encoded data and decodes it via XDR.

6. An RPC message is constructed and passed on the NFS server nfsd.

7. nfsd calls nfsd_read.

8. nfsd_read is translated into a disk read via ext2_read.

9. The data is read from the disk and passed back to nfsd.

10. nfsd passes the data back in the reverse order of all previous steps until in reaches the user process on the client.

In Sum

The Network File System allows users to share files among many machines seamlessly: users do not know if they are accessing files locally or remotely. NFS was designed to interoperate with many other systems so that users could get their files no matter where they were physically stored. That is one of NFS's greatest strengths and it is what contributed to its popularity—it is the most widely used remote-access file system.

The inner workings of NFS are complex. The system is broken into components that run on the client side and components that run on the server side. Both sides are layered on top of Remote Procedures Calls, which in turn are layered on top of XDRs, which is a method for encoding data in a consistent manner that can be interpreted identically by all clients and servers regardless of the operating system they run on. To add to this, primarily because of the original stateless design of the NFS server, there are many other components that are part of NFS. These include the following: an I/O daemon for improving performance, locking and status daemons for handling file and record locks, a portmapper for brokering all RPC services, a mount daemon for authenticating mount requests, and a quota daemon for providing quota information to NFS clients. Finally, the NFS system uses several configuration and state files. In this chapter, we only described a few. We describe all configuration and state files in more detail in the next chapter.

Despite its complexity, NFS is relatively simple to use. Administrators list file systems to export in one file, and file systems to mount in another configuration file. Restarting the NFS client's and server's programs and mounting remote file systems then allows users to access those remote volumes. The greatest benefit is to users—who notice no difference if the files are local or remote.

In this chapter, we described the various components of NFS and its protocols. We also showed a simple example of its basic use. In the following chapters, we show NFS's operation and configuration in greater detail. We will also cover important issues, such as performance optimizations, security, how to debug and correct problems in your NFS system, and how to add NFS support into your Linux system.

The Network File System

PART 1

.

2

Configuring NFS

The NFS system is simple to use but complex to configure. The system has a server side and a client side that must be configured separately. Moreover, both client and server must agree on various parameters such as protocol levels, network transports, access permissions, and more. While both the server and client have one configuration file each that administrators generally maintain, administrators must carefully choose among dozens of options and flags. The server-side configuration file for exported file systems must list the exact volumes available for access, whom to grant such access, and under what conditions to grant access. The client-side configuration file for mounted file systems must list remote NFS servers to mount, the file systems to mount, and local mount points. Additionally, this configuration file must choose among many mount options that can significantly affect behavior.

While on the surface administrators maintain only two primary configuration files, underneath, the NFS system maintains over a dozen more state files. These files are controlled automatically by several more daemons and tools, some of which are the side effects of administrator actions performed locally or remotely.

In this chapter we describe the primary files used by the NFS system, both configuration and state files. We describe their function and format and the tools that control them. In addition, we list all server-side and client-side configuration options for exporting and mounting file systems, respectively. We explain what each option does and when to use it. Our descriptions begin with the NFS server side, which must be configured first. We then proceed to discuss the NFS client side, which is configured afterward. By the end of this chapter, you will know how to configure a basic site with NFS clients and NFS servers.

Preparing to Configure NFS

The NFS system includes a client-side part and a server-side part. The first choice you must make is to decide which of the two you have to configure. This may seem like a trivial decision but it is a commonly confused one. Administrators configure a server when they need a client, or vice versa. Worse, they may configure both when only one is needed, or confuse which configuration parts belong to which side, resulting in a frustrating system setup that does not work and requires much debugging.

Configure your host as a server when your computer contains some local disks that you want other hosts to have access to; this is the NFS server-side configuration. Allowing another host to access a local disk is called *exporting* a file system.

Configure your host as a client when you want your computer to access some files on disks that physically reside on another computer; this is the NFS client-side configuration. Accessing a remote file server is called *mounting* a file system.

If your computer needs to allow other hosts to access its local files, as well as to access other hosts' files, then you should configure it both as an NFS server and as an NFS client. Either way, always set up your NFS servers first and then the clients. This is because you cannot test that your clients work before the servers are configured completely.

The next decision you need to make is which software you should have on your system. On an NFS server, the most important decisions are to ensure that your kernel supports the right NFS services and that you include the mount daemon `rpc.mountd`. On an NFS client, ensure that your kernel includes the NFS file system and that you have the right mount utilities, including `/bin/mount`. For more details on your software needs, refer to Chapter 1, "NFS Basics and Protocols." For details on how to build or install NFS software, refer to Chapter 7, "Building and Installing the Linux Kernel and NFS Software."

The NFS system uses many files. Some files are for the NFS server only, others are for the NFS client only, and some are for both. Some files are configuration files that users must edit, and others record the state of various tools. Table 2.1 lists all of these files. The table lists each file, which tools or subsystems use it, the parts of the NFS system that these files are used on, the type of file it is (configuration file or state file), and finally a brief description of the file. We describe the primary server-side and client-side files in this chapter. We defer detailed discussion of security-related files to Chapter 4, "Securing NFS."

Table 2.1   Files Used by NFS

File	Used By	Side	Type	Meaning
/etc/exports	exportfs, rpc.mountd	Server	Config	File systems to share and hosts allowed access to them
/etc/fstab	/bin/mount	Client	Config	File systems to mount
/etc/hosts	All	Both	Config	Names of other hosts (can also be configured in DNS)
/etc/hosts.allow	RPC services	Server	Config	Hosts to allow access
/etc/hosts.deny	RPC services	Server	Config	Hosts not allowed access
/etc/mtab	/bin/mount	Client	State	Currently mounted file systems
/proc/fs/nfs/exports	kernel, rpc.mountd, rpc.nfsd	Server	State	Kernel view of export list
/proc/mounts	Kernel	Client	State	Kernel view of mounted file systems
quota.group	rpc.rquotad	Server	Config	Quota information for groups in the root directory of each quota-enabled file system
quota.user	rpc.rquotad	Server	Config	Quota information for users in the root directory of each quota-enabled file system

Table 2.1   Files Used by NFS *(continued)*

File	Used By	Side	Type	Meaning
/var/lib/nfs/etab	rpc.mountd, rpc.nfsd	Server	State	Current high-level exports list
/var/lib/nfs/rmtab	rpc.mountd	Server	State	Lists of remote clients mounting exported file systems
/var/lib/nfs/sm/*	rpc.statd	Both	State	Status monitor state files
/var/lib/nfs/sm.bak/*	rpc.statd	Both	State	Backup of status monitor state files
/var/lib/nfs/state	rpc.statd	Both	State	State of the status monitor itself
/var/lib/nfs/xtab	exportfs, rpc.mountd	Server	State	Current low-level exports list

Interaction of Server Programs and Files

In this section we describe the complex interactions between the core components that run on the NFS server and the main files that they use. Figure 2.1 shows them. We recommend a good night's sleep before attempting to understand this figure and its accompanying description.

These interactions are complex for three reasons:

- The NFS server must coordinate efforts with potentially many NFS clients, by design.
- The Linux NFS implementation of exported volumes is more flexible and powerful than other systems. With this flexibility comes added complexity.
- The NFS system is split between user-level and kernel-level components. It is easier for each part to keep its own view of the configuration or the state files in its own level.

Figure 2.1   Files used on the NFS server and the programs controlling them

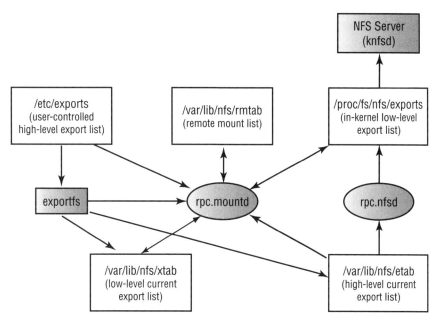

We begin by describing the meaning and use of each file in Figure 2.1. Then we describe how these files are used by the four program components in the same figure.

The */etc/exports* File

The /etc/exports file is a configuration file that administrators edit manually to describe file systems they wish to export to specific hosts or ranges of hosts (using net-groups, wildcards, or a subnet of hosts). The ability to export a single entry to a range of hosts allows more flexibility but must be handled securely and is one of the main reasons other files are needed.

The */var/lib/nfs/xtab* File

The /var/lib/nfs/xtab file is a state file that is considered the *low-level exports* list. It contains specific entries for each client host that actually requested NFS access to an exported file system. Suppose your /etc/exports file lists a wildcard export entry for *.example.com, such as the following:

```
/home        *.example.com(rw)
```

Many hosts could match this domain. If two hosts—`rens` and `timpy`—each ask for access to an exported file system, the `/var/lib/nfs/xtab` will contain two separate and almost identical entries for that file system:

```
/home        rens.example.com(rw)

/home        timpy.example.com(rw)
```

The reason a separate `/var/lib/nfs/xtab` file exists is to have fine-grained control over actual file systems exported to specific hosts, and to preserve the list of in-kernel mounts across reboots.

The /var/lib/nfs/rmtab File

When an NFS client wishes to mount a file system, it must first contact the `rpc.mountd` server using the MOUNTPROC_MNT RPC procedure. When the client is done, it can inform `rpc.mountd` using the MOUNTPROC_UMNT RPC procedure. Both procedures are described with the MOUNT RPC protocol in Chapter 1. When the mount daemon gets these two procedures, it updates the `/var/lib/nfs/rmtab` accordingly: a MOUNTPROC_MNT procedure adds an entry and the MOUNTPROC_UMNT procedure removes one.

Note that just because an NFS client checked for export permissions, or told the mount daemon that it intends to mount or unmount a file system, does *not* mean that it will do so. These RPC requests are advisory at best; NFS clients may not mount, use, or unmount the file systems they queried about. This is a deficiency of the NFSv2 and NFSv3 protocols—that intended actions and actual ones could differ. For these reasons, the `/var/lib/nfs/rmtab` file should not be considered authoritative; the information it has could be stale and otherwise completely inaccurate. On most well-maintained systems, however, the contents of this file could provide a reasonable approximation of which NFS clients have recently mounted the server's file systems.

The /var/lib/nfs/etab File

The `/var/lib/nfs/etab` file is a state file that is considered the *high-level exports* list. It contains all the entries listed in `/etc/exports` in the same format, but also entries that were manually exported by `exportfs -i`. The `-i` option tells `exportfs` not to use the `/etc/exports` file but to export the entry whose parameters are listed on the command line, as seen in Listing 2.6. The reason we have this separate file from `/etc/exports` is exactly because Linux allows you to add more exported entries without going through the `/etc/exports` file.

The /proc/fs/nfs/exports File

The `/proc/fs/nfs/exports` file represents the kernel's view of the low-level export list. The kernel keeps this list so it can update it quickly to verify export permissions. It is faster for the kernel-level NFS server (knfsd) to keep its own copy of this list so it does not have to access it from the disk in /var/lib/nfs/xtab. Note that the kernel's version of this information is volatile and goes away after the kernel is rebooted; the /var/lib/nfs/xtab file, on the other hand, contains the same information persistently since it is stored in a file on disk.

The *exportfs* Command

The exportfs command updates several files and informs other components of changes in the export list. If you run exportfs -a, it reads the /etc/exports file and then updates the low-level current export list file /var/lib/nfs/xtab for any single-host entry listed in /etc/exports. It does not do so for multihost specification (netgroups, wildcards, and network subnets) because /var/lib/nfs/xtab contains individual export entries, one per host.

For all entries listed in /etc/exports (single-host and multihost entries), exportfs informs rpc.mountd about them. The mount daemon, in turn, saves them in the /var/lib/nfs/etab file.

When you run exportfs -i to add a single entry to the export table, exportfs updates /var/lib/nfs/xtab with that entry and informs rpc.mountd to add an entry to the high-level export list file /var/lib/nfs/etab.

Finally, if you run exportfs -u, it removes individual host entries /var/lib/nfs/xtab and also informs rpc.mountd to remove entries from its respective state files.

The *rpc.mountd* Command

The rpc.mountd command has the most complex interaction with the rest of the NFS system. When rpc.mountd starts, it reads the user-controlled configuration file /etc/exports, the low-level export list /var/lib/nfs/xtab, and the high-level export list /var/lib/nfs/etab. The mount daemon reads all three files to find the most accurate export information and looks for entries in /etc/exports that may not have been exported manually. It looks in /var/lib/nfs/xtab and /var/lib/nfs/etab for entries that might have been exported manually using exportfs -i. Once rpc.mountd determines the most up-to-date export list, it updates /var/lib/nfs/xtab and /var/lib/nfs/etab as needed. It then provides the kernel an accurate list of exports by updating the /proc/fs/nfs/exports file directly.

The mount daemon listens for MOUNT protocol requests from NFS clients to add and remove entries in the remote mount table file /var/lib/nfs/rmtab and performs those operations. The rpc.mountd server also looks for entries in the /var/lib/nfs/rmtab file that are not recorded elsewhere and inserts those entries in the kernel's export list file /proc/fs/nfs/exports.

The rpc.mountd server is responsible for returning NFS handles to NFS clients. It also determines which version of NFS to return NFS handles for: NFSv2 or NFSv3. By default, Red Hat 7's rpc.mountd does not return NFSv3 file handles, only NFSv2. If you upgrade the Red Hat kernel on your system to include support for NFSv3 and you wish to run that system as an NFS server, you should edit the NFS startup script /etc/rc.d/init.d/nfs. Near the top of that file you will see two lines that read as follows:

```
# No NFS V3.
RPCMOUNTDOPTS="--no-nfs-version 3"
```

You should turn off that --no-nfs-version option. Edit those lines to read the following:

```
# Support both NFSv2 and NFSv3
RPCMOUNTDOPTS=""
```

Then restart your NFS service:

```
[root]# /etc/rc.d/init.d/nfs restart
Shutting down NFS mountd:                                  [  OK  ]
Shutting down NFS daemon:                                  [  OK  ]
Shutting down NFS services:                                [  OK  ]
Shutting down NFS quotas:                                  [  OK  ]
Starting NFS services:                                     [  OK  ]
Starting NFS quotas:                                       [  OK  ]
Starting NFS mountd:                                       [  OK  ]
Starting NFS daemon:                                       [  OK  ]
```

The *rpc.nfsd* Command and the *knfsd* Module

The NFS server proper has two components: the user-level startup daemon rpc.nfsd and the kernel-level module knfsd. The latter is of course the part that runs the actual NFS server code. The user-level program rpc.nfsd has several simple functions when it starts up: it reads the high-level export list /var/lib/nfs/etab and inserts it into the kernel's export list /proc/fs/nfs/exports. It then starts the in-kernel NFS server knfsd, which reads the export list from the in-kernel export list that is already available.

The */etc/hosts.allow* and */etc/hosts.deny* Files

The /etc/hosts.allow and /etc/hosts.deny files define which hosts are allowed to access particular services on the localhost. The files are part of the TCP wrapper system, a system to filter undesired hosts from accessing your system. We describe these files in more detail in Chapter 4.

The *quota.group* and *quota.user* Files

The quota.group and quota.user files are used by the quota system and are located in the root (top-level) directories of each quota-enabled file system. They list the quota information for Unix groups and users, respectively, for the file system in which they reside.

Files Used on the Client Side

Administrators only need to update a few configuration files on the NFS client. In comparison, an NFS server is more complex to configure: it uses many files and runs many programs. It is fortunate that an NFS client is simpler to configure because, typically, site administrators configure only a few NFS servers but many NFS clients.

The */etc/fstab* File

The /etc/fstab file lists the file systems (remote and local) that would be mounted at boot time, the servers they would mount from, the local mount points, the mount access options to use during a mount, and information on backup and file system checking options.

The */etc/mtab* File

The /etc/mtab file lists the names of the file systems that this host mounts and which servers it mounts them from. This file is updated by the /bin/mount tool, which is responsible for ensuring that the file is kept up-to-date with the actual list of mounts that the kernel knows about.

The */proc/mounts* File

The /proc/mounts file is a kernel-status file that shows the list of actively mounted file systems that the kernel knows about. This file is part of the /proc file system.

Files Used by Both Servers and Clients

A few files are used by both NFS servers and clients. These refer mostly to the definitions of hostnames and IP addresses and to the NSM protocol that NFS uses to store (lock) state about files.

The */etc/hosts* File

The /etc/hosts file lists the names and *Internet Protocol* (IP) addresses of all hosts that this computer needs to access. This is a local file on each host. However, most Linux systems probably use the *Domain Name System* (DNS) to resolve hosts' names and their IP addresses.

The Network File System

PART 1

The */var/lib/nfs/sm/* Directory

The directory /var/lib/nfs/sm/ contains files used by the status monitoring system, as explained in Chapter 1. Each file in this directory is named after the IP address of the host-name for which status is being monitored. The NFS system uses the status monitoring system to record file locks that NFS clients hold.

The */var/lib/nfs/sm.bak/* Directory

The directory /var/lib/nfs/sm.bak/ contains backup status files used by the status monitor. It uses backup files to ensure the consistency of this important state.

The */var/lib/nfs/state* File

The file /var/lib/nfs/state is an internal file used by the status monitoring system. It records the state of the rpc.statd program. When a host crashes and then reboots, this file helps rpc.statd determine what it was doing just prior to the crash.

Configuring an NFS Server

Before you can configure an NFS server, your system must already have the necessary NFS server-side software installed, as described in Chapter 1. Once the software is installed and running, configure your NFS server by following these two steps:

1. Edit your /etc/exports file to permit remote hosts to access your server.
2. Run the exportfs program to propagate changes in the exports file to the rest of the daemons on your server.

At this stage, do not concern yourself too much about performance or security. We cover those topics in the next two chapters. The NFS system is complex enough so that if you try to set up many configuration files all at once, you could easily make mistakes and waste time debugging erroneous configurations. Work one step at a time. While both performance and security are important, you should first get a basic NFS client-server working, and then worry about performance optimizations. Security, depending on your site's concerns, may be necessary to set up right away. In that case, we recommend that you first configure your NFS servers and clients on a private network. Once they work, secure your system. Only then should you expose your NFS servers to the rest of the world.

Configuring Exported Volumes

List the server's file systems that you want to allow NFS clients to access in the /etc/ exports file. This file identifies exported file systems and the access permissions for each file system. This text-based file is usually edited by the site's administrators. Blank lines and comments beginning with a "#" are ignored. Long entries may be broken over multiple lines using a backslash character. The syntax of an entry in this file is shown in Listing 2.1.

Listing 2.1   Syntax of an entry in the /etc/exports file

```
volname     hostspec1(opt1,opt2,...)  hostspec2(opt1,opt2,...) \
            hostspecN(opt1,opt2,...)
```

Each entry in the /etc/exports file begins with a volume name, a path name that lists the directory to export. Note that this directory does not have to be exactly the name of one of the host's file systems; it can be a subdirectory of those. This is why we call it a volume name, to avoid confusion with the file system's name. This feature allows NFS servers to grant access permissions to a subset of their file systems, thus providing finer-grained security and control.

After the volume name, you can list zero or more whitespace-delimited export specifications. Each export specification has two optional parts: the *hostspec* part and the parenthesized list of export options to apply to this *hostspec*. Either *hostspec* or the list of export options is optional, even both. Since whitespace delimits export specifications, it is important not to include whitespace between mount options or between the host specification and the parenthesized list of options.

If you only list a host specification without any options, the export options default to read-only. This means that NFS clients can only access files in this volume for reading, not for writing. If you only specify export options, the host specification part defaults to all hosts. If you list no export specifications after the volume name, you automatically export this volume to all hosts using the read-only export permissions.

The host specification is very flexible in what it can describe, anywhere from a single host to any number of hosts at once. You can describe hosts using four syntax styles:

A single host   To specify a single host, list either its short name or its fully qualified name; for example, earth or earth.example.com. You may also specify the IP address of a single host.

A netgroup   You can list a whole group of hosts as defined in your /etc/netgroup file or in your NIS netgroup map. Netgroup names begin with the @ symbol; for example, @laptops or @cpu-servers.

Wildcard hosts   You can list all the hosts within a domain, as they match the wildcard characters * and ?. The * matches zero or more characters, while the ? matches exactly one character. For example, to match all the hosts inside example.com, specify the host specification as *.example.com. Note, however, that these wildcards do not match dots in the hostnames. Therefore, *.example.com does not match moon.qa.example.com. To match the latter, you have to specify *.*.example.com.

Suppose your site contains several hosts named `linux-a.example.com`, `linux-b.example.com`, `linux-c.example.com`, etc. To match these specific hosts, you can use the export specification `linux-?.example.com`. This will match a single character but will not match a host that is named `linux-xy.example.com`.

A network of hosts   This export specification allows you to pick a particular subnet on your site, or even several subnets together, using the familiar *address/netmask* syntax. That is, you specify the IP address of your network, followed by a forward slash symbol, and then followed by the netmask number to apply. For example, the specification `128.59.18.0/255.255.255.0` will match all of the hosts whose IP addresses range from 128.59.18.0 through 128.59.18.255. (Note that in practice the all-ones .255 address is the broadcast address of the network and is never used as an actual IP address for a host on the Internet.)

The last part of the exports list we have yet to describe is the list of options. This list is comma delimited and must not include spaces. It can be of any length. The full list of options is shown in Table 2.2. We name the option, specify whether it is on or off by default, state whether it is a security- or performance-related option, and include a brief description of the option.

Most options are Boolean options: they turn a feature either on or off. Of those, the majority of options have a given name whose inverse is prefixed by `no` (e.g., `hide` and `nohide`).

Table 2.2   NFS Server Export Options

Option	Default	Type	Meaning
async	On	Perf	Write data to disk asynchronously (not when client asks for it).
sync	Off	Perf	Write data to disk as soon as client performs write operation.
wdelay	On	Perf	Delay synchronous writes to allow for aggregation.
no_wdelay	Off	Perf	Do not delay synchronous writes.
ro	On	Sec	Allow read-only access to this file system.
rw	Off	Sec	Allow read and write access to this file system.

Table 2.2   NFS Server Export Options *(continued)*

Option	Default	Type	Meaning
root_squash	On	Sec	Map UID 0 (root) requests to UID -2 (nobody).
no_root_squash	Off	Sec	Do not map UID 0 requests.
all_squash	Off	Sec	Map all UIDs and GIDs to -2 (nobody).
no_all_squash	On	Sec	Do not map all UIDs and GIDs.
anonuid=N	-2	Sec	Set the default UID of user nobody to N.
anongid=N	-2	Sec	Set the default GID of group nobody to N.
secure	On	Sec	Allow requests originating from ports smaller than 1024.
insecure	Off	Sec	Allow requests from originating ports greater than 1024.
secure_locks	On	Sec	Authenticate NLM protocol requests.
insecure_locks	Off	Sec	Do not authenticate NLM protocol requests.
auth_nlm	On	Sec	Synonymous with secure_locks.
no_auth_nlm	Off	Sec	Synonymous with insecure_locks.
subtree_check	On	Sec	Certify that a file handle belongs to an exported subtree of a whole file system.
no_subtree_check	Off	Sec	Do not certify that a file handle belongs to an exported subtree of a whole file system.
hide	On	Sec	Do not expose subsidiary mounted file systems below this mount point.
nohide	Off	Sec	Expose subsidiary mounted file systems below this mount point.

The options in Table 2.2 are server-side export options. In the upcoming section "Configuring an NFS Client," we describe the client-side mount options. Some of the server export options also exist as client mount options. In the case of conflicts, the server's options always take precedence. This policy is designed for better security, because the server is the ultimate controller of the actual local file system that NFS clients may mount.

The options in Table 2.2 relate either to performance or to security. We briefly survey these options next.

Performance Export Options

On the server side are only a handful of performance options, all relating to how the server handles writes that the client performs. If you use the sync option, the server will commit any write request it gets from the client immediately to disk. The server will not return a reply to the client until the write has completed. While this improves reliability, it slows performance. The async option tells the server not to write the data to disk right away, but to schedule it at a later time.

Even with the sync option in place, the server tries to improve performance by clustering related write requests for consecutive writes to the same file. When the server has to perform one write, it checks to see if there is another pending write request for the next chunk of data. If so, it may delay the first write request and then perform several write requests in one disk operation. This can improve performance, but it does decrease reliability, since not performing client-side write requests immediately can increase the chances for the server to go down and for data to be lost. For that reason, you can specify the no_wdelay option to turn off any write delay that the server may try to use.

Security Export Options

There are many more security options than there are performance options, because the server is in the best position to secure the data it exports to NFS clients.

The first two security options determine if the server allows clients to write to the file system or not: rw vs. ro. The next set of security options determines the handling of UID 0 (root), also called *squashing*. Squashing is the mapping of a UID to another by the server, to protect from client-side users trying to gain unauthorized access, especially as a superuser. The root_squash option does that by mapping the UID 0 to nobody, thus restricting root access. The all_squash option maps all UIDs (root and non-root) to nobody to prevent any user from accessing files using their UID. The value of the nobody mapped user is -2 by default and can be changed using the anonuid option.

The next set of options determines which port numbers NFS requests must come in on: a secure port that is less than 1024, or an insecure port over 1024. The secure_locks option forces authentication of NFS Lock Manager requests, a feature that not every NFS client supports.

The last set of options deals with the issues of exporting parts of file systems or their sub-mounts. In Linux, you do not have to export a whole file system but only a subset of it that we call a *volume*. However, an NFS server must authenticate all NFS client requests that arrive to a volume to ensure that the request does not attempt to access other unex-ported portions of the file system. This is called *subtree checking* and can be turned off using no_subtree_check. In addition, you may export a volume that may have other file systems mounted underneath it. The hide option ensures that NFS clients cannot see the second mounted file system under the exported one. The nohide option reverses this and descends into the second file system without the client knowing this.

An Example

We illustrate the configuration of a complex /etc/exports file in the example of Listing 2.2.

Listing 2.2   An example /etc/exports file

```
# exports file for server earth.example.com
/proj           moon
/scratch
/home           @workstations(rw) master(rw,no_root_squash)
/home/martha    winpc(rw,all_squash,anonuid=2301,anongid=90)
/usr            *.example.com(ro)
/usr/X11R6      128.59.0.0/255.255.0.0(ro) @masters(rw)
/n/ftp/pub      (ro,all_squash,no_auth_nlm,insecure)
```

The first line in the /etc/exports example of Listing 2.2 is a comment and is ignored. The meaning of the remaining lines is as follows:

/proj   This directory is exported to host moon. Since no export options were spec-ified, they default to ro, meaning that host moon can only read files under /proj but not modify them.

/scratch   Since no hosts are listed, this directory is exported to *all* hosts. Since no options were specified, they default to ro.

/home   This directory is exported to two host sets. The first is the netgroup @workstations, which can include any number of hosts listed in your NIS netgroup map or in your /etc/netgroup file. Hosts in this netgroup get read and write access. The next host set is the single host named master. This host gets read and write access as well as access as root; this is what the no_root_squash option does.

/home/martha   This directory is a subdirectory of /home and is exported with different options. The reason you may want this is to provide general options for a given file system and then override them for a subset of that file system. The /home/martha directory is exported to the host winpc, an MS-DOS PC acting as an NFS client. Often, such operating systems do not support multiple users and require special handling: mapping all UIDs and GIDs to a single number. This is done first by setting all UIDs and GIDs to the anonymous one (all_squash), and then by setting the anonymous UID and the anonymous GID to the preferred numbers that represent that user on the Linux NFS server (anonuid=2301 and anongid=90, respectively).

/usr   Here we export all of /usr with read-only permissions to all hosts that are part of the example.com domain.

/usr/X11R6   This entry specifically changes the export permissions of this subdirectory of /usr. First it allows all hosts in the class B network 128.59 read-only access. This is specified using the network/netmask syntax. Then it allows all hosts in the @masters netgroup read-write access.

/n/ftp/pub   This last entry does not provide a host specification and thus applies to all hosts. It is a public FTP directory that is exported to the world for NFS access. Therefore the export permissions are very strict: read-only, squashing all UIDs and GIDs, not performing NFS Lock Manager authentication (no_auth_nlm), and ensuring that NFS requests do not come from secure ports.

Careful Use of Whitespace in /etc/exports

When specifying export files, be careful about spaces. A single space character can make a very big difference. The following entry exports the /home partition to host titan with read-write and superuser access privileges:

```
/home titan(rw,no_root_squash)
```

A typical mistake administrators make is to place a space before the list of options:

```
/home titan (rw,no_root_squash)
```

This entry has a very different meaning: it exports the /home partition to host titan with read-only permissions. Then, it exports the same partition to the any host (worldwide) with read-write and superuser privileges.

Exporting Volumes

After setting all the exported volumes, hosts, and export options in your /etc/exports file, you should inform your NFS server of the changes you made. This is done using the exportfs command, whose usage is depicted in Listing 2.3.

Listing 2.3   Usage of the exportfs command

```
exportfs [-avi] [-o options,..] [client:/path ..]
exportfs -r [-v]
exportfs [-av] -u [client:/path ..]
exportfs [-v]
```

The usage of exportfs falls into four categories. You can specify a number of options that affect if you are exporting or unexporting volumes, as well as options to affect one volume, a few, or all volumes. We describe these options now.

-a   Apply the export or unexport option to all volumes.

-o *ARG*   List a number of comma-delimited export options in *ARG*. The options are the same as those listed in Table 2.2.

-i   By default, exportfs uses the information listed in the /etc/exports file. This option tells it to ignore the /etc/exports file and instead take the export information as specified on the command line.

-r   Export all volumes again. This is useful to reinitialize your NFS server's internal list of exports, adding new entries listed in /etc/exports, removing those that are no longer there, and changing the permissions of those volumes for which the export options have changed.

-u   Remove export information from your NFS server. If used with -a, removes all export information. If used with a command-line export option, only unexport that entry.

-v   Show what the exportfs command is doing verbosely.

We follow with a few examples. To export all volumes listed in your /etc/exports for the first time, run exportfs -a as seen in Listing 2.4.

Listing 2.4   Exporting all volumes

```
[root]# exportfs -av
```

If you are making changes to an existing /etc/exports file, re-export your volumes using exportfs -r, as seen in Listing 2.5.

Listing 2.5   Re-exporting all volumes

```
[root]# exportfs -rv
```

If you wish to export a volume to a single host temporarily, do not add it to your /etc/exports file. That would export it permanently. Instead, specify the host, volume, and export options on the command line, as seen in Listing 2.6.

Listing 2.6   Exporting a single volume

```
[root]# exportfs -v -i -o rw,no_root_squash earth:/usr/local
```

Listing 2.6 tells the mount daemon to export the /usr/local directory to host earth, with export permissions rw,no_root_squash. We use the -i option to tell exportfs to ignore the usual export information in /etc/exports, and only use the information specified on the command line.

To unexport the entry you added temporarily in Listing 2.6, run exportfs -u as seen in Listing 2.7.

Listing 2.7   Unexporting a single volume

```
[root]# exportfs -v -u earth:/usr/local
```

Now that we have seen the details of configuring NFS servers (exporting file systems), we can follow on to set up our NFS clients (mounting file systems).

Configuring an NFS Client

The procedure to configure an NFS client has two steps:

1. Exit your /etc/fstab file to specify client-side hosts, file systems, and mount options.

2. Run the /bin/mount command to mount the new volumes.

Configuring Mounted File Systems

To configure file systems so they can be mounted by hand or at boot time, place the information about those volumes in your /etc/fstab file. This file records file systems to mount, their mount points, mount options, file system types, and more. For NFS mounts, you must also specify the hostname of the remote NFS server. Blank lines and comments beginning with a "#" are ignored. The syntax of an entry in this file is shown in Listing 2.8.

Listing 2.8   Syntax of an entry in the /etc/fstab file

```
fspec    mntpt    type    options    freq    passno
```

Each line in the /etc/fstab file defines one mounted volume and has six components separated by whitespace. The meaning of each item is as follows:

fspec   This field specifies the file system name or device to mount. For NFS, list the hostname, followed by a colon, and then followed by the directory on the NFS server to mount; for example, earth:/b5/users/ezk.

mntpt   This field specifies the mount point on the local client to mount the file system; for example, /home/erez.

type   This field specifies the type of file system for the mount. Most often this is ext2 or nfs.

options   This field lists comma-delimited client-side mount options, as we detail shortly.

freq   This field lists the frequency in days at which file systems need to be backed up with the dump tool. NFS file systems do not get backed up remotely. Therefore, for NFS, set this value to 0, thus disabling it.

passno   This field determines the pass number for file system checking using fsck during boot time. NFS file systems do not get checked remotely. Therefore, for NFS, disable this by setting the value of this field to 0.

One of the important things that you get to list in the options field of your /etc/fstab file is NFS mount options. You could also specify mount options to the /bin/mount command by hand, as we show later in this chapter.

The mount options are listed in two tables. Both Tables 2.3 and 2.4 have four columns. The first column lists the name of the option, and the next column lists its default value; for Boolean options we list whether the option is on or off by default. The third column lists the general type of option: performance, security, or other. The last column provides a brief description of the option. Many options in these two tables have inverse options that are listed on the row following their counterparts.

Table 2.3 lists generic mount options that are applicable to all file systems.

Table 2.3   Generic Mount Options

Option	Default	Type	Meaning
async	On	Perf	Perform all writes asynchronously.
sync	Off	Perf	Perform all writes synchronously.
atime	On	Perf	Update file access times for each access.
noatime	Off	Perf	Do not update file access times for each access.
auto	On	Other	Allow mounting of this file system using mount -a.
noauto	Off	Other	This file system will not mount automatically on boot, but can be mounted manually.
defaults	N/A	Other	Use default options: async, auto, dev, exec, nouser, rw, and suid.
dev	On	Sec	Allow access to block and character devices.
nodev	Off	Sec	Disallow access to devices.
exec	On	Sec	Allow execution of binaries.
noexec	Off	Sec	Disallow execution of binaries.
suid	On	Sec	Allow setuid and setgid binaries to execute with those bits set.
nosuid	Off	Sec	Run setuid or setgid binaries, but with those set bits turned off.
broken_suid	Off	Sec	Support older binaries that assume superusers can write anywhere on the file system.
nouser	On	Sec	Allow only the superuser to mount the file system.
user	Off	Sec	Allow all users to mount the file systems.
remount	N/A	Other	Remount an already mounted file system.

Table 2.3   Generic Mount Options *(continued)*

Option	Default	Type	Meaning
ro	Off	Sec	Allow only read access to the file system.
rw	On	Sec	Allow read and write access to the file system.

Table 2.4 lists mount options that are only applicable to NFS mounts. However, when you specify mount options, you can mix both types of options (generic and NFS-specific) and list them in any order.

Table 2.4   NFS Client Mount Options

Option	Default	Type	Meaning
rsize=*N*	4096	Perf	Number of bytes to read from the NFS server.
wsize=*N*	4096	Perf	Number of bytes to write to the NFS server.
timeo=*N*	7	Perf	Number of tenths of seconds before re-transmitting RPC requests.
retrans=*N*	3	Perf	Number of timeouts and retransmissions before failing an RPC request.
acregmin=*N*	3	Perf	Minimum number of seconds for caching attributes of regular files.
acregmax=*N*	60	Perf	Maximum number of seconds for caching attributes of regular files.
acdirmin=*N*	30	Perf	Minimum number of seconds for caching attributes of directories.
acdirmax=*N*	60	Perf	Maximum number of seconds for caching attributes of directories.
actimeo=*N*	None	Perf	Timeout value for acregmin, acregmax, acdirmin, and acdirmax.

The Network File System

PART 1

Table 2.4 NFS Client Mount Options *(continued)*

Option	Default	Type	Meaning
retry=*N*	10000	Perf	Total number of minutes to retry NFS mount operations.
port=*N*	2049	Other	Contact NFS server on an alternate port *N*.
mountport=*N*	None	Other	Contact rpc.mountd on an alternate port.
mounthost=*ARG*	None	Other	Contact rpc.mountd on host *ARG*.
mountprog=*N*	100005	Other	Contact rpc.mountd using an alternate RPC program number.
mountvers=*N*	1	Other	Contact rpc.mountd using an alternate protocol version number.
nfsprog=*N*	100003	Other	Contact NFS server using an alternate RPC program number.
nfsvers=*N*	2	Other	Contact NFS server using an alternate protocol version number.
namlen=*N*	256	Other	Specify maximum length of file names that a remote NFS server supports.
addr=*N*	N/A	Other	Specify IP address of NFS server (ignored).
bg	Off	Other	Retry mount in the background.
fg	On	Other	Try mount in the foreground.
soft	Off	Other	Abort NFS operation if a major RPC timeout occurred.
hard	On	Other	Continue to wait for remote NFS server indefinitely, regardless of number of RPC timeouts.
intr	Off	Other	Allow users to interrupt hung processes.

Table 2.4   NFS Client Mount Options *(continued)*

Option	Default	Type	Meaning
nointr	On	Other	Disallow users from interrupting hung processes.
posix	Off	Other	Use POSIX semantics for this mount.
cto	On	Perf	Check attributes of files that were closed and reopened.
nocto	Off	Perf	Do not check attributes of files that were closed and reopened.
ac	On	Perf	Enable all attribute caching.
noac	Off	Perf	Disable all attribute caching.
tcp	Off	Perf	Use the TCP transport for this mount.
udp	On	Perf	Use the UDP transport for this mount.
lock	On	Other	Enable NFS locking.
nolock	Off	Other	Disable NFS locking.

Next, we will briefly describe performance- and security-related mount options. Following that, we describe all other options (those not specified as "perf" or "sec" in Tables 2.3 and 2.4) in detail.

> **WARNING**   Do not confuse client mount options and server export options. Some options are unique to the server, and some are unique to the client. Several options are shared: they have the same name and meaning. However, the options on the NFS server relate to its *export* permissions—or what it allows clients to do. The options on NFS clients relate to *mounting*—or what clients actually try to do.

Performance Mount Options

On the client side are many performance options. They fall into three categories: attribute caching control, writing behavior, and networking.

The attribute caching options control what happens to file attributes between the client and the server. In general, if you cache those attributes on the client and avoid changing them often on the server, you can improve your performance. The noatime option avoids updating the file access times on the server and can significantly improve performance. The acregmin, acregmax, acdirmin, acdirmax, and actimeo options determine how long the NFS client caches the attributes of files or directories and can be used to tune these caches to your particular needs. The noac option turns off all attribute caching and, thus, ensures that all client-side attributes are in sync with the server, at the cost of constant checking of attributes with the server. The nocto option avoids rechecking the attributes of a file that was closed and then reopened. This can be useful in case a new file with the same name had gotten created in between, and it uses different permissions modes.

The writing behavior options affect how often and how much data the client writes to the server at a time. The async option tells the NFS client (and possibly also the server) to write data asynchronously. This means that user processes do not have to wait for the data to be written to stable storage before continuing to run. The wsize and rsize options control the default sizes of writes and reads, respectively. On faster networks, raising these two parameters can improve performance by exchanging more data at once.

The networking options control RPC and IP features of NFS. The timeo, retrans, and retry options control the interval and number of minor and major RPC timeouts that the NFS client will use before retrying an operation or declaring it a failure. The tcp and udp options control the transport that the client will use to talk to the server. The TCP transport is available only for NFSv3.

Security Mount Options

The security options that the client uses prevent users from performing certain privileged actions. The nodev option prevents users from accessing block and character devices, which could let them read raw disk devices, possibly circumventing normal Unix security permissions. The noexec option disallows users from executing binaries. It is most useful when mounting partitions that contain data and text files, but not programs. The nosuid option prevents the activation of set-UID and set-GID bits in programs where those bits are set, thus ensuring that these programs will run as the users executing those binaries. The nouser option ensures that only the superuser could mount this file system. The ro option prevents users from changing any files or directories in the file system, thus ensuring its integrity against unwanted file deletions or modifications.

Other Mount Options

In this section we describe all other client-side NFS mount options. Many of these options work in pairs where one option has the opposite meaning from another; we describe those pairs together.

auto* and *noauto   The options auto and noauto make the most sense if used in the
/etc/fstab file instead of specified manually to /bin/mount on the command line. If you
specify auto, then this file system will be mounted automatically at boot time. If you specify noauto, then the file system will not be mounted automatically at boot time. Instead,
it would be mounted when you run the mount -a command to mount all file systems or
when you provide the mount command the name of the file system as an argument. The
noauto option is particularly useful when you have CD-ROMs or floppies that you wish
to mount. You cannot mount those file systems automatically, until their respective
devices are inserted. But it is useful nonetheless to prepare a mount entry for them in
/etc/fstab that can be mounted automatically using a single /bin/mount command.
Better yet, you could use an automounter to automate this process; see Part 2, "The Amd
Automounter," for more information.

defaults   The defaults option is simple shorthand for several other common options:
async, auto, dev, exec, nouser, rw, and suid. This is a useful option often used in /etc/
fstab files by default.

remount   The remount option is most useful when specified manually by the /bin/
mount command. Use this option when you have an already mounted file system with
some options and you wish to change the mount options for the mounted file system. One
way to achieve this would be to unmount the file system and then mount it again. However, with the remount option you can avoid the unmount and simply change the mount
options on the fly. The remount option is most often used when administrators wish to
make a read-only file system mounted with read and write permissions.

port=N   The port=N option allows the client to contact an NFS server that is listening on
a nonstandard port. It is sometimes useful to run an NFS server on a port other than the
default 2049. One reason is security: changing the port serves to prevent casual attempts
to probe your NFS server. Another reason is to run a second, experimental NFS server.

mountport=N, mounthost=ARG, mountprog=N,* and *mountvers=N   Before you can
use a file system over NFS, you must contact the rpc.mountd server to get authenticated
access to the file system you wish to use. Most commonly, the rpc.mountd server runs on
the same NFS server host. Also, the RPC parameters of the mount daemon are predeter-
mined: the mount port is retrieved from the portmapper, the RPC mount program number is 100005, and the RPC mount version is 1. However, you may wish to change any
one of these parameters. You could run a second, experimental mount daemon on an
alternate host. You could fix the port that the mount daemon uses without using a portmapper. You could also provide a mount daemon that services newer protocol versions:
2 and higher. In all of these cases, you could use one or more of the options mountport=N,
mounthost=ARG, mountprog=N, and mountvers=N to ensure that your NFS client can contact the remote mount daemon appropriately.

nfsprog=N   The `nfsprog=N` option allows you to contact an NFS server that is registered as an alternate RPC program. This could be useful if you run a second NFS server, perhaps for testing purposes.

nfsvers=N   The `nfsvers=N` option allows you to force the use of different NFS protocol versions. If you specify `nfsvers=3`, you will force your NFS mounts to use only version 3 of the protocol. By default, NFSv2 is used.

namlen=N   NFS clients and servers may work with each other, but the operating systems they run could actually support different features. In particular, the maximum number of characters that are allowed for file names may differ between the client and the server. If they do, use the `namlen=N` option to specify the maximum length that the NFS server should support for this client. This would ensure that the client would not send file names that are too long for the server to handle, and that the server would not send back file names that are longer than the client can handle.

addr=N   The `addr=N` option is not used. Its original intent was to allow users to specify the IP address of the remote host, but this is listed as part of the path name to mount (e.g., `earth:/usr/homes`).

bg* and *fg   The options `bg` and `fg` determine if mounts will be performed in the background or the foreground. With the `bg` option, `/bin/mount` will first try to mount in the foreground, and if that fails, it would continue to try in the background. This option is useful if you would like to mount a file system that is not crucial for your system's operation, and you do not wish to suspend the boot process of your system until that mount completes.

The `fg` option always performs mounts in the foreground. It is useful when the mount must complete before your system continues with its activities. For example, if you mount your `/usr` file system over NFS during the boot process, then your system will not function well if it does not have the `/usr` directory with its binaries available. For such a situation you should perform the mount in the foreground.

Regardless of the option, the mount program tries to mount a file system for a total number of seconds listed in the value of the `retry` option. If the mount did not succeed after that time, `/bin/mount` stops trying and returns an error code.

soft* and *hard   The options `soft` and `hard` determine how the NFS client will treat failures to contact the remote NFS server. The `soft` option tells the client to abort the operation immediately. This means that any small network failure, or even an NFS server that had crashed and is quickly rebooting, will result in user processes on the client getting error codes. These processes may abort unexpectedly and often. For that reason, the `soft` mount option is considered by many a dangerous option to be avoided.

The `hard` mount option is the default. It tells the NFS client to try indefinitely before aborting the operation. This allows time for partitioned networks to reconnect and for downed NFS servers to come back up. The NFS system was designed to survive such failures. Therefore it is a good idea for the client to wait for the NFS service to resume to normal status, rather than aborting the user process and potentially losing valuable data.

intr and *nointr*   The options `intr` and `nointr` determine if the user will be allowed to interrupt a hung process that is waiting for NFS service from a server. Suppose an NFS server is down and is not coming back up quickly enough. The `intr` option would allow the user to hit Ctrl+C on their keyboard or to send the INTR signal (using `kill -INTR`) to the process to interrupt it. The interrupted process will exit, and the user will have a chance to restart it or perhaps take corrective action to run their programs without depending on the hung NFS server.

The `nointr` option prevents users from interrupting their processes when they are hung on remote NFS servers. If you have an important program that must never be interrupted even if an NFS server is hung, and that program must wait indefinitely until the NFS server comes back up, then use the `nointr` option.

In general, administrators prefer a combination of the `hard,intr` options. That way, processes do not fail automatically on every small NFS failure, but users have the option to manually interrupt hung processes when they deem to have waited long enough for the NFS server to function again.

posix   In older versions, the NFS system had to be told manually if there were differences in maximum file name lengths, using the `namlen` option described previously. In newer versions, the NFS system can automatically exchange information about differences between clients and servers. This is done using the `pathconf` system call, which is part of an overall POSIX standard to support proper communications between heterogeneous clients and servers. If your server supports these POSIX semantics, specify the `posix` mount option; you can then avoid having to set the `namlen` option, among others. Note that the `posix` option is more powerful than just finding the maximum length of file names: it also finds the limits on many other system resources.

lock and *nolock*   Part of the NFS system includes the NFS Lock Manager protocol, which supports locking of files over NFS. The client and server must both agree on the level of NFS locking they support. Normally, they would find this automatically. Occasionally, however, they cannot agree on their level of support, or you know that the support code for locking is unstable and you may wish to turn it off, or you wish to turn on experimental new locking support explicitly. To force the client to use NFS locking with the server, use the `lock` option. To tell the client not to use NFS locking, use the `nolock` option.

Mounting File Systems

After setting all the desired mounted volumes and their options in your `/etc/fstab` file, mount them using the `/bin/mount` command. You could also reboot your system to allow boot-time mounted volumes to activate, but it is much safer to first try them one at a time manually. The usage of the `mount` command is depicted in Listing 2.9.

Listing 2.9 Usage of the `/bin/mount` command

```
mount [-lhV] -a [-fFnrsvw] [-t vfstype]
mount [-lhV] [-fnrsvw] [-o options [,...]] device | dir
mount [-lhV] [-fnrsvw] [-t vfstype] [-o options] device dir
```

Listing 2.9 shows that the usage of the `/bin/mount` command falls into three categories. The first form mounts all (`-a`) entries listed in the `/etc/fstab` file, or possibly only those that match a certain file system type. The second form mounts a file system and lets the `mount` command determine the proper file system type. The third form does the same but enforces a specific file system type to use. We list the mount flags now. Note that while we describe all flags, not all of them are applicable to NFS mounts.

-a This flag tells the `mount` command to mount all file systems listed in the `/etc/fstab` file. It can be combined with the `-t` option to mount all file systems that match a particular type. For example, `mount -a -t nfs` will mount all NFS file systems listed in your `/etc/fstab` file.

-f This flag "fakes" a mount. It performs all the actions needed to prepare for a mount but does not actually call the `mount(2)` system call to perform the mount. This can be useful in conjunction with the `-v` option to determine what the `mount` command is doing exactly without doing it.

-F This flag tells the `mount` command to fork a separate process for each mount. Doing mounts in parallel can speed operations. However, care must be taken to ensure that no two mounts depend on each other's order, since forked mounts could be done in an arbitrary order. In other words, if you have one file system to mount under `/usr` and another under `/usr/local`, do not use the `-F` option: if the `/usr/local` one mounts first, then the `/usr` mount will hide the `/usr/local` mount, making it inaccessible.

-h This flag prints a simple help message as seen in Listing 2.9.

-l This flag is used in conjunction with EXT2 file systems to add disk file system labels to the mount. See the `e2label` manual page for more details.

-L *LABEL*   This flag is useful for EXT2 file systems. It tells the mount command to mount a disk partition with a special *LABEL* that has been set using the e2label tool. It is most often useful to be able to mount a file system by a symbolic name given to it, not by the disk device and the partition it currently resides on. That way, even if the disk or partition move, the same file system can still be mounted, given its label.

-n   When the /bin/mount command successfully mounts a file system, it adds an entry to the /etc/mtab file. This file lists the currently mounted file systems. Occasionally, however, you may wish to mount a file system and not list it in the /etc/mtab file. The -n option does that. It is useful most often when the file system on which /etc/mtab resides is mounted read-only, as happens early in the boot process.

-o *OPTS*   This flag is followed by a comma-delimited list of mount options. You can use any of the mount options in Tables 2.3 and 2.4.

-r   This flag is the same as using -o ro: it tells the mount command to mount this file system read-only.

-s   This flag tells the mount command to ignore mount options that it does not recognize, rather than failing. It is sometimes useful to use this flag because not all file systems support all mount options. This flag is used primarily with Autofs, as described in Chapter 13, "Autofs."

-t *TYPE*   This flag is followed by a single name of a file system type to use. For example, mount -t nfs will force an NFS mount. The list of supported file systems to use is available in the /proc/filesystems file.

-U *UUID*   This flag tells the mount command to mount a disk (often EXT2) partition with a special *universal unique identifier* (UUID). This identifier is a 128-bit value that can uniquely identify a file system or partition even if it is moved from device to device. It is most often useful to be able to mount a file system by its logical identity, not by the disk device and the partition it currently resides on.

-v   This flag tells the mount command to produce verbose output showing what it is doing at each stage of the mount.

-V   This flag prints the version string of the /bin/mount command and exits.

-w   This flag is the same as using -o rw: it tells the mount command to mount this file system read-write.

In its simplest form, running /bin/mount without any options produces the list of currently mounted file systems as stored in /etc/mtab, shown in Listing 2.10.

Listing 2.10   Displaying mounted file systems using /etc/mtab

```
[ezk]$ /bin/mount
/dev/hda2 on / type ext2 (rw)
none on /proc type proc (rw)
```

```
usbdevfs on /proc/bus/usb type usbdevfs (rw)
/dev/hda7 on /homes type ext2 (rw)
/dev/hda6 on /usr type ext2 (rw)
none on /dev/pts type devpts (rw,gid=5,mode=620)
/dev/hda1 on /mnt/c type vfat (rw)
cricket:(pid693) /proj nfs (intr,rw,port=1023,map=/etc/amd.proj)
retro:/misc/mirror on /misc/mirror type nfs (rw,addr=128.59.16.150)
```

Running the mount command as in Listing 2.10 is similar to displaying the output of the mount table file manually using cat /etc/mtab. The /etc/mtab file must be updated by the /bin/mount command and all other tools that mount file systems, especially auto-mounters. In addition, you could use the -n option to the mount command to mount a file system without listing it in the /etc/mtab file. For these reasons, the contents of the /etc/mtab file should not be taken to be authoritative with respect to the actual mounts that the kernel supports.

Only the kernel knows with certainty which file systems are mounted. To get that list, display the contents of the /proc/mounts file, as seen in Listing 2.11.

Listing 2.11   Displaying mounted file systems using /proc/mounts

```
[ezk]$ cat /proc/mounts
/dev/root / ext2 rw 0 0
/proc /proc proc rw 0 0
usbdevfs /proc/bus/usb usbdevfs rw 0 0
/dev/hda7 /homes ext2 rw 0 0
/dev/hda6 /usr ext2 rw 0 0
none /dev/pts devpts rw 0 0
/dev/hda1 /mnt/c vfat rw 0 0
retro:/misc/mirror /misc/mirror nfs rw,v2,addr=retro 0 0
```

If you compare the output of Listings 2.10 and 2.11, you will see that the /etc/mtab file has one additional entry mounted on /proj that the kernel does not know about. Such spurious entries could occur for many reasons, often due to system overload or software bugs. Either way, to synchronize the contents of the /etc/mtab file with those of /proc/mounts, you need to remove that extra entry using the command umount /proj.

Listing 2.12 shows several entries in an /etc/fstab file for mounting some NFS disks.

Listing 2.12   Several example NFS entries in an /etc/fstab file

```
#HOST:/DIR          MNTPT      TYPE OPTIONS              FREQ PASSNO
earth:/homes        /home      nfs  default              0    0
retro:/misc/mirror  /mirrors   nfs  noauto,bg,intr,ro    0    0
moon:/u/test        /src/test  nfs  nfsvers=3,tcp,noatime 0    0
```

The first line in Listing 2.12 is a comment and is ignored. It is useful to place such a line in your /etc/fstab file to help you remember the meaning of each field. The meaning of the remaining three lines is as follows:

earth:/homes   This entry mounts home directories on /home, using the default mount flags. These default flags are useful for most common NFS file systems. Do not change them without a reason. This file system will get mounted automatically at boot time, because it is important to have access to one's home files before the system is fully up and users begin logging in.

retro:/misc/mirror   This file system contains mirrored files—in other words, files that are not crucial to have permanent access to, as they can be retrieved via FTP over the Internet. One common use is to mirror Red Hat's RPM software updates so they can be installed quickly from a local site copy. The four mount options we set for this mount reflect its type. The noauto option ensures that this file system will not be mounted at boot time. To mount it, we have to execute the mount command by hand:

```
[root]# mount /mirrors
```

The bg option tells us to mount this file system in the background. There is no need to wait for this mount before we can proceed with other uses of our system. The intr option lets us interrupt processing that might be hung if host retro is inaccessible; this is OK because we do not deem this mirrors file system to be crucial for system functionality. Finally, the ro option ensures that we mount this file system read-only. That way, there is no chance that the mirrored files could be changed inadvertently.

moon:/u/test   This file system is being tested. It runs on an experimental NFS server that runs the latest—and possibly unstable—NFSv3 server code that uses TCP as its transport. That is why we force the mount options to use NFS version 3 and the TCP transports, so we can test them. In this example, we also wanted to avoid updating file access times on the server, so we turned on the noatime option. The use of noatime with the other two options might be needed if we suspect that the code to update access times on NFSv3 is buggy and we wish to avoid it for the duration of our testing.

You will note that NFS file systems are neither backed up over NFS nor checked (using fsck) during boot time. That is why the last two fields for all NFS entries in Listing 2.12 have zeros in them.

Entering mounted file systems in your /etc/fstab file is useful if you wish them to be mounted permanently upon each reboot or to be available for such. For temporary one-time mounts, you could of course mount all NFS file systems by hand. Listing 2.13 shows the three commands you must run to mount the three file systems in Listing 2.12, respectively.

Listing 2.13   Mounting NFS file systems by hand

```
[root]# mount -t nfs -o default earth:/homes /home
[root]# mount -o noauto,bg,intr,ro retro:/misc/mirror /mirrors
[root]# mount -o nfsvers=3,tcp,noatime moon:/u/test /src/test
```

In the last two entries in Listing 2.13, we did not specify the type of file system as NFS. We actually do not need this for any of the hand-mounted entries, because the /bin/ mount command is smart enough to figure out from the name of the mounted file system that it is an NFS mount (since it contains a colon character, ":").

NOTE   Server export options take precedence over client mount options. For example, consider an NFS server that exports a file system with read-only per-missions. A client that tries to mount that file system with read-write permissions may succeed in mounting but will fail to write any files because the server will return the error message "Read-only file system."

Unmounting File Systems

So far we have concerned ourselves with mounting file systems. Occasionally, however, you will also need to unmount file systems you mounted, especially those mounted by hand temporarily. The /bin/umount command does that. The usage of the umount com-mand is depicted in Listing 2.14. You will find that most flags used by /bin/umount have the same meaning as those for the /bin/mount command.

Listing 2.14   Usage of the /bin/umount command

```
umount [-hV] -a [-nrv] [-t vfstype]
umount [-hV] [-nrv] device | dir [...]
```

WARNING   Do not confuse the name and the function of this command. The program name of this command is /bin/umount or simply umount. Its function is "the unmount command." Note that the program name does not include the first letter "n"!

-a   This flag tells the umount command to unmount all file systems currently mounted. It can be combined with the -t option to unmount all file systems that match a particular type. For example, umount -a -t nfs will unmount all currently mounted NFS file systems.

-f   This flag forces an unmount of an NFS file system whose file server is unreachable. This option works by indicating to the kernel that the NFS file system in question has timed out, thus accelerating and forcing a timeout procedure, leading to an eventual drop of this file system's mount. Note that this option is supported in Linux kernels 2.1.116 and higher. In practice, unfortunately, forcing the unmounting of NFS file systems does not always work reliably due to the complexity of the NFS system and current deficiencies in the Linux kernel.

-h   This flag prints a simple help message, as seen in Listing 2.14.

-n   When the /bin/umount command successfully unmounts a file system, it removes the corresponding entry from the /etc/mtab file. Occasionally, however, you may wish to unmount a file system and not remove its entry from the /etc/mtab file. This flag does that. Using umount -n is most often useful when the file system was originally mounted with mount -n; that is, it was mounted without adding an entry in the /etc/mtab file. In that case, there is no entry to remove in the first place.

-r   If an unmount attempt completely fails, this flag tells the umount command to try instead to remount the file system read-only. File systems will fail to unmount if they are busy: users are actively using the file system. If users are not actively writing files in that file system, it might be possible to remount the file system read-only. This is the first stage toward completely unmounting the file system. You could, for example, mount the file system read-only, ask the individual users to stop using the file system, and finally unmount the read-only file system.

-t *TYPE*   This flag is followed by a single name of a file system type to unmount. For example, umount -t nfs will perform an NFS unmount. This flag is most often used in conjunction with the -a flag to unmount all file systems of a given type.

-v   This flag tells the unmount command to produce verbose output showing what it is doing at each stage of the unmount.

-V   This flag prints the version string of the /bin/umount command and exits.

To unmount all NFS file systems, use the command and flags as seen in Listing 2.15.

Listing 2.15   Unmounting all NFS file systems

```
[root]# umount -a -t nfs
```

To unmount all three file systems hand-mounted in Listing 2.13, run the commands in Listing 2.16.

Listing 2.16   Unmounting NFS file systems by hand

```
[root]# umount /mirrors /home
[root]# umount -f -r /src/test
```

You will notice that we did not have to list the type of file system to unmount in Listing 2.16. The /bin/umount command will figure out the file system type automatically. Since the three mounted file systems each had an independent mount point, we could unmount them in any order. We show how to unmount several file systems at once by specifying them on the command line, as we do for the /mirrors and /home file systems. Finally, since /src/test is an experimental file system, it could hang due to software bugs. For that reason, we try to force it to unmount, and if forcing it fails, we at least try to remount it read-only.

TIP   If the number of NFS file systems you have to mount and unmount is small and does not change often, and the number of hosts you have to maintain NFS mounts for is small, you can list all of them by editing /etc/fstab files or even hand-mounting those file systems using /bin/mount. However, if the number of file system mounts or hosts you must maintain is large, you will find it very time-consuming to maintain them manually. Instead, use an automounter such as Amd: it can simplify NFS mounts considerably by centralizing them in one administrative location. We describe the automounter in Part 2 of this book.

In Sum

This chapter covered the configurations of NFS hosts in detail. It began with an overview of the configuration process, aimed at (mentally) preparing administrators for the tasks ahead, and continued with configuration of the NFS server. In particular, we covered the details of the /etc/exports file and the various export permissions that administrators can choose, and also showed how to use the various server-side tools to control the active export list. The discussion concluded the server-side configuration with a detailed explanation of the interactions between the various programs and daemons that run on the server and the files that they control.

Next, we described the configuration of the NFS client, starting with the syntax of the /etc/fstab file, which lists file systems to mount during boot time, and detailed the numerous mount options that are available to NFS clients. You can use two user-level tools to mount and unmount file systems: /bin/mount and /bin/umount, respectively.

This chapter focused on the basics: how to get your NFS client-server system functioning initially. We briefly described performance optimizations and security concerns. These two topics, while important, are not crucial to getting an NFS system working. The NFS system is complex and confusing for administrators; it is best to focus on basic functionality and then (quickly) move on to consider performance and security issues. These two important topics are described in the following two chapters.

3

NFS Performance

The NFS system uses the network to provide transparent file service. The network, however, is slower to access than local disks. For that reason, administrators have always sought to improve the performance of NFS. A disk-based file system such as EXT2 runs on a single host and generally contains a few parameters that could be tuned to improve its performance. NFS, however, has two parts: a client side and a server side. Because it has two parts, NFS has more than twice as many performance-tuning parameters. Understanding and properly adjusting these parameters can improve performance significantly.

There are many performance options you can use to affect system performance. Some of these options depend on others and because of this, they may have unexpected side effects on your system. When you begin experimenting with changing parameters, never change more than one parameter at a time. If you do, you will not be able to tell which parameter was responsible for the changes you saw. It is even possible for some parameters to undo the effects of others, thus making it appear as if no change was made to the system. The best techniques for improving the performance of your NFS hosts is to make one change at a time, run some benchmarks to verify that the change resulted in the desired effects, and let this stay for a few days before changing another parameter. Yes, this implies that it could take you weeks, even months, to try out many performance-tuning changes. That is indeed the nature of proper system administration: a never-ending string of small, careful changes applied to production systems.

> ***TIP***   Follow the instructions in Chapter 2, "Configuring NFS," to ensure that
> your system functions the way you intend before embarking on improving the
> performance of your NFS system. Let your system run for at least a week to guar-
> antee that it is stable, even if it does not perform as well as you would like. When
> you are satisfied that your NFS hosts are stable you can begin improving their
> performance.

This chapter will help you learn to understand and adjust these parameters. We begin by discussing the performance parameters that you can adjust on an NFS server; then we discuss those parameters that you can adjust on the client side. We continue by overviewing various tools that you can use to measure the performance of your NFS system, and we finish the chapter with additional information that can be used when all previous suggestions have been tried.

Server Performance

In this section, we list server-side performance options. There are four such options, which we listed in Table 2.2 of the previous chapter: async, sync, wdelay, and no_wdelay. These options are export options—those that the NFS server applies to all NFS clients that use it.

Aside from the export options that relate to performance, the most useful performance-improving feature you should use is the in-kernel NFS server. In Red Hat 6.1 systems and older, the NFS server was implemented in the user level as a part of the unfsd RPM. But because the user-level NFS server performed very poorly compared to the in-kernel one (knfsd), and because the user-level NFS server was also missing some vital functionality that made it less reliable and less secure, it should not be used anymore. Instead, make sure your Linux system uses the newer in-kernel NFS server, knfsd. See Chapter 7, "Building and Installing the Linux Kernel and NFS Software," for information on this topic.

Asynchronous vs. Synchronous Server-Side Writes

When a user process on an NFS client executes the write(2) system call, it expects that by the time the system call returns successfully, the data has been written to stable storage. This is because the original design of NFS called for the stateless server to commit all client-side data to its stable storage before returning a success code back to the client. This was done to ensure absolute reliability of the data. Should the NFS server crash immediately after the write system call returns, the data written would be guaranteed to be available. This design decision, to write all data immediately to disk, was called *synchronous writes*.

Unfortunately, writing all data synchronously to disk slows performance. An application that performs many writes over NFS could be slowed down considerably while it is waiting for these writes to complete. The alternative is for the server not to write that data immediately to disk, but to keep it in its kernel memory (the page cache), schedule it to be written to disk at a later time, and reply quickly to the client with a success return code. This is called *asynchronous writes*. Linux flushes those data pages to disk an average of five seconds after the write call is completed.

The problem with asynchronous writes is that if the NFS server or the host it is running on crashes before it had the chance to commit written data pages to disk, data is lost permanently. Worse, the NFS client now thinks that the data was written to stable media when, in fact, it was not. In practice, however, most Linux-based NFS servers remain running for long periods of time. While some risk remains, it is relatively small and often worth the improvement in performance.

On Linux NFS servers, asynchronous writes are the default. They are explicitly activated by the `async` option in your `/etc/exports` file on your NFS server.

If you wish to guarantee the reliability of your data at the expense of performance, turn on the `sync` export option in your `/etc/exports` file.

Write Delays

This option is another feature of Linux NFS servers aimed at improving performance, at the expense of reliability. Linux kernels, like many other operating systems, use a Virtual Memory (VM) system that is based on pages. This means that while user processes can perform read and write operations at arbitrary offsets and for any length of time, the operating system translates those into page-based operations. A typical page size on Linux is 4KB or 8KB, depending on the architecture. The VM system, along with its cache, was designed to work optimally for whole page operations.

For example, suppose a user process wishes to write 10 characters of data in a file, starting at byte 5000. Linux will actually retrieve the full second page of that file (bytes 4096 to 8191, assuming a 4KB page size), and fill in the 10 bytes in that page, appropriately adjusted for the starting offset of that page. Linux will then write all 4KB of that page to disk. Now, let us assume that a process on a NFS client issues another write request, this time to write 20 bytes starting at offset 5010 (right after the previous 10 bytes). Linux will have to repeat the whole process: retrieve the second page completely, fill in the 20 bytes in the appropriate location, and then write out the whole page.

This is a waste of resources and slows performance because many consecutive small writes arrive from an NFS client instead of fewer larger ones. If the NFS server waits before writing pages out, several small writes for the same physical data page can be clustered and only one actual page write is needed. This is what the wdelay option does.

The wdelay option, on by default, tells the NFS server to wait a little bit longer to see if additional writes come in that can be clustered together. Be aware, however, that delaying writes actually diverges from the original NFS specification. Write delays can improve performance, but they also increase the window of vulnerability for data loss. If the NFS server crashes before it can flush data pages for clustered writes, all those writes are lost.

NOTE The Linux NFS server waits 10 milliseconds when the wdelay option is used, but only if the previous write request was to the same file. This amount of time is not configurable. In general, this technique, and in particular the Linux implementation of it, are not very effective in improving the performance of the Linux NFS server.

If you do not expect your NFS server to see many consecutive writes, or if you are more concerned about the absolute reliability of your data, more so than performance, turn this feature off by putting no_wdelay in your /etc/exports file.

Client Performance

In this section, we list the many client-side performance options. These are mount options that NFS clients specify in their /etc/fstab file or manually to the /bin/mount command. The full list of options is available in Tables 2.3 and 2.4, in the previous chapter.

Asynchronous vs. Synchronous Client-Side Writes

Just as the server can decide whether to cache data that client-side user processes write, so can the NFS client. When an NFS client caches data that user processes write, that data is not transmitted immediately over the network to the NFS server. Instead, it remains in the NFS client's cache, often in a subsystem called the RPC I/O Daemon (rpciod), as we described in Chapter 1, "NFS Basics and Protocols."

When an NFS client caches data, it is said to be performing asynchronous writes. This feature, on by default on Linux, can also be activated by the async mount option. To turn this feature off, thus performing synchronous writes, use the sync mount option.

The same pros and cons that apply to the similar server-side export options are applicable here as well. If you use asynchronous writes, your NFS client will run faster, but you will risk losing data if your NFS client crashes. If you use synchronous writes, your data will be guaranteed reliable, but your NFS client will run slower, especially if it has to perform many writes.

There is one significant difference between server-side caching and client-side caching. If a client crashes before committing data to stable media, only that client's data is lost. If a server crashes before committing data to stable media, many clients' data could be lost. For that reason, client-side asynchronous writes are not nearly as risky as server-side ones. Most Linux systems perform well with client-side caching and rarely lose vital data. The benefit in performance is often worth the small added risk.

Access Times

In Unix, each file or directory has three time stamps that are associated with it: the time the file was created or its protection modes were last changed, the time that the file was last modified, and the time that the file was last accessed or read. That last time stamp is called the *last access time* or *atime*. This time stamp is updated each time a file is read or a directory is scanned. This means that even if you just casually browsed a directory by listing its contents, or if you read some files, the file system must update (write) some information on the disk that identifies the last time that those files or directories were accessed.

Updating the access times often seemed like a good idea to the original designers of Unix file systems. In practice, it turned out to be a feature seldom used but one that often consumed many disk resources. Users are far more interested in the last modification times of files than in their last access times. For that reason, Linux provides an option that, when turned on, skips the updating of the access times of files and directories. This improves performance significantly on busy file servers and News servers.

By default, Linux does update the access times of files. This can also be turned on by the `atime` mount option. To turn this option off so that access times are not updated, and thus improve performance, use the `noatime` option.

Read and Write Sizes

Unix file systems read and write files in fixed-size chunks, often called *pages*. Even when a user asks to read or write just one byte, the operating system internally will perform an operation on a whole data page. This was designed to simplify the code and improve performance by caching file system data pages that are used throughout the operating system. For the same reason, NFS performs actual reads and writes over the wire in units that have a fixed maximum size. These are called the *maximum read transfer size* and *maximum write transfer size*. These two values can be set by the parameters `rsize` and `wsize`, respectively.

The default values on Linux vary depending on the version of the Linux kernel and the support for NFSv3 that you may have. The original, and still the default on most Linux systems, is 4KB for both parameters. Newer kernels will negotiate this with the NFS server and may use values as high as 32KB.

The larger the read and write sizes are, the better the performance you can get from your NFS system since you can transfer more data at once. However, remember that NFS is built on top of RPC, which uses XDR. XDR, in turn, uses the Internet Protocol (IP) networking suite, most often over Ethernet networks. A large NFS transfer unit is likely to be broken into many small packets that are often as small as 1500 bytes (a typical Ethernet transmission unit). If you use NFS with UDP and just one of those packets is lost while all others arrive safely, the NFS system would be forced to resend the entire data chunk (as large as 32KB). If your network is unreliable and it loses packets often, you could get into a cycle of NFS retransmissions due to even the smallest network problem. Because of these reasons, you need to set up your rsize and wsize units to balance the speed vs. the reliability of your network.

The exact values that you should use can range from 1KB to 16KB for NFSv2, and up to 32KB for NFSv3 using TCP. While you can set any value in between, most users use whole kilobyte units, in powers of two: 1KB, 2KB, 4KB, 8KB, 16KB, or 32KB. You may have to experiment with different values to determine the optimal values for your network. We discuss tools and techniques for measuring your NFS performance in the upcoming section "Tools to Measure Performance." Use the following guidelines:

- If your network is fast and reliable, say a 100Mbps switched network with fast servers and clients, increase your rsize and wsize to 16KB or 32KB. You can do so by setting the mount options as follows:

      rsize=16384,wsize=16384

- If your network is slow, unreliable, or very busy, lower these values to 1KB or 2KB. For example, if you use NFS over dialup IP lines or DSL, you could set these mount options:

      rsize=1024,wsize=1024

- If you are not sure, or if your system is neither very fast nor very slow, leave the default options as they are. The defaults are most often sufficient for most users.

TIP   For typical networks, adjust your `rsize` and `wsize` so that they are at least as large as the smallest page size of your NFS servers and clients. This is most often 4KB. The reasons for using these values are twofold. First, operating systems and file systems will perform local disk operations using the native page size anyway. Second, file systems perform read–ahead to improve performance, so even if you read only 1KB, the system will ask to read more. Read-aheads are an optimization that assumes that users read files sequentially. When the operating system reads a given data block on behalf of a user, it assumes that the user would want to read the next block or two, and it retrieves them ahead of time.

TCP vs. UDP Transports

To TCP or to UDP: that is an age-old question. Conventional wisdom has taught us that UDP is always faster than TCP. But in practice, the choice between UDP and TCP is not that simple.

UDP is a connectionless and supposedly an unreliable protocol; packets are sent individually and without any requirement that they be acknowledged. *TCP* is a reliable protocol that automatically adjusts its capacity to match the behavior and reliability of the network and its bandwidth. TCP is a connection-oriented protocol, which means that it requires costly setup processing when the connection is made initially and equally costly tear-down processing when the connection is closed at the end of the transmission. In short, if you want a more reliable transmission protocol (TCP), it appears as if you have to pay a performance penalty.

In the early days of NFS, Sun Microsystems designed NFSv2 to use UDP only. The reasons for this were that machines had less memory, networks were slower, and CPUs were slower. Processing TCP imposed more resource demands on Unix systems. So Sun chose UDP. However, since UDP is not a reliable protocol, Sun designed an additional layer of reliability into NFS and RPC. They did this using retransmissions and acknowledgments at the RPC and NFS levels. This was a compromise solution that allowed Sun to use the less demanding UDP transport, yet still improve reliability through other methods.

Since then, networks have become faster, CPUs have become faster, and memory sizes have grown larger. This is why when Sun designed the NFSv3 protocol, they chose TCP as the default transport, while retaining UDP as an option. By choosing TCP, Sun benefited from all of the reliability and self-adjustment of that transport, and the need to depend on other special methods for improving NFS's reliability was reduced.

Much testing has been done since NFSv3 implementations first came out, to compare NFS using UDP vs. TCP. Many factors other than the transmission protocol itself weigh in to determine which one works better: speed of networks and machines, amount of memory, implementation details of NFS and the networking code in the kernel, and more. These results appear to be the consensus:

- If your network is fast and reliable, use UDP by setting your mount options to udp.
- If your network is slow or unreliable, use TCP by setting your mount options to tcp.
- If you are not sure, leave the default options as they are. They should work well for most users.

One interesting recent result that Brian Pawlowski (co-author of NFSv3) reported on Solaris systems is that TCP performance with NFS depends much on the default TCP transmission window size, a value that determines how much data the TCP transport exchanges. Brian experimented and showed that with a window size of 8KB (default on Solaris), NFS over UDP performed 50 percent better than TCP. With TCP's window size increased to 64KB, however, TCP beat the performance of UDP by about 10 percent.

On Linux, the default networking transmission and read sizes can be set in the /proc file system. You can read those values as shown in Listing 3.1.

Listing 3.1   Checking the default networking window sizes in Linux

```
[ezk]$ cd /proc/sys/net/core
[ezk]$ cat rmem_default
65535
[ezk]$ cat rmem_max
65535
[ezk]$ cat wmem_default
65535
[ezk]$ cat wmem_max
65535
```

The values in Listing 3.1 are all set to 64KB: rmem_default is the default read size; rmem_max is the maximum allowed read size; wmem_default is the default write size; and wmem_max is the maximum allowed write size. As you can see, these values are not small; therefore, they enable Linux to make the most out of NFS over TCP. Note that these values may need to be increased on busy NFS servers, as we describe in the upcoming section "Socket Input Queue Memory Limits."

So, which transport option should you use: UDP or TCP? The choice depends on your network conditions. It is best if you follow the advice given here and then test the performance to check to see if any one option makes a significant difference. Since both the transport protocol and the NFS read and write sizes can impact NFS's performance, change only one of them at a time before testing the performance.

Timeout Options

When NFS uses only UDP, additional mechanisms are needed to improve reliability. The timeout and retransmission counter options were added to improve RPC's reliability, when RPC runs over UDP.

When an NFS client sends an RPC message to an NFS server, it waits for a number of tenths of seconds as described in the `timeo` parameter. If it does not get a response in that time, the client sends the same message again and waits for another timeout period. It does this repeatedly until it either gets a response or the number of retransmissions exceeds the number defined in the `retrans` parameter. If, after waiting that many times, the NFS client still does not receive a response, it returns a failure message back to its caller. On Linux, these two parameters are set for 0.7 seconds timeout value, for a total of 2.1 seconds wait (three retransmissions).

The parameters set on Linux are relatively short, indicating an expectation that networks would be fast and reliable. On other operating systems, these parameters are set higher, causing longer waits. If your networks are slower, it may take longer than 0.7 seconds to transmit a packet from one end to another and receive a reply. In that case, you should increase the `timeo` value. If your networks are very busy or not very reliable, and thus tend to lose packets, you should also increase the number of retransmissions. For example, suppose you have a slow and busy network that is not very reliable. You can increase the total timeout to 10 seconds and then wait two seconds between each retransmission with the following mount options:

```
timeo=20,retrans=5
```

> **NOTE** The value of the `timeo` option is not given in seconds, but in tenths of a second.

The other timeout-related mount option is the `retry` one. This value determines the number of minutes to wait for a mount request. This is used only when the system boots up and mounts NFS partitions, or when you mount them by hand using the `/bin/mount` tool. This value's default is set pretty high, 10000, which is almost a whole week. This value seems unrealistically high for many administrators: will you really wait a week for a mount request to complete? Probably not. Your site administrators are likely to walk over to the server room and determine the nature of the problem that prevents users from mounting NFS servers. You could safely lower this value to something smaller, say three hours, by setting the following mount option:

```
retry=180
```

Attribute Caching

We described in the section "Access Times" how updating the last access times of files is an operation that happens often. In NFS, retrieving the attributes of files and directories (the NFS_GETATTR operation) is one of the most popular NFS procedures. This operation involves checking the owner and group of the file, the protection bits (readable, writable, executable), the set-UID and set-GID bits, and the time stamps. These attribute checks happen each time an NFS client wants to access a new file, read a directory, and more. However, the attributes of files do not change very often. Therefore, caching the attributes improves the performance of NFS while adding only a small chance of using stale attributes. For these reasons, there are many mount options that handle the caching of attributes.

First, determine if you want any attribute caching or not. Attribute caching is on by default, and is set with the ac option. To turn off all attribute caching, use the noac option. Turning off all attribute caching will slow your NFS system, but it is sometimes necessary on systems where files' attributes (owners, modes, etc.) do change often and must be in sync with all NFS clients that use them. (This is sometimes also a security concern, because one NFS client can change the permissions of a file on a server, and thus restrict the access to the same file for other NFS clients. We detail this situation in Chapter 4, "Securing NFS.")

Next, there are five specific attribute-caching parameters that you can set:

acregmin=N   This option sets the minimum number of seconds to cache the attributes of regular files (not directories). This means that the attributes remain in the cache for at least that long. It defaults to three seconds. If you set this value to zero, you turn off the caching of attributes of regular files. Setting this value higher (say, acregmin=30) will cache the attributes for longer. It could improve performance more, but then you will have to wait longer for attributes that have changed on the NFS server to become in sync with the client's view.

acregmax=N   This option sets the maximum number of seconds to cache the attributes of regular files. This means that the attributes remain in the cache for no longer than that value. It defaults to one minute. Setting this value to zero turns off the caching of attributes of regular files. Setting this value higher (say, acregmax=300) will cache the attributes for longer.

acdirmin=N   This is the minimum number of seconds to cache the attributes of directories. It defaults to 30 seconds—longer than for regular files—because directory attributes tend to change even less often than regular files.

acdirmax=N   This is the maximum number of seconds to cache the attributes of directories. It defaults to one minute. Setting either of the directory attribute cache parameters to zero disables caching of directory attributes.

actimeo=N   This mount option has no default value. If used, it sets the same timeout values for all four mount options: acregmin, acregmax, acdirmin, and acdirmax. The actimeo is shorthand for setting those four in just one option.

For example, to turn on attribute caching and to quadruple the default attribute caching timeouts, set these mount options:

```
ac,acregmin=12,acregmax=240,acdirmin=120,acdirmax=240
```

Close-to-Open Consistency

The NFS server is stateless: it does not know when NFS clients open or close files, only when they want to read or write the data of those files. The NFS client caches the attributes of files by default. These attributes determine if the NFS client is allowed to open, read, or write the file.

Suppose one NFS client opened a file it had access to, read or wrote some data, and then closed the file. The original attributes of that file remain cached in this client's memory for a period of time, for performance reasons. A few seconds later the same client tries to reopen the file to read some data off of it. The client will not recheck the attributes of that file, not by default. In that period of time, a second NFS client could have deleted the file and recreated it, or changed its protection modes. The first client cannot know this because its attributes, now stale and not in sync with the server, are cached. In other words, the attributes of the file (as the first client sees them) are not consistent when a file is closed and then reopened. This condition is known as not maintaining *close-to-open consistency*.

By default, Linux NFS clients maintain close-to-open consistency; this behavior can be set using the cto option. This means that when a file is closed, the NFS client removes its attributes from the cache. That way, when the same client tries to open the same file again, the NFS client will be forced to get its most up-to-date attributes at that time. This affects performance somewhat, but not very significantly for most applications.

The only applications that are affected by this are those that continually close and reopen the same file. For example, if you are delivering e-mail over NFS, the client would have to open users' mailboxes and append new mail to them; or if you are using tools that append information to log files that are stored over NFS. If you use such applications, and you know that the attributes of the NFS-stored files are not likely to change often, you can turn off the close-to-open consistency checks using the `nocto` mount option.

NOTE   The close-to-open consistency mount options are not purely performance options. Many administrators consider them to be security-related options just as much as they are performance options. This is because the `cto` option ensures that two clients that try to access or change protection modes of the same file on an NFS server would do so consistently. If one client changes the permissions of a file so that a second client should no longer be able to access it, that second client is denied access to that file if using the `cto` option; the second NFS client, however, could continue to use the file if the `nocto` option is used.

Tools to Measure Performance

So far, we have described the NFS server-side export options and client-side mount options and how they affect performance. In this section, we tell you how to check your performance. Checking performance is an art all by itself, and one that is often done incorrectly, leading to wrong or confusing results. There are several important guidelines you should follow when testing NFS performance:

- Ensure that your network and hosts are performing normally. It is important that your hubs, switches, routers, and networking infrastructure function well. If they do not, there is no point in testing NFS performance, especially when you cannot even get simple packets to traverse your network reliably.

- Run as many tests as possible while your hosts and networks are quiet. Do not run tests in the middle of the day or when many users are active at your site. Their causal (or heavy) use can skew your results significantly. Plus, your users will not be happy if you overload your site's servers and networks with testing.

- Be patient and follow the guidelines carefully. Running tests takes a long time and must be done repeatedly to ensure consistent results. Do not change more than one parameter at a time. If you do, and your new NFS performance tests show a difference (for better or worse), you will not be able to tell which of the parameters you changed was responsible for the change in performance and by how much. Worse, some parameters could have opposite effects, even canceling each other's effects partially or wholly, thus masking their individual contributions to overall performance.

- The science of performance measurement is complex. What is evident from years of research in this area can be summed in one phrase: your mileage may vary. In other words, performance test suites can be tuned to measure just about anything and they may report very different results: they are *never* free of bias. Do not take the results you get from these tools to be the most accurate values or the most representative figures of your site's behavior. Instead, consider them to be reasonable estimates.

- On a related note, do not waste too much time tweaking your site's performance for small gains. Your time as an administrator of your NFS hosts is valuable. Spending days to improve performance by just a few percentage points is not worth it.

- Consider security when changing the configuration of your site. Many performance options have some ramifications on security and vice versa. See Chapter 4 for details on security aspects of NFS.

Basic Networking Tests

We begin by describing basic networking tests. This is to ensure that your network is functioning well before going on to testing NFS. First, use ping from the NFS client to the NFS server to check the performance. This tool sends ICMP ECHO packets of a given size to another host, waits for replies, repeats sending them periodically, and measures packet loss rates as well as average round-trip transmission times.

By default, ping sends 56-byte packets every second until you stop the program using Ctrl+C. In the example of Listing 3.2, we use the -c option of ping to specify that we want to send no more than 10 packets.

Listing 3.2   Checking network performance using /bin/ping

```
[ezk]$ ping -c 10 cricket
PING cricket (128.59.1.2) from 128.59.1.2 : 56(84) bytes of data.
64 bytes from cricket (128.59.1.2): icmp_seq=0 ttl=255 time=67 usec
64 bytes from cricket (128.59.1.2): icmp_seq=1 ttl=255 time=38 usec
64 bytes from cricket (128.59.1.2): icmp_seq=2 ttl=255 time=32 usec
64 bytes from cricket (128.59.1.2): icmp_seq=3 ttl=255 time=30 usec
64 bytes from cricket (128.59.1.2): icmp_seq=4 ttl=255 time=38 usec
64 bytes from cricket (128.59.1.2): icmp_seq=5 ttl=255 time=31 usec
64 bytes from cricket (128.59.1.2): icmp_seq=6 ttl=255 time=32 usec
64 bytes from cricket (128.59.1.2): icmp_seq=7 ttl=255 time=29 usec
64 bytes from cricket (128.59.1.2): icmp_seq=8 ttl=255 time=30 usec
64 bytes from cricket (128.59.1.2): icmp_seq=9 ttl=255 time=29 usec

--- cricket ping statistics ---
10 packets transmitted, 10 packets received, 0% packet loss
round-trip min/avg/max/mdev = 0.029/0.035/0.067/0.012 ms
```

A good, fast, switched network would show the performance values as seen in Listing 3.2: no packets were lost, all packets were acknowledged in under one millisecond, and the standard deviation (mdev) was relatively small. The last parameter is just as important as having low latency. A low-latency network that exhibits high variance in round-trip times (RTTs) can destabilize TCP's congestion control algorithms and result in greater delays.

If your network is not very stable, ping will report a non-zero packet loss rate. A small, occasional packet loss is OK. Anything greater than 5 percent would result in poor NFS performance. Also, if the average RTT for such small packets is greater than 100 milliseconds, your network is probably not very fast.

Note that it is important to run ping first from the client to the server and then from the server to the client. Compare the two results you get. They should not vary by much. If they do, it might indicate that you have a general networking problem. This could be the result of asymmetric routes, bad hardware, misconfigured routers, or even buggy network drivers. Most often, if you get very different results between the two directions, it is because one host is using half-duplex Ethernet and the other host is using full-duplex Ethernet. This issue is often a problem with a network interface card (NIC) configuration or a switch port configuration. If you do get asymmetric ping results or you are not sure, consult your network administrator.

Unfortunately, ping sends very small packets by default, only 56 bytes long. On a busy NFS system, much larger data units will be exchanged—many kilobytes' worth. For that reason, and especially if you intend to adjust the rsize or wsize mount options as we described in "Read and Write Sizes," run ping with larger packet sizes. Listing 3.3 shows good results from sending 10 32KB packets.

Listing 3.3 Using /bin/ping to stress the network

```
[ezk]$ ping -c 10 -s 32768 cricket
PING cricket (128.59.1.2) from 128.59.1.2 : 32768(32796) bytes of data.
32776 bytes from cricket (128.59.1.2): icmp_seq=0 ttl=255 time=7.207 msec
32776 bytes from cricket (128.59.1.2): icmp_seq=1 ttl=255 time=7.081 msec
32776 bytes from cricket (128.59.1.2): icmp_seq=2 ttl=255 time=7.039 msec
32776 bytes from cricket (128.59.1.2): icmp_seq=3 ttl=255 time=7.056 msec
32776 bytes from cricket (128.59.1.2): icmp_seq=4 ttl=255 time=6.932 msec
32776 bytes from cricket (128.59.1.2): icmp_seq=5 ttl=255 time=7.032 msec
32776 bytes from cricket (128.59.1.2): icmp_seq=6 ttl=255 time=7.050 msec
32776 bytes from cricket (128.59.1.2): icmp_seq=7 ttl=255 time=6.926 msec
32776 bytes from cricket (128.59.1.2): icmp_seq=8 ttl=255 time=7.170 msec
32776 bytes from cricket (128.59.1.2): icmp_seq=9 ttl=255 time=6.902 msec
```

```
--- cricket ping statistics ---
10 packets transmitted, 10 packets received, 0% packet loss
round-trip min/avg/max/mdev = 6.902/7.039/7.207/0.126 ms
```

You will note that it took an average of seven milliseconds to send a 32KB packet to another host. That is to be expected, even on a fast network. The results in Listing 3.3 also show a very stable network: the standard deviation is pretty small, less than 2 percent difference from the mean.

Varying the size of the packets used with ping is important for your other NFS tests; doing so would give you a general idea of how much time your network takes to exchange a certain amount of data.

NFS Performance Benchmarks

Generally, when running performance tests, it is important to run two types of tests:

Micro-benchmarks   These tests are intended to isolate individual file system operations, such as read, write, or lstat. Since these tests are more focused on specific operations, they are easier to understand. Also, it is easier to see the impact of NFS configuration changes with micro-benchmarks.

General-purpose benchmarks   These are sometimes called *macro-benchmarks*. Such benchmarks test the overall performance of the file system and take into account many file system operations, which are distributed as closely as possible to what normal users would see in practice. A micro-benchmark may focus on, say, the performance of the mkdir operation. But usually, users do not create directories that often; only a small percentage of file system operations are directory creations. Therefore, even a tenfold improvement in the performance of mkdir over NFS may not be apparent to users of NFS. In other words, general-purpose benchmarks are the best tools to give users a feel for what performance they should expect from NFS in practice.

One crucial aspect of performance testing is the state of the operating system cache. Linux caches data pages and other parts of file systems. NFS can cache file data and their attributes on both the client and the server. Caches are useful in improving performance, but they can skew the results of benchmarks by making the file system appear faster than it really is. If your benchmarks, say, test the read performance of NFS, but you are reading data pages off of the page cache of the operating system, you are not really exercising the file system; instead, you are exercising the page caching system. For that reason, most benchmarks use a *cold cache*: they ensure that the cache does not contain any parts of the file system being tested. To ensure that our cache is cold, we will remove the files and directories that we use during the testing, and we may even unmount the file system between tests.

In contrast, a *warm cache* is one that is already populated with file system data pages and attributes. Warm-cache benchmarks are not useless; in fact, they can be useful when coupled with cold-cache tests. Warm-cache tests give the tester a good idea of how much the cache can improve file system performance when used under normal conditions.

In the next two benchmarking sections, we assume that we mount a home directory /home/ezk from host mars onto /mnt on the client.

Micro-Benchmarks

We show two types of micro-benchmarks: tests for read and write performance, and tests for attribute retrieval. We picked those two because they are popular NFS operations and they impact the users' perceived performance. To test the read and write performance, use the dd tool, as seen in Listing 3.4.

Listing 3.4   A micro-benchmark to test writing of files

```
[root]# mount mars:/home/ezk /mnt
[ezk]$ cd /mnt
[ezk]$ mkdir tests
[ezk]$ cd tests
[ezk]$ time dd if=/dev/zero of=test-file bs=4k count=8192
8192+0 records in
8192+0 records out

real    0m9.149s
user    0m0.020s
sys     0m0.450s
```

Listing 3.4 shows first how to mount the file system (as root), and then how to create a private test directory. The last command in Listing 3.4 times a single run of the dd command in the test directory. This command writes a file of a given total size using smaller defined units. We use the following options to dd:

if   The input file. We read values from /dev/zero. This device provides a very fast stream of zeros; thus, we know that this test is not impeded by the speed of the input file.

of   The output file. We write to a file named test-file, but this name can be changed to any other file name.

bs   The block size. Each data chunk that the dd command writes would be 4KB in size. You can specify any data chunk size you wish from a single byte to many gigabytes. See the manual page for dd for more details on this command. You might vary the bs parameter to simulate NFS clients that write more or less data all at once. Remember that NFS—and any file system—is more efficient when it writes more data at once. We picked 4KB because many applications write files using the native page size of the system, and 4KB is the page size of i386 machines.

count   How many blocks to write. We write 8192 blocks of 4KB each, resulting in the creation of a 32MB file.

The output of the dd command is the first two lines after the command run in Listing 3.4; these lines show the number of records dd read in and wrote out. The last three lines are the times reported by the time command, which measured the time it took to run our dd command. The most useful time value we are concerned with is the "real" time, also known as *elapsed* time. Our test shows that it took more than nine seconds to write that 32MB file over NFS. You should repeat this test at least 10 times, average the elapsed times you get from each run, and also compute the standard deviation to ensure that it is small. For each run, you must use a different file. Do not overwrite the same file because then you would be writing through the cache. Listing 3.5 shows how to create 10 such files.

Listing 3.5   Repeating a write benchmark several times

```
[ezk]$ n=1
[ezk]$ while test $n -le 10
> do
> time dd if=/dev/zero of=test-file-$n bs=4k count=8192
> let n=n+1
> done
```

You may wish to change any of the NFS mount parameters or export options as listed in this chapter; then you may want to rerun the write benchmarks. For example, if you suspect that your network is slow or not too stable, you could change the wsize mount option to the mount command in Listing 3.4 to read as follows:

```
[root]# mount -o wsize=2048 mars:/home/ezk /mnt
```

Afterward, repeat the tests in Listings 3.4 and 3.5. Other mount options to consider changing include those for asynchronous writes, choosing UDP vs. TCP transports, and choosing between NFSv2 and NFSv3. Also, you could change the export options described in the section "Server Performance."

The benefit of creating 10 test files in Listing 3.5 is that we can now use those to perform the next benchmark—reading files—as seen in Listing 3.6.

Listing 3.6   Repeating a read benchmark several times

```
[root]# cd /
[root]# umount /mnt
```

```
[root]# mount mars:/home/ezk /mnt
[ezk]$ cd /mnt/tests
[ezk]$ n=1
[ezk]$ while test $n -le 10
> do
> time dd if=test-file-$n of=/dev/null bs=4k count=8192
> let n=n+1
> done
```

In Listing 3.6, we first unmount and then remount the file system. This is important in order to flush the client-side file system cache. Then we run the dd command 10 times, this time reading each test file and writing it out to /dev/null (the Unix black hole). Again, you should average the elapsed times and compute a standard deviation to ensure that it is small. These read tests are useful if you plan on changing mount parameters, such as rsize.

The next set of tests practices attribute retrieval and caching. You could repeat this test multiple times while changing attribute-caching mount options as we described in the section "Attribute Caching." Listing 3.7 shows how we test the attribute cache.

Listing 3.7   Micro-benchmarks for file attributes

```
[root]# mount mars:/home/ezk /mnt
[ezk]$ cd /mnt/tests
[ezk]$ ncftpget ftp://ftp.am-utils.org/pub/am-utils/am-utils-6.0.5.tar.gz
[ezk]$ tar zxf am-utils-6.0.5.tar.gz
[ezk]$ cd /
[root]# umount /mnt
[root]# mount mars:/home/ezk /mnt
[ezk]$ cd /mnt/tests
[ezk]$ time ls -lR am-utils-6.0.5 > /dev/null
[ezk]$ time chmod -R o-r am-utils-6.0.5
```

In Listing 3.7, we mount the file system, unpack a recent distribution of am-utils, and then unmount the file system to ensure that all cached attributes are discarded. We then remount it and run two tests: one is the ls command to test the reading of attributes, and the other is the chmod command to change attributes. We picked am-utils-6.0.5 because it is a moderately large distribution that contains over 400 files and two dozen directories—a reasonable mix, and because it would be useful during the general-purpose tests. Remember to repeat the tests several times.

General-Purpose Benchmarks

A good general-purpose test performs a mix of file system operations that users are most often going to perform themselves: looking up and reading many files, writing a fair number of files (both new and old), and performing a few of the remaining file system operations (creating and removing directories, using symbolic links, etc.). One of the most popular methods for achieving this is to compile a large package inside the file system being tested. We will use the latest am-utils package, but you can substitute it with any other large package of your choice, such as the Linux kernel, X11R6, the GNU C compiler, GNU Emacs, etc.

We assume that you have already unpacked a distribution of am-utils as seen in Listing 3.8. To configure and build this package, use the `buildall` script that it comes with. Note that we remove any existing build directories starting with A. before we begin a new build.

Listing 3.8 General-purpose benchmarks using am-utils

```
[ezk]$ cd /mnt/tests/am-utils-6.0.5
[ezk]$ n=1
[ezk]$ while test $n -le 10
> do
> rm -fr A.*
> time ./buildall > /dev/null
> let n=n+1
> done
```

Be patient when running benchmarks with any large package. It could take minutes, even hours, to complete each test. For example, on a fast 600–700MHz Intel CPU, a single `buildall` command could run for 10 to 20 minutes.

Other Tests

The am-utils test is just one possible test, albeit a good one. If you are building a mission-critical NFS system and have lots of time (and money) to spare to optimize its performance, or if you are an NFS developer, you should consider several other NFS benchmarking tools. Note that some of these benchmarks may require a licensing fee, which is why they are not very popular in the Open-Source community. We provide references to these tools in Appendix B, "Online Resources."

nfsstone This is a portable C program developed in the late 80s. It executes many system calls intended to represent a typical server workload and measures the elapsed time to perform all of the operations. The `nfsstone` program has been ported to many operating systems. The tool reports a single figure—the average time it takes to execute a single operation. The main problem with this tool is that different NFS clients and servers are implemented differently, thus producing results that cannot be compared fairly, and that a single distribution of file system operations cannot accurately represent a large portion of NFS users' usage.

nhfsstone   This tool addresses `nfsstone`'s deficiencies by consulting `nfsstat` to gain statistics on the NFS client's and server's distribution of operations. The tool dynamically adjusts the kinds of system calls it performs so that it can reach a desired distribution of NFS calls.

SFS 1.1   The *System File Server* (SFS) benchmark, developed in the early 90s, further improved on previous benchmarks. SFS issues NFS calls directly to the NFS server, and because of this, it doesn't rely as much on operating system differences and NFS client implementations. SFS comes with its own standard user-level NFS client and provides accurate reporting that can be compared fairly among vendors. This version supported only NFSv2 over UDP.

SFS 2.0   This is the second major revision of SFS. It supports NFSv3 and NFS over TCP.

Checking Frequency of NFS Operations

After making any adjustments to your NFS clients and servers, let them run for at least a few days. Then use the `nfsstat` command to check on the distribution of NFS operations on servers, clients, and for different versions of NFS. Listing 3.9 shows the kind of numbers you might get from checking the NFS statistics on a client that uses NFSv3 primarily.

Listing 3.9   Checking NFS statistics for an NFS client

```
[ezk]$ nfsstat -c
Client rpc stats:
calls       retrans      authrefrsh
57443059    13687        0
Client nfs v2:
null        getattr      setattr      root          lookup        readlink
0        0% 82067     1% 0         0% 0          0% 5643649 98% 9142       0%
read        wrcache      write        create        remove        rename
0        0% 0         0% 0         0% 0          0% 0        0% 0          0%
link        symlink      mkdir        rmdir         readdir       fsstat
0        0% 0         0% 0         0% 0          0% 21       0% 58         0%


Client nfs v3:
null        getattr      setattr      lookup        access        readlink
0        0% 17637     0% 527012    1% 7801319  15% 38331065 74% 23079       0%
read        write        create       mkdir         symlink       mknod
```

```
1679413  3% 1073238  2% 246773  0% 39      0% 1285    0% 0        0%
remove      rmdir       rename     link      readdir    readdirplus
273901  0% 10       0% 488409  0% 8633    0% 297492  0% 0        0%
fsstat      fsinfo      pathconf   commit
369     0% 369      0% 0        0% 764996  1%
```

Listing 3.9 shows the number and percentage of the total number for each NFS operation performed on the NFS client. The figures are broken down for NFSv2 and NFSv3. As you can see, this client obviously performs many more NFSv3 calls than NFSv2. For NFSv3, you can see that the most popular operations are access and lookup. The access operation in NFSv3 checks to see if a user is permitted to use a file. In NFSv2, the lookup operation performed both a simple lookup and access checks; these were broken into two operations in NFSv3. Nevertheless, looking up and checking access to files on NFS clients takes the bulk of the operations. This is why so much effort has been devoted to caching of file attributes on NFS clients.

In Listing 3.9, you also see that all other operations represent a small portion of the overall number of operations. That is typical. If you see any other NFS operation taking an unusually large portion of the total, say more than 10 percent, you should investigate why. For example, if you see a large number of mkdir operations on your NFS client, there may be a runaway process or leftover cron job that may be creating directories repeatedly.

TIP Remember that NFS is always going to be slower than local EXT2 file systems. The ultimate solution to improving performance is to avoid using NFS for certain I/O–intensive programs and to run those programs directly on the NFS servers instead. In particular, do not run parallel makes (using, say, gmake -j) over NFS; this is because parallel compilations can create large load spikes on your NFS server. If you do run those parallel makes, you will find that the clients that run those compilations are not very busy compiling software. Instead, they are spending most of their time waiting for the busy (and now overloaded) NFS server to respond to them.

Also of interest in Listing 3.9 are the summary statistics of RPC calls used by NFS. That is seen in the first two lines of the output from nfsstat -c. You should ensure that the number of retransmissions is much smaller than the total number of RPCs performed.

Next, we want to check the NFS server statistics. We do that by running nfsstat -s, as seen in Listing 3.10.

Listing 3.10   Checking NFS statistics for an NFS server

```
[ezk]$ nfsstat -s
Server rpc stats:
calls       badcalls    badauth     badclnt     xdrcall
1943293     114         114         0           0
Server nfs v2:
null        getattr     setattr     root        lookup       readlink
647     17% 29      0%  0       0%  0       0%  221      5% 0          0%
read        wrcache     write       create      remove       rename
1939    50% 0       0%  945    24%  1       0%  1        0% 0          0%
link        symlink     mkdir       rmdir       readdir      fsstat
0        0% 0       0%  0       0%  0       0%  3        0% 17         0%

Server nfs v3:
null        getattr     setattr     lookup      access       readlink
196398  10% 416657  21% 22583   1%  811056  41% 136982   7% 316        0%
read        write       create      mkdir       symlink      mknod
114138   5% 116113   5% 15259   0%  917     0%  536      0% 0          0%
remove      rmdir       rename      link        readdir      readdirplus
9164     0% 482      0% 686     0%  284     0%  44335    2% 36366      1%
fsstat      fsinfo      pathconf    commit
8001     0% 1172     0% 432     0%  7613    0%
```

Listing 3.10 starts with the server RPC statistics. We see a large number of calls, as expected. We also see a small number of bad RPC calls; these calls indicate a problem. Often, this could be the result of a data corruption on the network, or buggy NFS clients that try to contact this server. Luckily, because NFS systems use retransmission, they are not bothered much by such problems. However, you should not see a large number of such bad calls. If you do, it could indicate a more serious problem with your NFS system.

Next in Listing 3.10, we see NFS server statistics for NFSv2 and NFSv3. This particular server is used primarily as an NFSv3 server. You will notice that the most frequent operations are for getting attributes and looking up files. This is typical for an NFS server. The access operation is not very frequent because the NFS client caches attributes by default. We also see that reads and writes take up about 5 percent each, which is typical of moderately busy NFS servers. Busy NFS servers may exhibit read and write frequencies that are as high as 10 percent. Anything significantly higher might indicate that it is time to upgrade your NFS server or spread its file systems into several servers.

We recommend that you check the server and client NFS statistics on all of your hosts, note any abnormalities, investigate, and then solve them. This may mean that you would have to run nfsstat on every host on your site.

> **NOTE** The high number of null calls seen in Listing 3.10 is due to the Amd automounter being used on NFS clients on the site where we measured these. Amd uses the NFS_NULL procedure to ping NFS servers for liveliness every few seconds, testing to see if the servers are alive and responding.

Improving Performance

To improve your NFS system's performance, start by understanding the various export and mount options and what impact they might have on your system. Then, get your network working and stable. After that, select a couple of simple benchmarks and run them to establish a base performance metric of your system given a vanilla, unchanged NFS system. Finally, make small changes to your NFS servers or clients, and repeat the performance benchmarks carefully to find out which change affects performance and how.

Changing mount options and export options are not the only ways to affect performance. Ultimately, it only takes a few NFS clients to overwhelm a single NFS server. That is why busy NFS servers are usually dedicated hosts that do nothing other than serve files. Such servers have large amounts of memory, several CPUs, and are attached to very fast networks. You should always endeavor to make your NFS servers more powerful than your NFS clients.

NFS Server Threads

To improve performance, the NFS server was designed to process multiple RPCs at the same time. The NFS server can fork multiple channels, each of which can handle a single NFS client at a time—much the same way that multithreaded applications do. By default, Linux NFS servers fork eight such threads, as we described in Chapter 1. Eight threads is enough for a small- to medium-size server. Larger servers may require more threads.

If you are running a Linux 2.2 kernel, there is no easy way to find out how busy your NFS server's threads are. You can check the overall load on your server using uptime. If you have a dedicated NFS server and your Unix load-average as reported by uptime is consistently higher than 1.00, your NFS server is too busy.

If you are running a newer Linux 2.4 kernel, you can check the NFS thread utilization as shown in Listing 3.11.

Listing 3.11   Checking the utilization of NFS server threads

```
[ezk]$ uname -r
2.4.0-test10
[ezk]$ grep th /proc/net/rpc/nfsd
th 8 0 0.000 0.000 0.000 0.000 0.000 0.000 0.000 0.000 0.000 0.000
```

The th line of the /proc/net/rpc/nfsd file shows the number of threads (8). The last 10 numbers of that line represent the number of seconds that the thread utilization was at that level. For example, if you see large figures at the last four numbers of the th line, it means that the average thread utilization had been greater than 60 percent. This would indicate a busy NFS server. (Listing 3.11 shows an NFS server that has not been used at all, since all 10 figures are zero.)

Regardless of the version of your Linux kernel, if you think that your NFS server is too busy and may need more threads, then you have to restart it with more threads. Edit the startup file /etc/rc.d/init.d/nfs and change the lines that say

```
# Number of servers to be started out by default

RPCNFSDCOUNT=8
```

so that the RPCNFSDCOUNT is higher, say 16 or 24:

```
# Number of servers to be started out by default

RPCNFSDCOUNT=16
```

Then restart your NFS server:

```
[root]# /etc/rc.d/init.d/nfs restart
```

Afterward, let your NFS server run for a while and check your thread utilization and load again. If it indeed went lower, you would know that your NFS server needed more threads. If it does not go lower, you can try and increase the number of threads again, but that may be insufficient; in fact, you may have to move some of the file systems on a busy NFS server to a new one.

Socket Input Queue Memory Limits

One additional concern with increasing the number of NFS server threads is how much buffer space Linux reserves for network requests. This is the location where Linux keeps network packets while they are being processed, also known as the *socket input queue*. You can find out the default size of the input queue, as seen in Listing 3.1. On Linux, this is relatively small for a busy NFS server, only 64KB. This means that if you are running eight NFS server threads (the default), and no other networking activity but NFS is running on the server (unlikely), then the maximum amount of data that each thread can support is only 8KB. So no matter how much you adjust mount options, such as `rsize` and `wsize`, Linux would only process a small amount of data at a time. On a busy NFS server, especially one where you had to increase the number of server threads, you should also increase the socket input queue size.

Unfortunately, increasing the socket input queue size permanently is not recommended. The Linux kernel has not been tested thoroughly with larger input queues, and your system may not be stable if you permanently increase the queue size. Therefore, it is important to increase the value only for the NFS server. Ideally, this would be done through socket options, such as those with the `setsockopt` system call. But the NFS server's code does not support such an option. Instead, you must increase the global size of the input queue before starting the NFS server and then bring it back down afterward.

The right amount to increase the global size depends on the load on your server. Eight kilobytes per thread is too small for a busy NFS server. You should increase this to 16KB or 32KB per thread. Suppose you also increased the number of threads to 20. Then you should up the input queue size to $20 \times 32\text{KB}$, or 655360.

Again, you must edit your NFS startup script, `/etc/rc.d/init.d/nfs`. Look for the two lines that read

```
echo -n "Starting NFS daemon: "
daemon rpc.nfsd $RPCNFSDCOUNT
```

and change them as seen in Listing 3.12.

Listing 3.12   Adjusting the NFS startup script with a larger socket input queue

```
echo 655360 > /proc/sys/net/core/rmem_default
echo 655360 > /proc/sys/net/core/rmem_max
echo -n "Starting NFS daemon: "
daemon rpc.nfsd $RPCNFSDCOUNT
echo 65536 > /proc/sys/net/core/rmem_default
echo 65536 > /proc/sys/net/core/rmem_max
```

The first two lines in Listing 3.12 increase the global socket input queue size to 655360 bytes. The third line prints a message on the console that indicates what happens next, and the fourth line actually starts the NFS daemon. The last two lines reset the global socket input queue size back to its original, smaller value of 64KB.

After you make those edits, you should restart your NFS server as follows:

```
[root]# /etc/rc.d/init.d/nfs restart
```

The Network File System

PART 1

Once the NFS server restarts, it will use the large socket input size, while the rest of the system will continue to use the regular, smaller socket input size.

Performance Improvements to IDE Disks

If you are using IDE disks on your NFS server, be sure to enable DMA access and 32-bit I/O support for those. By default, Red Hat systems do not enable these advanced features because not all IDE drives and IDE controllers support them. Nowadays, however, most systems do support these features. Turning these features on can significantly improve performance for local disk access—as much as 5–7 times faster for bulk disk writes. This can impact an NFS server's performance, especially for synchronous NFS operations.

To turn these features on, use the `hdparm` command as seen in Listing 3.13.

Listing 3.13   Improving disk I/O performance on the NFS server

```
[root]# hdparm -d1 -c1 -k1 /dev/hda
```

Assuming you only have one IDE disk named `/dev/hda`, the `hdparm` command in Listing 13.3 turns on DMA support (-d) and 32-bit I/O support (-c) and ensures that these options are kept on (-k) even after a disk reset or system reboot.

In Sum

There are many parameters that can affect the performance of your NFS system significantly. On the NFS server, there are a few export options that tell the server how to handle and cache writes. On the NFS client, there are many mount options that affect the reading and writing of files, attribute caching, network transports, and more.

We have listed a few methods and tools for testing the performance of your NFS system and grouped them in two categories: focused tests (micro-benchmarks) and general-purpose tests. Micro-benchmarks test individual NFS operations, while general-purpose benchmarks provide an overall performance metric. We have shown you how to run these tools carefully and methodically so that you can produce accurate results. Our recommendation is to be patient—make small changes, test them thoroughly, and let them remain in effect for a while before making new changes.

Some of the parameters that affect performance may also affect the security of your NFS system. We have mentioned those in this chapter wherever applicable. In the next chapter, we discuss the security of your NFS system in greater detail.

4

Securing NFS

Computer system security has become a greater concern in recent years. With the growing popularity of the Internet, the number of attacks on systems has increased. Not only is the number of vulnerable computers large, but the number of vulnerabilities within an individual computer is also large. Complex computer systems are made up of many components, and each component can easily compromise the security of the entire system. This chapter covers the security aspects of NFS—both from the server's perspective and the client's perspective. When appropriate, we mention how other security problems can also impact NFS's security.

How much security should you have? This question is constantly on the minds of administrators and users. The best answer I have heard is from Matt Blaze, a world-renowned security expert, who said that the amount of security you should have on your computer systems should be proportional to how much effort attackers will be willing to apply to break into your system. To that effect, a national military lab should have a different level of security from a public high school.

You should consider how important a target your system is, what you are protecting, and the ramifications to your site should it be compromised. One important factor in determining your level of security is the impact it has on your users. Higher security often results in decreased convenience to users:

- They may no longer be allowed to access certain services.
- They may have to authenticate themselves often (typing passwords and answering other challenges).

- They may have to go through intermediary systems to get to the final service.
- They may constantly have to justify to management and administrators why they need more access rights.

Choosing the right set of security features involves balancing many considerations: some security features reduce performance, some inconvenience users, and some make it hard for administrators to do their jobs. Take care to provide an appropriate level of security for both your systems and your users.

A common misconception about computer security is that you can have total security. There is no such thing, just as no amount of security alarms or protection devices can prevent a determined thief from stealing a car. Security is not all or nothing—black or white. Instead, security is a wide range of shades of gray. You cannot have total security, but you can have *more* or *less* security, by selectively applying small measures to increase or decrease the security of your system. Each measure you apply makes it more difficult for attackers to break into your system. Attackers who see a site that is reasonably protected are likely to move on to an easier target.

Several common security policies are used. Most experts would agree that the best policy is to turn off all access to a computer system, and then gradually and selectively turn on access to needed services. This way you avoid keeping access open to services for which vulnerabilities will be discovered and exploited in the future. We strongly recommend this policy, and we use it throughout this chapter.

This chapter covers many aspects of the security of the network file system. It begins with a discussion of security for NFS servers. A server-side security policy defines who can access the many services that make up an NFS server, who can access files that the server exports, and under what conditions these services and files can be accessed. We continue by examining the security of NFS clients: what users who run programs on these clients can do with files exported by NFS servers. After presenting the basic security features of NFS servers and clients, several common topics in NFS security are discussed. We close this chapter with a brief discussion of post-break-in actions you should take after your system has been compromised.

Server Security

Securing your NFS servers is the most important part of securing your NFS service. It is more important to secure your servers than your clients. A compromised server can impact the data and work of a whole site. A compromised client, on the other hand, often has a more limited impact. Your NFS servers are also the last barriers between attackers and the actual data that the servers protect. Clients can be compromised, but if your servers are relatively secure, you can limit how much damage attackers can do to your site.

There are two components to securing your NFS servers: access to RPC services, and export permissions on file systems. First, you should protect access to the various RPC services that make up an NFS server. Chapter 1, "NFS Basics and Protocols," describes the many services that are part of an NFS server: the portmapper, the `rpc.nfsd` daemon, the mount daemon, the locking daemon, the status daemon, the quota daemon, and more. We show how to secure access to these services using network access filters called *TCP Wrappers*. These wrappers can, for example, ensure that only hosts within your domain can access the portmapper.

The second component of NFS server security is the selection and use of the many export options that can impact what access NFS clients have. For example, an NFS server can enforce read-only access on certain exported directories and clients can try to write files in those directories, but the write actions will fail.

Access to NFS Server Services

The TCP Wrappers library (`libwrap`) contains a set of functions that consult two configuration files to determine who can access which services. The two files that the library uses to control access are `/etc/hosts.allow` and `/etc/hosts.deny`. These two files have a similar and simple text-based syntax: each line lists one or more comma-delimited service names, followed by a colon, and then followed by a comma-delimited list of hosts (a client list). A special keyword, `ALL`, can be used in place of a service name list or a host list as a wildcard, indicating that the line should be applied to all services or hosts respectively. As is usual with such files, blank lines, whitespace, and lines beginning with the "#" comment character are ignored.

The TCP Wrappers library performs these actions, in order, when a client tries to access a service on a host protected by these two configuration files:

1. If the hostname and IP address of the client match a service name that is listed in `/etc/hosts.allow`, then the client is allowed access.

2. If the hostname and IP address of the client match a service name that is listed in `/etc/hosts.deny`, then the client is denied access to that service.

3. Otherwise, the host is allowed to access the service. This is the default access rule and matches what normal Unix systems do: let everyone in. This unfortunate default behavior ensures the backward compatibility with previous (and insecure) Unix access permissions. It is therefore important that you use the `/etc/hosts.allow` and `/etc/hosts.deny` files and configure them correctly.

The values that you can use in the list of hosts that apply to the service are similar to the syntax of host access in /etc/exports files:

Hostnames   A string beginning with a period, such as .example.com, indicates that the service access should be applied to all hosts in the example.com domain.

Host addresses   A numeric string ending with a period indicates all the hosts that end with that IP address. For example, the string 128.59.17. includes all of the hosts from 128.59.17.0 to 128.59.17.255.

NIS netgroups   Any string starting with "@" indicates an NIS (the service formerly known as YP) network group. For example, the string @laptops applies to all of the hosts that are part of the laptops netgroup of your NIS server.

Network/netmask pairs   Any expression that includes a network number and network mask, delimited by a "/" character, indicates a subset of hosts from a particular network. For example, the designation 128.59.8.16/255.255.255.248 includes all of the hosts from 128.59.8.16 to 128.59.8.23.

The TCP Wrappers library is flexible and powerful. It can do more than what we have described, such as running arbitrary programs when matches are made. Additional details of using these two files can be found in the host_access(5) manual page.

TIP   While in this chapter we only consider NFS security, this library can be used to control access to many other services such as FTP and Web servers, rlogin, telnet, and more. Recall that any one component that is vulnerable can lead to a break-in of your site. If that happens, all other services—NFS included—can be compromised. Therefore, you should use TCP Wrappers to secure as many services as possible. Moreover, you should ensure that your site is up-to-date with respect to security patches from your software vendors. These are important because the TCP Wrappers library can only secure those programs that have been linked with it.

We begin by configuring our /etc/hosts.deny file such that, by default, it denies access to all hosts and all services. We use the special wildcard keyword ALL twice, as seen in Listing 4.1.

Listing 4.1   A sample /etc/hosts.deny file

```
ALL: ALL
```

Note that by denying access to all services, you will also prevent access to services that are not related to NFS, such as FTP and Web servers. Next, we gradually allow some access to NFS services. Listing 4.2 shows a mix of examples that enables all of the NFS-related services to be accessible for various parts of a site named example.com, whose class C network address is 128.59.10.0.

Listing 4.2   A sample /etc/hosts.allow file

```
portmap:         128.59.10.
lockd:           .example.com
nfsd:            128.59.10.0/255.255.255.0
mountd,rquotad:  @trusted-clients
statd:           128.59.10.,control.special.com
```

WARNING   Do not put RPC program names in your /etc/hosts.allow and /etc/hosts.deny files. Use their respective *service* names. For example, the service name for the mount daemon is mountd, but the program name is rpc.mountd. If you place the wrong service name in these configuration files, it will not match the service that you intended to control. As a result, you may inadvertently allow access to some RPC services that you intended to restrict.

The meaning of the five lines on Listing 4.2 are as follows:

portmap   We allow access to the portmapper only from the site's IP addresses. It is important not to put anything but IP numbers in the portmap lines of these files, to avoid the possibility of infinite loops. Hostname lookups can indirectly cause portmap activity, which can trigger hostname lookups, which can indirectly cause portmap activity, which will trigger...

lockd   We allow access to the locking daemon from all hosts that are part of the example.com domain.

nfsd   The NFS server itself permits access only for those hosts that are within the site's class C network.

mount,rquotad   Here we list two services that use the same access controls: the mount daemon and the remote quotas daemon. Both allow access to hosts that are listed in the trusted-clients NIS netgroup.

statd   We allow access to the status daemon from hosts in the site's network, as well as an additional, external host called control.special.com.

> **WARNING** Avoid placing the localhost name or IP address (127.0.0.1) in these configuration files. Many administrators think it is harmless and some even think it is necessary. You may only need to include localhost in these configuration files if you plan on NFS-mounting the server's partitions on the same host. Otherwise, opening access to 127.0.0.1 may decrease your security due to (a) the portmapper's ability to redirect RPC calls to other RPC services, and (b) IP spoofing attacks that show up as having arrived from localhost's address. Such attacks have been attempted in the past.

One of the nicest things about the use of /etc/hosts.allow and /etc/hosts.deny is that changes you make take effect immediately. New hosts that try to access these services are allowed or denied that access as soon as you save the changes in these two files. You do not need to restart any service, reboot, or send HUP signals to any daemon. Note, however, that previously allowed access that is ongoing will not be terminated by adding new restrictions. For that reason, check carefully if, say, a host you are now disallowing access has been able to gain that access prior to your changes. In that case, you may wish to terminate that host's access by killing the relevant daemons. The easiest and safest method, however, is simply to reboot your host.

Support for TCP Wrappers

You should ensure that your system comes with support for the TCP Wrappers library. Red Hat 7.0 and older systems do include the /usr/lib/libwrap.a library as part of the tcp_wrappers RPM. However, most of the RPC services that NFS uses were not linked with it. You should start by verifying that you have the TCP Wrappers library installed on your system, and which version of the NFS Utilities software you have. This is seen in Listing 4.3.

Listing 4.3 Checking for versions of the TCP Wrappers software and NFS utilities

```
[ezk]$ rpm -q tcp_wrappers
tcp_wrappers-7.6-15
[ezk]$ rpm -q nfs-utils
nfs-utils-0.1.9.1-7
```

Listing 4.3 shows that the sample Red Hat system has the TCP Wrappers package installed, as well as the NFS Utilities package. However, the version of nfs-utils is old. Install version 0.2.0 or newer; only those versions include TCP Wrappers support in all NFS programs. To get a newer version, either install one from Red Hat's FTP site (if available) or retrieve the sources to the nfs-utils package and build them yourself. Both procedures are detailed in Chapter 7, "Building and Installing the Linux Kernel and NFS Software."

When you are done updating the `nfs-utils` software, verify that it compiled with the TCP Wrappers library, as seen in Listing 4.4.

Listing 4.4   Checking for TCP Wrapper support in RPC services

```
[ezk]$ strings /usr/sbin/rpc.mountd | grep hosts
/etc/hosts.allow
/etc/hosts.deny
@(#) hosts_ctl.c 1.4 94/12/28 17:42:27
@(#) hosts_access.c 1.21 97/02/12 02:13:22
```

Listing 4.4 shows how to extract text strings' information out of the mount daemon's binary. In this case, it shows a binary that indeed includes support for the TCP Wrappers.

NFS Server Export Options

TCP Wrappers control access to the NFS service. Once access is granted, export options control the type of access granted to the NFS file systems. This section describes the NFS server-side export options that relate to security. The full list of export options is available in Table 2.2 in Chapter 2, "Configuring NFS." It is interesting to note that there are more security-related export options than all other types of options. The reason is that the NFS server is in the best position to enforce security restrictions on NFS clients. NFS clients can be compromised more easily, but the server is the one that stands between potentially malicious clients and access to the actual files stored on the server's local disks.

We divide the security export options into five categories and then describe each set of options:

- Read and write server access
- UID and GID squashing
- Port security
- Lock daemon
- Partial mounts and submounts

Read and Write Server Access

The two options, `ro` and `rw`, are the most common and familiar options. The `ro` option limits the NFS clients to read-only access. This means that clients cannot write files, delete or make directories, or otherwise perform any operation that changes the state of the file system. Read-only export access is the default.

The rw option allows user processes running on NFS clients to make those changes. However, there are exceptions for the root user, as explained next.

UID and GID Squashing

In Unix, the root user is dangerous because it can execute any command and change any file on the system. In an NFS client-server scenario, the server must be protected against malicious clients. Users can gain root access quite easily on NFS clients; for example, you can install Linux from scratch on your laptop and pick your own root password. If NFS clients are allowed root access to the NFS server, they can easily subvert the server, thus affecting a whole site that may depend on that NFS server's files. For these reasons, several NFS server export options can change the credentials of certain users and groups. This changing of credentials is known as *squashing*.

The most important option is root_squash. This option changes the effective UID of root processes from 0 (root) to –2 (nobody). That way, root processes running on NFS clients will execute as user nobody: a user ID with the least amount of privileges. In effect, trying to perform operations as the privileged root user on an NFS client reduces that user to one with fewer privileges than normal users. The default is root_squash.

There are cases where administrators wish to allow root access to NFS clients; for example, to allow a highly secured host to access all NFS servers as root. That secure client is often used to correct problems on NFS servers that cannot be corrected on the server itself. This is achieved using the no_root_squash export option. It is best to not turn off root squashing unless you really need it and there are no other ways to do what you want.

WARNING Do not use the nobody UID or nobody GID for anything on your system. Do not assign a password to either. Ensure that no files or directories are owned or group-owned by nobody. If you do, NFS clients using root privileges will be able to access any resource that is owned by nobody on your NFS server. Root squashing works well only if no resources are assigned to either the nobody UID or the nobody GID.

A stronger form of root squashing is squashing all UIDs and GIDs. This is off by default (no_all_squash) but can be turned on using the all_squash option. With this option, all UIDs and all GIDs—not just root—are mapped to the nobody UID and GID, respectively. This is useful when exporting read-only file systems that contain no executables but lots of data and text files such as manual pages or GNU info pages.

The UID and GID to squash to is that of nobody, which is –2 by default. The credentials of the nobody user can be changed to fit a particular site's needs or to interoperate with some systems on which it is not –2. The anonuid option can change the UID that the NFS server will map user requests to. Similarly, the anongid option can change the GID that the NFS server will use to squash group requests.

For example, to squash all UIDs to 60001 and all GIDs to 60002 (numbers that are popular on some SysV systems), use the following export option:

```
all_squash,anonuid=60001,anongid=60002
```

Whatever you change either anonuid or anongid to, ensure that these represent a user and group with the least privileges on your NFS server.

General-Purpose UID and GID Range Mapping

In the old days of the user-level NFS server (unfsd), there was support for general-purpose mapping of UID and GID ranges. For example, you could set the NFS server to map the UIDs 2301 through 2304 to 106 through 109, respectively. This kind of mapping can be useful when NFS-mounting across different administrative domains—where the same UIDs and GIDs have been assigned to different users over the years.

Support for range mapping is not available in the kernel-level NFS server, knfsd. It was easier to provide that support in a user-level process such as unfsd, but more difficult in the kernel. Support for this feature may be developed during the Linux 2.5 kernel series.

Port Security

NFS servers by default expect requests to arrive from port numbers that are no greater than 1024. These port numbers are often known as *secure* ports because only root users can use them. This default behavior can also be forced using the secure NFS export option. However, there are cases of NFS clients that send their requests on port numbers that are greater than 1024; these are known as *insecure* ports. A Linux NFS server that expects access from secure ports will refuse to serve requests from insecure ports. Clients that are known to do this are AIX and some BSD4.4 systems.

If your Linux server must interoperate with NFS clients that send requests from insecure ports, you should export your file systems using the insecure option. Unfortunately, using this option increases the chances that client-side non-root processes might gain unauthorized access to your NFS server. Usually, however, this is a small concern compared to clients that can easily become root. Furthermore, the `insecure` option may be necessary for your Linux server to interoperate with some non-Linux NFS clients.

Lock Daemon

The Network Lock Manager (NLM) handles file and record locking over NFS, as we described in Chapter 1. Over the years of NFS's existence, NLM has been known as the least-thought-out and buggiest piece of code. Some of the problems with NLM stemmed from the fundamental stateless design decision of the NFS server; NLM must keep state, and it was difficult to implement it reliably. Consequently, some NFS clients and servers have different implementations of the NLM subsystem; others may not even implement all of NLM. The following export options help you to interoperate your Linux NFS server with different NFS clients.

The `secure_locks` option, on by default, tells the NFS server to authenticate NLM requests so it can ensure who they came from. Some NFS clients (Compaq Tru64, SunOS 4, and others) send NLM requests from user `daemon`, instead of the root user. If you use the `secure_locks` option with those clients, you will get authentication errors when trying to perform any NLM operation. Instead, you have to turn off NLM authentication for any file systems exported to those clients, using the `insecure_locks` export option.

NOTE The `auth_nlm` option is the old name for, and is synonymous with, `secure_locks`. The `no_auth_nlm` option is the old name for, and is synonymous with, `insecure_locks`.

Partial Mounts and Submounts

Linux servers export a volume to a client. That volume does not have to be exactly a whole file system; it can be a subdirectory of it. Furthermore, other mounted file systems could be mounted on the server, below the exported directory. Special export options are available to handle situations that arise when part of a file system is exported, and when an exported file system may contain additional submounts.

NFS file handles are created by the NFS server. They contain information such as the file system ID, the inode number of the file, and more. One problem with NFS file handles is that they can be spoofed. If an attacker knows what to put in the NFS file handle, the attacker can create a fake file handle and send it in an RPC request to an NFS server. If the file handle matches an actual file on the NFS server, that server will grant access to the attacking client. When you export a subdirectory of a whole file system, it is easier to spoof file handles to other parts of the exported file system, because the file handles given to the client already contain much of the information needed to access the rest (and unexported) portions of the whole file system.

The `subtree_check` option, on by default, certifies that a file handle really belongs to the portion of the file system that has been exported. Suppose a Linux NFS server has a file system `/n/proj`, and it exports `/n/proj/kernel` to a certain client. Each time the client sends an NFS operation—and thus an NFS file handle—to the NFS server, the server will ensure that the file handle sent really belongs to the `/n/proj/kernel` directory (or anywhere below). If, for example, the server gets a file handle that points to a file `/n/proj/ids/main.c`, the NFS server will refuse the access to this file and return a "Stale File Handle" error message back to the client.

You can turn off subtree checking using the `no_subtree_check` export option. If you do, then the NFS server will not certify file handle validity for other parts of the file system. In the example just shown, the NFS server will grant access to a properly formatted file handle for the file `/n/proj/ids/main.c`. You should not turn off subtree checking unless absolutely necessary. If you export a whole file system, however, you can use `no_subtree_check` to speed up access to that file system a bit. Since there is no danger of accessing other parts of the whole file system, you can avoid these checks on each file handle that the server receives.

On the flip side of exporting parts of file systems, NFS servers must know how to handle additional file systems mounted below the exported directory. Normally, NFS servers do not show submounts below exported directories. This is the default and can also be enforced using the `hide` option. The reason for this default behavior is twofold. First, administrators are used to controlling each file system's export options individually; they will be confused if exporting one file system indirectly exports another. Second, and more serious, exporting submounts can cause infinite loops. Consider, for example, if the submount that the server exports is itself an NFS mount point that belongs to the actual client. Recall that NFS clients can also be servers. To satisfy file access of the submount to the NFS client, the NFS server must contact the NFS server for that submount. If that server is also the NFS client, the two hosts could get into an infinite loop trying to contact each other to resolve file requests.

If you are certain that no loops exist in your submounts, you can use the `nohide` export option to allow the NFS client transparent access to submounts on the NFS server. Note that the NFS client would not know that it is accessing a submount on the NFS server; to the client, this exported volume would seem just like one file system.

Client Security

So far we've discussed server-side NFS security. However, the server is only part of the total NFS security environment. In this section we consider client-side NFS security.

These are mount options that administrators can use to ensure that normal users running on the NFS client are restricted from performing certain dangerous actions.

Note that users with root access on NFS clients can easily bypass these restrictions by remounting the file system with other options. For that reason, you must first secure your NFS server. Nevertheless, using these client-side NFS mount options can still improve the security of your system. Recall that security is an ongoing effort to increase the level of security at your site, and every little bit can help.

Devices and Executables

The dev option, on by default, allows access to special block and character devices (often found under /dev). This option is needed primarily for diskless NFS clients. Otherwise, it should be turned off using the nodev mount option. Access to devices across NFS is dangerous; such access can, for example, allow NFS clients to read any parts of local disks if the access permissions of the exported device entries allow it. In other words, one poorly configured NFS server can easily open up vulnerabilities on all NFS clients that use that server.

Similar to preventing access to devices, the noexec option prevents the execution of binaries on the mounted file system. This option is off by default, therefore allowing the execution of binaries, which can also be explicitly enabled using the exec option. Disabling execution of binaries is useful if you are mounting a file system that contains data and text files such as manual pages, or if you are mounting a file system with binaries for a different operating system.

UIDs, GIDs, and User Access

The suid option, on by default, allows set-UID and set-GID programs to execute across NFS with the normal meaning of these set bits. That is, a set-UID binary from such a mounted file system would run with the effective UID of the owner of that executable. Set-UID binaries, especially set-UID root binaries, are dangerous because they can allow root access over NFS. For that reason, administrators concerned with security turn off this support using the nosuid option. Keep the setuid option on only if you know that you are mounting a file system that exports set-UID or set-GID binaries and you want these binaries to work with their permission bits set. To locate any set-bit binaries under, say, /n/path, run the find command as seen in Listing 4.5.

Listing 4.5 Finding set-UID and set-GID binaries

```
[ezk]$ find /n/path -perm -4000 -or -perm -2000 -ls
```

One additional problem with set-UID binaries is that newer Linux kernels are pickier about how they handle such binaries. Some older set-UID binaries were written to assume that, once executed, these binaries would gain full root privileges and be able to write everywhere on the system. This assumption is not always right when mixing local disks and remote NFS mounts. If you suspect that you are using such old set-UID binaries, and they do not appear to work correctly over NFS for your site, then you may have to set the mount option `broken_suid` for mounting the volume that contains those binaries. Ideally, however, you should avoid using such old set-UID binaries. Instead, use newer binaries from a newer Linux distribution, or rebuild these binaries from their latest stable sources.

Read and Write Client Access

The two options `rw` and `ro` control, from the NFS client's point of view, what kind of access it has to files on the mounted volume. With the `rw` option (the default), the client would be allowed to read and write files, as well as perform any operations that change the state of the file system (removing files, creating directories, etc.). The `ro` option only allows operations that do not change the state of the file system, such as reading files, listing directories, etc.

Interestingly, by default, the NFS client mount option is `rw`, while the default NFS server export option is `ro`. This means that if all options remain at their default values, NFS servers would not allow writing to exported volumes, while NFS clients would try to do so. If the clients try to write to such volumes, they would get back the NFS error "Read Only File System."

Securing Your NFS System

At this point, all the basic features and options that administrators can use to secure their NFS systems have been covered. We've discussed server-side and client-side security separately. Now it is time to examine general security tips that consider the overall site as one unit.

The Basics

We begin with the basics of NFS security: closing the biggest holes first. Start by securing your NFS servers, and then secure your NFS clients. The reason for this has been repeated throughout this chapter several times: your NFS servers are the last guardians that protect the files that the NFS servers export. When you secure your NFS hosts, address this check-list of topics:

- Consider the overall security policy: deny all access, and only give out access that is needed. That means, do not export your NFS volumes to any hosts other than those that explicitly need them. Export all file systems using read-only (ro) permissions unless the clients need to write to those file systems. Use root_squash as much as possible.

- Avoid exporting file systems to hosts that you do not trust. At any site are often a mix of hosts that are under full control of the site's administrators, as well as some hosts that are not (especially laptops). If you, the administrator, do not have full and exclusive control of some hosts, you should avoid exporting NFS volumes to them.

- Avoid giving out too many root accounts; the fewer the better. In particular, ensure that no users have root accounts on NFS clients. Since that is difficult to guarantee (anyone can reinstall a Linux laptop and give themselves a root account), use the root_squash and ro export options on your NFS servers. Users with local root access (especially with their own root IDs) can always use the su program to become any other user and see that user's file. For that reason, local root accounts should be avoided.

- Use restrictive NFS client-side mount options as much as possible; mount file systems read only (ro), and do not allow set-UID binaries (nosuid), devices (nodev), or executables (noexec) unless any of those are needed.

- If you have many NFS clients, consider using an Automounter such as Amd. Amd can ease the task of setting a fixed security policy via client-side NFS mount options; it can centralize all of these in one place. Otherwise, you will have to set and main-tain the correct mount options on each client's /etc/fstab file. We discuss the Amd Automounter in Part 2 of this book.

Mapping UIDs and GIDs

First, use the root_squash export option to ensure that no clients can access the servers' files as root. If you must use no_root_squash, consider why you need to do so. If you need to, say, install new software over NFS, and it must be done as root, then you should instead install that software directly on the NFS server.

Experienced system administrators often like to leave themselves multiple ways of getting into hosts (infamous back doors). The reason is that when something goes wrong on these hosts, one or more ways of getting in to fix the problem may not be possible; hopefully, at least one access method could still be available to the administrators. Suppose that somehow bad binaries got installed on your NFS servers, and you cannot log in to those servers remotely to fix the binaries, but you do have NFS access. If you could mount the server's partitions on a secure client and have root access through that client, then you could fix those binaries remotely. Some sites choose one host and secure it thoroughly using a firewall, packet filtering, TCP Wrappers, and other methods. Then, they export several important NFS partitions to that secure client, using the no_root_squash option. This way, that one secure client can be used as a last resort to fix some problems on the NFS servers.

Ports and Services

Use the TCP Wrappers library and configure your /etc/hosts.allow and /etc/ hosts.deny files to restrict access to the various NFS services so only those hosts that need access get it. Ensure that your NFS services are all built with the libwrap.a library as seen in Listing 4.4.

Recall that while the NFS server is stateless, many other RPC services are not. This means that they contain state—or information—that attackers might try to get. In particular, you should secure access to your portmapper. The portmapper controls access to many RPC-based services, not just the NFS ones. The portmapper can reveal the list of services running on your system via rpcinfo -p. It can redirect RPCs between services, so if one RPC service is broken, others can be too. Anyone who can send RPC commands to the portmapper can unmap (unregister) RPC services such as NFS or the mount daemon service from the portmapper, using the PMAP_UNSET portmapper RPC call; this is a typical denial-of-service attack and often requires a system reboot to fix.

Finally, do not forget that the security of the system is as good as its weakest link. Make sure that all other services you allow on any host are secure: NIS, DNS, FTP, HTTP, SMTP, NNTP, and so on. Look at your /etc/inetd.conf file, see which additional services are running, and turn them off if not needed. Plus, always keep up with the latest vendor-released security fixes and apply them as soon as they are available.

Security by Obscurity

A weak form of security known as *security by obscurity* advocates hiding various services in places where they are not usually found. For example, you can instruct your NFS server to run on a port other than the default port 2049. In that way, attackers who expect NFS to use port 2049 would not find it there and might assume that NFS is not running on the host.

There are two problems with obscuring methods such as these. First, they only stop novice attackers. Sophisticated attackers use port-scanning tools to check every port on your system for any available service. They are likely to discover the new port you are using with NFS relatively easily.

Second, if you change the nfsd port, you must make sure that all other services that work with the NFS server know of this port. While some of the tools in the nfs-utils package do support alternate ports (using a standard -p command-line switch), not all of the tools in that package do. It is expected that nfs-utils versions after 0.2.2 will begin supporting the -p option on all NFS programs.

RPC Security The RPC system allows for various authentication and security forms to be used, also known as Secure-RPC. When developers write RPC programs, they can choose one of these types of RPC security methods. The form of security is initialized when an RPC server begins running. This choice controls how RPC clients are allowed to communicate with a secure RPC server, what information would be exchanged, whether it would be encrypted, and so on. Usually, RPC systems support three types of security methods:

AUTH_NONE No authentication is used. Avoid this at all cost.

AUTH_UNIX Simple UID/GID credentials are passed between RPC servers and clients. This is a very simple and easily subverted authentication method. Unfortunately, it is also the default method and is available on most Unix hosts.

AUTH_DES This authentication method uses the DES encryption standard. It is much more secure. However, due to encryption export regulations and such, many systems, including Linux, do not support this authentication method natively.

Additional authentication methods available on some systems include Kerberos, Diffie-Hellman, and others. Unfortunately, none of those are readily available for Linux either. Since you cannot secure your RPC communications on Linux hosts very tightly, it becomes more imperative that you secure all other parts of your network communications: TCP/UDP transports and the NFS protocol.

NFSv4 holds great promise for better NFS security. For one thing, this is a stateful protocol that combines all of the NFS-related services into a single protocol that uses a single TCP port; therefore, a single resource can be secured more easily. Also, NFSv4 contains hooks for additional security mechanisms (authentication and encryption) not previously available. For more information on NFSv4, see Chapter 6, "NFS Version 4."

NFS Versions

Use NFS version 3 as much as possible. Not only is the NFSv3 protocol faster, but it supplies various security provisions. Among the most important features of NFSv3 is the doubling of the maximum NFS file handle size, from 32 to 64 bytes. The method of construction and exact contents of 32-byte file handles on some operating systems is well known and easily guessed. If the root file handle of a file system can be guessed, access to that whole file system becomes immediately available to the attacker. Such file handles can be guessed using brute-force methods using as little as an hour on a LAN and a few days on a WAN. (A student of mine wrote such a program a few years ago, and if you ask really nicely, I might give you the sources.)

Using NFSv3, you can decrease the chances that your file handles can be easily guessed. However, note the following two caveats:

- The NFSv3 protocol specifies that file handle sizes can be *up to* 64 bytes. They can be as small as 32 bytes. Therefore, the actual file handles depend on the implementation of your NFS server.

- Some poor implementations of the NFSv3 server use 64-byte handles, but only fill in the first 32 bytes of those, and pad the remaining ones with zeros. This is no more secure than having just 32-byte file handles. In a sense, it is even worse because it provides a false sense of security to users who think they are using longer and more secure file handles.

Transports

Use TCP with NFS. While TCP is often available only with NFSv3, some operating systems have TCP support for NFSv2 as well. The TCP transport is more secure than UDP. TCP packets contain sequence numbers; guarantee an ordered delivery of packets, making it harder to inject fake packets; and are more difficult to spoof. UDP packets require no acknowledgment, can be easily spoofed by changing the source or destination addresses in the packet headers, and contain no sequence numbers or handshaking mechanism that can validate who they came from.

UDP and NFS

You might be wondering, if UDP is so unsafe, why was it used with NFS all those years? When Sun initially developed NFS in the early eighties, CPUs were much slower and memory sizes smaller. At that time, the cost of using TCP was greater than UDP. TCP consumed much more memory and CPU resources than were available. Furthermore, security had not been such a large problem on the Internet back then, when the full list of hosts on the Internet could be easily enumerated; there simply were not very many attacks happening on Unix hosts in those days.

Fully-Qualified Host Names

Use Fully-Qualified Host Names (FQHNs) in all of your NFS configuration files: /etc/exports, /etc/fstab, /etc/hosts.allow, /etc/hosts.deny, etc. If you use short host-names, you open yourself to various attacks that exploit this, especially attacks via DNS or NIS. Details of the security of DNS and NIS are beyond the scope of this book. For more information on those, see Appendix B, "Online Resources," and *Linux DNS Server Administration* (Craig Hunt Linux Library) by Craig Hunt (Sybex, 2000).

Furthermore, do not export or NFS-mount via the localhost name or address (127.0.0.1). There is a myth among administrators that you should always include the localhost's address in permission on various configuration files, and that it is safe. Not only is it not needed, it is also not safe. Several clever IP spoofing attacks and RPC redirection attacks try to exploit those sites that allow NFS or RPC access to the localhost address.

Quotas

Whenever possible, use quotas on your exported file systems. Quotas are often ignored and much hated by users and administrators alike. Yet, if you do not use quotas, you open your NFS servers to denial-of-service attacks. Malicious users can fill up a remote file system, thus preventing other users, sometimes even administrators and root users, from writing any new files on that file system. In the extreme this can hang some hosts or even crash them.

Firewalls

Consider the use of firewalls on your system. TCP Wrappers can only prevent access to services that have been compiled with libwrap.a and configured in the relevant /etc/hosts.deny file. In contrast, a firewall works at a lower level and can control access to any service on any port. Firewalls are thus more powerful.

Most firewalls are used to protect a single site from outside attacks. You can set your firewall rules to deny all access to all ports, and then gradually allow some outgoing and some incoming access as needed. For example, you should allow SMTP (E-mail, port 25) to go in and out, as well as HTTP (port 80). You might also allow incoming SSH access (on port 22). In this fashion you can gradually allow more access through your firewall as needed.

If you choose not to deny all services first, but to allow everything in and out, then you will quickly have to deny access to these NFS-related services:

Portmapper   This is running on port 111.

NFS server   This is running on port 2049 by default.

Other RPC services   These get their own ports dynamically assigned by the port-mapper, and thus, you do not know which ports to deny. For this reason, it is best to deny all services first and grant access only to those that are needed.

If you plan to allow NFS *through* your firewall, ask yourself why. Are you really allowing file access of your site to a party outside your site? Can you trust everyone on that other site? Can you trust anyone on the way to that site to not sniff the packets and reconstruct your data files? Furthermore, be aware that due to the complex nature of NFS, being a mix of different services, some stateless and some stateful, it is difficult to configure firewalls to handle NFS reliably and securely.

If you are using a Linux-based firewall, you can use two forms of packet filtering. On Linux 2.2 kernels (such as Red Hat 7.0), you can use a system called *IPCHAINS*. On Linux 2.4 kernels, you can use a firewalling system called *NETFILTER*. Suppose that your site trusts a sister site with a class C network address of 128.59.8.0 and that your firewall's external IP address is 128.59.9.1. A typical set of IPCHAINS commands to use on a firewall is seen in Listing 4.6.

Listing 4.6   Firewalling commands using IPCHAINS (Linux 2.2)

```
[root]# ipchains -A input -f -j ACCEPT
[root]# ipchains -A input -s 128.59.8.0/255.255.255.0 \
>        -d 128.59.9.1/255.255.255.255 -j ACCEPT
[root]# ipchains -A input -s 0/0 -d 0/0 -p 6 -j DENY -y -l
[root]# ipchains -A input -s 0/0 -d 0/0 -p 17 -j DENY -l
```

A similar set of NETFILTER commands to use on a firewall is seen in Listing 4.7.

Listing 4.7   Firewalling commands using NETFILTER (Linux 2.4)

```
[root]# iptables -A INPUT -f -j ACCEPT
[root]# iptables -A INPUT -s 128.59.8.0/255.255.255.0 \
>        128.59.9.1/255.255.255.255 -j ACCEPT
[root]# iptables -A INPUT -s 0/0 -d 0/0 -p 6 -j DENY --syn \
>        --log-level 5
[root]# iptables -A INPUT -s 0/0 -d 0/0 -p 17 -j DENY --log-level 5
```

The general meaning of the commands in both Listing 4.6 and Listing 4.7 is as follows. The first line says to accept all packet fragments, except the first fragment; that one is treated as a normal packet (its headers are inspected to decide what to do with the rest of the packet's fragments). The second line says to accept only those packets that came from the trusted 128.59.8.0 network and were destined for this firewall's IP address, 128.59.9.1. The last two lines say to deny and log everything else.

WARNING Do not consider the commands in Listings 4.6 and 4.7 authoritative. There is much more science that goes into a proper setting and configuration of a good firewall. Before you use one, learn everything you can about firewalling. A full treatment of the use of firewalls is beyond the scope of this book. For more information on firewalls, see Appendix B and *Linux Security* (Craig Hunt Linux Library) by Rámon J. Hontañón (Sybex, 2001).

Recovering NFS after a Break-In

If you suspect that your site has been broken into, the first thing you should do is isolate the affected hosts and inspect them in turn. At the very least, turn off remote network access to those hosts. If you suspect that the attack came from within, or you do not want anyone to use the host remotely, then turn off its network interface using, for example, the command /etc/rc.d/init.d/network stop. You will have to log on to the host's console as root to be able to run these diagnostics.

You can use the rpm tool to verify the validity of your Red Hat Linux installation. This can help you to find out if any of the binaries on your system have been replaced, possibly with Trojan versions. However, verification through rpm works only if attackers did not also compromise the RPM installation database; if they did, your safest choice is to reinstall your system from scratch and restore all data from backup tapes (you do keep backups, right?).

To verify that, say, the nfs-utils package is valid, run the command as seen in Listing 4.8.

Listing 4.8 Verifying the validity of an installed RPM

```
[root]# rpm --verify nfs-utils
..5..... c /usr/sbin/rpc.mountd
```

The output line of Listing 4.8 shows a potentially clever attack: the rpc.mountd binary does not pass the MD5 checksum test that compares the current checksum to the one from when rpc.mountd was originally installed. This is indicated by the "5" in the output line. Note also that if all you see is an MD5 checksum difference, the attackers were able to replace your binary with one that has the same size and modification time; casual inspections would not have caught this—only MD5 checksum checks could. The rpm --verify command can alert you to various other differences on your system. For the full description, see the manual page for rpm(8).

If you suspect that, say, your `nfs-utils` package has been compromised, you should reinstall it from safe media such as vendor-supplied CD-ROMs. Detailed instructions on the use of the `rpm` tool are available in Chapter 7.

In Sum

This chapter covered many aspects of NFS security, such as how to restrict access to the services that run on your NFS server, and how to ensure that you provide only the access that is needed through export options. We discussed NFS client mount options that can further enhance the security of your site. In addition, we discussed general-purpose tips for improving your site's security and strategies for what to do if your site is broken into.

Security is a large field and an ongoing area of research that changes constantly. Responsible site administrators must be vigilant. Keep up with latest security advisories, apply security fixes as soon as they are available, and report attacks to the proper authorities (be a good citizen). Administrators must also balance the security requirements and policies of their site with their user community's needs; security should be as high as possible, but not so strict that it prevents your users from doing their work.

This chapter only discussed the security of NFS. There are many features that can be used on NFS servers and clients to improve security. If not configured correctly, NFS can easily compromise the security of an entire site. It is no wonder why some site administrator say that NFS sometimes stands for No File Security.

As software and systems continue to grow and become complex, more and more bugs and exploits will be discovered. Site administrators must secure a complete site, not just one component. Any one component of your site, such as NFS, can be compromised by any other part of your site. In Appendix B we provide several additional pointers to good resources on security.

5

NFS Diagnostics and Debugging

In the previous chapters we learned about the inner workings of NFS: the RPC components and tools it depends on and the protocols it uses, how to configure and use it under normal conditions, and how to improve the performance and security of your NFS system. However, we assumed that everything was working properly. As an administrator of a large site, you will find that setting and reconfiguring NFS on your hosts is an ongoing effort. Sometimes things do not work from the beginning or they stop working after a period of time.

This chapter discusses how to detect, diagnose, and correct problems with NFS. We begin by covering general tips and tools that are useful in diagnosing NFS problems, and gradually increase the complexity of our discussions from common problems to complex ones. As you shall see, most problems are easy to fix if you know how to interpret the error messages you get and use the tools described herein.

Linux is an ever-changing system; its NFS software and kernel are constantly being developed with new features. This sometimes produces changed behavior or even bugs that NFS users should be aware of. Furthermore, while the NFS specification is fixed, it is not always complete. Different vendor implementations can result in interoperability problems between Linux and non-Linux systems. The end of this chapter addresses such advanced topics and what to do in case you've exhausted all other diagnostics suggestions.

Diagnostic Tips

The first thing to do when you suspect a problem, or when a user reports one to you, is to verify it. It is important to be able to reproduce the problem on your own; that way you can use the same procedure to verify that the problem has gone away once you fixed it.

Even senior administrators are sometimes guilty of overlooking the obvious—the simplest problems that are often a matter of configuration. Start by ensuring that your NFS configurations are in place and correct. Do not assume they are fine just because "no one changed anything recently." While recent changes to configurations should be the first suspects for the cause of new problems, some problems could have existed for a long time and only been discovered or unmasked recently due to unforeseen side effects. If you suspect an undetermined NFS problem between your clients and servers, follow these procedures first:

- Check to see if both your NFS server and clients are up and running, that the load on them is not abnormally high, and that the network between them is functioning properly.

- Verify that your NFS server's /etc/exports file is syntactically correct and semantically correct: that it includes the export permissions you intend.

- Confirm that the NFS server is running all of the NFS software it needs. Restart it if needed by running the following command:

    [root]# **/etc/rc.d/init.d/nfs restart**

- Verify that your NFS client's /etc/fstab is correct: that it lists the proper NFS partitions to mount and that it contains no syntax errors.

- Confirm that your NFS client has NFS support in the kernel by listing the contents of /proc/filesystems and ensuring that nfs appears there. Restart the client-side NFS services if needed by running the following command:

    [root]# **/etc/rc.d/init.d/netfs restart**

Use the tools described in the next section to perform these tests and others. Also, look up any error messages you get in the upcoming section "Common Error and Log Messages" and follow the advice given in that section.

Diagnostic Tools

Administrators can employ several useful tools to debug NFS problems. These tools are very versatile: their usefulness goes well beyond just that of diagnosing NFS problems.

Familiarize yourself with these tools and their options by reading the tools' respective manual pages.

> **TIP** We describe the six most commonly used tools. Linux and Unix systems all come with these tools that you can use to diagnose various network problems. Consult your Linux system's documentation to see if your system provides additional tools.

We briefly explain the diagnostic tools next. These are general-purpose tools that we have seen and used in previous chapters. We proceed by explaining them from the simplest tool to the more complex ones.

> **WARNING** Make sure you do not have any firewalls or filtering routers between your NFS clients and servers. If you do, these devices may be filtering certain types of packets, especially ICMP ones, as well as disallowing access to certain ports. If that happens, these tools are not likely to work; do not confuse this situation with one in which the problem is with the NFS clients or servers.

ping

The ping program sends short ICMP ECHO messages from one host to another host and waits for replies. It also measures the round-trip-time (RTT) for such messages. Log in on your NFS client and ping your NFS server, then do the same in the reverse direction. Make sure that all packets sent arrive with zero loss. Also make sure that the RTT for these packets is sufficiently small. If you see any packet loss or abnormally high RTTs, check the stability and configuration of your network and routers. See Chapter 3, "NFS Performance," for more details on the ping tool.

Suppose you have an NFS server named earth and a client named moon. Log in to earth and run ping moon, then log in to moon and run ping earth.

traceroute

The traceroute tool determines the path that network packets take from one host to another. It works by sending ICMP messages with increasingly larger time-to-live (TTL) values and checking to see how far these messages reached. These TTL values are actually hop counts, so when traceroute increases the hop-count value, it ensures that the ICMP message could only reach that far. A router that is the last in such a chain of routers will respond with an ICMP "time exceeded" message. Then, traceroute increases the TTL by one and sends another ICMP message. This time, the message goes one hop further than before, and so on. Each time the client that runs `traceroute` gets back a response, it discovers the identity of one additional router on the path to the final host for which `traceroute` is tracing the path.

This tool is important because it ensures that the routes between your NFS servers and clients are *symmetric*. The RPC system does not work well on some systems if the routes between the hosts are asymmetric. In particular, you could have a problem if your NFS client or server are multihomed—they have more than one network interface—and packets go out one interface and arrive through another. In that case, your RPC system (and hence NFS) may not recognize the returned packets and may drop them. If the host drops packets, NFS connectivity will not be possible.

The `traceroute` tool also provides some additional pieces of information: how many routers are in between your NFS clients and servers, and how long it takes for packets to get from one to the other. The more routers you have in between, the longer the packets will take to reach their destinations, and the slower the performance will be. This is because each network hop adds another component that adds delay and could fail. Tracing the route paths can tell you, for example, if an intermediate router is down or misbehaving.

TIP Avoid having too many routers in between your NFS clients and servers. NFS was designed for—and works best—when the servers and clients are on the same subnet or Local Area Network (LAN). If you have one or two routers in between that, all using fast networking, you can still get good performance and behavior. But if you have more routers, or complex devices such as firewalls that introduce additional complexity, the chances of failure grow significantly higher.

To trace the route between two hosts (`earth` and `moon`), log in to `earth` and run `traceroute moon`, then log in to `moon` and run `traceroute earth`. The example in Listing 5.1 shows a good connectivity between two such hosts.

Listing 5.1 A good route traced between two hosts

```
[ezk]$ hostname
earth.example.com
[ezk]$ traceroute moon
traceroute to moon (128.59.35.142), 30 hops max, 40 byte packets
1 brooklyn.example.com (128.59.16.64)  11.854ms  6.624ms  107.660ms
2 edge.net.example.com (128.59.16.1)  4.642ms  5.053ms  4.695ms
3 moon.example.com (128.59.35.142)  4.912ms  1.354ms  4.230ms
```

Listing 5.1 shows that to get from earth to moon, packets traverse two routers: brooklyn.example.com and edge.net.example.com, in that order. If you trace the reverse route—from moon to earth—and your routes are symmetric, then you should see packets going in exactly the reverse order.

Listing 5.2 shows one of two typical route problems, a routing loop. This prevents packets from arriving at their destinations.

Listing 5.2   Tracing a routing loop

```
[ezk]$ traceroute moon
traceroute to moon (128.59.35.142), 30 hops max, 40 byte packets
1 brooklyn.example.com (128.59.16.64)   11.854ms   6.624ms   107.660ms
2 edge.net.example.com (128.59.16.1)   4.642ms   5.053ms   4.695ms
3 moon.example.com (128.59.35.142)   4.912ms   1.354ms   4.230ms
4 edge.net.example.com (128.59.16.1)   4.642ms   5.053ms   4.695ms
5 moon.example.com (128.59.35.142)   4.912ms   1.354ms   4.230ms
6 edge.net.example.com (128.59.16.1)   4.642ms   5.053ms   4.695ms
7 moon.example.com (128.59.35.142)   4.912ms   1.354ms   4.230ms
...
```

Here, two or more routers have routes that produce an infinite loop. Typically such routing loops fix themselves after a period of time (minutes to hours), but often it requires the intervention of the network administrators of those routers to reboot the routers or to remove the bad routes manually, thus breaking the loop.

Listing 5.3 shows what happens when an intermediary router is down.

Listing 5.3   Tracing a downed router

```
[ezk]$ traceroute moon
traceroute to moon (128.59.35.142), 30 hops max, 40 byte packets
1 brooklyn.example.com (128.59.16.64)   11.854ms   6.624ms   107.660ms
2 * * *
3 * * *
4 * * *
5 * * *
6 * * *
...
```

Again, whatever the problem may be, if packets cannot reach their destinations, NFS clients and servers cannot communicate with each other.

rpcinfo

The rpcinfo tool shows various pieces of information about the RPC system. Using the -p option, it displays the list of registered RPC services on a given host as we have seen in Listing 1.3 in Chapter 1, "NFS Basics and Protocols." Use this tool on the NFS client to ensure that your NFS server is running the required services.

Suppose your NFS server is called earth and your NFS client is called moon. Log in to moon and run rpcinfo -p earth: you should see at least the following list of services: portmapper, status, mountd, nfs, and nlockmgr; you may also see the rquotad service, but it is not necessary for proper functionality.

You should also run rpcinfo -p on the client, to check its own RPC services. You should see at least the status and nlockmgr services running.

nfsstat

The nfsstat tool provides statistics on the operation of NFS. As we have seen in Listings 3.9 and 3.10 in Chapter 3, nfsstat can list the number and frequency of NFS operations on the client side and on the server side. It can also separate them by protocol version: NFSv2 vs. NFSv3.

Run this tool both on your NFS servers and clients. If you compare the results among different hosts, you may find abnormalities. For example, while certain NFS operations are fairly popular (e.g., NFS_LOOKUP and NFS_ACCESS), you may find that certain hosts have a high incidence of other operations. This could indicate a problem such as runaway processes on clients or servers that perform these operations repeatedly or unintentionally.

tcpdump

The tcpdump tool captures packets (all packets, not just TCP) from the network and displays them in various degrees of detail. It is useful in determining the exact transport and NFS version in use between clients and servers. It can also show you if some packets go unanswered, packet fragmentation problems, and more. This extremely powerful tool should be in the arsenal of every network and system administrator.

Listing 5.4 shows you a typical packet capture using tcpdump. We show what NFS packets occur between an NFS client and server when a user executes a simple command to list the contents of an NFS-mounted directory using /bin/ls.

Listing 5.4   Using tcpdump to analyze NFS packets

```
[root]# hostname
earth.example.com
```

```
[root]# tcpdump -vv -s 1500 host moon
Kernel filter, protocol ALL, datagram packet socket
tcpdump: listening on all devices
17:48:23.636171 eth0 < moon.example.com.1833098338 > earth.example.com.nfs:
224 create fh 0,32/0 "newdir" (ttl 64, id 25170)
17:48:23.636414 eth0 > earth.example.com.nfs > moon.example.com.1833098338:
reply ok 248 create fh 0,1/4039115776 unk-ft 1269097360  0 ids 2/16877 sz 2
nlink 1 rdev 5a fsid 1000 nodeid 0 a/m/ctime 4096.000000 0.000000 2065.000000
(ttl 64, id 42978)
2 packets received by filter
```

Listing 5.4 shows what happens when client host moon tries to create a directory named newdir (using mkdir newdir), via NFS, on server host earth. Two packets are exchanged. The first packet asks the server to create the directory and the second packet acknowledges a successful creation of that directory. Spaces delimit the various fields in the output of each line from tcpdump. The > and < symbols indicate the direction in which packets flow.

The meaning of the various fields in the first packet is as follows:

17:48:23.636171   The time that this packet was sent in hours, minutes, seconds, and microseconds.

eth0 <   The interface that received the packet.

moon.example.com.1833098338 >   The hostname that sent the packet, followed by the RPC transaction ID number of this request.

earth.example.com.nfs   The host that received the request and the port that it received it on (NFS).

224   The number of bytes in this request.

create   The operation requested.

fh 0,32/0   The filehandle "requested" was for the device identified by the major and minor number pair <0,32>. The filehandle does not exist yet: that is the /0.

"newdir"   The name of the directory to create.

ttl 64   The TTL value for this packet.

id 25170   The unique ID number of this packet.

The reply packet is the second one in Listing 5.4. The meaning of most of this packet's fields is similar to the request packet:

17:48:23.636414   The time of the reply.

eth0 >   The interface that received the reply.

earth.example.com.nfs >   The host that sent the reply.

moon.example.com.1833098338   The host that received the reply and the transaction ID being replied to.

reply ok   The status of this NFS message: it is a reply and a successful one.

248   The length of this message in bytes.

create   The operation being replied to.

fh 0,1/4039115776   The filehandle that was created was on device ID <0,1>, followed by the filehandle number.

unk-ft 1269097360   This is printed when the overall file attribute is unknown, along with its actual value. That is, the number itself does not hold a special meaning.

0   The access modes of the new entry.

ids 2/16877   The UID/GID pair under which the new directory was created.

sz 2   The size of the file attribute's structure.

nlink 1   The number of links this new directory has.

rdev 5a   The hexadecimal device number on which NFS creates the directory.

fsid 1000   The file system ID.

nodeid 0   The NFS ID of the new node (directory).

a/m/ctime 4096.000000 0.000000 2065.000000   The access, modification, and last change times for this new directory, in seconds.

ttl 64   The TTL value for this packet.

id 42978   The unique ID number of this packet.

As the packet breakout clearly shows, tcpdump provides a detailed view of the inner workings of the NFS protocol. The tcpdump program can provide insight for troubleshooting the most difficult problems. Luckily, troubleshooting NFS does not normally require detailed packet analysis. It is generally enough to know that the client and server are talking and are exchanging the correct packets.

mount and *umount*

The tools to mount and unmount file systems—/bin/mount and /bin/umount—are useful in accessing remote NFS file servers. In particular, /bin/mount can use the numerous mount options that we have listed in Chapter 2, "Configuring NFS." If you cannot mount a certain file system, or you can but it does not behave as you would expect, you can always unmount the file system and then remount it using different mount options.

For example, suppose you are receiving a "permission denied" error when trying to mount a remote file server read-write. Try to mount it read-only using mount -o ro. Or, suppose you are using NFSv3 with TCP and are getting odd behavior. Try to mount using NFSv2 and UDP and see if that works better.

Other Tools

You might consider a few other Linux tools when debugging various NFS problems. We list them briefly here. Refer to their respective manual pages for more details.

ifconfig   This tool can show you the configuration of your network interfaces, as well as change it. For example, if your network mask (netmask) is wrong, ifconfig can fix that.

route, netstat, and ip   The route tool can set and remove network routes on your host. For example, if you are missing a default route, route can add it. You can view your existing routes using netstat. The ip tool is new and is a superset of the route tool.

tracepath   This tool can trace the path between two network hosts, similar to traceroute, but tracepath also performs Maximum Transmission Unit (MTU) discovery along the way. This is useful in debugging problems that may be the result of multiple and different networks (FDDI, ATM, Ethernet) between NFS clients and servers: each network type generally uses a different MTU and does not always interoperate properly with another.

arp   This tool lists the known mappings of Ethernet addresses to IP addresses. Run arp -a on NFS clients and servers to ensure that they both recognize the proper Ethernet address of each other. You can find the actual Ethernet address of each host by looking for the HWaddr part from the output of ifconfig -a.

One additional technique, often used by experts and kernel developers, is to turn on RPC debugging messages from the kernel. The old method of doing so was to use the rpcdebug tool that came with nfs-utils. It can turn on or off RPC debugging flags for various kernel modules: RPC, NFS (client and server), as well as NLM. Newer kernels allow you to turn debugging on or off for various subsystems, as seen in Listing 5.5.

Listing 5.5   Turning on kernel-level RPC debugging

```
[root]# cd /proc/sys/sunrpc
[root]# echo 65535 > nfs_debug
[root]# echo 65535 > nfsd_debug
[root]# echo 65535 > nlm_debug
[root]# echo 65535 > rpc_debug
```

In Listing 5.5, we turn on debugging for four different subsystems of the kernel by writing the value 65535 into the four /proc files in this order: the NFS client, the NFS server, the Network Lock Manager, and the RPC system in general. Of course, you can turn on individual debugging for just one of these components. To turn off debugging, write a 0 to the files you turned on (debugging is off by default).

Common Problems

In this section we list the more common error problems that administrators face when troubleshooting NFS problems. We list these from most common to least common and include a series of suggestions to solve each problem.

Cannot Mount a File System

By far, the inability to mount a file system is the most common problem, probably because there could be many reasons why this happens and also because this is one of the very first actions that administrators perform. The reasons for the problem, and its solution, depend on the type of error you get.

Permission Problems

If you receive a message from the NFS server that states "permission denied," it means that your NFS server is not allowing your client to mount the file system. Follow these suggestions one at a time and then try to mount the file system after each change:

- Inspect your /etc/exports file and ensure that it allows your NFS client to mount the file system you wish to mount.
- Run exportfs -ra on the NFS server to re-export all file systems with the various daemons and status files that the server maintains.
- If your NFS server is exporting file systems via an NIS netgroup, ensure that the NIS server lists the NFS client as part of that netgroup. One simple way to do so is to log in on the NFS server, run ypcat -k netgroup, and check that your NFS client's name is listed in the netgroup that the NFS server specifies in /etc/exports.
- Check your DNS records to ensure that your NFS client and server are listed with their proper IP addresses.
- Make sure that the /etc/hosts file on your NFS client does not have a different IP address for the NFS server.
- Similarly, make sure that the /etc/hosts file on your NFS server does not have a different IP address for the NFS client.
- Check the export permissions in /etc/exports on the NFS server for the NFS client. If, for example, it allows that client to mount the server using ro, but you are trying to mount it using rw, your client would not be allowed to do so.

NFS Services and Transports

An NFS server nowadays can support any subset of the combination of NFS protocol versions and transports: NFSv3 using TCP, NFSv3 using UDP, NFSv2 using TCP, and NFSv2 using UDP. The NFS client may support a different subset. To see what protocol versions and transports the server supports, you can run `rpcinfo -p` on the server. But it is not easy to check what the NFS client supports.

The am-utils package comes with a tool called `wire-test`, which can test this. If you are on a client and wish to check what combinations of NFS version and transport are supported by both the client and a server named `earth`, run `wire-test earth` on the client. This will list all successful combinations of protocol version and transport. We describe this tool and the am-utils package in great detail in Part 2 of this book, "The Amd Automounter."

RPC Services

If you are getting an error message stating "RPC: Program Not Registered," or any other RPC-related error message, the NFS services might not be running or functioning properly. Follow these suggestions in order, and try to mount the file system again after each change:

- Run `rpcinfo -p` on the server to see that it is running all of the necessary RPC services, especially `mountd` and `nfs`. This would also tell you which RPC versions and transports are available for each service.

  - If you see these services listed, then run `rpcinfo -p` for the server's name from the NFS client to ensure that you can see the same services from the client. If you can see the RPC services from both ends, try to vary the mount options you give to `/bin/mount` and see if that makes a difference. For example, you might try to mount using UDP or NFSv2, or try a read-only mount.

  - If you do not see these services listed in the output of `rpcinfo -p`, then restart them using `/etc/rc.d/init.d/nfs restart` and check again. If these services are still not listed, then you have a more serious problem with your NFS server's configuration: your kernel might be missing the right functionality, or you might not have the proper user-level tools installed. Refer to Chapter 7, "Building and Installing the Linux Kernel and NFS Software," for information on the software setup of your NFS system.

Service and Packet Filtering

If you are getting the error message "RPC: No Remote Programs Registered," or "RPC: Authentication error," it is likely that you have turned on TCP Wrapper support and that the server is denying access to your NFS client. Check the `/etc/hosts.allow` and

/etc/hosts.deny files on your NFS server to ensure that they allow your NFS client to access the RPC services on the server. See Chapter 4, "Securing NFS," for information on using TCP Wrappers. Use the traceroute and tracepath tools to ensure that your routes are symmetric, especially if either your NFS server or client is using an old Linux distribution or an older operating system.

If you are getting the error message "Remote system error - No route to host," or "Connection refused," then check to see if you have any firewalls or filtering routers between your NFS client and server. Such devices could be filtering RPC packets. Make sure that they are configured to allow RPC/NFS packets between the NFS server and clients. It is not easy to figure out if there is a firewall between your servers and clients, because by its very nature, a firewall filters the same packets that can be used to detect its presence. If you are not sure, contact your local network administrator for help. If you also maintain such a firewall, consult the manual page for ipfwadm and the links to resources given in Appendix B, "Online Resources."

Running Out of Mount Entries

If you've tried everything else and you still cannot mount a file system, check to see if you have exceeded the maximum allowed number of mounts. Linux keeps the number of existing mounts in the proc file system file /proc/sys/fs/super-nr and the maximum allowed number of mounts in /proc/sys/fs/super-max. The default maximum value is 256. While normally your hosts would not exceed this value, very busy NFS clients or servers can reach this maximum (especially if you use an automounter such as Amd). To check the current number of mounts, the maximum number of mounts, and then double the number of maximum allowed mounts, execute the commands as seen in Listing 5.6.

Listing 5.6   Increasing the maximum number of allowed mounts

```
[root]# cd /proc/sys/fs
[root]# cat super-nr
253
[root]# cat super-max
256
[root]# echo 512 > super-max
```

Cannot Access Files on a Mounted File System

The inability to access files from an NFS server can be the result of three possible conditions: mount problems, Unix file permission and ID mapping problems, and attribute caching problems.

Mounting Problems

If you cannot read, write, or see any files on a file system that is mounted, then first check to see if your NFS partition is indeed mounted. You can verify this by running /bin/ mount or cat /proc/mounts. If the remote file system is not mounted, mount it using /bin/mount. If the output from /bin/mount differs from that of cat /proc/mounts, it is likely that your file system is not mounted, but leftover entries remain in /etc/mtab (where /bin/mount may look for the list of currently mounted file systems). If your Linux system does not support the proc file system, then you cannot reliably determine which file systems are actually mounted because the /etc/mtab file may be out of sync with the list of actual mounts. In either case, run /bin/umount to unmount the file system, and then remount it again.

If the file system is indeed mounted, but you still cannot see the files you expect, do the following:

- Check on the NFS server to see that those files actually exist on the server. If they do not, perhaps the local EXT2 partition is not mounted. If that's the case, then your NFS server is exporting the underlying mount point—not the actual file system. Mount the local server partition and run exportfs -ra on the server, and then unmount and remount the file system on the client.

- If the files exist on the server, run exportfs -ra on it. It is possible that the file system on the server was mounted *after* the directory mount point was exported; in that case you are again exporting the underlying mount point and not the actual file system. If that is the case, re-export the file system on the server, and then remount it on the NFS client.

Unix File Permissions and ID Mapping Problems

If the file system is properly exported and mounted, but you are having problems accessing some files or directories, then follow these suggestions:

- If you are trying to write some files and getting an error saying "Read-only file system," then your NFS client might be mounting the file system with the ro flag. If the client appears to use the rw flag, then check to see if the NFS server exports the volume using the ro permission. If you change the /etc/exports file to correct the permission for the client, do not forget to run exportfs -ra to activate your changes.

- If you are getting a "Permission denied" error, first check the credentials of the directory in which you are trying to perform the operation. Ensure that you are indeed allowed to write to that directory by listing its modes using ls -l.

- Another problem that leads to denied permissions is related to UID and GID mappings. As we saw in Chapter 4, there are several "squashing" options that map UIDs and GIDs from one number to another. If you are running as the root user over NFS, and the NFS server is not setting the no_root_squash export option, then your root user will get mapped to the nobody user on the server. That user usually has little permission to access any files. Alternatively, your NFS server may use the all_squash export option, which maps all users, including root users. If that is the case, even normal users will be mapped to the nobody user, and trying to access remote files will produce a denied permission error message.

- The last problem that relates to permission access is if the UIDs or GIDs for your login ID are different on the server and the client. Log in to both the client and the server and run /usr/bin/id as follows:

      [ezk]$ **/usr/bin/id**
      uid=2301(ezk) gid=90(tech) groups=90(tech),0(root)

Ensure that your primary UID and all GIDs have the same name and number on both the NFS server and client. If they do not, check your NIS server (if you are using one) and the two files /etc/passwd and /etc/group for the mapping of user names and group names to their numbers.

Attribute Caching Problems

Occasionally, the permission modes of files appear correct but the system does not act in accordance with the modes you see. This scenario is seen when you change the attributes of files or directories in one place, but the attributes do not appear to change. The problem is that NFS clients can cache attributes of files for an undetermined length of time. See Chapter 3 for a detailed discussion of attribute caching.

Sometimes, when administrators wish to change the modes or ownerships of a large number of files, they run a recursive chmod, chgrp, or chown command on the NFS server to speed up the operation. If the operation is done over NFS on the NFS client, it could take many times longer than if done directly on the server. While these changes take hold on the server immediately, clients that previously accessed the changed files may still cache the older attributes of those files. Those clients continue to use the old attributes until a cache timeout occurs. The old attributes may be too restrictive or just plain wrong: it is important that all NFS clients use updated attributes as soon as they change.

Unfortunately, there is no easy way to flush the attribute cache on the NFS client. One way is to unmount the remote file system and then remount it. Alternatively, you just have to wait for the attributes to clear off of the cache. If you are facing repeated problems with cached attributes, change some of the relevant mount options as explained in "Attribute Caching" in Chapter 3.

NFS File Commands Time Out or Hang

Sometimes when you have an NFS file system mounted, a command stops working. Specifically, commands such as `ls` on directories or `cat` of files hang for a long time and then, possibly, time out. This is most likely the result of the NFS client's failure to access the remote NFS server and could be due to any of these causes:

- The NFS server is down.
- NFS software crashed or stopped running on the server.
- A router or firewall in between is down.
- The routes between your client and servers have become asymmetric due to the introduction of a new network, a new network interface, or even a misconfigured router or routing software daemon (such as `gated`).
- The network interface of the client or server is down.
- A bad Ethernet address was discovered by either client or server for each other. Use the `arp` command to find this.

The above are mostly software problems. An assortment of hardware problems could also affect the connectivity of your NFS system. See the section "Correcting Hardware Problems" later in this chapter for information on this possibility.

Serious Performance Degradation when Writing Large Files

Serious performance problems are often associated with older Linux kernels, especially the 2.2 kernels. The `fsync(2)` function in the 2.2 kernels was unfortunately implemented such that it has a quadratic performance degradation when a client tries to write very large files. This is not noticeable on small files; it is only apparent when file sizes exceed many megabytes.

One solution to this problem is to export the file system using the `no_wdelay` option. This forces the client-side program to open the file with the O_SYNC flag, which tells the kernel to synchronize the file's data with the disk and may improve performance. The superior solution, however, is to upgrade your kernel to 2.4 since this deficiency of the `fsync()` function was completely resolved in the 2.4 kernel.

Every Host Can Mount the Server's File Systems

Inappropriately exporting files systems to all remote computers is often a mistake in the server's `/etc/exports` file. As we mentioned in Chapter 2, the `/etc/exports` file is very sensitive to the use of whitespace. If you wish to allow the host `moon` to mount `earth:/home`, your exports entry should look like this:

```
/home        moon(rw)
```

If, however, you mistakenly inserted a space character between the client's name and the parenthesized list of options, your entry will look as follows:

```
/home       moon (rw)
```

This last entry has a very different meaning. It allows host moon to mount /home using the default export permissions (which, ironically, are read-only), and then it allows all other hosts on the Internet to mount this file system using rw permissions.

To fix this problem, simply edit out the extra space in this /etc/exports file and run exportfs -ra to synchronize the list of exports with the contents of the edited file.

Cannot Start NFS Services

If you cannot start NFS services on your NFS server, first check that you have the software installed. This is the nfs-utils RPM. Check that it is installed using rpm -q nfs-utils.

Then, check that your kernel has nfsd support. One way to check this is to run modprobe nfsd and then see if the nfsd kernel module is listed in the output of lsmod. However, if your NFS server was statically compiled into the kernel, it is difficult to figure this out. One way is to look for the string CONFIG_NFSD=y in your kernel configuration file, typically /usr/src/linux/.config.

The topic of ensuring that your system includes the proper kernel support and software for NFS is beyond the scope of this chapter. We devote a whole chapter to this: Chapter 7.

Cannot Unmount Busy File Systems

If you try to unmount a file system, say, /home, and you get the error message

```
umount: /home: device is busy
```

it means that some processes (or even kernel services) use that file system. Start by running lsof /home to list the processes that are still using files on that file system. You will have to kill all of these processes before you can unmount the file system.

On an NFS server, the kernel may hold certain resources and prevent the unmounting of any system that is exported in /etc/exports. This is to ensure that you could not unmount an exported file system that some NFS clients may be using. Before you can unmount such a file system, you have to unexport it using exportfs -u /home.

Common Error and Log Messages

In this section we list many common messages that you can see, and which of those messages indicate a problem. Some of these messages will appear on your console. Some will be displayed only on your current terminal, as a result of running a program. Other messages will only be appended to one of your system log files such as /var/log/messages or /var/log/all. Check the configuration of your /etc/syslog.conf file to see where system log messages go.

We ordered the list of error messages you get from the more common ones to the less common ones.

NFS Server Not Responding—Still Trying

If you get the message

```
    nfs: server host not responding, still trying
```

or

```
    nfs: server host not responding, timed out
```

where host is a name of a file server, it means that your NFS client cannot access that NFS file server. All user processes that use that server would be hung at this point. This could be the result of a downed network connection or remote file server. Often, if the server has crashed and is now rebooting, it would come back up in a few minutes and you will see (much to your relief) the message

```
    NFS server host OK
```

This indicates that the remote server is working again. If you do not get this message within a few minutes and your processes are still hung, check that the network connection to the server is working, that the remote host is up, and that the NFS server software is running on it.

Stale File Handle

If running any command causes the error message "stale file handle," then the NFS file handle that your client has received from the NFS server is no longer valid. The most common reasons you get this error are because the file system on which this file resided no longer exists on that NFS server, the file system was restored from backup tapes, or the file system's mount point has changed. This happens when administrators perform NFS maintenance on a server while some NFS clients still mount that server.

Other reasons why this could happen is that the remote file server changed either network interfaces (added or removed some) or IP address, or the server's hostname changed.

Unfortunately with this situation, you cannot do much on your client. First, try to unmount and remount the file system. If you cannot perform this because the file system is busy, try to kill all processes that may hold open files on that file system and then retry the unmount and remount. If that does not work either, you will have to reboot your NFS client.

Clock Skew Warnings from GNU Make

If you are building some software over NFS, and you are getting a warning message from GNU make such as in Listing 5.7, it means that the clocks on your NFS client and server are out of sync. Listing 5.7 shows a clock skew of one hour, a typical problem when hosts fail to adjust for daylight saving time.

Listing 5.7   Clock synchronization warning messages from GNU make

```
[ezk]$ make
make: *** Warning: File `foo.c' has modification time in the future (2001-02-
11 20:34:23 > 2001-02-11 19:34:35)
gcc     foo.c   -o foo
make: warning:  Clock skew detected. Your build may be incomplete.
```

This is a problem when building software using make because it determines when to build or rebuild certain targets based on the time stamps of the source files to those targets. Generally, make rebuilds a target when any of its source files have a newer time stamp than the target. When the clock on your NFS client is significantly off—more than a couple of seconds—from that of the NFS server's, this can throw off the dependency tracking that make uses. This can cause a target to be rebuilt over and over again. Worse, this can cause a target *not* to be rebuilt even if its sources have changed.

First, you must ensure that the clocks of all your site's hosts are in sync. The best way is to use the Network Time Protocol (NTP) package on all of your hosts. Install the ntp-4.0 RPM on all of your hosts and configure their /etc/ntp.conf file to synchronize with a reliable NTP server. See the documentation for the Linux NTP package in /usr/share/doc/ntp* for more details.

Once you have synchronized the clocks of your NFS client and server, you must now fix the sources of your package, since they still have the wrong time stamps. Start by removing all files that can be rebuilt, typically using make clean. Then, use the find and touch commands to force the time stamp of every file to the current time. Finally, rebuild the package. These three actions can be achieved as follows:

```
[ezk]$ make clean
[ezk]$ find . -print | xargs touch --time=now
[ezk]$ make
```

> **NOTE** The file /proc/fs/nfs/time-diff-margin contains the allowed time difference margin for NFS-mounted file systems. The default threshold is 10 seconds. It can be set to anywhere from 0 to 600 seconds by writing that number onto that time-diff-margin file. When the margin of difference between the times of the client and server is below the threshold listed in time-diff-margin, the system will ignore that difference. Generally, however, it is best not to increase this margin much beyond 10 seconds. In fact, it might even be better to lower it to, say, one second. It is much better to configure NTP on your system to synchronize the clocks of your site's hosts.

Mount Version Older/Newer than Kernel

When you mount a file system, you may get one of the following two warning messages:

```
nfs warning: mount version older than kernel
nfs warning: mount version newer than kernel
```

Both are harmless. They say that the program that is executing the mount(2) system call was compiled for a different version of the Linux kernel than is running: an older one or a newer one. The original intent of these warnings was to catch very old programs or very old kernels that may be expecting and using a different mounting API than the one available. However, the mount(2) system call has not changed in a long time on Linux and is not likely to change soon. Nowadays, these messages are more a nuisance than of real value.

Still, if you cannot sleep at night because of these warning messages, you will have to do one of two things:

- Install a kernel version that matches the mounting tools you have. It is generally not recommended to down-rev (reinstall older software on) a kernel version. See the sidebar "Downgrading Software and Software Stability," later in this chapter for general tips on updating software and when it might be appropriate to install an older piece of software.

- The recommended suggestion is to rebuild the mounting tools for your current kernel version. The most common mounting tools are /bin/mount, part of the nfs-utils RPM, and the Amd automounter, part of the am-utils RPM. Refer to Chapter 7 and to Chapter 14, "Building and Installing the Automounter Software," for information on rebuilding that software.

Can't Get a Request Slot

The following error message

```
kernel: nfs: task 12644 can't get a request slot
```

means that your network has some sort of problem or your NFS server is overloaded. Typically this is a network congestion problem. When the NFS client detects many RPC timeouts and failures, it throttles back the number of concurrent requests that it uses, so as to lower the load on the NFS server.

If you have not already optimized the performance of your NFS system, do so as advised in Chapter 4. Typically, problems such as this tend to be transient. If, however, they do not go away after a short period of time, a more serious problem may exist, and it could indicate possibly buggy software or bad networking hardware.

nfslock: rpc.lockd startup failed

Newer versions of the Linux kernel start the in-kernel NLM service automatically; older kernels required that it be started manually at boot time. System startup scripts such as /etc/rc.d/init.d/nfs start the locking daemon just in case. If the scripts run on a system with a newer kernel, they may print the error message "nfslock: rpc.lockd startup failed."

If you are running on an old Linux system, this error message may be real, indicating that the locking service was supposed to be started manually but didn't. In that case, you should investigate why rpc.lockd did not start. It is recommended, however, that you upgrade older Linux systems. The newer software is more reliable, and it fixes many security holes.

Silly Deletes and Renames

Unix file system semantics allow you to delete a file that any process has opened and is using. In that case, the file's name is removed from its directory, but the actual contents of the file remain on disk. When all processes that had the file open exit or close that file, the kernel will actually remove the file's data blocks on disk.

Linux complies with these semantics. Therefore, the first time you try to delete an open file, the delete will not take place and will be deferred. Linux NFS developers thought that these Unix semantics were silly (and I would agree), and therefore the kernel prints a harmless message such as this:

```
NFS: can't silly-delete filename, error=code
```

or

```
NFS: silly-rename(filename, count)
```

where *filename* is the name of the file being deleted, *code* is an error code from a delete (or rename) operation, and *count* is the number of other processes that have the file open.

fh_verify: permission failure

When you try to change the attributes of a file, you may get a message such as the following:

```
fh_verify: dan/staff permission failure, acc=4, error=13
```

This can be the result of using the chmod program, which gets translated into an NFS_ SETATTR operation on the NFS server. The error message you get is harmless. It tells you that you have tried to change the attributes of a file without having write permission to it.

This is another one of Unix's "silly" semantics: to change the mode or attributes of a file, you need to write to the inode of that file, not to the file itself or the directory that lists the file's name. So even if you do not have write permission to the file, you should be able to change its mode attributes. Linux is a bit safer in this respect and warns you when such a condition occurs. Often this is the result of users trying to change the modes of read-only files or directories that the users own. However, any excessive number of such "permission failure" warning messages could indicate a more serious problem, possibly even a security breach.

kmem_cache_create: forcing size word alignment - nfs_fh

Occasionally NFS displays the harmless error message:

```
kmem_cache_create: forcing size word alignment - nfs_fh
```

This message indicates that the system forced a value to be word-aligned. It means that the NFS system is using a file handle that is not an integer multiple of 4 bytes. The kernel's memory allocator must align such a file handle to the next multiple of 4 bytes. This message would most often occur when interacting with non-Linux NFS servers.

Advanced Problems

In this section we explore a few of the less common problems you may see. Depending on your site's conditions, these problems may not be uncommon to you. Furthermore, realize that this chapter is not an exhaustive list of every possible NFS problem, however common or uncommon.

Unstable Behavior and Poor Performance

This section discusses problems that manifest themselves as sudden poor performance or unstable behavior: when your NFS system functions well under normal conditions but occasionally exhibits bad behavior.

Read and Write Sizes

Suppose your NFS system seems to work under light or normal loads but fails when you use it heavily, such as when reading or writing a large number of files, recursively listing large directories, and so on. The most common cause of this is that your `rsize` and `wsize` parameters are too large: you are trying to transfer too much data across NFS all at once. While normally this would work, on slow or unreliable networks this could result in many packet losses and thus produce lengthy NFS and RPC retransmission times.

To fix this problem, remount your file system with smaller read and write sizes. For example,

```
[root]# mount -o rsize=1024,wsize=1024 earth:/home /home
```

With these, NFS will transmit fewer bytes each time it reads or writes files. Smaller transmission units are more likely to arrive at their destinations across unstable networks and overloaded systems.

Firewalls

A less common problem that could produce unstable behavior is if you have a firewall between your NFS server and client, and the firewall is not allowing fragmented packets through. In that case, you may see an error message such as this:

```
err msg: client denied from port 65535 to port 65535 on server
```

If you are using either the IPCHAINS system of Linux 2.2 or the IPTABLES system of Linux 2.4, do not forget to pass the `-f` flag to the firewalling tool to allow fragmented packets. Note, however, that blocking fragmented packets is considered better security against certain types of attacks. If you are using NFS through your firewall, you have to allow fragmented packets through, but doing so may lessen the security value of your firewall.

Fragmented Packets Overflow

When NFS uses UDP, it sends UDP packets whose size is determined by the `rsize` and `wsize` options. These UDP packets, in turn, may have to be fragmented into smaller units for transmission over the wire. This fragmentation occurs below the transport layer, at the IP layer. The Linux kernel collects fragmented packets and stores them in memory. When all fragments of a packet arrive, the kernel assembles them into a whole packet, and then it can process the packet. However, on really busy hosts, the number of unprocessed fragments may be very large. To ensure that this number does not grow beyond bounds, the Linux kernel keeps only a set number of such packets. If the total number of bytes of unprocessed fragments exceeds this threshold, Linux begins throwing away new packets. This would seem to an NFS client like a sudden failure of an NFS server. The idea is that the host that sent those packets would be responsible for resending them. After all, UDP is considered an unreliable transmission protocol.

The current threshold for the total, in bytes, for all unprocessed fragments is 192KB. It is listed in the file /proc/sys/net/ipv4/ipfrag_low_thresh. This value can be increased up to the maximum listed in /proc/sys/net/ipv4/ipfrag_high_thresh, which defaults to 256KB.

To find out if indeed you are losing fragmented packets, run the command in Listing 5.8.

Listing 5.8   Finding the number of packets that failed reassembly

```
[ezk]$ cut -d' ' -f17 /proc/net/snmp | head -2
ReasmFails
0
```

A value of zero as seen in Listing 5.8 indicates that no packet fragments were permanently lost and all packets were reassembled correctly. If you suspect that you are losing fragments, run the same command during heavy NFS activity times. If the value rises quickly to numbers larger than, say, 10, then you are losing packet fragments.

If your NFS host has enough capacity (CPU and memory) to hold more packet fragments, you may increase these two thresholds. One possible value to try is setting both to 512KB, as seen in Listing 5.9.

Listing 5.9   Increasing the threshold for unprocessed packet fragments

```
[root]# cd /proc/sys/net/ipv4
[root]# echo 524288 > ipfrag_low_thresh
[root]# echo 524288 > ipfrag_high_thresh
```

Packet Sizes

Sometimes, your network may be composed of hosts running different operating systems or versions thereof. The networks may use different routers or switches and may include a mix of Ethernet, ATM, and FDDI subnets. Some of the vendor equipment may not interoperate properly with other vendors' equipment, or the software on one unit may need special configuration to work with another. One possibility relates to a mismatch in transmission unit sizes: when different routers use Path MTU (PMTU) Discovery while others do not, or when different networks use different MTU numbers. Developing networking software that works well in all situations is difficult. Problems can easily be network software vendor bugs.

Occasionally, you may see a problem where some packets go through while others do not. Even stranger, you may see that, while packets of a certain size do not go through, smaller or larger packets do. These problems are indicative of PMTU problems—when some network entities do not negotiate the MTU correctly.

To identify such problems, use the `ping` program to send packets of a given size to a host. For example, default Ethernet MTU sizes are 1500. If you suspect that packets around that size may have a problem, run the example script in Listing 5.10.

Listing 5.10   Sending packets of different sizes to a host

```
[ezk]$ n=1400
[ezk]$ while test $n -le 1600
> do
>    ping -s $n -c 3 earth
>    let n=n+1
> done
```

This script will send three packets to host `earth` and increase the packet sizes from 1400 to 1600 bytes per packet. Under normal conditions, you should not lose any of those packets. If, however, you notice that packets of certain sizes are lost unexpectedly, it may indicate a problem with packets of that size.

Once you narrow down the range in which packets appear to be lost unexpectedly, use `ping -f` to flood the network with packets of that size, so you can ascertain the extent of the problem and get more detailed packet loss analysis. It may also help to run `tcpdump -s 1500 -vv host earth` in another window or shell so you can analyze the packets in detail as they are transmitted.

Asymmetric Performance Characteristics

Suppose you are using tools such as `ping` to measure the performance of your system, and you find that the performance when going from one host to another is much better than when going in the reverse direction. Or, suppose you are using fast 100Mbps networks between your client and server, and your networks are quiet and relatively unused, yet you cannot push more than about 10Mbps through the network. These two problems are indicative of problems with NIC auto-negotiation and duplex transmission settings (called *duplexity*).

Today's Fast Ethernet NICs support both 100Mbps and the slower 10Mbps Ethernet speeds. Also, these NICs can work in full-duplex or half-duplex modes. In full-duplex, packets can be sent and received in both directions at the same time. In half-duplex, packets can only be sent in one direction at a time. Modern networking hardware (NICs, routers, switches, and hubs) may include auto-negotiation features: the equipment on one end tries to negotiate the best possible performance features with the equipment that connects to it.

Unfortunately, auto-negotiation *only* works when both ends auto-negotiate, and do so correctly! Many older NICs, as well as inexpensive switches, do not auto-negotiate. Worse, many devices and even networking drivers are buggy and do not auto-negotiate properly. There is no way for one side to know when the other is or is not auto-negotiating. The result is that one entity finally settles on some configuration (often 10Mbps/Half-Duplex) while the other remains as it was before. When the two ends of a connection think that they are different speeds or duplexity, one side appears much slower than the other, or both end up being much slower than the maximum capacity of the network.

For this reason, many network administrators force the configurations of their NICs and switches to a fixed configuration, typically 100Mbps/Full-Duplex. That way they can be assured that all networking equipment will use the same configuration and utilize the network to its maximum capacity.

Interaction with Non-Linux Systems

Often, you may have to use non-Linux NFS clients or servers, with their Linux counterparts. While the NFS specification is standard, implementations vary considerably.

Use `rpcinfo -p` to compare the NFS versions (v2/v3) and transports (UDP/TCP) offered on each system. Then make sure that you use the most stable combination of implementations between the NFS client and server.

Do not confuse the syntax and names of configuration files for mount tables and export lists. For example, the exports file on Solaris is `/etc/dfs/dfstab` and uses an entirely different syntax. The mount table file on Solaris is `/etc/vfstab`, not `/etc/fstab`. Administrators of a large and heterogeneous site can confuse the syntax and file names between different operating systems.

If you are using SunOS or Solaris NFS hosts, set your `rsize` and `wsize` parameters no larger than 4KB to produce better performance. In general, your read and write sizes should match the smallest native page size between the client and the server.

If you are using SunOS 4.*x* or Digital Unix 4.*x* NFS clients with a Linux NFS server, use the `no_auth_nlm` or `insecure_locks` export options. This is needed because these clients send NFS locking requests from user `daemon`, not `root`.

If you are getting an error from a Solaris client such as

```
svc: unknown program 100227 (me 100003)
```

you may ignore it. It means that the Solaris client tries to get ACL information from your Linux server, which is not yet supported.

If you suspect that the problem is related to the interaction of your Linux NFS host with another non-Linux host, try to use an all-Linux configuration with the same versions of all software packages, even if just for a short period of time. That way you could determine if the problem has to do with the interaction of Linux with non-Linux systems. For more information, see the NFS-HOWTO document, located in `http://nfs.sourceforge.net/nfs-howto/`. It has a large section about the interoperability of your Linux NFS host with other non-Linux ones.

When All Else Fails

If you reached this section, you must be somewhat desperate. Before you assume that the problems listed here are indeed yours, make sure that you have correctly configured your NFS system as described in the previous chapters, and that you followed the advice in this chapter thus far. If you are certain that nothing else will help you solve the problems you are seeing, you can try a few suggestions listed here. Many of these suggestions could cause significant disruptions to your NFS service and to your users, and there is no guarantee that any of these tips will help. However, when nothing else works, these present the best course of action.

First, realize that the remaining reasons for your problems fall into two categories: bad software and bad hardware. Software is typically easier to fix and costs less than hardware.

Replacing Buggy Software

If you suspect bad or buggy software, try one or more of the following suggestions (not necessarily in order):

Reboot your system   Many bugs (but not all) can be fixed by a simple system reboot. If you reboot your system, and the problem goes away, wait a few hours or days and see if the problem comes back. If the problem does come back, consider another reboot to verify that a reboot indeed fixes it. If you are convinced that a reboot fixes the problem, you are most likely using buggy software that needs to be fixed.

Upgrade the kernel   Build and use a newer kernel. You should preferably upgrade to a newer stable kernel (such as 2.4.*x*), but sometimes even a development series kernel (such as 2.5.*x*) can fix bugs you have seen.

Upgrade kernel modules   If there is no newer kernel, check to see if there are updates to the in-kernel NFS server, any of its modules, or even NIC drivers. Check who the maintainers of that software are and whether they have released updates or fixes; sometimes individual maintainers release new software on their personal Web pages or limited-distribution mailing lists. If you can get those fixes, apply them to your kernel tree, rebuild it, and try the new kernel.

Upgrade router software   If your router or switch vendor uses complex software, or even just a small amount of firmware stored in a non-volatile RAM (NVRAM), check with your vendor for updates and apply them.

Upgrade user-level utilities   Check to see if there are any updates to user-level software such as `nfs-utils`, the C library, DNS, NIS, or anything that could possibly affect your NFS system (even if it appears unlikely). In general, it is good practice to keep up with vendor updates and apply them as soon as they are available.

Reinstall software   You may already have the latest software installed, but it still does not work. It is possible that some installed tools got corrupt on disk. A simple rebuild and reinstallation of that software (kernel, modules, and user-level utilities) from known uncorrupted sources could solve the problem.

Check the integrity of your installed software   It is possible that your system got broken into, and the intruders changed some of your software. This would be a poorly executed attack if it left behind traces, such as changed behavior and broken functionality. You can use `rpm --verify` to check that your system's software is as you installed it. We described this in Chapter 4.

Downgrading Software and Software Stability

One often-overlooked technique to fixing software is to revert back to an older version of it, sometimes known as *down-revving* software. New software typically contains two types of changes: bug fixes and new features. Introducing new features often also introduces new bugs. Worse, even fixing known bugs can introduce other bugs or expose existing ones.

For these reasons, many experienced administrators do not upgrade any software to a new major revision, the so-called *dot-zero* release (software versions such as *x*.0). They wait until the next release of that software (*x*.1).

Occasionally, you may be running software that exhibits problems, either immediately after upgrading the software or much later. In that case, consider installing a previous version of that software, one that used to work for you before an upgrade.

Everyone wants to run stable software but also to use the latest features, and these two goals often conflict. The right balance between these two depends on your site's needs. If you wish to maximize your chances of using stable software, follow these tips:

- Use vendor-approved software so that you can call customer support and get help with a problem using that software.

- Do not rush to install new software right away. Wait until a few weeks or months have passed or until the vendor releases a few fixes first. Do not believe any vendor who tells you that they do not have fixes for their software because it is stable!

- Ask others on the Internet for their experiences with the software. Many on the Web are eager to inform others about bad experiences they've had with software.

- Use software that many others use. Such software is likely to be more stable because more bugs have been discovered and (hopefully) fixed by the vendor.

- Avoid experimental software such as Linux kernel versions with an odd minor version number (2.1, 2.3, 2.5, etc.).

Correcting Hardware Problems

Hardware does not fail often, but when it does, it is usually difficult to detect. Some of the problem is perception: administrators get so used to reliable hardware that they refuse to acknowledge the possibility of bad hardware. At other times, bad hardware can produce symptoms similar to bad software. If you suspect bad hardware, follow these guidelines:

- Network cables do go bad occasionally, especially when they are located in an environment where lots of pulling and tugging occurs. This could happen if they are left on the floor where people might walk, if they are stressed when people move connected equipment around, or if your site has a particularly large and healthy population of rats and goats. Keep a set of known good cables around, and swap them with suspected bad cables. Sometimes just unplugging and re-plugging a cable helps.

- Ensure that all of your cabling, connectors, and terminators comply with specifications. For example, running Gigabit Ethernet (GigE) networks over copper-based wires requires expensive *Category-6* wires. If you are tempted to use your older 100Mbps-compliant Cat-5 wires with GigE, performance would be poor and unstable.

- Inexpensive hubs and switches, especially older ones, tend to break after a few years of honorable service. Give them the proper military-style burial and decommission them for newer units.

- Check that your disks are not failing. Completely dead disks might not even spin. Disks that are about to fail usually exhibit strange whirring and whizzing noises. Heed their last dying breaths, and replace them with newer disks. The sudden loss of a disk is usually a very costly problem. Even if you did keep perfect daily backups, you still have to get a new disk and populate it with the data.

- CPUs can die. Memory can begin to produce parity errors. CPU and computer fans could fail and cause the system to heat up, producing intermittent problems. Even a large accumulation of dust inside a computer can cause overheating and shorts.

- Extreme heat or cold, rapid changes in temperature, high humidity, exposure to direct sunlight, long-term accumulation of dust, corrosion, proximity to strong magnetic or electrical fields, vibration, and age can all affect hardware. Ensure that you use sufficiently new hardware under the conditions that the equipment vendor specified.

When in doubt, reboot. That is the motto of many administrators. Rebooting should be used as a last resort. If you can, perform a complete cold-boot: turn off the power to the computer system and all attached devices, wait a minute or two, and then turn everything back on. Sometimes a cold-reboot can clear up problems that a normal reboot cannot, such as bad state left in a peripheral device or an adapter.

Contacting the Experts

Finally, if even the suggestions above do not help, compose a detailed message listing your problem and post it to one of the proper NFS-related Linux mailing lists such as nfs@lists.sourceforge.net. Before sending a message, search the archives for the mailing list: it is possible that the problem had been seen and resolved by someone else; do not post messages to lists when the solution can be easily found by searching the Web a little. When you do post a message, include as much information as possible about the following:

- The operating system vendors and versions of your NFS servers and clients
- The versions of your NFS software
- Whether you're using UDP or TCP
- Whether you're using NFSv2 or NFSv3

- Any mount and export options you've used
- Relevant hardware types
- Any patches you have applied
- Any other tests you have performed and their results

The key to the ability of a software maintainer or vendor to fix a customer's problem is the *reproducibility* of the problem; that is, they have to be able to reproduce your problem repeatedly in their labs before they can fix it. The more detailed your message is, and the more you show your expertise and diligence in your attempts to solve the problem, the more likely it is that you will receive responses to your posts that include fixes or at least concrete suggestions for further tests. Of course, if you get no responses, consider hiring a consultant to help solve your problems. Even the author of this book is available for the right price.

In Sum

The NFS system is a complex client-server system. It includes many software and hardware components, each of which can fail in several ways. Fixing initial problems is usually difficult. Fixing problems that come up after a system has been working for a while tends to be even more difficult. We started this chapter by providing general tips and suggesting tools that you can use to diagnose NFS problems. We urge the readers to analyze configuration files and follow procedures carefully, as we described in previous chapters.

This chapter then listed a series of common problems, ranging from simple to moderately complex. Many of these are simple configuration problems such as wrong export options, but others are more difficult, such as kernel configuration problems. We continued by listing typical error messages and log messages you may receive and followed each message with a list of possible solutions to those problems. Some of these messages were harmless and could be ignored; a few were more serious and required actions such as remounting or rebooting hosts.

We next discussed advanced problems: those for which the solution is not simple and that may require lengthy analysis or the replacement of software and hardware. We concluded this chapter by providing advice to the desperate: what to do when every other suggestion fails. This included successive upgrading or replacement of hardware and software. Finally, if nothing else helped, we suggested that you reboot your systems or post the details of your problems on the appropriate mailing lists.

6

NFS Version 4

Sun engineers designed NFSv2 in the early 1980s, opening the protocol to other vendors to use, and even distributing a reference implementation. NFS has become a huge success since that time; it is the most popular distributed file system in use. Many vendors support NFS protocol versions 2 and 3 today. With such success and increased exposure, however, also came criticism regarding NFS's performance, security, flexibility, and interoperability with other systems.

When designing NFSv3 a decade later, Sun invited a few industry participants. The goals for developing NFSv3 were to complete the design and reimplementation in under a year and to address only the most important issues without making fundamental changes to the NFS protocol. These goals were achieved with the understanding that a further update of the protocol would be needed.

Because of NFS's popularity, it became apparent that the next revision of the protocol would be more significant than NFSv3 and needed to involve the larger Internet community in its design. A formal standardization process was needed. The *Internet Engineering Task Force* (IETF), a body of the *Internet Society*, had been very successful in producing quality protocol definitions for various Internet technologies. The IETF had in place a precise procedure for involving the community in the long process of proposing, defining, refining, and finally, publishing a document as a standard. These published standards are called *Request For Comments* (RFCs) and are available from www.ietf.org. The standardization process itself is a standard defined in RFC-2026, "The Internet Standards Process – Revision 3."

The IETF was the perfect choice to lead the charge for NFSv4. However, Sun Micro-systems had long held the "NFS" trademark. So before the IETF could begin this work, Sun had to relinquish control over the NFSv4 specification and its successors. This deci-sion is described in RFC-2339, "An Agreement Between the Internet Society, the IETF, and Sun Microsystems, Inc. in the matter of NFS V.4 Protocols."

The IETF then formed a *working group* (WG) for NFSv4, invited anyone who wanted to participate in the discussions, and ensured that the many working groups could meet at least three times a year during IETF meetings to report progress and discuss future work.

NFSv4 is very new. This chapter discusses the overall goals of the protocol and the new ideas or concepts that it introduces. We cover the new protocol messages that are exchanged in both directions between the NFS client and the server as well as the error codes that NFSv4 defines.

This chapter assumes a familiarity with NFSv2 and NFSv3 as described in previous chap-ters and especially in Chapter 1, "NFS Basics and Protocols." The discussion here focuses on the differences between NFSv4 and previous versions.

Finally, we report on the state of the NFSv4 implementation for Linux. Since the imple-mentation is only at its prototype stage, there is little that can be discussed regarding sys-tem administration activities related to NFSv4. Nevertheless, a general understanding of this new protocol and its operation should give system administrators familiar with pre-vious versions a feel for the effort involved in configuring and administering NFSv4.

Design Goals

Any good large-scale project begins with a requirements document to guide the project along. The IETF's NFSv4-WG started by declaring the overall goals of the project. These goals were outlined in RFC-2624, "NFS Version 4 Design Considerations." Published in June 1999, RFC-2624 states that the goals of the NFSv4-WG are to create a distributed file system that focuses on the following items:

> **Performance**   File system performance should be good especially when used over wide area networks (WANs). The protocol should handle the particular problems of the Internet: longer latencies, higher congestion, and increased packet loss when compared to a local area network. Previous NFS protocols always assumed that NFS would be used in a local area network, so when it was used on a WAN, it exhibited poor performance.

Scalability   NFSv2/NFSv3 servers typically can handle at most several hundreds of clients. A single NFSv4 server should be able to handle many thousands of clients.

Accessibility   The protocol should be easier to access through various network appliances such as firewalls, load-balancers, or caching devices, and application proxies such as those using SOCKS.

Reliability and high-availability   To improve reliability, the protocol should allow a client to use multiple replicas of file servers and to cache data in a coherent manner. See the sidebar "Load-Balancing NFS Mounts?" in Chapter 10, "Automounter Maps."

Strong security   The protocol should include strong security and built-in negotiation of security features. It should include a better security mechanism than the typical Unix UID/GID model, which includes simple bit-mode permissions.

Cross-platform interoperability   The protocol should be flexible enough for different systems to interoperate. It should not favor one operating system over another: Unix, MS-DOS and Windows, MacOS, VMS, etc., should all be treated equally.

Internationalization (I18N)   The protocol should allow clients and servers from different parts of the world to work with each other properly, especially if the server and client use a different character set or language.

Extensibility   The protocol should be extensible enough to evolve without a costly redesign for a new major version release. (Four versions of NFS is enough, thank you; we'd rather avoid a fifth.)

Much work proceeded after NFSv4's design goals were laid out. The WG worked diligently to detail the protocol's proposed specification, while various groups began implementing prototypes. These prototypes were tested for functionality and interoperability during several gatherings of interested parties at *Connectathon* meetings (`www.connectathon.org`). This event is designed to be a marathon of sorts, bringing together implementers of various protocols to test how well their systems implement a protocol and also to expose any deficiencies in the protocol.

Creating precise, accurate, and functionally complete protocols has always been very difficult. Often, protocols were ratified as formal specifications without much practical experience. Later—sometimes years after the fact—serious flaws in some protocols were uncovered but could not be corrected because the protocols had already been widely deployed. The Connectathon meetings proved very useful in preventing such problems. For the first time in the history of NFS, many groups worked together to create a detailed, comprehensive protocol. Prototypes were built and tested, and experiences from these tests helped further refine the protocol's description, leading to better prototypes. This process was repeated until everyone was satisfied that the protocol was adequately stable and that it addressed the goals outlined in RFC-2624.

A year and a half later, in December 2000, the NFS version 4 protocol specification moved from a *Draft Internet Standard* to a *Proposed Internet Standard*, and RFC-3010 was born. The next stage is to have the larger Internet community comment on this proposed standard. If it is accepted, it will become an Internet standard and be assigned a number in the IETF's "STD" series.

Overview

The IETF design and development process has created a new protocol with NFSv4. To support the stated design goals, NFSv4 substantially departs from previous NFS protocols in several ways. For example, NFSv4 servers maintain state; functions that previously occurred in separate "stateful" protocols are now integrated into the NFS server. In addition, security has been enhanced. Special filehandles and new filehandle types have been developed. New file attributes and concepts such as delegations, leases, and callbacks have been added to the protocol. Also, the protocol allows future developers to extend its functionality and includes facilities for clients and servers to agree on a common set of functions that they support. These extensive changes make NFSv4 a new challenge for even experienced NFS administrators. To put the protocol's new procedures in proper context, the next several sections overview the major features of NFSv4.

A Stateful Server

The NFSv4 server is no longer stateless. Chapter 1 showed how, while the NFSv2 and NFSv3 servers were indeed stateless, many other components were not. These extra protocols were folded into a single NFSv4 protocol: MOUNT, NLM, NSM, RQUOTA, and even the PCNFS protocol.

This consolidation of protocols helped to design a coherent interaction between clients and servers. Furthermore, now the NFSv4 server uses a single well-known port (2049) for all communication; this eases its transit across firewalls and proxies.

NFSv4 contains explicit OPEN and CLOSE operations. The OPEN operation provides clients with a single point where various open-time semantics can be controlled in a consistent manner, such as opening and locking a file atomically. The CLOSE operation helps clients to inform servers when the latter can discard the state that was associated with an opened file.

Security

Several mechanisms exist for securing network traffic. Two of the more popular ones are *Secure Socket Layer* (SSL) and *Internet Protocol Security* (IPSEC). The problem with these methods is that they only work with connection-oriented transport protocols such as TCP. They do not work with UDP, and NFS has to be able to use both UDP and TCP.

Over the years, Sun Microsystems has developed an RPC security mechanism called *RPC-SEC*. This is a secure method of exchanging network data but at the RPC layer, which is above the transport layer. Sun's efforts helped to evolve a general-purpose RPC-layer security protocol called RPCSEC_GSS, or the *Remote Procedure Call Security — Generic Security Services*.

RPCSEC_GSS was chosen as the security mechanism for use with NFSv4. Its advantage is that it works at the RPC layer and thus can support both UDP and TCP. Furthermore, it can be implemented for older versions of NFS.

The main features of RPCSEC_GSS that made it attractive for the NFSv4 designers were its ability to handle private keys such as those used in Kerberos 5. It supports public keys, encrypts data, includes strong authentication, and supports several security mechanisms, all of which improve the security of NFS.

NFSv4 added a special operation that allows clients to query a server for the methods of security that the server supports. This helps clients and servers negotiate automatically the types of security mechanisms that they wish to use. Such features need not be hard-coded into an implementation or have to require a complex and manual configuration. Servers and clients can implement any number of existing (or future) security methods, and the NFSv4 protocol is flexible enough to determine the best match of security features between the NFS clients and servers.

Compound Operations

Past analysis of NFSv2 traffic had shown that one of the most popular sequences of NFS messages was a READDIR followed by many GETATTR messages. This happened when users ran the common command to list a directory's contents: `ls -l`. This particular sequence was optimized in NFSv3 by the addition of a new protocol procedure called READDIRPLUS. This procedure saved the NFS client from having to exchange many RPC messages by returning the contents of a directory along with attributes for each entry—all in one RPC message.

Further analysis of NFS traffic suggested that many other sequences of procedures could be optimized. However, rather than create new procedures for each such sequence, NFSv4 introduces the concept of *compound operations*. An NFSv4 client can compose a compound operation by listing a series of NFS operations in one RPC message.

There are two advantages to compound operations. First, they save a lot of network traffic since only one RPC message is exchanged. Second, they alleviate some of the need for frequent protocol changes. Many past suggestions and some improvements to older NFS protocols involved the creation of new procedures that combined other procedures in different ways. With the compound procedure, protocol extensibility is improved.

NOTE NFSv4 actually defines only two primary procedures: NULL and COMPOUND. All other *operations* are defined in terms of the COMPOUND procedure. A client using even a single operation encapsulates it inside a COMPOUND procedure. See the upcoming section "Protocol Procedures and Operations."

One typical example of what NFSv4 clients might do would be to LOOKUP, OPEN, READ, and then CLOSE a file. This would let a client read a whole (presumably small) file in one message. These four operations would be combined into one COMPOUND procedure and sent to the NFSv4 server. The server interprets COMPOUND procedures by evaluating each composed operation in order until an error occurs or the end of the compound procedure is reached. The server then returns to the client the last success or error code, as well as the results for all of the successful operations.

The server evaluates each compound procedure independently, so that the same client or multiple clients can send different compound procedures and there is no confusion as to their interpretation. One way that the NFSv4 server achieves this is by using a *saved filehandle* for evaluating compounded operations. Evaluation of the operations in a compound procedure requires a temporary filehandle to avoid interfering with the primary filehandle that the server uses for the client, which is called the *current filehandle*. Additional details about filehandles are provided in upcoming sections.

File System Model

In NFSv4, a file system on the server is still represented as a hierarchy of files and folders. However, this is now decoupled from actual local file systems that exist on the server. Previous versions of NFS could export only one file system at a time, or a portion thereof. NFSv4 is able to create logical file system volumes that are composed of several physical file systems or their subdirectories.

The NFSv4 server is expected to provide *glue* between physical file systems where gaps in the namespace may exist. For example, if an NFSv4 server exports a single logical volume that combines /usr and /usr/local/bin, the server may have to create a glue filehandle for the local component, so that an NFS client can traverse from /usr down to local/bin transparently.

Filehandles

The NFSv4 filehandle, just as with all previous versions of NFS, is a unique file identifier that is constructed by the server and is opaque to the client. In previous versions of NFS, only one filehandle existed. This filehandle had to be exchanged many times between clients and servers. In addition, there were several ambiguities about the precise meaning of the filehandle on some systems. NFSv4 expands the definition of the filehandle by creating several filehandles, several types for each filehandle, and by creating new ways to save on repeated exchanges of these filehandles over the network.

Several special filehandles exist in NFSv4: current, saved, root, and public.

The Current Filehandle

Unix operating systems maintain a *current working directory* (CWD) for each running process on the system. This CWD is the default location from which all file access using relative path names is assumed to begin. Similarly, NFSv4 defines a *current* filehandle as the default filehandle that the server keeps on behalf of the client. That way the client does not need to include a filehandle for all operations; this saves on network use.

NFSv4 clients can reset this current filehandle using the PUTROOTFH operation, just as Unix users can cd to a new directory and begin working off of there.

The Saved Filehandle

The *saved* filehandle is another filehandle available on NFSv4 servers. It is used in various operations as temporary filehandle storage while manipulating the current filehandle.

For example, the COMPOUND procedure, described above, saves the current filehandle in the saved filehandle location while processing compound operations. The current filehandle typically gets restored from the saved filehandle when the compound operation finishes.

The Root Filehandle

The *ROOT* filehandle designates the root (top-level directory) of the exported volume. Recall that for the client, an exported volume appears as one directory hierarchy; on the server, this could be any combination of several physical file systems or subdirectories. That's why the root filehandle is often thought of as the logical head of the conceptual top-level filehandle of a directory tree: the server may have to create the root filehandle dynamically and there may not be an actual directory on the server that directly corresponds to this root filehandle.

In previous NFS protocols, clients authenticated to the server using a separate MOUNT protocol. This is not needed in NFSv4 since clients authenticate directly to the server.

When an NFSv4 client authenticates itself to a server, the client may instruct the server to set the value of the current (default) filehandle to that of the volume's root filehandle, using the PUTROOTFH operation. This operation sets the top-level directory entry from which the client can begin to access the server's files. Afterward, the client could begin traversing the entire directory tree of that volume using lookup operations and others.

The Public Filehandle

The *PUBLIC* filehandle is a special filehandle used by the server to authenticate clients, in lieu of the older MOUNT protocol. The server is responsible for the exact definition of the public filehandle and what file system objects it may be associated with.

Typically, the PUBLIC filehandle is a zero-length or all-zero filehandle. This special value cannot be a regular filehandle. When a server receives such a filehandle, it knows that a client is trying to authenticate for the first time. The server is then responsible for determining if the client should be allowed the access and, if so, for sending the client back a successful response. The client can then get the ROOT filehandle of the file system just authenticated for, or simply set to begin file access from the root of that file system (using the PUTROOTFH operation).

NFSv4 clients cannot assume anything about this association; they can, however, send a LOOKUP request using the predesignated public filehandle to an NFSv4 server—to request first-time access to the file server's volumes. Note that servers can choose to change the public filehandle's definition and hand it to a select set of clients; this can be useful in order to avoid causal attempts to attack an NFSv4 server by probing for access using the typical PUBLIC filehandle.

WebNFS

WebNFS is a protocol designed by Sun Microsystems as an extension to NFSv2 and NFSv3. Its main goal is to allow access to NFS servers across the Internet without the need for an explicit MOUNT protocol and without changing the existing protocols.

WebNFS achieves this goal by defining a special *PUBLIC filehandle* to be used with the NFS_LOOKUP procedure. The PUBLIC filehandle is defined as containing all zeros in NFSv2 and as having a zero length in NFSv3. A WebNFS client contacts a remote NFS server directly at port 2049 using standard-style Internet URLs and provides the remote NFS server with the PUBLIC filehandle. Upon receiving this filehandle, the remote NFS server authenticates the NFS client just as the MOUNT protocol does. The successful response from the NFS_LOOKUP call includes an actual filehandle to use for normal NFS operations.

Traditional NFS path traversal looked up each directory in a long path name for the component under that directory. This resulted in a series of NFS_LOOKUP requests sent over the network. A good Internet-wide protocol should endeavor to reduce the number of network messages used. To improve performance over the Internet, Web-NFS also supports multicomponent lookups. A client sends a whole path name to a server; the server interprets the complete path name and returns a filehandle for the final component.

The design of and the experimentation with WebNFS provided some useful feedback on the feasibility of NFS use over the Internet. The lessons learned from WebNFS were incorporated in the NFSv4 protocol.

Filehandle Types

Past NFS protocols assumed that filehandles were persistent: they must be valid at all times until the client is done with them. This became a problem for two reasons. First, some operating systems—especially non-Unix ones—lacked the information necessary to encode filehandles consistently. For example, their file systems may not use unique and constant inode numbers, or the file system ID could change after a reboot. Second, vendors who wanted to implement NFS replication (read-only), migration, or load-balancing faced serious obstacles since a filehandle on one server was not valid on another server, even for the same file.

NFSv4 defines two main types of filehandles: persistent and volatile. *Persistent* filehandles have the same semantics as filehandles in older NFS protocols. *Volatile* filehandles, on the other hand, may become invalid at any point. When that happens, the server returns the typical "stale filehandle" error code to the client. If the file system was renamed or migrated, the client can then query the file server for the new location of that file system. The client is then responsible for retrieving an updated filehandle for the file in question.

NFSv4 also supports expiration times on volatile filehandles. A server can issue timed file-handles to clients and be assured that clients could not use them after a certain period of time. The flexibility of filehandles in NFSv4 is neatly captured by the five different types that can be encoded as a type field bitmask in the filehandle itself:

FH4_PERSISTENT   This bit indicates that the filehandle is persistent.

FH4_NOEXPIRE_WITH_OPEN   This filehandle cannot expire while a client has the file open.

FH4_VOLATILE_ANY   This filehandle could expire at any time, especially during file system renaming or migration.

FH4_VOL_MIGRATION   This filehandle will expire during file system migration.

FH4_VOL_RENAME   This filehandle will expire during file system renaming.

One additional change to filehandles in NFSv4 was a semantic one. NFSv4 clarified the relationship between filehandles and files when it came to their equality or inequality. Two identical filehandles must represent the same exact file storage, even for files that are hard-linked. Two different filehandles must represent two different files.

File Attributes

Older versions of NFS defined a fixed set of mostly Unix-centric file attributes. There was no easy way to support non-Unix file servers or create new attributes. NFSv4 includes a flexible mechanism for supporting many platforms as well as creating new attributes.

NFSv4 defines three types of file attributes: mandatory, recommended, and named. We discuss these attribute types next.

Mandatory Attributes

Mandatory attributes are those that all servers and clients must define. The set of mandatory attributes is intended to be kept very small and forms a basis on which all NFSv4 systems can interact with each other.

Mandatory attributes include the type of a file (e.g., regular file, directory, symlink, etc.), the size of the file, a unique identifier for the file, and more. Some attributes are specific to a whole file system, such as a flag indicating whether the file system supports symbolic or hard links.

Recommended Attributes

Recommended attributes typically represent differences between various operating systems and file systems that need not be available in all NFSv4 implementations. An NFSv4 client has to query an NFSv4 server and find out which attributes (if any) are supported by both sides. The intent of this type of attributes is to allow servers to implement as many of them as possible, as long as it is simple to do so. Attributes that are difficult to implement should not be simulated or half done: it is better for a feature not to exist than to work inconsistently.

Recommended attributes include the "archived" and "hidden" file bits of MS-DOS file systems, Access Control Lists (ACLs), whether the file system is case-insensitive, quota information (thus subsuming the older RQUOTA protocol), and more.

Together, mandatory and recommended attributes represent the total set of file and file system attributes that exist on most systems used today. Both sets of attributes are defined and a bitmask is allocated for them, one bit per attribute.

Access Control Lists   *Access Control Lists* (ACLs) exist in some operating systems and file systems. They allow more flexible control than the simplistic Unix UID/GID model for who can access file system resources. Unfortunately, ACLs have been implemented in a variety of non-interoperable ways by different vendors. One of NFSv4's goals is to provide a flexible cross-platform way of specifying and using ACLs.

One special recommended attribute is the ACL attribute. This attribute specifies an array of *access control entries* (ACEs). ACEs define an access type, the files or directories it should apply to, and the actual access set (a single owner, a group, everyone, anonymous users, dial-up users, and more). Users, for example, could be represented in a universal fashion (such as an e-mail address). There are four types of possible ACEs:

ALLOW   Grant access as defined in the ACE.

DENY   Deny access as defined in the ACE.

AUDIT   Log any attempt to access any file or directory that uses the access method specified by the ACE.

ALARM   Generate an alarm on attempt to access any file or directory that uses the access method defined by the ACE.

Named Attributes

Named attributes allow NFSv4 to evolve and be extended easily. A named attribute has a simple string name and a value that is an arbitrary sequence of bytes. One use for these attributes is in the creation of application-specific file attributes. For example, a compression system could associate the type or compression algorithm used with the file, or a source-control system could attach version numbers to source files.

Named attributes are accessible to an NFSv4 client as an attributes directory for each file that has named attributes. The attributes directory contains files whose names are the named attributes' names and whose contents represent the values of the named attributes. In this way, named attributes can be listed, created, read, and modified easily with normal directory browsing tools (such as ls and cat).

Named attributes may themselves have attributes, even named ones. This allows for the creation of a whole hierarchy of attributes for a given file.

File Locking

File and byte-range locking methods used to be in a separate protocol, the Network Lock Manager (NLM), and included complex callback procedures. In addition, the PCNFS protocol included share reservation messages used typically by Windows-based systems. NFSv4 folds all locking and share-reservation support right into the protocol and does away with most of the locking-related callbacks. Since locks require that the server maintain state about the locked files, a simpler lease-based model was taken. This system allows for a wide range of locking semantics to be supported reliably—anywhere from advisory read-only locks to mandatory single-writer locks.

When the server creates any new state on behalf of a client, it provides the client a lease for that state for a period of time. This period of time is defined by the server globally for a given client. The client is responsible for renewing the lease, either explicitly by calling a RENEW procedure or implicitly by accessing the resource for which the lease was provided (such as reading from or writing to a file that is locked).

If the client does not renew the lease, the server may discard the state associated with that lease. A client that tries to access files with expired leases will get an error code.

Client Caching

NFSv4's primary goal is to provide good performance over the Internet. To that effect, the protocol minimizes the amount of communication that is needed. One method already mentioned is the COMPOUND procedure. Another obvious technique is caching. Previous versions of NFS also employed client-side caching to improve performance.

File data is cached by default. With such extensive caching, the chances for caches to get out of sync are increased. Older versions of NFS did not include cache consistency mechanisms; NFSv4, on the other hand, supports and describes cache consistency methods in detail. The client is responsible for ensuring cache consistency when it opens or closes a file. Applications that wish to enforce cache consistency at all times (and possibly bypass the cache) have to lock the byte ranges of the file in question.

Delegations

One important contribution to improving performance in NFSv4 is the concept of a *delegation*. An NFSv4 server can, upon opening a file, grant an NFSv4 client a read or write delegation, as well as several other types of delegations such as locks. This allows the client a measure of independence while manipulating the file. Clients can open, lock, read, write, and close files during a delegation—all without having to use costly network resources to communicate with the server.

With a read delegation, the server guarantees the client that no other client can write to that file during the lifetime of the delegation. With a write delegation, the server guarantees the client that no other client can read or write to that file.

Delegations, however, have a limited lifetime. Furthermore, delegations may be revoked or recalled by the server when it believes that a granted delegation conflicts with a more important request from a different client. In a marked departure from previous NFS protocols, NFSv4 servers may *themselves* initiate calls to NFS clients in order to recall a delegation. This reverse procedure-calling path is known as a *callback path*. If the callback path does not exist between the server and the client, servers will not grant that client any delegations. We describe the NFSv4 callback procedures later, under the section "Callback Procedures."

One possible problem with delegations, or for that matter, any state that either client or server maintains, is what happens when either party fails. If the server crashes, it will lose knowledge of any delegations it gave to clients. If a client crashes, it will lose any information about locks it held before. The problem is exacerbated by the Internet, where networks are less reliable and can become partitioned for a period of time. To address these situations, NFSv4 defines a method of *delegation recovery*. A server may, at any time, contact the client and ask it to relinquish its delegation. This could be useful, for example, for a server that crashed and came back up, to consolidate all of its known delegations before resuming regular file system activity.

Internationalization (I18N)

Older versions of NFS only supported the U.S. ASCII character set for file names. If NFSv4 is to cross international boundaries, the protocol must support character sets used throughout the world. This is particularly important because with NFSv4, a client could be accessing files that reside on a server in a different country, possibly one with a very different language and alphabet. Such a client would have to understand both the local and remote language character sets and possibly translate between the two sets, a process known as *internationalization* (I18N).

One proposed idea for I18N was for NFSv4 servers and clients to negotiate a locale before exchanging file names. Afterward, both parties could agree on a small subset of characters to use. This small set could be encoded in just 7 bits for most languages. However, several complications arose during the design of NFSv4, especially with multicomponent lookups where each pathname component could use a different locale. The idea of using a locale with each NFS operation was dropped in favor of a simpler method, albeit one that could consume more network bandwidth.

NFSv4 uses universal 16-bit or even 32-bit character sets, sometimes known as Unicode sets, or UTF-8. Sixteen-bit Unicodes have been determined to support all characters of all known languages. They are unique and simple and clearly identify the language to which the particular character belongs. Thirty-two-bit codes may be needed to support additional language character sets—perhaps when the intergalactic space station is completed (we may also have to revise I18N to support purely telepathic species).

Normalization is defined as the process by which a client and server agree on a base set of characters and then only use that set, thus saving on network bandwidth. For example, most NFSv4 clients and servers within the U.S. can easily fall back to using the ASCII character set. The first minor version of the NFSv4 protocol (version 0) does not specify how normalization should take place, nor does it require it. This is intended to be addressed in future revisions. Therefore, at this stage, NFSv4 clients and servers have to be able to handle un-normalized characters. If they choose to, or require it, such clients or servers can normalize the UTF-8 characters they get as needed.

Minor Versioning

Past NFS protocol revisions were *major*; the protocol procedures were changed significantly and were incompatible with previous versions. Typically, major revisions are assumed to be needed once a decade (yes, start worrying about NFSv5 come 2010).

In another departure from previous NFS versions, NFSv4 allows for *minor* revisions such as NFSv4.1, NFSv4.2, etc. Minor revisions are assumed to be standardized quicker, in about 1 to 2 years.

Many features of NFSv4 allow users to extend it without a formal change: compound operations and named attributes, for example. The IETF, however, recommends that the community using NFSv4 periodically reevaluate the need for small revisions since, in all likelihood, certain new features might turn out to be sufficiently useful that they should be standardized. Such features as named attributes should be standardized and given an official number through the *Internet Assigned Numbers Authority* (IANA).

The rules for minor revisions of the NFSv4 (and all future major versions) are as follows:

- New primary procedures may not be added or removed.
- No existing compound operations may be removed.
- New compound operations may be added. Since these compound operations may result in a semantically different NFS protocol for different minor versions, clients must not use filehandles or any objects returned from a compound procedure where the client's minor version was different from the server's minor version.

- Existing attributes may not be changed or removed. New attributes may be added by appending them at the end of the current list of attributes.

- No existing data structures, bit flags, attributes, returned results, or error codes may be changed or deleted.

- Semantics of all existing operations, returned results, and error codes must remain as is.

- New error codes can be defined.

- Minor versions can define an operation, an attribute, or a bit flag as "mandatory to not implement." All existing structure for the operation is kept intact, but the operation or object is obsoleted. This allows the reintroduction of the operation or object at a later date and avoids the possibility of reuse of the operation's or object's freed slot.

- Features may be downgraded from mandatory to recommended or from recommended to optional, or they may be upgraded in the reverse (but only one upgrade level at a time).

- No new features can be added as mandatory in a minor revision. They can be introduced as optional or recommended and then upgraded to mandatory in a subsequent revision.

- Clients and servers supporting a minor revision must support all previous minor revisions for the same major release.

Protocol Procedures and Operations

At the heart of any protocol are the procedures that make up the specification. Table 6.1 lists the procedures and operations of NFSv4. This protocol has only two primary procedures: NULL and COMPOUND, which are procedure 0 and procedure 1, respectively. Procedure 2 is undefined and reserved for future expansion. The rest are protocol operations that can only be encapsulated in a COMPOUND procedure.

Table 6.1   NFSv4 Protocol Procedures and Operations

Number	Operation	Meaning
Procedure 0	NULL	No operation.
Procedure 1	COMPOUND	Compound operations.
Procedure 2	N/A	(For future expansion.)

Table 6.1 NFSv4 Protocol Procedures and Operations *(continued)*

Number	Operation	Meaning
Operation 3	ACCESS	Check access rights.
Operation 4	CLOSE	Close file.
Operation 5	COMMIT	Commit cached data.
Operation 6	CREATE	Create a non-regular file object.
Operation 7	DELEGPURGE	Purge delegations awaiting recovery.
Operation 8	DELEGRETURN	Return delegation.
Operation 9	GETATTR	Get attributes.
Operation 10	GETFH	Get current filehandle.
Operation 11	LINK	Create link to a file.
Operation 12	LOCK	Create lock.
Operation 13	LOCKT	Test for lock.
Operation 14	LOCKU	Unlock file.
Operation 15	LOOKUP	Look up file name.
Operation 16	LOOKUPP	Look up parent directory.
Operation 17	NVERIFY	Verify difference in attributes.
Operation 18	OPEN	Open a regular file.
Operation 19	OPENATTR	Open named attribute directory.
Operation 20	OPEN_CONFIRM	Confirm open.
Operation 21	OPEN_DOWNGRADE	Reduce open file access.
Operation 22	PUTFH	Set current filehandle.
Operation 23	PUTPUBFH	Set public filehandle.

Table 6.1   NFSv4 Protocol Procedures and Operations *(continued)*

Number	Operation	Meaning
Operation 24	PUTROOTFH	Set root filehandle.
Operation 25	READ	Read from file.
Operation 26	READDIR	Read directory.
Operation 27	READLINK	Read symbolic link.
Operation 28	REMOVE	Remove file system object.
Operation 29	RENAME	Rename directory entry.
Operation 30	RENEW	Renew a lease.
Operation 31	RESTOREFH	Restore saved filehandle.
Operation 32	SAVEFH	Save current filehandle.
Operation 33	SECINFO	Obtain available security.
Operation 34	SETATTR	Set attributes.
Operation 35	SETCLIENTID	Negotiate clientid.
Operation 36	SETCLIENTID_CONFIRM	Confirm clientid.
Operation 37	VERIFY	Verify same attributes.
Operation 38	WRITE	Write to file.

Next, we describe the NFSv4 RPC messages shown in Table 6.1. For more details on each procedure, or for the precise source code definitions for these, see RFC-3010 and Appendix B, "Online Resources."

NULL   This is the standard ping procedure that takes and returns no arguments. It is intended to run very quickly because it is used more often by clients to test if a server is up and responding.

COMPOUND   The COMPOUND procedure combines several NFS operations into a single RPC message. As described above in "Compound Operations," the NFSv4 server evaluates each operation in the compound in order, until all operations have been evaluated or an error occurs. The server returns the last error status as well as the results for all intermediate operations.

ACCESS This is the first operation in the NFSv4 protocol. It verifies that a user, as specified by the user's credentials, has access to the file or directory in question. The NFS client can specify the bitmask of access rights to check, so that the NFS server can check only for those rights.

CLOSE This operation closes a file. The server releases any state information and share reservations that exist for the file. Clients are expected to release all locks held prior to closing a file. If they do not release locks, the server may try to free up the locks itself. If the server is unable to free all the locks, it returns an error message for the CLOSE operation.

COMMIT This operation flushes all unwritten data to stable storage, for a given file. Clients may specify the starting offset and length of bytes (a range) within the file to flush. If the offset and length are both zero, the server will flush the entire file.

One typical problem with asynchronous writes is the possibility of a server crash between an asynchronous write and a commit operation. Servers return a special identifier to clients upon a successful asynchronous write, called a *write verifier*. The same write verifier is returned to the client upon a successful commit. If clients receive a different write verifier, they know that, somehow, the previously written data was lost and not written to stable media. This can often happen when a server reboots between a write and commit operation.

CREATE This operation creates a non-regular file. To create regular files, clients must use the new OPEN operation. Clients must specify the type of object to be created: a directory, symbolic link, character device, or block device, etc.

DELEGPURGE Typically, when a server delegates access to a client, and either one of them crash, both parties have to recover their previous information about the delegations they provided or received. However, there are cases when not all delegations need to be recovered after a client or server crash. If a client determines that a delegation it lost was no longer needed, it can use the DELEGPURGE operation to tell the server to remove all of the delegations pending recovery for that client. This can happen when a client does not need to store information relating to the delegation into stable storage locally on the client. By purging such delegations, servers can clear up some of the state they hold and even unblock pending operations for other clients (possibly for the same shared resource).

DELEGRETURN Each delegation has a special *state identifier* (stateid) that the server hands back to the client. The DELEGRETURN operation simply returns to the server a delegation given its stateid. This operation is often the final stage in returning a delegation to a server that had recalled it from a client using the CB_RECALL callback operation (described below).

GETATTR   This operation returns the attributes for a given object. The client can specify the exact set of attributes it is interested in (because there could be many). The server returns a bitmap of the attributes for which it was able to get values, as well as the values for these attributes.

GETFH   This operation returns the current filehandle back to the client. This operation may be needed after a LOOKUP or CREATE since they do not automatically return new filehandles. See the section "Filehandles" above.

LINK   This operation creates a new name for a given file, known in Unix file systems as a hard-link. Of course, servers running on platforms that do not support hard-links will return an error code back to a client that requests the creation of a new link for an existing file.

LOCK   This operation requests a lock for a byte range in a file, specified using the starting offset and the length of the byte-range to lock. Clients can use special syntax to specify the locking of a file from a given offset through the end of the file, or the entire file. If a lock cannot be granted, the server returns as much information as it can about the conflict: the owner, offset, and length of the byte-range in the conflicting file. This way clients can tell which other client already has a lock on the file.

LOCKT   This operation does not set a lock; it tests to see if a lock exists for a file at a given offset and length. Note that the server does not guarantee that a different client may not acquire a lock shortly after a LOCKT.

LOCKU   This operation instructs a server to release (unlock) the locked resources specified by the given stateid for the file in question.

LOOKUP   This operation finds a file in a directory corresponding to the current filehandle. It supports multicomponent lookups, thus saving on repeated lookups for each component.

LOOKUPP   This operation specifically finds the parent directory of the current filehandle. Previous versions of NFS required special semantics to the LOOKUP procedure when looking up ".." or ".". However, this *dot-dot* concept is Unix-centric and does not exist on all operating systems. Therefore, the LOOKUPP operation must be used to ensure cross-platform compatibility; servers would implement this operation according to their own specifics.

NVERIFY   This operation can be used primarily to verify the validity of a cache. Suppose a client wants to find out if a cached file changed and, if so, return the new data bytes of the file. The client can send a sequence of <LOOKUP, NVERIFY, READ>, where the NVERIFY is asked to check for the size attribute of the file and the last modification time as the client knows them. If the file has not changed, NVERIFY will return an error indicating that the attributes checked for are still the same. If, however, the file did change, then NVERIFY will not return an error, and the compound procedure would proceed to process the READ operation—thus reading the updated bytes of the file.

OPEN   This complex operation opens a regular file, possibly creating it. The result of an OPEN leaves a state on the server, a state that is normally released using a CLOSE operation. Clients must issue an explicit GETFH operation to retrieve the filehandle to CLOSE. The OPEN operation, just as with the open(2) system call, can create files exclusively if they do not exist, or reopen existing files. One additional complication of this operation is the client's ability to claim to the server that it may have already held a previous lock or delegation.

OPENATTR   NFSv4 supports extensible attributes, designated as a hierarchy of named attributes and their values. To access these attributes, clients perform the OPENATTR operation. This operation returns a filehandle for a special virtual directory that contains the named attributes of the given file system object. The client can then issue normal READDIR, LOOKUP, READ, and WRITE operations on the attribute directory—since it appears as any other normal directory. This provides a very flexible method for extending and manipulating the attributes of a file.

OPEN_CONFIRM   During the time that a client opens and uses a locked file, the client may generate a lot of additional state information that the server is obligated to maintain. Each time a client generates such additional state information, it will typically include a sequence ID number along with the information. To help NFSv4 servers save on the amount of memory and resources consumed by possibly many such pieces of state data, the client may periodically issue the OPEN_CONFIRM operation. The client passes a sequence ID number to the server; the server may then discard much of intermediate state information for that client's use of the file.

OPEN_DOWNGRADE   This operation is used to reduce a client's access to an open file. It may be necessary if a client that locked a file has the file opened multiple times and possibly is using different access or deny permissions. When one of the opened references is closed, the file's permanent access restrictions may be changed in such a way as to conflict with some of the remaining opened references. This procedure is useful to instruct a server to replace the access and deny bits of an opened file with those specified by the client.

PUTFH   This operation replaces the current filehandle with the handle specified by the client. It is useful, for example, when clients change to different directories or other operations where the clients wish to change the context for the following operations.

PUTPUBFH   This operation replaces the current filehandle with the one that represents the server's public filehandle. This operation is often the first NFSv4 operation used, to set the initial context for future operations. Recall that the public filehandle can be different from the root filehandle, as detailed in "Filehandles" above.

PUTROOTFH   This operation replaces the current filehandle with the one that represents the server's root filehandle. This operation is also often the first NFSv4 operation used, to set the initial context for future operations. See "Filehandles" above.

READ   This operation reads a number of bytes, starting at a given offset, for the file represented by the current filehandle.

READDIR   This operation returns a number of entries in a directory, starting from a given offset in that directory (which is often the last place where a previous READDIR left off). The client may specify a list of attributes to return for each entry. This operation in NFSv4 subsumes the capabilities of NFSv3's READDIRPLUS procedure.

READLINK   This operation reads the value of a symbolic link, or what the symlink points to. If the server does not support symlinks, it returns an error.

REMOVE   This operation deletes a file system object from the directory corresponding to the current filehandle. If that is the last reference to the object, the server may destroy any information associated with that file object. This operation can remove files, directories, or any other type of file.

RENAME   This operation renames a file. The old and new names of the file are given as UTF-8 strings. The old directory where the file resides is stored in the current filehandle, and the new directory location is stored in the saved filehandle.

RENEW   When clients receive a lease from a server, for example, a lease to write a file exclusively, that lease expires after the designated period of time. Clients must issue the RENEW operation as needed to renew their lease; otherwise the server may timeout the lease and free it.

RESTOREFH   This is one of several operations that are used to manipulate the various filehandles that servers can have; such operations include setting and copying values of filehandles between different handles. This operation copies the saved filehandle contents into the current filehandle.

SAVEFH   This operation copies the current filehandle into the saved filehandle location. It is in essence the opposite of the RESTOREFH operation.

SECINFO   This operation returns a list of valid available RPC authentication techniques that the server supports for a given filehandle. In this fashion, clients and servers can negotiate the most suitable forms of security for their needs.

SETATTR   This operation changes a set of attributes for a given file system object. The client provides the server with a bitmask of attributes to change along with their values.

SETCLIENTID   Each NFSv4 client is identified to a server using a *client ID*, which includes a possible callback path: an RPC program number and a port number. This operation tells a server that the client wants to use a different client ID for subsequent operations. It can be used, for example, by NFSv4 clients that act as proxies, caching devices, or load-balancers.

SETCLIENTID_CONFIRM This operation confirms that a client identifier given in a previous SETCLIENTID operation is still valid. It may be necessary to use this operation if the server holds state for a given client ID because that state should not be released for a client that has changed its ID.

VERIFY This operation is used to ensure that the attributes of a file are the same before proceeding with the next operation. For example, a client can issue a sequence <LOOKUP, VERIFY, PUTFH, REMOVE> to remove a file. However, the client issues the VERIFY before removing the file to check, for example, that the file's size and owner are what the client expects. If the attributes are not the same, the VERIFY operation would return an error and the file would not be removed: the compound procedure will terminate before completing all operations.

WRITE This operation writes data to a regular file represented by the current file-handle. The client can specify the offset and length of bytes to write to the file.

An NFSv4 Implementation RFC

Past NFS protocols attempted to specify design and implementation information in the same RFC. Worse, often many implementation recommendations were not discussed at all, leading vendors to implement past protocols in incompatible ways.

The NFSv4-WG left many implementation details unanswered in RFC-3010. This was intentional, so that the main RFC would only concern itself with the design and specification of the NFSv4, not how it might be implemented. For example, for callbacks to work through firewalls and NAT boxes, these devices will have to be modified to be aware of NFSv4, so they can properly allow such access through the firewall and into a secure site. In addition, load-balancers will have to figure out how to migrate or replicate NFSv4 files for use with this new protocol. These implementation details, and many more, are the subject of an upcoming NFSv4-WG RFC—an *implementation* RFC—that the working group is scheduled to work on next.

Callback Procedures

Because of the complexity of NFSv4, the server may require access to the client. That is, the client itself must act as a server under certain conditions. The client's ability to service requests is done via the NFS4_CALLBACK program. This program is just another RPC program: it has a set of procedures and operations. However, there is no preassigned RPC program number and port number for the callback program. The client provides the server with its callback program number and port numbers via the SETCLIENTID operation.

In a similar fashion to the NFSv4 server program, the NFS4_CALLBACK client program also defines only two primary procedures: CB_NULL and CB_COMPOUND. All other callback operations are defined in terms of the CB_COMPOUND procedure. Table 6.2 lists all callback procedures and operations.

Table 6.2   NFSv4 Callback Procedures and Operations

Number	Operation	Meaning
Procedure 0	CB_NULL	No operation.
Procedure 1	CB_COMPOUND	Compound operations.
Procedure 2	N/A	(For future expansion.)
Operation 3	CB_GETATTR	Get attributes.
Operation 4	CB_RECALL	Recall an open delegation.

Next, we describe the NFSv4 callback RPC messages shown in Table 6.2. For more details on each procedure, or for the precise source code definitions for these, see RFC-3010 and Appendix B.

CB_NULL   This is the standard ping procedure. The server uses this procedure to verify that a callback path to the client exists.

CB_COMPOUND   This procedure is a wrapper for any number of operations. Its behavior is similar to the NFSv4 COMPOUND procedure.

CB_GETATTR   This is the first callback operation. When a client holds a delegation on a file, it can perform read and write operations that change the attributes of the file—such as its size. If another client asks the server for the attributes of that file, the server has to call the original client using the CB_GETATTR operation to find out the most up-to-date attributes of the file before responding to the second client.

CB_RECALL   Using this operation, a server asks a client to relinquish a delegation. The client has to process the recall as soon as possible and then return the delegation using the DELEGRETURN operation.

Error Messages

One of the ways to understand any protocol is to look at the error conditions that can occur. Many of the NFS error messages in this and previous protocols resemble standard error conditions such as those listed in the header file /usr/include/asm/error.h. In this section we summarize the error conditions of the NFSv4 protocol. Note that these errors can be returned by servers to clients, as well as by clients to servers (in response to a call-back procedure).

NFS4_OK   The operation completed successfully.

NFS4ERR_ACCES   The caller does not have the proper permission to perform the operation requested.

NFS4ERR_BADHANDLE   The server could not decode the filehandle, possibly due to an internal consistency failure.

NFS4ERR_BADTYPE   The server does not support the type of object that the client tried to create.

NFS4ERR_BAD_COOKIE   The *cookie* (an internal identifier) of a READDIR operation is invalid.

NFS4ERR_BAD_SEQID   Each locking request must identify itself using a sequence number that is either the last one or a new one that is one more than the last one used. If a different sequence number is used, the server responds with this error.

NFS4ERR_BAD_STATEID   Each state that either clients or servers maintain has a unique identifier (stateid) that is exchanged between them. If a stateid was used that the other party does not recognize, it returns this error.

NFS4ERR_CLID_INUSE   A client tried to use the same client ID (via SETCLIENTID) that another client already uses.

NFS4ERR_DELAY   Occasionally, a client will send a request to a server and the server will begin processing it. However, the server may realize that the request is taking a long time to process; for example, when retrieving a file that has been stored on a backup tape as part of a Hierarchical Storage Management (HSM) system. In that case, the server responds with this error, telling the client that the request is taking longer and that the client should retry it later.

NFS4ERR_DENIED   Trying to lock a file failed. This could be a temporary condition and the client should try again later, since the other client who held the lock might release it.

NFS4ERR_DQUOT   The hard quota limits have been exceeded.

NFS4ERR_EXIST   The file already exists. This could happen when a client tries to create a file exclusively and the file already exists.

NFS4ERR_EXPIRED   The client's lease has expired.

NFS4ERR_FBIG   The server is unable to perform the operation because it would result in growing the file beyond the server's limits.

NFS4ERR_FHEXPIRED   A volatile filehandle has expired.

NFS4ERR_GRACE   When a server crashes and then restarts, there is a period of time when it is initializing and cannot respond to some operations. During that time and similar times, the server will return this error.

NFS4ERR_INVAL   The client passed an operation that included an invalid argument, or the server cannot support the operation requested.

NFS4ERR_IO   A hard I/O error (such as a failing disk) occurred.

NFS4ERR_ISDIR   A non-directory operation was applied to a directory.

NFS4ERR_LEASE_MOVED   The lease has moved or migrated to a new server.

NFS4ERR_LOCKED   The client tried to read or write a file that is locked by another client.

NFS4ERR_LOCK_RANGE   This error occurs when a client requests a lock for a portion of a file that overlaps a portion locked by another client.

NFS4ERR_MINOR_VERS_MISMATCH   The server does not support the minor revision of the protocol requested.

NFS4ERR_MLINK   The file has too many hard-links.

NFS4ERR_MOVED   The file system was moved or migrated to another server. The server can find out the new location for the file system by requesting the `fs_locations` attribute of the current filehandle.

NFS4ERR_NAMETOOLONG   The name of the file is too long.

NFS4ERR_NODEV   The device does not exist.

NFS4ERR_NOENT   The file or directory does not exist.

NFS4ERR_NOFILEHANDLE   The current filehandle has not been properly set.

NFS4ERR_NOSPC   The file system is full.

NFS4ERR_NOTDIR   The directory operation was applied to a non-directory.

NFS4ERR_NOTEMPTY   Cannot remove the directory because it is not empty.

NFS4ERR_NOTSUPP   The operation is not supported.

NFS4ERR_NOT_SAME   The attributes requested in the VERIFY operation do not match those on the server.

NFS4ERR_NXIO   The device or address does not exist or had an I/O error.

NFS4ERR_OLD_STATEID   An older state identifier was used.

NFS4ERR_PERM   The operation is not permitted because it was not performed by the superuser or the file's owner.

NFS4ERR_READDIR_NOSPC   The space provided by the client for filling in a READDIR request is not sufficient.

NFS4ERR_RESOURCE   While processing a COMPOUND procedure, the host ran out of resources (such as memory).

NFS4ERR_ROFS   A file system–modifying operation was attempted on a read-only file system.

NFS4ERR_SAME   The attributes requested in the NVERIFY operation match those on the server.

NFS4ERR_SERVERFAULT   An unknown error occurred on the server and it cannot be mapped to any predefined NFS error code.

NFS4ERR_SHARE_DENIED   Cannot open a file with a share reservation because a share is already reserved by another client.

NFS4ERR_STALE   The filehandle is invalid, the file referenced by it does not exist, or access to that file was revoked.

NFS4ERR_STALE_CLIENTID   The server does not recognize the client ID sent to it by a locking request or a confirmation request for setting a client ID.

NFS4ERR_STALE_STATEID   The state ID used was generated by an earlier or older server.

NFS4ERR_SYMLINK   This error is returned if the client tries to open a symlink file or look up a file in a directory that is specified by a symlink. The client is supposed to recursively traverse symlinks by getting their values explicitly (using READLINK) and then passing the non-symlink value to a LOOKUP or OPEN operation.

NFS4ERR_TOOSMALL   The space provided in a buffer or request is too small.

NFS4ERR_WRONGSEC   The client used a security mechanism that is not supported by the server's security policy.

NFS4ERR_XDEV   The client tried to create a hard-link across a different device.

Linux Implementations

The Center for Information Technology Integration (CITI) at the University of Michigan has been working on a prototype implementation of an NFSv4 server and client for Linux and NetBSD. CITI's first goal for the Linux port was to support the most mandatory NFSv4 features; this goal was achieved in early 2000. The group then went on to complete the Linux port, based on the 2.2.*x* kernel and the existing NFSv3 client/server code. The status of these ports is available from CITI's NFSv4 Web page at `www.citi.umich.edu/projects/nfsv4/`.

This section describes the procedures for retrieving, configuring, installing, and running the prototype implementation of NFSv4 for Linux. Note that the procedures described here are likely to change often, and the NFSv4 support in Linux is highly experimental—alpha quality at best. If these procedures do not work for you, refer to CITI's Web site and the NFS mailing list at nfs@nfs.sourceforge.net. For general guidelines of how to build and install a Linux kernel and user-level software, refer to Chapter 7, "Building and Installing the Linux Kernel and NFS Software."

1. Start by downloading the following three packages from CITI's download page: www.citi.umich.edu/projects/nfsv4/download/. Store them in /usr/src.

   linux_nfsv4.tar.gz   Linux 2.2.14 kernel source and the NFSv4 additions.

   redhat_mount.tar.gz   Linux mount-2.9o source that contains the NFSv4 additions.

   rpcsec_gss.tar.gz   Linux RPCSEC_GSS user-level library and the GSS daemon.

2. Then download the server side utilities from www.citi.umich.edu/projects/nfsv4/sept_2000_rel/server_util/server_utils.tar.gz.

3. Unpack the sources:

   ```
   [root]# cd /usr/src
   [root]# tar xzf linux_nfsv4.tar.gz
   [root]# tar xzf redhat_mount.tar.gz
   [root]# tar xzf rpcsec_gss.tar.gz
   ```

4. Configure and build the kernel in /usr/src/linux_nfsv4. When configuring the kernel, make sure you select the SUNRPC, NFS_FS, and NFSD modules, but not NFSv3 support.

   ```
   [root]# cd /usr/src
   [root]# mv linux linux.old
   [root]# ln -s linux_nfsv4 linux
   [root]# cd linux
   [root]# make menuconfig
   [root]# make dep
   [root]# make clean
   [root]# make bzImage
   [root]# make modules modules_install
   ```

5. Manually enable NFSv4 in your kernel configuration file:

   ```
   [root]# echo "CONFIG_NFS_V4=y" >> .config
   [root]# make bzImage modules
   [root]# cp arch/i386/boot/bzImage /boot/vmlinuz-nfsv4
   [root]# cp System.map /boot/System.map-nfsv4
   ```

6. Add a new kernel boot entry to the end of your /etc/lilo.conf file, which looks as follows:

   ```
   image=/boot/vmlinuz-nfsv4
           label=linux-nfsv4
           read-only
           root=/dev/hda1
   ```

   Of course, /dev/hda1 is just an example. Make sure that your root entry matches your host's root disk.

7. Run /sbin/lilo.

8. Configure and build the linux mount program that supports NFSv4.

   ```
   [root]# cd /usr/src/redhat_mount
   [root]# ln -s ../setproctitle.o lib/setproctitle.o
   [root]# make
   [root]# install -s -c -m 755 mount /usr/sbin/mount-nfsv4
   ```

9. Install MIT's Kerberos version 5. If you are using Red Hat 7, insert the installation CD-ROM and install the following RPMs:

   ```
   [root]# cd /mnt/cdrom/RedHat/RPMS
   [root]# rpm -Uvh krb5-server-1.2.1-8.i386.rpm
   [root]# rpm -Uvh krb5-devel-1.2.1-8.i386.rpm
   [root]# rpm -Uvh krb5-libs-1.2.1-8.i386.rpm
   [root]# rpm -Uvh pam_krb5-1-19.i386.rpm
   [root]# rpm -Uvh krb5-workstation-1.2.1-8
   ```

10. Build and install the GSS server:

    ```
    [root]# cd /usr/src/rpcsec_gss
    [root]# ./configure
    [root]# make
    [root]# make install
    [root]# install -s -c -m 755 gssd/gssd /usr/sbin/gssd
    ```

Server-Side Support

Unpack and install server-side utilities (only needed for NFSv4 servers):

```
[root]# mkdir /usr/src/server_utils
[root]# cd /usr/src/server_utils
[root]# tar xzf ../server_utils.tar.gz
[root]# install -c -m 755 exportfs /usr/sbin/exportfs
[root]# install -c -m 755 rpc.nfsd /usr/sbin/rpc.nfsd
[root]# install -c -m 755 nfsv4 /etc/rc.d/init.d/nfsv4
```

Turn on NFSv4 services and start the servers:

```
[root]# chkconfig nfsv4 on
[root]# /etc/rc.d/init.d/nfsv4 restart
```

Client-Side Support

Follow the general instructions to build and install the NFSv4 software and utilities, and then start the GSS server and load up the proper modules.

```
[root]# /usr/sbin/gssd &
[root]# insmod sunrpc
[root]# insmod nfs
```

Now you can use the special /usr/sbin/mount-nfsv4 program to mount an NFSv4 server:

```
[root]# /usr/sbin/mount-nfsv4 server:/home /mnt
```

NOTE NFSv4 was designed to work across many platforms, including Windows. The Windows world uses the *Server Message Block* (SMB) protocol to share files and printers with other Windows systems. Also, through the use of SAMBA—a Unix-based SMB server—Windows and Unix systems can share files and printers. While NFSv4 is expected to integrate file access in a better way between all Unix and non-Unix systems, NFSv4 was not designed to share printers.

In Sum

NFSv4 is a major redesign of the NFS protocol. The goals of this protocol are to provide good performance over the Internet, work well with many clients, work across firewalls and network appliances, be highly reliable and available, include strong security, interoperate with any platform, support international character sets, and extend easily.

This complex new protocol subsumes all previous protocols. It includes lots of support for clients and servers to maintain caches and share state, as well as checking those for consistency and coherency.

Great care was taken to allow for many possible optimizations. Since the Internet is a wide area network and subject to high latency and greater loss of packets, the protocol ensures that only the bare essential information is exchanged over the network. The protocol allows servers to delegate access to clients for a duration of time, so the servers need not be involved with the client at all for that time.

The protocol also defines a new concept of a compound procedure: a wrapper routine that encapsulates many other operations. Such a composition is sent as a single RPC message to the server and processed all at once.

To avoid having to redesign this protocol again in just a couple years, extensibility methods were built into the protocol. Clients and servers can, for example, create new named attributes for file system objects. Through minor revisions of the protocol, new operations and attributes can be created, and much more functionality can be changed, as long as it complies with the rules set forth for minor revisioning.

The NFSv4 protocol is the first NFS protocol on its way to becoming an Internet standard. For the first time in its history, an NFS protocol design was opened to the whole community and is guided by the IETF's strict rules for creating new protocols. The full detailed description of NFSv4 is available in RFC-3010 and spans over 200 pages. Happy reading.

7

Building and Installing the Linux Kernel and NFS Software

Linux is a popular operating system. Different vendors package Linux with their own set of user tools and features, and release them periodically. Some of these features are maintained by a handful of people around the world. Often, core Linux software must change: new features are added or bugs are fixed. Unfortunately, vendors of Linux systems cannot track these changes quickly enough or release updates to their distributions as soon as software maintainers release new code. Therefore, the task of updating software on Linux systems often falls to the site administrators.

NFS is kernel-level software that includes client-side and server-side components; these components must be compiled into the kernel to use the latest NFS protocols. Amd uses Linux file systems, all of which also have to be compiled into the kernel for Amd to use them. Furthermore, most kernel-level file systems require corresponding user-level administrative tools; these must be compiled and installed as well. To use the latest NFS software and other file systems, site administrators often have to configure and install those themselves.

This chapter describes the process of configuring, building, and installing the Linux kernel to add or change NFS and features that Amd uses. It also describes how to update user-level tools that may be required to handle new kernel features.

Linux kernels and user-level software come in two forms: pre-built binaries and sources that you have to build by hand. Pre-built binaries are managed by the Red Hat Package Manager (RPM) tool, rpm. In this chapter, we describe the usage of RPM packages first. Afterward, we describe how to retrieve kernel and user-level sources, unpack them, patch the sources to provide additional features or fixes, configure the kernel, build the kernel and user-level tools, install them, and finally test them.

The state of NFS in the Linux world has been in flux for some time now and is likely to continue to change all the time. New features are added or changed every day, and more appear in the mainline Linux kernels as well as the Red Hat–supplied ones. We suggest you use the information provided in this chapter and in Appendix B, "Online Resources," to verify the status of NFS as described herein. Appendix B also provides up-to-date errata for material that may have changed since writing this book.

We introduce many new procedures in this chapter, but we focus on those applicable to the topics of this book. This chapter is not a general-purpose tutorial on Linux kernels, RPM, and other tools. We will, however, tell you where to find additional documentation about these. Furthermore, you can always refer to Appendix B for pointers to extra sources of useful up-to-date information on all of this book's topics.

NOTE   We assume that users use Red Hat Linux version 7.0 in this chapter and we describe the procedures accordingly. However, these procedures may not match your usage perfectly for three reasons. First, you may use newer versions of Red Hat Linux, which are out every few months. Second, some administrators continue to use older, and more stable, releases of Red Hat Linux. Third, some users use Debian, SuSE, and other Linux distributions. We explain the process of building and installing Linux kernels and NFS software to be understood by all Linux users. Nevertheless, if you face difficulties, please refer to the documentation for your Linux distribution and seek the assistance of your local administrators.

Using RPMs

The *Red Hat Package Manager* (RPM) is an integral part of Red Hat Linux. The RPM software itself cannot be removed from Red Hat systems because it maintains the rest of the installed system. RPM files (RPMs) can contain binaries, libraries, text files, and even scripts that execute before or after the RPM is installed. RPMs contain an MD5 checksum that the rpm tool uses to verify the integrity of the RPM. RPMs can even certify the authenticity of the creators of the RPM, using PGP-based encryption. These facilities ensure that the RPM did not get corrupted or subverted somehow. Furthermore, for each

RPM that contains software to install (often binaries), Red Hat releases a *Source RPM* (SRPM) that contains all the sources needed to build its binary version.

The `rpm` tool is very flexible and comes with many features. The tool is used often to install, remove, and update packages. But it can do much more: rebuild and repackage software from sources, manage RPM installation databases, and more. To see a brief usage listing of `rpm`, run it without any arguments:

    [ezk]$ **rpm**

To get more detailed help, run it with the `--help` flag:

    [ezk]$ **rpm --help**

For a full description of `rpm`, see the `rpm` manual page.

RPM files usually end with the extension `.rpm` and have the following common format:

> *name-version-release.arch*.rpm
>
> *name*   Is the full name of the package, for example, `am-utils`.
>
> *vers*   Is the version number of the package, for example, `6.0.3`.
>
> *release*   Is the Red Hat release number of the same package and version. If the release number is 1, then Red Hat used the original sources for the package unmodified. Red Hat, however, often adds additional features or fixes bugs in common packages. Each time they do so, they increase the release number by one. If the release number is greater than 1, then the SRPM corresponding to the binary RPM includes additional patches applied by Red Hat.
>
> *arch*   Is the host architecture of the machine, for example, `i386`.

In the next three sections, we outline three categories of common `rpm` commands:

- Commands to query RPMs
- Commands to install RPMs
- Commands to remove RPMs

Querying RPMs

To query RPMs, use the basic `-q` option with any other option. To list all the RPMs installed on the system, run `rpm -qa`. To check if an RPM is installed on the system, for example, `am-utils`, run

    [ezk]$ **rpm -q am-utils**
    am-utils-6.0.4s5-8

This means that the `am-utils` package is installed and gives its full name. If the package is not installed, you will get a different message:

```
[ezk]$ rpm -q am-utils
package am-utils is not installed
```

To query the list of files that belong to a given installed RPM, use it with the -l option, as seen in Listing 7.1.

Listing 7.1 Querying the list of files in an installed RPM

```
[ezk]$ rpm -ql ypbind
/etc/rc.d/init.d/ypbind
/etc/yp.conf
/sbin/ypbind
/usr/share/doc/ypbind-1.6
/usr/share/doc/ypbind-1.6/NEWS
/usr/share/doc/ypbind-1.6/README
/usr/share/man/man5/yp.conf.5.gz
/usr/share/man/man8/ypbind.8.gz
/var/yp/binding
```

You can also query the list of files in an RPM file that may not have been installed already, using the -p option, as seen in Listing 7.2.

Listing 7.2 Querying the list of files in an RPM file

```
[ezk]$ ls -l rusers-0.17-6.i386.rpm
-rw-r--r-- 1 root   root      16090 Aug 30 18:16 rusers-0.17-6.i386.rpm
[ezk]$ rpm -qlp rusers-0.17-6.i386.rpm
/usr/bin/rup
/usr/bin/rusers
/usr/share/man/man1/rup.1.gz
/usr/share/man/man1/rusers.1.gz
```

Listing 7.3 shows how you can display detailed package information, including the RPM's name, version, and description, using the -i option.

Listing 7.3 Displaying the detailed package information of an RPM

```
[ezk]$ rpm -qi am-utils
Name        : am-utils      Relocations: (not relocateable)
Version     : 6.0.4s5       Vendor: Red Hat, Inc.
Release     : 8             Build Date: Sat 15 Jul 2000 02:09:46 PM EDT
Install date: Tue 03 Oct 2000 11:45:19 PM EDT
```

The Network
File System

PART 1

```
Build Host  : porky.devel.redhat.com
Group       : System Environment/Daemons
Source RPM  : am-utils-6.0.4s5-8.src.rpm
Size        : 1492186                      License: BSD
Packager    : Red Hat, Inc. <http://bugzilla.redhat.com/bugzilla>
URL         : http://www.cs.columbia.edu/~ezk/am-utils/
Summary     : Automount utilities including an updated version of Amd.
Description :
Am-utils includes an updated version of Amd, the popular BSD
automounter.  An automounter is a program which maintains a cache
of mounted filesystems.  Filesystems are mounted when they are
first referenced by the user and unmounted after a certain period of
inactivity. Amd supports a variety of filesystems, including NFS, UFS,
CD-ROMS and local drives.


You should install am-utils if you need a program for automatically
mounting and unmounting filesystems.
```

You can also check which RPM a file belongs to, if any, as shown in Listing 7.4.

Listing 7.4   Finding out which RPM contains installed files

```
[ezk]$ rpm -qf /etc/passwd
setup-2.3.4-1
[ezk]$ touch /tmp/foo.c
[ezk]$ rpm -qf /tmp/foo.c
file /tmp/foo.c is not owned by any package
```

The next section shows how to query RPMs for their dependencies when installing
new RPMs.

Installing RPMs

Before installing RPMs, you should have access to a repository of RPMs. The Red Hat
CD is a perfect choice. To start, mount it and cd to the directory with the RPMs on it:

```
[root]# mount -t iso9660 /dev/cdrom /mnt/cdrom
```

```
[root]# cd /mnt/cdrom/RedHat/RPMS
```

To install an RPM, use the -i option:

```
[root]# rpm -i bash-2.04-11.i386.rpm
```

A better way would be to see the package name being installed (-h option) and to view a progress monitor as the package is being installed (-v option):

```
[root]# rpm -ivh bash-2.04-11.i386.rpm

bash2##############################################
```

The -i option will install RPMs for the first time. If you want to install or upgrade an RPM to a newer version, use the -U option. This option will install an RPM if it does not exist already but will also upgrade an existing RPM to a new one. It is therefore a useful substitute often used instead of the -i option.

Some RPMs depend on others. So before you can install a given RPM, you must install all the RPMs it depends on. For example, if you tried to install the am-utils RPM, you might get an error such as

```
[root]# rpm -ivh am-utils-6.0.4s5-8.i386.rpm

error: failed dependencies:

        liblber.so.1 is needed by am-utils-6.0.4s5-8

        libldap.so.1 is needed by am-utils-6.0.4s5-8
```

Now you have to find out which RPMs contain the two missing libraries. To do so, first install a special RPM database that contains a full mapping of RPM package names and their contents:

```
[root]# rpm -Uvh rpmdb-redhat-7.0-0.20000830.i386.rpm

rpmdb-redhat##################################################
```

This RPM installs its database in /usr/lib/rpmdb/i386-redhat-linux/redhat. Now you can query the special database for the two missing libraries using the -q and --whatprovides options. Note that you also have to tell rpm to use the special database for this query. Listing 7.5 shows this.

Listing 7.5 Finding which RPMs provide given files

```
[root]# rpm -q --whatprovides --dbpath \
> /usr/lib/rpmdb/i386-redhat-linux/redhat liblber.so.1
openldap-1.2.11-15
[root]# rpm -q --whatprovides --dbpath \
> /usr/lib/rpmdb/i386-redhat-linux/redhat libldap.so.1
openldap-1.2.11-15
```

Since the same openldap package provides both libraries, we can now install it and then install am-utils, as Listing 7.6 shows.

Listing 7.6   Installing multiple RPMs and their dependencies

```
[root]# rpm -ivh openldap-1.2.11-15.i386.rpm
openldap            ###############################################
[root]# rpm -ivh am-utils-6.0.4s5-8.i386.rpm
am-utils            ###############################################
```

You can also specify several RPMs on one command line and the rpm tool will install all of them:

```
[root]# rpm -ivh openldap-1.2.11-15.i386.rpm am-utils-6.0.4s5-8.i386.rpm
openldap            ###############################################
am-utils            ###############################################
```

This is particularly useful if some of the RPMs you list depend on others listed. The rpm tool will determine those dependencies regardless of their listing order on the command line and will install them properly without warning the user to install individual RPMs in dependency order.

You could also force the installation of a package even if its dependencies are not installed, using the --nodeps option:

```
[root]# rpm -ivh --nodeps am-utils-6.0.4s5-8.i386.rpm
```

That, however, is not recommended; the am-utils package would be installed but its binaries would not function properly.

If some files that were installed got damaged, you can reinstall that RPM, but you would have to force that installation:

```
[root]# rpm -Uvh --force am-utils-6.0.4s5-8.i386.rpm
```

Removing RPMs

To remove RPMs, simply use the -e flag. For example, to remove the am-utils package, run

```
[root]# rpm -e am-utils
```

If a package is a prerequisite for other packages, you cannot remove it before removing the packages that depend on it. For example, to remove the openldap package, you would have to remove the am-utils package first:

```
[root]# rpm -e am-utils
[root]# rpm -e openldap
```

You can, however, force the removal of a prerequisite package using the --nodeps option:

```
[root]# rpm -e --nodeps openldap
```

Of course doing so is not recommended, for it will remove vital components that the am-utils package needs: its binaries will no longer function.

WARNING If other packages depend on openldap, you will not be able to remove it unless you specify the --force option. If you do so, however, you may break not just Amd but other packages that depend on openldap.

Deciding What to Build and Install

RPM is a great tool for installing precompiled and prepackaged software. However, sometimes you need to install software that is not available as RPMs: user-level tools, additional kernel file systems, or even whole new kernels. Modifying system software such as the kernel is not something to be taken lightly. Careful planning is needed. In this section we outline the overall procedure to get the right kernel features installed on your system—features such as NFS, Autofs, other file systems, and any associated user-level tools that might be needed. In general, the process follows these steps:

1. Determine which kernel features and user-level tools you need.
2. Inspect what you have on your system.
3. Decide if you have to rebuild your kernel and, if so, which kernel to use.
4. Configure and build your kernel.
5. Install the kernel and update related system boot configuration files.
6. Reboot your system to start with a new kernel.
7. Determine which user-level tools you need to use, if any.
8. Retrieve sources for user-level tools, build, install, and test them.

We begin by determining which features you need. In this chapter, we assume that you want to include as many kernel features in your system that would support NFS and be detected and used by Amd. These include the following:

- NFS client-side code:
  - Protocol version 2 (NFSv2) and 3 (NFSv3)
  - Using UDP and TCP transports
- NFS server-side code:
  - Both NFSv2 and NFSv3
  - Using UDP and TCP transports

- File systems that Amd can use:
  - NFS
  - EXT2
  - VFAT or FAT
  - ISO9660
  - Autofs (version 3 and version 4)

As you will see shortly, some of those features may already exist on your system. Furthermore, for every new kernel feature you add, you may have to get one or more of the following user-level tools:

- An updated /bin/mount program that can handle NFSv3 and TCP mounts
- Updated NFS utilities, documentation, scripts, and various daemons: locking, mounting, status, and quota processing over NFS

You should retrieve all the software you need before compiling or trying any of it. In particular, if you depend on new NFSv3 features but have not updated your user-level utilities, you may be unable to make NFSv3 mounts until you have installed new mount utilities and NFS utilities. If you depend on NFS to access those sources, you may not be able to retrieve them—a deadlock. While you should retrieve all sources, you should first install and test a new kernel before trying new user-level tools.

TIP   Avoid using the kernels that came with older Red Hat releases. The kernels that were distributed in Red Hat releases 6.1 and older did not include in-kernel NFS server support, only in-kernel NFS client support. The user-level NFS server (RPM package unfsd) that was included was slow due to context switches and lacked important functionality, such as the Network Lock Manager (NLM) protocol and the Network Status Monitor (NSM) protocol. The user-level tools that came with this kernel worked in conjunction with unfsd but only with that one. Later on, the mainline Linux kernel began supporting the NFS server in the kernel, but the user-level tools Red Hat included no longer worked with it. Instead, the user-level support tools had to be replaced with a new package of user-level tools called knfsd. These days, in Red Hat 6.2 and newer, the default Red Hat kernel includes a kernel-level NFS server, and all user-level tools work with it.

Using the Red Hat Kernels

The Red Hat–supplied kernels provide almost all the features one might want. Most of those features are supplied as loadable modules so their components could be loaded and unloaded as needed to customize individual installations. Red Hat kernels, however, almost always include additional features and fixes that are not available in the corresponding mainline kernel. To see this, check the version of your installed Linux kernel:

```
[ezk]$ rpm -q kernel
kernel-2.2.16-22
```

The above tells you that you have installed Red Hat's modified version of the 2.2.16 kernel. The 22 implies that Red Hat has included that many additional patches to the vanilla 2.2.16 kernel.

Mainline vs. Red Hat Linux Kernels

Linus Torvalds releases the only official Linux kernels, also known as the *mainline* or *vanilla* kernels. Linus often concentrates on the latest kernel series, say, 2.3 and 2.4. However, the latest kernels are often the least stable ones, as new features are added constantly, and major changes take place. At the same time, Linus also delegates much of the release responsibility for the older and more stable kernels to others, such as Alan Cox. Red Hat's kernels are based on these stable mainline kernels, since Red Hat is committed to providing the most stable Linux system. In addition, Red Hat will often take fixes and new features that are in a newer kernel and add them to Red Hat's own released kernel. Red Hat does this to provide features that users request and include critical fixes, especially security fixes.

The features that Red Hat kernels include are

- NFSv2 client and server support, UDP only
- Autofs version 3
- EXT2, V/FAT, and ISO9660 file systems

The implication of using the Red Hat kernels, however, is twofold. If you are using precompiled Red Hat kernels, you will get lots of features already built in and perhaps even some features that are unavailable in the vanilla kernel. On the other hand, if you have to add features to a Red Hat kernel, you will have to apply patches to the Red Hat kernel SRPM. These patches are often produced for vanilla kernels and may not apply cleanly or work correctly if applied to a Red Hat kernel source. For that reason, we recommend that if the sets of features supplied by Red Hat kernel are insufficient for your needs, use one of the two vanilla Linux kernels, as described in the next two sections. This is particularly true if you wish to use NFSv3 in general, or with Amd.

If you insist on rebuilding the Red Hat Linux kernel from sources, then first install the following RPM from your Red Hat distribution CD:

```
[root]# mount -t iso9660 /dev/cdrom /mnt/cdrom
[root]# cd /mnt/cdrom/RedHat/RPMS
[root]# rpm -Uvh kernel-source-2.2.16-22.i386.rpm
kernel-source###################################################
```

After doing so, follow the instructions in the upcoming section, "Patching the 2.2 Kernel."

Using the Official 2.2 Kernels

Use the official 2.2 kernel if you cannot use the Red Hat–supplied 2.2 kernel and you want the most stable of Linux kernels but you also want to add NFSv3 features. The first few steps you must accomplish are

1. Get the appropriate Linux kernel sources.
2. Unpack them.
3. Retrieve any patches you may need.
4. Apply patches to your kernel.

The next few steps are to configure and build the kernel, described later in this chapter.

To retrieve the sources to the Linux kernel, FTP them from `ftp://ftp.kernel.org` or one of its mirror sites.

```
[root]# cd /usr/src
[root]# ncftpget ftp://ftp.kernel.org/pub/linux/kernel/v2.2/linux-
2.2.16.tar.gz
```

Note that I retrieved the 2.2.16 kernel. At any given time, you should check which is the latest stable kernel and preferably use that one. To find out which is the latest kernel, look for a file named LATEST-IS-$X.Y.Z$, where $X.Y.Z$ would be the revision of the latest kernel; this file exists in the same directory as the kernel tarballs of the same series.

Next, we unpack the sources into /usr/src/linux, but first we make sure that we rename any existing sources:

[root]# **mv -f linux linux.old**

[root]# **tar zxf linux-2.2.16.tar.gz**

You will need about 75 to 80MB of free disk space to unpack this kernel.

Patching the 2.2 Kernel

Now we have to find and retrieve patches for the 2.2.16 kernel we just unpacked. The official Web site that maintains that information is http://nfs.sourceforge.net. You should check that site to ensure that you use the latest patches that match the kernel you plan on using. There, you get instructions for adding two sets of patches. The first set of patches is mostly for the NFS client side, maintained by Trond Myklebust:

[root]# **cd /usr/src**

[root]# **wget http://www.fys.uio.no/~trondmy/src/linux-2.2.16-nfsv3-0.22.0.dif.bz2**

If you cannot find the above patches in that directory, it is probably because newer patches exist for newer kernels, and the ones you are looking for were moved to the subdirectory nfsv3-old:

[root]# **wget http://www.fys.uio.no/~trondmy/src/nfsv3-old/linux-2.2.16-nfsv3-0.22.0.dif.bz2**

The next set of patches is for the NFS server side, maintained by Dave Higgen:

[root]# **wget http://download.sourceforge.net/nfs/kernel-nfs-dhiggen_merge-3.0.tar.gz**

Next, we want to apply those patches to the 2.2.16 kernel we unpacked:

[root]# **cd /usr/src**

[root]# **bunzip2 linux-2.2.16-nfsv3-0.22.0.dif.bz2**

[root]# **cd linux**

[root]# **patch -s -p1 < ../linux-2.2.16-nfsv3-0.22.0.dif**

To use the second set of patches, we must first untar that distribution:

[root]# **cd /usr/src**

[root]# **mkdir dhiggen**

[root]# **cd dhiggen**

[root]# **tar xzf ../kernel-nfs-dhiggen_merge-3.0.tar.gz**

```
[root]# /bin/ls -l
total 460
-rw-r--r--   1 ezk     fist         7825 Jun 12 19:06 README
-rw-r--r--   1 ezk     fist         3329 Jun 12 18:43 README.trond
-rw-r--r--   1 ezk     fist       218839 Jun 12 18:45 dhiggen-over-0.21.3
-rw-r--r--   1 ezk     fist       219242 Jun 12 18:47 dhiggen-over-0.22.0
-rw-r--r--   1 ezk     fist         4396 Jun 12 19:06 ext3-nfs
```

As per the README in that directory, use the dhiggen-over-0.22.0 file:

```
[root]# cd /usr/src/linux
[root]# patch -s -p2 < ../dhiggen/dhiggen-over-0.22.0
```

You now have a patched 2.2.16 kernel containing all the new NFSv3 features as well as many fixes to make that kernel stable and work well especially if used as a busy NFS server. Note that the NFSv3 support in the 2.2 kernels does not include NFS server support over TCP and is not likely to include that support in the near future. If you also want TCP support for NFS, use the 2.4 kernel series.

Using the Official 2.4 Kernels

Use the official 2.4 kernel if you cannot use either the Red Hat–supplied 2.2 kernel or the vanilla 2.2 kernel and getting the very latest of features is important to you. Note that the 2.4 kernels are newer and contain many new features, but 2.4 kernels are not as stable as the 2.2 kernels. The main new features that the 2.4 kernels support and that are of interest for this chapter are

- NFSv3 using TCP, both client and server side
- Autofs version 4

To get the latest 2.4 kernel, you should first find out which one it is. The latest kernel has the highest revision number. Also, a special text file whose name starts with LATEST-IS-points to the latest version of the kernel. You can use wget to first find the latest version of the 2.4 kernel and then retrieve it:

```
[root]# cd /usr/src
[root]# wget ftp://ftp.kernel.org/pub/linux/kernel/v2.4/LATEST-IS-*
[root]# ls -l LATEST-IS-*
```

```
-rw-r--r--   1 root      wheel      0 Sep  8 13:26 LATEST-IS-2.4.0-test8
[root]# wget ftp://ftp.kernel.org/pub/linux/kernel/v2.4/linux-2.4.0-
test8.tar.bz2
```

Next, we unpack the 2.4 kernel, similar to how we did for the 2.2 kernel in the previous section:

```
[root]# cd /usr/src
[root]# mv -f linux linux.old
[root]# tar Ixf linux-2.4.0-test8.bz2
```

You will need about 110 to 120MB of free disk space to unpack this kernel. You are now ready to configure your Linux kernel.

Configuring the Linux Kernel

In the previous sections we learned how to retrieve and unpack Linux kernel distributions and even apply source patches to them so they support additional features. In this section we will describe how to configure the Linux kernel prior to building it. Since the 2.4 kernel series is likely to become the default stable series soon, we will show the kernel configuration procedure using the 2.4 kernel. The procedure is identical when using the 2.2 kernel, except some features may not be supported in the (patched) 2.2 kernel. Note also that this section describes the procedure for configuring the Linux kernel as it applies to this book; this is not a general-purpose kernel-configuration manual.

Linux kernels need configuration to balance two needs: to get all the features you need but, at the same time, keep the kernel's size small so it consumes less memory and (generally) will run faster. You could take the Red Hat approach and turn on every feature, but that increases the kernel size significantly, even if you configure most features as loadable modules. Plus, loadable modules still consume disk space. In this chapter we describe only those kernel features that are applicable to this book.

Before you begin configuring the Linux kernel, you have to make two important choices: whether to use experimental kernel features and whether to compile kernel features as loadable modules or not.

Turning on Experimental Features

Every Linux kernel contains features that are well tested and considered stable (but *not* bug-free), as well as features that have not been tested thoroughly or at length, or are relatively new. The latter set of features is known as *experimental*. If you turn on these experimental features, which is done early in the Linux-kernel-configuration process, then you will see additional features offered and marked `experimental`. At this stage in the 2.4-kernel-development phase, some of the features we need are marked experimental, and so to use them we have to turn on the configuration option for experimental features.

Modules vs. Statically Compiled Features

You can configure most of the features in the Linux kernel to one of three states:

N **or** No   Turn off that feature.

Y **or** Yes   Turn on that feature and compile it statically into the kernel.

M **or** Module   Turn on that feature and compile it as a loadable kernel module.

If you compile a feature as a module, then the feature is not immediately available in the kernel. The module file corresponding to that feature must first be loaded into the kernel using the `insmod` or `modprobe` commands. Modules are good because they decrease kernel sizes and are used only when needed, thus saving on memory and CPU cycles. Modules are useful for features that you do not use often. If your kernel contains features that you know you will use all the time and constantly, then you can configure them not to build as modules—statically compiled into the kernel. Also, if any kernel features are crucial to the booting of your system, then you *must not* configure them as modules. See the upcoming section, "Configuring the RAM Disk Boot Loader," for more details.

Therefore, in addition to turning on experimental features, we separate the rest of the features into two groups: statically compiled and modules.

The features we statically compile into the kernel are used all the time:

- EXT2 file system: mandatory
- ISO9660 file system: used often
- NFS client: most machines need to access NFS servers

The features we compile as modules are not used all the time:

- NFS server: most machines are not NFS servers
- MSDOS and VFAT
- Autofs

Of course, if your needs differ, then you can decide to compile features differently.

Next, there are three methods to configure the Linux kernel:

Text-Based Configuration   Each kernel option is listed in turn, and the user must decide whether to turn on or off each feature. This can take a long time, especially since there are several hundred options to configure. However, this method works from anywhere, in X-terminals (xterms), text-based consoles, remote logins over slow networks, etc. Furthermore, if you are configuring a Linux kernel for the first time, this option is useful in taking you through every possible kernel option.

Curses-Based Full-Screen Configuration   This is a menu-based method, using basic colors but no graphics. This method works inside any text terminal. It is easier to navigate with this method using keyboard keys, and this is the option most often used by people configuring Linux kernels.

X11-Based Graphical Configuration   This is a graphical configuration method, based on the TCL/Tk graphics system, and works with a remote X11 display. While it is easy to navigate this method using the mouse alone, it requires that your system have all the TCL/Tk graphical libraries.

Text-Based Configuration

The text-based configuration option lists each of the several hundred Linux kernel configuration options and asks the users to select those they want. Since the list is long, we show only the parts relevant to our discussion.

To use this option, run make config from /usr/src/linux, and answer the questions displayed. For each question, you will see possible answers appear in square brackets ([]) and the default answer (if you simply hit the Enter key) appearing first, in uppercase. Listing 7.7 shows the beginning of that process.

Listing 7.7   Linux kernel configuration using a text-based interface

```
[ezk]$ make config
rm -f include/asm
( cd include ; ln -sf asm-i386 asm)
/bin/sh scripts/Configure arch/i386/config.in
#
# Using defaults found in arch/i386/defconfig
#
*
* Code maturity level options
*
Prompt for development and/or incomplete code/drivers (CONFIG_EXPERIMENTAL)
[N/y/?] y
```

```
*
* Loadable module support
*
Enable loadable module support (CONFIG_MODULES) [Y/n/?] y
  Set version information on all module symbols (CONFIG_MODVERSIONS) [Y/n/?]
  Kernel module loader (CONFIG_KMOD) [Y/n/?]
*
* Processor type and features
*
```

In the above kernel configuration section, we turned on CONFIG_EXPERIMENTAL so the configuration script will prompt us to select among those. We also turned on loadable module support (although it is on by default). Next, we turned off the forcing of module version checks. This means that we will not allow modules to be loaded into our kernel if they were not compiled for that kernel. This is usually a good idea and ensures that your kernel will not use modules built for other kernels. Then, we leave on the use of an automatic kernel module loader, by simply hitting Enter and moving on. The kernel module loader is very useful: it will automatically load modules as needed, so you will not have to do so manually.

TIP   You can always select the ? option to get a brief help message on each feature.

Each section of configuration options is usually preceded by a section name indicated by three lines that begin with an * symbol. The sections we are interested in are labeled File Systems and Network File Systems. To reach those sections you must answer all of the intervening configuration questions until you get to the section on configuring file systems shown in Listing 7.8. Be patient; there may be *hundreds* of questions in between. However, it is often safe to accept the default answers for those questions by hitting the Enter key when prompted.

Listing 7.8   Configuring the general file systems section of the Linux kernel

```
*
* File systems
*
Quota support (CONFIG_QUOTA) [N/y/?]
Kernel automounter support (CONFIG_AUTOFS_FS) [N/y/m/?] m
Kernel automounter version 4 support (also supports v3) (CONFIG_AUTOFS4_FS)
[Y/m/n/?] m
ADFS file system support (CONFIG_ADFS_FS) [N/y/m/?]
```

```
Amiga FFS file system support (EXPERIMENTAL) (CONFIG_AFFS_FS) [N/y/m/?]
Apple Macintosh file system support (EXPERIMENTAL) (CONFIG_HFS_FS) [N/y/m/?]
BFS file system support (EXPERIMENTAL) (CONFIG_BFS_FS) [N/y/m/?]
DOS FAT FS support (CONFIG_FAT_FS) [N/y/m/?] m
  MSDOS FS support (CONFIG_MSDOS_FS) [N/m/?] m
    UMSDOS: Unix-like file system on top of standard MSDOS FS
    (CONFIG_UMSDOS_FS) [N/m/?]
  VFAT (Windows-95) FS support (CONFIG_VFAT_FS) [N/m/?] m
EFS file system support (read only) (EXPERIMENTAL) (CONFIG_EFS_FS) [N/y/m/?]
Compressed ROM file system support (CONFIG_CRAMFS) [N/y/m/?]
Simple RAM-based file system support (CONFIG_RAMFS) [N/y/m/?]
ISO 9660 CDROM file system support (CONFIG_ISO9660_FS) [Y/m/n/?]
  Microsoft Joliet CDROM extensions (CONFIG_JOLIET) [N/y/?]
Minix FS support (CONFIG_MINIX_FS) [N/y/m/?]
NTFS file system support (read only) (CONFIG_NTFS_FS) [N/y/m/?]
OS/2 HPFS file system support (CONFIG_HPFS_FS) [N/y/m/?]
/proc file system support (CONFIG_PROC_FS) [Y/n/?]
/dev file system support (EXPERIMENTAL) (CONFIG_DEVFS_FS) [N/y/?]
/dev/pts file system for Unix98 PTYs (CONFIG_DEVPTS_FS) [Y/n/?]
QNX4 file system support (read only) (EXPERIMENTAL) (CONFIG_QNX4FS_FS)
[N/y/m/?]
ROM file system support (CONFIG_ROMFS_FS) [N/y/m/?]
Second extended FS support (CONFIG_EXT2_FS) [Y/m/n/?] y
System V and Coherent file system support (read only) (CONFIG_SYSV_FS)
[N/y/m/?]
UDF file system support (read only) (CONFIG_UDF_FS) [N/y/m/?]
UFS file system support (read only) (CONFIG_UFS_FS) [N/y/m/?]
```

In the section shown in Listing 7.8, you see the option for selecting a feature to compile as a module. We selected five features to be modules and one to be statically compiled in the kernel. The next section, shown in Listing 7.9, immediately follows the one above and is for configuring network-based file systems.

Listing 7.9 Configuring the network file systems section of the Linux kernel

```
*
* Network File Systems
*
Coda file system support (advanced network FS) (CONFIG_CODA_FS) [N/y/m/?]
NFS file system support (CONFIG_NFS_FS) [Y/m/n/?]
  Provide NFSv3 client support (EXPERIMENTAL) (CONFIG_NFS_V3) [N/y/?] y
NFS server support (CONFIG_NFSD) [Y/m/n/?] m
  Provide NFSv3 server support (CONFIG_NFSD_V3) [N/y/?] y
```

```
SMB file system support (to mount Windows shares etc.) (CONFIG_SMB_FS)
[N/y/m/?]
NCP file system support (to mount NetWare volumes) (CONFIG_NCP_FS) [N/y/m/?]
```

We selected NFS client code to compile statically and NFS server side (both NFSv2 and NFSv3) to compile as a module.

Continue to select options, or pick the default ones, until you reach the very end. You will then see the following:

*** End of Linux kernel configuration.

*** Check the top-level Makefile for additional configuration.

*** Next, you must run 'make dep'.

You can now invoke the same configuration procedure, or a different one, to reconfigure the kernel. When you are done configuring the kernel, you can begin building it.

Curses-Based Full-Screen Configuration

The curses-based full-screen configuration option is based on simple menus. To start it, run the following commands:

[ezk]$ **cd /usr/src/linux**

[ezk]$ **make menuconfig**

Basic help commands appear at the top of each screen. Use the following keys to navigate the menus and control selections:

N   Turn off a configuration option.

Y   Turn on a configuration option.

M   Turn on a configuration option as a module.

+   Move down in the menu of options.

-   Move up in the menu of options.

Enter   Select a submenu.

Escape   Exit a menu and get back to its parent.

?   Get help on this configuration method or option, including more key shortcuts.

The first menu you will see is the top menu:

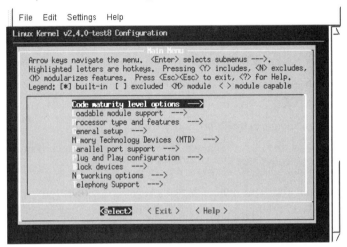

1. Hit Enter to select that menu:

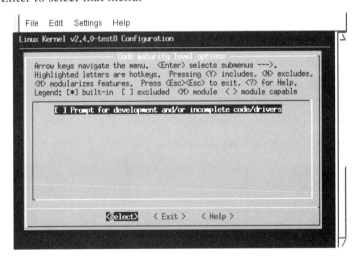

2. Then hit **Y** again to select the Prompt For Development And/Or Incomplete Code/ Drivers (Experimental) option. When the option is selected, you will see an * inside the []:

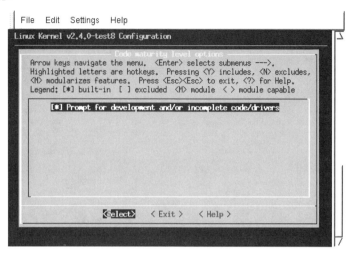

3. Now hit Escape to exit that menu and go back to the previous (main) menu. Next type + to scroll down the main menu options until you reach the File Systems submenu. Submenus are marked with a ---> next to their descriptions.

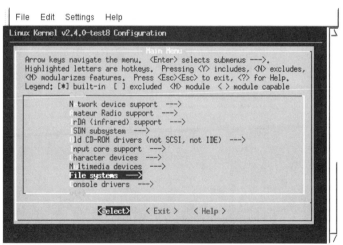

4. Then select the File Systems submenu by hitting Enter. You will now be inside that menu:

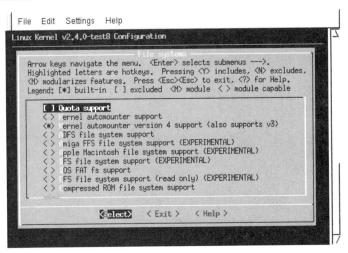

5. Now we will scroll up and down using the - and + keys, respectively. Each time we see a kernel option highlighted, we will hit **Y** to turn it on, or **M** to turn it on as a module. The first two options (Autofs) should look like the following:

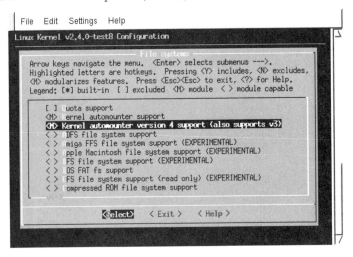

6. Then we select the three DOS file system options on:

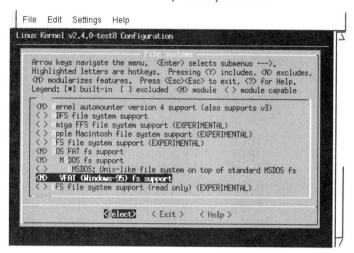

7. Scrolling down, we see that the ISO9660 option is already selected:

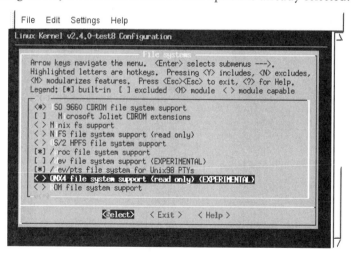

8. Also, the EXT2FS (Second Extended FS Support) option is already selected. Next move the highlighted line to the Network File Systems submenu option:

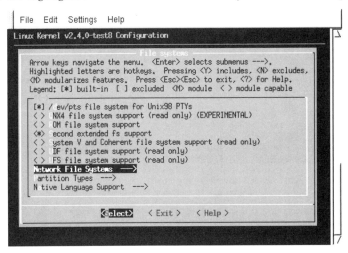

9. Hit Enter to select this menu and see the following:

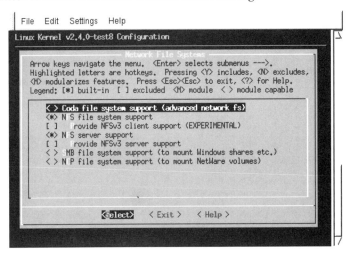

10. Now, scroll a bit down to the NFS File System Support option, and select it by hitting **Y**. Do not forget to select its sub-option: NFSv3 client support. Just below, go to NFS Server Support and hit **M** to select it as a module. Also select its sub-option, Provide NFSv3 Server Support. When done, you should see the following:

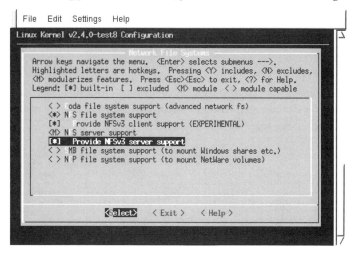

11. You are done configuring the kernel. Now hit Escape once to exit the Network File Systems menu, a second time to exit the File Systems menu, and one last time to exit the whole configuration tool. You will be prompted to save or discard the configuration.

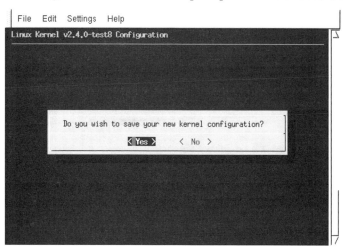

12. Hit **Y** to save the configuration.

13. All kernel configuration options are saved in the file named .config inside /usr/ src/linux.

X11-Based Graphical Configuration

The graphical configuration tool requires that you have installed the `tcl` and `tk` RPMs. To use this configuration option, run the following commands while setting your `$DISPLAY` environment variable to a suitable X11 display:

```
[ezk]$ cd /usr/src/linux
[ezk]$ export DISPLAY=:0
[ezk]$ make xconfig
```

The procedure here is very similar to the previous section, only this time it is completely graphical, and you can achieve all configuration options using the mouse. The first main menu you will see is the following:

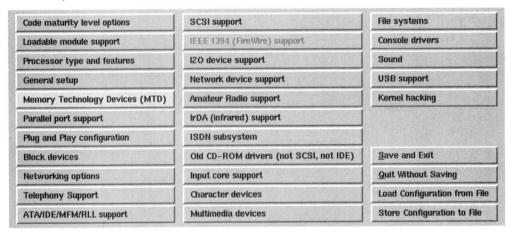

1. Click Code Maturity Level Options (upper-left) to get the following window, then click **Y** to select prompting for experimental code:

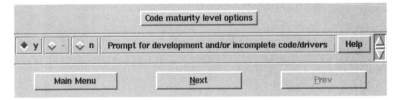

2. Click the Main Menu option to close this small window, then click the File Systems menu:

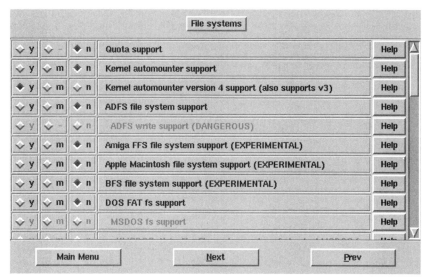

3. You can stretch your window to enlarge or shrink its height as needed, and scroll using the scrollbar on the right side. Set the two Autofs options to M (build as a module), as well as the three DOS options:

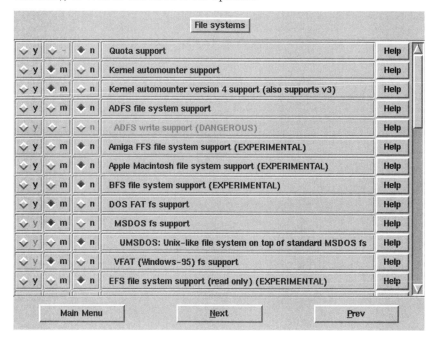

4. You will see that some options are already turned on: ISO9660 and EXT2 (Second Extended FS Support):

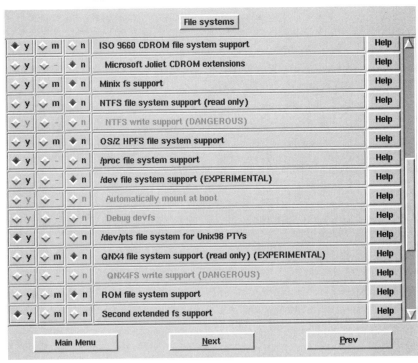

5. Now scroll to the bottom of the File Systems window:

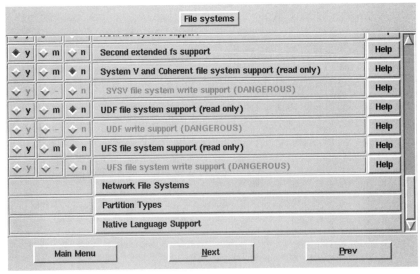

and click the Network File Systems option. A new window will pop up:

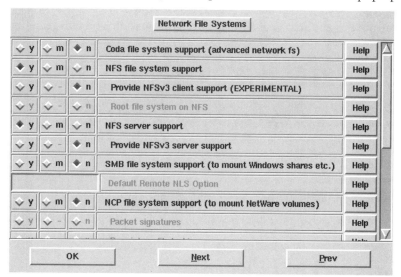

6. Now select the NFS File System Support option and its NFSv3 Client Support sub-option. Then select the NFS Server Support option (as a module) and its NFSv3 Server Support sub-option. Your window should look like the following:

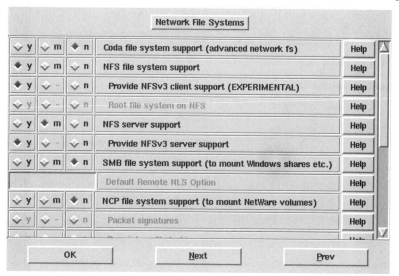

7. Click OK to close the Network File System menu. Then click Main Menu to close the File Systems window. Finally, click the Save And Exit option to save this configuration and exit the graphical kernel configuration tool. You will get an informational window:

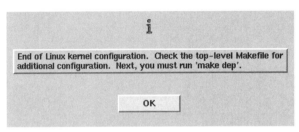

8. Click OK in that window. The graphical configuration tool will exit.

You are now done. Continue to the next section for building the Linux kernel.

Building the Linux Kernel

Before building the kernel, make sure you have about 40 to 60MB of free disk space. The build process is relatively simple but can take a very long time, especially on slow machines. You start by building the dependency files, then cleaning any leftover files from a previous build, then building a compressed kernel image, and finally building modules:

```
[root]# cd /usr/src/linux
[root]# make dep
[root]# make clean
[root]# make bzImage
[root]# make modules
```

If you face any compilation errors, do not continue and do not try to install that kernel. Check that you have followed the proper procedures for unpacking and configuring the kernel. Also check that you have enough disk space in /usr/src/linux. If you are using an experimental kernel, check with the linux-kernel mailing list (see Appendix B) to see if anyone had seen this problem. You may have to back out to an older, more tested kernel version, or use a newer kernel release that fixes the problems you are seeing.

If all build stages completed without any errors, continue to the kernel installation.

Installing the Linux Kernel

To install the Linux kernel, execute the following commands in order:

```
[root]# cd /usr/src/linux
[root]# make install
[root]# make modules_install
```

The make install command installs the kernel in the /boot directory. The make modules_install command installs modules in /lib/modules. If the two make commands proceeded successfully, proceed to configure the RAM disk boot loader and the Linux kernel boot loader, LILO.

The RAM disk boot loader is a program that allows you to load dynamically loadable kernel modules with the kernel at boot time, as if they were linked with it statically. LILO is a boot loader that allows you to configure multiple kernel images to choose from at boot time. We describe these two components next.

WARNING   Do not reboot your system after installing a new kernel until you have updated your RAM disk boot loader, edited your /etc/lilo.conf file, and ran lilo. Many Linux users forget one of these extra steps, reboot, and find that their system will not longer come up. Then they have to reinstall the Linux system from scratch.

Configuring the RAM Disk Boot Loader

As we mentioned earlier, loadable kernel modules are convenient because they decrease the kernel's image size and can provide additional functionality when it is needed. However, modules can only be loaded after the kernel starts and the root file system is mounted. So what happens when the kernel code needed to mount the root file system is in a module on that file system? What you get is an unbootable system! You must avoid this situation at all cost by carefully configuring your kernel and modules so they are all available when needed.

In particular, you must ensure that all modules that are needed for the kernel to continue its boot process and mount the root file system are available at boot time. A special tool, mkinitrd, creates a RAM disk image that the kernel can load at boot time. This image must contain all the modules the kernel needs at boot time.

One typical example of where an initial RAM disk is needed is on systems with two types of disks: IDE and SCSI. If your Linux system used to reside on the IDE drive but now is installed on the SCSI drive (second disk), then your kernel may not have support for SCSI drivers and may not be able to boot into the second (SCSI) disk.

If you already installed your system using the Red Hat CD, then it configured the initial RAM disk as needed in the file /etc/conf.modules. If not, then you will have to configure it yourself. On a system with both IDE and SCSI disks, and booting off of the SCSI disk, the contents of your /etc/conf.modules file might be as follows:

```
[ezk]$ cat /etc/conf.modules
alias scsi_hostadapter aic7xxx
```

The above tells the system to load the Adaptec SCSI driver module aic7xxx at boot time. Once you have configured your /etc/conf.modules as needed, you have to run the mkinitrd command to create the RAM disk image file. Recall that we built a 2.4.0-test8 kernel earlier.

```
[root]# mkinitrd /boot/initrd-2.4.0-test8.img 2.4.0-test8
```

The above command will create the file /boot/initrd-2.4.0-test8.img containing the modules listed in /etc/conf.modules. For more information, see the manual page for mkinitrd. Next, you should refer to this RAM disk image in the Linux boot loader configuration file.

Configuring the LILO Linux Boot Loader

When you installed your Linux kernel, it installed its image file in /boot/vmlinuz-2.4.0-test8. The RAM disk image was installed in /boot/initrd-2.4.0-test8.img. Now you have to tell the Linux boot loader, lilo, where these two images are.

You also have to find out which partition your kernel is installed on. Run df /boot and see which device it resides on. The following means that your kernels boot off of the second partition of the primary IDE drive:

```
[ezk]$ df /boot
Filesystem          1k-blocks      Used Available Use% Mounted on
/dev/hda2             124443      69337     48680  59% /
```

while the following means that you are booting off of the first partition of the first SCSI drive:

```
[ezk]$ df /boot
Filesystem          1k-blocks      Used Available Use% Mounted on
/dev/sda1             879078     819618     14047  98% /
```

Whichever partition it happens to be, it must also be listed in the LILO configuration file, /etc/lilo.conf. Start by adding an entry as shown in Listing 7.10 to the *end* of your /etc/lilo.conf file.

Listing 7.10 A new kernel image configuration section in /etc/lilo.conf

```
image=/boot/vmlinuz-2.4.0-test8
        label=linux-2.4.0t8
        root=/dev/sda1
        initrd=/boot/initrd-2.4.0-test8.img
        read-only
```

The above adds another boot image to your system. The meaning of these five lines is as follows:

image   Selects the file containing the kernel image. There cannot be more than 19 image names.

label   Gives this image a symbolic name. This name cannot be longer than 15 characters.

root   Selects the device of the root file system.

initrd   Is optional and points to the name of the RAM disk image.

root-only   Specifies that the root file system should be mounted read-only initially. The rest of the system startup sequence will remount that file system read-write anyway.

When the system boots the next time, the LILO boot: prompt will list another image named linux-2.4.0t8 and you will be able to select it and boot that image.

The reason we asked you to add this new entry to the end of your /etc/lilo.conf file is so you keep the rest of the entries in that file untouched. This is crucial to your ability to recover the system in case the new kernel you built is not working. In that case, you could simply reboot the system and pick another kernel image to boot from. In particular, you should keep any older working kernels, such as the default Red Hat kernel you installed initially.

Once you have updated your /etc/lilo.conf file, run lilo to update the actual boot loader code. This is an important step that, if forgotten, will result in an unbootable system:

```
[root]# lilo
Added linux *
Added dos
Added linux-2.4.0t8
```

The above tells you that `lilo` added three kernel images to boot from. The first two were there before: your default Linux kernel and a `dos` boot image (for systems that have a Windows or DOS partition). The third boot image is the one we just added. Note that the * after the first boot image also indicates that this is the default boot image.

This means that when the system boots next, it will boot your original kernel by default, not the one you just installed. This is intentional. We want to make sure that we can boot an original working kernel and manually specify the new kernel we wish to test.

Finally, we are ready to reboot. First make sure no users are on your system, and close all applications. Then reboot as follows:

    [root]# **reboot**

When the system starts booting, you will be prompted with a `LILO boot:` prompt for (typically) five seconds. At that time, you can hit the Tab key to see a list of all available images, or type **linux-2.4.0t8** and hit Enter to boot your new kernel. If the system comes back up, then install and test the user-level tools as described in the next section. After you are confident that both the new kernel and the new user-level tools work correctly, set this new kernel to become the default boot kernel by adding the following line to the top of your /etc/lilo.conf file:

    default=linux-2.4.0t8

Then rerun `lilo` to make sure that this image is now the default boot image and, finally, reboot one last time:

    [root]# **lilo**

    Added linux

    Added dos

    Added linux-2.4.0t8 *

For more information on LILO, see the manual pages for `lilo` and `lilo.conf` and the documentation files in the directory /usr/share/doc/lilo-21.4.4.

Additional NFS Software

After building and rebooting your Linux system with a new kernel, you should quickly proceed to get any additional user-level tools configured and installed. You may not be able to take advantage of your new kernel features without these tools, especially new NFSv3 features. Just as with kernel patches, you should find out which of the latest user-level packages you need that work with your chosen kernel version. Generally, follow the instructions in http://nfs.sourceforge.net, especially if you try to use your system as an NFSv3 client or server and these features do not appear to work. These instructions will tell you to get these tools:

- An updated /bin/mount program that can handle NFSv3 and TCP mounts
- Updated NFS utilities, documentation, scripts, and various daemons: locking, mounting, status, and quota processing over NFS

User-Level Mount Utilities

The new /bin/mount program is available in several distributions. This stems from the fact that the package maintainer maintains it as a small mount-only distribution called mount-2.10 and as part of a larger distribution called util-linux.

To make things more complex, Red Hat distributes these as two separate packages: a mount-2.10 RPM containing the /bin/mount program and a util-linux RPM that contains various utilities but no /bin/mount program. Nevertheless, here we will retrieve and build the full package:

```
[root]# cd /usr/src
[root]# wget ftp://ftp.kernel.org/pub/linux/utils/util-linux/util-
linux-2.10o.tar.gz
[root]# tar xzf util-linux-2.10o.tar.gz
```

NOTE As is always the case with any software you download, there could be a newer version of this package on ftp.kernel.org. Always check download sites for the latest version.

Next, configure the package and install it:

```
[root]# cd /usr/src/util-linux-2.10o
[root]# ./configure
[root]# make
[root]# make install
```

After doing so, try out your new /bin/mount program to see if it is capable of performing NFSv3 mounts. For example, if you have an NFS server named shekel running NFSv3 server software and exporting the file system /u/zing to this client, you can try the following mount command:

```
[root]# mount -t nfs -o nfsvers=3 shekel:/u/zing /mnt
```

If the command succeeds, then your kernel and mount utilities correctly support NFSv3 client-side code.

If you are rebuilding NFS for use with Amd, then you may choose to proceed and rebuild am-utils as described in Chapter 14, "Building and Installing the Automounter Software." Then you can run amd -v to see that the new Amd recognizes NFSv3, and then start your new Amd and verify that it performs NFSv3 mounts correctly. Note, however, that if the above mount command succeeded when run manually, there is a very good chance that Amd will work as well.

User-Level NFS Utilities

User-level NFS utilities are needed to support new NFSv3 server-side code. If your Linux system will act as an NFS server, then you will need these utilities. Before installing new ones, check to see if your current Red Hat utilities support NFSv3 (as of Red Hat 7.0, they do not, but newer Red Hat distributions are likely to support NFSv3).

Start by getting the latest nfs-utils package as shown in Listing 7.11 from http://nfs.sourceforge.net, then unpack, build, and install it.

Listing 7.11   Getting and installing additional user-level NFS software

```
[root]# cd /usr/src
[root]# wget http://download.sourceforge.net/nfs/nfs-utils-0.2.1.tar.gz
[root]# tar xzf nfs-utils-0.2.1.tar.gz
[root]# cd nfs-utils-0.2.1
[root]# ./configure
[root]# make
[root]# make install
```

Then, you must restart all of your NFS daemons but run these two initialization scripts in order:

```
[root]# /etc/rc.d/init.d/nfslock restart
```

```
[root]# /etc/rc.d/init.d/nfs restart
```

If you are running a sufficiently newer kernel (e.g., 2.4), then the NFS locking service is part of the kernel, as we described in Chapter 1, "NFS Basics and Protocols." However, the nfslock startup script distributed with Red Hat Linux does not know that and attempts to start the service as a user-level one. In that case, you may get the error message "lockdsvr not implemented," which you can ignore.

Now you are ready to try your new kernel and user-level utilities. To do so, try to NFS-mount an exported partition of this Linux system from another Unix system that supports NFSv3. See Chapter 2, "Configuring NFS," for details on setting your NFS servers and clients and performing basic client/server testing.

In Sum

In this chapter we learned how to configure and build the Linux kernel from sources. We also learned how to find out, retrieve, and apply source patches that add new kernel features such as NFSv3. We learned how to pick the set of kernel features most suitable for our needs and we saw three different methods for configuring the kernel.

We then learned how to configure our system to boot the new kernel properly and how to configure, install, and test user-level utilities that may be necessary to activate the new kernel features.

Installing new kernels is not an option that should be taken lightly. A mistake could result in permanent loss of all data on a system with a bad or misconfigured kernel and may require a complete system reinstallation—a lengthy process. That is why you should follow the procedures in this chapter carefully. Keep in mind, also, that Linux kernels and associated procedures tend to change often. So before you embark on installing a new kernel, ensure that you understand any changed procedures. For that, consult Appendix B for any updates to the procedures described in this chapter.

Part 2

The Amd Automounter

Featuring:

- An introduction to the Amd automounter

- The Amd runtime startup configuration file

- The automounter maps

- Dynamic query and control using Amq

- Testing and debugging Amd configurations

- Advanced examples

- Using Autofs with Amd

- Other tools in the am-utils package

- Building and configuring the am-utils package

8

Overview of the Amd Automounter

The Network File System (NFS) protocol defines a method for connecting remote hosts together. For clients to access files on remote file servers, they have to mount those NFS partitions locally. To maintain reliability, the NFS protocol was designed such that if an NFS server becomes inaccessible, all file activity on the client mounting the downed server is suspended until the server becomes available again. This ensures that all unsaved data remains in memory until it can be saved reliably to the server. The problem is that if the NFS server does not come back up quickly, the client remains hung all that time, resulting in rather unhappy users marching down to the system administrators' offices, muttering unkind words.

A large site may have many file servers, and oftentimes, even single-user workstations serve files over NFS. This results in many hosts serving as NFS file servers to many others. The easiest way for administrators to provide access to all servers is to NFS-mount each server on all clients. The larger the site, the higher the chances are that at least one machine will be down at any given time. Unfortunately, with such a cross-mounting configuration, all it takes is for one machine to be down to hang all the other hosts. That was indeed the situation before automounters came into being.

An *automounter* automates the mounting of NFS servers; administrators do not have to fix the set of mounts on each client. An automounter will mount remote NFS servers on demand, only when a user accesses a path name that is not mounted yet. Over time, however, the number of automounted NFS file systems may grow to a point where so many are mounted that even one of their respective NFS servers going down could hang the host. That is why automounters also unmount servers that have not been used recently.

Automounters add two more benefits. First, they allow administrators to centralize the management of mounts. Without automounters, static mounts have to be edited in the /etc/fstab file on each host. Automounters allow administrators to define *mount maps* in a single location and distribute them to many clients using network-wide services such as the *Network Information Service* (NIS). Second, automounters help administrators provide uniform naming for all file systems. For example, the path names /home/ezk and /home/martha can always be available and valid from any host, even if they physically reside on the NFS locations shekel:/n/jin/u/zing/ezk and opus:/raid1/users/ martha, respectively.

In this chapter we discuss the basics of the Amd automounter: how it works, its relationship to NFS, and its interaction with the rest of your system. We describe the basic information components that Amd manipulates: hostnames, file systems, as well as multiples or subsets of file systems. We detail some of the main functional concepts of Amd and show how it processes a user request to mount a file system. We follow with an example for configuring Amd and defining its maps: the configuration files that determine how Amd mounts file systems. Finally, we also show how to control Amd using the Amq query and control tool.

The Structure and Operation of Amd

To understand how Amd works, see Figure 8.1, which shows it in relation to the other components running on the system. Amd is a user-level NFS server that communicates with the kernel using *Remote Procedure Call* (RPC) messages. The RPC system allows one host to execute functions on another host. A typical user process begins by issuing a system call to, say, open a file. The system call traps into the kernel; the kernel suspends the running process and begins executing the code for the system call on behalf of the user process. The kernel begins by calling the *Virtual File System* (VFS). The VFS realizes that in order to resolve the path name of the file, it must traverse through an NFS server. Normally NFS servers are remote hosts. In Figure 8.1 the NFS server happens to be local to the host, but it is still contacted in the same manner as a remote server—by sending an RPC message to the server.

The NFS client portion of the kernel issues RPC messages compliant with the NFSv2 protocol on the IP address and port of the registered NFS server (the Amd process), as follows:

1. Amd receives RPC messages and, in turn, uses the mount(2) system call to mount the specific file system that would satisfy the user's request.

2. A system call traps into the kernel, which then performs the mount operation—in this figure, mounting an EXT2FS partition.

3. The kernel replies back to Amd with a successful return code from mount(2).

4. Amd sends the kernel the proper RPC messages to tell the NFS client code that the mount had succeeded.

5. The kernel returns back from the original process's system call, and the user process unblocks and resumes running.

Figure 8.1   Amd is a user-level NFS server that communicates with the kernel using RPC messages.

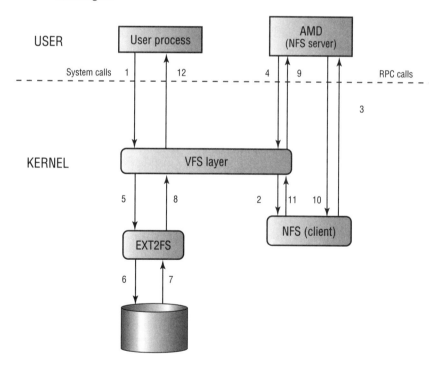

Amd Performance

Typically, file server code resides in the kernel. This ensures that file systems run very quickly and that they have more control over their own resource allocations. Amd, being a user-level file server, must exchange several messages with the kernel. Each time it exchanges a message, an operating system context switch occurs.

Context switches are costly and slow, resulting in slow performance for Amd (or any other user-level file server). For example, a typical mount request using Amd takes 1 to 3 seconds the first time and 0.1 to 0.5 seconds for subsequent times; this is often much slower than in-kernel code. Furthermore, as a user process, Amd must contend for CPU and memory resources with all other processes running on the system. This means that if the system is busy with many users running many jobs, Amd may become even slower, resulting in mounts taking many seconds to complete.

For these reasons and more (discussed in Chapter 13, "Autofs"), a helper file system called Autofs was created by Sun. Autofs performs the operations most critical to automounters in the kernel. Amd can work with or without Autofs. Additional information on optimizing the performance of Amd is given in Chapter 12, "Advanced Amd Uses."

Hosts and File Systems

The structure of components within Amd itself is shown in Figure 8.2. Amd manages a set of automounted directories (Amd mounts). Each automounted directory has an associated *mount map* that describes the various mounts to manage under that directory. The set of automounted directories and their mounts is listed in the Amd configuration file *amd.conf*. To manage all of its mounts, Amd maintains information about three additional items: *hosts*, *file systems*, and *volumes*. A host is a file server containing file systems that could be mounted. These file systems often correspond to whole, physical, exported partitions on the host. NFS servers can also export subdirectories within file systems. NFS clients, however, cannot tell the difference between a whole exported partition and just a subdirectory that was exported by the NFS server. Amd treats all exported file systems as if they were complete file systems.

Figure 8.2   The components of a running Amd

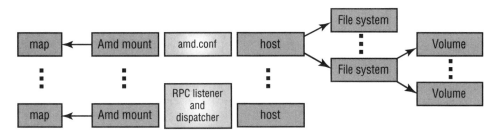

For example, consider an NFS server that has the following file systems (see Listing 8.1).

Listing 8.1   An example list of partitions on an NFS server

```
[ezk]$ df
Filesystem          1k-blocks    Used Available Use% Mounted on
/dev/hda2             124443     67484     50533  57% /
/dev/hda8            9471868   8517412    473312  95% /homes
/dev/hda7             497829        13    472114   0% /n/fist
/dev/hda6            2016016   1010060    903544  53% /usr
```

The server exports the /homes partition (/dev/hda8) to everyone with read and write permissions, and the /n/fist/src subdirectory of the /n/fist partition (/dev/hda7) to a host named "whitestar." The NFS server records this export information in the file /etc/exports (see Listing 8.2).

Listing 8.2   Contents of a sample /etc/exports file for an NFS server

```
/homes            (rw)
/n/fist/src       whitestar(rw)
```

Note that while /n/fist is a whole partition on the NFS server, it exports only its src subdirectory. Amd does not distinguish between whole file systems exported by the server and partially exported file systems. Amd mounts these file systems from the NFS client's perspective that considers the two exported file systems in Listing 8.2 as whole file systems. In other words, Amd's notion of file systems treats /homes and /n/fist/src as two complete units. Amd, however, can automount portions of those file systems. For example, it can automount /home/ezk separately from /home/martha, even if both reside physically in the exported /homes file system on the NFS server.

The Amd
Automounter

PART 2

Volumes

A volume gives administrators more flexible control over file systems. A volume can be one or more subparts (subdirectories) of an exported file system, several different file systems treated as one unit, and even *replicated* or *replacement* volumes. A replicated volume is one defining several identical file systems. Amd can choose one of them at random when mounting the volume. This allows administrators to configure automounted volumes that can survive even if one or more of the file systems in the volume are down: Amd will pick one of the volumes out of those that are up and running. A replacement volume is a similar concept, only here, a volume that was mounted and working stopped working because the remote file server could not be reached. In this case, Amd will mount another volume in place of the non-working one. (Chapters 10, "Automounter Maps," and 12 show several examples of using volumes that are either subsets of file systems, or a collection of several file systems.)

Consider the following exported file systems:

- `opus:/usr/local`
- `titan:/usr/local` (identical to `opus:/usr/local`)
- `earth:/usr/local` (identical to `opus:/usr/local`)
- `kosh:/n/fist/src`. Let us also assume that this directory contains the following subdirectories:
  - `/n/fist/src/crypto/` contains sources for an encryption package.
  - `/n/fist/src/gzip/` contains sources for a compression package.

Listing 8.3 lists an Amd map example of a replicated volume.

Listing 8.3 An example of a replicated volume

```
binaries        -type:=nfs;rfs:=/usr/local \
                rhost:=opus   rhost:=titan   rhost:=earth
```

The above example tells Amd that the three hosts, `opus`, `titan`, and `earth`, provide the same files. When a user accesses the `binaries` entry, Amd will try to mount the three file servers and will use the one that responds first to the user's mount request.

The example in Listing 8.3 combined several file systems into a single volume. Amd supports a few more methods of joining file systems into a single volume, such as mounting two or more file systems together. This type of mount is called `nfsx`; it and all others are described in detail in Chapter 10.

The example in Listing 8.4 shows how to create two volumes that are subsets of a single file system.

Listing 8.4   Examples of volumes that use subsets of file systems

```
/defaults          type:=nfs;rhost:=kosh;rfs:=/n/fist/src

encryption         sublink:=crypto

compression        sublink:=gzip
```

In the example in Listing 8.4, we use the Amd map variable sublink to tell Amd to create two distinct volumes named encryption and compression. Each of those comes from a subdirectory within the actual file system kosh:/n/fist/src. Recall that the latter is actually a subdirectory on the NFS server that exported a portion of /dev/hda7 as seen in Listing 8.1.

With these three pieces of information in place—hosts, file systems, and volumes—Amd can separate the naming of files based on their desired usage, not on their physical location on the network. Let us assume that the Amd map example in Listing 8.4 is part of the /src map. Users should not have to remember that the encryption sources reside on an NFS server named kosh that exports a file system /n/fist/src, that /n/fist/src is only a subset of one of its devices, and that the sources are located in a subdirectory further down named crypto. Instead, users need only remember one easy path name: /src/encryption. This powerful abstraction gives users the stability of naming, as they can refer to site-wide files and directories in the same manner; at the same time, this gives administrators the flexibility to change the physical location of servers and their file systems without impacting users. After such changes, administrators need only update the site's Amd maps.

Amd uses RPC messages to communicate with several components of the system: automount points, non-blocking mounts and unmounts, keep-alives, and portmapper registration. These are handled by the RPC Listener and Dispatcher component of Amd, seen in Figure 8.2.

Automount Points

Amd's own automount points are NFSv2 mounts on the local host. The kernel issues NFS RPCs to Amd, asking Amd to look up names inside the automounted directory. When Amd receives such a lookup request, it consults its mount maps for the automounted directory, trying to match the name with a key in its map. If found, Amd then mounts the volume that corresponds to the key. When the mount is successful, Amd returns back to the kernel an RPC that tells the kernel that the requested path name is available. In addition, Amd tells the kernel that the path name represents a symbolic link (symlink). That symlink points to the directory where Amd mounted the specific volume.

Non-Blocking Mounts and Unmounts

The Amd process must never block or hang because it serves many user requests. In particular, one specific lookup of an automounted path name should not hang the Amd process and cause problems for other users. For that reason, all mounts and unmounts performed by Amd are done in the background: Amd forks a separate process to perform them. Before it forks the process, Amd sets up an RPC listening callback channel that would be invoked when the *backgrounded* (run in the background) mount is finished.

Amd can set up many such listening channels, one per mount or unmount. When a backgrounded operation completes, a signal is sent from the child process to the parent process. The parent process, or master Amd process, finds the listening channel corresponding to the child's task and continues the work in that channel. In that fashion, any hung child process that could not complete its mount will not hang the master Amd process.

NOTE If many backgrounded operations fail, many background-mount processes could accumulate on a long-running system. These can take up memory and swap space on the system. Luckily, Amd performs various non-blocking checks before attempting to mount a volume, contacting the remote portmapper and the remote mount daemon. These checks decrease the chances that even backgrounded mounts could hang.

Keep-Alives

Amd periodically pings mounted file servers to check if they are still alive. If several successive pings fail, Amd considers the remote file server down and then tries a replacement volume. If a replacement volume is not available, Amd blocks this automounted path name from being accessed by new processes by sending an "Operation Would Block" (EWOULDBLOCK) error code, in the hopes that the remote file server will come back up eventually. Amd continues to ping remote servers periodically until they come back. Once they are up again, Amd unblocks any waiting processes.

Keep-alives are only performed for NFS mounts that use UDP as their transport. Amd uses the NFS NullProc (procedure 0) RPC message to ping the remote server. TCP mounts do not need keep-alives because TCP is a reliable transport mechanism that includes its own methods for checking the liveness of a connection.

Portmapper Registration

RPC servers register themselves with the host's portmapper, an RPC service broker that can tell other programs which RPC services are running on that host and how to contact them. Amd also registers itself with the local host's portmapper.

Amd comes with a query and control tool called *Amq*. This tool communicates with Amd, through the portmapper, to check the current state of the automounter or to change that state. For example, Amq can list actively automounted file systems, turn on verbose logging in Amd, force Amd to flush its cache, and more. Amq is described in more detail in Chapter 11, "Runtime Automounter Administration."

Mounting a Volume

A volume is described in the Amd mount map as a *key* followed by one or more *locations*. There is no limit imposed by Amd on the number of locations that can exist in a single map entry. A key is the name of the looked-up pathname component inside of the auto-mounted directory. A location is a description of one optional way to satisfy the mount of the key:

```
key    location1  location2  location3  locationN
```

Amd begins inspecting locations one at a time from first listed to last. A volume may contain selectors such as os==linux. These selectors tell Amd to use a location only if all listed selectors match (evaluate to True). In this example, the location will be selected only if Amd is running on a Linux system. Amd therefore ignores locations that do not satisfy all of their selectors and goes on to process the next one. Amd then mounts the locations that matched their selectors.

A mount can fail for one of four reasons:

No location matched its selectors.   To solve this problem, the particular map must be revised to include selectors that match the conditions of the running system. For example, if your map listed the two selectors os==linux;osver=2.0, they will match if you are running on a Linux system *and* your kernel version is 2.0.*x*. If you upgrade your system to one that uses Linux kernel version 2.2 (e.g., Red Hat 7), this location will fail because the kernel version would no longer match. To correct this problem, you could either change the location that lists the 2.0 version in your map or add a new location that starts with os==linux;osver=2.2 instead.

All matched locations resulted in a mount error. For example, the error code "permission denied" (EPERM) is returned if the remote file server does not permit the host to mount its file systems. In this case, the error returned to the user process looking up the key is the error code from the last mount request. To solve this problem, ensure that your network is functioning, that the remote hosts are up and running, that the file system in question permits the client host to mount it, and that you have no syntax errors in the Amd map.

TIP A useful way to find out if a mount problem of this sort is the result of map errors or remote host failures is to hand-mount the remote file system using /bin/mount. If it succeeds, then the problem is in the Amd maps; if it fails, then the problem is with the remote host or the network.

Another, identical mount is already in progress and in the background. Since Amd performs mounts asynchronously and in the background, multiple users can access the same unmounted volume at once. Amd dispatches only one backgrounded mount request and blocks all others until that mount completes. This problem often happens in systems with heavy constant use of automounter maps, and especially if mounted map entries time out too fast, resulting in repeated concurrent user requests to mount the volume. To alleviate this problem, ensure that Amd mounted volumes do not time out too fast on busy systems by using the dismount_interval configuration parameter described in Chapter 9, "The Amd Configuration File."

The mount is deferred. A deferred mount is one that cannot complete for lack of information. Once Amd collects that information, it will try the mount. When a mount is deferred, Amd continues to try the next available location. For example, before Amd mounts a file system, it first checks to see if the remote portmapper is alive, and then it communicates with the remote host's mount daemon (rpc.mountd) to find out which versions of NFS are supported by both client and server. That information is needed so Amd can ensure that the remote server is behaving normally and so Amd can use the most suitable (and often the latest) version of NFS supported by both. During this time, however, the actual mount(2) system call is not started and Amd marks the mount as "deferred." If the additional information does not become available to Amd within six seconds (a value that is hard-coded in the Amd sources), Amd will timeout that mount attempt and mark it as a failed mount. If a mount is deferred, users have no choice but to wait for the information to be available. If the information is not available and the mount is marked as failed, administrators should investigate why Amd could not contact the remote host. It is often the result of a severed network or a downed NFS server.

A Quick Example: */home map*

In this section you can see a complete but simple example of configuring and using Amd. Consider a mount map used to consolidate users' home directories. We have three users:

- Martha, whose home directory is /raid1/users/martha on host opus
- Erez, whose home directory resides on /n/jin/u/zing/erez on host shekel
- A dummy user X11, whose home may reside in one of two directories: /usr/X11R6 on Linux hosts, or /usr/openwin on Solaris hosts

---

TIP It is often useful for administrators to define dummy user homes such as X11 for their user community to use in search paths. Users do not have to know where X11 binaries reside exactly on each host. Instead, they can simply add ~X11/bin to their *PATH* environment variable.

A Sample *amd.home* Map File

The mount map containing the information about the above three user homes is called amd.home, and Amd will serve it under the automounted directory /home, as shown in Listing 8.5.

Listing 8.5 Contents of map file /etc/amd.home

```
/defaults   type:=nfs;opts:=nosuid,quota,intr,rw

martha      -rhost:=opus;rfs:=/raid1/users;sublink:=${key} \
            host!=${rhost};type:=nfs \
            host==${rhost};type:=link

erez        -rhost:=shekel;rfs:=/n/jin/u/zing;sublink:=${key} \
            host!=${rhost} \
            host==${rhost};type:=link

X11         os==linux;type:=link;fs:=/usr/X11R6 \
            os==solaris2;type:=link;fs:=/usr/openwin
```

Listing 8.5 contains four keys, each with its own set of locations. The first key, /defaults, is a special one. It sets default values to use in the rest of the map, such as mount options, mount types, and more:

type:=nfs   Says that the default mount type is NFS

opts:=   Sets several NFS mount options:

nosuid   Is a security option set so that no set-UID binaries can execute with their set-UID bit set

quota   Turns on file system quotas over NFS

intr   Allows processes to interrupt access to the mounted file system using Ctrl+C

rw   Allows both reading and writing of files in mounted file systems

Entry for User Martha

The entry for Martha has three lines. These three lines constitute one entry: the backslash (\) tells Amd that these lines are part of the same entry.

- The first line starts with a dash (-) and lists entry-specific defaults. These override defaults specified for the whole map in /defaults. The defaults we set here are the name of the remote host (*rhost*) and the name of the remote file system on that host (*rfs*); we also state that the actual directory of Martha's home is a sub-directory (*sub-link*) of the remote file system, and that the value of that subdirectory is the same as that of the key "martha" (*${key}*). This will make Amd use the path name /raid1/users/martha to resolve the automounted path name /home/martha.

- The second line says that if the current hostname (*host*) is not the same as the remote host, you should use an NFS mount.

- The third line handles the case of accessing /home/martha on the local host and says to use a simple symbolic link (type:=link) without having to perform a remote NFS mount, because the /raid1/users file system is locally mounted.

Entry for User Erez

The entry for Erez is similar to that of Martha's with two exceptions:

- We list the remote host and remote file system for this user's home.

- We do not state explicitly that the second line should use an NFS-type mount, because this is the default for the whole map.

Entry for User X11

The entry for user X11 uses symbolic links to one of two directories:

- The first line of this entry says that if we are running on a Linux host, /home/X11 will resolve to /usr/X11R6. This is the meaning of the os==linux selector.

- The second line will be interpreted only if the first line failed to match. It says that if we are running on a Solaris host, we should resolve /home/X11 to /usr/openwin.

> **TIP** In accordance with volume mounting rules, if neither location matches its selectors, an error is returned to the user trying to access /home/X11. It is useful in such cases to provide a catch-all location that contains no selectors: `type:=link;fs:=/usr/X11`.

Starting Amd

To start Amd with this map, we can run

```
[root]# amd -l /var/log/amd -a /n /home /etc/amd.home
```

This tells Amd to log any messages in the file /var/log/amd, to perform temporary mounts under /n, and to serve an automounted map in /home whose entries are defined in the file /etc/amd.home.

> **TIP** Name automounted maps in relation to the automounted directories they will be served on. The most common naming convention is amd.*foo* for a map served under */foo*.

A better method of starting Amd is to place all startup options in a configuration file /etc/amd.conf, as shown in Listing 8.6.

Listing 8.6 Contents of the /etc/amd.conf file for the above Amd startup options

```
# define global options
[global]
auto_dir =  /n
log_file =  /var/log/amd

# define one map
[ /home ]
map_name =  /etc/amd.home
```

Then you can start Amd with

```
[root]# amd -F /etc/amd.conf
```

Since the default configuration file is looked for in /etc/amd.conf, you can even omit the -F argument and start Amd with the simple command

```
[root]# amd
```

The Amd
Automounter

PART 2

> ***TIP*** The use of a configuration file is preferred because it supports many more startup options and features than are available by using Amd's command line options. Also, when the number of startup options grows large, it is impractical to list all of them on one line. Administrators often prefer to use a configuration file where they can also insert comments and experiment with alternatives.

Checking Amd's Built-In Support

A useful way to find out which features Amd supports on a local host and what it detected about them is to ask Amd to provide verbose information, as shown in Listing 8.7.

Listing 8.7   Finding out about compiled support in Amd

```
[ezk]$ amd -v
Copyright (c) 1997-2000 Erez Zadok
Copyright (c) 1990 Jan-Simon Pendry
Copyright (c) 1990 Imperial College of Science, Technology & Medicine
Copyright (c) 1990 The Regents of the University of California.
am-utils version 6.0.3 (build 5).
Built by ezk@vir.cs.columbia.edu on date Sat Aug 28 21:29:58 EDT 2000.
cpu=i686 (little-endian), arch=i386, karch=i686.
full_os=linux, os=linux, osver=2.2, vendor=redhat.
Map support for: root, passwd, union, nisplus, ldap, hesiod, nis, ndbm,
                 file, error.
AMFS: nfs, link, nfsx, nfsl, host, linkx, program, union, inherit, ufs,
      cdfs, pcfs, auto, direct, toplvl, error.
FS: iso9660, nfs, vfat, ext2.
Network 1: wire="lab-net.cs.columbia.edu" (netnumber=128.59.10).
Network 2: wire="wireless.cs.columbia.edu" (netnumber=128.59.8).
```

After wasting four lines on copyright information, we get to the useful stuff. In order of each line, they are as follows:

1. The version of the am-utils package and how many times it was built.

2. Who built this version and when.

3. The CPU type, general architecture, kernel architecture, and endianess of the host.

4. The name of the operating system, its version, and the OS vendor.

5. List of map services supported by this Amd. These describe the different types of input Amd can use to read map information, such as YP, NIS+, LDAP, Hesiod servers, plain files, and more.

6. List of automounted file systems (AMFS) supported. These usually include generic names for file systems, such as NFS and UFS (Unix File System), and are mapped to the physical file systems listed in the next line. Also included here are special file systems supported entirely within Amd, such as multi-NFS (nfsx), NFS and symlink (nfsl), link with target validation (linkx), and more. All are described in detail in Chapter 10, "Automounter Maps."

7. Physical file systems supported: iso9660 used for the generic mount type cdfs, nfs, vfat for pcfs, and ext2 used for ufs.

8. Finally, a list of all detected active networks on the host running Amd, with their network names and numbers.

> **WARNING** Make sure your system runs Amd from the am-utils 6.0.2 distribution or newer. *All* older versions of Amd (from am-utils, the UPL series, or original version) contained several serious security holes that allow remote attackers to gain root access on systems running a vulnerable version of Amd! You can find out more information about this problem in the CERT advisory and incident notes, available from http://www.am-utils.org/.

Amd is an RPC server that registers itself with the local host's portmapper. This allows other programs to access Amd's services using the RPC system. One such program is Amq, a tool that can check, report, and change the status of a running Amd process.

Using Amq to Check Amd's Status

To check the status of a running Amd, use Amq:

```
[ezk]$ amq
/                root    "root"              shekel:(pid291)
/home            toplvl  /etc/amd.home       /home
/home/X11        link    ./usr/X11R6         /usr/X11R6
/home/martha     nfs     opus:/raid1/users   /n/raid1/users/martha
```

Amq shows the information about the current running automounter. The first line shows the topmost (root) entry that Amd maintains. This is a virtual entry from which Amd instantiates specific automounted directories such as /home, listed in the second line. The first line also includes the hostname on which this Amd process runs (shekel), and its process ID (291). The second line says that /home is an automounted path name served by the contents of the file /etc/amd.home.

The remaining two lines say that two automounted entries inside /home are active—for users X11 and Martha, respectively. The former is found locally in /usr/X11R6 and is a simple symlink. The latter is NFS-mounted off of host opus's partition /raid1/users, but the actual entry is satisfied by the full path name /n/raid1/users/martha. The /n path component comes from definition of the temporary mount directory (-a command line option or auto_dir in the amd.conf file), and the last component is due to the use of *sub-link* in that map entry's definition.

To check on the status of a specific entry, give Amq the path name of the entry on the command line:

```
[ezk]$ amq /home/martha
What          Uid  Getattr Lookup RdDir RdLnk Statfs Mounted@
/home/martha 0    71768   0      0     462   0      99/09/18 23:42:49
```

This tells us when the entry was initially mounted and some additional file statistics such as the number of times the entry was traversed (readlink) and the number of times its attributes such as permission mode bits were retrieved (get attributes).

Using Amq to Change Amd's State

Often, administrators wish to add new entries to mount maps. For example, if you have a new user, David, whose home directory is opus:/n/opus/u/foria/david, then you can edit the amd.home file and add this entry:

```
david      -rhost:=opus;rfs:=/n/opus/u/foria;sublink:=${key} \
           host!=${rhost};type:=nfs \
           host==${rhost};type:=link
```

Now that you have edited the amd.home file, you can tell Amd to re-read the map file so it finds the new entry. To do so, use the -f option to Amq:

```
[ezk]$ amq -f
```

The -f option instructs Amd to flush its current maps and re-read them. After Amd flushes and re-reads the maps, you can access David's home directory as /home/david.

> **WARNING** Amd can take an arbitrarily long time to re-read its maps, as it may have to contact remote servers such as NIS or Hesiod. After you issue the flush command (amq -f), wait a few seconds before attempting to access new entries. To be sure, check the Amd log file for entries such as "reload #2 of map amd.home succeeded."

Amd does not touch any existing mounts after it reads an updated map, even if some entries were removed. In addition, a map's key may have stayed the same, but the volume that satisfies it could have changed. This can happen, for example, when a user's home directory is moved (as often happens when disks fill up and administrators move some users' home directories to new disks). If Amd had the user's old home already mounted, it will not remount it from the new location, even if you reloaded the maps using the Amq flush command. To change the mounted entry to the new location, Amd must first unmount it. This can be done by sending Amd an unmount command for a given entry:

```
[ezk]$ amq -u /home/ezk
```

Amq is a useful tool. It can check the state of a running Amd and report a variety of information. Amq can force Amd to load new maps, flush old ones, turn on/off debugging and logging at various levels of verbosity, and more. With Amq, you will rarely have to restart Amd. Amq will help you see what Amd is doing and debug it when necessary. More details about Amq are given in Chapter 11, "Runtime Automounter Administration."

In Sum

Amd is a useful tool that helps administrators centralize and automate the mounting of many NFS servers. Administrators maintain Amd maps in one place and can distribute them throughout a site using services such as NIS, LDAP, and more. Amd mounts remote servers on demand and unmounts unused ones after a period of disuse. With Amd, administrators can provide uniform naming for common locations, such as users' home directories, irrespective of the physical locations of those directories on the network.

Amd reads startup configuration parameters from a configuration file and manages a set of mount points, each with an associated mount map. Mount maps tell Amd which servers and file systems to mount, how, and what name to give them on the local system. To speed up its performance and improve its reliability, Amd performs many actions in the background. Amd's asynchronous RPC component dispatches requests to local and remote kernels, as well as replies to RPC messages from the kernel and remote users.

Amq is Amd's query and control tool. It can be used to find out about features supported by Amd, list active mounts, reload mount maps, force the unmounting of existing mounts, and much more.

The Amd Automounter

PART 2

9

The Amd
Configuration File

Amd began its development much like other Unix programs, with few features available. At the time, command-line interface (CLI) options were popular methods to select different behavior for the same program. Often, the name of the CLI option or switch was related to its meaning: -d for debugging, -h for help, -f for input file, etc. However, as programs increase in complexity and new features are added, CLIs quickly reach their practical limitations; you run out of one-letter options and begin assigning options whose meaning is not immediately obvious from the option letter selected.

Also, during the development years of Amd, many options were available only by compiling special code. There were no runtime options to turn such features on or off. For these reasons I decided to create a runtime configuration file for Amd. This has several benefits:

- The file lists all of the configuration parameters for a running Amd process. You may use multiple files for different configurations.

- The names of the options are full (but short) phrases that are much easier to remember than single letters.

- Administrators may place comments explaining particular choices of options.

- It is easier to extend the syntax of such a configuration file and add newer parameters.

- You no longer have to compile special features into Amd. A single binary includes all available features, and those can be turned on or off and configured as needed by the configuration file.

TIP For backward compatibility, all of the older CLI options are supported by the configuration file. However, many new features are only available via the configuration file. Therefore, I highly recommended that administrators use Amd configuration files exclusively.

This chapter covers the syntax and features in the Amd configuration file. This file is used to set default parameters for the running Amd process, to define mount maps and their locations, and more.

Creeping Featurisms (or *"Freeping Creaturisms"*)

Software continues to get more complex every day. Software engineering experts who object to the ever-growing list of features in programs, and the way they "sneak up" on you, coined the term *creeping featurisms*. A field of software engineering called *runtime configuration management* advocates simplifying the configuration of large and complex software systems using mechanisms such as configuration files (i.e., amd.conf) and command-line query and control tools (such as Amq). Remembering many command-line options is hard. Typing them all on one line is even harder. Often, administrators resort to creating startup wrapper scripts that execute complex programs and list all of their options in the script. In a sense, this is no different from having a configuration file. The latter, however, is much more manageable.

As food for thought, I leave you with this story of an IT recruiter interviewing a candidate:

Recruiter: "Can you list all the options used by /bin/ls and their meaning?"

Candidate: "BSD options or System V?"

Recruiter: "You got the job!"

Mixing Command-Line Options with a Configuration File

Amd supports many features as command-line interface (CLI) options. The command in Listing 9.1 prints Amd's typical usage.

Listing 9.1   Amd's command-line options

```
[ezk]$ amd -H
Usage: amd [-nprvHS] [-a mount_point] [-c cache_time] [-d domain]
[-k kernel_arch] [-l logfile|"syslog[:facility]"]
[-t timeout.retrans] [-w wait_timeout] [-C cluster_name]
[-o op_sys_ver] [-O op_sys_name]
[-F conf_file] [-T conf_tag] [-y nis-domain]
[-x {no}{all,debug,error,fatal,info,map,stats,user,warn,warning}]
[-D {no}{all,amq,daemon,fork,full,info,mtab,str,test,trace}]
[directory mapname [-map_options]] ...
```

Since more options are available using the runtime configuration file, those can be stored in a file that Amd will read at startup time. The simplest form of starting Amd is to give it no options on the command line. The following command will look for an Amd configuration file in /etc/amd.conf and use it if it exists. Otherwise, Amd will print the usage string shown in Listing 9.1 and exit:

```
[root]# amd
```

To tell Amd to use any other configuration file at start time, specify it using the -F option:

```
[root]# amd -F /usr/local/lib/myamu.conf
```

You may specify both command-line options and an Amd configuration file at startup time. For consistency, however, Amd will always process all CLI options first, then process the configuration file. For example, the following two commands produce the same behavior, regardless of the arbitrary list of options listed as *options1* and *options2*:

```
amd options1 -F /etc/amd.conf options2

amd options1  options2 -F /etc/amd.conf
```

For example, if your /etc/amd.conf file contains this text:

```
[global]
log_file = /var/log/amd
```

The Amd Automounter

PART 2

and you start Amd as follows:

    [root]# **amd -F /etc/amd.conf -l /tmp/amd.log**

or

    [root]# **amd -l /tmp/amd.log -F /etc/amd.conf**

then the actual log file used would be /var/log/amd because the path name specified in the configuration file supersedes the one specified on the command line.

> *TIP*   Avoid mixing CLI options and an Amd configuration file, as it can become confusing. The Amd configuration file supports all CLI options, and then some. Your life as an administrator will be considerably easier if you just use the Amd configuration file—only one place to look to see how your Amd is configured.

Structure of the Amd Configuration File

The syntax of the Amd configuration file was modeled after the Samba configuration file smb.conf. Major sections that correspond to the same item begin with a keyword enclosed within square brackets:

    [global]

or

    [/home]

Individual configuration parameters are of the form

    key = *value*

where *key* is a predefined name of a parameter and *value* is the value assigned to that parameter. Additional key-value pairs must appear on their own line. The following parsing rules apply to the configuration file:

- Comment lines begin with the "#" character and are ignored.
- Blank lines are ignored.
- Lines containing only *whitespace* (spaces and Tab characters) are ignored.
- The term *global* and the mount point names must appear on a separate line, surrounded by square brackets.
- The entry for [global] must appear only once in the Amd configuration file.
- The same mount point (specified inside a []) may not be defined more than once.

- Whitespace inside the square brackets is ignored.
- Mount point names must be absolute path names beginning with the "/" character.
- All other lines must be of the form *key = value:*
  - Whitespace around either side of the "=" character is ignored.
  - Consecutive whitespace characters in *value* are treated as one space character.
  - To include whitespace verbatim in value, it must be double-quoted with a pair of " " characters.
- Only predefined keys are allowed.
- Some keys have a limited set of allowed values (i.e., yes or no). Only recognized values are allowed.

Any key-value pairs that appear after the term [global] (but before the next set of []) define parameters that apply globally to the running Amd. Any key-value pairs that appear after a mount point term such as [/home] define values that apply only to the /home mount point.

> **TIP** Place your [global] section first. It is possible for the [global] entry and its key-value pairs to appear after one or more mount point sections. This will cause the parameters defined in [global] to affect only those mount points that appear afterward. Since this can be confusing—especially if coupled with a mix of command-line options and a configuration file—it is best avoided.

The rules for where and how many times key-value pairs appear are as follows:

- Some keys can only appear in the [global] section.
- Some keys can appear only in mount point sections.
- Some keys may appear in either section. In this case, the entry in the map-specific section supersedes the global one, but only for that mount point.
- All keys may be listed more than once. In that case, the last one within the same section supersedes the previous ones.

To ensure consistent and reliable behavior, Amd checks that the above rules are obeyed when starting up. If Amd detects a syntax error, it will print a detailed error message specifying the line number in the configuration file where the error occurred and the nature of the error, and it will refuse to run.

In the rest of this chapter, we describe all possible Amd configuration file parameters. We first break parameters into the categories based on their availability: common, global, or map-specific parameters. Since most parameters are global, we further subdivide those into sets of related parameters. We begin each set of related parameters with a short table summarizing the parameters' default value and possible values, and then we describe each parameter in detail.

TIP   It is not easy to remember the default values for all of the configuration parameters. It is useful, therefore, to list keys with their default values in your amd.conf file, even if those values would not change Amd's behavior. Alternatively, you could leave commented-out entries explaining what the default behavior is. The am-utils distribution (available from www.am-utils.org) includes a scripts directory containing a sample template configuration file called amd.conf-sample that can be used as a starting point to write your own.

Common Configuration Parameters

Common parameters are those that may appear in either the [global] section or any mount-point-specific section (see Table 9.1). If they appear in both, then the value in the map-specific section overrides the one in the global section, for that mount point only.

Table 9.1   Common Parameters

Parameter	Default	Possible Values
browsable_dirs	no	yes, no, full
map_options	None	cache:=all
map_type	Search all types in the order of Possible Values	passwd, hesiod, ldap, union, nisplus, nis, ndbm, file, error
mount_type	nfs	nfs, autofs
search_path	None	/local:/etc:/usr/share/amdmaps

browsable_dirs

The directory that Amd manages is the automount point, say, /home. This mount point appears like a normal directory, but what is special about it is that the entries within it cannot be resolved until they are accessed—or automounted. Because entries do not appear before they are mounted, those entries cannot be listed by programs such as /bin/ ls. Users often like to see the entries inside directories, automounted or otherwise, so they can use file browsers such as Midnight Commander or Gnome. If the entries are not visible, however, users cannot naturally browse those entries that represent directories.

Amd, the automounter, knows which entries are supposed to appear under /home, because those are the keys listed in the *map file* that is attached to the /home mount point (e.g., amd.home). Since Amd is acting as a file server for the automounted points, it can satisfy directory-listing requests from users by returning a list of known entries in its maps. The browsable_dirs flag determines if and how Amd lists directory entries to users. By default, entries are not listed. If the flag is set to yes, then Amd will list entries to users.

Consider the amd.src map in Listing 9.2, mounted on /src.

Listing 9.2   Sample map mounted on /src

```
/defaults    type:=nfs;sublink:=${key}

X11          rhost:=shekel;rfs:=/proj/X11R6

Kernel       rhost:=opus;rfs:=/src2/linux

projects/*  rhost:=iron;rfs:=/usr/src;sublink:=${/key}
```

The important parts to note about the map in Listing 9.2 are not the values of the keys, but the keys themselves. Note that two keys contain the "/" character, a character that is illegal in Unix file names because it is the default directory character separator. When browsable_dirs is off, trying to list entries in /src yields only the listing for the current and parent directories:

```
[ezk]$ ls -a /home
.  ..
```

If you set browsable_dirs to yes in your amd.conf, you can see all entries that represent true single entries within /src:

```
[ezk]$ ls -a /src
.  .. X11   kernel      projects
```

Note that you did not see the entry for /defaults, nor the "/*" component of the projects/* entry (that entry is called a wildcard entry, and its use is described in detail in Chapter 10, "Automounter Maps"). That is because the browsable directories flag, when set to yes, only shows single real entries corresponding to Unix directory entries. To see all entries in a map, regardless of their Unix validity, set browsable_dirs to full. With the full listing option on, you see all entries:

```
[ezk]$ ls -a /src
.  .. X11   kernel     projects/*  /defaults
```

Note that setting this option to full can confuse directory listing and browsing programs such as /bin/ls, because single directory entries are not supposed to include "/" characters. For that reason, browsable_dirs is best set to yes.

WARNING   Mount storms! If you turn on browsable_dirs and then try to list all the entries in an automounted directory, Amd may attempt to mount all the entries at once. This condition is known as a _mount storm_ and can overwhelm your system. For more information, see the section titled "Mount Storms" in Chapter 11, "Runtime Automounter Administration."

Despite the possibility of mount storms, browsable directories can be very helpful, especially in automounted directories where the number of entries is small. Fewer entries minimize the chances of mount storms. One particularly useful application for browsable automounted directories is in shell expansions such as bash. For the example in Listing 9.2, you could simply type

```
[ezk]$ ls /src/k
```

and then hit the Tab key to complete the entry to /src/kernel.

map_options

Map options are parameters that affect the behavior of Amd for a given map or automount point. The default value of map_options is

```
type:=toplvl;cache:=mapdefault;fs:=${map}
```

This means the following:

type:=toplvl   Is a top-level map, an Amd mount point attached to a map file. Only Amd automount points can be of this type.

cache:=mapdefault   Defines the caching policy for entries in this map, for this mount point. This value is defined by the precompiled behavior for that type of map. For example, NIS maps' default caching policy is to cache all entries, while NIS+ maps' default caching policy is to cache entries incrementally. The default caching type for all maps is described in Chapter 10. The types of caching policies available are described shortly below in "Map Caching Options."

fs:=${map} Specifies that the default file system to mount is listed in the map file itself. The *fs* variable, described in detail in Chapter 10, denotes the path name of the file system for a given type. For example, for an NFS file system (type:=nfs), the *fs* variable may have the value /n/fist/src, which is the NFS path name to mount in a given map entry.

Options specified in map_options override the precompiled default (the latter cannot be changed). Amd prepends options listed in map_options to the precompiled default. Amd's parsing rules look for the first matching entry in a list of options. Therefore, prepended entries override the default ones.

In practice, only a handful of options are useful for use with map_options, because only a few options are meaningful for the automount point itself, which is of type NFS and is served by Amd:

type The type of the automount point, always toplvl (a top-level mount)

cache Caching policy options, described below in "Map Caching Options"

fs The file system that serves this top-level mount point

opts NFS mount options, such as rw (read-write), ro (read-only), and more, described in Chapter 10.

TIP Do not confuse map_options with /defaults options. Options specified in map_options affect only the automount point, which is always a special NFSv2 mount served by Amd. Options specified in the /defaults map entry affect mounts performed by Amd as specified in the map itself—usually below or outside the automount point. These can be many types of mounted file systems: NFS, ext2fs, iso9660, vfat, and more. If you make a mistake, however, and list options in map_options that do not apply to the automount map itself, Amd will ignore those and print a warning message in its logs.

Map Caching Options

The following six values can be given to the cache parameter, and define different caching policies:

- all
- inc
- sync
- re or regexp
- none
- default or mapdefault

all   When Amd starts, it reads the complete map into memory and caches all key-value pairs listed in the map. This means that when a user process looks up a path name in an automount point, Amd already knows what it has to do to satisfy the lookup request; Amd does not have to consult the map to find the path name.

With this option, all entries are cached ahead of time. The problem is how to find out when the administrator made changes to the map's source. Amd was designed such that it can find out about new entries that were added to the source map after Amd cached the map. If a new entry was added to a map, Amd will find out about it even with the cache policy of all. This is done by searching the cache, and if an entry is not found there, Amd tries to look it up in the source of the map. If found in the source of the map, Amd then uses this new entry and adds it to the cache. If Amd fails to find an entry in its cache, and the cache type was all, Amd checks the modification time of the map with the information service providing the map (say NIS, Hesiod, etc.). If the modification time is newer than the cached map, Amd flushes its map and reloads it from its source.

Reloading Maps Safely

Whenever Amd has to reload a map, whether the action was the result of human intervention or an automatic behavior, Amd endeavors to ensure the validity of the data being reloaded. When the map is served by a service such as NIS, Amd depends on the network and the NIS server (ypserv) to function perfectly. When they do not, it is possible for corrupt maps to be reloaded in place of good ones. For this reason, Amd performs the following safety checks when reloading maps:

1. "Ping" the map service to see if it is up and responding. This involves the following:

   - For file maps, try to lstat the file.

   - For NIS maps, check if the *map order* (version number) can be retrieved.

   - For Hesiod maps, perform a sample query for /defaults.

   - For other maps, Amd skips this test. Future versions of Amd may add ping tests to other map services.

2. Amd begins loading the map one entry at a time. New entries are loaded into a temporary buffer.

> **3.** If any error, however minute, occurred during the loading of the map's entries, Amd discards the temporary buffer.
>
> **4.** If no errors occurred, Amd discards the current map and replaces it with the values from the temporary buffer.

The problem is that with all, Amd cannot find out when an *existing* entry has changed in the map: only new entries that were not cached before can trigger a map reload. Amd, however, will always find cached entries when they are looked up again, even if they have changed (or been removed) in the source map. To fix this problem, Amd's cache must be flushed manually. To flush the cache, you have two options:

- Send Amd a HUP signal: `skill -HUP amd`. (The `skill` tool is similar to the `kill` program, only that `skill` can find the PID of the program symbolically, given its name.)
- Use Amq to instruct Amd to flush its caches and reload all maps: `amq -f`.

Amq is the preferred method to flush caches and reload maps because it does not depend on having the `skill` program handy or figuring out what the process ID (PID) of the master running Amd is. With `skill`, you run the danger of sending a HUP signal to all running Amd processes. If, say, Amd were in the process of mounting several other file systems, there would be multiple Amd processes in the background, each handling a single mount. Sending a HUP signal to all of the backgrounded processes will terminate them, resulting in failed mounts.

> **NOTE**   With the all option, Amd will pre-load all entries in the map. If you have particularly large maps, this can consume a lot of memory on each host. Specifically, Amd may read and cache many entries that may never be accessed. In that case, a better caching option may be inc.

inc   Here, Amd does not cache any entries from the map ahead of time, but incrementally. Amd does not read any entries from the map until a lookup request occurs. When a user process looks up a path name, Amd searches the map for an entry matching that of the looked-up entry. For example, consider an automount point /home, whose corresponding Amd map is served by an NIS map named amd.home. If a user process looks up the path name /home/tom, Amd will first look to see if the entry is already in the cache. Initially, the entry would not be in the cache. This is called a *cache miss*. Amd will then contact the NIS server bound to the local host and ask for the value string matching a key named tom. If the entry is found, Amd will cache it in its internal map cache and then proceed to process the entry based on the value of the key.

After the first lookup of the key, subsequent lookups are satisfied from the cache without consulting the map information service (NIS in this example). This is also called a *cache hit*.

The incremental caching option has the same problem as the all option: Amd cannot tell when cached entries have changed in the source map. This is where the next option, sync, comes in handy.

sync   This option tells Amd to synchronize the cache with the map each time a cached entry is used. Amd will check the modification time of the map before using cached entries. If a newer map exists, Amd will flush its cache and look up the entry in the newer map.

The options inc and sync are particularly useful together. Using both, you can instruct Amd to create a synchronized, incremental cache. Note, however, that with the sync option, Amd will contact your map service (say, NIS) each time it looks up an entry. If your map service provider (e.g., the ypserv program for NIS maps) is down or slow, Amd will be slow too, or hang.

To Cache or Not to Cache?

That is an age-old question. If you cache, you do not need to look up entries in the source of the cache. This can speed up lookups as they are served from fast in-memory cache. However, if the source of the data has changed, your cache may become incoherent, resulting in the use of stale cache entries.

If you do not cache, you are guaranteed to use valid information at all times. However, you pay a penalty in accessing the (usually slow) source of the cache each time an entry is looked up. These penalties accumulate even if the cache's source rarely changes and you get the same data each time you look up an entry in the cache's source.

What should you do? It depends on your site's conditions. If your maps rarely change, and your networks and services are reliable, use the all caching option. If your machines have limited amounts of memory and your maps are large, or your maps change often, you may choose the combination options inc,sync instead.

re and *regexp*   If one of these two synonymous options is used, then Amd treats map keys as egrep-style regular expressions. If it is not specified, then Amd performs regular string matching on the keys. With the regexp option, Amd enumerates the entire map and loads it into the cache first. Amd then performs key lookups using the system's regexp library. Using regular expressions in Amd maps is an advanced topic, which we discuss in more detail in Chapter 12, "Advanced Amd Uses."

none   This option tells Amd not to cache any entries. Each time an entry is looked up, Amd will query the map service for it. Use this option if your maps change very often or your machines do not have enough memory to cache the maps, but your networks are reliable.

default and *mapdefault*   These two options are synonymous. They tell Amd to use the caching options that were predefined (and precompiled) for the given map type. These can be any combination of the five options listed above: all, inc, sync, re (or regexp), and none. Note that some combinations may not make much sense, such as none,all. In that case, later options take precedence.

An Example Using *map_options* to Set Caching Policy

The syntax for map_options is as follows:

    map_options = *options;options;…;options*

where *options* is a semicolon-delimited list of options, each of which may use Amd's map syntax for assigning options (described in Chapter 10). For example,

    map_options = cache:=all;browsable

Note that the leftmost "=" symbol separates the map_options key from its value, while the second ":=" sequence separates the cache variable from its own value, all. The semi-colon separates the cache variable and its value from the next map option, browsable. The latter is an alternate form of turning on browsable directories, which is also described earlier in this chapter in the section "browsable_dirs."

As mentioned above, the default value of map_options is

    type:=toplvl;cache:=mapdefault;fs:=${map}

So if you, say, use the following in your amd.conf file:

    map_options = cache:=inc,sync;opts:=intr

then Amd will prepend that string to the default one, thus using the following map options:

    cache:=inc,sync;opts:=intr;type:=toplvl;cache:=mapdefault;fs:=${map}

The Amd
Automounter

PART 2

Note that `cache` appears twice in that string. However, Amd parses options from left to right so it will always find the first set of cache options and will never use the second one (which is also the default). This will instruct Amd to use an incremental, synchronized cache.

We also added the option `opts:=intr`. This tells Amd to allow users to interrupt (hit Ctrl+C) when automounting entries. The `intr` option is an NFS mount option.

map_type

The `map_type` parameter specifies the source information service that provides the data for maps to Amd. This section introduces the types of maps that Amd can use. Chapter 10 provides more details on map services: examples using each map, and how to populate an information source with a given list of map keys and their values. In addition, Chapter 14, "Building and Installing the Automounter Software," shows how to include additional support for these information services in your Amd.

Amd recognizes the following sources of information:

passwd   Map entries are specially configured based on the home directory entries in the site's `/etc/passwd` file.

hesiod   Maps are read from a Hesiod server. Hesiod is an information service system developed at MIT and based on DNS.

ldap   Maps are read from a Lightweight Directory Access Protocol server. LDAP is a new information service intended to replace Hesiod, NIS, and NIS+.

union   A special map that works in conjunction with the Union file system (described in Chapter 10). This map can join the contents of two or more directories through the automounter, making them appear as one.

nisplus   Maps are read from an NIS+ server. NIS+ is a hierarchical information service developed by Sun Microsystems and is mostly available for Solaris hosts.

nis   Maps are read from an NIS (formerly YP or Yellow Pages) server. While NIS was also developed by Sun Microsystems, it is very popular and is available on Linux as well as many other systems.

ndbm   Maps are read from DBM, NDBM (New DBM), or GDBM (Gnu DBM) files. DBM is a fast indexing system that hashes keys in a binary format, so they can be looked up much faster than a simple scan through the whole file.

file   Maps are read from simple files. This parameter is often used with the `search_path` parameter described below.

By far, file and nis maps are the most popular types of maps used by Amd. An additional map type, error, is used internally by Amd. It indicates that an information service for the map could not be found. Users of Amd cannot assign the error type to Amd maps.

The map_type parameter is optional. If not specified, Amd will try to read the map from each of the above information services until one succeeds, in the following order: passwd, hesiod, ldap, union, nisplus, nis, ndbm, file, and error. Note that error is the last one in the list, because if Amd was unable to initialize any of the other map information services, an error must have occurred. This can indicate, for example, that the maps are missing from the system, that the network is down, or that the remote information servers are not functioning properly.

With an amd.conf file you can specify the map information service type separately for each map. You can also choose not to list the map_type parameter, in which case all possible types will be tried in order. You cannot, however, list a subset of map types to use in a map: it must be one of the listed types, or all of them when map_type is not used.

To find which map information services your Amd supports, run Amd with the -v option and check for the line starting with "Map support for" (see Listing 9.3).

Listing 9.3   Checking which map information services Amd supports

```
[ezk]$ amd -v
Copyright (c) 1997-2000 Erez Zadok
Copyright (c) 1990 Jan-Simon Pendry
Copyright (c) 1990 Imperial College of Science, Technology & Medicine
Copyright (c) 1990 The Regents of the University of California.
am-utils version 6.0.3 (build 5).
Built by ezk@vir.cs.columbia.edu on date Sat Aug 28 21:29:58 EDT 2000.
cpu=i686 (little-endian), arch=i386, karch=i686.
full_os=linux, os=linux, osver=2.2, vendor=redhat.
Map support for: root, passwd, union, nis, ndbm, file, error.
AMFS: nfs, link, nfsx, nfsl, host, linkx, program, union, inherit, ufs,
      cdfs, pcfs, auto, direct, toplvl, error.
FS: iso9660, nfs, vfat, ext2.
Network 1: wire="lab-net.cs.columbia.edu" (netnumber=128.59.10).
Network 2: wire="wireless.cs.columbia.edu" (netnumber=128.59.8).
```

In this example, we see that Amd was compiled with map support for five actual information services: passwd, union, nis, ndbm, and file. The error map type appears in the end as usual. An additional internal map service, root, appears first; it is a placeholder for the very top automount node that Amd uses to instantiate actual maps underneath. The root map type is for internal use only and cannot be used directly by users. Note also that the order in which the map types are listed in the output of amd -v is the same order in which they are searched when the map_type parameter is not specified in the amd.conf file.

In the example of Listing 9.4, we illustrate a typical setup for an amd.conf file: using file-type maps for maps that do not change often and using NIS for a map that changes often.

Listing 9.4 An amd.conf file mixing file and NIS maps

```
[global]
map_type = file

[/src]
map_name = /usr/share/maps/amd.src

[/software]
map_name = /usr/share/maps/amd.soft

[/home]
map_name = amd.home
map_type = nis
```

Listing 9.4 shows a useful mix of file and NIS maps. The default map_type is set to file in the [global] section. This applies to the maps for /src and /software. The /home map, however, overrides the default and uses NIS for the information service. The reasons for doing so are twofold and stem from the expectation that maps containing users' home directories change much more often than maps for sources and software packages:

- File maps are more reliable; files exist on a local disk and can always be read, while NIS maps depend on the network and the remote ypserv daemon to function properly. However, file maps must be distributed to all machines that need them, using file distribution mechanisms such as rdist or rsync. Whenever maps change, they must be distributed as quickly as possible to all machines running Amd to ensure that those machines have the most up-to-date maps. Therefore, to minimize the number of file distributions necessary, maps that change infrequently are more suitable for use as file maps.

- Maps that change often are more suitable for distribution using NIS. If they were distributed as files, the administrators would have to ensure they are updated on all machines running Amd rather frequently. This is impractical in large sites. Instead, to ensure that users' home directories are available to Amd as soon as the users' accounts are created, such large and often-changing maps are better distributed using a network-wide service such as NIS.

mount_type

The `mount_type` parameter specifies what basic file service Amd will use for a given map. There are only two options here: `nfs` or `autofs`. The default mount type is `nfs` and is the traditional method that Amd operates—as an NFS server for the local host. This was introduced in Chapter 8, "Overview of the Amd Automounter." In this mode, each automounted entry is represented by a symbolic link to another directory where a file system was mounted (often a remote NFS partition).

With Autofs, Amd uses an advanced in-kernel file system called *autofs*. This file system has several benefits:

- Mounts are faster because they are handled mostly in the kernel.
- Unmounts are more reliable because the kernel avoids situations that can lead to partially unmounted directories or deadlocks.
- Mounts are performed in-place, directly *inside* the automounted directory.

The use of Autofs with Amd is explored in greater detail in Chapter 13, "Autofs." Chapter 14 shows how to include Autofs support with Amd and your Linux system.

The main reason to set `mount_type` to `nfs` over `autofs` is stability. Amd's NFS service code is old and reliable, albeit limited; Amd's Autofs support is relatively recent and the Autofs protocols in Linux may still be changing. If your Linux system supports Autofs, you can take advantage of its advanced capabilities with Amd. If you are not sure, check www.am-utils.org for the latest information relating to Autofs support in Amd.

The most likely scenario for setting the `mount_type` parameter is one time in the [global] section. That is, if you decided on using `autofs` over `nfs`, you might as well use it for all of your maps. Listing 9.5, however, shows an example mixing the two.

Listing 9.5   Mixing `autofs` and `nfs` in the `mount_type` parameter

```
[global]
mount_type = nfs
map_type = nis

[/src]
map_name = amd.src

[/home]
map_name = amd.home
```

```
[/atest]
map_type = file
map_name = /tmp/amd61.testautofs
mount_type = autofs
```

In this example, we define the default mount_type as nfs, even though it is the default Amd built-in type. Then we use NFS automounts for the /src and /home maps. Finally, we set a test automounted directory, /atest, that uses Autofs style mounts and reads its map from the file /tmp/amd61.testautofs. This example was useful to us while adding Autofs support to Amd: we wanted most maps to work normally and run well, and we just used one test map for Autofs.

NOTE Do not confuse the type of mount set in mount_type with the types of mounts specified in the Amd maps themselves. The mount_type parameter sets the type of mount that Amd serves to the local host's kernel—the automount point. The type of mounts set in the Amd maps, often set with type:=, specifies the type of mount to use when user processes access directories that are *inside* the automount point.

---

search_path

The search_path parameter is often used in conjunction with file maps. This parameter specifies a search path for locating maps in several directories. It is similar to how shells use the $PATH variable to locate programs executed by users: a colon-delimited list of directories.

The search_path parameter is used only when Amd looks for maps in regular files. This can happen in two cases. First, the map_type parameter was set to file. Second, the map_type parameter was not set, and Amd has searched all other map information services that are tried before files.

For security reasons, the search_path parameter may list only absolute path names—those starting with the "/" character. Amd will look for file maps in each directory listed in the search_path parameter, starting with the leftmost directory. If a search path is not specified, and the map is of type file, then the map's name must also be an absolute path name (as shown in Listing 9.4).

> **TIP** Do not use file maps and place the maps on an NFS server partition that is automounted. All maps must be available before Amd starts. Obviously, before Amd starts, automounted directories are not yet available. (This is a typical chicken-and-egg scenario.)

The example in Listing 9.6 shows a combination of several file maps and several search paths.

Listing 9.6 An amd.conf file using the search_path parameter

```
[global]
map_type = file
search_path = /usr/share/maps:/usr/local/share

[/src]
map_name = /usr/lib/amd.src

[/software]
map_type = file
map_name = amd.soft

[/home]
map_name = amd.home
map_type = nis

[/local]
search_path = /etc/local:/usr/share
map_name = amd.local
```

Listing 9.6 illustrates several uses for maps and their search paths:

global Sets the default map type as file, and the search path as /usr/share/ maps/, followed by /usr/local/share/.

/src Gets its map directly from the file /usr/lib/amd.src and, thus, ignores the global search path.

/software Will look for its map in the global search path. Setting the map_type to file here is redundant, because it is also set in [global].

/home Gets its map from NIS directly, because it specifies nis as the map_type.

/local   Will look for the map named amd.local in the directory /etc/local/ and then in the directory /usr/share/. This scenario is particularly useful in large sites with multiple groups, each group controlling its own machines. Administrators can set general-purpose maps such as /src and /home. At the same time, the administrators can allow individual groups to have some control over the Amd maps. In this example, any group that wants to have additional automounted path names can place its own Amd map in, say, /etc/local/amd.local. If that file exists, Amd will start a new automount point under /local. Otherwise, Amd will only start the generic automount points, but not /local.

Global Configuration Parameters

Global parameters are those that may only appear in the [global] section. The vast majority of Amd configuration parameters are global. We categorize them into five groups:

System information   These are parameters of the system that are compiled when the am-utils package is built.

Debugging and logging   These are parameters that can help administrators track the behavior of Amd.

Performance and tuning   These are parameters that administrators can use to improve the performance and stability of Amd.

Information services   These are parameters that affect one or more map information services.

Map-related globals   These are parameters that affect the overall default behavior of Amd for all maps.

The parameters in these five categories are fully explained in the following sections. Each group of parameters opens with a table that shows their typical use and default values. Each parameter explained includes some examples showing how to use them in an Amd configuration file and how that affects the interpretation of Amd's maps.

System Information

System information parameters are automatically detected by am-utils when it is first built. These parameters (see Table 9.2) include the name and version of the operating system, the hardware architecture, and more. These parameters are compiled into the Amd binary, as we describe in Chapter 14.

Sometimes, however, it is necessary to change them. This is useful because all of the parameters in Table 9.2 have equivalent selectors that administrators can use in Amd maps. Amd uses these selectors to pick among several locations in an Amd map entry.

One way to change these configuration parameters is to rebuild the `am-utils` package so it detects the new parameters. However, that may not be possible or desirable for the administrators. It is simpler in such situations to override the compiled-in value in the `amd.conf` file. This section includes useful examples for changing each of the parameters in Table 9.2.

Table 9.2   Global Parameters—System Information

Parameter	Default	Some Possible Values
arch	Host architecture	i386, sparc, alpha
karch	Kernel architecture	i586, i686, sparc64
os	Name of operating system	linux, solaris2, freebsd
osver	Operating system (short) version	2.0, 2.2, 2.3, 2.4
full_os	Full name of operating system with version	linux2.0.36, linux2.2.16, linux2.4.0
vendor	Operating system vendor	redhat, sun, unknown

arch

The host architecture of the running system is often the name of the CPU. For example

i386 For Intel and its derivatives

sparc For Sun's SPARC machines

alpha For DEC's (make that Compaq's) AXP chips

Older versions of Amd used i586 for Pentium-class machines, and i686 for Pentium-PRO machines. If you have such an old Amd binary and cannot rebuild it, you can simply put this in your `amd.conf`:

```
[global]
arch = i386
```

Now you are able to write a single map entry for all Intel-based systems:

```
X11bin      os==linux;type:=link;fs:=/usr/X11.${arch}/bin
```

This example may be part of a /packages map. In this case, users need only put /packages/X11bin in their $PATH environment variable. The map will ensure that the correct host architecture is used for Linux hosts: /usr/X11.i386/bin for Intel-based systems, /usr/X11.sparc/bin for SPARC systems, and so on.

karch

Some systems distinguish between the user-level host architecture (arch), and the kernel-level host architecture (karch). The reason for this difference is that some systems' user-level binaries are binary-compatible with other versions of the operating system, but kernel-level modules are not. On those systems, the value of karch may be different from that of arch.

NOTE This book focuses on Linux. However, Linux is a very homogeneous system even though it runs on many different hardware platforms. Due to that homogeneity of Linux, some Amd examples are better illustrated using other systems. In this section and throughout the rest of this chapter, we use a few such examples.

For example, Sun Microsystems produces many SPARC machines. Most binaries execute across the range of platforms; for these, the host architecture is sun4. Some binaries and kernel modules, however, can run only on the kernel architecture they were designed for:

- sun4u binaries for SPARC Ultra systems
- sun4m binaries for older SPARC multiprocessor systems
- sun4d binaries for packet-switching backplane systems

The karch Amd configuration parameter has its equivalent map variable ${karch}. One typical method to use it is with maps that automatically create paths to kernel-specific binaries without the knowledge of users:

```
kbin      type:=link;fs:=/platform/${karch}
```

If the above example is part of the /binaries map, then the directory /binaries/kbin will point to the correct kernel-architecture directory of binaries on different systems.

Next, let us assume that you have an Amd binary compiled on an Intel-based Pentium system where arch is i386 and karch is i586. You want to run this binary on a Pentium-PRO system where the kernel architecture should be i686, but Amd's compiled-in default is i586. While the Amd binary from an older architecture will work on a newer one, it may report the wrong kernel architecture in your Amd maps, and that can result in incorrect values for the ${karch} variable. To solve this problem, you could rebuild Amd. Easier, however, is to use the same Amd binary on the Pentium-PRO system and set the correct kernel architecture in your amd.conf file:

```
[global]
karch = i686
```

os

The os parameter specifies the name of the operating system as detected by GNU configure during the build of am-utils. The name of the operating system is often close or identical to the value reported by the command uname. When this parameter is changed in the amd.conf file, it affects its equivalent variable in Amd maps, ${os}.

Occasionally, the GNU configure script may pick an undesirable name for the operating system:

- lignux or linux-gnu for some Linux systems
- sunos for Solaris 2 systems

In addition, older versions of Amd used to hard-code the name of the operating system and did not detect it automatically. For example, SunOS 4.*x* systems used sos4 for the os parameter and sos5 on SunOS 5.*x* (Solaris 2) systems. You can override the value of the os parameter on those and other systems to suit your particular needs.

For example, suppose you have a mixture of regular Linux systems and some that are configured in a Beowulf cluster. The cluster may be running very different software tools intended to run in a distributed or parallel environment. Administrators who control all systems might want to create common Amd maps that distinguish between standard and cluster Linux systems. In that case, you can put the following in your amd.conf file on the clustered systems:

```
[global]
os = beowulf
```

With the above in your amd.conf file, you can write a map, for example, that will treat tools used to build and run distributed programs on the cluster, as if they were standard tools. Let us assume that a special version of the GNU C compiler, pgcc, can build binaries that can run on distributed or parallel systems, and that pmake is the parallel version of make that can run on the same cluster. Normally these tools are located in /usr/bin, but on the cluster, they may have been built by hand and installed in /usr/local/cluster /bin. You can write a single map, automounted under /binaries, that will make all tools appear under /binaries, whether running on the cluster or elsewhere, as shown in Listing 9.7.

Listing 9.7   A map example using the overridden amd.conf os parameter

```
/default    type:=link

cc          os==linux;fs:=/usr/bin/gcc \
            os==beowulf;fs:=/usr/local/cluster/bin/pgcc

make        os==linux;fs:=/usr/bin/make \
            os==beowulf;fs:=/usr/local/cluster/bin/pmake
```

The example in Listing 9.7 would create symbolic links to cc and make that point to their standard location on regular Linux systems, and to their special location on clustered Linux systems.

osver

The configuration parameter osver names the version of the operating system. This value is often similar or identical to the value reported by running uname -r. This configuration parameter has an equivalent Amd map variable, ${osver}.

One reason to use this configuration parameter to override the Amd compiled-in default is that you have upgraded your kernel but not the version of Amd running on the system. For example, suppose you upgraded your kernel from version 2.2.16 to 2.4.7. You can tell Amd that the kernel's version is newer in your amd.conf file:

```
[global]
osver = 2.4.7
```

Then you could write an Amd map entry, say, automounted under /sys, which can point to the right location of kernel-loadable modules:

```
/default    type:=link

kmod        os==linux;fs:=/lib/modules/${osver} \
            os==solaris2;fs:=/platform/${karch}/kernel \
            os==freebsd;fs:=/modules
```

Another reason to override the osver parameter is that it may be too specific and you wish to use it more generally. For example, you may have many Linux systems running kernel versions from 2.2.10 to 2.2.16, but you do not wish to write Amd maps that handle each operating system version separately: that is cumbersome and requires constant updating to the maps. Instead, you can override the `osver` parameter to a more generic version, 2.2, in your `amd.conf` file:

```
[global]
osver = 2.2
```

Now you can write more generic maps that select on this operating system version, say, as part of a `/src` map:

```
/defaults    type:=nfs


build        os==linux;osver==2.2;rhost:=lynn;rfs:=/usr/src \
             os==linux;osver==2.4;rhost:=ltest;rfs:=/usr/src \
             os==solaris2;osver==2.7;rhost:=titan;rfs:=/misc/sunsrc
```

The above example is useful in consolidating all builds of software packages in a single location. That way, anyone who builds new software need only remember one directory to unpack and compile software in. The path name `/src/build` will always point to the right location where packages are built, regardless of their physical location:

- Linux 2.2.*x* hosts are served by `lynn:/usr/src`.
- Linux 2.4.*x* hosts are served by `ltest:/usr/src`.
- Solaris 7 hosts are served by `titan:/misc/sunsrc`.

full_os

The `full_os` parameter combines the name and version of the operating system in a concise form. The equivalent variable for use in Amd maps is `${full_os}`.

It might not be immediately apparent why this parameter is needed; one might be able to concatenate the contents of the `os` and `osver` variables in a map as follows:

```
${os}-${osver}
```

The problem, however, is that `${os}` sometimes contains the version of the operating system. For example, on Solaris 2 systems, `${os}` is `solaris2`, so if you were to concatenate these two variables in a map, say in Solaris 8, you will get the value `solaris2-2.8`, which is not the desired result. Instead, the variable `${full_os}` is already configured to include the name and an abbreviated version of the operating system. On Solaris 8 systems the value of `${full_os}` is `solaris2.8`.

One reason to change the value of the parameter `full_os` is that it may not fit your needs. For example, Sun Microsystems used to number the versions of their operating system 2.4, 2.5, and 2.6. After that 2.6 release, Sun began numbering their operating system with single digits: 7, 8, etc. However, the ${full_os} variable would still show the full name and version of the operating system as solaris2.7, solaris2.8, etc. If you work for Sun and do not wish to offend your employer, you may override the value of this variable by setting the full_os parameter in the amd.conf file as follows:

```
[global]
full_os = solaris8
```

Now you can write an Amd map, say, part of the /binaries map, to help users find the locations of the LDAP binaries on the system, as shown in Listing 9.8.

Listing 9.8   A map example using the overridden amd.conf full_os parameter

```
/defaults    type:=link

ldap         os==linux;fs:=/usr/ldap \
             full_os==solaris8;fs:=/opt/SUNWldap/bin \
             os==solaris2;osver==2.7;fs:=/usr/bin \
             fs:=/usr/local/ldap
```

The above map example shows how you can find LDAP binaries always using the common /binaries/ldap path name:

- On Linux systems, the binaries are actually located in /usr/ldap.
- On Solaris 8 systems, when Sun began including a full LDAP distribution, they are part of a package installed in /opt/SUNWldap.
- On Solaris 7 systems, when Sun distributed LDAP partially, they are in /usr/bin.
- On all other systems, including older Solaris systems, it is assumed that the LDAP package was hand built and installed in /usr/local/ldap.

vendor

The vendor configuration parameter also has an Amd map equivalent, ${vendor}. This parameter is the name of the vendor of the system and is detected by the configuration part of am-utils during its build.

For Linux systems running the Red Hat software distribution, the vendor parameter is set to redhat. For Solaris systems running on Sun's SPARC hardware, this parameter is set to sun. For many systems, unfortunately, this parameter is simply set to unknown. The reason for this is often a limitation of the GNU configure script that detects this parameter. The problem is that there could be two or more vendors for many systems: one being the vendor of the operating system software and the other being the vendor of the hardware. For example, it is unclear who the vendor should be for a Red Hat Linux system running on an ALPHA hardware: `redhat`, `dec`, or `compaq`? Because of this potential confusion, you can override the vendor parameter as needed.

Suppose you have an Amd binary from a SuSE Linux system, and you wish to run it on a Red Hat Linux system. However, you want that binary to report its vendor name as `redhat`, not `suse` (perhaps you own some RHAT stocks and feel obligated). You can do so in your `amd.conf` file as follows:

```
[global]
vendor = redhat
```

With this parameter set, you can write an Amd map that sets the name of the release file as follows:

```
release     type:=link;fs:=/etc/${vendor}-release
```

Debugging and Logging

This set of configuration parameters, listed in Table 9.3, allows administrators lots of control over the behavior and tracking of what Amd does. In particular, you can select many different options of verbosity for Amd's normal run mode (logging) and extended verbosity (debugging).

Table 9.3   Global Parameters—Debugging and Logging

Parameter	Default	Possible Values
`log_file`	`/dev/stderr`	`/dev/stderr`, `/var/log/amd`, `syslog`, `syslog:`*facility*
`log_options`	None	`all`, `fatal`, `error`, `user`, `warn`, `info`, `map`, `stats`. (Logging options prepended with no are excluded from being listed.)
`debug_options`	None	`all`, `amq`, `daemon`, `fork`, `full`, `hrtime`, `info`, `mem`, `mtab`, `str`, `readdir`, `test`, `trace`, `xdrtrace`. (Debugging options prepended with no are excluded from being listed.)
`print_version`	no	`yes`, `no`
`pid_file`	`/dev/stdout`	`/dev/stdout`, `/var/run/amd.pid`

The Amd
Automounter

PART 2

Table 9.3 Global Parameters—Debugging and Logging *(continued)*

Parameter	Default	Possible Values
print_pid	no	yes, no
portmap_program	300019	300019, 300020, ..., 300029

Next we describe the parameters in Table 9.3. We briefly describe the following three parameters: log_file, log_options, debug_options, and portmap_program. A more detailed treatment of these three options is provided in Chapter 11.

log_file

The log_file parameter specifies one of three possible methods for Amd to output logging and debugging information:

- /dev/stderr: Amd will log information to the standard error.
- syslog: Amd will log its information using the system logger daemon, syslogd. If you use the syntax syslog:*facility*, Amd will log to the specific facility (sub-type) of the syslog daemon. For more information, consult the manual page for syslog.conf.
- If the log_file parameter is set to an absolute file name, Amd will log all information into that file. This is the most popular method.

For example, Linux systems place logs in the directory /var/log. To be consistent with this standard, set your Amd to log messages in the file /var/log/amd as follows:

```
[global]
log_file = /var/log/amd
```

log_options

Amd can log information about its activities to a designated logging target specified by the log_file parameter. The type of information logged is determined by the value of the log_options parameter. This parameter can control how much information is logged and at what level of verbosity. For example, you can choose to see only critical errors, messages about map-parsing activities, and more. You can choose to see all possible information, or none at all.

Amd logs particular types of activities based on keywords listed in the `log_options` parameter. Those are as follows:

all   This option instructs Amd to log all messages.

debug   This option includes very detailed debugging messages.

error   This option will log non-fatal system errors such as failure to contact a map service or mount an entry.

fatal   These report fatal errors that prevent Amd from functioning normally.

info   These represent informational messages about major activities that Amd performs, such as reloading maps, contacting information servers, etc.

map   This option provides information about map errors such as parsing errors, as well as information about selectors being evaluated.

stats   This option provides a little bit of additional statistical information: remote server uptimes and downtimes.

user   This option provides non-fatal user errors such as map-parsing errors.

warn and **warning**   These are warning messages that are serious, but not fatal enough to warrant shutting down Amd.

The full list of all the logging messages that Amd produces is in Appendix C, "Amd Log and Debug Messages."

The syntax for the value of `log_options` is a comma-delimited list of logging keywords. Each keyword can be prefixed by the string **no** to negate its meaning; this can be used to log all information excluding a certain type.

To log all serious messages through `syslogd`, use this in your `amd.conf` file:

```
[global]
log_file = syslog
log_options = fatal,error,warn
```

debug_options

Amd includes extensive facilities for debugging its operation. These include changing its behavior through debugging options, as well as logging extra information verbosely. The target that Amd uses to log this extra debugging information is specified by the `log_file` parameter. The type of debugging information logged or debugging options turned on is determined by the value of the `debug_options` parameter.

Note that to use any debugging options with Amd, you must build Amd with debugging code, as we describe in Chapter 14.

The Amd
Automounter

PART 2

The values possible for the debug_options parameter and their meaning are as follows:

all This option instructs Amd to include all debugging messages and turn on all debugging options.

amq This action option tells Amd to register itself with the portmapper.

daemon This action option tells Amd to enter daemon mode, or *daemonize* itself.

fork This action option currently is used only by a special automounter called hlfsd.

full This informational option shows the full names and arguments of the commands used to mount and unmount file systems in maps of type:=program.

hrtime This informational option prints high-resolution time stamps with each logged message on systems that support a high-resolution clock.

info This informational option logs debugging messages that are specific to a map service.

mem This informational option traces the allocation and freeing of memory within Amd.

mtab This action option tells Amd to update the list of mounted file systems in a file named ./mtab, located in the current directory where Amd starts. If it is not used, Amd will default to using the Linux /etc/mtab file.

readdir This informational option traces the execution of directory reading operations within Amd.

str This informational option traces string manipulations in great detail.

test This debugging option is shorthand for all options but the following four: daemon, mem, str, and xdrtrace.

trace This informational option turns on tracing of RPC protocol message exchanges between Amd and the kernel, as well as NFS mounts.

xdrtrace This informational option turns on tracing of XDR messages that Amd exchanges with the kernel and Amq.

The full listing of all the debugging messages that Amd produces is in Appendix C.

The syntax for the value of debug_options is a comma-delimited list of debugging keywords. Each keyword can be prefixed by the string no to negate its meaning; this can be used to debug all information excluding a certain type or option.

To turn on full debugging of everything, use this in your amd.conf file:

```
[global]
debug_options = all
```

In practice, however, administrators are often overwhelmed by the amount of debugging information that Amd can produce. Instead, they find it useful to turn on debugging for all useful services, without changing Amd's behavior and excluding options that produce a lot of information:

```
[global]
debug_options = all,nomtab,notrace,noxdrtrace
```

print_version

The print_version option simply displays the output of amd -v on the terminal and then continues to run as usual. The output of amd -v includes version information, system configuration, compiled in support for various features, and a network interfaces list; this was shown in Chapter 8, "Overview of the Amd Automounter."

Note that whenever Amd starts, the first thing it logs on its logging file is the same information seen from amd -v. Therefore the print_version configuration option may not be of much use under normal circumstances. One possible use for it is to start Amd and at the same time get this configuration information stored in a different file than the standard log file. For example, if you set your /etc/amd.conf file as follows

```
[global]
print_version = yes
log_file = /var/log/amd
```

then you can start Amd as usual but also put the output of amd -v in a separate file, say, /tmp/amd-support-info, as follows:

```
[root]# amd -F /etc/amd.conf > /tmp/amd-support-info
```

pid_file

The pid_file parameter specifies the name of a file to store the process ID (PID) of the master Amd program when it starts. Many systems include this option for long-running daemons such as Amd. The intent is to store the PID of a daemon in a file, so it is easier to find it when the daemon needs to be shut down. At that time, the administrator can easily find the PID of the process to send a signal to by looking at the stored PID in the file.

For example, if the PID of the Amd process was stored in the file /tmp/amd.pid, you could terminate it as follows:

```
[root]# kill -TERM `cat /tmp/amd.pid`
```

This command sends a TERM signal to the PID whose number is stored in the file /tmp/amd.pid.

The Amd Automounter

PART 2

On Linux systems, PIDs are often stored in the /var/run directory, using file names that begin with the program's name and end with the suffix .pid. To tell Amd to store its PID in such a file, use the pid_file parameter in your amd.conf file:

```
[global]
print_pid = yes
pid_file = /var/run/amd.pid
```

> **NOTE**   In the above example, it is insufficient to specify the PID file alone. You also have to tell Amd to output the PID number in the given file by turning on the Boolean keyword print_pid.

Unfortunately, the technique of saving PIDs in files is not very reliable. The reason is that the program may abort unexpectedly, or the computer may crash, leaving behind a stale PID file. It is possible to start the system or the daemon again and have a PID file containing the wrong PID. In that case, attempting to send a signal to that PID may not signal the desired process but rather a completely different one. You may wind up killing a different program than you intended.

Moreover, the PID file technique is useful for storing one PID for one daemon. It does not scale well if you wish to store multiple PIDs for several programs. As you will see later in this section and also in Chapter 11, it is possible to run multiple Amd processes. This is often useful for running one production automounter and one or more test versions. In these cases, it is highly undesirable to use the same PID file for all instances of the same program because only one PID could be recorded in the PID file—the PID of the process that started last.

For these reasons, Amd provides a better mechanism for finding its PID: an RPC query initiated from Amq, Amd's query and control tool. Using Amq, you can find out the actual PID of any running instance of Amd. Amq will contact the running Amd and report the actual PID of that instance of Amd. There is no need to rely on prior storage of the PID in a separate file. To find out the PID of a running Amd, run

```
[ezk]$ amq -p
1347
```

In this example, Amq reported that the PID of the current running Amd was 1347. To send a signal to that Amd, say, the HUP signal that instructs Amd to re-read its maps, run the following shell command:

```
[root]# kill -HUP `amq -p`
```

Chapter 11 discusses this and other options of Amq, how to get the PID of other instances of Amd, and how other scripts in the am-utils package take advantage of this feature.

print_pid

The print_pid keyword tells Amd to print the PID of the Amd process into the file named by the pid_file parameter. If pid_file is not specified, Amd will use the special path name /dev/stdout for the PID file. This tells Amd to output its PID to the stdout file descriptor, not to a file or device named /dev/stdout. Either way, print_pid must be set to yes for Amd to output its PID anywhere.

For example, to tell Amd to print its PID to a file named /tmp/.amdpid, use this in your file:

```
[global]
print_pid = yes
pid_file = /tmp/.amdpid
```

portmap_program

The portmap_program parameter allows you to run several instances of Amd concurrently. The main reason to run more than one version of Amd is so that you can keep one production version of Amd running and have a second one for testing of new features or maps. This parameter provides an RPC identity to each running copy of Amd; only one may exist for each running program.

The default value for portmap_program is 300019. To run a second Amd with a different RPC program number, set the program number in a different Amd configuration file, say, /tmp/test-amd.conf, as follows:

```
[global]
portmap_program = 300020
```

To start the second Amd with the new program number, run

```
[root]# amd -F /tmp/test-amd.conf
```

Now that you have a second version of Amd running, you can contact it using Amq as follows:

```
[ezk]$ amq -P 300020
```

The Amd Automounter

PART 2

Performance and Tuning

The set of parameters listed in Table 9.4 can be broken into two groups: numeric parameters that affect timing events, and general Boolean flags that affect overall performance. This section describes these performance and tuning parameters in the Amd configuration file. Chapter 11 covers general-purpose optimizations and performance tuning for Amd maps.

Table 9.4   Global Parameters—Performance and Tuning

Parameter	Default	Possible Values
cache_duration	300	Number of seconds
dismount_interval	120	Number of seconds
nfs_retransmit_counter	11	Number of retransmission attempts
nfs_retry_interval	8	Tenths of seconds
plock	no	yes, no
restart_mounts	no	yes, no
unmount_on_exit	no	yes, no

cache_duration and *dismount_interval*

The two parameters cache_duration and dismount_interval are related to each other. As was explained in Chapter 8, Amd maintains lists of file servers, file systems, and volumes. Volumes are subsets of file systems or collections of file systems mounted from one or more file servers. Amd maintains mappings of volumes to file systems and mappings of file systems to file servers. One of Amd's main features is automatic unmounting of volumes that are no longer in use.

The cache_duration parameter tells Amd what is the length of time, in seconds, to keep used or cached volume names. Each time a reference is made to a volume, Amd resets the counter to zero. Once that time exceeds and no additional references to the volume have been made, Amd discards the volume to file system mapping for that name.

Since volumes may use several file systems, Amd may keep several volume references to the same file system. Therefore, discarding one volume to file system mapping does not mean that the file system as a whole is no longer in use. Amd also keeps a count of the number of references a file system has. Once the last volume reference to a file system is discarded, Amd can try to unmount that file system.

Amd can only try to unmount file systems. It is not guaranteed to succeed, because Amd does not control what happens below the actual NFS mount points where Amd mounts remote file systems. Amd can control everything below its own automount points, but not those of other NFS mounts. For example, if a user process keeps a file open somewhere inside the mounted NFS partition, trying to umount(2) will fail with a File System Is Busy (EBUSY) error code.

If Amd tries to unmount a file system for which all volume references were discarded, and that unmount fails for any reason, Amd waits for the number of seconds listed in the dismount_interval parameter, then tries again. This continues until the file system is unmounted successfully or is referenced again. A new reference, say, by a user accessing the volume, will create a new volume to file system mapping.

In general, the defaults of five minutes for the cache_duration and two minutes for the dismount_interval parameters are sufficient. There are two typical scenarios where you might want to change them: a busy multiuser server and a small workstation with very little resources.

If you have a large and busy multiuser machine, it is possible that Amd will have to work hard on that machine, mounting and unmounting many file systems. More so, however, Amd will be busy replying to lookup requests for volumes that are already mounted. Amd replies to an already-mounted volume lookup request much faster than it does to a mount request for a volume not yet mounted. The former can be done within a few milliseconds, while the latter can take several seconds while Amd contacts remote information servers, remote RPC servers, and remote file servers. Therefore it is desirable to keep in the cache entries that will be used often. At the same time, entries that will not be used often should not be cached.

On a busy large machine, you will want to increase both parameters to ensure that entries remain cached for longer periods of time. This assumes that your server has lots of memory and fast CPUs. To increase the values of these parameters, you could, for example, set the cache duration to one hour and the dismount interval to 10 minutes. You can configure these two parameters by inserting this in your amd.conf file:

```
[global]
cache_duration = 3600
dismount_interval = 360
```

On the other hand, on a small workstation mostly used by one person, you would usually prefer to remove unused entries faster and keep the list of mounted volumes small to consume as little memory and CPU resources as possible. Remember that as the amount of mounted volumes you have increases, not only does Amd have to work harder, but your /etc/mtab file contains more entries, and thus, programs such as df run slower. Plus, the fewer mounted file systems your system has, the less chance you will have of hanging your system when just one of those file servers goes down. To achieve these goals on a smaller workstation, reduce the values of the cache duration and the dismount interval to, say, 60 and 15 seconds, respectively, as follows:

```
[global]
cache_duration = 60
dismount_interval = 15
```

Ping-Pong Mounts

Be careful when lowering the values of the cache_duration and dismount_interval parameters. If you unmount entries too fast, and they will be needed shortly afterward, Amd will have to remount those file systems again. But since you have lowered the cache duration and dismount intervals, that file system will be unmounted shortly afterward. Then when it is needed again, it will be remounted once more. This constant cycle of unmount and remounts is called *ping-pong mounts*. It can happen, for example, if you set a user's personal cron job that runs every minute from your automounted home directory and lower the cache_duration and dismount_interval to under a minute. The cron job will ensure that Amd will use, and remount as needed, your home directory. Let us assume that your cron job runs for 10 seconds. This means that for the 50 seconds after the job completes, your home directory can be unmounted. If you lowered the cache_duration and dismount_interval parameters to less than 50 seconds, your home directory will be deemed unused and get unmounted before the next cron job runs, forcing a remount.

An alternative to setting these timers is to tell Amd never to unmount that volume. This can be done with the nonmount mount parameter, described in Chapter 10.

nfs_retransmit_counter and nfs_retry_interval

The two parameters nfs_retransmit_counter and nfs_retry_interval are also related to each other. As explained in Chapter 1, "NFS Basics and Protocols," the RPC system was designed to handle some amount of network failures. When an RPC client tries to access an RPC server on another host, the client sends the server a network message. Due to bad network conditions, possibly temporary, that message could be lost. The RPC system on the client side automatically resends the message again every few seconds, configured by a parameter known as the *retry interval*.

This works well if the network conditions that resulted in the lost message are corrected quickly: a dead server comes back up, network congestion is cleared, etc. However, if the network conditions persist and the RPC client cannot contact the remote RPC server for a long period of time, it stops trying and reports an error to its caller. RPC clients retry, sending unacknowledged messages several times. That number of times is known as the *retransmission counter*. After that many messages were sent and not acknowledged, the RPC client declares the original operation a failure and reports an error.

Since NFS was designed on top of RPC, it behaves in a similar manner. An NFS client sends RPC messages to a remote NFS server. These messages are, for example, to list files, read file contents, delete files, etc. If these messages fail to reach the file server, the NFS client will retry them every few seconds, up to a given number of times.

When an NFS client mounts a remote file server, it can configure these two values using mount options. The `retrans` mount option controls the number of retransmissions, and the `timeo` option controls the interval between retransmissions.

Amd is a user-level NFS server, and it uses RPCs to communicate with the local host's kernel. The kernel acts as the RPC client and Amd is the RPC server. The two Amd configuration parameters, `nfs_retransmit_counter` and `nfs_retry_interval`, control the number of retransmissions and the intervals between them when Amd communicates with the kernel.

Note that Amd is an NFS server running on the local host. So why would it need retransmissions if the chances that network packets will be lost on the local host are very slim? The reason is that Amd depends on the kernel RPC retransmission mechanism for other reasons. Amd is both an NFS server (to the kernel) and an NFS client (to other hosts). While Amd is processing a user request to list the contents of an automounted directory, it may have to perform many actions to satisfy that request:

1. Contact an information server such as NIS.
2. Download maps from it.
3. Parse map entries.
4. Contact remote portmappers.
5. Contact remote mount daemons.
6. Contact remote NFS servers.

The Amd Automounter

PART 2

These actions can take as long as several seconds. All the while, the kernel is still waiting for Amd to respond to the original query. Amd knows that it may not be able to reply fast enough to the kernel, so when it gets an RPC message from the kernel that it sees could not be processed in time, Amd simply discards (drops) the message. Amd relies on the kernel to retransmit that message to it, hopefully in time for Amd to respond to it in a timely fashion. Note that the actions Amd had to take to satisfy the original request continue to run even after Amd discards one or more RPC messages. Amd expects to get retransmitted messages and hopes that they will arrive just after it finishes performing the actions requested by the first RPC message.

Generally, the default values that Amd sets for these two parameters are sufficient. Do not change them unless you face a particular situation that calls for it. One typical situation where you would need to change these parameters is if your site is composed of a mixture of slow and fast networks, slow and fast hosts, and your networks are busy and not too reliable. In that case, it may take longer for packets to reach their destinations, and some may be lost on the way. It would be possible to lose enough packets for the RPC client side (the kernel) to declare the whole message a failure, whereas if you had waited a little longer, some packets would have gone through.

The default value for the nfs_retransmit_counter is 11 retransmissions. The default value for nfs_retry_interval is 8, but the units for this parameter are in tenths of a second. So the total default time the kernel will wait for Amd to complete a mount request is 8.8 seconds. Let us consider a site where the networks are slow but reliable. In that case, packets are not likely to be lost; they'll just arrive later. So you can lower the retransmission counter to 5 and increase the retry interval to 2 seconds:

```
[global]
nfs_retransmit_counter = 5
# interval is given in tenths of seconds
nfs_retry_interval = 20
```

With that amd.conf in place, you have increased your total timeout time to 10 seconds and changed the parameters to better suit your site.

If, on the other hand, your site is characterized by many failing servers, then you want to time out faster and detect those conditions quickly. So you could, for example, set a total timeout of two seconds as follows:

```
[global]
nfs_retransmit_counter = 4
# half a second interval
nfs_retry_interval = 5
```

Setting the right values for these parameters may take a bit of experimentation. If you set them too low, the kernel may time out good mounts before they complete and declare them a failure. If you set these parameters too high, the kernel may take too long to detect truly downed servers because it will have to wait longer to time out those mount attempts.

plock

On Linux and most other operating systems, file system code runs in the kernel. This guarantees its reliability because it runs in high-priority mode. Amd, however, is a user-level file server: it is just another process competing for system resources like any other process. When system conditions worsen, the kernel may deschedule (swap out) some processes. If the system decided to swap out the Amd process, Amd will get less of a chance to serve the system. This, ironically, can get the system into a locked-up state: the same process that is needed to serve users is prevented from serving them.

By all rights, the code that Amd runs should be running inside the kernel. That is why the automounter-assisting file system, Autofs, was created. It is described in Chapter 13.

Without Autofs, Amd must still run as a user-level NFS server. However, with the `plock` (Process Lock) parameter, you can ensure that Amd will not be descheduled by the system and would otherwise be given a better chance of running. If you set the `plock` parameter to `yes` in your `amd.conf` file, as follows:

```
[global]
plock = yes
```

then Amd will instruct the system to lock its process pages in place. The kernel will reserve enough memory for Amd and will ensure that both text and data pages of Amd are locked in place by the `mlock` system call. In general, this results in a faster-running Amd.

WARNING Do not use the `plock` option to lock process memory pages on a system that does not have a lot of available memory. This will reserve memory for Amd and may leave very little left for the rest of the system.

---

restart_mounts

When Amd starts, it is likely that some file systems have already been mounted. This happens most often when Amd starts after some system partitions are mounted already: `/`, `/usr`, `/home`, and `/usr/local`. This could also happen if Amd was stopped or died unexpectedly, or if you start a second copy of Amd. The `/etc/mtab` file may list mounts that remain on the system. In that case you may want Amd to resume its previous state—when it knew about those mounts. To do so, set the `restart_mounts` parameter to `yes` in your `amd.conf` file:

```
[global]
restart_mounts = yes
```

If this parameter is set to `yes`, Amd will read the contents of the `/etc/mtab` file and create internal data structures for every file server and file system listed in there. Then, when Amd has to mount new volumes that use those file servers, it will not have to mount those volumes because they are already mounted. This can speed up starting and running Amd.

This option is very useful and used by most administrators. However, if you are planning to run a second version of Amd, you should not set that one to restart mounts as well. Having more than one Amd restarting mounts can cause confusion: both Amd processes will attempt to manage, and even unmount, the same file systems.

Internally, the way Amd handles restarted file systems is by assigning their type to the inheritance (`type:=inherit`) file system. This tells Amd that this file system was inherited by reading existing mounted file systems from `/etc/mtab`. Chapter 10 describes this internal file system in more detail.

unmount_on_exit

The parameter `unmount_on_exit` is a cleanup option. If the `unmount_on_exit` parameter is set to `yes`, then Amd will try to unmount all of the file systems it knows about before it exits. To turn on this parameter, place this in your `amd.conf` file:

```
[global]
unmount_on_exit = yes
```

As we have seen during the discussion for the other parameters in this section, unmounts may not always succeed. That is why Amd will try only once to unmount these file systems upon exit. Nevertheless, there is a good chance that Amd will succeed in unmounting most of them. That is because user processes that might be keeping mounted file systems busy are usually terminated before daemons like Amd are shut down.

This option is useful when the system shuts down completely. During system shutdown, processes are usually terminated in the reverse order that they started, as governed by the scripts in the subdirectories of the `/etc/rc.d` directory. All file systems must be unmounted before a clean shutdown can be achieved. The system will try to unmount all remaining mounted file systems right before the end of the shutdown. However, it would be better to let Amd try and unmount those file systems that it was responsible for mounting in the first place, because it is done more cleanly by a party that knows more about those mounts. For example, Amd knows if certain file systems have to be unmounted in a particular order to succeed; the system in general simply unmounts all file systems in the order of their listing in the /etc/mtab file.

Information Services

Amd can read maps from various sources of information: NIS servers, Hesiod servers, LDAP servers, and more. Table 9.5 lists configuration parameters that affect how Amd interacts with these services. This section provides basic information about Amd's use of these services. Chapter 10 provides more information about using these information services with Amd.

Table 9.5   Global Parameters—Information Services

Parameter	Default	Possible Values
local_domain	Local DNS domain	example.com, cs.columbia.edu, am-utils.org
fully_qualified_hosts	*no*	yes, no
nis_domain	Local NIS domain name	Any arbitrary string
normalize_hostnames	no	yes, no
hesiod_base	automount	automount, amd, auto
ldap_base	None	"ou=Marketing, o=AMD Ltd, c=US"
ldap_hostports	None	ldap.example.com:389
ldap_cache_maxmem	131072	Number of bytes
ldap_cache_seconds	0	Number of seconds

local_domain

Amd detects the hostname of the local host at runtime. Amd also needs to know the DNS domain of the local host. That is often part of the Fully Qualified Host Name (FQHN) of the host. For example, for a host whose FQHN is titan.example.com, titan is the (short) hostname and example.com is the DNS domain name.

The Amd Automounter

PART 2

Amd maps can refer to these three name representations as follows:

${**host**}   Is the short hostname, often the first component of the FQHN

${**domain**}   Contains the remaining parts of the FQHN after the first one

${**hostd**}   Is the fully qualified hostname and is a synonym for the concatenation of ${host}.${domain} (with a single period in between)

When Amd starts, it does its best to figure out all three parameters. However, depending on how the host was named and how DNS was configured on that host, it may not be possible to find the proper value for the ${domain} variable. If that happens, then Amd cannot find the proper value for ${hostd} either, and it defaults to the same value assigned to ${host}.

If Amd cannot tell what value to assign to ${domain}, you can set that value using the local_domain configuration parameter. Another reason to do so is if your host belongs to one DNS domain based on its IP address but to another DNS domain based on its name. For example, say you own the class C network 204.17.100 for your example.com DNS domain, but you host a different domain internally: addresses 204.17.100.16 through 204.17.100.31 belong to the ulkesh.net domain. If you run Amd on hosts inside the ulkesh.net domain, and you share a single set of Amd maps across all of your class C, you may want to tell Amd that the hosts inside the ulkesh.net domain are part of the example.com DNS domain. To do so, set the following in your amd.conf file used on the ulkesh.net hosts:

```
[global]
local_domain = example.com
```

Without the above change, you might have had to write Amd maps that handled both domains separately:

```
extrabin    domain==example.com;rhost:=titan;rfs:=/usr/local \
            domain==ulkesh.net;rhost:=titan;rfs:=/usr/local
```

With the above change to your amd.conf file, however, you could simplify the map as follows:

```
extrabin    domain==example.com;rhost:=titan;rfs:=/usr/local
```

and you could run it on all the hosts in your class C network.

fully_qualified_hosts

The Boolean parameter fully_qualified_hosts determines if Amd will use fully qualified host names when authenticating NFS mounts in the RPC system. Normally, Amd uses the name of the current host that it retrieves from the gethostname system call. That can be either a short hostname or a fully qualified one. There is nothing wrong with either, until you try to use them in RPC authentication, especially that involving NFS, because the RPC system tries to authenticate the RPC client that tries to access services on the server. Some RPC servers are more secure than others and require that hostnames exchanged during the authentication phase be fully qualified.

If your site contains several RPC servers that require FQHNs during authentication, you will find out because Amd will not be able to mount remote NFS file systems. Instead, Amd will log an error message in its log (see the preceding section "log_file"). To avoid this problem, set the fully_qualified_hosts parameter to yes in your amd.conf file as follows:

```
[global]
fully_qualified_hosts = yes
```

With this parameter turned on, Amd will use the value of the ${hostd} variable during RPC authentication. Note that if your system does not detect the value of your DNS domain correctly, you are hosting other domains inside your domain, or you perform NFS mounts across different DNS domains, then you may have to set the local_domain parameter as well (described above).

If you have only a small number of remote hosts that require fully qualified hostnames, you do not have to set the global fully_qualified_hosts or local_domain parameters. Instead, you can simply use the FQHN for that remote host in the specific Amd maps:

```
extrabin    rhost:=titan.example.com;rfs:=/usr/local
```

Amd will use the value of the ${rhost} variable during authentication, which is already fully qualified.

TIP When you configure new hosts, set their hostnames to be fully qualified: not whitestar, but whitestar.example.com. Novice administrators often set hostnames to the short form for two reasons. First, it appears easier for some users to use (often due to a misconfigured /etc/resolv.conf file). Second, the administrators know that they are already in the example.com domain, and there does not appear to be a reason to qualify names fully. Amd, RPC systems, and many other services work more securely if they use fully qualified hostnames. If you use short names, attackers can more easily break into your system through vulnerabilities in DNS, NIS, and NFS. See Appendix B, "Online Resources," for information on related security advisories.

The Amd Automounter

PART 2

nis_domain

The nis_domain parameter is only used or needed if you are reading Amd maps from the Network Information System (NIS, formerly Yellow Pages, or YP). NIS defines a server domain name that clients must join to access NIS databases. If the client host sets the NIS domain correctly (see the nisdomainname man page), Amd will find it when it starts up. Amd will use this name when it needs to access NIS servers (ypserv) to download Amd maps.

The NIS system was designed to allow a site to configure multiple NIS domains. A client host can join different NIS domains, but it has to know the names of the NIS domains to join. In practice, most sites use only one NIS domain and there is no need to use the nis_domain parameter to set a different parameter than that of the client host. There are two cases where you might want to set the nis_domain for use by Amd:

- You are in the process of changing your NIS domain, perhaps due to security concerns, and you wish to test to see if your Amd will work with the new domain. In that case, you can combine setting the nis_domain parameter in your amd.conf file and running a second Amd as follows:

  ```
  [global]
  nis_domain = NuN2oBvious_dooh-maNE
  portmap_program = 300020
  ```

- You may indeed be running multiple NIS domains at your site, and each client host is set to use the correct NIS domain. However, you distribute a common set of Amd maps over a single NIS domain. For example, your client host is part of the shadow.vessels NIS domain, but you want Amd to download its maps from the vorlon.empire NIS domain. To do so, set the following in your amd.conf file:

  ```
  [global]
  nis_domain = vorlon.empire
  ```

WARNING Do not confuse the NIS domain with the DNS domain, and do not set both to the same name. The NIS domain name can be any arbitrary string, while the DNS domain is almost always a part of your fully qualified hostname. Unfortunately, novice administrators often set the NIS domain to be the same as the DNS domain. This not just confuses the understanding of which domain is which but is also very insecure. The NIS system can be easily subverted if attackers can find out your NIS domain name. If you use the same NIS domain name as your DNS name, attackers can guess that easily and try to break into your site, download your NIS password maps, run password-cracking tools on those, break into user accounts, and launch attacks on other sites. A couple of days later, you may get angry calls from administrators of sites attacked from your site and, if you're unlucky enough, perhaps even a visit from a friendly man in black. ...

normalize_hostnames

The normalize_hostnames parameter ensures that Amd uses the official fully qualified hostname when contacting remote hosts. The official hostname is not always the one used in the Amd maps, because hosts can have multiple names. In DNS, a canonical name (CNAME) is an alias for an official name. Sites often assign CNAMEs to hosts based on their function: www, ftp, and mailhost are often CNAMEs for the actual hostname.

If you let Amd use CNAMEs instead of official hostnames, you may face two problems:

- RPC authentication could fail if the remote hosts demand official hostnames.
- Amd could get confused and think that the CNAME and the official name refer to two different hosts, resulting in multiple entries in /etc/mtab for the same mounted file system.

To avoid these problems, you can either ensure that you are using official names in all of your Amd maps, or, simply set the normalize_hostnames parameter to yes in your amd.conf file:

```
[global]
normalize_hostnames = yes
```

For example, suppose the host bester.psycorps.gov has a second (canonical) name, garibaldi, and you have two volumes from the same physical host in your Amd map:

```
X11bin       rhost:=bester;rfs:=/usr;sublink:=X11/bin

TeXbin       rhost:=garibaldi;rfs:=/usr;sublink:=teTeX/bin
```

If you access both of these volumes and set normalize_hostnames to yes, you can ensure that RPC authentication and Amd will understand that these different names refer to the same physical host.

> **TIP**   If your Amd maps contain any CNAMEs, set the normalize_hostnames configuration parameter to yes.

hesiod_base

Hesiod is a name service based on DNS and developed at MIT. Amd can read automount maps from Hesiod servers. Maps must be prefixed with the string hesiod to be used as Hesiod maps, unless the map_type parameter is set to hesiod.

The Amd
Automounter

PART 2

For example, if your Hesiod map is named `users`, and Amd was asked to look for the entry `martha` in that map, Amd will contact your Hesiod server and ask it to look up the entry `martha.users.automount`:

- `martha` is the volume that Amd is trying to resolve.
- `users` is the name of the map.
- `automount` is the default Hesiod base name.

If your Amd entries in the Hesiod server use a different base name, say, `amdents`, set your `hesiod_base` parameter in your `amd.conf` file as follows:

```
[global]
hesiod_base = amdents
```

This will ensure that Amd looks up entries such as the one above using the full Hesiod string `martha.users.amdents`.

Note that the `hesiod_base` parameter is only used by Amd for Hesiod maps. Chapter 10 provides more details about Amd's use of Hesiod servers.

ldap_base

The following four Amd configuration parameters relate to the *Lightweight Directory Access Protocol (LDAP)* system. They are used only when Amd downloads maps from LDAP servers. LDAP is a general-purpose information service that tries to act as a database of sorts: you can define arbitrary fields, types, and values.

The `ldap_base` parameter specifies the base search value for LDAP servers; in LDAP, this is also called the *DN parameter*. This parameter must be specified if you are using LDAP with Amd. The syntax of this parameter is a comma-delimited list of *key=value* pairs. For example, you can set this in your `amd.conf`:

```
[global]
ldap_base = "c=US, o=Am-Utils Ltd, ou=Engineering"
```

Note that since the value of the `ldap_base` parameter contains spaces, it must be double-quoted. The three *key-value* pairs in the above example tell Amd to pass this to the LDAP search functions:

`c=US`   The country is the United States.

`o=Am-Utils Ltd`   The organization is Am-Utils Ltd.

`ou=Engineering`   The subgroup within the organization is Engineering.

> **NOTE** LDAP is no more "lightweight" than SNMP is a "simple" network management protocol. If you plan on using LDAP with Amd, make sure you investigate the different distributions, and carefully follow build, configuration, and installation instructions before using LDAP with Amd. For more information, see www.ldap.org.

ldap_cache_maxmem and ldap_cache_seconds

The two parameters ldap_cache_maxmem and ldap_cache_seconds are related. Amd uses them when setting LDAP caching policies. The ldap_cache_maxmem parameter gives LDAP the maximum number of bytes to use for its cache. This is a cache used by LDAP, not Amd. The default size of the cache is 128KB.

The ldap_cache_seconds tells LDAP how many seconds to keep entries cached. The default value for this parameter is 0, meaning that the cache is limited only by its size, not by the length of time entries remain in the cache.

If you set the ldap_cache_maxmem value to 0, then the LDAP cache will be restricted only by length of time, not by an upper-bound size.

For example, if you run Amd on a large machine with enough memory, and your Amd maps are large, you can place the following values in your amd.conf file to improve caching behavior by increasing the cache size to 1MB and the cache timeout to one hour:

```
[global]
ldap_cache_maxmem = 1048576
ldap_cache_seconds = 3600
```

ldap_hostports

LDAP servers run on specific hosts and ports. If you use LDAP with Amd, you must specify this parameter. The syntax of this parameter is a hostname, followed by a single colon, followed by the port number. If, for example, you want Amd to contact a special LDAP server running on port 639 on host control.bureau13.gov, then set this in your amd.conf file:

```
[global]
ldap_hostports = control.bureau13.gov:639
```

Map-Related Globals

This section contains Amd configuration parameters that affect the overall behavior of all Amd maps globally. These parameters can only appear in the [global] section, and thus, they impact all maps. Some of the features that these parameters control can be changed in individual maps. However, it is easier to control them in a single place that affects all Amd maps; that is why they are here. Table 9.6 lists those parameters.

Table 9.6 Global Parameters—Map-Related Globals

Parameter	Default	Possible Values
auto_dir	/a	/tmp_mnt, /n
selectors_on_default	no	yes, no
show_statfs_entries	no	yes, no
nfs_proto	All available transport protocols	tcp, udp
nfs_vers	All available versions	2, 3

auto_dir

Amd performs various mounts, mostly NFS mounts, of remote file servers. Amd mounts those in a temporary location and returns a symbolic link to their location inside the auto-mounted directory. For example, consider this map entry, part of the /home map:

```
ezk    rhost:=shekel;rfs:=/usr/homes;sublink:=${key}
```

Amd must mount the file system shekel:/usr/homes somewhere and then return to the calling process a symbolic link to the ezk subdirectory within it. (This process is described in greater detail in Chapter 10) The default location where Amd mounts file systems temporarily is defined by the value of the ${fs} variable. The default value for ${fs} is ${autodir}/${rhost}${rfs}. The value of ${autodir} is defined by the Amd configuration parameter auto_dir.

For the above example, Amd will mount the remote file system under /a/shekel/usr/homes:

- /a is the default value of ${autodir}.
- shekel is the remote hostname, ${rhost}.
- /usr/homes is the name of the remote file system.

After the mount is successful, Amd will return a symbolic link to a subdirectory within the mount point, since the map entry defined the `sublink` parameter to be equal to the key. You can check what it did using `ls -l`:

```
[ezk]$ ls -l /home/ezk
lrwxrwxrwx 1 0  0 11 Aug 17  /home/ezk -> /a/shekel/usr/homes/ezk
```

Amd will perform all mounts somewhere under the /a directory. If you wish to change it to, say, /tmp_mnt, set the following in your `amd.conf` file:

```
[global]
auto_dir = /tmp_mnt
```

After setting that, the home directory example will be mounted under that directory:

```
[ezk]$ ls -l /home/ezk
lrwxrwxrwx 1 0  0 11 Aug 17  /home/ezk -> /tmp_mnt/shekel/usr/homes/ezk
```

Normally, there is no need to change the value of this configuration parameter. When administrators do change it, it is often due to a conflict with another directory. For example, they may want to use the /a directory for something other than Amd.

selectors_on_default

Each Amd map may contain a list of default options and default values for some variables. These map-specific defaults are listed in a special map entry: `/defaults`. Amd treats this entry specially. For example, Amd does not treat it as a normal volume entry: you cannot list multiline values or use selectors unless you set `selectors_on_default` to yes.

For example, without setting `selectors_on_default` to yes, a normal Amd map (part of /home) might look like Listing 9.9.

Listing 9.9 An example without using `selectors_on_default`

```
/defaults    type:=nfs;opts:=nosuid,quota,intr,rw

martha       -rhost:=opus;rfs:=/raid1/users;sublink:=${key} \
             host!=${rhost};type:=nfs \
             host==${rhost};type:=link

erez         -rhost:=shekel;rfs:=/n/jin/u/zing;sublink:=${key} \
             host!=${rhost} \
             host==${rhost};type:=link
```

```
X11        os==linux;type:=link;fs:=/usr/X11R6 \
           os==solaris2;type:=link;fs:=/usr/openwin
```

The opts listed in /defaults are the default NFS options used for all mounts in this map. Consider now what might happen if you needed to change these default options but only under certain conditions:

- Part of your site's network is running over a slow wireless network. For that network, you wish to improve the performance of NFSv2 mounts by reducing the default read and write size used by NFS. They are 8192 bytes by default, which works well for fast and reliable networks but poorly for slower, unreliable networks. A better value is 1024 bytes.

- Your site contains a few IRIX machines. Those machines support NFSv3 mounts, but the implementation of NFSv3 under IRIX is not very stable and does not interoperate well with the rest of your site. You want to turn off NFSv3 mounts for IRIX hosts only.

You can accomplish these two goals by adjusting each and every volume entry listed in your map, but that would be a lot of work and would be difficult to maintain. Instead, you can turn on selectors_on_default in your amd.conf file as follows:

```
[global]
selectors_on_default = yes
```

and once done, you can update the /defaults entry in your /home map as follows:

```
/defaults   in_network(wireless-net);type:=nfs;\
                 opts:=nosuid,quota,intr,rw,rsize=1024,wsize=1024 \
            os==irix;type:=nfs;\
                 opts:=nosuid,quota,intr,rw,vers=2,proto=udp \
            type:=nfs;opts:=nosuid,quota,intr,rw
```

The above entry has only three total lines. Note the difference between a "\" character that is preceded by a space, and one that is not preceded by a space. The one preceded by a space delimits a whole location in the /defaults entry. The one not preceded by a space is a simple line continuation.

The above /defaults entry means the following:

- If your host is part of the wireless-net network, then set the mount type to NFS, and the default mount flags to the following:
  - nosuid, meaning do not allow set-UID binaries to execute
  - quota, meaning turn on quota processing over NFS

- intr, meaning allow interrupting mounts in progress using Ctrl+C
- rw, meaning allow processes to read and write files in the file system
- rsize=1024, meaning read file chunks over the network that are no bigger than 1KB
- wsize=1024, meaning write files over the network in chunks that are no bigger than 1KB

- If this Amd is running on an SGI IRIX host, then set the default mount to NFS, use the same basic NFS mount options, and also turn off NFSv3 mounts as follows:
  - vers=2 tells Amd to set the NFS mount version to version 2 instead of version 3.
  - proto=udp tells Amd to set the transport protocol for NFS to UDP instead of TCP.
- The last entry has no selectors, so it always matches if neither of the previous ones matched. It sets the default mount type to NFS and sets the same basic four NFS mount flags: nosuid, quota, intr, and rw.

Using selectors_on_default can be a very useful feature, especially for sites with heterogeneous networks and hosts. You can run the same set of Amd maps everywhere, yet have the control you need to affect subsets of these hosts so they behave differently as desired. Administrators who use this feature often optimize behavior of slow networks, turn special mount flags to provide better security to some of their hosts, or turn off special features for a subset of operating systems and operating system versions, and more.

show_statfs_entries

The df program uses the statfs system call to find out status information about file systems: total size of the file system, how much of it is used, and how much of it is free. It makes sense to find out the size and remaining capacity for physical file systems, those that have backing storage such as disks, floppies, and CD-ROMs. However, an automounter file system is a virtual one. It has no persistent storage; therefore, it cannot report maximum and current capacity. That is why automounters such as Amd often report all zeros for these values.

Suppose /home is an Amd automount point. Running df on it yields the following:

```
[ezk]$ df /home
    Filesystem       1k-blocks  Used Available Use% Mounted on
    beetle:(pid2536)         0     0         0 100% /home
```

There is, however, some information that Amd can report to statfs: the number of entries that it knows about for that map, and the number of entries in that map that are in use. Indeed, that is what this Amd configuration parameter does. If you turn it on as follows in your `amd.conf` file

```
[global]
show_statfs_entries = yes
```

and, say, your /home map has 117 entries, of which 35 are mounted, then running `df` will show you this:

```
[ezk]$ df /home
    Filesystem        1k-blocks   Used Available Use% Mounted on
    beetle:(pid2536)        117     35        82  29% /home
```

Note that this is only a tricky way for Amd to pass some useful information back to the `statfs` system call. It does not mean that the size of the /home file system is 117KB or that it is "29% full."

NOTE   GNU df, used on Linux systems, automatically skips listing of file systems that report all zeros in their `statfs` output. This often results in skipping the listing of Amd mount points. You must use `df -a` to list all file systems regardless of their capacities or types.

nfs_proto and nfs_vers

The two options `nfs_proto` and `nfs_vers` are related. They affect the overall use of NFS protocol versions and transports for all Amd maps used by this instance of Amd. When you build Amd as part of the `am-utils` package, the automatic configuration process will detect if your operating system supports NFS version 3 and which transports it supports: UDP, TCP, or both. Amd will then compile in support for all recognized NFS versions and transports. However, sometimes the operating system in question may have a client-side implementation of NFSv3 that is not very reliable. Moreover, it could be that the server side is not too reliable either, and thus, you may not want to use NFSv3 on this host at all.

Disabling NFSv3 support by recompiling Amd without it is not very easy because of the automated build process that am-utils uses. Alternatively, you can put the proper options to turn off NFSv3 (`opts:=vers=2,proto=udp`) in your Amd maps, as seen in the `selectors_on_default` configuration parameter described above. However, making such a change requires changing the Amd maps. That may not be administratively possible, or it might be undesirable if it affects other systems. Furthermore, you would have to put those changes in each and every map.

An easier way to turn off NFSv3 support globally is to use these two configuration parameters in your amd.conf file:

```
[global]
nfs_proto = udp
nfs_vers = 2
```

The above change tells Amd to force use of NFS to the older NFSv2 protocol and use the original UDP transport. Note that you do not have to use both options. Some systems have a fairly stable NFSv3 implementation using UDP, but not TCP. In that case, you can set the protocol transport to UDP but leave the version to its default, version 3.

> **NOTE** When Amd detects that your system supports NFSv3 and the TCP transport, it will attempt to use those when mounting remote file systems. However, at compile time, Amd does not know what each of your NFS servers support. Both NFS client and server must support the same protocol version and transport. That is why Amd will try the following four combinations, in order, until one succeeds: NFSv3 using TCP, NFSv3 using UDP, NFSv2 using TCP, and finally NFSv2 using UDP.

The Amd Automounter

PART 2

Map-Specific Configuration Parameters

Map-specific parameters are those that may only appear in the map section. There are only a few such parameters and they are described in Table 9.7.

Table 9.7 Global Parameters—Map-Specific Parameters

Parameter	Default	Possible Values
map_name	Any string	amd.home, /usr/share/maps/amd.src
tag	None	Any string

map_name

The name of the map must be specified. The only necessary parameter is map_name. The name can be any string, but each map must have a separate name. The name of the map also affects its type or the information source that will be used to retrieve the map.

If you set the map_type parameter (described earlier in this chapter), then the map will be loaded from that type exactly. If you did not specify the type of the map, then its name as specified in map_name will affect its type under the following rules:

- Names beginning with a "/" parameter are loaded from files.
- Names that begin with the string hesiod. are loaded from Hesiod maps.
- Other maps are most likely to be loaded from NIS.

The amd.conf example in Listing 9.10 shows several maps.

Listing 9.10   Setting map names in amd.conf files

```
[global]
map_type = nis

[/src]
map_name = amd.src
map_type = file
search_path = /etc/amdmaps:/usr/local/share/amd

[/home]
map_name = amd.userhomes

[/projects]
map_name = hesiod.prj

[/packages]
map_name = /etc/local/am.pkg
```

The above amd.conf file has four maps:

- The /src map will be loaded from a file located either in /etc/amdmaps/amd.src or /usr/local/share/amd/amd.src.
- The /home map will be loaded from the NIS map named amd.userhomes.
- The /projects map will be loaded from your Hesiod server using the postfix .prj.automount (see the hesiod_base parameter, described earlier in the chapter).
- The /packages map will be loaded from the file /etc/local/am.pkg.

tag

The tag configuration parameter is optional and works in conjunction with the amd -T flag. This parameter is useful to start certain automount points optionally. Any automount point that does not use the tag parameter is started always. Automount entries that use the tag parameter are not started automatically by Amd unless the tags are specified on the command line when Amd starts.

For example, a particularly interesting use for this parameter is to distribute a fixed set of amd.conf files and Amd maps to all hosts, but to allow some hosts to start new maps. These could be used for customization or testing by individuals, while allowing the site's system administrators to control the main amd.conf file and the main Amd maps. Consider the amd.conf file in Listing 9.11.

Listing 9.11   A sample amd.conf file utilizing map tags

```
[global]
map_type = nis

[/home]
map_name = am.users

[/src]
map_name = amd.src

[/local]
tag = testing
map_type = file
map_name = /etc/local/amd.test
```

When Amd runs using the amd.conf file in Listing 9.11, it will always start automount points on /home and /src but not necessarily the /local map. To start the /local automount point, Amd must be started as follows:

[root]# **amd -T testing**

This tells Amd to also start all automount points that have the testing tag. You can distribute an Amd startup script that runs at boot time as shown in Listing 9.12.

Listing 9.12   A sample Amd startup script utilizing map tags

```
#!/bin/sh
# allow hosts to start a host-specific automount point
if test -f /etc/local/amd.test
then
    amd -T testing
else
    amd
done
```

The Amd Automounter

PART 2

The script in Listing 9.12 tests to see if the file `/etc/local/amd.test` exists. If it does, it starts Amd with the `testing` tag, telling Amd to start the `/local` automount point. Otherwise, Amd starts normally without the `/local` automount point.

Configuration Parameter for Other Unix Systems: *cluster* (HP-UX)

This section lists the only Amd configuration parameter that is not applicable to Linux. It is listed in this book for the sake of completeness.

The HP-UX operating system defines the concept of *clusters*. All hosts in a cluster use services from a master server and can share files and file systems from a set of replicated file systems. When Amd runs on an HP-UX host, it will try to determine the name of the local cluster automatically. If that name cannot be determined automatically, or you wish to change it, set the `cluster` configuration parameter in your `amd.conf` file to another value:

```
[global]
cluster = mailservers
```

Changing this configuration parameter affects the `${cluster}` map selector. You can write maps that will behave differently under different HP-UX clusters:

```
srv    cluster==mailservers;rfs:=/var/spool/mail \
       cluster==fileservers;rfs:=/homes
```

NOTE   Interestingly enough, the powerful idea of clusters did not catch on very much outside HP-UX for years. Only recently, in the Linux world, have we started seeing a renewed practical effort for building large and inexpensive clusters of hosts, for example *beowulf* clusters. This `cluster` configuration parameter may yet have a use under Linux in the future.

A Complete *amd.conf* Example

So far in this chapter, we have seen many configuration parameters, each with examples ranging in size. In this section, we show one complete example and analyze it line by line. The example in Listing 9.13 is actually used in our department.

Listing 9.13   A complete amd.conf example

```
# -*- text -*-

# GLOBAL OPTIONS SECTION
[ global ]
normalize_hostnames =   no
print_pid =             no
restart_mounts =        yes
auto_dir =              /n
log_file                /var/log/amd
log_options =           all
#debug_options =        all,nomtab,noxdrtrace
plock                   no
selectors_on_default =  yes
#os =                   sos5
#karch =                sun4c
arch =                  i386
osver =                 2.2
# if you print_version after setting up "os",
# it will show it.
print_version =         no
map_type =              file
search_path =           /etc/amdmaps:/usr/lib/amd:/usr/local/AMD/lib
browsable_dirs =        yes

# DEFINE AN AMD MOUNT POINT
[ /u ]
map_name =              amd.u

[ /proj ]
map_name =              amd.proj

[ /src ]
map_name =              amd.src

[ /misc ]
map_name =              amd.misc

[ /import ]
map_name =              amd.import
```

```
[ /tftpboot/.amd ]
tag =                    tftpboot
map_name =               amd.tftpboot


[ /home ]
map_name =               amd.home
browsable_dirs =         no
```

We now analyze the `amd.conf` file in Listing 9.13, one line at a time:

```
# -*- text -*-
```

All comments start with the "#" symbol. This particular comment is used by Emacs to set the editing mode to text-mode when editing this file with Emacs. You might find it useful to make sure that plaintext files use Emacs's text-mode so that certain features are activated by default: commenting styles, spelling styles, Tab definitions, and more.

```
# GLOBAL OPTIONS SECTION
```

This is another comment. It never hurts to place lots of comments in configuration files, because it helps other administrators understand what is going on. This comment is useful to understand that what follow are global options. Even an administrator that is not familiar with Amd's configuration syntax could at least get a hint of what this section means.

```
[ global ]
```

Now the global section starts.

```
normalize_hostnames =  no
```

We like our hostnames abnormal. Actually, we do not need to tell Amd to try to expand hostnames and to find their official names, because our maps use all official names. Also, when we set names of hosts, we fully qualify them.

```
print_pid =            no
```

We do not print the PID of Amd upon startup. We do not need to because we use the `amq -p` option to find out the PID of Amd, if and when we need it. Note that the default value for `print_pid` is no anyway, but we set it here nonetheless, because it is easier for others reading the file to know exactly what might or might not happen with this feature.

```
restart_mounts =       yes
```

We definitely like to restart existing mounts when Amd begins running. This way, Amd has a better view of the rest of the system.

```
auto_dir =              /n
```

We want to create all temporary mount points under /n, not /a. This was mostly done for historical reasons, a decision some system administrator made many years ago.

```
log_file =          /var/log/amd
```

We want to log Amd information in the file /var/log/amd, where all other log files reside.

```
log_options =       all
```

We have enough space to log all messages and find it useful to keep them around. We also use logrotate to rotate and compress logs nightly.

```
#debug_options =        all,nomtab,noxdrtrace
```

We do not want to turn on any sort of debugging unless we are investigating a serious problem. However, we find it useful to keep a commented-out entry for the usual debugging options we do want to turn on when we need debugging: all options but changing the /etc/mtab file and without all the really verbose XDR traces.

```
plock =             no
```

Linux does not support the plock call, although it could, since it does support the mlock system call (which plock often uses).

```
selectors_on_default =      yes
```

We have a large site with many hosts and networks. We use selectors on /defaults entries to turn off NFSv3 on some systems and use more optimal NFS options for slow networks.

```
#os =               sos5
#karch =            sun4c
```

These are commented-out entries that remain from an old Solaris amd.conf file. This illustrates the point that if you are not sure how to configure your amd.conf file, copy an existing one and start modifying it.

```
arch =              i386
```

We run a mixture of Amd versions on our Linux systems. Some older versions of Amd report the arch as i486, i586, etc. So we want to force the arch to be i386 no matter what.

```
osver =             2.2
```

We run Amd on machines with newer test Linux kernels such as 2.3. We want to make sure that we treat those machines as 2.2 for now.

```
# if you print_version after setting up "os",
# it will show it.
print_version =    no
```

We do not need to print the version information of Amd on the terminal because it will be added to the log file by default anyway. Note the comment above this entry: Amd will log the version information that included the overridden values for arch and osver.

```
map_type =        file
```

We like file-type maps because they are the most reliable: we do not have to depend on network services such as NIS for Amd to function.

```
search_path =     /etc/local/amdmaps:/usr/lib/amd
```

This is our search path for Amd maps. We allow users to override maps in their host-specific /etc/local/amdmaps directory.

```
browsable_dirs =  yes
```

This is useful for file browsers to be able to list all entries that can be automounted, but it can also cause mount storms with Gnome's file browser and others that run the lstat system call on each Amd entry, thus causing it to mount the entry.

```
# NEXT WE DEFINE SEVERAL AUTOMOUNT POINTS
```

It is a good idea to start the section that lists actual automount points with a comment.

```
[ /u ]
map_name =          amd.u
```

The /u automount point mounts whole disks that contain user home directories. For example, /u/staff is the home directory for all of the technical staff, /u/admin is for all of the administrative staff, /u/guest for all guests, and so on. User home directories at our site are used for storing login scripts, e-mail and its archives, and some documentation, but not for large source repositories.

```
[ /proj ]
map_name =          amd.proj
```

Each research group at our (university) department has several project disks where they store sources, binaries, and other files. The /proj automount point has those.

Another interesting fact about the separation of /u and /proj disks is administrative: /u disks are managed by the system administrators' group, while /proj disks are managed by their individual groups. This allowed our administrators to impose quotas on user home directories, so everyone gets a fair share of that space. Project disks do not have quotas, and that allows individual research groups to expand as their funding allows.

```
[ /src ]
map_name =              amd.src
```

The /src automount point contains links to various project sources. Some of these are for general use to everyone (/src/linux-kernel and /src/X11R6), while others are used by individual research groups (/src/graphics, /src/nlp, /src /fist, etc.).

```
[ /misc ]
map_name =              amd.misc
[ /import ]
map_name =              amd.import
```

These two automount points have the same function; they are for miscellaneous automount points that otherwise do not fit well anywhere else. The reason we have two is historical: years ago, /import was intended for diskless workstations, but diskless technologies are not popular these days since disk sizes have grown and prices dropped significantly in the past decade.

```
[ /tftpboot/.amd ]
tag =                   tftpboot
map_name =              amd.tftpboot
```

This is a clever map that uses an automount point inside a chroot(2)-ed directory. Chapter 12 describes this particular example in detail.

```
[ /home ]
map_name =              amd.home
browsable_dirs =        no
```

The /home map lists every user with a home directory. This map consists almost entirely of links to subdirectories with the /u map, the one that mounts whole user disks. Note that since this map is pretty large, we turn off browsable_dirs on it, so an occasional ls -l in there will not try to automount several thousand entries.

As you can see from the above example, Amd maps are simple to read and maintain: plain text with spaces and comments as you see fit. Each automount map has its own clearly marked section. One global section lets you place parameters that affect the overall behavior of Amd and all the maps it uses. Each parameter configuration line in the amd.conf file has a simple *key = value* syntax, where keys use names that are easy to understand.

In Sum

The Amd configuration file, typically stored in /etc/amd.conf, provides a powerful mechanism to control the behavior of Amd on each host. Many options can be defined or redefined in this file, options that affect how Amd starts and ends, where it gets maps and how it interprets them, how much logging and debugging information it produces, caching policies, ways to tune the performance of Amd, parameters to control the use of information services, and more.

The syntax of Amd configuration files is simple: plaintext files. You can use comments and white space as needed. Each automount node has its own section, as well as a special section that determines global options. The syntax for configuration parameters is also very simple: short key names and values, separated by an equal sign (=).

Amd configuration files can be extremely helpful but should be used with care. If you have one already, start with a copy of it and modify it to suit your needs for another system. If you do not have one, the am-utils package comes with a sample amd.conf file that you can use as a starting point. If you are testing many new features with Amd, you can run multiple Amd binaries: one production automounter for use by your users, and one or more test versions until you are satisfied that your new configuration file and new maps do what you need.

While many of the Amd configuration options are also available as command-line options, not all are. Old users of Amd may be inclined to use command-line options, but that will not work for newer features that are only available in amd.conf files. Moreover, it is better to place all of your configuration options in one simple file than to type many of them on the command line where the command will become very long and difficult to maintain or type each time.

Many of the features available in Amd configuration files affect the interpretation of Amd maps. This chapter showed many examples of amd.conf files and some examples of Amd maps that behave differently depending on the contents of the Amd configuration file. Next, Chapter 10 details the syntax and use of Amd maps.

10

Automomounter Maps

A*utomounter maps* provide the core definitions of Amd's dynamic file system views. Amd reads these maps from various input sources and creates a virtual file system at each automount point corresponding to a map. What the maps describe will be seen by users as a directory hierarchy with entries that can be mounted upon access. The exact conditions under which Amd will mount these entries are described precisely in the automounter maps, also called *Amd maps*.

Some of what we describe in this chapter also relates to Chapter 9, "The Amd Configuration File," because many features placed in Amd configuration files affect the overall behavior of Amd's maps. We will identify these whenever appropriate in this chapter. In Chapter 9 we discussed parameters individually. But in this chapter we discuss those and other parameters in related groups, with the intent of emphasizing the relationships and dependencies between the many components that make up Amd maps.

While the syntax of these maps is simple, you can use many features to perform automounting. Often, there is more than one way to achieve an automount goal. In this chapter we describe the syntax of Amd maps in detail. We then cover each of the many variables and selectors you can use in Amd maps. Following that, we cover many of the options used for mounting file systems. Finally, we discuss each of the file systems recognized by Amd: native file systems as well as meta file systems. As is usual with this book, we provide practical examples with the descriptions of each feature.

Map Syntax

The syntax of Amd's map is relatively simple: it is a list of key-value pairs. We begin by listing the formal specification for the syntax of the map language, seen in Listing 10.1.

Listing 10.1 Formal syntax specification for Amd's maps

```
map : entries

entries : entry NL
        | entry NL entries

entry : key WS location-list

key : | /defaults
      | non-WS

location-list : -entry-defaults location
              | location
              | location location-list
              | location || location-list

entry-defaults : assignment-list

location : assignment-list
         | selector-list ; assignment-list

assignment-list : assignment
                | assignment ; assignment-list

selector-list : selector
              | selector ; selector-list

assignment : varname:=value

selector : selname==value
         | selname!=value
         | selname(value)
         | !selname(value)
```

The rules for parsing an Amd map are as follows:

- A map is a list of entries, separated by newlines (NL).

- An entry is a key-value pair, separated by whitespace (WS).

- Whitespace is defined as any sequence of consecutive Tab and Space characters.
- A key can have one of two values:
  - The special value `/defaults`.
  - Any non-whitespace sequence of characters.
- The value of an entry is a list of locations (or volumes) to satisfy the request for *key*.
- The list of locations (volumes):
  - Is one or more locations, usually separated by whitespace.
  - Can begin with a special default value list, entry-defaults.
  - Can use special lazy-evaluation (| |), which we describe in detail in Chapter 12, "Advanced Amd Uses."
- An entry-defaults is a list of variable assignments, separated by semicolons.
- A location (volume) can be one of the following:
  - A list of variable assignments.
  - A list of selectors, followed by a semicolon, followed by a list of variable assignments.
- An assignment-list is a semicolon-delimited list of variable assignments.
- A selector-list is a semicolon-delimited list of selectors.
- An assignment is a variable name, followed by :=, followed by the value to assign.
- A selector includes the name of the selector and its value and can have one of four forms:
  - Equality test, using ==.
  - Inequality test, using !=.
  - Boolean function evaluation using ().
  - Negated Boolean function evaluation using !().

In addition to the above rules, certain additional rules apply to the handling of file maps only. The reason for this additional syntax is that it is often useful to write the maps as regular files, where using multiple lines for each entry and inserting comments can clarify the intent of that entry:

- Blank lines are ignored.
- Comment lines, beginning with the # symbol, are also ignored.
- Line continuation: the backslash symbol (\) may appear at the end of the line, in which case the backslash, the following newline (NL) character, and any subsequent whitespace are ignored. Amd imposes a limit of 2048 characters for all continuation lines within a single map entry.

The Amd Automounter

PART 2

That last line-continuation rule has subtle ramifications, illustrated by these examples. The map entry

```
key    val1  val2;  \
       val3
```

specifies three locations and is identical to

```
key    val1  val2;  val3
```

That is because the backslash, following newline, and following whitespace up to val3 are ignored. The space before the backslash is not ignored. This is why the entry

```
key    val1  val2;\
       val3
```

specifies only two locations, and is identical to

```
key    val1 val2;val3
```

Note that blank lines, comments, and continuation lines are supported only for file maps. However, from file maps you can generate maps in various other formats, as described in Chapter 11, "Runtime Automounter Administration."

The simple map example in Listing 10.2, part of a possible /home map, shows some of the syntax of an Amd map.

Listing 10.2   A simple Amd map example illustrating the basic map syntax

```
/defaults    type:=nfs;opts:=nosuid,quota,intr,rw

# this is the home entry for Erez
ezk    -rhost:=shekel;rfs:=/n/jin/u/zing;sublink:=${key} \
       host!=${rhost} \
       host==${rhost};type:=link
```

The meaning of each part of the text in Listing 10.2 is as follows:

- All of Listing 10.2 is a single Amd map.
- The map has two entries, with keys /defaults and ezk.
- The first entry, /defaults, lists some default values that will be used for the rest of the entries in this map.
- The value of the /defaults entry contains two assignments:
  - The type variable is set to the value nfs.
  - The opts variable is set to the value nosuid,quota,intr,rw.

- The blank line after the /defaults entry is ignored.
- The next line (starting with #) is a comment line and is also ignored.
- The second entry, ezk, has three lines continued with the backslash character—each line becoming a separate whitespace-delimited component of that entry.
- The first line in the ezk entry starts with a -, listing the defaults for the rest of this entry, and contains three assignments:
  - The rhost variable is set to the value shekel.
  - The rfs variable is set to the value /n/jin/u/zing.
  - The sublink variable is set to the value ${key}.
- The second line in the ezk entry contains only one thing, a single selector:
  - The host selector is checked for inequality against the value of ${rhost}.
- The third line in the ezk entry contains a single selector followed by one assignment:
  - The host selector is checked for equality against the value of ${rhost}.
  - The type variable is assigned the value link.

We now proceed to describe more specific rules for key lookup, default values, and variable expansions.

How Keys Are Looked Up

A user types in a file or directory to lookup inside an automounted directory. Amd tries to find that input string in the corresponding map, matching it against the keys in the map. Keys are looked up using the information service servicing the map: file maps, NIS, Hesiod, LDAP, etc. We describe map information services in more detail in Chapter 11. The simplest form of key lookup is an exact string match. Four conditions could affect the lookup of keys: variable expansions, map prefixes, regular expressions, and pathname components.

Variable Expansion

If the user input contains any variables, they will get expanded before matching. For example, if the user looks up an entry /src/${os}-${osver}-kernel, and /src is an automount point, and Amd is running on a Linux 2.2.16 system, then Amd will look up the map entry /src/linux-2.2.16-kernel.

Another use for this would be to set several automount entries, each pointing to a different set of binaries for an operating system and architecture, and then place pathname components with Amd variables in your ${PATH} shell environment variable. For example, consider the map in Listing 10.3, part of the /packages automount point.

Listing 10.3 A sample map illustrating pathname lookup variable expansion

```
/defaults        type:=nfs

linux-i386       rhost:=lynn;rfs:=/usr/bin

linux-alpha      rhost:=alef;rfs:=/usr/local/bin

linux-sparc      rhost:=sparkee;rfs:=/usr/test

solaris-sparc    rhost:=sun;rfs:=/bin
```

With the map in Listing 10.3 in place, you can set your ${PATH} as follows:

[ezk]$ **export PATH=${PATH}:/packages/\\${os}-\\${arch}**

Note that because $ is a special character in most shells, it must be escaped using a backslash (\) to ensure that the $ remains in the ${PATH} variable. After you set your ${PATH} as described, each time you look up a program in your shell, the proper path name in /packages will be used:

- /packages/linux-i386 on Linux systems running on Intel architectures
- /packages/linux-sparc on Linux systems running on the SPARC architectures
- And so on

The nice thing about this feature is that you only have to set your ${PATH} component once. Amd will expand the variables in your ${PATH} when it searches inside automount points, and the expansion will occur locally on the running host. In other words, a single pathname component can be translated directly on multiple hosts, saving you from typing or setting up special cases for your ${PATH} depending on the system you are running on.

Map Prefix

A map prefix is a string whose value gets prepended to keys before they are looked up in a map. The variable ${pref}, if set to non-NULL, defines the prepended value. You can set this variable in the amd.conf file for a given automount point, in the map_options parameter. You can also set this variable in a map that defines one or more subsidiary automount points.

For example, if ${pref} is set to local/, and a user looks up the entry bin in a map with that prefix, then Amd will search the corresponding map for the entry local/bin. Map prefixing is an advanced feature of Amd. We provide more information about it further in this chapter, under the section "Variables," and we also show one advanced example using ${pref} in Chapter 12.

Regular Expressions

If the map cache is of type `regexp` or `re`, then key lookups are treated as egrep-style regular expressions. You can set the map cache type in your `amd.conf` file using the following:

```
map_options = cache:=regexp
```

Say your `/binaries` map uses regular expressions and contains the following entry:

```
X11.*       exists(/usr/${key});type:=link;fs:=/usr/${key}
```

If a user looks up the directory `/binaries/X11R6`, Amd will match the key `X11R6` with the regular expression `X11.*`. It will match because the regular expression syntax `.*` (dot-star) will match anything after the `X11` part. (Consult the manual page for `egrep` for details on regular expression syntax.) Since the key matched, Amd will process the value of the entry, which says that if the directory `/usr/X11R6` exists, then set a symbolic link to it.

Such a map entry can work in places where you have a mix of various versions of the X11 windowing system: `/usr/X11R5`, `/usr/X11R6`, `/usr/X11R6.3`, etc. The usefulness of such a map is that it need only be written once, and it will work automatically based on which X11 directories you have installed under `/usr`.

Pathname Component Lookup

If Amd looks up a key and cannot find it in the map, it will then apply the *wildcard* matching rules and try again. In particular, Amd will strip the last component from a looked-up key, add `/*` to it, and try again. Finally, Amd will try the match-all wildcard entry `*`. Wildcards are restricted forms of regular expressions, not as powerful as regular expressions. Wildcards are often used by shells to match file names. Consult the manual page for `bash` for explanations of the wildcard syntax.

The intent of these wildcard rules is to allow administrators to specify maps that contain various catch-all or catch-some defaults, and override them as needed. For example, a lookup for the entry `/home/staff/martha` will proceed to match the following, until one or none match:

1. `home/staff/martha`
2. `home/staff/*`
3. `home/*`
4. `*`

Note that these lookup rules apply regardless of the actual order of entries in your map. The map in Listing 10.4 illustrates the use of wildcards for a `/home` map.

Listing 10.4 A map sample illustrating wildcards

```
/defaults        type:=nfs

*                rhost:=globo;rfs:=/praid/sales;sublink:=${key}

staff/*          rhost:=ober;rfs:=/users/admin;sublink:=${/key}

staff/martha     rhost:=opus;rfs:=/u/staff;sublink:=martha
```

The meaning of this map is as follows:

/defaults This entry specifies that the default mount type is NFS.

* All users by default are assumed to be sales personnel whose home directories reside on the globo:/praid/sales disk. Each salesperson's home directory is a subdirectory inside /praid/sales. That is what the sublink variable means, and it will be explained further in this chapter, under the section "Variables."

staff/* If the key specified matched the wildcard staff/*—meaning anything under staff/—then find the home directory for those users in the ober:/users/admin disk. The actual home directory would be a subdirectory of /users/admin whose name is the last component of the matched key. The special syntax ${/key} (described in the upcoming section "Variable Expansion") is similar to the basename command: it tells Amd to strip everything but the last component of a path name. That way, whichever string matched the * in staff/* will be assigned to the sublink variable, the variable denoting the user's home directory under /users/admin.

staff/martha This entry will match specifically for user martha before any other entry would. This way we allow for exceptions: only this user needs to get her home directory from opus:/u/staff.

What makes a map such as the one in Listing 10.4 so useful is that you can specify general map entries that can match most of the time for a certain class of directories (in this case, directories representing users' home directories) and, at the same time, specify overrides for a few exceptions. These exceptions, such as staff/martha, will be matched first; only if they do not match will Amd proceed to look up more general wildcards such as staff/* or even *.

Defaults

Three kinds of defaults affect the interpretation of maps:

Amd configuration file defaults These are defaults specified in your amd.conf file such as those that override the values of certain variables. These were described in Chapter 9.

Defaults per map   These are default values that are specified in a special entry /defaults, as seen in Listing 10.1. Only one such entry may exist in each map. Amd processes any variable assignments specified there before processing any entry in the map. Normally, only variable assignments may be used in /defaults. However, if you turn on selectors_on_default=yes in your amd.conf file, you can also include selectors in your /defaults entry. Amd will evaluate these selectors each time it parses the /defaults entry. The assignments listed for the location in the /defaults entry for which all selectors matched will be used as the default assignments before evaluating other entries. We have shown a few simple examples using selectors_on_default in Chapter 9. We show more advanced examples in Chapter 12.

Defaults per location list   In any given Amd entry, a list of locations may be preceded by defaults applicable to that list alone. These were specified as *-entry-defaults* in Listing 10.1. These defaults start with the - (minus) symbol. Consider the example in Listing 10.5, part of a /home map.

Listing 10.5   An example with defaults per map and per location list

```
/defaults    type:=nfs

ezk    -rhost:=shekel;rfs:=/homes2;opts:=suid,quota \
       host!=${rhost} \
       host==${rhost};type:=link

tim    -rhost:=biker;rfs:=/u/foria \
       host!=${rhost} \
       host==${rhost};type:=link
```

Here, we see the usefulness of defaults: they save you typing and they simplify your maps so they are more readable. First, we set the default mount type to be nfs. We specify this only once in the /defaults, and then we do not have to list this again in the rest of the map.

Next, we see that the actual location list of both entries (ezk and tim) remains the same. Only the default parts change and those list the remote hostname, remote file system, and possibly mount options. It is easy to edit such a map and add new user home entries by copying the three lines of any user entry and just changing the key and the per-entry default portions.

Variable Expansion

In this section we describe the rules for parsing and evaluating variables in Amd maps. The basic syntax for a variable is

> ${*varname*}

where *varname* is a name of a variable.

Many variables are predefined by Amd and all are described in the upcoming section "Selectors and Variables." Amd will first evaluate variables that are predefined—whose names are reserved. If they are not found, Amd will search the environment under which Amd started to see if an environment variable was exported. For example, consider the map in Listing 10.6, part of the /misc map.

Listing 10.6   A map example showing environment variables

```
temp  -type:=link \
      exists(${TMPDIR};fs:=${TMPDIR} \
      fs:=/tmp
```

Now, suppose you started Amd as follows:

> [root]# **TMPDIR=/usr/local/bigtmp amd -F /etc/amd.conf**

The map in Listing 10.6 will evaluate /misc/temp to /usr/local/bigtmp if that directory exists. Otherwise, Amd will evaluate /misc/temp to /tmp. In this way you can have users use /misc/temp exclusively and it will be redirected to /usr/local/bigtmp on systems that contain that directory (presumably that directory has plenty of available space).

Quoting and Special Characters

As we have seen in Listing 10.1, whitespace holds a special meaning in Amd maps: it separates keys from their values, and locations from each other. If you have to include a space character verbatim in the value of a variable, then quote it using double quotes, as follows:

```
docs  type:=link;fs:="/msdos/My Documents"
```

In that example, we evaluate the docs key to be a symlink to the path name

```
/msdos/My Documents
```

including the single space character between My and Documents, but not including the actual double-quote characters.

As you might have noticed already, several characters have special meanings in Amd maps: the semicolon, colon, equal sign, and others. If you need to include them verbatim in Amd maps, use the special codes listed in Table 10.1.

Table 10.1 Special Characters in Amd Maps

Special	Meaning
\\	A literal backslash
\b	Backspace
\e	Escape
\f	Form Feed
\g	Bell
\n	Newline
\r	Carriage Return
\t	Horizontal Tab
\v	Vertical Tab
NNN	Any other ASCII value, specified in octal

There is one exception to the entries in Table 10.1: including a literal dollar symbol. That symbol is very special in Amd maps, as it prefixes variables. The usual escaping rules in Table 10.1 do not work for the dollar symbol because Amd performs multiple passes over map entries, especially for expanding variables that may be listed in the values of other variables. A literal dollar will confuse Amd into thinking that it is a prefix for a variable's name. Instead, you should include dollar symbols using the special variable ${dollar}. For example, if you have a file system named /disk/fire$c on an NFS server named brimstone, you can set an Amd map to mount it as follows:

```
cdisk type:=nfs;rhost:=brimstone;rfs:=/disk/fire${dollar}c
```

Pathname and Hostname Operators

Four special operators can further help to post-process the value of a variable. These operators can retrieve a subset of the value of a variable. Two are pathname operators and two are hostname operators.

The pathname operators can retrieve the basename of the path name or the directory-name part of a path name. For example, if the value of ${var} is /u/class/jazz, then

> ${/var} is jazz
>
> ${var/} is /u/class

Similarly, if the value of a variable is a dot-separated hostname, then you can retrieve the short hostname or the domain name of the fully qualified hostname using the hostname operators. For example, if the value of ${var} is titan.filesystems.org, then

> ${.var} is filesystems.org
>
> ${var.} is titan

Selectors and Variables

Variables are the basic components that hold information in Amd maps. Some variables' values are fixed, while others can change. Variables' values can change by setting the variable to a different value, or by overriding it globally in the amd.conf file, as described in Chapter 9. Amd's maps support many variables, each of which has a different meaning and use in the general scheme of automounting volumes.

Selectors are special kinds of read-only variables. Primarily they are used for comparisons of their current values against other values. Some variables (variable selectors) can also be used in the value assignments of other variables. Selectors can therefore guide the automounting actions based on specific conditions of the system or site. They allow administrators to capture multiple needs for a given automounted volume and ensure that the volume is mounted correctly under each different set of conditions.

Two kinds of selectors exist: variable selectors and function selectors. Variable selectors are those that match a selector for equality or inequality against a given value. Function selectors are functions that take a single argument and evaluate to true or false based on the value passed to them. For example

> host==titan will evaluate to TRUE if the current hostname is titan.
>
> host!=titan will evaluate to TRUE if the current hostname is not titan.
>
> exists(/u/fonic) will evaluate to TRUE if the path name /u/fonic exists.

`!exists(/u/fonic)` will evaluate to TRUE if the path name `/u/fonic` does not exist.

The values of variables can be used in the assignment of other variables or in the comparison of selectors against other values. Variables and other values listed together form an automatic string concatenation. For example, the code

`fs:=/n/${rhost}/${path}-tmp`

will assign to the variable `${fs}` the value that is the concatenation of the following five components:

- The string `/n/`
- The value of the `${rhost}` variable
- The string `/`
- The value of the `${path}` variable
- The string `-tmp`

Selector Variables

In this section we discuss the selector variables used by Amd. Because many of the selectors are related to each other, we discuss them in common groups and also provide examples utilizing them together. Table 10.2 lists these selectors in alphabetical order along with their default values. The table lists whether the selector is compared case-sensitively or case-insensitively. In the third column, the table states one of the five general places where a selector can exist:

Amd run   These are selectors whose value is generally constant throughout the run of Amd.

Each map   These are selectors that are specific to the information service used to load the map: file, NIS, Hesiod, LDAP, etc.

Each user   These are selectors that change for *each* user that invokes an automounted path name.

Non-Linux   These selectors work for systems other than Linux.

Deprecated   These selectors are replaced with newer, generally better selector functions.

Table 10.2 Selector Variables

Name	Case Sensitive?	Specific To	Default Value
arch	Yes	Amd run	Host architecture.
byte	Yes	Amd run	Byte order (endianess).
cluster	Yes	Non-Linux	Host cluster (HP-UX only).
domain	Yes	Amd run	Hostname (pseudo-DNS) domain.
full_os	Yes	Amd run	Operating system name version.
gid	No	Each user	Effective group ID making request.
host	Yes	Amd run	Short hostname.
hostd	Yes	Amd run	Full hostname.
karch	Yes	Amd run	Kernel architecture.
netnumber	No	Deprecated	Same as in_network (see Table 10.3).
network	No	Deprecated	Same as in_network (see Table 10.3).
os	Yes	Amd run	Operating system name.
osver	Yes	Amd run	Operating system version.
uid	No	Each user	Effective user ID making request.
vendor	Yes	Amd run	Vendor of the system.
wire	No	Deprecated	Same as in_network (see Table 10.3).

Note also that the default values for most of the selectors listed in Table 10.2 can be overridden in your amd.conf file, as described in Chapter 9. The variables that can be overridden in this way are arch, cluster, domain, full_os, karch, os, osver, and vendor.

arch and *karch*

The arch and karch selectors check the host architecture and the host kernel architecture of the machine Amd is running on. The architecture is often the CPU system type: i386, SPARC, Alpha, etc. The kernel architecture is often the kernel CPU architecture: i486, i586, i686, sun4u, sun4m, etc. The karch selector often provides more specific information about the architecture of the machine.

A typical use for arch is to select directories containing files specific to the CPU type. Consider an automount map /packages that provides a link to the keyboard key-maps on Red Hat 7.0 systems. Intel key-maps are installed in /usr/lib/kbd/key-maps/i386, while Sun (SPARC) key-maps are installed in /usr/lib/kbd/key-maps/sun:

```
keymaps     -type:=link \
            arch==i386;fs:=/usr/lib/kbd/keymaps/i386 \
            arch==sparc;fs:=/usr/lib/kbd/keymaps/sun
```

The above map will set a symbolic link from /packages/key-maps to /usr/lib/kbd/key-maps/i386 on Intel systems, and to /usr/lib/kbd/key-maps/sun on SPARC systems.

The assembly header files that are part of the Linux kernel source tree are often specific to the kernel architecture of the host. In particular, all Intel systems use headers from /usr/src/linux/include/i386. However, 32-bit SPARC systems use /usr/src/linux/include/sparc, while 64-bit SPARC systems use /usr/src/linux/include/sparc64. To set a single location pointing to the right headers, you may use a map such as follows:

```
asm    -type:=link \
       karch==sparc;fs:=/usr/src/linux/include/sparc \
       karch==sparc64;fs:=/usr/src/linux/include/sparc64 \
       karch==i386;fs:=/usr/src/linux/include/i386 \
       karch==i486;fs:=/usr/src/linux/include/i386 \
       karch==i586;fs:=/usr/src/linux/include/i386 \
       karch==i686;fs:=/usr/src/linux/include/i386
```

The Amd Automounter

PART 2

In the preceding map, we set the link name based on the specific kernel architecture. However, such a map would be better written as follows:

```
asm    -type:=link \
       karch==sparc;fs:=/usr/src/linux/include/sparc \
       karch==sparc64;fs:=/usr/src/linux/include/sparc64 \
       arch==i386;fs:=/usr/src/linux/include/i386
```

Here, we take advantage of the arch selector that is always set generically to i386 on Intel machines, and the fact that the link name always points to /usr/src/linux/include/i386.

byte

The byte selector differentiates machines based on their byte order, often called the *endianess* of a machine: whether the machine is big-endian or small-endian. One possible use for this is to select the correct binary-formatted *New Data-Base Map* (NDBM) files such as those stored by NIS servers in /var/yp. These are files that are written based on the host byte order and, therefore, cannot be easily shared between hosts of different endianess. The following map will give you access to the right set of those files:

```
ypfiles    -type:=nfs;rfs:=/var/yp/2easy.dom.ain \
           byte==little;rhost:=intelligent \
           byte==big;rhost:=sparky
```

In this example, the NIS files come from an Intel host named intelligent if the host is little-endian, and from the SPARC server sparky if the host is big-endian.

host, domain, and hostd

The hostd selector always contains the Fully Qualified Host Name (FQHN), for example, titan.filesystems.org. The host selector often contains the short hostname of the host, for example, titan. The domain selector contains the domain of the host, for example, filesystems.org. The latter is sometimes incorrectly referred to as the DNS domain, when it is only the FQHN sans the first component.

The most common use of the host selector is to select between an NFS mount and a simple symbolic link. Suppose the host shekel exports the /n/zing file system, and you want to automount it under /homes/staff. On the shekel host, you can simply use a symlink to /n/zing; on all other hosts, however, you must use an NFS mount:

```
staff -rhost:=shekel \
      host==${rhost};type:=link;fs:=/n/zing \
      host!=${rhost};type:=nfs;rfs:=/n/zing
```

You can use the `hostd` selector when you need to select on the FQHN of the host. Often, however, administrators use the `domain` selector to select based on multiple domains. This is useful when your Amd maps are shared across several domains, which can happen in hosting sites. In this example, you can set a symlink to the home directory of the `httpd` server (your HTML content) based on your domain:

```
html    -type:=link \
        domain==filesystems.org;fs:=/n/zing/fs-html \
        domain==buy-filesystems.com;fs:=/secure/shtml \
        domain==example.com;fs:=/n/teaching-content
```

os, osver, and full_os

The `os` selector contains the short name of the operating system, for example, `linux`. Sometimes, it will also include the major version number of the operating system, for example, `solaris2`. The `osver` selector includes the full version of the operating system, for example, `2.2.16`. The `full_os` selector contains the name and version of the operating system. It is needed separately because sometimes the major version of the operating system is part of the `os` selector, and if you tried to concatenate `os` and `osver`, you would get duplicate version digits.

A typical use for these selectors is to pick binaries for different operating systems and versions:

```
X11lib        os==linux;osver==2.2.16;fs:=/usr/X11R6/lib \
              os==solaris2;osver==2.6;fs:=/usr/openwin/lib
```

The above example will point the X11lib automount node to `/usr/X11R6/lib` on Linux 2.2.16 hosts, and to `/usr/openwin/lib` on Solaris 2.6 hosts.

vendor

The `vendor` selector can help you pick files based on the operating system vendor of the current host. For example, to set a specific message of the day (MOTD) for different hosts, you could store different `motd` files for each vendor on one server, and refer to them as follows:

```
msg    -type:=nfs;rhost:=muttered;rfs:=/etc/global/motd-files \
       vendor==redhat;sublink:=motd.rh \
       vendor==sun;sublink:=motd.sun \
       sublink:=motd.generic
```

The Amd Automounter

PART 2

In this example, we set the `msg` automount node to `muttered:/etc/global/motd-files/motd.rh` on Red Hat Linux hosts, and to `/etc/global/motd-files/motd.sun` on Sun hosts. Last, we set it to `/etc/global/motd-files/motd.generic` on all other hosts. Note that we did not need a selector for that last location because we want it to match always if the first two locations failed to match.

uid and *gid*

The `uid` and `gid` selectors change upon each invocation of Amd, especially if different users invoke Amd at the same time. These useful selectors can help you create maps that are only used for a given user or set of users. For example, suppose we have several collections of sources on the system and we want them all to be accessible under a single automounted name, `/src/sys`, in the following manner:

`/usr/src/crypto` can be used only by user `bill`, whose UID is 2301.

`/usr/src/linux` can be used by all users in the `kernel` group, whose GID is 1784.

`/usr/src/public` can be used by all others.

The following map can accomplish that:

```
sys   uid==2031;fs:=/usr/src/crypto \
      gid==1784;fs:=/usr/src/linux \
      fs:=/usr/src/public
```

Note in this example that the user whose UID is 2301 can also be a member of the group whose GID is 1784. Amd's selector evaluation rules, however, test one location at a time. If the first location's selectors match, Amd will neither test the selectors of the second location (second line) nor process the second location, even if subsequent locations could match if tested.

WARNING Do not depend on the `uid` and `gid` variables for serious security reasons. These two variables can easily be subverted by hackers. Amd uses the AUTH_UNIX authentication style for RPC, a very simple form of authentication. The UID and GID values can be changed by anyone who holds a root account on the machine, can inject packets onto the machine, and more.

Deprecated Selectors: *wire, network,* and *netnumber*

These selectors are deprecated in favor of the new, all-encompassing selector function `in_network`, described in the upcoming section "Selector Functions."

> **_WARNING_** Avoid using the wire, network, and netnumber selectors because they will be removed from future distributions. Use the in_network selector function, which subsumes the functionality of these three selectors.

Non-Linux Selector: *cluster*

The only non-Linux selector is the cluster selector, used by HP-UX. This selector can pick a host that is part of a distributed file system cluster. For example, you can set your main NFS server for /usr/local files for each cluster to be the master server of that cluster:

```
binaries    cluster==media-lab;rhost:=tele;rfs:=/usr/local \
            cluster==dbms-lab;rhost:=sun;rfs:=/opt
```

Selector Functions

Table 10.3 lists selector functions supported by Amd. Selector functions are selectors that use the form of a function by accepting arguments.

Table 10.3 Selector Functions

Name	Case Sensitive?	Argument It Takes	Default Value/Test
in_network	No	Network name or address	Existence of this host/ network on any available interface
netgrp	No	Netgroup name	Membership of this host (${host}) in the netgroup
netgrpd	No	Netgroup name	Membership of full hostname (${hostd}) in the netgroup
exists	Yes	File name	Existence of file
true	N/A	N/A	Always TRUE
false	N/A	N/A	Always FALSE

The Amd Automounter

PART 2

in_network

The in_network selector function matches a network name or network number against any of the active interfaces that are available on the host running Amd. You can also use partial network names or partial network numbers. The intent of this selector function is to allow Amd to select a better service based on network closeness to the network service. For example, a multihomed host with three interfaces on three different networks can get to either of those networks directly. Getting to any other network would require going through at least one hop.

This selector subsumes the previous functionality of the following selectors: wire, network, and netnumber. These three used to match the network name (wire and network) or the network number (netnumber), but only for the first active interface on the host. The in_network selector functionality matches against any of the active interfaces on the host and is thus more flexible.

WARNING   Multihomed hosts still require that you install network routes to each of the networks to which your multihomed host is attached. This is necessary to ensure that routing will get you to those networks directly. Furthermore, it is needed to avoid *asymmetric routes*—when packets go through one interface and their replies come through another. Asymmetric routing can cause serious problems with many networking subsystems, especially those based on RPC (such as Amd). Amd does not verify the validity of your routes, only whether your host is a member of any of those networks. It is the network administrator's responsibility to ensure that valid routes are installed. For more information, see the manual page for the route command.

To find out which network names and network numbers your host belongs to, run amd -v, as seen in Listing 10.7.

Listing 10.7   Inspecting what your Amd supports

```
[ezk]$ amd -v
Copyright (c) 1997-1999 Erez Zadok
Copyright (c) 1990 Jan-Simon Pendry
Copyright (c) 1990 Imperial College of Science, Technology & Medicine
Copyright (c) 1990 The Regents of the University of California.
am-utils version 6.0.1s11 (build 5).
Built by ezk@holstein.cs.columbia.edu on date Sat Aug 28 21:29:58 EDT 1999.
cpu=i486 (little-endian), arch=i386, karch=i486.
full_os=linux, os=linux, osver=2.2, vendor=pc.
```

```
Map support for: root, passwd, union, nisplus, nis, ndbm, file, error.
AMFS: nfs, link, nfsx, nfsl, host, linkx, program, union, inherit,
      ufs, cdfs, pcfs, auto, direct, toplvl, error.
FS: iso9660, nfs, vfat, ext2.
Network 1: wire="cs-net" (netnumber=128.59.10).
Network 2: wire="wireless-net" (netnumber=128.59.8).
```

The above host is a member of two networks, listed in the last two lines. The first network's name is cs-net. This would be its short name. Its full name is cs-net.cs .columbia.edu (run the command dnsdomainname or dig localhost to find out what your DNS domain is). The network number of the first network is 128.59.10 (short version) or 128.59.10.0 (full IP network version, padded with zeros).

The second network's name is wireless-net, whose full name is wireless-net.cs .columbia.edu; its network number is 128.59.8, or full-length number 128.59.8.0.

Since the in_network selector function can match against either the long or the short versions of either the network name or the network number, and match against any active interface, the following eight selector functions will all evaluate to TRUE:

- in_network(cs-net)
- in_network(cs-net.cs.columbia.edu)
- in_network(128.59.10)
- in_network(128.59.10.0)
- in_network(wireless-net)
- in_network(wireless-net.cs.columbia.edu)
- in_network(128.59.8)
- in_network(128.59.8.0)

This flexibility of the in_network selector function is what allowed us to deprecate the older three selector variables. As you can see, you can use any valid form to represent one of your networks, and this selector function will match against it.

As an example, consider the situation where you have a mix of a slow and a fast network. On the slow network, say the wireless network, typical NFS service may not work as optimally as on faster networks. On slower networks, typically administrators lower the unit sizes for reading and writing files over NFS. The default is 8192-byte read/write chunks. On slower networks, it is best to lower those to 2048 or 1024 bytes. You can accomplish this with the following map:

```
bins  -rhost:=servy;rfs:=/usr/local;type:=nfs \
      in_network(wireless-net);opts:=rsize=1024,wsize=1024 \
      !in_network(wireless-net)
```

The Amd
Automounter

PART 2

In this example, we set the NFS mount options `rsize` and `wsize` to 1024 bytes each, but only for NFS mounts on the `wireless-net`.

Another typical example of using `in_network` is to ensure that the file servers closest to your network will be used. Suppose you have three networks: 128.59.10.0, 128.59.11.0, and 128.59.12.0. And let us assume that each network has a file server that can serve the same /usr/X11R6 files to all the hosts on that network: server `earth` on the 128.59.10.0 network, server `wind` on the 128.59.11.0 network, and server `fire` on the 128.59.12.0 network. Ideally, you'd like each file server to be used on its own network and not on other networks, so as to optimize your NFS traffic. The following map can achieve this:

```
X11dist     -type:=nfs;rfs:=/usr/X11R6 \
            in_network(128.59.10.0);rhost:=earth \
            in_network(128.59.11.0);rhost:=wind \
            in_network(128.59.12.0);rhost:=fire \
            rhost:=earth    rhost:=wind    rhost:=fire
```

The last line in the above example will ensure that if none of the first three `in_network` lines matched—in other words, you were not on any of these three networks—Amd will pick one of those three servers at random. See the description for the `delay` map option in the upcoming section "Options," as well as Chapter 12 for more examples of configuring replicated volumes.

netgrp and *netgrpd*

The `netgrp` selector function matches the current hostname against a netgroup. Network groups are often described in the file /etc/netgroup or in an NIS map called `netgroup`. The `netgrp` selector function will use the short hostname to perform the match—the one described in the ${host} variable. The `netgrpd` selector function will use the full hostname to perform the match—the one described in the ${hostd} variable.

Administrators can add and remove hosts from network groups as needed. Suppose your administrators set up a netgroup called `servers` that is permitted more liberal NFS access to various file systems, and a netgroup called `dmz` for hosts that are allowed only restricted NFS access. Then you can use the following Amd map throughout your site:

```
binaries    -rhost:=servy;rfs:=/usr/local \
            netgrp(servers);opts:=suid,rw,noquota,devs,intr \
            netgrp(dmz);opts:=nosuid,ro,quota,nodevs,nointr \
            opts:=rw,quota,intr
```

The above map will allow hosts in the `servers` netgroup to access `servy:/usr/local` liberally: execute set-UID binaries, allow read-write access, turn off quota restrictions, allow access to device files over NFS, and allow you to interrupt pending mounts. Hosts in the `dmz` netgroup have almost opposite restrictions: not allowed to execute set-UID binaries, read-only access, quotas enforced, no access to device files, and not allowed to interrupt pending mounts. Finally, all other hosts are allowed a default set of mount options more suitable for regular user workstations: read-write access, quotas enforced, and the ability to interrupt pending mounts.

exists

The `exists` selector function returns TRUE if the file (or directory) name specified as its argument exists. This selector function uses the `lstat` system call to check for the path name's existence. This is a simple way to ensure that you provide automount links to files or directories that exist. A typical use might be the following:

```
X11files    -type:=link \
            exist(/usr/X11R6);fs:=/usr/X11R6 \
            exist(/usr/openwin);fs:=/usr/openwin
```

The above example will set up a symlink to /usr/X11R6 if that directory exists. If not, it will set up a symlink to /usr/openwin if that directory exists. If neither directory exists, trying to resolve the `X11files` automount node will result in an error "No such file or directory."

> **WARNING** Do not specify automounted path names to the `exists` selector function, especially not automounted path names that belong to the same map. If you do, you will deadlock Amd, have to kill the Amd process, and possibly need to reboot. Amd does not attempt to check to see if the path names given to the `exists` function are automounted ones because that test cannot be performed reliably.

true and false

The two selector functions `true` and `false` are there mostly for completeness. Amd ignores any arguments passed to these two functions. The `true` selector function can be used to temporarily force a location to match regardless of the rest of selectors in the entry. At the same time, you can use the `false` function to skip an entry without too much editing of your Amd map. For example, you will not have to comment out an entry you want to skip for a short period of time. (Recall also that commenting entries using the #

character only works for file maps, not NIS, Hesiod, etc.) For example, suppose you have an Amd entry such as the following:

```
TeX    -type:=nfs \
       osver==2.2;rhost:=stable;rfs:=/usr/tex \
       osver==2.3;rhost:=testy;rfs:=/usr/test/teTeX
```

If you want to skip the first location, but always make sure that the second one succeeds, you can make a permanent edit to that map and make it look like the following:

```
TeX    -type:=nfs \
       rhost:=testy;rfs:=/usr/test/teTeX
```

Since there are no selectors in this revised map, it always succeeds. However, if you wanted to preserve the overall structure of the entry (perhaps because the change you are making is only temporary and will be reverted in a few days), you could then use the true and false selector functions as follows:

```
TeX    -type:=nfs \
       false(osver==2.2);rhost:=stable;rfs:=/usr/tex \
       true(osver==2.3);rhost:=testy;rfs:=/usr/test/teTeX
```

This entry will ensure that the first location will be skipped, while the second one always matches. Note how we saved the old selector variable comparison as arguments to the true and false selector functions; that way we can change it back easily.

Variables

Variables are those information holders in Amd maps that you can assign values to, or refer to in the value of other variables. Note also that all the variable selectors seen so far can be used in the values of other variables. In this section we will show both assignments of variables and assignments to them. Table 10.4 lists these variables in alphabetical order, their default values, and the meaning of these variables. In the rest of this section, we group the variables and discuss several of them together in related examples.

Table 10.4   Map Variables

Name	Default Value	Meaning
addopts	None	Additional options to add or override the existing options
autodir	/a	Temporary directory for NFS mounts
cache	None	Map cache style for auto-mounter file systems
cachedir	None	The directory where the cache is stored (Solaris)
delay	None	Number of seconds to delay a mount
dev	None	Name of device to mount for some file systems (must be specified)
dollar	$	A literal dollar symbol
fs	${autodir}/${rhost}${rfs}	Full path name of local (temporary) directory mount point
host*	Local hostname	Often determines local vs. remote mounts
key	Key looked up by user	The key that Amd will look for in this map
map	Path name where map is auto-mounted	Directory that Amd automounts
maptype	None	Source type for the map: file, NIS, Hesiod, etc.
mount	None	Arbitrary program to mount a file system

The Amd
Automounter

PART 2

Table 10.4   Map Variables *(continued)*

Name	Default Value	Meaning
opts	rw	Mount options for use with the file system being mounted locally
path	${map}/${key}	Full path name to the auto-mounted node, or path name being looked up by user
pref	None	Prefix prepended to user key lookup before searching in map
remopts	${opts}	Mount options for remote NFS mounts only
rfs	${path}	Remote file system name to mount
rhost	${host}	Name of remote hostname to NFS-mount
sublink	None	The name of a subdirectory within the mounted remote file system to point the auto-mounted node to
type	None	Type of file system to mount (must be specified)
unmount	None	Arbitrary program to un-mount a file system
var0...var7	None	Eight arbitrary placeholders

* The host **selector was also discussed in the preceding section "Selectors and Variables."**

Note that we have briefly covered some of these variables in Chapter 9, when we discussed those parameters whose defaults can be overridden in the amd.conf file. In particular, these were as follows:

- The autodir variable, using the autodir configuration parameter

- The map variable, which is controlled by the name of the map in square brackets in your amd.conf

- The type variable, which is controlled by the map_type Amd configuration parameter

- The cache variable, which is controlled by the map_options Amd configuration parameter

autodir, key, map, host, rhost, path, rfs, fs, and *sublink*

The set of nine variables autodir, key, map, host, rhost, path, rfs, fs, and sublink form the core group of variables used most often in Amd maps. In addition, these variables depend on each other very closely. As you can see from Table 10.4, the default value for some of these variables is actually a combination of values of other variables.

NOTE If you change the values of these variables, the change will only affect these variables for the duration of the processing of the given map entry. Furthermore, the change will only be seen if you use these variables in the values of other variables. In particular, changing these values does *not* have the side effects you might expect: changing key does not rewrite the map, changing host or rhost will not change the actual hostname of any machine, changing map will not change Amd's automount point, and so on.

To understand how Amd uses these variables, we will use a detailed example. Suppose you have a /home map with several users. One of the entries in that map is for user ezk. To get to that user's home directory, you must contact host sunny, NFS-mount the file system /u/nic of that host, and then find the home directory for this user in the subdirectory zadok18 under /u/nic. The map to satisfy these requirements would be as follows:

    ezk   type:=nfs;rhost:=sunny;rfs:=/u/nic;sublink:=zadok18

In particular, this map says that

- The type of file system mount is nfs.

- The remote host to mount is sunny.

- The remote file system to mount is /u/nic.

- The actual home directory is in the subdirectory named zadok18.

Let us also assume that the autodir was set to /n. If you inspect the path name /home/ezk and your mounted file systems after referencing /home/ezk, you will see an NFS mount of host sunny and a symbolic link inside the automount point:

    $ df /home/ezk
    sunny:/u/nic   2060846   1963245   76993 96% /n/sunny/u/nic

The Amd Automounter

PART 2

```
$ ls -l /home/ezk

lrwxrwxrwx   1 root     root     15 Sep 21 09:12 /home/ezk ->
    /n/sunny/u/nic/zadok18
```

The nine steps that Amd took when /home/ezk was invoked, and which resulted in the above mount and symlink, were as follows:

1. Check to see if /home/ezk is already mounted and in the cache. If so, use it.

2. Otherwise, evaluate and normalize the rhost variable. This means also that the short hostname is used for rhost.

3. Evaluate the remaining variables in the map in order of appearance in the map.

4. If not evaluated already, evaluate the values of these variables: autodir, key, map, host, rhost, path, rfs, fs, and sublink.

5. Check to see if the directory specified by ${fs} exists and make it if necessary. This prepares the mount point /n/sunny/u/nic before NFS-mounting on top of it. This is the same as running the following command:

    ```
    [root]# mkdir -p ${fs}
    ```

    or

    ```
    [root]# mkdir -p /n/sunny/u/nic
    ```

6. Contact the remote host listed in ${rhost} and see if it is up. This ensures that the sunny file server is ready to receive NFS requests.

7. Ask the remote host for a file handle to the file system specified in ${rfs}. This makes sure that we could NFS-mount /u/nic.

8. NFS-mount ${rfs} from host ${rhost} on top of ${fs}, using the remote mount options specified in ${remopts}. This is similar to executing the following command:

    ```
    [root]# mount -t ${type} -o ${remopts} ${rhost}:${rfs} ${fs}
    ```

    or

    ```
    [root]# mount -t nfs -o rw sunny:/u/nic /n/sunny/u/nic
    ```

    Note that the value of ${remopts} was computed to be rw, the default used for ${opts}.

9. Return a symbolic link to the user, pointing the ${key} name to the ${fs}. This is similar to executing the following:

    ```
    [root]# ln -s ${fs} ${path}
    ```

    or

    ```
    [root]# ln -s /n/sunny/u/nic /home/ezk
    ```

WARNING Ensure that you always set ${rhost} to the proper value. If you forget to set it, it will default to the local host's name and Amd will attempt to perform an NFS-mount from local host onto local host. This can cause kernel deadlocks or even trigger bugs in older operating systems.

---

type

The type variable specifies the type of file system mount to perform in the given location. This variable is also closely related to the nine variables described in the previous section. The list of file systems that you can mount using Amd is given in the output of amd -v as seen in Listing 10.7. You can mount all the file systems listed under FS as well as AMFS. Because of the amount of detail involved, we describe those separately in the sections "Native File Systems" and "Meta File Systems," later in this chapter.

The type variable must be defined. It has no default. You may set a default for it in your map, under /defaults. You may set a per-map default as well as set it for each volume. As you will see later in this chapter, under "Native File Systems," the type of file system you mount can also impact the location as a whole, and in particular, which map variables you have to use.

dev

The variable dev specifies the physical device to mount and is used for those file systems listed later in this chapter, under the section "Native File Systems." For example, when you mount an ISO-9660 CD-ROM on a Linux system where the CD-ROM device is the master device on the second IDE chain, that device would be named /dev/hdc. To set up an automount point for that CD-ROM, use the following:

```
cdrom  type:=cdfs;dev:=/dev/hdc;opts:=ro
```

The above says to mount /dev/hdc as an ISO-9660–type file system and mount it read-only.

pref

The pref variable sets a prefix for the entry to look up in the Amd map. This is better explained with an example. Suppose /home is an automount point, and a user types **cd /home/jms**. The kernel will get a request to resolve the jms component in the NFS file system mounted under /home. Recall that Amd appears to the kernel as an NFS server. The kernel will send an RPC message to the NFS server (Amd) to resolve the lookup. Amd will receive an RPC lookup request, but before looking jms up in its maps, it will prepend the contents of the ${pref} variable to the lookup string, and then look up all of that.

The following example illustrates how the ${pref} variable works. Let us say you have this amd.conf map:

```
[/home]
map_name = amd.home
map_options = pref:=sales/
```

and you use it with this amd.home map:

```
/defaults    type:=nfs;rhost:=blue;rfs:=/users/quest


sales/dan    sublink:=daniel_lionden


sales/alice sublink:=alice_wunderland
```

If a user tries to access /home/dan, Amd will look up sales/dan in the amd.home map, not just the name dan. That is because the prefix in ${pref} is prepended to the looked-up name before the map lookup takes place.

The above is a simple example. The pref variable is explained with a more practical example in the upcoming section "Automount File System (auto)."

cache

The cache parameter determines how Amd caches entries are seen in a map. It is typically set when a map is configured, either in the amd.conf file or when using a type:=auto file system. Since most maps are configured in an amd.conf file, we described these options in Chapter 9. Some automounter maps can also be set inside an existing Amd map—as a subsidiary map. At that point, you can also set caching parameters. We describe this later in the chapter, under "Automount File System (auto)."

maptype

The maptype variable sets the type of the input source to use for the map: file, NIS, Hesiod, etc. The full list of possible map types can be seen by running amd -v, as in Listing 10.7. If not specified, Amd will search all the maps available in the order listed in the output of amd -v.

mount and umount

The two variables mount and unmount are used with the type:=program mount. This file system can mount any arbitrary program by simply specifying the programs to mount and unmount it. The mount variable specifies the name and arguments to a program that can mount a specific file system. The umount variable specifies the name and arguments to a program that can unmount the specific file system. We describe this file system in detail later in this chapter, under the section "Program File System (program)" and also in Chapter 12.

opts, remopts, and addopts

The three variables opts, remopts, and addopts affect the mount options used when Amd mounts file systems. We describe the basic use of these three variables here. Later in this chapter, under the section "Options," we detail the actual mount options available.

opts   The opts variable specifies the basic mount options used for all mounts. These mount options are often specified in the /defaults entry for the whole map, or in the default entry for a specific mount entry or volume. Each time opts is specified, it overrides any previous default for this variable.

For example, suppose you use the map in Listing 10.8.

Listing 10.8   An example for overriding mount options

```
/defaults    type:=nfs;opts:=rw

play         rhost:=gamer;rfs:=/usr/games

oxygen       -rhost:=air;opts:=proto=udp,vers=3 \
             host!=${rhost};rfs:=/usr/lists
             host==${rhost};fs:=/usr/lists

lists        -rhost:=dept \
             host!=${rhost};rfs:=/usr/lists;opts:=quota,nosuid \
             host==${rhost};fs:=/usr/lists

test         -rhost:=qaserv;opts:=suid,noquota,rw,intr \
             host!=${rhost};rfs:=/usr/local/qa;opts:=devs,posix \
             host==${rhost};fs:=/usr/lists
```

For the play entry, the options used would be rw, because they are defaulted from the /defaults entry. The oxygen entry will use the options proto=udp,vers=3 because that entry's default overrides the map default. The lists entry will use the quota,nosuid defaults but only when on a host other than dept, because this specific location overrides the map defaults. Finally the test entry specifies both an entry and a location default for one of the locations. When the host is other than qaserv, Amd will use the options devs,posix. When the host is qaserv, Amd will use the options in the entry default, suid,noquota,rw,intr.

remopts The `remopts` variable specifies the mount options to use for remote NFS mounts. If not specified, it defaults to the options listed in `${opts}`. Sometimes, however, there are specific options that may be useful or desired only for remote NFS mounts. For example, suppose you want all local mounts—disk, floppy, and CD-ROM—to allow the owner of the workstation to write to those devices that are locally attached. At the same time, however, you want to protect your main NFS file servers, and so you can specify that all NFS mounts should be read-only and disallow set-UID binaries. You can accomplish this with the map seen in Listing 10.9.

Listing 10.9 A map sample using remopts

```
/defaults   opts:=rw,noquota,devs,suid;\
            remopts:=ro,quota,nodevs,nosuid

binaries    type:=nfs;rhost:=binmaster;rfs:=/usr/local

floppy      type:=pcfs;dev:=/dev/fd0H1440

cd          type:=cdfs;dev:=/dev/cdrom
```

This example will ensure that the `binaries` entry will use the options `ro,quota,nodevs,nosuid`, while the `floppy` and `cd` entries will use the `rw,noquota,devs,suid` options.

addopts The `addopts` variable specifies additional mount options to add for a given mount. The `opts` variable always overrides any previously set options, as we saw in Listing 10.8. However, with `addopts` you can add or override options only for a given entry. The `addopts` variable also affects the values specified in the `remopts` variable for remote mounts.

Options that start with `no` will override those with the same name that do not start with `no` and vice versa. Special handling is given to inverted mount options such as `soft` and `hard`, `bg` and `fg`, `ro` and `rw`, etc.

For example, if the default options specified were

```
opts:=rw,nosuid,intr,rsize=1024,wsize=1024,quota,posix
```

and the ones specified in a map entry were

```
addopts:=grpid,suid,ro,rsize=2048,quota,nointr
```

then the actual options used would be

```
wsize=1024,posix,grpid,suid,ro,rsize=2048,quota,nointr
```

This is because some options in `addopts` override what the original `opts` had:

- `suid` overrides `nosuid`.
- `ro` overrides `rw`.
- `quota` overrides `quota`, but that does not change the outcome.
- `nointr` overrides `intr`.
- `rsize=2048` overrides `rsize=1024`.

As an example combining these options, suppose that for security reasons, you set all default mount options to read-only. However, you wish to allow a select set of file systems to have read-write access, in particular those containing users' home directories. In addition, you want to use all other default mount options.

You can accomplish this as follows:

```
/defaults    opts:=ro,quota,nodevs,nosuid


users        type:=nfs;rhost:=raider;rfs:=/uhomes;addopts:=rw
```

In this example, the `users` entry will mount with `rw` options, as well as `quota,nodevs,nosuid`. All other entries in this map will use the options specified in the `/defaults` entry, including the read-only option.

delay

The `delay` option causes some NFS mounts to be postponed by a number of seconds. This is useful in a replicated server environment, where Amd can mount any one of several replicated volumes to satisfy a mount request. The syntax for replicated volumes is to specify the list of remote hosts without any selectors, therefore selecting all of them.

Suppose you have this map:

```
X11dist     -type:=nfs;rfs:=/usr/X11R6 \
            rhost:=earth    rhost:=wind    rhost:=fire
```

What Amd will do is fork a copy of itself to mount `earth` in the background, then another background copy to mount `wind`, and then another to mount `fire`. You would have four Amd processes at that given time: one master Amd process and three backgrounded mount processes. The master process will wait until one of the backgrounded mounts succeeds (or all time out or fail). Once any one of the backgrounded mounts succeeds, the master Amd process will use that file server and ignore the other two. In that way, the first one to answer will be used.

However, oftentimes administrators have server preferences. They might want the wind server to be used primarily, the fire server secondarily, and the earth server as a last resort. One way to achieve this is with the delay option, as follows:

```
X11dist      -type:=nfs;rfs:=/usr/X11R6 \
             rhost:=earth;delay=4   rhost:=wind   rhost:=fire;delay=1
```

In this case, the mount for the earth server will not be attempted for four seconds, the mount for the fire server will be delayed by one second, and the wind server's mount will proceed without delay. These delays force an order of sorts on NFS mounts by delaying them by different amounts of time.

Load-Balancing NFS Mounts?

In practice, the delay option is not that useful nowadays. If you do not use delays, and all your servers are up, it is most likely that the first one listed will be used. This is because Amd is not multithreaded: it forks background mounts for servers in the order that they are listed in the map. Since networks and servers are pretty fast these days, by the time Amd gets to fork the second mount, the first one most likely had already responded.

In addition, the granularity of the delay option is in seconds. One second is too long a delay in today's sites, with fast hosts and networks. Delaying a mount by even as little as one second is likely to ensure that those entries not delayed, or delayed by fewer seconds, will answer first.

Even if the delay option could use a microsecond resolution clock for its delays, a larger problem still exists: how do you know ahead of time what delay values to set such that all mounts are truly attempted at the same exact time? Administrators would have to measure the responsiveness of servers and networks to compute proper delay values. But that does not help to account for temporary network and server conditions that may make some servers more or less available than they were just a second ago.

What administrators often want is a true load-balancing solution for NFS servers: a way to find out accurately the performance and availability of a set of NFS servers, and distribute NFS requests to NFS servers based on that availability, avoiding downed servers until they come back up. This technology is not available with NFSv2 or NFSv3; some of the specification in NFSv4 makes allowances for replicated servers but does not provide all the details for load-balancing NFS servers.

Consequently, the delay option is useful today only to order a list of NFS servers such that a given server in the ordered list of servers will be used only if all the servers listed earlier are down.

dollar

The dollar variable is used for one thing: to insert a literal $ symbol anywhere in an Amd map. As we explained in the section "Variable Expansion" at the beginning of this chapter, Amd performs multiple passes over Amd entries, until it can resolve all variables. However, since the $ symbol is a special character that indicates the beginning of a variable's name, it cannot be inserted easily in Amd maps, for Amd will incorrectly consider that symbol to begin another variable's name. Other methods for quoting or escaping characters do not work because Amd processes them before evaluating variable values.

As an example, suppose you have an NFS server that exports a file system named /projects/xy$z4. To mount it, you cannot specify the following:

```
bigp  type:=nfs;rhost:=mortal;rfs:=/projects/xy$z4
```

If you do, Amd will report a syntax error that it cannot resolve the variable $z, and what it will try to mount is /projects/xy4. That is because the value of any variable that cannot be resolved becomes NULL or empty. Instead, you must specify this entry as follows:

```
bigp  type:=nfs;rhost:=mortal;rfs:=/projects/xy${dollar}z4
```

Spare Variables: *var0* through *var7*

The eight variables ranging from var0 to var7 do not have any particular meaning and can be used as placeholders for any values. One particular use for these is to simplify maps and make them more readable, especially if you have long names or strings that must be repeated. Suppose you have a file server that contains several user file systems, all starting with the string /export/raiddisks/user-homes/staff, and you wish to mount several of them. If you specify each file system, your map entries will be long and harder to understand. But if you recorded the prefix of these file systems in a separate variable, you could simplify such a map as follows:

```
/defaults   type:=nfs;rfs:=fserv1;\
                    var3:=/export/raiddisks/user-homes/staff


admin       rfs:=${var3}/admin


tech        rfs:=${var3}/tech
```

This way, when you access admin, you will actually mount the file system /export/raiddisks/user-homes/staff/admin, and when you access tech, you will mount the file system /export/raiddisks/user-homes/staff/admin.

Non-Linux Variable: *cachedir*

The only non-Linux variable is cachedir. It is used on Solaris systems with the CacheFS file system, a caching file system that can cache files from a remote slow NFS server to a local faster disk. CacheFS works by storing cached data in a special formatted cache directory. Cached files are not directly accessible from that cache directory, but from a *front file system* mount point. Suppose you want to cache the contents of the directory /usr/local into /import and use /cdat for the cache directory data. The following Amd entry achieves that:

```
copt   type:=cachefs;cachedir:=/cdat;rfs:=/usr/local;fs:=/import
```

Options

Amd supports many mount options, spanning a large number of file systems and operating systems. Mount options are specified as a comma-delimited list of strings. Options are listed as the values for the variables opts, remopts, and addopts, described above under the section "opts, remopts, and addopts."

Options come in three flavors:

- Boolean options are those that can turn a feature on or off, such as intr and nointr.
- Numeric options are those that take a number as their value, such as rsize=2048.
- String options are those that take a word as their value, such as proto=tcp.

In addition, options can be classified into groups of file systems they affect:

- Options that affect the automounter file system (Amd) as a whole
- Generic mount options that affect all mounts that Amd performs
- Native file system options: NFS, EXT2, ISO9660, VFAT, etc.

Automounter options are options that are implemented by Amd, not by the operating system or any other file system. These options are meaningful only for Amd.

The mount system call takes several arguments. One of the arguments specifies generic mount options. These are options that are applicable to every file system type being mounted. In addition, the mount system call takes an additional argument for file system–specific parameters. This argument is typically a pointer to a file system–specific data structure that the mount system call passes to the kernel. One or more of the fields in this data structure declare mount options that are only applicable to the file system type being mounted.

Amd can take any list of mount options, mixing all types of options together. The user listing these options can specify them in any order, delimited by commas. Amd does the hard work: it determines what category the mount option belongs to and how to apply it. Since there are many mount options and more than half of them apply to specific file systems or operating systems, Amd takes a liberal approach in processing unknown mount options: it logs a warning message and otherwise ignores unknown mount options. This allows administrators to specify all the mount options they wish to use, and let Amd use those that are implemented and applicable. The downside, however, is that administrators must check the log files to ensure that mount options they do want applied are not ignored.

In this section we describe the automounter mount options in detail. We then list generic mount options and file system–specific mount options, but we do not describe them in detail since they were covered in Chapter 2, "Configuring NFS." Then we briefly list mount options for systems other than Linux. For more details about all these options, refer to the manual page for mount.

Automounter Mount Options

The options listed in Table 10.5 are implemented by Amd and are meaningful only for Amd. Some of these options relate to specific Amd configuration file parameters.

Table 10.5   Automounter Mount Options

Option	Default	Description
browsable	Off	Allow listing of Unix directory entries in automount file systems.
fullybrowsable	Off	Allow listing of all entries in automount file systems.
nounmount	Unmount	Keep this file system mounted all the time.
ping=*N*	4	Set the keep-alive ping interval to *N* seconds.
retry=*N*	2	Retry the mount(2) system call *N* times at most.
utimeout=*N*	300	Extend a mount's TTL by *N* seconds after a failed unmount attempt.

The Amd Automounter

PART 2

browsable and *fullybrowsable*

A file system is browsable when you can list the names of files and directories in it. Most Unix file systems are browsable, so users can search for and find their files. Automounter file systems do not have to be browsable to allow administrators greater control over naming and access to volumes that can be automounted.

The options `browsable` and `fullybrowsable` turn on browsability of Amd's automounter file system, allowing entries to be listed by programs such as `ls`. Normally, these two options are set in the `amd.conf` file for any given map. See Chapter 9 for details.

The main reason to allow these two options here is for `type:=auto` file system mounts, which provide a subsidiary Amd automount directory under an existing one. See the related discussion later in this chapter, under "Automount File System (`auto`)," for more information.

nounmount

As we saw in Chapter 9, Amd keeps mounts for a period of time, called the *time-to-live* (TTL) interval. When that TTL timer expires, Amd tries to unmount the volume. Certain pathological timer configurations could result in repeated sequences of unmounts and remounts, a condition we described in Chapter 9 under the sidebar titled "Ping-Pong Mounts." If your file system really needs to remain mounted all the time, then you can set this option.

For example, suppose you automount your shared libraries on diskless workstations. Shared libraries such as those in `/usr/lib` must be available all the time for binaries to function, since those binaries were dynamically linked with those shared libraries. You can ensure that such a file system would remain mounted all the time as follows:

```
shlibs      rhost:=bootsrv;rfs:=/usr/lib;addopts:=nounmount
```

WARNING Do not use this parameter unless absolutely necessary. If you use it too much, your system will include many file systems that will never unmount even if they are no longer used. This defeats the purpose of one of the primary functions of the automounter: to unmount unused file systems. See Chapter 8, "Overview of the Amd Automounter."

---

ping

As we described in Chapter 8, Amd tests to see if remote file servers are up or down by sending them small RPC messages, or *pings*, using the NFS NullProc message (procedure 0). The `ping` option specifies the interval, in seconds, between those keep-alive messages.

When four consecutive pings have failed, the mount point is marked as hung. The interval between pings is 30 seconds and cannot be changed by users. If the ping interval is less than zero, no pings are sent and the host is assumed to be always up. Furthermore, by default, pings are not sent for NFS mounts using the TCP transport, since TCP comes with its own keep-alive mechanism.

Suppose you have a slow and busy network. On such a network, four consecutive pings may be lost even if the remote server is still up. If that happens, Amd may incorrectly consider working file servers as being down. In such a case, doubling the value of this counter may improve performance:

```
/defaults    addopts:=ping=8
```

In this example, we set the number of pings to 8 in the /defaults entry, thus affecting all mounts for that map.

retry

The retry mount option specifies the number of times that the mount system call will execute. This value defaults to 2. Amd will try twice to mount a given file system. If both tries fail, Amd will consider the whole mount as failed. Generally, by the time Amd gets to perform the mount system call, enough information has been gathered and validated that the mount is likely to either succeed or fail on the first try; a second try is not likely to change that. This is why the default value for this parameter is small, only 2.

If your systems and networks are fairly reliable, you can avoid trying these extra mounts by setting this parameter to 1, as follows:

```
/defaults    addopts:=retry=1
```

utimeout

The utimeout option specifies the interval, in seconds, by which the mount's TTL is extended after an unmount attempt has failed. In fact, the interval is extended before the unmount is attempted to avoid thrashing. The default value is 120 seconds (two minutes) or as set by the dismount_interval Amd configuration parameter.

While the amd.conf file can control this parameter globally, you can use the utimeout mount option to affect this value for a single volume. If you have a busy file system, say for user homes, then you might wish to increase this value:

```
homes   type:=nfs;rhost:=largo;rfs:=/homes;addopts:=utimeout=3600
```

This example increases the unmount TTL to one hour.

Generic Mount Options

Generic mount options are those that apply to all file systems. We described these and other options in detail in Table 2.3 in Chapter 2. Amd uses the same names for generic mount options that the system's /bin/mount program uses. Here, we list the options that Amd uses and briefly remind you what each option does. Recall that most Boolean mount options have an opposite option that often starts with no.

async Perform all I/O asynchronously.

atime Update the inode access times for this mount.

dev Allow character or block special devices on the file system.

exec Permit execution of binaries in this file system.

grpid Create new files with the group ID of the directory in which they are created.

noatime Do not update the inode access times for this mount.

noauto Do not list the mount of this file system in the output of df.

nodev Disallow character or block special devices on the file system.

noexec Disallow execution of binaries in this file system.

nogrpid Create new files with the effective group ID of the process that creates them.

noquota Do not process or enforce quota limitations.

nosuid Disallow executions of set-UID binaries. This is generally considered more secure.

quota Process and enforce quota limitations for this mount.

ro Mount this file system read-only.

rw Mount this file system read-write, allowing destructive operations such as file removals.

suid Allow executions of set-UID binaries. This is generally considered less secure.

sync Perform all I/O synchronously. Increases reliability of file systems but lowers performance.

File System–Specific Mount Options

File system–specific mount options are those that apply to just one specific native file system. We describe some of these options here, seen in Table 10.6. However, the bulk of these are NFS options, which we described in detail in Chapter 2. Amd uses the same names for these mount options that the system's /bin/mount program uses.

Table 10.6   Disk and CD-ROM–Specific Mount Options

Option	File System	Default	Meaning
norock	ISO-9660	Off	Disable Rock Ridge extensions.
grpid	EXT2	Off	Create files with group ID of parent directory.
nogrpid	EXT2	On	Create files with group ID of running process.
noquota	EXT2	On	Do not enforce quotas.
quota	EXT2	Off	Enforce quotas.

ISO-9660 Mount Option

The only mount option for ISO-9660 (`type:=cdfs`) file systems is the `norock`. This option turns off Rock Ridge extensions for CD-ROMs. The Rock Ridge extensions allow ISO-9660 file systems to include symbolic links, devices, and more. To use this option, you can set it in an entry such as this:

```
localcd      type:=cdfs;dev:=/dev/hdc;addopts:=norock
```

EXT2 Mount Options

Amd supports the four EXT2FS mount options listed in Table 10.6. Depending on your version of Linux, it may allow you to specify these four options for all file systems, or only to EXT2FS file systems. In either case, their meaning is identical to what we described above in the section "Generic Mount Options."

NFS Mount Options

This section briefly describes the meaning of those NFS mount options that Amd supports. All of these options and others were described in detail in Table 2.4 in Chapter 2.

acdirmax=N   Set the maximum time for caching the attributes of a directory to N seconds.

acdirmin=N   Set the minimum time for caching the attributes of a directory to N seconds.

acregmax=N   Set the maximum time for caching the attributes of regular files to N seconds.

acregmin=N Set the minimum time for caching the attributes of regular files to N seconds.

actimeo=N This is a shortcut option that sets the four values acdirmin, acdirmax, acregmin, and acregmax to N.

hard If an NFS server is not accessible, try to access it indefinitely. During this time, all processes with open files on the downed file server remain hung until the file server comes back up. This improves reliability but can annoy users whose processes are stuck.

intr If the file server is not responding, your file system was hard-mounted, and your user process is hung, this allows you to abort that process by sending it the INTR signal (often generated using Ctrl+C).

mounthost=S Specify the name of the host running the rpc.mountd server as S. Normally this is the same host that runs the NFS server.

mountport=N Specify the port that the rpc.mountd server runs on as N. Normally this port is found by contacting the remote host's portmapper.

mountprog=N Use an RPC mountd program number other than the default (100005). This is useful if you are running multiple rpc.mountd servers or purposely run them on different RPC program numbers.

mountvers=N Use a mount protocol version number different from the default, 1. This is useful if you want to force usage of newer protocol versions or experimental ones, or if your remote NFS server does not support version 1 of the protocol.

namlen=N Force the maximum length of file names to N. This is useful with older mount protocols.

nfsprog=N Use an NFS program number other than the default (100003). This is useful if you are running multiple NFS servers or purposely run them on different RPC program numbers.

noac Disable all forms of attribute caching. This can slow performance significantly but provides up-to-date values for the attributes of all files for this mount.

nocto Do not necessarily maintain close-to-open consistency by not retrieving new attributes for a file that may have been deleted and then recreated.

nointr If the file server is not responding, your file system was hard mounted, and your user process is hung, do not allow users to send signals to abort hung processes.

nolock Do not start the rpc.lockd process and do not support file locking over NFS. This can result in file corruption when two or more processes try to update the same file but can speed up file access.

port=N   Connect to an NFS server running on port *N*, instead of the default 2049. This is useful if you run multiple NFS servers or special-purposes ones, or if you start them on a different port (for security reasons).

posix   Mount the file system using the POSIX semantics. Among other things, this allows the client and server to exchange *pathconf* information correctly to determine the maximum file name length supported by both client and server.

proto=S   Mount the file system using protocol transport type *S*, currently either udp or tcp.

retrans=N   Set the number of allowed minor RPC timeouts to *N*, defaults to 3. When 3 minor timeouts occur, a major timeout is triggered and an error is returned to the user process.

rsize=N   Read files from the server in chunks of *N* bytes. This value defaults to anywhere from 1024 to 32768, depending on your Linux kernel version. Larger values provide better throughput on faster networks, while smaller values are better for slow or unreliable networks.

soft   If an NFS server is not accessible, timeout the request and report a failure, thus unlocking otherwise hung processes. This can result in serious data corruption, since most user applications do not handle this case gracefully.

tcp   Use the TCP transport for this NFS mount.

timeo=N   Set the interval between minor RPC retransmissions to *N* tenths of a second.

udp   Use the UDP transport for this NFS mount.

vers=N   Mount the file system using protocol version *N*, currently either 2 or 3.

wsize=N   Write files onto the server in chunks of *N* bytes. This value defaults to anywhere from 1024 to 32768, depending on your Linux kernel version. Larger values provide better throughput on faster networks, while smaller values are better for slow or unreliable networks.

As a simple example, if you are running NFS over slow or unreliable networks, you should use protocol version 3 because it is more efficient and use the TCP transport because it is more reliable, and you should lower the default read and write buffer sizes to 1024 bytes. You can achieve this with the following set of options in your Amd map:

```
/defaults   opts:=vers=3,proto=tcp,rsize=1024,wsize=1024
```

The Amd Automounter

PART 2

Non-Linux Mount Options

This section lists all of the mount options that Amd supports on non-Linux systems. We list them briefly in Table 10.7. For more information, consult the am-utils user manual on www.am-utils.org, as well as your host's mount manual pages.

Table 10.7   Non-Linux Mount Options

Option	File System	Meaning
automntfs	Generic	Ignore this mount in df (bsdi4).
cache	Generic	Allow data to be cached from a remote server for this mount.
compress	NFS	Use a proprietary NFS compression protocol.
deadthresh	NFS	Set dead server retry threshold.
defperm	CDFS	Ignore the permission mode bits, and set default file permissions to 0555, UID 0, and GID 0.
dumbtimr	NFS	Turn off the dynamic retransmit timeout estimator. This may be useful for UDP mounts that exhibit high retry rates, since it is possible that the dynamically estimated timeout interval is too short.
extatt	CDFS	Enable extended attributes in ISO-9660 file systems.
fsid	Generic	Set ID of file system.
fsname	NFS	Provide the name of the server's file system to the kernel.
gens	CDFS	Enable generations in ISO-9660 file systems. Generations allow you to see all versions of a given file.
grpid	NFS	Use BSD directory group-ID semantics.

Table 10.7   Non-Linux Mount Options *(continued)*

Option	File System	Meaning
hostname	NFS	Provide the name of the server's hostname to the kernel.
ignore	Generic	Ignore this mount by df.
ignore	NFS	Ignore this mount by df.
int	NFS	Allow keyboard interrupts (signals) on hard mounts.
jfs	Generic	Use the Journalling file system (AIX).
leaseterm	NFS	Set the lease term (for NQNFS, Not Quite NFS).
maxgroups	NFS	Set the maximum number of groups to allow for this mount.
maxgrps	NFS	Set the maximum number of groups to allow for this mount.
multi	Generic	Perform multi-component lookup on files.
nfsv3	NFS	Perform an NFS version 3 mount.
nocache	Generic	Do not allow data to be cached from a remote server for this mount.
noconn	NFS	Do not use connected UDP sockets on datagram transports.
nodefperm	CDFS	Do not ignore the permission mode bits.
nodevs	Generic	Do not allow local special devices on this file system.
noint	NFS	Do not allow keyboard interrupts (signals) on hard mounts.

Table 10.7 Non-Linux Mount Options *(continued)*

Option	File System	Meaning
nomnttab	Amd	This option is used internally to tell Amd that a Solaris 8 system using mntfs is in use.
norrip	CDFS	Turn off the Rock Ridge Interchange Protocol (RRIP) extensions to ISO-9660.
nosub	Generic	Disallow mounts beneath this mount.
noversion	CDFS	Strip the extension ;# from the version string of files recorded on an ISO-9660 CD-ROM.
nqnfs	NFS	Use the Not Quite NFS server extensions, which provide a non-RFC–compliant state-full NFS server.
optionstr	Generic	Under Solaris 8, provide the kernel a string of options to parse and show as part of the special in-kernel mount table file system, mntfs.
overlay	Generic	Overlay this mount on top of an existing mount, if any.
pgthresh=N	NFS	Set the paging threshold to N KB.
rdonly	Generic	Mount this file system read-only.
readahead	NFS	Allow NFS to read ahead of the current read pointer of the process.
resvport	NFS	Use a reserved port (smaller than 1024) for remote NFS mounts. Most systems assume that, but some allow for mounts to occur on non-reserved ports. This causes problems when such a system tries to NFS-mount one that requires reserved ports. It is recommended that this option always be on.

Table 10.7   Non-Linux Mount Options *(continued)*

Option	File System	Meaning
ronly	Generic	Mount this file system read-only.
ronly	NFS	Mount this file system read-only.
rrip	CDFS	Use the Rock Ridge Interchange Protocol (RRIP) extensions to ISO-9660.
spongy	NFS	Like soft for status requests, and hard for data transfers.
symttl	NFS	Turn off the symbolic link cache TTL (a must if using hlfsd).
synchronous	Generic	Perform synchronous file system operations on this mount.
ver3	NFS	Perform an NFS version 3 mount.

File Systems

Amd supports a variety of file systems. Administrators specify the exact file system to mount, in the maps, as the argument to the type variable.

In the next four sections, we describe these file systems in the following order:

- Native file systems that the operating system implements
- Meta file systems that Amd implements using native file systems
- Internal file systems that Amd implements for bookkeeping purposes
- Non-Linux file systems that may already be available for Linux

To find out which file systems your system supports, run amd -v as seen in Listing 10.7. Native file systems are listed under FS, while non-native file systems are listed under AMFS.

Table 10.8 alphabetically lists all the file systems that Amd can use (if support is compiled into the kernel, not all of them are in the kernel by default). Since native file systems have a specific name on the operating system, sometimes different from that used by Amd, we list both when they differ. We classify each file system into the group that best describes it. We also include the list of variables that must be properly defined for each file system.

The Amd
Automounter

PART 2

Table 10.8 File Systems Supported by Amd

Amd Name	Linux Name	Group	Variables Needed
auto		Meta	cache, fs, pref
autofs		Native	N/A
cachefs	N/A	Non-Linux	cachedir, rfs, fs
cdfs	ISO-9660	Native	dev
direct		Meta	An automount point
efs	EFS	Non-Linux	dev
error		Internal	N/A
host		Meta	rhost
inherit		Internal	N/A
link		Meta	fs
linkx		Meta	fs
lofs	LOFS	Native	rfs
nfs	NFS	Native	rhost, rfs
nfsl		Meta	rhost, rfs, fs
nfsx		Meta	rhost, rfs
pcfs	VFAT, FAT	Native	dev
program		Meta	mount, umount
root		Internal	N/A
toplvl		Internal	N/A
ufs	EXT2	Native	dev

Table 10.8   File Systems Supported by Amd *(continued)*

Amd Name	Linux Name	Group	Variables Needed
union		Meta	Automount point and list of directories
xfs	XFS	Non-Linux	dev

Since we have covered the various Amd map variables throughout this chapter, we have already seen several examples of most of these file systems. A few of the file systems that Amd implements are advanced and used for special situations. We give an example of those but defer a detailed discussion to Chapter 12.

Native File Systems

Amd users primarily use two types of file systems that Amd supports: native and non-native. Native file systems are those that are supported by the operating system. Amd uses them as is. Non-native (meta) file systems are those that Amd implements internally, often by using native file systems.

In this section we describe each native file system and give an example of its use: nfs, ufs, cdfs, pcfs, and lofs. In the next section we describe non-native file systems.

Network File System (*nfs*)

The network file system (nfs) is based on Sun's NFS, and is the most popular file system in use by Amd. NFS provides access to a remote file system over the network. You should carefully configure two variables for this file system:

rhost   This is the name of the remote file server. The name must exist. The default value for this variable, if not specified, is ${host}. It is important to set this variable because otherwise Amd will perform a localhost NFS mount, a process that can occasionally lock up the system.

rfs   This is the name of the remote file system to mount. If not specified, it defaults to ${path}. Again, this is important to set up to avoid deadlock problems with Amd mounting on top of itself.

Recall that much of Amd's support revolves around NFS file systems. Amd keeps a cache of known working file servers, obtains handles for using them, mounts and unmounts file servers in the background, monitors their uptime, retries failed operations, and more.

The Amd Automounter

PART 2

The most typical use of NFS is in conjunction with the `type:=link` file system. A file system is exported by an NFS server. On the host that exports the file system itself, you need only provide a symbolic link to the location of the file system (and avoid a `localhost` NFS mount). On all other hosts, however, you perform an NFS mount. Here is an example entry:

```
demo  -rhost:=mars;addopts:=ro,suid \
      host!=${rhost};type:=nfs;rfs:=/usr/demo \
      host==${rhost};type:=link;fs:=/usr/demo
```

> **NOTE** Note that to improve performance, we order the locations in this example such that the most likely location will match first. That is the case when mounting the file system remotely.

Unix File System (*ufs*)

The Unix file system (`ufs`) provides access to a disk-based file system. This is often the most commonly used disk-based file system on the operating system Amd runs on. On Linux, Amd uses the EXT2 file system. Note, however, that regardless of the operating system name of the file system, it is always accessed by Amd as `type:=ufs`.

For example, suppose you have a test partition that you do not wish to mount all the time, perhaps because you are constantly reformatting it. This is a typical scenario at sites that *burn in* disks for mass production of preinstalled Linux systems. In this case, you can set up the following entry to automount the first partition of your second SCSI drive onto `/mnt/test`:

```
test  type:=ufs;dev:=/dev/sdb1;fs:=/mnt/${key}
```

> **WARNING** Do not use this file system for Amd mounts of disks that you also want to export for NFS use. Most operating systems will not allow you to NFS-export a partition before it is mounted. If you do, your file system could be mounted locally but could not be mounted remotely. Users will get a "Permission Denied" error code. For more information, see the jukebox example in Chapter 12 under the section "Automounting a Jukebox (CD Changer)."

CD-ROM File System (*cdfs*)

The CD-ROM file system (cdfs) can mount an ISO-9660 CD-ROM. One of its most popular uses is to mount a CD-ROM correctly on different operating systems, since each uses a different device:

```
cdrom       -type:=cdfs;addopts:=ro \
            os==linux;dev:=/dev/hdc \
            os==sunos4;dev:=/dev/sr0 \
            os==sunos5;dev:=/dev/dsk/c0t6d0s2 \
            dev:=/dev/cdrom
```

The above example will mount the CD-ROM as device /dev/hdc (master drive on second IDE bus) on Linux systems and use the proper devices for other operating systems. As a last resort, the map entry tries to mount a generic name used by many vendors, /dev/cdrom.

Floppy File System (*pcfs*)

The floppy file system (pcfs) provides access to an MS-DOS FAT file system or one of its newer variants such as VFAT (the Windows 95 file system). Like cdfs, this file system is also often used as a way to mount floppies on different operating systems. A typical entry looks as follows:

```
floppy      -type:=pcfs;fs:=/msdos/a \
            os==linux;dev:=/dev/fd0H1440 \
            os==sunos4;dev:=/dev/fd0 \
            os==sunos5;dev:=/dev/diskette
            dev:=/dev/floppy
```

Note that this file system does not care if the device used is a floppy or not, only what the type of the file system is: FAT or VFAT. Many Linux laptop users install their systems as dual-booted: one partition contains Linux, and another contains Windows. It is very useful to have automatic access to your Windows partition when running Linux. Assuming the Windows partition is /dev/hda8, you can tell Amd to automount the partition as follows:

```
win    type:=pcfs;dev:=/dev/hda8;fs:=/mnt/c-drive
```

Loopback File System (*lofs*)

The loopback file system (lofs) mounts a local directory on another, thus providing mount-time binding to another location (unlike symbolic links). Another way to think of lofs is as a cross-file-system hard-linked directory.

The loopback file system is particularly useful within the context of a chroot-ed directory, to provide access to directories otherwise inaccessible. A chroot-ed process runs inside a directory, but no files outside that directory are accessible normally; this is mostly a security precaution. However, there are cases when you do want to provide access to a select set of external directories inside the chroot-ed directory.

To use lofs, you must specify the rfs variable. While normally this variable names the path of the remote file system, for lofs it names the directory to mount on top of the target directory, specified in ${fs}.

Usually, an FTP server runs in a chroot-ed environment, for security reasons. In this example, we use lofs to provide a subdirectory within a user's home directory, also available for public FTP:

```
ezftp        type:=lofs;rfs:=/home/ezk/myftp;fs:=/usr/ftp/pub/ezk
```

In that example, we run a chroot-ed FTP server in /usr/ftp. User ezk wants to provide some files available under the FTP server in /pub/ezk. A nice way to do so is by allowing the user to place files in a directory of his choosing, somewhere in the home directory, in this case /home/ezk/myftp. If you made a symbolic link from /usr/ftp/pub/ezk to /home/ezk/myftp, it would not work because the symlink points outside of the chroot-ed directory. Instead, you can use the above map to loopback-mount the user's FTP files into the chroot-ed FTP environment.

The above trick works for one simple reason: Amd runs outside the chroot-ed environment and, thus, has access to all local files and directories. In Chapter 12, we show more advanced examples using the lofs file system.

NOTE While the lofs file system is integral to some operating systems, it is not to Linux. To use lofs, you will have to apply special kernel patches and rebuild your kernel. See Appendix B, "Online Resources," for pointers to instructions on how to do so.

Meta File Systems

Meta file systems are those that Amd implements by building on top of native file systems. Meta file systems often provide semantics that are not available anywhere and help users to write more concise Amd maps.

Several file systems build on top of NFS. For those, all of the usual NFS mount options may apply. We described those options earlier in this chapter, under "NFS Mount Options."

Network Host File System (*host*)

The network host file system (host) NFS-mounts all possible file systems that a certain host exports. This file system is very similar to Sun's /net file system.

When you install am-utils on Red Hat Linux 7.0 systems, Amd is configured with one map and one entry using the host file system:

```
/defaults    fs:=${autodir}/${rhost}/root/${rfs};opts:=nosuid,nodev


*            rhost:=${key};type:=host;rfs:=/
```

This map is mounted under /net. The * matches any name as the key, and that key is then assigned as the remote hostname. So if you have a host, say shekel, and you try to access it via this map, you will get all (five) file systems mounted from that host:

```
[ezk]$ ls /net/shekel
n/
[ezk]$ df
Filesystem              1k-blocks       Used Available Use% Mounted on
/dev/sda1                  879078     820034     13631  98% /
kosher:/home              6224742    4955202    952258  84% /home
shekel:/n/shekel/misc/shekel
                          8705501    7051733   1566713  82%
                 /.automount/shekel/root/n/shekel/misc/shekel
shekel:/n/shekel/proj/amd
                          2044038    1230300    752417  62%
                 /.automount/shekel/root/n/shekel/proj/amd
```

```
shekel:/n/shekel/proj/bank
                    4125390    2541318    1542819  62%
            /.automount/shekel/root/n/shekel/proj/bank
shekel:/n/shekel/proj/fist
                    8735855    2906989    5392074  35%
            /.automount/shekel/root/n/shekel/proj/fist
shekel:/n/shekel/u/zing
                    4179366    3316251     821322  80%
            /.automount/shekel/root/n/shekel/u/zing
```

The host file system starts by querying the rpc.mountd server on the remote host to retrieve its export list. Amd then obtains NFS file handles for each of the exported file systems. If Amd is unable to get a file handle for any particular file system, it ignores it because it could be that the particular file system is down at that time, or that it does not allow this client to NFS-mount it. Then, Amd mounts each of the file systems it received file handles for. Any mount errors are logged but ignored.

One typical reason for Amd to fail to mount any of these file systems is that the mount point does not exist. Although Amd tries to create mount points automatically, the directory creation may be on another file system that Amd doesn't have access to, or its name conflicts with an existing file server's mount.

When Amd has to unmount a host file system, it has to unmount each of the individual file systems that were exported and mounted in order. If one or more of those unmounts fails, Amd remounts any file systems that had been successfully unmounted. Before doing so, Amd queries the rpc.mountd server again and obtains an updated export list. Only then does Amd try to complete the list of mounted file systems by mounting those file systems that are not currently mounted.

Network Group File System (*nfsx*)

The network group file system (nfsx) mounts a set of NFS file systems as one group. It is different from the host file system because you can configure the specific list of file systems that you want to mount together.

For the nfsx file system, you should specify the following variables:

rhost   This is the name of the remote file server that exports the file systems.

rfs   This is the list of file systems to mount. The list is a comma-delimited set of path names. The first entry in this list is special: it is treated as a prefix file system name for the rest of the file systems. Amd tries to ensure a consistent layout of a tree of mounts by using a parallel operation to determine the local mount points. Nevertheless, it is best to specify the ${fs} variable to avoid name conflicts.

fs   This specifies the local mount point. The default local mount point will not work correctly in the general case because it will conflict with any of the file systems listed in ${rfs}, if they are mentioned in another map entry.

Suppose your site mirrors other FTP servers around the Internet, but you do not have enough disk space for all the mirrored directories on one partition. In the absence of RAID, one way is to configure several partitions, each one holding a few mirrors. Let us say that you have three such file systems, named /usr/ftp/mirrors/Security, /usr/ftp/mirrors/GPL, and /usr/ftp/mirrors/texts. You can write an Amd entry that would mount all three at once as follows:

```
archives     -rhost:=lol;fs:=${autodir}/${rhost}/root \
             host!=${rhost};type:=nfsx;\
                 rfs:=/usr/ftp/mirrors,/Security,/GPL,/texts \
             host==${rhost};type:=link;fs:=/usr/ftp/mirrors
```

Note that we have set ${fs} to ${autodir}/${rhost}/root explicitly. This adds the component /root to the name of the local mount point. This guarantees that these nfsx mounts would use a different local mount point from the one that Amd uses by default.

Symbolic Link File System (*link*)

The symbolic link file system (link) provides a simple symbolic link to another path name. That path name can be automounted or not, but you should avoid using links to the same automount node; this can lead to deadlocks.

One of the most typical uses of the link file system is to provide alternate names for common directories, making it easy for users to find directories based on their contents. This allows administrators to change actual locations of files without affecting users. For example, suppose you have a large partition, /import/packages, that contains some Linux kernel sources under linux-src, TeX binaries under teTeX, and X11 libraries under X11R6/lib. The following map, mounted under /misc, can achieve this:

```
pkg          type:=nfs;rhost:=serv2;rfs:=/import/packages


src          type:=link;fs:=/misc/pkg/linux-src


TeX          type:=link;fs:=${map}/teTeX


X11lib       type:=link;fs:=${map};sublink:=X11/lib
```

In that way, administrators can change what TeX points to, or even where pkg is, and users can continue to use the same path name to reach those files: /misc/TeX.

Verified Symbolic Link File System (*linkx*)

The verified symbolic link file system (linkx) is similar to the link file system. The only difference is that Amd checks if the symlink exists before pointing to it. This test is done using the lstat system call.

One of the uses for the linkx file system is with wildcard map entries. There, Amd can provide targets only for those directories that exist locally. For example, if you have a large partition with many user homes under /n/users, you can list each and every user in your Amd map, but an easier way is to use linkx as follows:

```
*  type:=linkx;fs:=/n/users/${key}
```

Assume this map is mounted under /home. Here, Amd will provide the symlink /home/joe only if the directory /n/users/joe exists.

NFS-Link File System (*nfsl*)

The NFS-link file system (nfsl) is a combination of two others: link and nfs. If the local hostname is equal to the value of ${rhost}, or if the target path name listed in ${fs} exists, nfsl will behave exactly as type:=link and refer to the target as a symbolic link. If the local hostname is not equal to the value of ${rhost}, or if the target of the link does not exist, Amd will treat it as type:=nfs and will mount a remote path name for it.

The nfsl file system type is particularly useful as a shorthand for the more cumbersome and yet one of the most popular Amd entries. Many maps have the form that uses NFS for remote mounts and symlinks for local mounts:

```
zing  -fs:=/n/shekel/u/zing \
      host!=shekel;type:=nfs;rhost:=shekel;rfs:=${fs} \
      host==shekel;type:=link
```

Other maps have the form that uses a symlink if the entry exists, and a remote NFS mount if it does not:

```
zing  -fs:=/n/shekel/u/zing \
      exists(${fs});type:=link \
      !exists(${fs});type:=nfs;rhost:=shekel;rfs:=${fs}
```

You can simplify both of the above entries with a single, simpler nfsl type entry:

```
zing  type:=nfsl;fs:=/n/shekel/u/zing;rhost:=shekel;rfs:=${fs}
```

Not just does it make the maps smaller and simpler, but it avoids possible mistakes that often happen when you forget to set up the two entries (one for `type:=nfs` and the other for `type:=link`) necessary to perform transparent mounts of existing or remote mounts.

Program File System (*program*)

The program file system (`program`) can mount any arbitrary file system. Its primary use is as an extension mechanism for Amd, when Amd is unable to mount the file system directly but another user-level tool can. This happens often on Linux systems when you want to mount a file system that Amd does not have support for.

To use the `program` file system, you must define at least these two variables in the map entry:

mount This variable defines the program that can mount the given file system. Specifically, the mount variable needs the absolute path name of the program or script that can mount the file system, followed by the name of that program, followed by any optional arguments. You may pass Amd map variables to the mount program.

umount This variable defines the program that can unmount the given file system. Specifically, the unmount variable needs the absolute path name of the program or script that can unmount the file system, followed by the name of that program, followed by any optional arguments. You may pass Amd map variables to the unmount program.

TIP If the program file system does not appear to work for you, check carefully the arguments you are passing to the mount and umount variables. They *must* first list the absolute path name of the program, followed by its name, then followed by optional arguments. Administrators often forget to include the second argument: program name. Experienced Unix programmers would notice that the values of these two variables closely resemble the arguments of the execv system call.

Suppose you have an NTFS partition on your /dev/hdb1 partition. Currently you cannot mount it natively using Amd. But you can use the /bin/mount program on Linux to mount it on /mnt/winnt as follows:

```
[root]# mount -t ntfs /dev/hdb1 /mnt/winnt
```

You can automount this partition using the program file system as follows:

```
nt    type:=program;dev:=/dev/hdb1;fs:=/mnt/winnt;\
      mount="/bin/mount mount -t ntfs ${dev} ${fs}";\
      umount="/bin/umount umount ${fs}"
```

The Amd Automounter

PART 2

In this example, we use ${dev} as a temporary variable just to hold the value of the device to mount. We do not have to use this variable; we could have used ${var4}, for example, or we could have hard-coded the device name directly in the mount command. Note also that the above example has only one volume: the backslash characters are not preceded by whitespace, making them continuation lines for the same location.

Automount File System (*auto*)

The automount file system (auto) creates a new Amd automount point below an existing one. It appears as a subdirectory inside a top-level automount point. The main use of the auto file system is to provide for additional, deeper directory structure provided by Amd.

You can specify these options:

cache This variable determines caching behavior of the map, for example, to cache all entries, none, incrementally, synchronized, etc. See Chapter 9 for the details of this variable.

fs This variable names the mount map to use for the new mount point. A dot (.) is a special name referring to the current map. If you, say, specified /etc/amd.spec, then that file would be read and used as the list of entries for this automount point.

maptype This variable sets the type of the input source to use for the map: file, NIS, Hesiod, etc. The full list of possible map types can be shown by running amd -v, as seen in Listing 10.7. If not specified, Amd will search all the maps available in the order listed in the output of amd -v.

pref This variable sets the lookup prefix for the automount node. When a single automount map is shared among several type:=auto nodes, you often have to tell Amd how to look up for entries under that node, so they can be found in the map.

opts This variable specifies any options that are often useful for automount maps. These options are listed in Table 10.5.

As an example, let us take a large site with many working groups. One possible working group is the engineering department, and they may have several file servers and several disks each. The engineers want to automount all of their disks. You could set up a regular automount entry for each of those disks, but if you have lots of those disks and lots of groups in your large site, your Amd map can become very flat and long. Instead, you can designate a sub-automount called eng, under which you will mount each of the engineering department's disks.

Suppose the site administrators automount everything under /grp. The engineering department's disks would be automounted under /grp/eng, the sales department's under

/grp/sales, the staff's under /grp/staff, and so on. Also let us assume that the engineering department wants to have access to the following disks:

sharon:/n/sources automounted as src

sharon:/n/hraid automounted as homes

folk:/proj/packaging automounted as pkg

rice:/misc/jukebox automounted as mp3

The map in Listing 10.10 achieves this.

Listing 10.10   A sample map using a subsidiary automount file system

```
/defaults    type:=nfs

eng          type:=auto;fs:=${map};pref:=${key}/

eng/src      rhost:=sharon;rfs:=/n/sources

eng/homes    rhost:=sharon;rfs:=/n/hraid

eng/pkg      rhost:=folk;rfs:=/proj/packaging

eng/mp3      rhost:=rice;rfs:=/misc/jukebox
```

This example sets eng as a subsidiary automount point. The map, listed in ${fs}, is read from the current map. We set the prefix for this map to be eng/. That way, when a user tries to cd to /grp/eng/src, Amd will get a lookup request for src, under the automount node for /grp/eng. Since that automount node has a prefix of eng/, Amd will look up the key eng/src in the automount map in Listing 10.10.

The auto file system is rather advanced. We provide additional examples in Chapter 12.

Direct Automount File System (*direct*)

The direct automount file system (direct) mounts a file or directory *directly* on top of the automount point. In other file systems, Amd creates an automount point, under which all entries can be mounted one at a time. With the direct file system, Amd mounts the entry right on top of the mount point.

The direct file system is often useful if you have only one entry to mount in a map and you want to mount it exactly on top of a mount point, not under. For example, suppose you wish to automount all your manual pages from one host but automount them directly on top of /usr/man. You can do so with the amd.conf file seen in Listing 10.11 and the Amd map seen in Listing 10.12.

Listing 10.11   Amd configuration file for a direct automount file system

```
[ /usr/man ]
map_name = /etc/amd.man
map_options = type:=direct
```

Listing 10.12   Amd map /etc/amd.man for the direct file system example

```
usr/man     type:=nfs;rhost:=spring;rfs:=/usr/share/man
```

The amd.conf file lists /usr/man as the automount point and specifies that the map file is in /etc/amd.man and that this is a direct automount point. The /etc/amd.man map file lists only one entry, stating that /usr/man should be NFS-mounted from spring:/usr/share/man. When Amd starts with these two files, it automounts itself on top of /usr/man on the local host. Amd then overlays the mount point /usr/man with a symlink. The symlink is there just to provide an automount trigger. When you cross that symlink, Amd replaces it with the real (NFS) mount of spring:/usr/share/man. At that point you get to see a normal NFS mount on top of a mount point /usr/man.

WARNING   Do not use the direct automount type excessively. Each time you use it, you add another automount file system to Amd, which is a real operating system mount that exists as soon as Amd is started. Unix operating systems were designed with the expectation that there would not be many mounts on each host. If you do use it, you can slow down the system considerably, especially for any command that deals with file systems, such as mount or df. Kernels use a simple singly linked list to search through mounted file systems' data structures. Commands such as mount or df degrade quadratically with the number of mounted file systems. One Amd user told me he uses 179 direct type mounts on his system. I was only half kidding when I asked him if he has to go to lunch each time someone runs df on his systems.

Union File System (*union*)

The union file system joins the contents of several directories. It creates a special automount directory and populates it with symbolic links to the entries in the list of directories to unify.

The most important issue when dealing with unifying file systems is how to handle duplicates. The policy Amd uses is that directories later in the list take precedence over those listed before.

This file system does not need an Amd map. You can specify all the information you need in the amd.conf file or on the command line when starting Amd. We will show both ways.

One example is to merge the contents of several system directories that can hold temporary binaries. If you start Amd as follows

[root]# **amd /bigtmp union:/tmp:/var/tmp:/mnt/C/TEMP -type:=union**

then Amd will join the contents of /tmp, /var/tmp, and /mnt/C/TEMP, with files in the latter directory taking precedence over former ones.

Another example could be to override binaries with newer versions. On Linux, most GNU binaries are located in /usr/bin. Let us say that you hand-built some new GNU binaries and installed them in /usr/local/gnu/bin. You want to use binaries in /usr/local/gnu/bin first; only if a binary does not exist there do you want to look it up in /usr/bin. One way to achieve this is to force all users to change their login shell ${PATH} variable so it lists both of these directories, and /usr/local/gnu/bin before /usr/bin. Another, easier alternative is to use Amd to unify the contents of these two directories and then just let users use the usual /usr/local/bin directory that is already likely in their search path.

The following amd.conf example uses /usr/local/bin as the automount point. It merges the contents of /usr/bin and /usr/local/gnu/bin onto this automount point, with the same named binaries in /usr/local/gnu/bin taking precedence:

```
[ /usr/local/bin ]
map_type = union
map_name = union:/usr/bin:/usr/local/gnu/bin
```

Internal File Systems

In this section we briefly discuss the internal file systems used by Amd. None of these can be assigned or used directly. However, they do show up in the output of amq when Amd uses them and it is important to understand what each one means.

Root File System (*root*)

When Amd starts, it creates a master node from which it instantiates sub-nodes for each mount point. This master node is the root node, and it shows up as the first entry in the output of amq, as shown in Listing 10.13.

Listing 10.13   root and toplvl internal file systems

```
[ezk]$ amq -h earth
/            root     "root"                   earth:(pid676)
/src         toplvl   /etc/amdmaps/amd.src     /src
/misc        toplvl   amd.misc                 /misc
```

As you can see from Listing 10.13, the root node is /, it is called root, and its mount point is the hostname and process ID of the running Amd process: earth:(pid676).

Top-Level File System (*toplvl*)

Amd creates a toplvl automount file system for each map that is listed on the command line or the amd.conf file. In Listing 10.13, you can see two: one on /src and the other on /misc. Both are of type toplvl. The /src map is mounted under /src and its contents come from the file /etc/amdmaps/amd.src. The /misc file map is mounted under /misc and its contents come from the NIS map amd.misc.

Inheritance File System (*inherit*)

When you start Amd with the amd.conf global parameter restart_mounts set to yes, Amd reads in the contents of your /etc/mtab file to see which file systems are already mounted. Amd then creates special inherit nodes for each of those mounted file systems. These nodes tell Amd that if a user tries to access Amd such that a mount would be requested for the same file server and file system that is already mounted, Amd should take advantage of the fact that the file system is already mounted and report a successful "mount" of that file system.

Note that no real mount is performed. Amd just inherits that mount from the existing system. When that happens, Amd changes the status of an inherit node to the type of mount that it is currently: nfs, ufs, cdfs, etc.

Error File System (*error*)

When Amd starts, it looks up the information service used to read the contents of the map. If, for one reason or another, Amd could not contact the information server and download the map, it sets its state as error.

The error type file system is also set for any node that failed to mount. This can happen if permission to mount the file system was denied, the remote file server is down, etc. Error file systems show up in the output of amq. They remain there until you remove the entry using amq -u, a ping timer expires and Amd detects that a previously downed server is now back up, or when you restart Amd.

Autofs File System (*autofs*)

If you use Amd with Autofs, you can set individual maps to use Autofs instead of a user-level NFS service. This is done in the amd.conf file with the mount_type parameter as described in Chapter 9. Amd marks those automount nodes that use Autofs as autofs.

Non-Linux File Systems

In this section we briefly describe file systems that are not always available for Linux.

Caching File System (*cachefs*)

Solaris defines a caching file system called CacheFS. The `cachefs` file system caches files from one location onto another, presumably providing faster access. It is particularly useful to cache from a larger and remote (slower) NFS partition to a smaller and local (faster) UFS directory.

The following options must be specified:

    `cachedir`   This specifies the directory where the cache is stored.

    `rfs`   This lists the path name to the *back-file system* to cache from.

    `fs`   This names the *front-file system* mount point to the cached files, where Amd will point a symbolic link to.

A CacheFS entry for, say, the `/import` Amd mount point, might be as follows:

```
copt  type:=cachefs;cachedir:=/cache;rfs:=/import/opt;\
            fs:=/n/import/copt
```

Access to the path name `/import/copt` will follow a symbolic link to `/n/import/copt`. The latter is the mount point for a caching file system that caches from `/import/opt` to `/cache`.

There are several caveats when using the `cachefs` file system:

- This file system is currently only implemented for Solaris 2.*x*.

- Before being used for the first time, the cache directory must be initialized with `cfsadmin -c cachedir`. See the manual page for `cfsadmin` for more information.

- The back file system mounted must be a complete file system, not a subdirectory thereof; otherwise you will get an error "Invalid Argument."

- If Amd aborts abnormally, the state of the cache may be inconsistent, requiring running the command `fsck -F cachefs cachedir`. Otherwise you will get the error "No Space Left on Device."

SGI File System (*efs, xfs*)

The file systems `efs` and `xfs` are both popular and available on SGI Irix systems. Amd can only use one native file system when you specify `type:=ufs`. Since both may be available on Irix systems, Amd cannot always tell which one to use. In that case, you can force it using `type:=efs` or `type:=xfs`. All other rules that apply to `type:=ufs` apply for these two as well.

The Amd
Automounter

PART 2

The EFS file system is even available on newer Linux 2.4 systems. Ports of the XFS file system to Linux are under way. See Appendix B, "Online Resources," for information on the XFS port to Linux.

In Sum

We started this chapter by describing the exact parsing rules for Amd maps. We showed how Amd looks up keys in maps, how and when variables are evaluated, how to write your specific rules in Amd maps, how to set default values per map or per map entry, and how to quote or escape certain text.

We then discussed the many selectors and variables that Amd maps can specify. Selectors are used to guide Amd into mounting the right location given certain conditions: existence of files, membership in lists, system names or versions, network conditions, and much more. We described selector variables, those that can be matched for equality or inequality against a given value. We also showed selector functions, those that return a TRUE or FALSE value based on the arbitrary argument passed to the function. We saw how to combine multiple selectors to allow for conjunction or disjunction of conditionals.

We covered many Amd variables and their special meanings. These variables determine what will be mounted, from where, when, and onto which mount point. We discussed many of the mount options that are available: some were generic, while others were specific to a given file system.

We discussed the file systems that Amd can use. Some were native file systems such as NFS and EXT2. Others were meta file systems, those implemented by Amd on top of other native file systems. These meta file systems provide unique functionality not readily available in Linux without the Amd automounter. We saw which variables and other parameters affect the behavior of these file systems: which are mandatory and which are optional.

We covered a lot of material in this chapter. Together, Chapters 9 and 10 describe the core of all of Amd's functionality; they cover every basic Amd function from what goes into the Amd configuration file, to how to write Amd maps. In the next chapter, we cover the runtime administration of Amd, especially the management of the Amd map sources for different information services.

11

Runtime Automounter Administration

Building and installing Amd, however difficult, need only be done once for most sites. Configuring Amd to run for the first time and writing the initial maps are also daunting tasks but are usually performed only once. However, maintaining Amd on a daily basis can easily take more effort overall in the long run. Administrators must update Amd maps all the time, occasionally changing Amd's configuration files. They have to check Amd when things go wrong, debug its behavior, and attempt to recover when it fails. That is why the am-utils package includes many additional tools and scripts. Some of these tools contain many options to assist administrators with the daily tasks of automounter maintenance.

In this chapter we cover various administration issues relating to Amd. We discuss tools, scripts, and files that come with the am-utils package, many of which help in administering an automounter system. We describe how you can trace what Amd is doing on your system and how to debug your Amd configurations. We cover the maintenance of the various map services that contain the source maps: NIS, NDBM, LDAP, etc.

We begin by listing all the files that come with the am-utils package, shown in Table 11.1. Throughout this chapter we will discuss several of those tools in the appropriate context. We cover the remaining tools that we do not discuss in any particular section in the last section in this chapter, under "Other am-utils Tools."

Table 11.1   Utilities and Scripts in the am-utils Package

File	Usage
am-eject	Unmount floppy or CD-ROM and try to eject it.
amd	Amd automounter.
amd.conf-sample	Sample Amd configuration file.
amd2ldif	Convert Amd file maps to LDAP input files.
amd2sun	Convert Amd maps to Sun Automounter maps.
amq	Amd query and control tool.
automount2amd	Convert old Sun Automounter maps to Amd.
ctl-amd	Control starting and stopping of Amd.
ctl-hlfsd	Control starting and stopping of HLFSD.
expn	Expand mail aliases.
fix-amd-map	Update old syntax of Amd maps to newer one.
fixmount	Delete bogus remote mount entries.
fixrmtab	Invalidate remote host entries from local /var/state/ nfs/rmtab file.
fsinfo	Generate Amd maps and other system files from a high-level language.
hlfsd	Redirect users' mail to their home directories.
lostaltmail	Resend any lost mail.
lostaltmail.conf-sample	Sample configuration file for lostaltmail.
mk-amd-map	Convert an Amd map file to an NDBM/DB file.
pawd	Display automounter-adjusted directory.
wait4amd	Perform an action once Amd starts on a host.

Table 11.1   Utilities and Scripts in the am-utils Package *(continued)*

File	Usage
wait4amd2die	Wait until a local Amd process terminates completely.
wire-test	Check NFS and RPC connectivity with a host.

Controlling Amd's Run

To start Amd, you can simply run the amd binary. To stop it, you can send a termination signal to it. This had been a standard mode of operation for managing daemons on many Unix systems. Nowadays, however, wrapper scripts do this work more reliably and consistently. These scripts know the proper way to start, stop, restart, and even check the status of a running daemon.

There are two such scripts for am-utils:

/etc/rc.d/init.d/amd   This is Red Hat's startup script for Amd. If you have installed the am-utils RPM from your Red Hat distribution, this is the startup script you should use.

ctl-amd   This is the script that gets installed when you build and install am-utils from original sources. This script is a superset of the Red Hat script and often does more. It was written to work for many Unix and Linux systems, but particularly well with Red Hat Linux. In fact, you may replace the Red Hat startup script with the am-utils one as follows:

[root]# **cp /usr/local/sbin/ctl-amd /etc/rc.d/init.d/amd**

The above command assumes that you have built and installed am-utils in /usr/local. Furthermore, if you use ctl-amd instead of your Red Hat–supplied Amd startup script, it will work with the chkconfig runtime configuration tool, described in Chapter 14, "Building and Installing the Automounter Software." Nevertheless, in this section we will assume that you have installed the am-utils-supplied script, ctl-amd.

To see the usage of the ctl-amd script, run it without any arguments:

[root]# **ctl-amd**

Usage: ctl-amd [start|stop|status|restart|condrestart|reload]

As you can see, you can take six actions, described next.

Starting Amd

To start Amd, run

> [root]# **ctl-amd start**

The script will use an amd.conf file and would look for it in the following locations, in order. The script uses the first one found:

/etc/local/amd.conf   This allows local users to use a custom amd.conf file on their local machine.

${prefix}/etc/amd.conf   This is a configuration file located under the installation tree where am-utils was configured. If you configured am-utils with --prefix=/usr/local/AMD, then this configuration file will be looked for in /usr/local/AMD/etc/amd.conf. See Chapter 14 for more details.

/etc/amd.conf   This is the default location for installing Amd configuration files.

NOTE   An older, alternate method of starting Amd was to run amd `ypcat -k amd.master`. This method assumed that NIS was running but had the advantage that the list of Amd maps to automount came from a special NIS map named amd.master. That way, administrators did not have to define the actual list of automount points in their amd.conf file. However, since amd.conf provides many more advantages, it is the recommended way of starting Amd these days.

WARNING   Do not start a second Amd with the same amd.conf file, or you will hang both Amd processes. Instead, use the restart option to ensure that you terminate the previous Amd process before starting a new one.

Stopping Amd: *ctl-amd* and *wait4amd2die*

To stop Amd, run

> [root]# **ctl-amd stop**

The ctl-amd script stops Amd by sending a TERM signal to the Amd process. First, however, the script has to find the process ID of Amd. It does so by executing amq -p (which we describe later under "Amq Options").

If Amq is unable to locate the PID (process ID) of Amd, the ctl-amd script then tries to run the ps axc command to list all of the processes on the system, and pipe the listing through grep to get the PID of any processes named amd.

This second method is not as reliable, especially if there are multiple Amd processes on the system, because the script may attempt to terminate the wrong Amd process. In practice, however, the first method (amq -p) works well enough that these problems are rare. Either way, the stop option is intended to stop only the primary Amd process. If you are running more than one Amd, this script will not stop the second one. To do so, see later in this chapter, under "portmap_program: Running Multiple Automounters."

One of the advantages of using ctl-amd to stop Amd is that it takes better measures to ensure that Amd has terminated cleanly, and it also finds out more quickly when Amd terminates compared to other Red Hat scripts. The way ctl-amd does so is by invoking a second script called wait4amd2die.

As its name states, this script waits for Amd to die (terminate). This configurable script waits a few seconds and checks to see if Amd is not running. If it is, the script waits a few seconds more and then checks again, up to a configurable maximum number of tries. This way, the script does not have to wait too long for Amd to terminate, but it also does not wait indefinitely in case Amd is hung and cannot terminate cleanly.

The wait4amd2die script is important because it guarantees that when ctl-amd stop returns control back to the invoking parent process (say, a shell), Amd has indeed terminated. When you send signals to processes, they are sent asynchronously: the kernel is not guaranteed to deliver the signal immediately (although it often does), and the process receiving the signal is not guaranteed to terminate right away. In our case, Amd has to perform many actions before it can terminate, especially unmounting its automount points and possibly other mounted file systems.

Checking Status and Restarting Amd

The ctl-amd script comes with four more options intended for use when Amd is already running. Administrators use these options often for controlling Amd's behavior on a daily basis. While you can achieve the same results by using Amq and other shell commands by hand, using the ctl-amd script is better and easier: it is guaranteed to work consistently and the script provides a single command that administrators need to remember.

Checking Amd's Runtime Status

To check Amd's runtime status, use ctl-amd with the status argument. If Amd is running, you will get back a message with the PID of the running Amd:

```
[root]# ctl-amd status
amd (pid 1765) is running...
```

If Amd is not running, you will get back the message

```
[root]# ctl-amd status
amd is stopped
```

Restarting Amd

To restart Amd, run

```
[root]# ctl-amd restart
```

This action is equivalent to executing the `stop` action immediately followed by the `start` action. Since the `ctl-amd` script executes both actions in order, it is imperative that the script will start the new Amd process only if it could terminate the previous one cleanly. To that effect, `ctl-amd` relies on the `wait4amd2die` script to tell it if Amd had indeed terminated cleanly. If Amd did not terminate cleanly, `ctl-amd restart` will not start a new Amd process and will report the error message "NOT restarting amd!"

Conditional Restarting of Amd

Red Hat Linux also comes with a special option that will restart Amd only if it is already running:

```
[root]# ctl-amd condrestart
```

The way the script tells if an Amd is already running on Red Hat is by checking for the existence of the lock file `/var/lock/subsys/amd`. Otherwise, this conditional restarting option works the same as the regular restarting option: `ctl-amd restart`.

Reloading Amd's Maps

Finally, to reload Amd's maps, run

```
[root]# ctl-amd reload
```

This simply executes `amq -f`, which instructs Amd to flush its maps and reload them from the source of these maps (files, NIS servers, Hesiod servers, LDAP servers, etc.). See later in this chapter, under "Amq Options" for more details.

Signals

Amd accepts three signals. Signals are the old Unix way of telling running daemons to perform certain actions. You can send a signal to Amd using the `kill` program. Note, however, that the kernel may not necessarily deliver the signal to Amd right away. Furthermore, once Amd receives a signal, it can take arbitrarily long to process it.

Terminating Amd Signal

To terminate Amd, send it the TERM (terminate) signal. This is similar to running `ctl-amd stop`, only that the latter is guaranteed to wait until Amd actually terminates. To find out the PID of the running Amd, use `amq -p`:

```
[root]# kill -TERM `amq -p`
```

Terminating Amd and Unmounting Signal

If you send Amd the INT (interrupt) signal, it will terminate Amd just as if you sent it the TERM signal but will also attempt to unmount all existing mounts. The latter is equivalent to setting `unmount_on_exit=yes` in your `amd.conf` file:

```
[root]# kill -INT `amq -p`
```

The advantage of this method is that it also tries to clean up as many of the (NFS) mounts that Amd automounted during its run, thus leaving the system in a cleaner state. This could be useful because after Amd stops running, there is no longer an automounter that can unmount file systems that may no longer be in use.

Note also that Amd cannot guarantee that it will be able to unmount file systems that it mounted, because they could be in use. Therefore, Amd tries to unmount them using the `umount(2)` system call but does not fail if the unmount fails.

Reloading Amd Maps Signal

If you send Amd the HUP (Hangup) signal, it will not hang up on you. Rather, it will flush its maps and reload them anew from the information service of the maps. This signal's action is identical to running `amq -f`:

```
[root]# kill -HUP `amq -p`
```

Recovering from a Hung Automounter

It would be a stretch to say that Amd is the most stable and reliable program ever written. As we explained in Chapter 8, "Overview of the Amd Automounter," Amd is a user-level file server, which makes it dependent on various system conditions. Arguably, Amd should be running in the kernel like all other file systems. Also, Amd depends on the health of your DNS system, services such as NIS or LDAP, general networking, and how loaded is your system. Furthermore, administrator mistakes in Amd maps or `amd.conf` files can deadlock Amd. Finally, bugs in Amd or incompatible Linux kernel changes can cause it to abort unexpectedly.

When Amd hangs for any reason, its process may have died. Furthermore, its automount points may be hung as well. This means that *any* access attempt to these automount points could hang the user process trying to access them. This is particularly bad for shells like

The Amd
Automounter

PART 2

bash. If your ${PATH} environment variable includes any automounted directory, or even a directory with one or more symbolic links to binaries on automounted volumes, and any of those automounted volumes are hung, your shell will hang if you tried to search for those binaries!

Before you can attempt to recover from a situation where your Amd and your automount points may be hung, you should ensure that you would not further hang your own working shell in the process. Start by changing your working directory away from a possible automounted one, unsetting your environment variable, becoming root, and then again changing your working directory and unsetting the ${PATH} variable:

```
[ezk]$ cd /
[ezk]$ unset PATH
[ezk]$ /bin/su root
Password:
[root]# cd /
[root]# unset PATH
```

The simplest thing to do at this stage is reboot your system:

```
[root]# /sbin/reboot
```

However, if your system cannot reboot cleanly, it may hang midway through the reboot. If you suspect that is the case, it is better to issue a more forceful reboot:

```
[root]# /sbin/reboot -n -f
```

The -n option tells reboot not to synchronize unwritten data to disks, and the -f option tells it to force a reboot without an orderly shutdown of services. When you use these two options, your system is sure to reboot even if Amd is hung. However, it may leave your system in an inconsistent state where some users' data could be lost and the disks are not left clean. The latter means that your system will have to execute lengthy boot-time file system checks using fsck to correct any EXT2 file system status problems before coming back up.

Unfortunately, rebooting is a luxury that not every administrator can afford. If your Linux system is used by many users, or runs important services such as the NIS or DNS master servers, an Oracle DBMS, etc.—you cannot simply reboot your system at will. In that case, you have to do all you can to ensure that your system continues to run as you try to fix it.

WARNING Some of the procedures I am about to describe now are considered by most administrators as *evil hacks*. I suggest you keep a full bottle of Mylanta handy before proceeding to read further.

First, you must make sure that any leftover Amd processes are terminated. Start by killing Amd using the startup script. Note that since I have no guarantee that these will work, I always run them in the background:

> [root]# **/etc/rc.c/init.d/amd stop &**

Then wait a few seconds, and see if the Amd process has died:

> [root]# **/bin/ps auxcn | /bin/grep amd &**
>
> ```
>     0   795   0.0  0.6  1736   840  ?            D      Oct03    0:01 amd
> ```

The above means that Amd is still running. Note the process is in an uninterruptible sleep (D), which is usually due to some (network) I/O wait. Next, we send it a TERM signal explicitly (since the ctl-amd stop command may not have succeeded in doing so):

> [root]# **kill -TERM 795**

Note that we did not give the full path name to kill because it is a built-in command to the bash shell. Now check again with ps to see if Amd died. If it did not, send it the infamous -9 kill signal, which cannot be ignored:

> [root]# **kill -9 795**

There are conditions under which not even a kill -9 will kill a process, if that process is deadlocked in the in-kernel network subsystem, or low enough in the kernel interrupt table. Either way, you should now proceed to unhang the mount points.

You have to know ahead of time which automount points Amd used. These are listed in your amd.conf file. For our example, we will assume that you have two automount points: /home and /src. Start by forcing an unmount of those two:

> [root]# **/bin/umount /home &**
>
> [root]# **/bin/umount /src &**

Wait a few seconds, then check to see if any of those entries are still listed in your /etc/ mtab file.

> [root]# **/bin/egrep '/home|/src' /etc/mtab &**
>
> ```
> lorien:(pid795) /home nfs
> intr,rw,port=1023,timeo=8,retrans=110,toplvl,map=amd.home,
> dev=00000003 0 0
> ```

The above means that you were able to successfully unmount /src but not /home. You should try the umount commands a few more times. Also try umount -f to force the unmounting of NFS mounts. If the entries you try to unmount are still not removed from your /etc/mtab file, edit them out:

> [root]# **/bin/egrep -v '/home|/src' /etc/mtab > /etc/mtab.tmp**
>
> [root]# **/bin/mv /etc/mtab /etc/mtab.orig**
>
> [root]# **/bin/mv /etc/mtab.tmp /etc/mtab**

With luck, you should be able to start a new Amd and it would run:

> [root]# **/etc/rc.c/init.d/amd start &**

If that does not work, and your system must run Amd to function properly, your only recourse is to reboot.

Planning to Recover from a Hung Automounter

With some forethought, you can increase your chances of being able to restart a new Amd, even if the previous Amd has not terminated cleanly. The trick is to set the automount points so they reside *inside* another directory.

For example, suppose you normally use two automount points: /home and /src. If they are hung, you cannot mount a new Amd on them. You might try to remove them or rename them, so you could create new mount points, but you cannot do so if the existing ones are hung. If, instead, you used /am/home and /am/src, and both hung, you could recover more gracefully. The reason is that the actual directories that are hung are the home and src subdirectories of /am. The /am directory itself is *not* hung. It can be renamed or moved away easily. Therefore, if the two actual automount nodes got hung, and all your efforts to clear them failed, simply rename the /am parent directly, make a new one, and restart Amd:

> [root]# **/bin/mv /am /am.bad**
>
> [root]# **/bin/mkdir /am**
>
> [root]# **/etc/rc.c/init.d/amd start**

Before doing so, you should ensure that no previous entries were left in /etc/mtab; clear them as we described above.

The only problem with the above procedure is that you still have a couple of directories that have hung processes mounted on them: /am.bad/src and /am.bad/home. You cannot clear those until you reboot your system. After you do, you should remove the bad directories manually:

> [root]# **/bin/rmdir /am.bad/src /am.bad/home**
>
> [root]# **/bin/rmdir /am**

Forced Unmounts

When an NFS server dies, we do not want to terminate processes on the client that may be waiting for it because we could lose data. But when Amd—a user-level NFS server—dies, we can almost always kill and restart it without losing user data. That is because user processes are usually hung on the actual remote NFS mounts, not on Amd's own NFS mounts. The latter do not have any persistent storage requirements: Amd's automount points can be recovered completely by restarting Amd using its maps.

For this reason, it should be possible to kill automount nodes such as Amd's without much concern. Unfortunately, most Unix systems do not allow you to force an un-mount of Amd's mount points. Some Linux systems have a special system call umount2(2) that is intended to do just that. It forces an NFS timeout of all in-progress NFS operations on a mount point and then tries to unmount it. Unfortunately, this does not always succeed either.

In most kernels the list of mounted file systems is a simple singly linked list starting from a global kernel variable often called rootvnode. A long time ago, I wrote a pro-gram that opened /dev/kmem, searched for that head of the list, and followed it care-fully until it reached an Amd mount point. It was able to identify Amd mount points by their "host" name: always the name of the current host followed by the Amd PID. It then unlinked the offending data structure from the mounted file systems' linked list by setting the pointer of the previous cell to the one following the unlinked cell. While such a program can be written for most Unix systems, it still does not solve the fundamental problem of leaving processes that are hung because they are tied to one particular mount.

A better method is needed for recovery, one that will allow you to gracefully switch all hung processes from one bad NFS server to another. This is a difficult problem in the area of fail-over NFS servers.

The Amd
Automounter

PART 2

Amq Options

Amq is Amd's command and query tool. To find out which options Amq supports, run it with the -H argument, as seen in Listing 11.1.

Listing 11.1   Amq's usage information

```
[ezk]$ amq -H
amq [-fmpsvwHTU] [-h hostname] [-l log_file|"syslog"]
    [-x log_options] [-D debug_options]
    [-P program_number] [[-u] directory ...]
```

A brief description of each option is seen in Table 11.2. In the following, we describe each of Amq's options in more detail.

Table 11.2   Amq Command-Line Options

Option	Usage
-D *opts*	Set debugging flags to *opts*.
-f	Flush Amd caches and reload all maps.
-h *host*	Contact *host* instead of localhost.
-H	Print usage information.
-l *logtarget*	Set logging file or target to *logtarget*.
-m	Show extended status (server up/down times).
-p	Return PID of Amd.
-P *prognum*	Contact Amd at RPC program *prognum*.
-s	Show status of Amd's NFS operations.
-T	Use TCP to contact Amd.
-u *path*	Force unmount of *path*.
-U	Use UDP to contact Amd.
-v	Display version string.
-w	Print current working directory via Amd.
-x *opts*	Set logging flags to *opts*.

The syntax of the Amq program is relatively straightforward: a list of options, some of which take a single argument. After you specify all options, you can list one or more directories on which Amq will operate. By default, Amq will list the status of these automounted directories. However, if the -u option was specified before the list of directories, Amq will attempt to unmount each of those.

Amq Default Information

The default output that Amq lists is seen in Listing 11.2 and includes the following four columns:

The automount point   This can be the special "/" for the top-level Amd's root node, a top-level automount point where a map is served, or any other automounted file system.

The file system type   This can be one of Amd's internal file systems or any of the native file systems it implements.

The mount map or mount information   This provides information about the source of information for this mount and can be a remote file server, an Amd map, etc.

The internal or system mount point   This is the physical mount point where Amd mounted the file system.

Listing 11.2   Default output from Amq

```
[ezk]$ amq
/               root    "root"                       beetle:(pid1846)
/mnt            toplvl  /etc/local/amd.mnt           /mnt
/u              toplvl  amd.u                        /u
/home           toplvl  amd.home                     /home
/home/ezk       link    ./u/zing/ezk                 /u/zing/ezk
/u/zing         nfs     shekel:/n/shekel/u/zing      /n/shekel/u/zing
/mnt/G          auto    /etc/local/amd.mnt           /mnt/G
/mnt/G/bin      link    ./usr/i386-redhat-linux      /usr/i386-redhat-linux
```

If you run Amq with one or more arguments representing directory names, it will list the status of those automount directories, and any subdirectories, as seen in Listing 11.3.

Listing 11.3   Checking the status of an automount point using Amq

```
[ezk]$ amq /home
What           Uid Getattr  Lookup RdDir RdLnk  Statfs Mounted@
/home          0   1360129  5566   0     0      25     00/09/21 02:18:47
/home/martha   0   145317   0      0     1488   0      00/09/26 00:48:27
/home/ezk      0   1152156  0      0     2493   0      00/09/21 02:19:03
```

The meaning of each of the columns in Listing 11.3 is as follows:

What Is the volume name.

Uid Is not currently used.

Getattr Counts the number of times the GETATTR NFS operation executed on the node.

Lookup Counts the number of times the LOOKUP NFS operation ran on this node. This counter should be non-zero for directory nodes, and zero otherwise.

RdDir Counts the number of times the READDIR NFS operation ran on this node. This counter is often non-zero for directory nodes, and zero otherwise.

RdLnk Counts the number of times the READLINK NFS operation ran on this node; this operation is executed each time a symlink is followed. This counter should be zero for directory nodes.

Statfs Counts the number of times the STATFS NFS operation ran on this node. This counter should be non-zero for top-level nodes.

Mounted@ Lists the time and date that the volume was first referenced.

Amq Status Options

In this section we list Amq options that relate to the overall status of Amd.

amq -s

The -s option displays Amd's overall status counters, as seen in Listing 11.4.

Listing 11.4 Displaying Amd's global status using Amq

```
[ezk]$ amq -s
 requests stale     mount   mount    unmount
 deferred fhandles  ok      failed   failed
 1111     0         1363    6        622
```

The meaning of each of the five columns in Listing 11.4 is as follows:

Deferred requests This counter shows the number of times RPC requests were deferred—those for which Amd could not provide an immediate reply. This happens most often when a background mount is needed. Since Amd is likely to perform many background NFS mounts, this number tends to be large.

Stale filehandles This counter shows the number of times that the kernel sent Amd a stale NFS file handle. Usually this value would be small. If it is large, this could indicate a problem with the communication between Amd and the kernel.

Mount ok   This counter shows the number of times that Amd successfully completed a mount. The higher this number is compared to the other numbers, the healthier your system is.

Mount failed   This counter shows the number of times that Amd was unable to perform an automount. This could happen for various reasons but most often because a remote file server was down or did not permit the mount. This number should be small. If it is large and keeps growing, check your Amd logs and see if you have a particular set of mounts that keep failing.

Unmount failed   This counter shows the number of times that Amd was unable to unmount a file system whose volume was not recently used. Unmounts can fail when the actual remote mounted NFS file system is busy because a user process is using it, while not accessing it directly through Amd. A large busy server could have large numbers here. However, large numbers would indicate that Amd should cache active volumes for a longer period. See the discussion for "`cache_duration` and `dismount_interval`" in Chapter 9, "The Amd Configuration File."

amq -f

The -f option forces Amd to flush its map cache and reload all the maps from their sources—even if the source of the map has not changed. Normally, Amd will check every hour to see if any of its maps changed at the source, and will reload only those that changed. However, with the -f option, Amd will unconditionally reload all maps. When you force a reload, Amd will log information to its log file, which looks as follows:

```
[ezk]$ amq -f
[ezk]$ tail -7 /var/log/amd
amd[345]/info:  amq says flush cache
amd[345]/info:  reload #7 of map /etc/amdmaps/amd.misc succeeded
amd[345]/info:  reload #3 of map /etc/amdmaps/amd.src succeeded
amd[345]/info:  reload #4 of map /etc/amdmaps/amd.proj succeeded
amd[345]/info:  reload #3 of map /etc/amdmaps/amd.import succeeded
amd[345]/info:  reload #4 of map /etc/amdmaps/amd.u succeeded
amd[345]/info:  reload #19 of map /etc/amdmaps/amd.home succeeded
```

For further discussion on the subject of map caches, see "Map Caching Options" in Chapter 9.

The Amd
Automounter

PART 2

amq -u

The -u option takes one or more directory names as arguments. This option must be specified after all other options, as implied by the usage information in Listing 11.1. Amd then removes any cached entries for each of those directories and attempts to unmount the file systems that are mounted for those entries. Note that while Amd can remove an entry from its own cache, it cannot force a remote mounted NFS file system to unmount because the latter can be busy due to user processes on the current client host.

This option is often useful in conjunction with the -f option. Suppose you have an automounted entry /proj/ectile that is currently automounted, and you had to change it in the source Amd map. If you only reload Amd's maps, the entry will still be mounted and cached with the old value. If you only unmount the entry, Amd may still have the whole map cached internally. To ensure that Amd actually starts using the new value for this automounted node, use both options as follows:

```
[root]# amq -f -u /proj/ectile
```

amq -m

The -m option shows extended status information about mounted file systems, over that which the -s option provides. Listing 11.5 shows an example of such output.

Listing 11.5   Displaying Amd's extended status using Amq

```
[ezk]$ amq -m
"root"                    shekel:(pid345)      root    1   localhost is up
/etc/amdmaps/amd.home     /home                toplvl  1   localhost is up
/etc/amdmaps/amd.u        /u                   toplvl  1   localhost is up
opus:/n/opus/u/admin      /n/opus/u/admin      nfs     2   opus is up
opus:/n/opus/u/staff      /n/opus/u/staff      nfs     2   opus is up
orion:/n/orion/u/tah      /n/orion/u/tah       nfs     0   orion is down
ober:/n/ober/u/zer        /n/ober/u/zer        nfs     0   ober is up (Permission
                                                               denied)
```

The meaning of each column in the output of Listing 11.5 is as follows:

- The name of the mounted volume.
- The local mount point where the volume is mounted.
- The type of file system.
- The number of references to the file system. When this reference count is zero, it means that the file system is no longer mounted. However, Amd caches information about the state of the remote file server, so it can be used more quickly should this file server be needed again.

- The hostname of the server.

- The state of that file server: up, down, and any error that might have occurred.

Amq Logging and Debugging

This section lists Amq's options relating to logging and debugging. Not surprisingly, these options relate directly to the Amd configuration file logging and debugging options, described in Chapter 9.

amq -l

Most Unix systems use some form of log rotation tools. These tools can rename older log files on a daily basis, compressing old ones and even purging log files older than, say, one week. If your system uses a log rotation tool, you have to tell the log rotation tool (logrotate on Red Hat Linux systems) how to initialize a new log file after an existing one was renamed. To do so, use the Amq tool as follows:

```
[root]# amq -l /var/log/amd
```

You must specify the exact log file name listed in the amd.conf file, or Amd will refuse to initialize the new log. The -l option to Amq was initially intended to tell Amd to use a newly named log file, but it was deemed a serious security risk to allow remote users to change Amd's log file. That is why Amq compares the argument to the -l option with the log file set in the amd.conf file and uses this only to reinitialize an existing log file for the purpose of nightly log rotations.

amq -x

The -x option allows Amq to change Amd's logging options dynamically. The list and syntax for the logging options used is the same as specified in the section "log_options: Controlling Amd's Logging Details" later in this chapter.

One particular use for this option is to change the logging options temporarily while inspecting a potential problem. After you change logging options dynamically, you can let Amd run and check the logs as needed. In the following example, we turn on all logging, then turn off map-related messages, then turn off all logging, and finally turn on just fatal and user errors:

```
[ezk]$ amq -x all
[ezk]$ amq -x nomap
[ezk]$ amq -x noall
[ezk]$ amq -x fatal,user
```

The Amd
Automounter

PART 2

Note that in between changing Amd's logging options, we can run for any length of time with Amd and check the logs for any pertinent information.

amq -D

The -D option allows Amq to change Amd's debugging options and debugging actions dynamically. The list and syntax for the debugging features used is the same as specified in "debug_options: Controlling Amd's Debugging Details" later in this chapter.

Amd's debugging information can be very verbose. It is often useful to keep all debugging options off until needed, then turn them on for the period of time when you are, say, investigating a problem. When done, you can turn back off those debugging options. In the following example, we turn on readdir debugging so we can check how Amd constructs and lists automounted directory entries. When we are done, turn off all debugging.

```
[ezk]$ amq -D readdir
[ezk]$ amq -D noall
```

Note that if you did not build Amd with debugging support, trying to set debugging options using Amq will produce an error message indicating this.

Other Amq Options

In this section we list all remaining miscellaneous Amq options.

amq -h

The -h option allows Amq to apply its operation to a remote host running Amd. For example, to list the status of the Amd running on host cosmos, run the following:

```
[ezk]$ amq -h cosmos -s
requests   stale      mount      mount      unmount
deferred   fhandles   ok         failed     failed
53059      5          150235     211        8802
```

amq -H

The -H option prints a brief usage string of Amq, as seen in Listing 11.1.

amq -p

The -p (lowercase) option returns the PID of a running Amd. This is most often useful for sending Amd a signal. For example, one way to terminate Amd is to send it the TERM signal. Normally you would have to find the PID of Amd before you could send it the signal. With amq -p, this is easier:

```
[root]# kill -TERM `amq -p`
```

amq -P

The -P (uppercase) option tells Amq to contact an alternate running Amd that had registered itself on a different RPC portmap_program number and apply all other operations to that instance of the automounter. This is useful when you run multiple copies of Amd and need to manage each one separately. If not specified, Amq will use the default program number for Amd, 300019. For security reasons, the only alternate program numbers Amd can use range from 300019 to 300029, inclusive.

For example, to kill an alternate running Amd on the local host, use

```
[root]# kill -TERM `amq -p -P 300020`
```

To flush the maps of a remote, second Amd on host twinp using program number 300027 and also unmount /home/kyle, run

```
[root]# amq -f -h twinp -P 300027 -u /home/kyle
```

amq -T and -U

The -T option causes Amq to contact Amd using the TCP transport only (connection oriented). The -U option causes Amq to contact Amd using the UDP transport only (connectionless). Normally, Amq will use TCP first and, if that failed, it will try UDP.

Usually TCP is slower because it has to set up a connection for the network socket. However, TCP is guaranteed reliable. UDP is faster but not guaranteed to be as reliable as TCP.

Furthermore, while UDP can in theory use packet sizes as large as 64KB, in practice most RPC implementations that use UDP impose a limit of 8800 bytes. This remains so for historical reason from the initial design of NFSv2 by Sun Microsystems. On very busy hosts, Amd may have hundreds of active automount points that may be reported to Amq. The total size of data Amd has to transfer to Amq on such hosts can exceed 8800 bytes. On such hosts, it is necessary to use the -T option to guarantee that Amq can transfer large buffers from Amd.

Finally, if you are mixing an old Amd with a newer Amq or vice versa, there is a chance that either UDP or TCP may not work, because older implementations did not support both UDP and TCP. In those cases, you may have to use a newer Amq and pick the correct transport that interoperates with the Amd version you use.

The Amd Automounter

PART 2

amq -v

The -v option retrieves the Amd version string just as amd -v does. To get the version string from a remote host named retro, run Amd with the -v and -h options, as seen in Listing 11.6.

Listing 11.6   Checking version information of a remote Amd

```
[ezk]$ amq -v -h retro
Copyright (c) 1997-2000 Erez Zadok
Copyright (c) 1990 Jan-Simon Pendry
Copyright (c) 1990 Imperial College of Science, Technology & Medicine
Copyright (c) 1990 The Regents of the University of California.
am-utils version 6.0.4s4 (build 1).
Built by ib42@cs.columbia.edu on date Tue May 16 05:40:37 EDT 2000.
cpu=i686 (little-endian), arch=i386, karch=i586.
full_os=linux, os=linux, osver=2.2, vendor=pc.
Map support for: root, passwd, union, nisplus, nis, ndbm, file, error.
AMFS: nfs, link, nfsx, nfsl, host, linkx, program, union, inherit, ufs,
      efs, cdfs, pcfs, auto, direct, toplvl, autofs, error.
FS: autofs, iso9660, efs, nfs, nfs3, vfat, ext2.
Network: wire="16-net" (netnumber=128.59.16).
```

amq -w

The -w option translates a full path name as returned by getpwd(3) into a short Amd path name that goes through its mount points. This option requires that Amd be running. Often, the problem with Amd (when not using Autofs) is that the automounted path name is not the same as the location where Amd mounted a remote file system.

For example, my /home/ezk automounted path name is actually located on the file server shekel in the file system /n/shekel/u/zing, with the subdirectory ezk inside of it. If I cd to my home and print the working directory, I do not get what I expect:

```
[ezk]$ /bin/pwd
/n/shekel/u/zing/ezk
```

However, with Amq's -w option I get the correct (shortest) automounter path name:

```
[ezk]$ amq -w
/home/ezk
```

This works because Amq passes to Amd the full path name /n/shekel/u/zing/ezk and asks Amd to translate that long path name recursively based on the list of existing automounted volumes. Amd continues to translate the path name until it can no longer shorten it, and finally returns the shortest automounted path name back to Amq, which merrily displays it to the user.

Debugging Amd

In this section we discuss how to handle Amd when things go wrong: your file systems will not mount or Amd performs actions other than what you intended. In most cases the problems can be traced to two sources:

- Mistakes in the Amd maps
- Remote file server problems

In all cases, if Amd does not behave the way you expected, you should start by inspecting the log files. You can gradually increase the level of logging to get more detailed information. If that information is not enough, you can then turn on debugging to get much more verbose information. If needed, you can even run multiple versions of Amd so you can keep experimenting with alternate copies and not interfere with your production automounter.

Four `amd.conf` parameters can help you track what Amd is doing, as shown in Table 11.3. We described those briefly, along with all other configuration parameters in Chapter 9. Next, we describe these four parameters in more detail.

Table 11.3   Debugging and Logging Configuration Parameters

Parameter	Default	Possible Values
`log_file`	`/dev/stderr`	`/dev/stderr`, `/var/log/amd`, `syslog`, `syslog:`*`facility`*.
`log_options`	None	`all`, `fatal`, `error`, `user`, `warn`, `info`, `map`, `stats`. (Logging options prepended with `no` are excluded from being listed.)
`debug_options`	None	`all`, `amq`, `daemon`, `fork`, `full`, `hrtime`, `info`, `mem`, `mtab`, `str`, `readdir`, `test`, `trace`, `xdrtrace`. (Debugging options prepended with `no` are excluded from being listed.)
`portmap_program`	300019	300019, 300020, …, 300029.

log_file: Setting Amd's Log File

The log_file parameter specifies one of three possible methods for Amd to output logging and debugging information:

- If set to the string /dev/stderr, Amd will log information to the standard error file descriptor, *stderr*. Note that Amd will not actually attempt to write to a file or device named /dev/stderr.

- If set to the string syslog, Amd will log its information using the system logger daemon, syslogd. This daemon reads its commands from a configuration file named /etc/syslog.conf. That configuration file defines how different classes of logging messages are logged: written to regular files, displayed on the terminal of some users, or even forwarded to a syslogd server on another host.

In addition, log_file may be set to print to a specific class of messages, better known as a *facility* by syslog, using the syntax syslog:*facility*. The list of facilities is defined by your system. Consult the manual page for syslog.conf for more details. Typically, *facility* can be one of the following:

- auth (or security) for security and authorization messages
- authpriv for private security and authorization messages
- cron for messages from the clock daemon
- daemon for messages from other system daemons
- ftp for the file transfer program
- kern for messages initiated by the kernel
- lpr for the line printing subsystem
- mail for the e-mail system
- mark is for internal use and should not be used by users
- news for the network news subsystem
- syslog for messages generated internally by syslogd
- user for random user-level messages
- uucp for the UUCP subsystem, for those unfortunate enough to be using it
- local0 through local7 are reserved for local use

If you plan on using a facility for logging messages from Amd, choose one that is appropriate: daemon or one of the local0 through local7 ones. If the facility is not specified, Amd uses daemon.

- The third and last method for logging information from Amd is actually the most popular form of logging—regular files. If the `log_file` parameter is set to an absolute file name, Amd will log all information into that file.

For example, Linux systems place logs in the directory /var/log. To be consistent with this standard, set your Amd to log messages in the file /var/log/amd as follows in your `amd.conf` file:

```
[global]
log_file = /var/log/amd
```

You can also exert some control over the log file via Amq, as we described above in the section "`amq -l`." For example

```
[root]# amq -l /var/log/amd
```

log_options: Controlling Amd's Logging Details

Amd can log information about its activities to a designated logging target specified by the `log_file` parameter. The type of information logged is determined by the value of the `log_options` parameter. This parameter can control how much information is logged, and at what level of verbosity. For example, you can choose to see only critical errors, messages about map-parsing activities, and more. You can choose to see all possible information or none at all.

Amd logs particular types of activities based on keywords listed in the `log_options` parameter. Those are as follows:

all   Instruct Amd to log all messages.

debug   This includes conditional debugging messages. This option must be turned on for any debugging messages to appear. Debugging messages are described below in the section "debug_options: Controlling Amd's Debugging Details." In addition, if you build Amd yourself from the am-utils package, you must configure it with the `--enable-debug` option for debugging code to be compiled in. See Chapter 14 for details on building special support into Amd.

error   This option will log non-fatal system errors such as failure to contact a map service or mount an entry. These are non-fatal because Amd can continue to run even after the failure occurred and may recover from it later. Nevertheless, these are often problems that administrators wish to know, and so they are useful to log.

fatal   These report fatal errors that prevent Amd from functioning normally, such as running out of memory, the inability to establish network connections with the local host, or an unsuccessful RPC registration. Often, but not always, Amd will shut down after such errors. If Amd continues to run, it is because there may be a chance that it could continue to function for a while longer. However, if you see any such errors, it is best to correct the problems reported and restart Amd.

info   These represent informational messages about major activities that Amd performs, such as reloading maps, contacting information servers, executing commands as instructed by Amq, mounting remote NFS servers, and more.

map   This option provides information about map errors such as parsing errors, as well as information about selectors that matched or mismatched their values. This option can produce a lot of logging information, since Amd processes maps and their entries each time it looks up a new entry.

stats   This option provides a little additional statistical information: notices of remote servers that are still up after a timeout period, and when remote servers are deemed down and tested to verify that they are still down.

user   This option provides non-fatal user errors such as map parsing errors, when maps neglect to list all necessary information to complete a given mount type, or when the regular expression library failed to process regular expressions used in a map. These errors are not critical and often affect a single map entry. Amd can continue to run correctly indefinitely.

warn and warning   These are warning messages that are serious but not fatal enough to warrant shutting down Amd: NFS protocol errors, missing NFS mount options, TTY errors, and more. These messages are often useful to see.

The full list of all the logging messages that Amd produces is in Appendix C, "Amd Log and Debug Messages."

You can get a quick listing of all Amd's logging options by running amd -H and looking for the options available to amd -x, as shown in Listing 11.7.

Listing 11.7   Finding which logging options Amd supports

```
[ezk]$ amd -H
Usage: amd [-nprvHS] [-a mount_point] [-c cache_time] [-d domain]
       [-k kernel_arch] [-l logfile|"syslog[:facility]"]
       [-t timeout.retrans] [-w wait_timeout] [-C cluster_name]
       [-o op_sys_ver] [-O op_sys_name]
       [-F conf_file] [-T conf_tag] [-y nis-domain]
       [-x {no}{all,debug,error,fatal,info,map,stats,user,warn,warning}]
       [-D {no}{all,amq,daemon,fork,full,info,mtab,readdir,str,test,
            trace,xdrtrace}]
       [directory mapname [-map_options]]
```

The syntax for the value of log_options is a comma-delimited list of logging keywords. The special keyword all tells Amd to log all information. Each keyword can be prefixed by the string no to negate its meaning; this can be used to log all information excluding a certain type.

To log all serious messages through syslogd, use this in your amd.conf file:

```
[global]
log_file = syslog
log_options = fatal,error,warn
```

To log all but casual debugging messages and also ignore verbose map-related log messages, use this in your amd.conf file:

```
[global]
log_options = all,nodebug,nomap
```

Note the prefix no to debug and map, which tells Amd to exclude these two types of log messages from all messages.

If you are not sure what to log, try to log everything first. Then inspect your Amd logs and decide which messages are important to keep and which are not, based on the log type (which is put in the log along with the log message itself). To log all messages to the file /var/log/amd, put this in your amd.conf file:

```
[global]
log_file = /var/log/amd
log_options = all
```

You can also control the logging options via Amq dynamically, as we described above in "amq -x." For example, to turn off all logging options but fatal messages, use this:

```
[root]# amq -x noall,fatal
```

debug_options: Controlling Amd's Debugging Details

Amd includes extensive facilities for debugging its operation. These include changing its behavior through debugging options, as well as logging extra information verbosely. The target that Amd uses to log this extra debugging information is specified by the log_file parameter. The type of debugging information logged or debugging options turned on is determined by the value of the debug_options parameter.

Before you can use any debugging options, you must ensure that your Amd was built with debugging support. To check that, run amd -H and look for the options available to amd -D, as shown in Listing 11.8.

Listing 11.8 Finding which debugging options Amd supports

```
[ezk]$ amd -H
Usage: amd [-nprvHS] [-a mount_point] [-c cache_time] [-d domain]
       [-k kernel_arch] [-l logfile|"syslog[:facility]"]
       [-t timeout.retrans] [-w wait_timeout] [-C cluster_name]
       [-o op_sys_ver] [-O op_sys_name]
       [-F conf_file] [-T conf_tag] [-y nis-domain]
       [-x {no}{all,debug,error,fatal,info,map,stats,user,warn,warning}]
       [-D {no}{all,amq,daemon,fork,full,info,mtab,readdir,str,test,
            trace,xdrtrace}]
       [directory mapname [-map_options]]
```

If no options are listed there, it means that Amd was not built with debugging support. To build Amd with debugging options, configure it with one of these two options:

--enable-debug=yes This tells the build process to include debugging code and options. The resultant Amd binary will be larger and run slower since it may have to process and report extra information.

--enable-debug=mem This option tells the build process to include the usual debugging options and, in addition, to include memory-debugging options. This turns on extra checking for memory allocations and freeing of data buffers. Again, this option will also increase the Amd binary size and slow its execution.

For information about building and configuring Amd, see Chapter 14.

The values possible for the debug_options parameter and their meanings are as follows:

all This option instructs Amd to include all debugging messages and turn on all debugging options.

amq This action option tells Amd to register itself with the portmapper. Using noamq tells Amd not to register itself with the portmapper. This feature was useful when administrators wanted to run multiple copies of Amd. However, it is not necessary these days with the portmap_program parameter, described in the upcoming section, "portmap_program: Running Multiple Automounters."

daemon This action option tells Amd to enter daemon mode, or to *daemonize* itself. That is, Amd will fork a copy of itself, detach itself from the controlling terminal, and place its running process in the background. The option nodaemon is useful to ensure that Amd remains running in the foreground; this is needed when debugging Amd using a source code debugger such as gdb. Note that while the master Amd process can remain in the foreground with the nodaemon option, Amd will still fork background processes for each mount and unmount request. This is needed to ensure that the master Amd process will never hang because a remote server is down.

fork   This action option is listed here but currently is not in use by Amd. It is used by a special automounter called hlfsd, which is part of the am-utils distribution. Near the end of this chapter we provide a brief description of this program.

full   This informational option shows the full names and arguments of the commands used to mount and unmount file systems in maps of type:=program. These special *program* type mounts allow Amd to execute arbitrary mount and unmount programs to satisfy a mount and are useful when Amd does not have built-in support for a mount type. Chapter 10, "Automounter Maps" describes this and other map types in detail.

hrtime   This informational option prints high-resolution timestamps with each logged message on systems that support the clock_gettime function. It is useful when debugging many events that Amd may process in a short period of time and trying to get an accurate timing for each event. Unfortunately, Linux does not yet support this function.

info   This informational option logs debugging messages that are specific to a map service. In particular, it turns on resolver debugging (RES_DEBUG) for the Hesiod map service.

mem   This informational option traces the allocation and freeing of memory within Amd. It is usually a debugging option used by Amd's maintainers and is intended to identify memory leaks. That is why memory debugging information is not compiled in by default with other debugging options: you have to configure am-utils with --enable-debug=mem to include code for tracing memory allocations. Compiling in this code will slow Amd's run somewhat.

mtab   This action option tells Amd to update the list of mounted file systems in a file named ./mtab, located in the current directory where Amd starts. Amd maintains a list of mounted file systems in the standard mount-table file /etc/mtab. This file is used by programs such as df and /bin/umount to list or unmount file systems, respectively. The mtab debugging option redirects Amd to a different mount-table file, so that administrators can inspect Amd's actions in writing and updating the mount-table file, without affecting the main file used by the system, /etc/mtab.

NOTE   This option may not be needed in the future on Linux systems, because the *proc* file system maintains a file /proc/mounts that provides an accurate listing of all mounts recognized by the kernel. On those systems, /etc/mtab could become a symlink to /proc/mounts. In fact, the mtab option is not useful on systems that already maintain mount tables in the kernel (BSD-4.4 systems, Solaris 8, AIX, Ultrix, and others).

The Amd Automounter

PART 2

readdir   This informational option traces the execution of directory reading operations within Amd. This debugging option is particularly useful when using the browsable_dirs option (described in Chapter 9); that option, when used carelessly, can lead to a massive succession of unintended automount operations, also known as a *mount storm*.

Mount Storms

Amd is capable of listing entries in automounted directories. This means that the system call getdents(2), often executed by commands like /bin/ls, returns to the user process a listing of all the entries in a directory. However, most users do not just run /bin/ls but also ls -l or ls -F. When these options are used, /bin/ls also inspects each entry returned by getdents(2). This inspection is performed by the lstat(2) system call. When /bin/ls tries to lstat(2) an entry, Amd must mount the entry first before it can return information to the lstat(2) system call about the entry—information such as owner, group, and mode bits. If /bin/ls -l lists and lstats entries, they will all be automounted.

This condition is known as a *mount storm*: many entries are mounted all at once. Worse, since Amd avoids hanging the master automounter process, it forks a process for each mount that it performs in the background. A mount storm results in many processes forked in a short period of time and a flurry of RPC messages exchanged between Amd and the kernel. All the while, the user process that initiated the storm is hung, waiting for all automounted entries to be mounted.

Mount storms can easily overwhelm even powerful systems but often will disappear on their own minutes later. One possible solution to the mount storm problem is use of Autofs with Amd, described in Chapter 13, "Autofs." Since Autofs is an in-kernel file system designed to assist automounters, it can defer mounting of entries until after they are needed, which is often after the entries are lstat(2)ed.

---

str   This informational option traces string manipulations in great detail and is alone responsible for much of the debugging text that appears when all debugging options are turned on. With the str option you can debug string parsing when strings are broken into smaller components given their delimiters, when variables are expanded and to which values they are expanded, and more.

test   This debugging option is shorthand for all options but the following four: daemon, mem, str, and xdrtrace. This option is useful to keep Amd running normally and to trace a lot of activity, but not to trace the most verbose activities.

trace   This informational option turns on tracing of RPC protocol message exchanges between Amd and the kernel, as well as NFS mounts. For NFS mounts, this option shows all of the flags and parameters Amd passes to the mount(2) system call when mounting remote NFS file systems. This is very useful if you suspect that Amd may be mounting NFS volumes differently from the /bin/mount program.

xdrtrace   This informational option turns on tracing of *eXternal Data Representation* (XDR) messages that Amd exchanges with the kernel and Amq. XDR messages are part of the RPC system, and form the basis for a portable method for exchanging data between RPC services. This option can produce vast amounts of debugging information but is useful if you suspect that Amd is not communicating correctly with other RPC services.

The full listing of all the debugging messages that Amd produces is in Appendix C.

The syntax for the value of debug_options is a comma-delimited list of debugging keywords. The special keyword all tells Amd to turn on all debugging options. Each keyword can be prefixed by the string no to negate its meaning; this can be used to debug all information excluding a certain type or option.

To turn on full debugging of everything, use this in your amd.conf file:

```
[global]
debug_options = all
```

In practice, however, administrators are often overwhelmed by the amount of debugging information that Amd can produce. Instead, they find it useful to turn on debugging for all useful services, without changing Amd's behavior, and excluding options that produce a lot of information:

```
[global]
debug_options = all,nomtab,notrace,noxdrtrace
```

Note the prefix no to mtab, trace, and xdrtrce, which tells Amd to exclude these three types of debugging options from all options.

The Amd Automounter

PART 2

You can also dynamically control the debugging options via Amq, as we described above in the section "amq -D." For example, to turn off all debugging options but NFS mount traces, use this:

```
[root]# amq -D noall,trace
```

portmap_program: Running Multiple Automounters

The portmap_program parameter allows you to run several instances of Amd concurrently. It is useful to run more than one version of Amd for two reasons:

- You can keep a production version of Amd running and try a significant change in your maps, amd.conf file, or information services, all without affecting your production automounter.

- You can run newer versions of Amd, perhaps experimental ones, while maintaining your original Amd running unhindered. This ability proved very useful during the development cycle of am-utils, including the experimentation with many of the examples listed in this book.

Amd is an RPC-based service and registers itself with the portmapper, as was explained in Chapter 8. The portmapper allows only one program to register with the same ID. This RPC ID is known as a *program number*. Due to design limitations of the RPC system, only one program may hold the same ID. If a second program tries to register itself with the same program number as an existing one, it will be allowed to do so, but the first program would lose its RPC identity. To solve this problem, use the portmap_program parameter to set a different RPC program number for additional instances of Amd.

The default value for portmap_program is 300019. This is the assigned RPC program number of Amd. You can check to see what RPC services are running on your system and what their assigned program numbers are by running the rpcinfo program, as shown in Listing 11.9.

Listing 11.9   Finding RPC information on a running Amd

```
[ezk]$ rpcinfo -p
program vers proto   port  service
 100000    2   tcp    111  rpcbind
 100000    2   udp    111  rpcbind
 100024    1   udp    997  status
 100024    1   tcp    999  status
 100011    1   udp    742  rquotad
 100011    2   udp    742  rquotad
 100005    1   udp    749  mountd
```

```
100005   1   tcp    751   mountd
100005   2   udp    754   mountd
100005   2   tcp    756   mountd
100005   3   udp    759   mountd
100005   3   tcp    761   mountd
100003   2   udp   2049   nfs
100003   3   udp   2049   nfs
100021   1   udp   1026   nlockmgr
100021   3   udp   1026   nlockmgr
100021   4   udp   1026   nlockmgr
100001   3   udp    782   rstatd
100001   2   udp    782   rstatd
100001   1   udp    782   rstatd
100002   3   udp    795   rusersd
100002   2   udp    795   rusersd
100007   2   udp    825   ypbind
100007   2   tcp    827   ypbind
300019   1   tcp    842   amd
300019   1   udp    843   amd
```

Here you can see that Amd's program number is 300019, the RPC implementation version number supported is 1, both UDP and TCP transports are available, and Amd listens to requests on ports 842 and 843. Chapter 1, "NFS Basics and Protocols," provides more information about the RPC system and the properties of RPC-based programs.

To run a second Amd with a different RPC program number, set the program number in a different Amd configuration file, say, /tmp/test-amd.conf, as follows:

```
[global]
portmap_program = 300020
```

To run the second Amd with the new program number, run

```
[root]# amd -F /tmp/test-amd.conf
```

Now if you run rpcinfo and look for program numbers with the string 3000 in them (using the grep command), you will see output such as the following:

```
[ezk]$ rpcinfo -p | grep 3000
  300019   1   tcp    842   amd

  300019   1   udp    843   amd

  300020   1   tcp   7937

  300020   1   udp   7938
```

In other words, two versions of Amd are running. Note that the RPC system cannot identify the second instance as Amd because program number 300020 is not an officially assigned program number given to Amd. Official RPC program numbers are listed in the file /etc/rpc, but only 300019 is listed in that file as belonging to Amd.

Amq depends on the RPC program number to query and control Amd. If you run multiple copies of Amd, you can use the -P option to Amq to access an alternate running Amd. For example, to query the list of mounts of the default Amd, run

```
[ezk]$ amq
```

However, to query an alternate Amd running as program number 300020, run

```
[ezk]$ amq -P 300020
```

Debugging Individual Mounts

Suppose you have a problem where Amd is not performing the action you wish to achieve. Say you wish to automount titan:/n/gin on /home/train, yet it does not work. In this section we describe the actions you can take to gradually debug this problem. Generally these are as follows:

- Turning on logging and debugging options and inspecting the logs
- Looking for and correcting map syntax errors
- Making sure NFS clients and servers can communicate properly
- Flushing all of Amd's cached information and reloading maps
- Restarting Amd
- Rebooting the machine
- Trying a new version of Amd
- Checking the various Amd mailing lists
- Hiring Erez on a consulting basis

First, start by turning on the appropriate logging and debugging options as we described in the previous section, "portmap_program: Running Multiple Automounters." Then look at the log file. In Appendix C, we list all of Amd's log and debug messages.

If you see any parsing error messages, it is likely that you have a typo in your Amd map for the train entry in amd.home. For example, a typical error administrators often make is to forget a line continuation mark (backslash), or to use the = sign for assignments instead of :=. Fix the error in the source of the map, unmount the entry, and reload your maps using Amq as follows:

[root]# **amq -f -u /home/train**

If you see a mount error message, it is likely that for one reason or another, your NFS client cannot mount the remote server. One very useful way to check to see if an NFS mount problem is due to a problem with Amd is to try and hand-mount the partition temporarily:

[root]# **/bin/mount titan:/n/gin /mnt**

If this command fails, you have a general NFS mount problem between your client and your server and you must fix it first. Amd cannot succeed in mounting any volumes if you cannot mount them by hand. This can happen for several reasons:

- Your NFS server is down. You must bring it back up first.
- The network to your NFS server is not reachable. You must ensure proper network connectivity.
- Your NFS server does not permit this client to mount the remote server. This is often seen as a "Permission Denied" error message in Amd's logs. Make sure your NFS server permits this client host to mount the given file system, reload or restart your NFS server's rpc.mountd program, and then try to mount the file system via Amd again. You may have to flush all cached entries in Amd first, using amq -f.

If, however, the above command succeeds, then there is a possible problem with Amd.

If the Amd logs say that it cannot find the host to mount, check that the host is listed in your /etc/hosts or DNS maps. If it is there, make sure that your DNS resolver configuration file, /etc/resolv.conf, is set correctly.

To be sure, use the wire-test program. This program checks that Amd can communicate with a remote host and whether the client and host agree on which NFS versions to use. A successful run of wire-test is seen in Listing 11.10.

Listing 11.10   Successful run of wire-test

```
[ezk]$ wire-test titan
Network 1: wire="net1.dev.hydraweb.com" (netnumber=172.29.1).
Network 2: wire="172.29.17.0" (netnumber=172.29.17).
My IP address is 0xac1d0141.
NFS Version and protocol tests to host "titan"...
        testing vers=2, proto="udp" -> found version 2.
        testing vers=3, proto="udp" -> found version 2.
        testing vers=2, proto="tcp" -> failed!
        testing vers=3, proto="tcp" -> failed!
```

Listing 11.10 shows that this host was able to communicate with host titan using NFS versions 2 and 3, but for UDP only. That is OK. Listing 11.11 shows an unsuccessful run of wire-test.

Listing 11.11   An unsuccessful run of wire-test

```
[ezk]$ wire-test titan
Network 1: wire="net1.dev.hydraweb.com" (netnumber=172.29.1).
Network 2: wire="172.29.17.0" (netnumber=172.29.17).
My IP address is 0xac1d0141.
NFS Version and protocol tests to host "titan"...
        testing vers=2, proto="udp" -> failed!
        testing vers=3, proto="udp" -> failed!
        testing vers=2, proto="tcp" -> failed!
        testing vers=3, proto="tcp" -> failed!
```

Here, we can see that the client could not agree with the server on any version or transport for NFS. This could be for two reasons:

- The remote host is not configured as an NFS server, or its kernel does not support NFS. If the latter, you may have to build a new kernel for that host, as we described in Chapter 7, "Building and Installing the Linux Kernel and NFS Software."

- The current client host does not support NFS's client-side code. If that is the case, you may also have to build a new kernel for this host, as we described in Chapter 7.

It is also possible that Amd is not performing NFS mounts exactly the way /bin/mount does. To see the exact data and flags that Amd passes to the kernel using the mount(2) system call, turn on debug_options=trace and check the logs for what Amd prints when it performs your specific mount. Listing 11.12 shows the trace log information for a typical successful NFS mount on Linux.

Listing 11.12   Traces of an NFS mount log in Amd

```
Generic mount flags 0xc0ed0002
NA->addr {sockaddr_in} (len=16) = "02000801803b14640000000000000000"
NA->addr.sin_family = "2"
NA->addr.sin_port = "264"
NA->addr.sin_addr = "803b1464"
NA->hostname = "titan"
NA->namlen = 255
NA->filehandle =
    "008000f400000002000a0000000000026e065b6c000a0000000000026e065b6c"
NA->version = 3
```

```
NA->flags = 0x0
NA->rsize = 4096
NA->wsize = 4096
NA->bsize = 0
NA->timeo = 7
NA->retrans = 3
NA->acregmin = 3
NA->acregmax = 60
NA->acdirmin = 30
NA->acdirmax = 60
```

If your mount varies significantly from that listed here, it could indicate a problem with the flags you set in your Amd map, or with Amd. At this stage you should consider simply restarting Amd:

[root]# **/etc/rc.d/init.d/amd restart**

If you cannot interrupt your users to restart Amd, you may wish to run a second Amd as we described above in "portmap_program: Running Multiple Automounters."

Sometimes, complex system interactions can place your system in an unstable state. This can be particularly true if you are running an experimental version of the Linux kernel. If you suspect that is the case, try and reboot your system.

If that does not help, check with your Linux vendor for any system patches to any component that could affect NFS behavior: new kernels, new RPC daemons, etc. Red Hat often distributes these as RPM updates from ftp://updates.redhat.com.

Your very last resort, before calling me at home, would be to check the linux-kernel and linux-nfs mailing lists for any known bugs that may have already been fixed and the amd-dev or amd-workers mailing lists for the same. You may have to download and build a new version of your kernel, user-level tools, or the automounter. We described those procedures in Chapters 7 and 14.

Maintaining and Using Map Information Services

In Chapter 10, we discussed the syntax of Amd's maps. We also outlined the additional syntax of maps when their source are regular files: comments, blank lines, and continuation lines. In Chapter 9, we discussed how you can tell Amd to read those maps from various *information services*—servers that Amd can query to locate map keys and their values. But so far we have not told you how to maintain your maps under these various servers. That is the role of this chapter. Next, we tell you how to maintain your maps under the various possible sources, as well as how to populate your servers with Amd maps for the first time.

Table 11.4 shows you all the map types supported by Amd, the default caching type for entries in such maps, and any utility programs that am-utils has to assist in maintaining these map types.

Table 11.4 Map Types Supported by Amd and Their Default Caching Behavior

Map Type	Caching	Conversion Utility
error	None	N/A
file	all	N/A
hesiod	inc	None
ldap	all	amd2ldif
ndbm	all	mk-amd-map
nis	all	Part of YP Makefile
nisplus	inc	None
password	all	N/A
root	root	N/A
union	all	N/A

Some of the map types in Table 11.4 do not require any maintenance because they are special, and we have described them elsewhere before:

error This is the default map name when no other map service could be initialized. You can tell Amd to use a particular map service, or all of the map services as listed in the output of amd -v. If no map initialized successfully, Amd sets the map type to error, which you can see in the output of amq.

root Amd instantiates this very special map once, as the top-level map for the running automounter. You can see this as the very first instance in the output of amq:

```
[ezk]$ amq -h shekel
/              root     "root"                        shekel:(pid345)
/u             toplvl   /etc/amdmaps/amd.u            /u
/home          toplvl   /etc/amdmaps/amd.home        /home
/home/martha   link     ./u/admin/martha             /u/admin/martha
/home/ezk      link     ./u/zing/ezk                 /u/zing/ezk
/u/admin       nfs      opus:/n/opus/u/admin         /n/opus/u/admin
/u/zing        link     ./n/shekel/u/zing            /n/shekel/u/zing
```

File Maps

File maps are the most popular maps that administrators use. File maps support continuation lines, comment lines, and blank lines, as well as the basic map syntax as described in Chapter 10.

Maintaining these maps is very easy: just edit them with your favorite text editor, change what you need, and then save the files. When done, you may run amq -f to force a reload of all maps.

We depend on file maps to support the other map types. The reason for this is that file maps are very flexible, and we can convert them into the corresponding representations for the other types. In fact, am-utils comes with scripts that help you with this task.

> **NOTE** This section does not teach you how to maintain network information servers such as NIS, LDAP, or Hesiod—only how to produce Amd maps for those services. You should refer to the manual pages for these services for specific information on setting and configuring these services.

Hesiod Maps

When the map name begins with the string hesiod., or you set the map_type=hesiod in your amd.conf file, Amd performs key lookups using a Hesiod name server. The string following the dot in the map name is treated as a name qualifier and is prepended to the key being located. Amd then resolves the entire string in the automount *context*. This context can be changed using the amd.conf parameter hesiod_base.

For example, if the key is ezk and the map name is hesiod.home, then Amd will ask Hesiod to resolve the string ezk.home.automount. If your Hesiod server has the following entries:

```
ezk.home.automount HS TXT "rhost:=shekel;rfs:=/u/zing;sublink:=ezk"

martha.home.automount HS TXT "rhost:=ape;rfs:=/u/staff;sublink:=martha"
```

then Amd will point the key ezk to the directory /u/zing/ezk of host shekel. Listing 11.13 shows a sample set of shell commands to convert an amd.home map into a list of Hesiod entries, stored in a file amd.home.hesiod.

Listing 11.13   Converting file maps to Hesiod maps

```
[ezk]$ mk-amd-map -p amd.home |
> while read a b
> do
> echo $a.home.automount HS TXT \"$b\"
> done > amd.home.hesiod
```

LDAP Maps and *amd2ldif*

Am-utils comes with a script called amd2ldif to convert Amd maps to LDAP Directory Interchange Format (LDIF). Suppose you have an Amd map amd.home that looks as follows:

```
/defaults     opts:=rw,intr;type:=link


zing          -rhost:=shekel \
              host==shekel \
              host!=shekel;type:=nfs
```

To convert this file map to LDAP's format, run amd2ldif as seen in Listing 11.14.

Listing 11.14   Converting file maps to LDAP maps

```
[ezk]$ amd2ldif amd.home CUCS < amd.home > amd.home.ldif
[ezk]$ cat amd.home.ldif
dn: cn=amdmap timestamp, CUCS
cn              : amdmap timestamp
objectClass     : amdmapTimestamp
amdmapTimestamp: 873071363

dn: cn=amdmap amd.home[/defaults], CUCS
cn              : amdmap amd.home[/defaults]
```

```
objectClass : amdmap
amdmapName  : amd.home
amdmapKey   : /defaults
amdmapValue : opts:=rw,intr;type:=link

dn: cn=amdmap amd.home[], CUCS
cn          : amdmap amd.home[]
objectClass : amdmap
amdmapName  : amd.home
amdmapKey   :
amdmapValue :

dn: cn=amdmap amd.home[zing], CUCS
cn          : amdmap amd.home[zing]
objectClass : amdmap
amdmapName  : amd.home
amdmapKey   : zing
amdmapValue : -rhost:=shekel host==shekel host!=shekel;type:=nfs
```

The first argument to amd2ldif is the map name. The second argument is the LDAP base.

After converting the file map to LDIF, you can feed the amd.home.ldif file to your LDAP server. See the manual page for slapd.

NDBM Maps and *mk-amd-map*

An NDBM map can be used as a fast access form of a file map. Am-utils comes with a program called mk-amd-map that converts a normal map file into an NDBM database. Note that NDBM format files may not be sharable across machine architectures. NDBM maps are generally faster only for large maps; a small map, less than a single disk block, is more likely to process faster as a plain file map.

On systems that support the Berkeley DB database format, mk-amd-map converts file maps into DB format files.

For example, to convert a map file amd.home into NDBM format, run

```
[ezk]$ mk-amd-amp amd.home
[ezk]$ ls -l amd.home*
-rw-r--r--   1 ezk     tech       76638 Oct 14 02:03 amd.home
-r--r--r--   2 ezk     tech        4096 Oct 14 02:03 amd.home.dir
-r--r--r--   2 ezk     tech      206518 Oct 14 02:03 amd.home.pag
```

As you can see, mk-amd-map created the two standard NDBM files, one with the .dir extension and one with the .pag extension.

You can also run mk-amd-map with the -p option to print the map on the standard output instead of generating a database. This is usually used to merge continuation lines into one physical line.

NIS Maps

NIS maps are a form of NDBM maps that are used by the NIS server ypserv. To convert file maps to NIS maps, you have to add an automatic conversion rule to /var/yp/ Makefile on your master NIS server host. A code snippet for that Makefile is seen in Listing 11.15; this one is used to convert an Amd map file $(YPSRCDIR)/amd.src (often /etc/amd.src) to its NIS equivalent.

Listing 11.15   A Makefile snippet for converting file maps to NIS maps

```
AMD_SRC     = $(YPSRCDIR)/amd.src

amd.src: $(AMD_SRC) $(YPDIR)/Makefile
        @echo "Updating $@..."
        -@sed -e "s/#.*$$//" -e "/^$$/d" $(AMD_SRC) | \
        $(AWK) '{\
              for (i = 1; i <= NF; i++)\
                if (i == NF) { \
                  if (substr($$i, length($$i), 1) == "\\") \
                    printf("%s", substr($$i, 1, length($$i) -1)); \
                  else \
                    printf("%s\n",$$i); \
                } \
              else \
                printf("%s ",$$i);\
            }' | $(DBLOAD) -i $(AMD_SRC) -o $(YPMAPDIR)/$@ - $@
        -@$(NOPUSH) || $(YPPUSH) -d $(DOMAIN) $@
```

If you have several Amd file maps, duplicate the amd.src example in Listing 11.15 and change it for each map.

NIS+ Maps

Red Hat Linux supports NIS+ client calls but not NIS+ servers. Populating NIS+ maps must be done on the server. This machine is most likely to be a Sun Solaris machine. To create an NIS+ table named `homes`, of type `amd_tbl`, with two fields, `amdkey` and `locations`, run the following:

```
[root]# nistbladm -c amd_tbl amdkey=S,a+r,o+m locations=S,a+r
    homes.example.com.
```

The above command creates the `homes` map in the `example.com` NIS+ directory. The latter often corresponds to your domain name. The two columns of the table are of type string (`S`). Their modes are set such that only the owner can modify this table; all other users can only read the table.

To add entries to the table we just created, you can use the `-A` option to the `nistbladm` command. The small shell script in Listing 11.16 reads an Amd file map named `amd.home` and creates the corresponding NIS+ table.

Listing 11.16   Converting file maps to NIS+ maps

```
[ezk]$ mk-amd-map -p amd.home |
> while read a b
> do
> nistbladm -A amdkey=$a locations=\"$b\" homes.example.com
> done
```

Password Maps

Password maps are different from other map types. When the map name is the special string `/etc/passwd`, or when you set `map_type=passwd` in your `amd.conf`, Amd will look up a username in the password file and rearrange the home directory field to produce a usable map entry.

Amd assumes the home directory has the format

/anydir/dom1/.../domN/login

Amd breaks this string into a map entry as follows:

- `${rfs}` has the value */anydir/domN*
- `${rhost}` has the value that is the reverse concatenation of *domN* through *dom1* with a period in between each domain component
- `${sublink}` has the value of the *login* component

For example, if the password file entry was /home/titan/ezk, then the map entry Amd would use is

```
rfs:=/home/titan;rhost:=titan;sublink:=ezk
```

The Amd Automounter

PART 2

Similarly, if the password file entry was /home/edu/columbia/cs/sunny/martha, then the map entry used by Amd would be

```
rfs:=/home/sunny;rhost:=sunny.cs.columbia.edu;sublink:=martha
```

Union Maps

Union maps are another unusual type of map: they do not even have any physical map to store their entries. Rather, they form their entries automatically by merging the contents of several directories as listed in the map's name. Union maps are for use with the type:=union Amd file system only.

The following amd.conf example uses /usr/X11 as the automount point. It merges the contents of /usr/X11R6 and /usr/openwin onto this automount point. If any binaries have the same name in both locations, those in /usr/openwin take precedence.

```
[ /usr/X11 ]
map_type = union
map_name = union:/usr/X11R6:/usr/openwin
```

For more details, see "Union File System (union)" in Chapter 10.

Other am-utils Tools

In this section we discuss any other programs, tools, or files that come with am-utils, and which we have not already discussed. We discuss these briefly here, because they are not used often. Table 11.1 lists the full contents of the am-utils package.

We group these into five categories:

- Administrator scripts and files related to Amd
- Programs that control Amd maps
- Programs that control mount tables
- Files that are part of the special hlfsd automounter
- The fsinfo utility

Administrator Scripts

These scripts and files are used by administrators and relate directly to Amd.

am-eject

The shell script `am-eject` unmounts a floppy or CD-ROM that is automounted and then attempts to eject the removable device. The script is needed because you cannot eject a removable device that is mounted. To eject a CD-ROM, run

[ezk]$ `am-eject cdrom`

To eject a floppy disk, run

[ezk]$ `am-eject floppy`

This script is fairly simple and can only eject floppies and CD-ROMs.

amd.conf-sample

The script `amd.conf-sample` is a sample Amd configuration file and is a good starting point for writing your own `amd.conf` file. This file lists every possible Amd configuration parameter along with comments, so you can pick and choose those options that suit your needs.

pawd

The `pawd` program works similarly to `amq -w`. It prints the current working directory, adjusted to reflect proper paths that can be reused to go through the automounter for the shortest possible path. In particular, the path printed back does not include any of Amd's local mount points. Using them is unsafe, because Amd may unmount managed file systems from the mount points, and thus, including them in paths may not always find the files within managed directories.

Without any arguments, `pawd` will print the automounter-adjusted current working directory. With any number of arguments, it will print the adjusted path of each one of the arguments.

wait4amd

The `wait4amd` script waits for Amd to start on a particular host before performing an arbitrary command. The command is executed repeatedly, with one-second sleep intervals in between. You may interrupt the script using Ctrl+C (or whatever keyboard sequence your terminal's `intr` function is bound to).

Examples include the following:

[ezk]$ `wait4amd saturn amq -h saturn`

When Amd is up on host `saturn`, get the list of available mounts of that running Amd.

[ezk]$ `wait4amd pluto ssh pluto`

Securely log in to host `pluto` when Amd is up on that host. It is generally necessary to wait for Amd to start properly and initialize on a remote host before logging in to it, because otherwise user home directories may not be accessible across the network. Using `wait4amd` to log in to another host is particularly useful.

```
[ezk]$ wait4amd pluto
```

This is a shorthand version of the previous command, but using `rlogin`, since the most useful reason for this script is to log in to a remote host. I use it very often when testing new versions of Amd or while doing kernel development, and need to reboot hung hosts.

wait4amd2die

The `wait4amd2die` script is used internally by `ctl-amd` when restarting Amd as we described earlier in this chapter. It waits for Amd to terminate after Amd had been sent a termination signal (the script will not cause Amd to terminate). If it detected that Amd terminated cleanly, this script will return an exit status of zero. Otherwise, it will return a non-zero exit status.

By default, the script tests for Amd's existence once every five seconds, six times, for a total of 30 seconds. It will return a zero exit status as soon as it detects that Amd dies. To wait for Amd to terminate for a total of one minute, but check every two seconds, run it as follows:

```
[root]# wait4amd2die 2 30
wait4amd2die: delay 2 sec (1 of 30)...
wait4amd2die: delay 2 sec (2 of 30)...
wait4amd2die: amd is down!
```

Map Control

The map-control scripts manipulate Amd maps. In particular, they convert maps between different formats.

amd2sun

The `amd2sun` script converts Amd maps to (old) Sun Automounter maps. Use it as follows:

```
[root]# amd2sun < amd.home > /etc/auto_home
```

> **WARNING** Amd maps support syntax and features that are much more complex than that of Sun's Automounter maps. This script will not be able to convert all Amd maps completely. Inspect the resulting Sun Automounter maps carefully before using them.

automount2amd

The script `automount2amd` converts (old) Sun Automounter maps to Amd maps. Since Sun's old automounter maps are simpler than Amd, this script achieves a high success rate in converting Sun's maps to Amd's. Nevertheless, you should inspect the resulting Amd maps carefully before using them. Note also that `automount2amd` does not understand newer Sun Automount map syntax, such as those used by Autofs.

Say you have the Sun Automounter file /etc/auto_src, with these two lines:

```
home                    earth:/home
moon    -ro,intr        server:/proj/images
```

To convert this map to an Amd map, run

[root]# **automount2amd /etc/auto_src > amd.src**

The script will produce the Amd map `amd.src` with the content as seen in Listing 11.17.

Listing 11.17   A Sun Automounter map converted to an Amd map

```
# generated by automount2amd on Sat Aug 14 17:59:32 US/Eastern 1999

/defaults \
    type:=nfs;opts:=rw,grpid,nosuid,utimeout=600

home \
    host==earth;type:=link;fs:=/home \
    rhost:=earth;rfs:=/home

moon \
    -addopts:=ro,intr \
    host==server;type:=link;fs:=/proj/images \
    rhost:=server;rfs:=/proj/images
```

This `automount2amd` script will use the following /default entry:

```
type:=nfs;opts:=rw,grpid,nosuid,utimeout=600
```

If you wish to override that, define the ${DEFAULTS} environment variable or modify the script. If you wish to generate Amd maps using the hostd selector variable instead of the host selector variable, then define the environment variable ${DOMAIN} or modify the script.

fix-amd-map

Am-utils changed some of the syntax and default values of some variables. For example, the default value for ${os} for Solaris 2.*x* (aka SunOS 5.*x*) systems used to be sos5. It is now more automatically generated from config.guess and its value is sunos5.

The script fix-amd-map converts older Amd maps to new ones. Use it as follows:

```
[root]# fix-amd-map < old.map > new.map
```

Mount-Table Control

The mount-table-control programs manipulate the contents of remote and local mount-table files, since with Amd, the contents of these files can get out of sync with the list of actual mounted file systems on the host.

fixmount

When an NFS client mounts a remote server, the server's mount daemon records who mounted its file systems in a file called /var/state/nfs/rmtab. Often, however, clients crash or reboot without informing remote servers that they no longer mount that server. This leaves the server with lots of stale entries in its /var/state/nfs/rmtab file.

The fixmount program is a variant of showmount(8), which can delete these bogus mount entries in remote mountd(8) daemons. You can list several hosts on the command line to fixmount; the actions specified by the options are performed for each host in turn. The following options are supported:

-a, -d, -e Work as in showmount(8) except that only entries pertaining to the local host are printed.

-r Removes those remote mount entries on hosts that do not correspond to current mounts. Those are often left over from a crash or are the result of improper handling of the mount protocol. The fixmount program verifies that the mounts actually exist in /etc/mtab.

-v Verify remote mounts. Similar to -r except that only a notification message is printed for each bogus entry found. The remote mount table is not changed.

-A Issues a command to the remote mountd declaring that *all* of its file systems have been unmounted. This should be used with caution, as it removes all remote mount entries pertaining to the local system, whether or not any file systems are still mounted locally.

-q   Be quiet. Suppresses error messages due to timeouts and "Program not registered" messages—those due to remote hosts not supporting RPC or not running mountd.

-h *name*   Pretend the local hostname is *name*. This is useful after the local hostname has been changed and /var/state/nfs/rmtab entries using the old name remain on a remote machine. Unfortunately, most mount daemons will not be able to handle removal of such entries successfully, so this option is useful in combination with -v only. This option also saves time as comparisons of remotely recorded and local hostnames by address are avoided.

A typical use for this program is as follows:

```
[root]# fixmount -r titan earth
```

There are several limitations to the fixmount program:

- No attempt is made to verify the information in /etc/mtab itself.

- Since swap file mounts are not recorded in /etc/mtab, a heuristic specific to SunOS is used to determine whether such a mount is actual (replacing the string swap with root and verifying the resulting path).

- Symbolic links on the server will cause the path in the remote entry to differ from the one in /etc/mtab. To catch those cases, a file system is also deemed mounted if its local mount point is identical to the remote entry. That is, on a diskless client, server:/export/usr/share.i386 could actually be /usr/share. Since the local mount point is /usr/share as well, this will be handled correctly.

- There is no way to clear a stale entry in a remote mountd after the local hostname (or whatever reverse name resolution returns for it) has been changed. To take care of these cases, the remote /var/state/nfs/rmtab file has to be edited and mountd restarted.

- The RPC timeouts for mountd calls can only be changed by recompiling. The defaults are two seconds for client-handle creation and five seconds for RPC calls.

fixrmtab

The fixmount program can fix stale entries remotely, from the client. The fixrmtab script can invalidate /var/state/nfs/rmtab entries on the local host for the hosts named. This script also restarts mountd for changes to take effect. Use it, for example, to affect these two hosts:

```
[root]# fixrmtab shine moon
```

The Amd Automounter

PART 2

The HLFSD Automounter

The `hlfsd` program; the `ctl-hlfsd`, `expn`, and `lostaltmail` scripts; and the sample configuration file `lostaltmail.conf-sample` relate to the *Home-Link File System Daemon*, HLFSD. This special automounter was designed to deliver users' e-mail directly to their home directories.

hlfsd

The `hlfsd` daemon implements a file system containing a symbolic link to a subdirectory within a user's home directory, depending on the user who accessed that link. It was primarily designed to redirect incoming mail to users' home directories, so that the mail could be read from anywhere along with the users' home files.

HLFSD operates by mounting itself as an NFS server for the directory containing *linkname*, which defaults to `/hlfs/home`. Lookups within that directory are handled by `hlfsd`, which uses the password map to determine how to resolve the lookup. The directory will be created if it does not already exist. The symbolic link will be to the accessing user's home directory, with *subdir* appended to it. If not specified, *subdir* defaults to `.hlfsdir`. This directory will also be created if it does not already exist.

For more information on HLFSD, follow the pointers in Appendix B, "Online Resources."

ctl-hlfsd

The script `ctl-hlfsd` controls the starting and stopping of the `hlfsd` automounter, the same way that `ctl-amd` controls Amd.

expn

The `expn` script expands mail aliases and is part of the `lostaltmail` script, a program that can resend mail that was misdirected (lost). See the manual page for `expn` for all usage options.

For example, to check the full expansion of my e-mail ID, step by step and verbosely, run

```
[ezk]$ expn -v ezk@cs.columbia.edu
ezk@cs.columbia.edu ->
        ezk@shekel.mcl.cs.columbia.edu
ezk@shekel.mcl.cs.columbia.edu ->
        Erez Zadok <"| /usr/mh/lib/slocal -user ezk || exit 75>
        Erez Zadok <\ezk>
        Erez Zadok </home/ezk/.mailspool/backup>
```

lostaltmail

The script `lostaltmail` is used with HLFSD to resend any misdirected mail. HLFSD redirects mail that cannot be written into the user's home directory to an alternate directory. This is useful to continue delivering mail, even if the user's file system was unavailable, full, or over quota. However, the mail that gets delivered to the alternate directory needs to be resent to its respective users once their home directories are available again, so that those users can read their mail. This is what the `lostaltmail` script does.

Use it as follows:

    [root]# **lostaltmail**

This script is suitable for placing in a daily or even hourly `cron(8)` job.

lostaltmail.conf-sample

The `lostaltmail` program needs a configuration file `lostaltmail.conf` set up with the right parameters to work properly. This file is a sample of such a configuration file and contains descriptive examples and comments.

FSinfo

FSinfo is a file system management tool. It has been designed to work with Amd to help system administrators keep track of the ever-increasing file system namespace under their control.

The purpose of FSinfo is to generate all the important standard file system data files from a single set of input data. Starting with a single data source guarantees that all the generated files are self-consistent. One of the possible output data formats is a set of Amd maps that can be used among the set of hosts described in the input data.

FSinfo implements a declarative language. This language is specifically designed for describing file system namespace and physical layouts. The basic declaration defines a mounted file system including its device name, mount point, and all the volumes and access permissions. FSinfo reads this information and builds an internal map of the entire network of hosts. Using this map, many different data formats can be produced, including `/etc/fstab`, `/etc/exports`, Amd mount maps, and `/etc/bootparams`.

Unfortunately, FSinfo is rarely used by administrators. The vast majority of administrators prefer to edit Amd maps directly. FSinfo also has not been kept up-to-date for several years, while more and more features have been added to Amd's maps.

The Amd Automounter

PART 2

In Sum

In this chapter we learned how to administer Amd. We started by covering the basics of how to start and stop Amd, how to check its status, and how to signal it to perform certain actions.

We then covered Amq, Amd's query and control tool. Amq can retrieve information from Amd: global status information, state of automounted volumes, and more. Amq can also control Amd's behavior: changing logging and debugging options, flushing maps, unmounting volumes, etc.

We learned about the various ways of tracing Amd's behavior through logging options, debugging flags, and running multiple automounters. We covered techniques for debugging Amd's maps and recovering from problems, especially a hung automounter.

Throughout this chapter we showed the use of assorted tools that come with am-utils. We saw programs and scripts that can help administrators maintain their Amd maps using various information services such as NIS, Hesiod, LDAP, etc. We also learned about scripts used to maintain mount information consistency between clients and servers, converting between Amd and Sun Automount maps, and others.

12

Advanced Amd Uses

Writing Amd maps to do simple tasks is easy, as we have seen in previous chapters. Amd also comes with many advanced features, which we also mentioned in previous chapters. However, we covered some of those features individually or only briefly. In this chapter, we discuss those features in more detail and illustrate them with full-length examples. It is easier to discuss advanced features here because the reader already understands many of the basics of Amd and NFS.

We always advocated writing maps so that they are easy to understand and modify. Often, there are several ways to write the same map entry. In this chapter, we also discuss how to write maps more optimally—so they are shorter or they run faster.

Finally, we also provide a few complex map examples to solve problems that stress even Amd's abilities to the limit. In a few of those examples, we show two ways to write the map: the first being the more obvious one, and the one that does not generally work; the second being a revision of the first, and the one that works. These advanced examples were designed to let you appreciate Amd's abilities as well as its limitations.

Simple Optimizations

We begin by discussing some of the most obvious and simple optimizations to Amd. While each of the items we discuss next may not produce a significant improvement alone, combining several of them certainly does.

Turning Off Debugging Support

If you do not need debugging support in Amd, then do not compile it in. By default, when you build am-utils, debugging is not included unless you configure the package with --enable-debug. If you do not compile debugging support in Amd, the resulting binary will run faster because it will not have to process debugging options and debugging messages. Furthermore, the size of the Amd binary will be smaller, which further speeds up running because smaller binaries generally run faster.

Debugging, however, is a useful feature many administrators like to have available. The Red Hat–distributed am-utils package, for example, does include debugging support. One alternative you can take is the best of both worlds. Build two versions of am-utils: one to use when you are debugging maps and Amd in general, and another to use when you are using it in production once all debugging is done.

If you must include debugging support, then you should turn it off. This is the default behavior for debugging as long as debug_options is not specified in your amd.conf file. You could also turn off debugging dynamically using amq -D noall.

When you do need to debug your maps and Amd, turn on only those debugging options that you need at that time. For example, if you are debugging how Amd processes directory reading, do not turn on all debugging options, but only those related to directory reading: amq -D readdir.

For more information on debugging, see Chapter 11, "Runtime Automounter Administration."

Reducing the Number of Maps and Entries

Avoid using too many maps, and also avoid making too many entries in each map. If you have to make a choice between more maps or more entries, however, it is preferable to have more entries in each map and fewer maps than more maps. The reason why this solution is preferable is that each Amd map is generally automounted on a separate mount point, and each map carries a fair amount of additional overhead and state associated with it in Amd. Each mount also increases the number of in-kernel data objects and the size of your /etc/mtab file, slowing programs such as df.

In general, today's workstations can support up to about a dozen automount maps without any noticeable degradation in performance; servers can support between 10 and 30 automount maps comfortably. Each Amd map can easily include several hundred entries, but you may notice a degradation in performance if you have more than a thousand entries in any given map. Note that these estimates are based on today's hardware. With faster CPUs and networks, and larger memories, you can easily increase the loads on Amd for your system with no performance penalty.

Avoiding Regular Expression Maps

Use regular expressions only if you have to. Most administrators do not need regular expression processing in Amd maps. While they are indeed powerful, the regular expression processing functions are expensive to use: they consume more memory and many more CPU cycles than Amd's standard key lookups.

Caching Everything for Longer Periods

Cache as much as possible and for as long as possible. If you do nothing, Amd will cache some items automatically: names of file servers and volumes, NFS file handles, map entries, and more. One of the most obvious items to cache is the map entries, using the cache:=all per-map parameter, as we described in Chapter 9, "The Amd Configuration File," under "Map Caching Options." Also in Chapter 9, under "Performance and Tuning" and "Information Services" we discussed other parameters that affect the length of time Amd keeps certain pieces of information.

Using File Maps

File maps work the fastest because reading files off of the local disk does not involve the network. When you use maps that reside on NIS, Hesiod, or LDAP servers, your Amd will always depend on the speed of your network to get map information and to reload maps.

Locking Process Pages

Use the plock=yes parameter in your amd.conf file. Locking down the text and data pages of your Amd can ensure that these parts of your running Amd binaries will never get swapped to disk or page out. This can happen if your system becomes busy with many active user processes vying for CPU cycles and real memory.

Avoiding *selectors_on_default*

If you turn on selectors_on_default in your amd.conf file, Amd will have to process selectors for each line specified in your /defaults entry. This processing is interpreted and happens *each* time an Amd map entry is looked up. The more selectors and lines you have in your /defaults entry, the longer Amd will take to process each entry in that map.

Therefore, you should use `selectors_on_default` only if you need it. Ironically, one of the most popular uses of this exact feature is to set more optimal NFS tuning parameters that would be used under different conditions. See below under "Using Selectors on `/defaults`" for a discussion on its use for optimization.

Turning Off Browsable Directories

If you set `browsable_dirs` in your `amd.conf` file, you will not notice any performance degradation until a user tries to list the entries in that map. If the map has many entries, listing all of them will take longer. Worse, if not used carefully, browsable directories can lead to a serious performance condition called a *mount storm*, as we described in Chapter 11.

WARNING   Do not avoid useful features just to make Amd run faster. These days, CPUs continue to get faster and memory and disk space larger. While you should be aware of the impact of any feature you use, if you see a feature that you think best suits your need, use it. Furthermore, do not obfuscate your Amd maps so that they run faster. A clean, readable, and well-commented map is important so that others can read, understand, and edit it as needed.

Complex Optimizations

In this section, we cover several more complex performance optimizations for Amd. These optimizations involve using better map syntax, tuning several parameters, or avoiding typical administrator mistakes. These tips are not the only possible optimizations available, but they are the most common ones, and they are intended to illustrate the types of optimizations you might consider.

Distinguishing Between File Servers and Using Sublinks

Amd caches the names of remote file servers and information about file systems that those servers export. The reason Amd caches that information is that it takes time and resources to gather it for a new file server or file system that Amd is trying to mount for the first time.

Suppose you have a file server named `titan` that exports a `/homes` file system, and that file system contains the home directories for three users: `larry`, `curly`, and `moe`. A typical, but suboptimal, map for mounting these is seen in Listing 12.1.

Listing 12.1   A suboptimal /homes map that does not use sublinks

```
larry        type:=nfs;rhost:=titan;rfs:=/homes/larry
curly        type:=nfs;rhost:=titan;rfs:=/homes/curly
moe          type:=nfs;rhost:=titan;rfs:=/homes/moe
```

The problem with the map in Listing 12.1 is that each entry uses a different `rfs`, or remote file system name. Amd will consider all three `rfs` entries to represent different file systems on the remote host. For each file system, Amd retrieves NFS file handles and mounts that file system separately. This results in slower access to those users' home directories, as well as three NFS mounts of essentially the same physical file system: `/homes`.

A better map is seen in Listing 12.2. It uses the same `rfs` value, but distinguishes the entries based on the subdirectories—or sublinks—inside.

Listing 12.2   An optimal /homes map that uses sublinks

```
larry        type:=nfs;rhost:=titan;rfs:=/homes;sublink:=larry
curly        type:=nfs;rhost:=titan;rfs:=/homes;sublink:=curly
moe          type:=nfs;rhost:=titan;rfs:=/homes;sublink:=moe
```

When any one of the three entries in the map in Listing 12.2 is first accessed, Amd will retrieve and cache the file server information about the `titan:/homes` file system. Upon subsequent accesses to other entries, Amd will reuse the cached information about `titan:/homes`. All Amd would have to do in those cases would be to append the value of the `sublink` variable to the symbolic link pointing to the map key's resolution.

Slow vs. Fast Networks

There are several (mostly numeric) Amd configuration parameters you can use to tune Amd's behavior for different network conditions. We have described those in detail in Chapter 9, but we'll briefly mention them here:

dismount_interval   Describes the number of seconds to wait for another attempt to dismount a possibly unused file system. Increase it on busy networks.

nfs_retransmit_counter and **nfs_retry_interval**   Control Amd's behavior as a local NFS server for the localhost. Increase those if your localhost has to process lots of packets or is rather busy.

rsize and **wsize**   Control the default NFS read and write buffer sizes, respectively. On slow or very busy networks, you should decrease these values.

The Amd Automounter

PART 2

Ordering Entries in Maps and Using the NFS-Link File System

The most typical entries in Amd maps are of the form that NFS-mounts a remote file system on most hosts and uses a symbolic link to it on the local host. The latter is done to avoid localhost NFS mounts, which are not just slow, but can hang the kernel on some systems. Those entries typically appear as seen in Listing 12.3.

Listing 12.3   A suboptimal map entry using NFS and link

```
ezk   -rhost:=shekel;sublink:=${key} \
      host==${rhost};type:=link;fs:=/homes \
      host!=${rhost};type:=nfs;rfs:=/homes
```

The problem with the entry in Listing 12.3 is that in most cases, Amd will fail to match the first line where we are checking if we are on the local host named shekel. Since there are many more hosts other than shekel who wish to mount that file system, Amd has to fail to match the first line before it can match the second. A better map would rearrange the lines such that the more likely matches occur first, as seen in Listing 12.4.

Listing 12.4   A better map entry using NFS and link

```
ezk   -rhost:=shekel;sublink:=${key} \
      host!=${rhost};type:=nfs;rfs:=/homes \
      host==${rhost};type:=link;fs:=/homes
```

WARNING Be careful when editing file maps and simply cutting and pasting text lines casually. A single Amd map entry can span multiple lines, and those lines must use the backslash continuation symbol. A very common administrator error is to move the last line in an Amd map entry such as in Listing 12.3, a line without a continuation symbol, so that it appears earlier in the map entry. The earlier line without a continuation backslash results in terminating the map entry too early, and because of this, all the lines that follow the line without the continuation backslash are ignored by Amd.

A much better organization for the entries in Listings 12.3 and 12.4 is seen in Listing 12.5.

Listing 12.5   An optimal map entry using NFS and link

```
ezk   type:=nfs;rhost:=shekel;sublink:=${key};rfs:=/homes;fs:=/homes
```

Using the NFS-Link File System, you can avoid any possible problems of forgetting to add one of the selector cases in Listing 12.4, or the need to optimize the map in Listing 12.3; the type:=nfsl Amd file system takes care of these issues automatically.

Double Automounts

A subtle yet sinister problem is when a local Amd must inadvertently cause a remote automount to satisfy a local request. You should avoid this situation because it creates a chain of dependencies between Amd processes: a local Amd process functions well only as long as a remote Amd process works.

To illustrate this problem, consider the following situation. A client named clio and a server named iron both run the same Amd maps. The server named iron exports a file system named /n/iron/import/pkg. An Amd map, mounted on /import, contains an entry to automount that file system under /import/pkg, as shown in Listing 12.6.

Listing 12.6   A map entry causing double automounts

```
pkg    -rhost:=iron \
       host!=${rhost};type:=nfs;rfs:=/import/pkg \
       host==${rhost};type:=link;fs:=/n/iron/import/pkg
```

The map in Listing 12.6 says that iron should use a symbolic link to /n/iron/import/pkg, and all other hosts (clio included) should NFS-mount iron:/import/pkg. But watch what happens when Amd contacts the host iron to mount /import/pkg. The remote server, iron, also runs Amd, and /import/pkg is an automounted path name for it as well as for clio. Therefore, before iron can respond back to clio's mount request, it must resolve the /import/pkg path name locally on iron. In other words, before clio can automount /import/pkg, iron must automount it first—hence the double automount!

The simplest thing you can do to avoid double automounts is to avoid specifying automounted path names in the value of the rfs variable. Instead, list the actual, absolute path name of the remotely exported file system in your map, as seen in Listing 12.7.

Listing 12.7   A map entry avoiding double automounts

```
pkg    -rhost:=iron;rfs:=/n/iron/import/pkg;fs:=${rfs} \
       host!=${rhost};type:=nfs \
       host==${rhost};type:=link
```

Note that the map in Listing 12.6 *does* work, albeit slower than the map in Listing 12.7. Most administrators who write maps that cause double automounts do not notice it until the remote Amd process is down or malfunctioning: only then does the map in Listing 12.6 stop working, while the one in Listing 12.7 continues to work unimpeded.

Automatic Generation of */home* Maps

Amd maps to serve user homes are very popular. Often, administrators have to maintain those by hand. However, maintaining those maps by hand is a process fraught with problems: administrators can easily make mistakes in the maps. In particular, the information about a user's home directory is split between /etc/passwd and the Amd map that serves /home, some of which must be duplicated. It would be better to put all of that information in one place and document it only once.

One idea is to use the GCOS field in the /etc/passwd file to store extra information. The GCOS field is a general-purpose informational field that often contains just one thing, the user's full name. When additional information is added to the GCOS field, it is usually delimited by commas. Following the user's full name, you can add in the server's name and the file system's name where the user's home directory resides.

For example, if the home directory for user ezk is on the server named shekel and the file system is named /u/zing, then the corresponding /etc/passwd entry for this user could be

```
ezk:*:2301:90:Erez Zadok,shekel,/u/zing:/home/ezk:/bin/bash
```

You can use the Perl script in Listing 12.8 to convert an /etc/passwd file containing this special GCOS information into an amd.home map.

Listing 12.8   A script to auto-generate a /home map

```
#!/usr/bin/perl
# read passwd-format file, get file server information from
# the GCOS field, and write out a /home map on stdout.
while (<>) {
    chop;
    @pwent = split(/:/);
    $gcos = $pwent[4];
    ($fullname, $host, $fserver) = split(/,/, $gcos);
    next unless (defined($host) && defined($fserver));
    $name = $pwent[5];
    $name =~ s:^.*/::g;
    printf STDOUT "$name\t-sublink:=$name \\
\thost!=$host;type:=nfs;rhost:=$host;rfs:=$fserver \\
\thost==$host;type:=link;fs:=$fserver\n\n";
}
```

Assume the script in Listing 12.8 is named mk-home-map; then run it as seen in Listing 12.9.

Listing 12.9   Auto-generating /etc/amd.home from /etc/passwd

```
[root]# mk-home-map /etc/passwd > /etc/amd.home
[root]# cat /etc/amd.home
ezk    -sublink:=ezk \
       host!=shekel;type:=nfs;rhost:=shekel;rfs:=/u/zing \
       host==shekel;type:=link;fs:=/u/zing
```

Note that the script generates an Amd map with hard-coded values in entries. The map
does not refer to variables in other variables. For example, we could have used
sublink:=${key}, but since the whole /etc/amd.home file gets autogenerated, we prefer
it to be generated so that it can be processed the fastest: that means we need to eliminate
as much extra variable processing as possible.

Automounter Map Submounts

Automounter submounts allow you to create an Amd automount directory under another
Amd automount directory. They allow administrators to create a deeper hierarchy of
Amd nodes, not just a flat one under a single node. We showed one example of this in
Chapter 10, "Automounter Maps." Here, we will show a few more.

Automount Directory Delegation

One use for these sub-automounts is to collect several groups' automounted names under
a single directory. Suppose your site has a Quality Assurance (QA) group with lots of its
own automounted file systems. As the site's main administrator, you can maintain those
yourself and change them each time the QA group asks for a change. But you can also delegate control over a portion of that site to individual groups. The map in Listing 12.10
shows that.

Listing 12.10   Delegating automounted directories to individual groups

```
qa     type:=auto;fs:=amd.qa;maptype:=ldap

sales  exists(/etc/local/am.sale);type:=auto;fs:=/etc/local/amd.sale
```

You, the site administrator, can control the Amd map in Listing 12.10. However, you can
let the QA group control their own amd.qa map through an LDAP server and let the sales
group control their own automount nodes through the map file, /etc/local/amd.sale.
If the map in Listing 12.10 is automounted under /groups, then the QA group will control everything under /groups/qa/, and the sales group will control everything under the

/groups/sales/ directory. For example, the QA group can have an Amd map that contains entries such as the following:

```
tests        type:=nfs;rhost:=q1;rfs:=/usr/tests
```

```
results      type:=link;fs:=/proj/qa-dated/res
```

In that case, the QA group would access these two Amd entries as /groups/qa/tests and /groups/qa/results.

Consolidation of Several Maps

When you install the am-utils that comes with Red Hat Linux, it creates a single automount node called /net, which uses the type:=host Amd file system type to access all exported file systems from a remote host. Suppose you have your own set of Amd maps, and you do not want to waste another directory just for this host style automount. You can include this automounted entry in another map, say, the one mounted under /import, as seen in Listing 12.11.

Listing 12.11 Consolidating a /net map inside another

```
html   -rhost:=cosmos;rfs:=/n/${rhost}/import/${key};fs:=${rfs} \
       host!=${rhost};type:=nfs \
       host==${rhost};type:=link

net    type:=auto;fs:=.

net/*  host==${/key};type:=link;fs:=/ \
       host!=${/key};type:=host;rhost:=${/key}
```

The first entry in the map of Listing 12.11 is for a regular NFS mount of a file system from a host called cosmos. This map is there as part of /import already. The second entry creates an automount node of type host under /import/net/. That way, if you access, say, /import/net/daffy, Amd will NFS-mount all of the file systems that host daffy exports under /import/net/daffy/.

The net entry (second) is the one that creates the automount node /import/net; this node, or directory, is just a placeholder. Note that it sets the fs variable to just a single dot (.). This tells Amd that the content of this new automount node is served from this local /import map. That is why the third entry is in the same map.

The wildcard (third) entry net/* does all the hard work. When accessing /import/net/daffy, Amd will be asked to look up the entry net/daffy, which will match the wildcard entry. The special operator ${/key} chops the last component of the string net/daffy, resulting in just daffy. Then the two selectors try to match against this host named daffy. If it is this host, then Amd simply creates a symlink to the root directory "/" so that it can access all of that host's files. On any other host, Amd will NFS-mount all exported file systems from daffy and automount them so that they are accessible under /import/net /daffy.

Using Selectors on */defaults*

Earlier, we discussed some performance optimizations that advocated not using selectors_on_default because it slows down parsing of maps. But we also mentioned that selectors_on_default is one of the main methods for optimizing performance under certain conditions. One of the most popular ways to optimize performance is by setting NFS parameters that are more suitable for different network conditions; this is done by picking parameters that improve performance, as well as by avoiding the use of poor or buggy implementations of certain NFS servers and clients.

Under normal circumstances, NFSv2 using UDP and default configuration works well. However, NFSv3 using TCP is often superior to NFSv2 using UDP; this is because the NFSv3 protocol is more optimal and TCP can handle varying network conditions more gracefully. On the other hand, NFSv3 is not used as widely as it could be because support is not very stable on many platforms, so administrators try to avoid using NFSv3 on these. To add to that, on systems that can only support NFSv2 using UDP, administrators like to optimize performance so that it matches better with slow or unreliable networks.

If you do not handle all of these conditions correctly, some of your NFS hosts will behave poorly or even badly because they might use suboptimal NFS options or unstable code. All of these conditions require using different NFS-mount options at different times. You can set those options individually for each map entry that they are relevant for, but that would make your maps too complex and difficult to maintain. What you want is a way to affect the whole map in one central location: that is what selectors_on_default is for.

Listing 12.12 shows an example of the power of selectors on /defaults.

Listing 12.12   A complex /defaults entry with selectors

```
/defaults    os==linux;osver==2.4;opts:=proto=tcp,vers=3 \
             os==linux;osver!=2.4;opts:=proto=udp,vers=3 \
             os==solaris2;opts:=proto=tcp,vers=3 \
             os==bsd44;opts:=proto=tcp,vers=2 \
             os==irix;opts:=proto=udp,vers=3 \
             in_network(wireless-net);opts:=rsize=1024,wsize=1024 \
             in_network(atm-backbone);opts:=rsize=32768,wsize=32768 \
             opts:=rsize=8192,wsize=8192,proto=tcp,vers=3 \
```

The meaning of the /defaults entry in Listing 12.12 is as follows:

- On Linux 2.4 systems, use NFSv3 using TCP. This is because the 2.4 kernel has a fairly stable NFSv3 and TCP implementation.

- On other Linux systems, use NFSv3 but with UDP only. This is because the TCP support in NFSv3 did not become very stable until 2.4. Note that saying vers=3 does not mean that we will only force usage of NFSv3. If NFSv3 is not available, Amd will try NFSv2. So the proto and vers options only set an upper bound on the NFS features used.

- On Solaris 2 systems, use NFSv3 with TCP. This is because Sun Microsystems had the first and most stable implementation of NFSv3.

- On BSD 4.4 systems, use NFSv2 but with TCP. NFSv3 on some of those systems is not very robust, but they had a TCP implementation over NFSv2 that was stable years ago.

- On Irix systems, avoid TCP with NFSv3. Irix has a working NFSv3 but not when used with TCP.

- On all machines that are on the wireless-net network, reduce the NFS read and write buffer sizes to 1KB. This is because wireless networks are slower and more prone to packet loss. If you try to send large buffers through NFS on slow networks, you are more likely to lose a small portion of the large buffers, requiring a full retransmission of the whole large buffer. Lowering the size of the read and write buffers for NFS increases the chances that they would arrive at their destination without any loss, avoiding expensive retransmissions.

- For machines that are on the fast ATM backbone, we increase the NFS read and write buffer sizes to 32KB. Since these are more reliable and dedicated networks, often used by servers, we can be sure that these networks are more reliable. Increasing the read and write buffer sizes improves performance by sending more data at once.

- The last entry uses no selectors, and sets the default options for all other systems.

Replication and Failover

Amd is capable of defining a set of replicated file servers such that it will pick the most responsive one of them to use first. Amd can also define a set of volumes to use in series: when or if one volume fails to mount, Amd tries the next one in the list, and then the next one, until one succeeds. This allows you to create more complex maps that provide better and more reliable file service to your users.

Replicated File Servers

Most Amd map entries contain multiple locations, each one with a set of selectors, as seen in Listing 12.13.

Listing 12.13   An Amd map to illustrate serial location matching

```
cdrom   -type:=cdfs \
        os==linux;dev:=/dev/cdrom \
        os==solaris2;dev:=/dev/rdsk/c0t6d0s0 \
        os==sunos4;dev:=/dev/sr0
```

In the map of Listing 12.13, Amd will mount the CD-ROM from `/dev/cdrom` on Linux systems, if the `os` selector matches `linux`. If the selector does not match, Amd then goes on to check the next location, matching against `solaris2`. If that does not match, Amd goes on to the next location, and so on. In other words, Amd serializes its selector checks for various volumes, checking each volume's selectors one line at a time, until one matches. When it finds a match, Amd will try and mount that volume, and it will not proceed to check the rest of the locations in this map entry.

There is, however, one exception to the serialized checks: NFS. Recall that in Chapter 8, "Overview of the Amd Automounter," we explained how Amd performs NFS mounts in the background, and how it uses asynchronous RPC calls to find out when a back-grounded mount has been completed. We explained that this was for reliability, to ensure that the main Amd process does not hang because Amd cannot complete a mount of a remote file server. But there is another reason for this: to support replicated NFS servers.

When Amd sees an NFS mount, it forks a copy of itself and starts the mount in the background. That mount can take an undetermined length of time to complete. Under normal conditions, that mount can be as quick as under a second, but it can take longer on busy systems. Furthermore, it can take as much as a minute or more to time out a hung mount. For that reason, after Amd backgrounds an NFS mount, it sets a callback to process that mount should it succeed, but then Amd *continues* to look at the map entry for additional NFS mounts.

Consider a map such as that in Listing 12.14.

Listing 12.14   A map illustrating replicated file servers

```
X11R6  type:=nfs;rhost:=earth;rfs:=/usr/X11R6 \
       type:=nfs;rhost:=wind;rfs:=/usr/X11 \
       type:=nfs;rhost:=fire;rfs:=/opt/testing/X11R6
```

The Amd Automounter

PART 2

When Amd is asked to look up X11R6, it will start a backgrounded NFS mount for earth:/usr/X11R6. Amd will then continue to parse the map and start a second back-grounded NFS mount for wind:/usr/X11. But Amd will not stop there. It will conclude with a third and last backgrounded mount of fire:/opt/testing/X11R6. As soon as the first of those three backgrounded mounts completes successfully, Amd will use that one to resolve the X11R6 key, and Amd will discard the other two backgrounded mounts. In this fashion, Amd can perform three backgrounded mounts almost in parallel and use the most responsive one.

Unfortunately, because current networks and hosts are relatively fast, the first back-grounded mount is more likely to be picked first. You can use the delay parameter to force a certain order on the hosts. This parameter has a granularity of only one second, and it is thus a rather crude method of ordering mounts. Listing 12.15 shows this.

Listing 12.15 A map illustrating replicated file servers with delay

```
TeX    -type:=nfs;rfs:=/usr/TeX \
       rhost:=bet;delay:=1
       rhost:=gimel;delay:=2
       rhost:=aleph
```

When Amd resolves the TeX entry in Listing 12.15, it will indeed fork three backgrounded NFS mounts. However, the backgrounded mount for host bet will not start for one sec-ond, the one for host gimel will be delayed by two seconds, and the mount for host aleph will not be delayed at all. This forces an ordering of mounts that prefers first host aleph, then bet, and finally gimel.

Volume Failover

As we saw in the previous section "Replicated File Servers," Amd performs all non-NFS mounts serially. What this means is that once Amd matches the selectors for a particular location within an entry, Amd will try to mount that location and no more. If that mount failed, Amd will fail the whole entry and will *not* go on to try the next mount.

Consider the map in Listing 12.16.

Listing 12.16 A map entry illustrating the problems of non-failover

```
cd   -dev:=/dev/cdrom;rfs:=/cdrom \
     type:=ufs;opts:=rw \
     type:=ufs;opts:=ro \
     type:=cdfs;opts:=rw \
     type:=cdfs;opts:=ro
```

In Listing 12.16, you wish to mount a CD-ROM, but you do not know ahead of time what the format of that CD-ROM is. It can have a UFS (EXT2) file system on it, or it can have an ISO-9660 file system on it. It can be a read-only CD-ROM, or a rewritable one. Since there are no selectors in the map of Listing 12.16, Amd will proceed to try the first location, assuming that this is a rewritable CD-ROM with an EXT2FS file system on it. (Even if this map had selectors, the point is still the same: multiple locations can all match, if Amd only continues to try other locations in an entry.)

If the CD-ROM has an ISO-9660 file system on it, this first entry will fail to mount, and Amd will return a failure for the whole cd entry. This is an unfortunate behavior that some administrators dislike (a new feature to allow failover location will be added to Amd in a future version of am-utils). The only current solution to this problem is to use the program type mount as seen in Listing 12.17.

Listing 12.17   Using a program type mount for failover

```
cd  -type:=program;rfs:=/cdrom;dev:=/dev/cdrom \
    mount:="/etc/cdmount cdmount ${dev} ${rfs}";\
    unmount:="/bin/umount ${rfs}"
```

The trick in the map of Listing 12.17 is to use a special script to perform failover CD-ROM mounts and a simple unmount command to unmount /cdrom. The cdmount script is shown in Listing 12.18.

Listing 12.18   A shell script to perform failover CD-ROM mounts

```
#!/bin/sh
/bin/mount -t ext2 -o rw $1 $2     &&  exit $?
/bin/mount -t ext2 -o ro $1 $2     &&  exit $?
/bin/mount -t iso9660 -o rw $1 $2  &&  exit $?
/bin/mount -t iso9660 -o ro $1 $2  &&  exit $?
exit 1
```

The script in Listing 12.18 tries to perform four mounts in order and exits as soon as one of them succeeds. If none of the four mounts succeeds, the script returns a failure code. The four mounts that it does try in order are the same as those listed in Listing 12.18: a read-write mount of an EXT2 file system, a read-only mount of an EXT2 file system, a read-write mount of an ISO9660 file system, and finally, a read-only mount of an ISO9660 file system.

The Amd
Automounter

PART 2

The || Cut Operator

The || operator acts as a cut operator (Prolog fans rejoice). Its effect is to prevent use of locations to its right if any of the locations on its left were selected, regardless of whether Amd was able to mount any of them successfully. Without the || operator, Amd would continue to parse and mount other locations in the background. Note that this only happens with NFS mounts, because only NFS mounts happen in the background.

The cut operator provides *syntactic sugar*—it does not provide any new syntax that cannot be accomplished with other syntax. Consider the example in Listing 12.19.

Listing 12.19 An example not using the || operator

```
/defaults    -type:=nfs
lbin         os==linux;osver==2.4;arch==i386;rfs:=/usr/local \
                  rhost:=h1  rhost:=h2 \
             os==linux;osver==2.2;arch==sparc;rfs:=/usr/local \
                  rhost:=h3  rhost:=h4 \
             os!=linux;osver!=2.4;arch!=i386;rfs:=/usr/local \
                  rhost:=h5  rhost:=h6 \
             os!=linux;osver!=2.2;arch!=sparc;rfs:=/usr/local \
                  rhost:=h5  rhost:=h6
```

Here, we want to use either hosts h1 or h2 for Linux 2.4 systems running on the i386 architecture. For systems that run Linux 2.2 on SPARC architectures, we want to use hosts h3 or h4. For all other systems, we want to use one of the h5 or h6 servers. As you can see in Listing 12.19, the last two locations need to contain the negated selector conditions of the first two in order to mean the opposite.

Note that if we took away the last two selector lists, Amd will always try to mount hosts h5 and h6 in the background, and if one of them replies first, Amd will use it. That may be an undesirable behavior.

Listing 12.20 shows a simplified version of the map in Listing 12.19.

Listing 12.20 An example simplified by using the || operator

```
/defaults    -type:=nfs
lbin         os==linux;osver==2.4;arch==i386;rfs:=/usr/local \
                  rhost:=h1  rhost:=h2 || \
             os==linux;osver==2.2;arch==sparc;rfs:=/usr/local \
                  rhost:=h3  rhost:=h4 || \
             -rfs:=/usr/local \
                  rhost:=h5  rhost:=h6
```

Here, we use cuts to ensure that if the first set of selectors matches, Amd will use one of the first two hosts and not try any subsequent hosts. If the first condition does not match, only then will Amd go on to see if the second set of selectors matches.

If neither of the two sets of selectors matches, then Amd goes on to try one of the h5 or h6 hosts. Listing 12.20 shows how we simplified a complex map, making it more readable.

Using Regular Expressions

If you set your map cache parameter to `cache:=regexp` (or `cache:=re`), then Amd treats map keys as `egrep`-style regular expressions. If not specified, Amd performs regular string matching on the keys. With the `regexp` option, Amd enumerates the entire map and loads it into the cache first. Amd performs key lookups using the system's regexp library.

For example, let us consider a map `amd.src` served off of /src. In this example, you maintain many Linux kernel source distributions online, unpacked into directories corresponding to the kernel's version: `linux-2.0.36`, `linux-2.2.16`, `linux-2.3.99`, `linux-2.4.0`, etc. All of these are subdirectories under /usr/src, and you want these kernel versions to show up as Amd entries right under /src. Without the `regexp` option, you would have to write this map, as shown in Listing 12.21:

Listing 12.21   A map for Linux kernel sources, without regular expressions

```
/defaults        type:=link;fs:=/usr/src
linux-2.0.36     sublink:=${key}
linux-2.2.16     sublink:=${key}
linux-2.3.99     sublink:=${key}
linux-2.4.1      sublink:=${key}
```

While this map is simple, it has to be updated each time a new kernel distribution is unpacked under /usr/src. With regular expressions, this map can be written once as shown in Listing 12.22.

Listing 12.22   A map for Linux kernel sources, using regular expressions

```
/defaults                 type:=link;fs:=/usr/src
linux-[0-9]\.[0-9]+\.[0-9]+   sublink:=${key}
```

The particular regular expression matches as follows:

1. Look for a string starting with `linux-`,
2. followed by a single digit from the range of 0–9,

3. followed by a literal dot (the backslash escapes characters that are considered special by the regular expression library),

4. followed by one or more digits: the + symbol says to match the previous character one or more times,

5. followed by another literal dot,

6. ending with another sequence of one or more digits.

In this next example, seen in Listing 12.23, we use regular expressions in a map that gets local software first, if available. Otherwise, the map gets the software from one of two replicated NFS servers.

Listing 12.23   An example for getting local software using regular expressions

```
X11.*  exists(/usr/${key});type:=link;fs:=/usr/${key} \
       -type:=nfs;rfs=/usr/${key}  rhost:=server1  rhost:=server2
```

In regular expression syntax, the sequence of ".*" matches everything: a dot matches any single character, and the asterisk matches zero or more instances of the previous character. So the sequence X11.* will match any string that begins with X11. Suppose a user looks up the key X11R6. The map in Listing 12.23 will match this key and Amd will check if the directory /usr/X11R6 exists. If it does, Amd will set up a symlink to it. If the directory does not exist locally, Amd will try to NFS-mount one of the two NFS servers.

TIP   The order in which a cached map is searched does not correspond to the ordering in the source map. Write your regular expressions so that they are mutually exclusive within each map. This will avoid confusion when matching regular expression entries.

Advanced Mounting

In this section, we list several complex automounting examples using Amd. Each example solves a real problem that administrators have faced before. These examples push Amd's capabilities to its limits. That was intended in order to illustrate the most advanced uses of Amd. A few of those examples are sufficiently advanced so that we show more than one solution for them.

Mounting an NFS Bridge to DFS Using per-UID Passwords

Suppose you have a DFS (Distributed File System) server, and you want to NFS-mount it on machines that do not have DFS support. You can do so using the NFS bridge to DFS.

That bridge is a server that exports DFS disks as NFS volumes. For all intents and purposes, the NFS bridge acts as an NFS server but with one crucial exception: users must authenticate themselves to it by providing their passwords interactively.

So, if you are to automount these DFS partitions using the NFS bridge, you must provide passwords to it. Unfortunately, automounters such as Amd do not work interactively: they cannot stop and prompt a user for a password. The way to solve this involves a bit of a security compromise. We can use the `type:=program` file system and pass it the relevant mount information, including the UID of the invoking user. We pass those to a special script that can mount the file system after providing the authentication non-interactively. This of course assumes that the NFS bridge to DFS allows non-interactive mounts that can provide the password.

The Amd entry to mount this file system is shown in Listing 12.24.

Listing 12.24   An Amd entry to mount a special NFS bridge using per-user access

```
brg   type:=program;rfs:=/exported/data;rhost:=kwai;\
      mount:="/etc/brg-mount ${rhost}:${rfs} ${fs} ${uid}";\
      unmount:="/bin/umount ${fs}"
```

The script `brg-mount` takes three arguments: the mounted file system, the mount point, and the UID of the calling process. The script is shown in Listing 12.25.

Listing 12.25   A shell script to mount the NFS bridge with user authentication

```
#!/bin/sh
case $3 in
    2301 ) passwd="mypeL2,Q" ;;
    # insert other passwords here
    * ) passwd="***NONE***" ;;
esac
/usr/dfs/bin/mount -u $3 -p $passwd $1 $2
exit $?
```

The script in Listing 12.25 sets the password for the user based on their UID, and then calls the DFS mount program to perform the mount as that user. Note that this script is terribly insecure, because it encodes passwords in the clear. At the very least, this script would have to be protected, and the passwords that are used should be different from the users' other (login) passwords. Nevertheless, this example shows you how you can use `${uid}` in Amd to perform the next best thing to interactively authenticated automounts.

CD-ROM Images

Red Hat distributes CD-ROM images as ISO-9660 files. For example, the Red Hat 7.0 first disk image is named 7.0-i386-disc1.iso. Normally, you can mount an actual CD-ROM using Amd's type:=cdfs file system. However, there is nothing that prevents you from mounting an ISO-9660 image file as such. In Linux, you can mount an ISO-9660 image file as follows:

```
[root]# mount -t iso9660 -o loop /tmp/zoot-i386.iso /mnt/disk1
```

To achieve the same using Amd, you can use a type:=program map and execute the above command, or use type:=cdfs more directly as follows:

```
d1  type:=cdfs;addopts:=loop;dev:=/tmp/zoot-i386.iso;rfs:=/mnt/disk1
```

Automounting in a *chroot-ed* FTP Environment

The FTP daemon runs inside an environment that uses the chroot(2) (Change Root) system call. The daemon can run, say, under /proj/bank/ftp. This means that the process (in.ftpd) running inside /proj/bank/ftp cannot access any files from outside /proj/bank/ftp.

Suppose you want each of your users to have their own personal directory for storing anonymous FTP files. One way is to create subdirectories under /proj/bank/ftp/users with the name of each user, and let each user write to those directories. Users, however, like to store their public Web page files in locations such as ~/public_html.

So let us say that you want to let your users store their FTP files in ~/public_ftp. It's best to let users store their FTP files in their home directories for several reasons:

- If they have quotas on their home directories, those quotas will include their FTP files.

- Users do not have to waste space from the /proj/bank/ftp disk.

- Administrators do not have to maintain directories for many users under /proj/bank/ftp/users.

In addition, you would like a system that allows FTP to show private directories for users only if those users' home FTP directories exist. That way, users who do not create the ~/public_ftp directory will not be seen under the anonymous FTP server.

The problem is that users' home directories reside outside the chroot-ed /proj/bank/ftp directory and are, thus, inaccessible by default. The solution to this problem is to use Amd to automount the users' own public_ftp directories *inside* the chroot-ed environment. That is possible because the Amd process works from *outside* the chroot-ed directory.

Listing 12.26 shows an example of such an Amd map entry for one user.

Listing 12.26   ~ftp/users/* in a chroot-ed environment, take 1

```
martha        -rhost:=opus;fs:=/proj/bank/ftp/.a/${key} \
              host!=opus;type:=nfs;rfs:=/home/${key}/public_ftp \
              host==opus;type:=lofs;rfs:=/home/${key}/public_ftp
```

Assuming that the map in Listing 12.26 is stored in the file /etc/local/amd.ftp, we can start it as follows:

```
[root]# amd /proj/bank/ftp/users /etc/local/amd.ftp
```

The intent of that map is to mount Martha's private FTP files under /proj/bank/ftp/.a/ martha. Martha's home directory files reside on host opus. If the FTP server is running on any host other than opus, then we NFS-mount Martha's public_ftp directory onto /proj/bank/ftp/.a/martha. If the FTP server is running locally, there is no need for an expensive NFS mount, and we can use a loopback mount using lofs.

Amd will indeed perform the mount inside the chroot-ed FTP directory, and then it will create a symbolic link from /proj/bank/users/martha to /proj/bank/ftp/.a/martha. However, notice what the target of the Amd symlink is: it is /proj/bank/ftp/.a/martha, which, while valid outside the chroot-ed FTP directory, is not valid inside of it! One way to circumvent this is by faking the directory structure needed to cause that symlink to resolve to the right mounted directory. You can do so by manually running the following commands:

```
[root]# cd ~ftp
```

```
[root]# mkdir -p proj/bank/ftp/proj/bank/ftp
```

```
[root]# ln -s ../../../.a proj/bank/ftp/proj/bank/ftp
```

The above solution in Listing 12.26 is not satisfactory. Amd is not capable of completely handling chroot-ed environments using native mounts because the symlinks it creates point to directories that could reside outside the chroot-ed environment. Instead, Amd needs to create a different symlink than normal inside the chroot-ed environment.

We solve this problem using the type:=program mount style in Amd, and a mount command that directly mounts the needed directories inside the chroot-ed environment. This is seen in Listing 12.27.

The Amd Automounter

PART 2

Listing 12.27 ~ftp/users/* in a chroot-ed environment, take 2

```
martha -rhost:=opus;type:=program;\
        fs:=/.a/${key};\
        rfs:=/home/${key}/public_ftp;\
        var1:=/proj/bank/ftp;\
        unmount:="/bin/umount umount ${var1}/${fs}"; \
      host==${rhost};\
        mount:="/bin/mount mount -F lofs ${rfs} ${var1}/${fs}" \
      host!=${rhost};\
        mount:="/bin/mount mount -F nfs ${rhost}:${rfs} ${var1}/${fs}"
```

Here, we essentially perform the same mounts as in Listing 12.26, but we explicitly set
${fs} to /.a/martha, which is the correct path name that will resolve correctly inside the
chroot-ed environment. Note that we had to mount Martha's home directory in one
place, but we had to provide the symlink to another place, because the mount occurs from
outside the chroot-ed FTP environment while the symlink resolution occurs within.

NOTE This example uses a loopback file system called lofs. Currently, the
lofs file system is not part of the mainline Linux kernel. You can get an implementation of lofs for Linux from yours truly. See Appendix B, "Online
Resources," for pointers to sources for such a file system.

Automounting a Jukebox (CD Changer)

In this example, we consider how to automount a CD changer, also called a *jukebox*. This
device often contains many platters, a robotic disk changer, and a few drives. The key part
is that there are fewer drives than there are physical CDs. Therefore, the CD changer can
access only a few CDs at once.

In this example, we consider a jukebox with 32 optical platters, two sides each, and a
total of two drives. Each platter's side is formatted as EXT2FS. Only two CDs may be
accessed at the same time. When the jukebox is asked to access a third, the hardware must
evict one of the CDs and put the new one in its place. The device driver for the jukebox
provides 64 devices for the jukebox: /dev/jb/{1a,1b,2a,2b,...,32a,32b}. This device
driver can mount more than two such platters at once, even if the physical jukebox can
access only two at a time.

Our first attempt to mount the jukebox platters uses EXT2FS mounts of the physical
devices, as seen in Listing 12.28.

Listing 12.28   Jukebox automount example, take 1

```
juke        type:=auto;fs:=${map};pref:=${key}/
juke/*      -rhost:=fork;opts:=nosuid,rw,intr \
            host!=fork;type:=nfs;rfs:=/misc/${key}/. \
            host==fork;type:=ufs;addopts:=nounmount;\
                dev:=/dev/jb/${/key};fs:=/${key}
```

In this case, to mount, say, the first platter, we mount /dev/jb/1a in /juke/1a. We perform a type:=ufs mount on the local host, and a type:=nfs for remote hosts. While everything seems to work, there is a subtle problem: you cannot export NFS entries before they are mounted because of security reasons. This means that you must first mount the platter physically, then NFS-export it, and only then can you NFS-mount it remotely. In Listing 12.28, we perform both local and remote mounts indiscriminately and without any NFS-exports in between.

The solution to this problem is to statically mount all 64 jukebox platters first: each /dev/jb/* is mounted on the corresponding /n/juke/*. You can put all of those entries in your /etc/fstab, then add the appropriate entries in /etc/exports, and after that, you can start Amd. The proper Amd map entry is seen in Listing 12.29.

Listing 12.29   Jukebox automount example, take 2

```
juke/*      -opts:=nosuid,rw,intr;rhost:=fork \
            host!=fork;type:=nfs;rfs:="/n/${key}" \
            host==fork;type:=link;fs:="/n/${key}"
```

This simpler map works because the file system is already mounted somewhere, and all we have to do is provide a symlink to it locally, or NFS-mount it remotely—just the same as any other disk partition.

Samba Mounts

The *Server Message Block* (SMB) protocol is a complex protocol used by Microsoft to share access between machines, especially file access. Linux comes with a popular Samba server implementation that can allow Windows machines to access Unix files as Samba folders. The SMB protocol requires user-specific authentication (passwords) to complete a mount. The Unix Samba implementation also requires that a client-side daemon (smbmnt) remain running in the background in order to access files from the actual SMB server. In particular, this smbmnt program supports reconnecting to the main SMB server so that users do not have to worry about servers going up and down.

This last requirement is an important one because it does not fit the usual model of mounting file systems. A normal mount(2) system call runs in the kernel, which changes

The Amd
Automounter

PART 2

some internal kernel state but leaves nothing more behind. To mount Samba shares, you must execute a command such as the following:

```
[ezk]$ /usr/bin/smbmount //shekel/u_zing /mnt \
> -o username=ezk,password=mypass
```

The above command says to mount the u_zing share from the host shekel, using the user ezk and password mypass. If the password is not specified on the command line, smbmount will prompt you for it. For security reasons, we are going to use a guest login with a fixed password. See above, under "Mounting an NFS Bridge to DFS Using per-UID Passwords," for an example that involves user-specific passwords.

Listing 12.30 shows our first attempt to perform SMB mounts through Amd. Since Amd does not support Samba mounts natively, we must use the program file system.

Listing 12.30 Samba mounts, take 1

```
s1  type:=program;fs:=/smb;\
    mount:="/usr/bin/smbmount smbmount \\\\shekel\\u_zing ${fs}\
        -o username=guest,password=mypass";\
    unmount:="/bin/umount umount ${fs}"
```

Note that in Listing 12.30, we escape the backslash characters by prefixing them with the shell escape character, also a backslash; this is needed because the backslash character is a special character in Amd maps. Listing 12.30 tries to mount the Samba share as if we mounted it by hand. But if you run this example, the backgrounded mount Amd performs will never return. Eventually it will time out, and Amd will declare it a failure to mount. This is ironic, especially considering that for Samba mounts to succeed, the smbmount command must leave something running behind.

Our next attempt, in Listing 12.31, does not call smbmount directly; instead it calls a helper script called /etc/smb.sh. The helper script is shown in Listing 12.32.

Listing 12.31 Samba mounts, take 2

```
s2  type:=program;fs:=/smb;\
    mount:="/etc/smb.sh smb.sh ${fs}";\
    unmount:="/bin/umount umount ${fs}"
```

Listing 12.32   `/etc/smb.sh` Samba mount helper script

```
#!/bin/sh
PATH=/usr/bin:${PATH}
export PATH
(smbmount //shekel/u_zing $1 -o username=guest,password=mypass &)
sleep 4
exit 0
```

The script ensures that `smbmount` remains running by forcing it to run in the background of the shell script. The script then waits a few seconds, and finally it signals back to the caller (Amd) that the mount succeeded. The main problem with this technique is that, through this script, there is no easy way to inform Amd of any failure codes from `smbmount`.

Not being able to handle complex mount protocols, such as SMB, is a deficiency of Amd, and it will be addressed in a future version of Amd. For a full treatment of Samba, see Roderick W. Smith's *Linux Samba Server Administration* (Sybex, 2001), which is part of the Craig Hunt Linux Library.

In Sum

Writing Amd maps involves using Amd's own language, with many possible features. As with any system that offers many features, it is possible to achieve the same results in multiple ways. Often, some ways are better than others. In this chapter, we discussed how to write things more concisely, so that your maps would be more readable and understood by others.

We also discussed various performance optimizations. Some were trivial, such as not compiling in debugging code. Others were more complex, such as avoiding double-mounts in your map specifications. Whatever optimizations you apply, our recommendation is to make sure that your maps are clean and easily understood by others. That way, anyone can update them as needed, and problems can be easily corrected.

The bulk of this chapter provided an assortment of advanced Amd examples. Each example was intended to show something different about Amd that was not covered in depth in earlier chapters. With each example, we endeavored to explain the thought process that goes into writing such a map and how a new map could solve a problem you have.

The key to understanding any topic is knowing when you have reached its limitations—when you find yourself struggling to use a system because it cannot easily support your needs. In the last three examples, we showed you just what happens when you reach this point. Using three complex examples, we started by showing the most obvious solution to an automount problem. As it turns out, that first solution does not work for various reasons, some of which are Amd's limitations. Trial and error are typical parts of developing complex Amd maps. The second try of each of these three examples shows a solution that does work, even though it tasks Amd's capabilities to the max.

13

Autofs

The automounter is a user-level program that acts like an NFS server for the local host. The automounter serves a mount point like any other in-kernel file server. This mount point is called the *automount directory*. When users list the contents of the auto-mounted directory or look up files in it, the file server is invoked to service this request. The automounter services such requests by mounting other file systems and providing a symbolic link to the location where the automounter mounted those other file systems. Each subsequent access to the newly mounted file system must also pass through the auto-mounter.

The main problem with automounters such as Amd (in am-utils 6.0 and earlier) and Sun's original Automounter was that they were implemented as user-level servers. As we explained in Chapter 8, "Overview of the Amd Automounter," Amd must be involved in many user actions that access the file system. This slows down performance considerably since the user process must invoke the kernel, which then invokes another user-level tool (Amd) to service the user's request. This results in a large number of context switches. Furthermore, if Amd aborts abnormally, or is delayed by a busy system or misbehaving network service, users experience long delays accessing files, and their shells and processes hang indefinitely.

Another problem that plagued user-level automounters was that they distinguished between the mount point and the automounted directory. Suppose /home is an auto-mount point, /home/ezk represents my home directory, and the home directory comes from the NFS server path name titan:/users/faculty/ezk. Typically, Amd will mount that remote NFS server in a separate location on the local host, say, /n/users/faculty/ ezk, and create a symlink to this location from /home/ezk. When users ran /bin/pwd anywhere inside their home directory, they were given the path name /n/users/faculty/ ezk and not /home/ezk. This was confusing to users. That's why am-utils comes with the pawd program that attempts to normalize the actual mount path name so it can recover the desired automounted path name. The reason Amd has to use a separate directory to mount remote hosts is that Amd cannot mount other file systems *in place* (inside the automounted directory). If Amd tried to mount in place, it will deadlock with itself since Amd will be asked to serve the very same request that it will be waiting to process.

To address these and other problems, Sun Microsystems designed a special in-kernel helper file system called Autofs. The purpose of Autofs is to offload the most critical functions of the user-level automounter and move this functionality into the kernel—where it can run faster and more reliably.

This chapter describes the Autofs automounter file system, its user-level tools, and how Amd uses them. The latest version of am-utils (version 6.1, under development) fully supports Autofs and thus benefits from it. This chapter will describe the Autofs in-kernel file system and briefly discuss the user-level automounter utilities that are part of the autofs-3.1.5 RPM. Primarily, the chapter focuses on using the latest Amd that supports Autofs. As you shall see, it is very simple to use Autofs with Amd.

WARNING Do not confuse automount, Amd, and Autofs. Autofs is the in-kernel file system that can help any automounter tool-suite. automount is the user-level daemon on Linux that uses Autofs. Users of Solaris or Irix systems may also note that there are two different versions of user-level automounters on those systems, and both are also named automount. The first is an older NFS-based automounter that did not use Autofs; the second is a newer automounter that uses Autofs exclusively. Finally, there is Amd, which can behave as either a user-level, NFS-based automounter, or one that uses Autofs. Amd is even able to work in both modes concurrently. However, only the Amd that comes in am-utils versions 6.1.*x* and newer supports Autofs; older versions of am-utils can only work as an NFS-based user-level automounter.

Syntax of Autofs's Automounter Configuration Files

The Autofs system on Linux is initialized by running /etc/rc.d/init.d/autofs start, which starts the /usr/sbin/automount user-level daemon. This automount program reads a configuration file located in /etc/auto.master. The configuration file is similar to Amd's /etc/amd.conf: it defines automount points, the sources of information that provide entries for each automount point, and options applicable to the mount point.

A typical syntax for entries in the /etc/auto.master file is shown below:

    mountpoint   mapsource   [options]

An entry in the /etc/auto.master file contains up to three fields: the name of the mount point, the source of the map file, and possibly a list of options. A typical example for /etc/auto.master is seen in Listing 13.1.

Listing 13.1   A sample /etc/auto.master file

```
/home    /etc/auto.home    --timeout=60
/misc    yp:misc.map
```

Listing 13.1 shows the contents of a small auto.master file. The file contains the following two lines:

/home   This entry directs the Autofs automounter to mount the file systems defined in /etc/auto.home on the /home mount point. This entry also defines the default timeout for entries mounted under this mount point to one minute. /home is the typical mount point for users' home directories, and automount is typically configured to read the map used to mount these directories from the /etc/auto.home file. You will find an entry identical to this one in most auto.master files.

/misc   The /misc mount point reads its entries from an NIS (YP) server map named misc.map. automount will contact this network server and download the entries from the misc.map map one at a time. Each entry will serve as a single automount entry under /misc. Both Automount and Amd support a variety of map types: files, NIS, LDAP, Hesiod, etc.

Automount map files have a syntax that includes features similar to Amd. The syntax of Automount maps is the following:

    key   [-options]   location

The map syntax includes a key representing an automounted entry within the automount point, a list of options, and the source file system that is mounted to satisfy the resolution of the key. For example, if /misc is an automount point and a user accesses /misc/bob, then automount will try to resolve the key bob inside the /misc map. An example map is shown in Listing 13.2.

Listing 13.2 A sample Automount map file

```
homes           -rw,intr                titan:/usr/homes
testdisk        -fstype=ext2            :/dev/hda5
share           -fstype=smbfs           ://win2k/c
floppy          -fstype=auto            :/dev/fd0
cdrom           -fstype=iso9660,ro      :/dev/hdc
jukebox         -fstype=changer         :/dev/sda1
```

Listing 13.2 shows an automounter map file. Each entry in the file lists a mount node point name (key) followed by its mount options, and the source of the data accessed through the mount point. The entries in Listing 13.2 have the following meaning:

homes   This is an NFS mount of host titan's /usr/homes file system, using the mount options rw,intr. Note that the file system type defaults to NFS; hence, -fstype=nfs is not necessary for this entry. It is similar to Amd's type:=nfs mount type.

testdisk   This is a native EXT2 file system mount of the /dev/hda5 partition. This entry is similar to Amd's type:=ufs mount type. Note that the location information starts with a colon to indicate that there is no hostname component as there is with an NFS mount.

share   This entry mounts an MS-DOS partition named //win2k/c using SMB. Amd can mount such file systems directly using the type:=pcfs mount type. Also, in Chapter 12, "Advanced Amd Uses," we showed how to mount remote SAMBA shares using Amd's type:=program mount type.

floppy   This mounts a floppy disk from /dev/fd0 and will automatically look for its type. Most floppies are formatted as MS-DOS file systems, which Amd can mount using the type:=pcfs mount type. Amd users can also write maps that will try several types of mounts until one succeeds. See the section "Volume Failover" in Chapter 12.

cdrom   This entry mounts an ISO-9660 CD-ROM from /dev/hdc. Amd can do the same using the type:=cdfs file system.

jukebox   This entry mounts a CD-ROM jukebox changer, a SCSI device named /dev/sda1 with several CDs and fewer drives.

As you can see, Automount shares many features with Amd. The syntax of the configuration files that both systems use, however, is different.

How Autofs Works

Two different versions of Autofs exist: one used on Sun Solaris systems and another used on Linux. They both provide similar features. Autofs is only a helper file system: it does not do all of the work. A user-level program or daemon parses the automounter maps and exchanges information with the in-kernel Autofs component. In Solaris, the kernel and the user-level automounter communicate using RPCs. In Linux, they communicate by sending ioctls over a simple Unix socket.

When the system starts, /usr/sbin/automount runs. It reads /etc/auto.master and calls the autofs file system to mount any entry listed in that configuration file. The user-level /usr/sbin/automount daemon then establishes a socket that it shares with the in-kernel autofs module. Both parties talk to each other over that socket, and communication can be initiated by either side (user-level or kernel).

Automounters that use Autofs have five distinct advantages over ones that use a user-level NFS server (such as older versions of Amd): in-place mounts, improved performance, robustness, automatic timeouts, and safe directory browsing.

In-Place Mounts

One of the problems with NFS-based automounters is that they cannot mount the remote file servers inside the automounted directory. For example, consider an automounted directory /home with the node /home/ezk that is mounted from titan:/users/staff/ezk. NFS-based automounters will create a symlink from /home/ezk to a local mount point, typically /a/titan/users/staff/ezk. When users change the directory to their home directory /home/ezk, then run the pwd command to print the working directory, they get an unexpected result: /a/titan/users/staff/ezk instead of /home/ezk.

This has two problems. First, the users see a directory that is different from their home directory. Novice users get confused about the relationship between the two directories. Second, and worse, users tend to place non-automounted path names in their environment variables. For example, they would put /a/titan/users/staff/ezk/bin in their $PATH variable instead of /home/ezk/bin, the automounted path. Using non-automounted paths is bad because the automounter can unmount them unexpectedly and the user's search directory would not be accessible.

The reason for having two directories is that an NFS-level automounter is the file server that serves /home. It cannot distinguish between a lookup for /home/ezk and an attempt to mount a file system in /home/ezk. Consider what happens when a user looks up /home/ezk for the first time. The automounter will look it up in its maps and issue an NFS request to mount the volume that satisfies it. Meanwhile, the user process that made the initial call is waiting. Now, the automounter is waiting for the mount request to complete. But if that mount request will invoke the automounter's own mount point—to mount /home/ezk *inside* the automounted directory—a deadlock will happen! That is, Amd will hang itself, and hence the user process that made the initial call will be blocked indefinitely.

Over the years there have been several suggestions to solve this problem, from special automounter-aware tools like pawd to modified C runtime libraries. These solutions were suboptimal at best. It was not until Autofs came into being that this problem was solved once and for all. The reason is that Autofs is separate from the user-level automounter, and Autofs controls the automounted file system hierarchy completely. In that fashion, Autofs is able to mount titan:/users/staff/ezk directly onto /home/ezk. This is called an *in-place* mount. With in-place mounts, users do not see separate directories for the automounted directory vs. the NFS-mounted directory.

Performance

Autofs improves performance considerably. The first reason for the improved performance is that traversing path names that are already automounted does not invoke the user-level automounter. Reducing the number of times the kernel has to call the user-level daemon reduces the number of context switches. Path names that are already mounted exist in the kernel and are maintained by the Autofs file system. The only time Autofs needs to call the user-level daemon is to look up a new entry that is not yet mounted. After that entry is mounted, all subsequent access remains in the kernel.

Since Autofs performs in-place mounts, it does not have to use symlinks from the automounted node to the actual location of the mounted file system. That also improves performance because the kernel does not have to look up and traverse these symlinks.

Robustness Despite User-Level Daemon Failures

One of the most serious problems with NFS-based user-level automounters is that of reliability. If such an automounter failed, crashed, or aborted for any reason, it left its automount points hung: all user access to those nodes resulted in the user processes being hung. Most often this required a system reboot to correct.

Furthermore, the user-level automounter is a regular process and has to contend for system resources: CPU, memory, disk, etc. The operating system could deschedule the automounter or swap it out when it needs more resources. Also, the automounter depends on other network services such as NIS and DNS, so if they are busy, the user-level automounter is too. All of these problems caused user-level NFS-based automounters to slow down and perform poorly at a time when they were expected to serve files like any other file system.

Autofs solves this problem because it keeps the automounter file system service in the kernel and lets the user-level daemon handle only map lookups for new mounts. This way, the kernel can continue serving automounted files even if the user-level automounter dies. Furthermore, this makes it relatively easy to restart the user-level daemon for any reason: to include new functionality or fix bugs, to install new automount nodes, and more.

Automatic Kernel-Initiated Timeouts

The older user-level NFS-based automounters were also responsible for scheduling the time when the automounted node should be unmounted. After a period of disuse, they attempted to unmount the file system. One problem with this was that user-level NFS-based automounters could not know reliably when a file system was no longer used. This was because users could access the mounted file system via two distinct paths, as the $PATH variable example in the "In-Place Mounts" section demonstrated. Only one of these paths was the automounted path. User-level automounters were unaware of file system access through the other path. Such automounters simply tried to unmount file systems periodically, and often this failed. Moreover, these older automounters could not determine the dependency order of a hierarchical automounted structure of file systems such as that used with Amd's type:=nfsx maps; they could not unmount a tree of mounted file systems in the proper order—from leaves to parent nodes.

Autofs consolidates all the file system functionality of the automounter in one place, the kernel. As such, Autofs is able to determine accurately when a remote file server is no longer used and the proper order to unmount file systems in a hierarchical structure. Autofs waits for a period specified by the --timeout flag as shown in the example /etc/auto.master in Listing 13.1. When that period expires, Autofs unmounts unused file systems and informs the user-level automount server about this activity.

Browseable Directories

Older versions of Amd had an additional problem in supporting browseable directories and causing mount storms. As explained in Chapter 11, "Runtime Automounter Administration," Amd is able to provide a list of all entries it has in a map without mounting them. But when users run typical commands like ls -l, the users' actions result in mounting all of the entries at once—a mount storm. The reason for the storm is that Amd is unable to tell if a single lookup of an entry to automount came from a user who wanted to look up only that entry or from a user who tried to look up all of the entries.

Autofs solves this problem because it consolidates all file system access into the kernel. Autofs is able to distinguish between a lookup for an entry that is not mounted yet and a lookup for an entry below it. For example, suppose /home is an Autofs-automounted directory, and a user looks up the directory /home/ezk. Autofs returns an entry for ezk for this lookup that satisfies user-level tools like ls and cd. Autofs defers the actual auto-mounting of /home/ezk until someone tries to look up something further down, say /home/ezk/.bash_profile. This means that casually running ls -l /home will not produce a mount storm because none of the entries under /home will be automounted. Note, however, that Autofs cannot prevent storms entirely. It is possible for a user to run ls -l /home/*/* and produce a mount storm inside /home.

Autofs Support in Amd

So now that you know how great Autofs is, you are probably wondering what you have to do to use it with Amd. The answer is "very little."

Start by ensuring that your system supports Autofs: try to load the autofs.o module and then check to see if your kernel supports Autofs. This is seen in Listing 13.3.

Listing 13.3 Checking for kernel support for Autofs

```
[root]# modprobe autofs
[root]# cat /proc/filesystems
        ext2
nodev   proc
        iso9660
nodev   devpts
nodev   autofs
```

As you can see in Listing 13.3, Autofs is supported on this sample system. If your Linux system does not support Autofs, you will have to rebuild your kernel as detailed in Chapter 7, "Building and Installing the Linux Kernel and NFS Software."

Next, check if your Amd supports Autofs, as seen in Listing 13.4.

Listing 13.4 Checking for Autofs support in Amd

```
[ezk]$ amd -v
Copyright (c) 1997-2001 Erez Zadok
Copyright (c) 1990 Jan-Simon Pendry
Copyright (c) 1990 Imperial College of Science, Technology & Medicine
Copyright (c) 1990 The Regents of the University of California.
am-utils version 6.1a3 (build 9).
Built by ezk@earth.example.com on date Sun Feb 18 16:22:11 EST 2001.
cpu=i686 (little-endian), arch=i386, karch=i686.
full_os=linux, os=linux, osver=2.2.18-1cucs, vendor=pc.
```

```
Map support for: root, passwd, ldap, union, nisplus, nis, ndbm,
                 file, error.
AMFS: nfs, link, nfsx, nfsl, host, linkx, program, union, inherit,
      ufs, efs, cdfs, pcfs, auto, direct, toplvl, error.
FS: autofs, iso9660, efs, nfs, nfs3, vfat, ext2.
Network: wire="16-net" (netnumber=128.59.16).
```

Listing 13.4 shows that this version of Amd does support Autofs: it is listed as part of the native file systems (FS) in the output of amd -v. If your Amd does not support Autofs, you will have to rebuild am-utils as described in Chapter 14, "Building and Installing the Automounter Software."

Next, edit your /etc/amd.conf file to specify which Amd automount points you would like to use with Autofs. Do this using the mount_type Amd configuration parameter, as seen in Listing 13.5.

Listing 13.5   Mixing Autofs and non-Autofs mounts in /etc/amd.conf

```
# GLOBAL OPTIONS SECTION
[ global ]
restart_mounts =        yes
auto_dir =              /.automount
log_file =              /var/log/amd
log_options =           all
search_path =           /etc

# DEFINE AN AMD MOUNT POINT
[ /net ]
map_name =              amd.net
map_type =              file
mount_type =            nfs

[ /home ]
map_name =              amd.home
map_type =              nis
mount_type =            autofs
```

Listing 13.5 shows two automount points. For the /net automounted directory, Amd will use a standard NFS-based automount style. For the /home automounted directory, Amd will use Autofs. Typically, users will mix Autofs and non-Autofs automount points only when testing Amd's Autofs functionality. Once testing is done, you can have Amd use Autofs for all entries by placing mount_type = autofs in the [global] section of your /etc/amd.conf file.

The Amd Automounter

PART 2

Finally, restart Amd using /etc/rc.d/init.d/amd restart. That's it! You do not have to change your Amd maps at all. Amd will now use Autofs on your Linux system, with all the benefits that Autofs has.

Removing User-Level Autofs Support

Red Hat 7 comes with an Autofs RPM named autofs-3.1.5-5, which includes all of the user-level utilities needed to run an Autofs-only automounter. This RPM does not include the kernel-level Autofs module. Therefore, if you are using Autofs with Amd, you can safely turn off, disable, and remove this RPM as follows:

```
[root]# chkconfig autofs off
[root]# /etc/rc.d/init.d/autofs stop
[root]# rpm -e autofs
```

Amd or Automount?

One choice administrators are often faced with is when to use Amd and when to choose Automount (whether the latter is running on Linux, Solaris, or any other system that includes an Autofs-based automounter). Note that the choice is not between an Autofs-enabled automounter or not, but between two different user-level automounters, both of which can use Autofs.

The reasons for choosing Automount over Amd are as follows:

- You run a small, homogeneous site. For example, if your site is composed entirely of Linux machines, and you do not have many of them, then using Automount is simpler.

- The syntax and features of Automount are sufficient for you. Automount's map files use a simple syntax. If you make frequent changes to your automounter maps, or the features you need are pretty basic, choose Automounter.

There are several strong reasons for choosing Amd over Automount:

- If your site is heterogeneous or large, Amd is the only automounter that you can use. Amd is supported on dozens of platforms and variants. Nowadays, with decreased prices for computer hardware and ever-changing operating systems software, administrators find themselves supporting more types of hosts. Using Amd guarantees that you can use the same automounter with the same map syntax on all of your hosts, no matter what they run.

- You can run Amd on sites where some hosts support Autofs and others do not. You will not have to change your Amd maps at all to use Autofs, only your /etc/ amd.conf file on those hosts that support Autofs. This is also an advantage for sites that use Amd when they are small and homogeneous: as the site grows and becomes heterogeneous, administrators do not have to switch from Amd to Automount. In other words, Amd can support your growing site needs.

- Amd's support is more comprehensive. It supports many native file systems and meta file systems such as nfs-link, multi-nfs mounts and hierarchical mounts, replicated volumes, direct mounts, union mounts, and more. These were described in Chapter 10, "Automounter Maps."

- Amd's map syntax is very powerful. It supports many static and dynamic variables, powerful selectors and facilities to choose among different conditions for mounting file systems, and more. These were described in detail in Chapter 10. Furthermore, am-utils comes with the `automount2amd` script that can convert simple Automount maps to Amd maps, as we described in Chapter 11.

NOTE To support Autofs, /bin/mount includes a special flag –s. The "sloppy" flag tells Autofs to ignore mount options that it may not recognize. It is needed with Autofs because users tend to mount many different file systems that support different sets of options. With this option, Autofs will ignore flags that it does not recognize, rather than failing the entire mount. Amd has used this policy since its inception: you can specify any number of mount options in your Amd maps, and all Amd will do is print a warning message about any option it does not recognize.

Deficiencies of Autofs

There are two versions of the Autofs protocol supported by recent Linux kernels (2.2 and 2.4): Autofs v3 and v4. Amd can use both, but it is better to enable Autofs v4 because it is more powerful. Still, there are a few deficiencies in all existing versions of Autofs as they are used with Amd:

- Autofs does not support restartable mount points. If Amd exits, previous mount points are still accessible. But once Amd restarts, these mount points become inaccessible until they are unmounted. This means that with the current Autofs behavior, if Amd exits, dies, or is stopped, your system will have to be rebooted for Amd to recognize these mount points again.

- The support for automatic expiration of mount points in Autofs requires that the user-level daemon (`automount`) listen to an Autofs-supported socket synchronously. This means that the user-level daemon has to wait for the kernel module to reply and cannot do anything else during that time. Amd was designed as an asynchronous automounter so it will not block due to external events. Therefore, Amd currently uses its own internal mechanism for timing out and unmounting mount points that have not been used recently; Amd listens to unmount requests from the in-kernel Autofs-initiated expiration mechanism but does not use them.

- Autofs v4 does not yet support browseable directories without causing mount storms.

The developers of Autofs and the maintainers of am-utils have been discussing these issues. It is expected that Autofs v5—currently under development—will fix these problems. To find out more information about Autofs, such as related mailing lists and the latest sources, see Appendix B, "Online Resources."

In Sum

Autofs is a powerful in-kernel file system that takes much of the burden from user-level NFS-based automounters. By consolidating all automounter file system–related functions in one place—the kernel—Autofs achieves many benefits over NFS-based automounters, especially in improved performance and reliably.

Autofs supports in-place mounts, which produce the same path name for users whether going through the automounter or not. Autofs avoids using symlinks, which increases the speed of resolving directory names. Autofs continues to run even if the user-level daemon aborts or is restarted; also, Autofs does not depend on user-level networking services to function properly. Autofs can also control when and in what order automounted directories should be unmounted. Finally, Autofs can provide a safe mechanism for browsing automounted directories while avoiding the most obvious mount storms that could ensue.

The latest version of am-utils (6.1 and higher) supports Autofs for several platforms: Linux, Solaris, and Irix. This support was carefully integrated into Amd without requiring users to make any changes to their Amd maps. Only a small configuration change is needed on the host's `/etc/amd.conf` file. In this fashion, administrators can use Amd throughout their sites, use the same set of unmodified Amd maps, and take advantage of Amd's comprehensive support and powerful map syntax.

This chapter introduced the new in-kernel Autofs file system and the configuration that is needed for Amd to use it. Next, in Chapter 14, we describe how to include support for Autofs and other features into Amd.

14

Building and Installing the Automounter Software

On most Linux systems, administrators can install Amd as part of the initial system installation. This is done by installing the am-utils package, which includes Amd, Amq, and other related utilities. Administrators also have the option to install the am-utils package after an initial system setup. Often, however, this is not enough. Linux vendors cannot track thousands of software packages and release updates each time those packages change. Furthermore, Linux vendors build am-utils generically—it includes support for basic services, but not all possible services. Therefore, administrators need to know how to build and install the am-utils package on their own, from original sources. This can be very useful for updating your Amd software to fix bugs, add new features, include any additional support your site needs, and most importantly, to close potential security holes.

This chapter describes how to install am-utils from precompiled binaries, as well as how to build am-utils from original sources. It also discusses how to add support for new features to Amd and how to address common build and installation problems.

In addition, this chapter explains the process of building and installing Amd in a generic manner that, at a conceptual level, applies to all versions of Linux. Our examples, however, must be based on something more specific; most examples have been centered on

Red Hat Linux version 7. Of course, you may be using a different version of Red Hat, or a different distribution of Linux (SuSE, Debian, etc.), which means the specific details may vary. If you face difficulties, please refer to the documentation for your Linux distribution and seek the assistance of your local administrators.

Because our examples are based on Red Hat Linux, we used the Red Hat Package Manager tool, rpm. See Chapter 7, "Building and Installing the Linux Kernel and NFS Software," for more information about RPM. Chapter 7 also describes how to turn on support for new features in the Linux kernel. These features may be desired for use by Amd.

Checking Installed Software on Your Site

Most Linux distributions come with some version of am-utils that may be suitable for your needs. The first question you must ask yourself is whether you need to rebuild am-utils from sources or simply use precompiled binaries that came with your distribution. If you can use precompiled binaries, you can save yourself a lot of time. However, that may not be possible at your site for several reasons:

- Your system did not come with a precompiled version of Amd.
- Your precompiled version of Amd is missing support for some features that you wish to use, such as support for LDAP or Hesiod maps.
- A new version of Amd is available that adds new basic features or fixes bugs that you have faced.
- You are just the kind of administrator who likes to run the very latest version of every package for which you can get a prerelease, early-alpha, maintainers-only tarball....

The Amd that comes with Red Hat 7.0 is am-utils-6.0.4s5, built on a Red Hat 7.0 system. To find out what it supports, run amd -v, as seen in Listing 14.1.

Listing 14.1 Checking the built-in Amd support in Red Hat Linux

```
[ezk]$ /usr/sbin/amd -v
Copyright (c) 1997-2000 Erez Zadok
Copyright (c) 1990 Jan-Simon Pendry
Copyright (c) 1990 Imperial College of Science, Technology & Medicine
Copyright (c) 1990 The Regents of the University of California.
am-utils version 6.0.4s5 (build 1).
Built by prospector@porky.devel.redhat.com on date Sat Jul 15 13:50:32 EDT
2000.
```

```
cpu=i386 (little-endian), arch=i386, karch=i686.
full_os=linux, os=linux, osver=2.2.5-22smp, vendor=redhat.
Map support for: root, passwd, ldap, union, nisplus, nis, ndbm, file,
              error.
AMFS: nfs, link, nfsx, nfsl, host, linkx, program, union, inherit, ufs,
      cdfs, pcfs, auto, direct, toplvl, error.
FS: iso9660, nfs, vfat, ext2.
Network: wire="ezknet.cs.columbia.edu" (netnumber=128.59.8).
```

The Red Hat–distributed Amd supports the following map services:

root, passwd, union, and file   These are native map services that are supported by all versions of Amd and were described in Chapter 10, "Automounter Maps."

nis and nisplus   These are Network Information System maps (NIS, formerly YP) and NIS+ maps. Support for these two map services is integral to Red Hat 7 and is built into the GNU C library, glibc. This library comes with the glibc-devel RPM and cannot be removed.

ndbm   Another integral map service that comes with the glibc-devel RPM is the New DataBase Manager, NDBM.

ldap   These maps support the Lightweight Directory Access Protocol (LDAP). LDAP support is part of a separate RPM, openldap. Since the Red Hat–distributed Amd was built with LDAP support, the am-utils RPM depends on the openldap RPM; both RPMs must be installed together.

The Red Hat precompiled version of Amd also supports the following file systems:

NFS   The Network File System, without which there is no point in running Amd in the first place. Note that this is the client-side NFS. While Amd is an NFS server by itself, it does not need a server-side NFS to work. You will only need an NFS server running on your machine if you plan to export file systems to other hosts or you plan to make local NFS mounts such as localhost:/usr/local. The latter are relatively rare and can be accomplished using better mechanisms such as loopback mounts, as described in Chapter 3, "NFS Performance."

ISO9660   This is the most common file system used to mount CD-ROMs.

VFAT   This is an MS-DOS–based file system that also supports long file names. It is often called the Windows 95 file system.

EXT2FS   This is the main disk-based file system used on Linux. It is mandatory.

One file system that was missing from the (older) Red Hat 6.2–distributed Amd was VFAT. If you wanted Amd to mount MS-DOS–formatted disk partitions or floppies on those older systems, you had to rebuild Amd as described later in this chapter or use the program type as described in Chapter 10. Either way, even if your Amd was compiled with VFAT support, your kernel may not necessarily support it. This can happen often when new kernels are installed on an existing system or when modules are damaged.

To check to see if your system supports a given file system, say, VFAT, start by checking the current list of file systems that the kernel supports. You do so by listing the contents of the special *process-file-system* file /proc/filesystems:

```
[ezk]$ cat /proc/filesystems
        ext2
nodev   proc
        iso9660
nodev   devpts
nodev   nfs
```

The above listing tells you that the running kernel supports the EXT2, proc, ISO9660, and NFS file systems. It does not support MS-DOS (VFAT). However, many Linux file systems are not precompiled into the kernel but, rather, are available as loadable kernel modules. Support for those file systems is not available until their respective modules are loaded.

To see if you can load up support for the MS-DOS file system, run the modprobe command. If you do not have support, you will get an error message, as follows:

```
[root]# modprobe vfat
modprobe: Can't locate module vfat
```

If your system indeed does not support a file system that you want Amd to use, you must rebuild that module for the Linux kernel to support it. Amd does not, for example, implement native file systems such as VFAT and ISO9660; Amd uses them when and if they are available. Chapter 7 provides that information on reconfiguring your Linux kernel for additional file system support.

If your system does include the loadable modules for the VFAT file system, you will not get an error message:

```
[root]# modprobe vfat
```

Afterward, you will be able to display the current list of supported file systems, including VFAT, as follows:

```
[ezk]$ cat /proc/filesystems
        ext2
nodev   proc
        iso9660
```

```
nodev    devpts
nodev    nfs
         vfat
```

You can also check to see which kernel modules are currently loaded onto your system with the lsmod (List Modules) command:

```
[ezk]$ lsmod
Module          Size   Used by
vfat            9276   0 (unused)
fat             30400  0 [vfat]
nfs             28896  1 (autoclean)
lockd           31496  1 (autoclean) [nfs]
sunrpc          53028  1 (autoclean) [nfs lockd]
```

You will notice in the above listing that two related modules are loaded: fat and vfat. FAT is the old MS-DOS file system that supported short uppercase-only file names of the 8.3 format (up to eight characters for the name and up to three characters for the file's extension). VFAT is also known as the Windows-95 file system; it is similar to MS-DOS but also supports mixed-case and long file names. In Linux, the code base for both FAT and VFAT is so similar that the vfat module uses much of the code in the fat module. Therefore, when we ran the modprobe command above to load the vfat module, it automatically loaded the module that it depends on: fat. For more information about modules, see the manual pages for lsmod, rmmod, insmod, and modprobe.

By now you should have decided if you can use the precompiled version of Amd that came with Red Hat or you have to build some software yourself. If you only need to install existing precompiled RPMs, continue reading this chapter. If you need to rebuild your kernel, consult Chapter 7. If you need to rebuild Amd, skip to the section "Building Software from Sources" later in this chapter.

Installing Precompiled Software Packages

Before you install the RPM for am-utils and any additional binary RPMs, you should check what you have installed. This section will show you several simple options to use with the rpm tool, the program you can use to manage the packages installed on your Red Hat system. For a more detailed description of this tool, refer to the section "Using RPMs" in Chapter 7 and to the rpm manual page.

Start by checking to see if Amd is installed. If it is installed, it would be installed in /usr. You can use ls to find it:

```
[ezk]$ ls /usr/*/amd
ls: /usr/*/amd: No such file or directory
```

This tells you that Amd is not installed on this system. To install the RPM that includes Amd, install the am-utils RPM from the Red Hat CD. We start by inserting the Red Hat 7 CD into the CD-ROM drive and mounting it under /mnt/cdrom:

```
[root]# mount -t iso9660 /dev/cdrom /mnt/cdrom
```

Then we cd to the directory where the RPMs are on the CD-ROM, list the am-utils package, and install it using the rpm -ivh command. Note that in this case we assume you are installing on an i386 platform running Linux.

```
[root]# cd /mnt/cdrom/RedHat/RPMS
[root]# ls am-utils*
am-utils-6.0.4s5-8.i386.rpm
[root]# rpm -ivh am-utils-6.0.4s5-8.i386.rpm
error: failed dependencies:
        liblber.so.1 is needed by am-utils-6.0.4s5-8
        libldap.so.1 is needed by am-utils-6.0.4s5-8
```

As you can see, the RPM installation command failed! This is because it has a dependency on the LDAP libraries. You must install the LDAP package first. Start by finding which one it is, and then install it before trying to reinstall am-utils. This is seen in Listing 14.2. See Chapter 7 for general instructions on using RPMs.

Listing 14.2 Checking and resolving RPM dependency conflicts for am-utils

```
[root]# rpm -q --whatprovides --dbpath \
> /usr/lib/rpmdb/i386-redhat-linux/redhat liblber.so.1
openldap-1.2.11-15
[root]# rpm -q --whatprovides --dbpath \
> /usr/lib/rpmdb/i386-redhat-linux/redhat libldap.so.1
openldap-1.2.11-15
[root]# cd /mnt/cdrom/RedHat/RPMS
[root]# rpm -ivh openldap-1.2.11-15.i386.rpm
openldap             ###############################################
[root]# rpm -ivh am-utils-6.0.4s5-8.i386.rpm
am-utils             ###############################################
```

Note that when I installed these two RPMs, I used the -v and -h options; these list the base name of the RPM being installed and print out hash marks (#) as progress indicators as the rpm tool proceeds to install the packages.

Now we can verify that Amd is installed:

```
[ezk]$ ls /usr/*/amd
/usr/sbin/amd
```

Removing and Upgrading Precompiled Packages

If you ever have to remove the RPM for am-utils, use the rpm -e command. Since the am-utils RPM depends on LDAP, you cannot remove the openldap RPM first. Also, you may wish to remove am-utils but keep the openldap package installed, perhaps because you use an LDAP server for other functions. In this example, we remove both:

```
[root]# rpm -e am-utils
[root]# rpm -e openldap
```

Far more likely is that you will be updating or upgrading your version of Amd by installing a newer RPM. Suppose Red Hat releases an update to the am-utils RPM: am-utils-6.0.5-1.i386.rpm. If you have not installed am-utils before, you can install this new RPM with the usual rpm -ivh command. If you have installed the am-utils RPM before, you can upgrade it using the *freshen* command to RPM. In this example, we give the full URL to the new RPM as it might exist on Red Hat's RPM-updates FTP server. The RPM command will ftp the RPM file and then install it locally, upgrading the existing version of am-utils:

```
[root]# rpm -F ftp://contrib.redhat.com/redhat/updates/7.0/i386/am-
utils-6.0.5-1.i386.rpm
```

Starting Precompiled Packages

Now that you have installed or upgraded your version of Amd, you have two choices:

- Start it by hand one time.
- Configure the system to start Amd at boot time, then reboot.

When you install the Red Hat am-utils package, you also install startup scripts, an /etc/amd.conf file, and a single Amd map /etc/amd.net. The latter uses the type:=host Amd file system to mount all file systems for remote hosts based on their names.

If you do not wish to use the Amd configuration file or map that comes with Red Hat, you will first have to write your own or distribute existing ones from other hosts. In the rest

The Amd Automounter

PART 2

of this section, however, we assume that you keep the existing setup that comes with Red Hat 7's am-utils package.

To run Amd once by hand, start it using its startup script, as seen in Listing 14.3.

Listing 14.3 Starting Amd using the Red Hat startup script

```
[root]# /etc/rc.d/init.d/amd start
Starting amd:                                          [ OK ]
```

Now you can run amq to see what has started:

```
[root]# amq
/      root     "root"        lorien:(pid10555)
/net   toplvl   /etc/amd.net  /net
```

Next, you can use the /net automount point to mount file systems from various hosts, as we see in Listing 14.4. For example, the host shekel exports five file systems, all of which start with the /n path name, and all of which were mounted at the same time:

Listing 14.4 Testing Red Hat's Amd

```
[root]# ls /net/shekel
/n
[root]# amq
amq
/            root    "root"       lorien:(pid10555)
/net         toplvl  /etc/amd.net /net
/net/shekel  host    shekel:/     /.automount/shekel/root
[root]# df -t nfs
Filesystem            1k-blocks    Used Available Use% Mounted on
shekel:/n/shekel/misc/shekel
                      8705501   6628106   1990340  77% /.automount/shekel/
root/n/shekel/misc/shekel
shekel:/n/shekel/proj/amd
                      2044038   1199182    783535  60% /.automount/shekel/
root/n/shekel/proj/amd
shekel:/n/shekel/proj/bank
                      4125390   2524431   1559706  62% /.automount/shekel/
root/n/shekel/proj/bank
shekel:/n/shekel/proj/fist
                      8735855   2504227   5794836  30% /.automount/shekel/
root/n/shekel/proj/fist
shekel:/n/shekel/u/zing
                      4179366   3152733    984840  76% /.automount/shekel/
root/n/shekel/u/zing
```

Now that we started Amd by hand and verified that it works, we can configure the Linux system to start Amd by default at boot time. When you install the am-utils RPM, Amd is not configured to start automatically at boot time. To check its boot time status, use the chkconfig (Check Configuration) command as follows:

```
[ezk]$ chkconfig --list amd
amd                0:off   1:off   2:off   3:off   4:off   5:off   6:off
```

The chkconfig command reports the name of the program and its status in all seven run levels (0–6). These run levels correspond to various stages or states of the boot sequence, as seen in Table 14.1. The string of offs next to each of the run levels indicates that Amd is turned off at all levels.

Table 14.1   Linux Boot Sequence Run Levels

Run Level	Meaning
0	System halt or shutdown
1	Single-user mode
2	Multiuser run level, but without NFS (same as level 3 if you do not have networking on)
3	Full multiuser mode
4	Unused
5	Full multiuser mode with X11
6	System reboot (an ordered full shutdown followed by a normal reboot)

To turn Amd on for starting at boot time and recheck its startup status, use the commands seen in Listing 14.5.

Listing 14.5   Turning on boot-time startup support for Amd in Red Hat

```
[root]# chkconfig amd on
[ezk]$ chkconfig --list amd
amd                0:off   1:off   2:off   3:on   4:on   5:on   6:off
```

As you can see, after turning the Amd service on, it is now configured to start at various run levels. Do not be concerned that it is not on at all levels: Amd does not have to be. It is quite normal for a service to start at boot time only in a few run levels. For example, Listing 14.5 shows that Amd is on at run levels 3 through 5, but not at level 1. That is because normally Amd does not need to be running in single-user mode. The most important thing to ensure is that Amd is turned on in the two most important and practical normal run levels: 3 and 5. What the chkconfig program does not show is that when you shut down the system, Amd gets killed in run levels 0, 1, 2, and 6. You can find out which levels Amd gets killed in by running the following:

```
[ezk]$ cd /etc/rc.d
[ezk]$ ls */K*amd
rc0.d/K28amd   rc1.d/K28amd   rc2.d/K28amd   rc6.d/K28amd
```

The reason Amd is killed in these four run levels is that they represent states in which the system is rebooted or brought out of full multiuser mode, and Amd must not be running when the system reaches any one of these four run levels.

Now you can reboot your system:

```
[root]# reboot
```

If you watch the boot messages as your system starts, it should show you a line as follows:

```
Starting amd:                                          [  OK  ]
```

The OK status (appearing in green on your console) indicates that Amd started at boot time correctly. If Amd could not start correctly at boot time, you will see instead the following message:

```
Starting amd:                                          [FAILED]
```

If you get that failure message (FAILED printed in red on your console), let the system finish booting, and then try to start Amd by hand. If it does not start, check the error message that Amd prints and correct it. If Amd starts by hand, then most likely your problem is that your networking or some other service that Amd depends on is not ready by the time Amd starts. This often happens when Amd reads its maps from NIS, which needs the network to be up fairly early, but your network comes up late because it starts from a PCMCIA Ethernet card. On older Red Hat systems, PCMCIA services do not always start early enough to initialize properly before they are needed by other network services such as NIS and Amd. One solution to this problem is to move the start of your PCMCIA services earlier in the boot process and possibly also to move the start of Amd later in the boot process. For more information on this, see the manual pages for init and chkconfig.

NOTE   You can also use a curses-based system configuration tool called linuxconf for turning system services on and off. While linuxconf simplifies various complex network setups, I find it quicker and more efficient to use commands such as chkconfig to check and turn on/off various system services such as Amd.

Building Software from Sources

If you have determined that using precompiled am-utils software is not sufficient for your needs, then you will have to build it yourself. Before doing so, ensure that you have the following tarballs:

- The linux kernel, if you need to rebuild it
- Any additional map services you wish to support, such as Hesiod or LDAP
- The am-utils version you wish to build

Next, ensure that you have enough disk space left on your system to accommodate the unpacking and building of your software. Table 14.2 shows the expected disk-space utilization for retrieving, unpacking, and fully building various packages. It is always safer to have more space available than you need, in case you need to build multiple versions of a package.

Table 14.2   Approximate Disk Space Needed for Unpacking and Building Various Distributions (in MB)

Distribution	Tarball	Unpacked	Built	Total
linux-2.2.16 (Red Hat SRPM)	21.1	91.8	37.3	150.2
hesiod-3.0.2	0.1	0.2	0.5	0.8
am-utils-6.0.4	1.4	7.5	13.7	22.6

Once you have allotted enough disk space, start by rebuilding your kernel as needed. If you have installed the Linux kernel that came with Red Hat (version 2.2.16 for Red Hat 7), it includes most features that Amd could use and therefore you would not need to rebuild your Linux kernel. Such features are support for NFS, EXT2, ISO9660, VFAT, and

The Amd
Automounter

PART 2

Autofs file systems. If you require additional support, or if you are building a newer kernel, say 2.4.0, refer to Chapter 7 for details. Additional kernel support you may wish to have prior to rebuilding Amd includes new file systems: Autofs version 4, NFS version 3, etc. If you are rebuilding your kernel, do so before embarking on a rebuild of am-utils. Also, restart your Linux system with any new kernel before moving on.

The next step is to install any additional user-level software that Amd will need. This almost always includes support for new map services. In this example, we wish to install support for LDAP and Hesiod map services. We illustrate this example by showing two different install methods: installing LDAP from precompiled Red Hat binaries and installing Hesiod support by rebuilding the sources for it from scratch.

You can use any tool you wish to ftp files to your local machine. Some of the FTP tools that come with Red Hat Linux 7 include the following:

- /usr/bin/ftp, the original interactive client
- ncftp and ncftpget, improved command-line clients
- gftp, a Gnome-based graphical client
- Netscape Navigator and any other Web browser
- wget, GNU's WebGet non-interactive client

Note that not all of these tools may be installed on your Red Hat system. You may have to install them from the Red Hat distribution CD as described earlier in this chapter, in "Installing Precompiled Software Packages."

If you know the location of a software you wish to ftp, it is quicker to use command-line tools to get it. If you know what you are looking for but do not know where to get it, you can use any of the FTP search engines listed in Appendix B, "Online Resources."

Installing LDAP RPMs before Rebuilding Amd

Red Hat includes all the libraries and header files necessary to rebuild am-utils with LDAP support. These are part of the openldap-devel RPM. This RPM must be installed separately before rebuilding am-utils. Note that the openldap-devel RPM, unlike the openldap RPM, is not needed to run the Amd that came from the am-utils RPM.

To install the LDAP RPM, follow a similar procedure as used when installing other RPMs off of your Red Hat CD, as seen in Listing 14.6.

Listing 14.6   Installing LDAP RPMs

```
[root]# mount -t iso9660 /dev/cdrom /mnt/cdrom
[root]# cd /mnt/cdrom/RedHat/RPMS
```

```
[root]# ls *ldap*.rpm
auth_ldap-1.4.3-2.i386.rpm
nss_ldap-113-2.i386.rpm
openldap-1.2.11-15.i386.rpm
openldap-clients-1.2.11-15.i386.rpm
openldap-devel-1.2.11-15.i386.rpm
openldap-servers-1.2.11-15.i386.rpm
php-ldap-4.0.1p12-9.i386.rpm
[root]# rpm -ivh openldap-devel-1.2.11-15.i386.rpm
openldap-devel        ##################################################
```

Note again that we listed several LDAP-related RPMs from the distribution CD but only installed the openldap-devel one.

You have now installed all the files that am-utils needs to recognize and include support for LDAP. Next, we do the same for Hesiod.

Installing Hesiod before Rebuilding Amd

The official sources to Hesiod are located at MIT's official ATHENA FTP server (Hesiod was part of a larger project called Athena). You can use GNU wget to retrieve Hesiod and store it in /usr/src, as seen in Listing 14.7.

Listing 14.7   Getting Hesiod sources

```
[ezk]$ cd /usr/src
[ezk]$ wget ftp://athena-dist.mit.edu/pub/ATHENA/hesiod/hesiod-3.0.2.tar.gz
--19:53:40--  ftp://athena-dist.mit.edu:21/pub/ATHENA/hesiod/hesiod-
3.0.2.tar.gz
           => `hesiod-3.0.2.tar.gz.1'
Connecting to athena-dist.mit.edu:21... connected!
Logging in as anonymous ... Logged in!
==> TYPE I ... done.  ==> CWD pub/ATHENA/hesiod ... done.
==> PORT ... done.    ==> RETR hesiod-3.0.2.tar.gz ... done.
Length: 31,974 (unauthoritative)

   OK -> ......... ......... ......... .                 [100%]

19:53:41 (600.47 KB/s) - `hesiod-3.0.2.tar.gz.1' saved [31974]
```

To unpack the distribution, use the tar x command. Since the Tape Archive (TAR) file is compressed with GNU Zip, you must use the z flag to decompress the file first. I also like to see the files as they unpack, using the v flag: it gives me a visual indicator of progress and a general feel for the number of files that have to be compiled, as seen in Listing 14.8.

Listing 14.8 Source files for the Hesiod package

```
[ezk]$ tar xzvf hesiod-3.0.2.tar.gz
hesiod-3.0.2/
hesiod-3.0.2/Makefile.in
hesiod-3.0.2/NEWS
hesiod-3.0.2/README
hesiod-3.0.2/acconfig.h
hesiod-3.0.2/config.h.in
hesiod-3.0.2/configure
hesiod-3.0.2/configure.in
hesiod-3.0.2/hescompat.c
hesiod-3.0.2/hesinfo.1
hesiod-3.0.2/hesinfo.c
hesiod-3.0.2/hesiod.3
hesiod-3.0.2/hesiod.c
hesiod-3.0.2/hesiod.conf.5
hesiod-3.0.2/hesiod.conf.sample
hesiod-3.0.2/hesiod.h
hesiod-3.0.2/hesiod_end.3
hesiod-3.0.2/hesiod_free_list.3
hesiod-3.0.2/hesiod_free_passwd.3
hesiod-3.0.2/hesiod_free_postoffice.3
hesiod-3.0.2/hesiod_getpwnam.3
hesiod-3.0.2/hesiod_free_servent.3
hesiod-3.0.2/hesiod_getmailhost.3
hesiod-3.0.2/hesiod_getpwuid.3
hesiod-3.0.2/hesiod_getservbyname.3
hesiod-3.0.2/hesiod_init.3
hesiod-3.0.2/hesiod_p.h
hesiod-3.0.2/hesiod_resolve.3
hesiod-3.0.2/hesiod_to_bind.3
hesiod-3.0.2/hesmailhost.c
hesiod-3.0.2/hespwnam.c
hesiod-3.0.2/hesservbyname.c
hesiod-3.0.2/hestest.c
hesiod-3.0.2/hestest.conf
hesiod-3.0.2/install-sh
hesiod-3.0.2/mkinstalldirs
hesiod-3.0.2/resscan.h
```

Next, cd into the hesiod-3.0.2 source directory, run the GNU configure tool to configure the package, and then run make to build the package. Normally, GNU configure sets up software to install under /usr/local. In the example in Listing 14.9, we give the configure script the --prefix option to tell it that we wish to install Hesiod in a nonstandard location, /usr/local/hesiod.

Listing 14.9   Configuring, building, and installing the Hesiod package

```
[ezk]$ cd /usr/src/hesiod-3.0.2
[ezk]$ ./configure --prefix=/usr/local/hesiod
creating cache ./config.cache
checking for gcc... gcc
checking whether we are using GNU C... yes
checking whether gcc accepts -g... yes
checking for a BSD compatible install... /usr/local/gnu/bin/install -c
checking for ranlib... ranlib
checking how to run the C preprocessor... gcc -E
checking for res_mkquery... no
checking for -lresolv... yes
checking for strerror_r... yes
updating cache ./config.cache
creating ./config.status
creating Makefile
creating config.h
[ezk]$ make
gcc -c -I. -DSYSCONFDIR=\"/usr/local/hesiod/etc\"  -g -O hesiod.c
gcc -c -I. -DSYSCONFDIR=\"/usr/local/hesiod/etc\"  -g -O hesmailhost.c
gcc -c -I. -DSYSCONFDIR=\"/usr/local/hesiod/etc\"  -g -O hespwnam.c
gcc -c -I. -DSYSCONFDIR=\"/usr/local/hesiod/etc\"  -g -O hesservbyname.c
gcc -c -I. -DSYSCONFDIR=\"/usr/local/hesiod/etc\"  -g -O hescompat.c
ar cru libhesiod.a hesiod.o hesmailhost.o hespwnam.o hesservbyname.o
hescompat.o
ranlib libhesiod.a
gcc -c -I. -DSYSCONFDIR=\"/usr/local/hesiod/etc\"  -g -O hesinfo.c
gcc  -o hesinfo hesinfo.o libhesiod.a -lresolv
gcc -c -I. -DSYSCONFDIR=\"/usr/local/hesiod/etc\"  -g -O hestest.c
gcc  -o hestest hestest.o libhesiod.a -lresolv
[root]# make install
./mkinstalldirs /usr/local/hesiod/lib
mkdir /usr/local/hesiod/lib
./mkinstalldirs /usr/local/hesiod/bin
mkdir /usr/local/hesiod/bin
```

The Amd
Automounter

PART 2

```
./mkinstalldirs /usr/local/hesiod/include
mkdir /usr/local/hesiod/include
./mkinstalldirs /usr/local/hesiod/man/man1
mkdir /usr/local/hesiod/man
mkdir /usr/local/hesiod/man/man1
./mkinstalldirs /usr/local/hesiod/man/man3
mkdir /usr/local/hesiod/man/man3
./mkinstalldirs /usr/local/hesiod/man/man5
mkdir /usr/local/hesiod/man/man5
/usr/local/gnu/bin/install -c -c -m 644 libhesiod.a /usr/local/hesiod/lib
ranlib /usr/local/hesiod/lib/libhesiod.a
chmod u-w /usr/local/hesiod/lib/libhesiod.a
/usr/bin/install -c -c -m 555 hesinfo /usr/local/hesiod/bin
/usr/bin/install -c -c -m 444 ./hesiod.h /usr/local/hesiod/include
/usr/bin/install -c -c -m 444 ./hesinfo.1 /usr/local/hesiod/man/man1
/usr/bin/install -c -c -m 444 ./hesiod.3 /usr/local/hesiod/man/man3
/usr/bin/install -c -c -m 444 ./hesiod_end.3 \
        /usr/local/hesiod/man/man3
/usr/bin/install -c -c -m 444 ./hesiod_free_list.3 \
        /usr/local/hesiod/man/man3
/usr/bin/install -c -c -m 444 ./hesiod_free_passwd.3 \
        /usr/local/hesiod/man/man3
/usr/bin/install -c -c -m 444 ./hesiod_free_postoffice.3 \
        /usr/local/hesiod/man/man3
/usr/bin/install -c -c -m 444 ./hesiod_free_servent.3 \
        /usr/local/hesiod/man/man3
/usr/bin/install -c -c -m 444 ./hesiod_getmailhost.3 \
        /usr/local/hesiod/man/man3
/usr/bin/install -c -c -m 444 ./hesiod_getpwnam.3 \
        /usr/local/hesiod/man/man3
/usr/bin/install -c -c -m 444 ./hesiod_getpwuid.3 \
        /usr/local/hesiod/man/man3
/usr/bin/install -c -c -m 444 ./hesiod_getservbyname.3 \
        /usr/local/hesiod/man/man3
/usr/bin/install -c -c -m 444 ./hesiod_init.3 /usr/local/hesiod/man/man3
/usr/bin/install -c -c -m 444 ./hesiod_resolve.3 \
        /usr/local/hesiod/man/man3
/usr/bin/install -c -c -m 444 ./hesiod_to_bind.3 \
        /usr/local/hesiod/man/man3
/usr/bin/install -c -c -m 444 ./hesiod.conf.5 /usr/local/hesiod/man/man5
```

At this stage we have installed Hesiod's libraries, headers, and even manual pages into the proper subdirectories under /usr/local/hesiod. We are finally ready to begin unpacking and building am-utils.

Getting am-utils Sources

You can get sources for the am-utils package from two sites:

- Red Hat's FTP site
- The official am-utils Web site, www.am-utils.org

Using am-utils Sources from Red Hat

To get Source RPMs (SRPMs) from Red Hat's FTP server, we use any FTP client. In this example, we use a different tool, ncftpget. This tool, like wget, also produces output that tracks the download progress.

```
[root]# cd /usr/src/redhat/SRPMS

[root]# ncftpget -v ftp://ftp.redhat.com/redhat/current/SRPMS/SRPMS/
am-utils-6.0.4s5-8.src.rpm

am-utils-6.0.4s5-8.src.rpm:                    1.28 MB   168.96 kB/s
```

Note that we retrieved the SRPM into /usr/src/redhat/SRPMS. That is the standard directory where SRPMs should be stored. Next, we unpack or install this SRPM:

```
[root]# rpm -ivh am-utils-6.0.4s5-8.src.rpm

am-utils
####################################################
```

After installing this SRPM, you will find several new files in /usr/src/redhat/SOURCES and /usr/src/redhat/SPECS, as shown in Listing 14.10.

Listing 14.10   Files belonging to the Red Hat am-utils source RPM

```
[root]# cd /usr/src/redhat/SOURCES
[root]# ls -l
total 1336
-rw-rw-r--  1  root   tech   1346429 Jun 16 02:09 am-utils-6.0.4s5.tar.gz
-rw-r--r--  1  root   tech       688 Feb 16 2000 am-utils.conf
-rwxr-xr-x  1  root   tech      1535 Jul  6 12:51 am-utils.init
-rw-r--r--  1  root   tech       105 Mar 21 1999 am-utils.net.map
-rw-r--r--  1  root   tech        56 Mar 21 1999 am-utils.sysconf
[root]# cd /usr/src/redhat/SPECS
[root]# ls -l
total 8
-rw-r--r--  1  root   tech      5999 Jul 15 13:47 am-utils.spec
```

Most of those files are used by the rpm tool itself to rebuild am-utils and even repackage the built Amd back as a binary RPM. However, we are not interested in this here. Rather, we want to unpack the am-utils main tarball (am-utils-6.0.4s5.tar.gz) and build it by hand. The reason we want to build it by hand is that we have previously installed specialized support for Hesiod in a non-standard directory. If we attempt to build am-utils from RPM sources using the default build mode, the Amd we will build will not include all the support we want it to have.

Next, we unpack the sources into /usr/src/am-utils-6.0.4s5. This is seen in Listing 14.11.

Listing 14.11   Unpacking the sources for am-utils

```
[root]# cd /usr/src
[root]# tar xzvf redhat/SOURCES/am-utils-6.0.4s5.tar.gz
am-utils-6.0.4s5/
am-utils-6.0.4s5/aux/
am-utils-6.0.4s5/aux/macros/
am-utils-6.0.4s5/aux/macros/HEADER
am-utils-6.0.4s5/aux/macros/TRAILER
am-utils-6.0.4s5/aux/macros/c_void_p.m4
am-utils-6.0.4s5/aux/macros/cache_check_dynamic.m4
am-utils-6.0.4s5/aux/macros/check_amu_fs.m4
          .
          .
          .

rest of output from tar suppressed
```

Note that we have only listed part of the sources in am-utils. See Appendix A, "Sources in the am-utils Package," for the full listing.

Using am-utils Sources from *www.am-utils.org*

It is probably more likely that you will want to install Amd from a newer source distribution than that which Red Hat distributes. Red Hat gets their am-utils sources directly from the same location you can too: www.am-utils.org. For example, Red Hat 7 distributes am-utils-6.0.4s5, which does not include support for Autofs. To get an Autofs-aware Amd, you have to build am-utils-6.1. To retrieve it, we use wget again, and then we unpack the distribution. See Listing 14.12.

Listing 14.12   Getting the latest am-utils sources

```
[root]# cd /usr/src
[root]# wget ftp://ftp.am-utils.org/pub/am-utils/am-utils-6.1.tar.gz
output of wget suppressed
```

Next, we unpack the sources into /usr/src/am-utils-6.1:

```
[root]# cd /usr/src
[root]# tar xzvf am-utils-6.1.tar.gz
am-utils-6.1/
am-utils-6.1/aux/
am-utils-6.1/aux/macros/
am-utils-6.1/aux/macros/HEADER
am-utils-6.1/aux/macros/TRAILER
am-utils-6.1/aux/macros/c_void_p.m4
am-utils-6.1/aux/macros/cache_check_dynamic.m4
am-utils-6.1/aux/macros/check_amu_fs.m4
.
.
.

rest of output from tar suppressed
```

Note that we had to unpack the sources as user root. It is best to perform as few system administration tasks as root, so as to avoid mistakes and errors from damaging the system. Therefore, after unpacking the am-utils sources, we change the owner of the unpacked tree to a non-root user, ezk:

```
[root]# chown -R ezk /usr/src/am-utils-6.1
```

At this stage, you have accomplished the following steps prior to the actual building of am-utils from sources:

1. Rebuilt and rebooted your new kernel with additional support, if it was necessary

2. Installed support for additional map services such as LDAP and Hesiod

3. Unpacked an am-utils distribution

Building am-utils from Sources

We are now ready to build am-utils from sources. The procedure is the same regardless of which version of am-utils you have unpacked. Therefore, we will show the examples in this section using am-utils-6.1. First, we must cd to the source directory. Then we list the files in the top-level source directory of am-utils, as seen in Listing 14.13.

Listing 14.13 Top-level contents of the am-utils source tree

```
[ezk]$ cd /usr/src/am-utils-6.1
[ezk]$ ls -F
AUTHORS          aclocal.m4         fixmount/
BUGS             amd/               fsinfo/
COPYING          amq/               hlfsd/
ChangeLog        aux/               include/
INSTALL          aux_conf.h.in      install-sh*
LSM.am-utils     buildall*          libamu/
MIRRORS          conf/              ltconfig*
Makefile.am      config.guess*      ltmain.sh
Makefile.in      config.guess.long* missing*
NEWS             config.h.in        mk-amd-map/
README           config.sub*        mkinstalldirs*
README.autofs    configure*         scripts/
README.y2k       configure.in       stamp-h.in
acconfig.h       depcomp*           tasks
acinclude.m4     doc/               wire-test/
```

The contents of the top-level source directory fall into one of three groups:

- Informational files: README, BUGS, NEWS, INSTALL, ChangeLog, etc.
- Software autoconfiguration tools: configure, config.guess, and all of the *.m4, *.in, and *.am files
- Source directories: libamu, amd, amq, scripts, etc.

There are two stages to the build process:

1. Configure the package using configure or buildall.
2. Compile it using make.

Autoconfiguration Options Using *configure*

The am-utils package uses GNU Autoconf, a system of shell scripts that can configure a package before building it. Autoconf does so by running many small tests that detect various system features accurately. It also allows you to set user-specified configuration options. For example, you can set the target installation directory, control building of shared or static libraries, pick a compiler and compile options, tell the compiler to look for additional headers and libraries elsewhere, and more.

Since Autoconf is a generic package configuration tool, it has many options, not all of which are immediately useful to am-utils. We list only a few of those options that are most popular and useful for am-utils. To find out all of the options for the configure script, run it with --help, as can be seen in Listing 14.14.

Listing 14.14   Options available to am-utils's GNU configure script

```
[ezk]$ ./configure --help
Usage: configure [options] [host]
Options: [defaults in brackets after descriptions]
Configuration:
  --cache-file=FILE       cache test results in FILE
  --help                  print this message
  --no-create             do not create output files
  --quiet, --silent       do not print `checking...' messages
  --version               print the version of autoconf that created configure
Directory and file names:
  --prefix=PREFIX         install architecture-independent files in PREFIX
                          [/usr/local]
  --exec-prefix=EPREFIX   install architecture-dependent files in EPREFIX
                          [same as prefix]
  --bindir=DIR            user executables in DIR [EPREFIX/bin]
  --sbindir=DIR           system admin executables in DIR [EPREFIX/sbin]
  --libexecdir=DIR        program executables in DIR [EPREFIX/libexec]
  --datadir=DIR           read-only architecture-independent data in DIR
                          [PREFIX/share]
  --sysconfdir=DIR        read-only single-machine data in DIR [PREFIX/etc]
  --sharedstatedir=DIR    modifiable architecture-independent data in DIR
                          [PREFIX/com]
  --localstatedir=DIR     modifiable single-machine data in DIR [PREFIX/var]
  --libdir=DIR            object code libraries in DIR [EPREFIX/lib]
  --includedir=DIR        C header files in DIR [PREFIX/include]
  --oldincludedir=DIR     C header files for non-gcc in DIR [/usr/include]
  --infodir=DIR           info documentation in DIR [PREFIX/info]
  --mandir=DIR            man documentation in DIR [PREFIX/man]
  --srcdir=DIR            find the sources in DIR [configure dir or ..]
  --program-prefix=PREFIX prepend PREFIX to installed program names
  --program-suffix=SUFFIX append SUFFIX to installed program names
  --program-transform-name=PROGRAM
                          run sed PROGRAM on installed program names
Host type:
  --build=BUILD           configure for building on BUILD [BUILD=HOST]
  --host=HOST             configure for HOST [guessed]
  --target=TARGET         configure for TARGET [TARGET=HOST]
Features and packages:
  --disable-FEATURE       do not include FEATURE (same as --enable-FEATURE=no)
  --enable-FEATURE[=ARG]  include FEATURE [ARG=yes]
```

The Amd
Automounter

PART 2

```
        --with-PACKAGE[=ARG]      use PACKAGE [ARG=yes]
        --without-PACKAGE         do not use PACKAGE (same as --with-PACKAGE=no)
        --x-includes=DIR          X include files are in DIR
        --x-libraries=DIR         X library files are in DIR
--enable and --with options recognized:
  --enable-debug[=ARG]      enable debugging (yes/mem/no)
  --enable-cppflags=ARG     configure/compile with ARG (-I) preprocessor flags
  --enable-libs=ARG         configure/compile with ARG (-l) library flags
  --enable-ldflags=ARG      configure/compile with ARG (-L) library flags
  --enable-am-cflags=ARG    compile package with ARG additional C flags
  --enable-shared[=PKGS]    build shared libraries [default=no]
  --enable-static[=PKGS]    build static libraries [default=yes]
  --enable-fast-install[=PKGS]
                            optimize for fast installation [default=yes]
  --with-gnu-ld             assume the C compiler uses GNU ld [default=no]
  --disable-libtool-lock    avoid locking (might break parallel builds)
```

For more information on the GNU autoconfiguration suite of tools, make sure you have the following three RPMs installed on your system: autoconf, automake, and libtool. Then, use the info command to view detailed instructions of those three tools:

```
[ezk]$ info autoconf
```

```
[ezk]$ info automake
```

```
[ezk]$ info libtool
```

When building the am-utils package, the most useful configuration options that you can pass to the ./configure script are described in the following sections.

--help   The --help option reminds you of all the other options. If there is one option you should always remember, this is the one.

--prefix=PREFIX   The --prefix=PREFIX option sets the installation directory to PREFIX. The default value for this is /usr/local. After the package is configured and built, installing it (via make install) will place headers in PREFIX/include, libraries in PREFIX/lib, binaries in PREFIX/bin and PREFIX/sbin, and so on. Since I build and install Amd on many systems with different needs, I often configure am-utils with --prefix= /usr/local/AMD. That way all the files in my package get installed in a separate unique directory and do not get mixed with files from other packages.

--srcdir=DIR   If you plan on building am-utils for more than one different system, you should build the binaries in separate directories. To avoid mixing binaries for different systems, you should build am-utils anywhere other than inside the unpacked source directory. If you do so, however, you have to tell the configure script where your sources actually reside by setting DIR to the relative or absolute path name where the top-level am-utils source directory is.

> **NOTE** In a newer version of GNU Autoconf, the --srcdir=*DIR* option is not always necessary. If you execute a configure script from the place it was unpacked and you are in a different directory, it would automatically assume that the sources are located where the configure script is.

--enable-debug[=*ARG*] The --enable-debug[=*ARG*] option tells am-utils to include code for debugging and tracing Amd's actions, as we discussed in Chapter 9, "The Amd Configuration File." The value of *ARG* can be as follows:

- Left empty, which is the same as yes
- yes, to include debugging options useful for administrators
- mem, to include additional memory debugging options useful for am-utils maintainers
- no, to exclude debugging code

--enable-cppflags=*ARG* The --enable-cppflags=*ARG* option tells am-utils to include additional search directories for C headers during both the configuration and the compilation phases. This is useful, for example, to look for Hesiod headers in a non-standard directory. Standard header directories where gcc searches are /usr/include and /usr/local/include.

--enable-libs=*ARG* The --enable-libs=*ARG* option tells am-utils to link with additional libraries during both the configuration and the compilation phases. You can use this option, for example, to build with a non-standard C library (libc) that may be installed in a location other than /usr/lib.

--enable-ldflags=*ARG* The --enable-ldflags=*ARG* option tells am-utils to include additional search directories for libraries during both the configuration and the compilation phases. This is useful, for example, to look for Hesiod libraries in a non-standard directory. Standard library search directories where gcc searches are /usr/lib and /usr/local/lib.

--enable-am-cflags=*ARG* The --enable-am-cflags=*ARG* option tells am-utils to turn on additional compile flags, but *only* during the compilation phase. For example, suppose you want to turn on strict compilation options for gcc: -Wall -Werror. You can use the --enable-am-cflags configuration option to turn these two options on. However, if you turn on these -W options during the configuration phase, even the slightest warning will result in a configuration error and am-utils will not configure correctly: many valid features might get missed.

If you wish to turn on additional C flags for both the configuration and the compilation phases, set the CFLAGS environment variable to those flags before configuring. For example, to turn on maximal compile optimizations, you can use the following:

```
[ezk]$ CFLAGS=-O6 ./configure
```

--enable-shared[=*PKGS*] and --enable-static[=*PKGS*]   Packages that can build libraries have the option to build and install shared libraries, static libraries, or both. Shared libraries are useful when you have several binaries that need to link with the same library, as they save disk space. Also, you can replace a shared library with one that fixes bugs and adds additional features without recompiling or relinking executables. However, binaries linked with shared libraries can take slightly more time to start the first time. Static binaries are bigger, but they start a little faster and are mostly useful if you wish to distribute a single working binary without having to include additional shared libraries as well.

You can set *PKGS* to yes or no to turn on or off the building of static or shared libraries. The am-utils package includes only one library. When your package contains multiple libraries, you can control exactly which of the libraries will be built as static and which will be built as shared.

The following are a series of progressively more complex configuration examples. They all assume that you have unpacked am-utils-6.1 into /usr/src/am-utils-6.1 and your current working directory is there.

The simplest configuration option, for installing am-utils in /usr/local, is seen in Listing 14.15.

Listing 14.15   Simple configuration of am-utils

```
[ezk]$ ./configure
creating cache ./config.cache
*** INITIALIZATION:
*** SYSTEM TYPES:
checking host system type... i686-pc-linux-gnu
checking host cpu... i686
checking vendor... pc
checking host full OS name and version... linux
checking host OS name... linux
checking host OS version... 2.2.16-22
checking host OS architecture... i386
checking host name... lorien.cs.columbia.edu
```

```
checking user name... ezk
.
.
.
```
rest of configure output suppressed

We omitted the rest of the output from the configure script (and subsequent examples in this section) because it is rather long. See the upcoming section "Excerpts from a Full Run of buildall" for a more detailed explanation and a longer configuration example.

To configure for installing in a different directory, say /usr/local/AMD, use the --prefix option:

```
[ezk]$ ./configure --prefix=/usr/local/AMD
```

To enable debugging, disable building of static libraries, and enable building of shared libraries, use the following --enable options:

```
[ezk]$ ./configure --enable-debug=yes --enable-static=no \
>        --enable-shared=yes
```

A shorter version of the above example is to use the --disable option and omit yes when it is obvious:

```
[ezk]$ ./configure --enable-debug --disable-static --enable-shared
```

Recall in the preceding section "Installing Hesiod before Rebuilding Amd" that we built and installed Hesiod in /usr/local/hesiod. Since that directory is not a standard one where gcc looks for headers and libraries, you must tell am-utils's configure script to search there as well:

```
[ezk]$ ./configure --enable-cppflags=-I/usr/local/hesiod/include \
>        --enable-ldflags=-L/usr/local/hesiod/lib
```

Suppose you want to build two copies of am-utils, one for Linux on i386 systems and one for SPARC systems. Start by creating two build directories, say, under your home directory, and then use the --srcdir configure option to tell the build process where to locate sources. Assuming you logged first into an i386 Linux system and that /usr/src is shared over NFS (unpacked sources are available to both systems), run the following on the i386 system:

```
[ezk]$ cd ~
[ezk]$ mkdir linux-i386
[ezk]$ cd linux-i386
[ezk]$ /usr/src/am-utils-6.1/configure --srcdir=/usr/src/am-utils-6.1
```

The Amd Automounter

PART 2

Now log on to your SPARC system and execute the following:

[ezk]$ **cd ~**

[ezk]$ **mkdir linux-sparc**

[ezk]$ **cd linux-sparc**

[ezk]$ **/usr/src/am-utils-6.1/configure --srcdir=/usr/src/am-utils-6.1**

The actions performed on the two systems are independent: you can even run them concurrently. This can save you time, as you can unpack the am-utils sources once and then build am-utils multiple times concurrently—one build per system.

Note that we have only shown a few of the options available to `configure`. You might get a sense by now that combining a lot of these options together can result in long and tedious commands typed at the shell prompt. For that reason, am-utils comes with a simpler script that can configure and build am-utils for most common cases, `buildall`.

Autoconfiguration Options Using *buildall*

The `buildall` script comes with am-utils and simplifies common build operations. This script is a wrapper script around `configure` and others. To find out the options that this script recognizes, run it with the -h flag, as seen in Listing 14.16.

Listing 14.16   Options available to am-utils's `buildall` script

```
[ezk]$ ./buildall -h
Usage: buildall [-b] [-[cCdD][s]] [-K] [-q] [-h] [-- makeopts]
    -b: build only
    -c:  configure (debugging)
    -cs: configure (debugging, shared libs)
    -C:  configure (strict compile, debugging)
    -Cs: configure (strict compile, debugging, shared libs)
    -d:  configure in /usr/local/AMD (debugging)
    -ds: configure in /usr/local/AMD (debugging, shared libs)
    -D:  configure in /usr/local/AMD (strict compile, debugging)
    -Ds: configure in /usr/local/AMD (strict compile, debugging, shared libs)
    -K: run mkconf to update *.in files (developers only)
    -q: quick configure only (run config.status)
    -h: print usage
    makeopts: options to pass to make (must be last and after a --)
You may pass variables: CFLAGS for build, MAKE for your make program
and AM_CFLAGS for additional build flags.
```

The `buildall` script always builds am-utils in separate build directories. It runs the `config.guess` script that comes with am-utils to generate a unique signature for the system; for example, `i386-pc-linux-rh7.0` or `sparc-pc-linux-rh7.0`. Then the `buildall` script creates a subdirectory under the source directory named A.*GUESSED-CONFIG* where *GUESSED-CONFIG* is the output from the `config.guess` script. The `buildall` script passes `--srcdir=..` to the `configure` script, to tell it to find the am-utils sources in the parent directory.

The options `buildall` provides almost always turn on debugging support in am-utils. This is because most administrators like to compile that support in, even if they do not plan on using it often. The rest of the options fall into various categories:

-b Only compile the package. This is akin to running `make` in the A.* directory.

-c, -C, -d, and -D options   These options only configure (without building) am-utils under different conditions.

-cs, -Cs, -ds, -Ds   These options, ending with s, turn on building of shared libraries.

-c vs. -C and -d vs. -D   Uppercase configuration options include strict compilation options for `gcc`: `-Wall -Werror`.

-c and -C vs. -d and -D   The `-c` and `-C` options configure am-utils for installation in `/usr/local` (the default). The `-d` and `-D` options configure am-utils for installation under `/usr/local/AMD`.

-q   This option skips a full reconfiguration (after at least one run of `configure` took place) and only runs the `config.status` script. This script regenerates `Makefiles` and other files needed to run `make` but does not run a full `configure` script.

With these options in place, you run a typical configuration and building of am-utils as follows:

```
[ezk]$ ./buildall
```

My favorite options turn on debugging support, use strict compilation options to ensure that code compiles correctly, build shared libraries instead of static ones, and prepare am-utils to install in `/usr/local/AMD`:

```
[ezk]$ ./buildall -Ds -b
```

Up until now, we have only seen how to configure am-utils for various options. Next we see how to compile it after configuration.

Compiling am-utils

To compile am-utils, you must first configure it. Then, you should run make in the same directory where you configured it. If you configured for building a single copy of am-utils, then you can compile it in the same directory:

```
[ezk]$ ./configure
[ezk]$ make
output of make command elided
```

We removed the output of the make command in this and subsequent examples because it is long. See the upcoming section "Excerpts from a Full Run of buildall," for more build details.

If you configured am-utils for building in a separate directory, run make there as well:

```
[ezk]$ cd ~
[ezk]$ mkdir linux-i386
[ezk]$ cd linux-i386
[ezk]$ /usr/src/am-utils-6.1/configure --srcdir=/usr/src/am-utils-6.1
[ezk]$ make
```

If you use the buildall script, then depending on the options you gave it, the script may have compiled the sources. See Listing 14.17. Regardless, we can run make clean to clean up any built binaries, and rerun make. Note that buildall automatically generates an A.* directory that we must cd to first.

Listing 14.17 Building am-utils using the buildall script

```
[ezk]$ ./buildall -Ds -b
Configuring/building am-utils in directory ./A.i386-pc-linux-rh7.0 ...
cd ./A.i386-pc-linux-rh7.0
AM_CFLAGS="-Wall -Werror"
export AM_CFLAGS
../configure --prefix=/usr/local/AMD --enable-debug=yes --prefix=/usr/local/
AMD --enable-shared --disable-static --enable-am-cflags=-Wall -Werror
creating cache ./config.cache
*** INITIALIZATION:
*** SYSTEM TYPES:
checking host system type... i686-pc-linux-gnu
   .
   .
   .
```

```
[ezk]$ cd A.i386-pc-linux-rh7.0
[ezk]$ make clean
[ezk]$ make
```

Note in the above example that we have only shown a part of the output from `buildall` but enough to see how it invoked the `configure` script and which A.* directory it used to build am-utils.

WARNING Do not mix building am-utils with `buildall` and `configure` directly. It can cause the make program to confuse the location of the sources. In particular, this can happen if you first build am-utils directly inside the unpacked source directory and then you build it in an alternate directory (using `buildall` or `configure --srcdir`). It is therefore best to use the `buildall` script for most builds of am-utils.

Excerpts from a Full Run of *buildall*

In this section we show a full run of `buildall -Ds -b`. Since it is long, however, we excerpted it and show only a few lines from each configuration and build section. We show each excerpt and then explain briefly what each portion does.

```
Configuring/building am-utils in directory ./A.i386-pc-linux-rh7.0
...
cd ./A.i386-pc-linux-rh7.0
AM_CFLAGS="-Wall -Werror"
export AM_CFLAGS
../configure --prefix=/usr/local/AMD --enable-debug=yes --prefix=
/usr/local/AMD --enable-shared --disable-static --enable-am-cflags=
-Wall -Werror
```

The `buildall` script shows what it is doing first: which directory it is building am-utils in and how it invokes `configure`. Until otherwise noted, the rest of the output comes directly from the `configure` script.

```
creating cache ./config.cache
*** INITIALIZATION:
*** SYSTEM TYPES:
checking host system type... i686-pc-linux-gnu
checking host cpu... i686
```

```
checking vendor... pc

checking host full OS name and version... linux

checking host OS name... linux

checking host OS version... 2.2.16-22

checking host OS architecture... i386

checking host name... lorien.cs.columbia.edu

checking user name... ezk

checking configuration date... Sat Sep  2 20:33:43 EDT 2000
```

Each major configuration section starts with ***. First, we find out system configuration parameters.

```
*** PACKAGE NAME AND VERSION:

checking package name... "am-utils"

checking version of package... "6.1"

checking for a BSD compatible install... /usr/bin/install -c

checking whether build environment is sane... yes

checking whether make sets ${MAKE}... yes

checking for working aclocal... found

checking for working autoconf... found

checking for working automake... found

checking for working autoheader... found

checking for working makeinfo... found
```

Verifying the name of the package and some tools needed to build it.

```
*** OPTION PROCESSING:

checking for debugging options... yes

checking for configuration/compilation (-I) preprocessor flags...
none

checking for configuration/compilation (-l) library flags... none

checking for configuration/compilation (-L) library flags... none

checking for additional C option compilation flags... -Wall -Werror

checking a local configuration file... no
```

Processing compilation options such as --enable ones.

*** PARTICULAR PROGRAMS (part 1):

checking for gcc... gcc

checking whether the C compiler (gcc) works... yes

checking whether the C compiler (gcc) is a cross-compiler... no

checking whether we are using GNU C... yes

checking whether gcc accepts -g... yes

checking if libtool supports shared libraries... yes

checking whether to build shared libraries... yes

checking whether to build static libraries... no

creating libtool

Find out tools used to compile, link, and assemble binaries—either shared or static executables.

*** EXTRA OPTION PROCESSING:

Checking for additional flags passed to configure for use when compiling (but not for configuring) am-utils.

*** UNIX VARIANTS:

checking host headers version... 2.2.16-22

Unix-specific options. Here, we check the version of the Linux system headers, compare it to the running kernel, and ensure that all system header files exist. This is a necessary check on Linux systems, where it is possible to have many kernel versions, different header versions, and packaging (Red Hat, SuSE, Debian, Slackware, etc.).

*** PARTICULAR PROGRAMS (part 2):

checking for a BSD compatible install... /usr/bin/install -c

checking for bison... bison -y

checking for flex... flex

*** GENERIC PROGRAMS:

checking for perl... /usr/bin/perl

Checking for more programs needed to build am-utils, as well as programs needed to install Perl scripts.

```
*** LIBRARY FILES:
checking for clnt_sperrno in -lrpc... no
checking for xdr_fhandle in -lrpcsvc... yes
checking for yp_all in -lnsl... yes
checking for ldap_open in -lldap... -lldap -lber
```

Checking for the existence of various functions and libraries. Note, for example, that the ldap_open function was found to require two LDAP libraries. This would be useful to tell am-utils (later on) to compile LDAP support.

```
*** PARTICULAR LIBRARY FUNCTIONS:
checking for alloca... yes
checking for 8-bit clean memcmp... yes
checking for a file-descriptor leakage clean yp_all... yes
```

This section checks the validity of various functions that are known to be broken on some systems.

```
*** GENERIC LIBRARY FUNCTIONS:
checking for bcopy... yes
checking for bzero... yes
checking for clnt_create... yes
checking for clnt_create_timed... no
```

This long section checks for the existence of many library functions. The compile phase will compile code for these functions only if these functions are found.

```
*** SAVING CONFIGURE STATE:
updating cache ./config.cache
```

After each major section of configuration parameters, we save a cache of the results of those configuration tests. That way, if we have to stop and restart the long configure process, it will be sped up significantly by reading previously computed cached results.

```
*** PARTICULAR HEADER FILES:
checking for dirent.h that defines DIR... yes
checking for sys/wait.h that is POSIX.1 compatible... yes
*** GENERIC HEADER FILES:
checking for arpa/nameser.h... yes
checking for arpa/inet.h... yes
checking for bsd/rpc/rpc.h... no
checking for isofs/cd9660/cd9660_mount.h... no
checking for linux/fs.h... yes
checking for machine/endian.h... no
```

This long section checks for the existence of many system header files. Their existence tells am-utils to include or exclude certain functionality.

```
*** PARTICULAR STRUCTURES:
checking whether stat file-mode macros are broken... no
checking whether time.h and sys/time.h may both be included... yes
checking whether struct tm is in sys/time.h or time.h... time.h
*** GENERIC STRUCTURES:
checking location of NFS protocol header files... linux
checking for struct mntent... yes
checking for struct mnttab... no
checking for struct nfs_args... struct nfs_args
checking for struct nfs_gfs_mount... no
checking for the name of the nfs filehandle field in nfs_args_t...
root
checking for type/structure of NFS V2 filehandle... nfs_fh
checking for type/structure of NFS V3 filehandle... notfound
```

Checking for the existence of various data structures in system headers and whether certain header combinations are allowed. This section includes some of the most vital tests, that if failed, will prevent am-utils from compiling: nfs_args, mntent, and mnttab. The nfs_args data structure must be found and one of mntent or mnttab should be found.

```
*** PARTICULAR TYPEDEFS:
checking for uid_t in sys/types.h... yes
checking type of array argument to getgroups... gid_t
checking for mode_t... yes
*** GENERIC TYPEDEFS:
checking for time_t... yes
checking if plain fhandle type exists... yes
checking type of mount type field in mount() call... char *
checking printf string to print type field of mount() call... %s
checking pointer type of 3rd argument to yp_order()... int
checking non-pointer type of 6th (fromlen) argument to recvfrom()...
int
checking argument type of 5rd argument to authunix_create()... gid_t
```
Checking for C type definitions.

```
*** PARTICULAR COMPILER CHARACTERISTICS:
checking whether byte ordering is bigendian... no
checking for working const... yes
checking for inline... inline
*** GENERIC COMPILER CHARACTERISTICS:
checking if compiler can handle void *... yes
```
Checking for some specific compiler characteristics.

```
*** EXTERNAL DEFINITIONS:
checking if external definition for sys_errlist exists... yes
checking if external definition for optarg exists... yes
checking external function definition for clnt_spcreateerror... yes
checking external function definition for getccent... no
checking external function definition for getdomainname... yes
```

Checking for C extern definitions for various functions and variables. This is to ensure that only one extern definition is used.

*** FIELDS WITHIN STRUCTURES:

checking if mntent_t field mnt_ro exist... no

checking if cdfs_args_t field norrip exist... no

checking if pcfs_args_t field gid exist... no

checking if nfs_args_t field acdirmin exist... yes

checking if nfs_args_t field acregmin exist... yes

checking if struct ifreq field ifr_addr exist... yes

checking if struct ifaddrs field ifa_next exist... no

Many systems define data structures with the same name but containing a different number and name for fields in that data structure. This section runs configuration tests to find these differences so they can be accounted for in the compiled sources.

*** MAP TYPES:

checking for file maps... yes

checking for hesiod maps... no

checking for ldap maps... yes

checking for dbm_open... yes

checking for ndbm maps... yes

Checking for Amd map support. Note that since we installed the LDAP RPMs, am-utils found it. Since we installed Hesiod binaries but did not tell this configure process where to find the headers and libraries for Hesiod, am-utils cannot find support for Hesiod maps.

*** FILESYSTEM TYPES:

checking for autofs mntent definition... yes

checking for cdfs (from: cdfs hsfs cd9660 iso9660 isofs cdrom) mntent definition... yes

checking for nfs mntent definition... yes

```
checking for nfs3 mntent definition... no
```

```
checking for pcfs (from: vfat pcfs pc msdos msdosfs fat) mntent
definition... yes
```

```
checking for tmpfs mntent definition... no
```

```
checking for ufs (from: ext2 ffs ufs 42 efs xfs jfs ultrix) mntent
definition... yes
```

Checking for support for several native file systems. Note that am-utils could not find support for NFSv3 here, because it could not find the NFSv3 data structure in the preceding GENERIC STRUCTURES section.

```
*** AUTOMOUNTER FILESYSTEM TYPES:
```

```
checking for automounter filesystem (auto)... yes
```

```
checking for direct automount filesystem (direct)... yes
```

```
checking for top-level filesystem (toplvl)... yes
```

Checking for non-native file systems, those defined and implemented by Amd. Most of the time they are all available. Where they are not, it is usually the result of failure to locate one or more native file systems in the preceding section.

```
*** MOUNTING TYPES:
```

```
checking for mount(2) type/name for nfs filesystem... MNTTYPE_NFS
```

```
checking for mount(2) type/name for nfs3 filesystem... notfound
```

```
checking for mount(2) type/name for ufs filesystem... "ext2"
```

Finding the file system type (string or macro) that we have to pass to the mount system call, to tell it to perform a mount of that file system.

```
*** MOUNTING TABLE NAMES:
```

```
checking for mnttab name for nfs filesystem... "nfs"
```

```
checking for mnttab name for nfs3 filesystem... notfound
```

```
checking for mnttab name for ufs filesystem... "ext2"
```

Checking for the type and name of file systems, as they are recorded in the mount table file /etc/mtab.

```
*** MOUNT TABLE OPTION NAME STRINGS:
checking for mount table option acdirmax... notfound
checking for mount table option nosuid... "nosuid"
checking for mount table option ro... "ro"
checking for mount table option rw... "rw"
```

Checking how to record mount table option names in /etc/mtab.

```
*** GENERIC MOUNT(2) OPTIONS:
checking for generic mount(2) option nocache... notfound
checking for generic mount(2) option nosuid... 0x2
checking for generic mount(2) option rdonly... 0x1
```

Checking for codes that we have to pass to the mount system call to turn on special mount options. These options are generic because they apply to all types of mounts: EXT2, NFS, ISO9660, etc.

```
*** NFS-SPECIFIC MOUNT(2) OPTIONS:
checking for NFS-specific mount(2) option intr... 0x2
checking for NFS-specific mount(2) option noac... 0x20
checking for NFS-specific mount(2) option posix... 0x8
checking for NFS-specific mount(2) option resvport... notfound
checking for NFS-specific mount(2) option soft... 0x1
Checking for NFS-specific file system mount options.
*** SYSTEM-SPECIFIC TESTS:
checking mount table style... file
checking for mount type to hide from df... nfs
checking for mntctl... (cached) no
checking for getmntinfo... (cached) no
checking for getmountent... (cached) no
```

The Amd
Automounter

PART 2

```
checking where mount table is kept... file
checking for name of mount table file name... /etc/mtab
checking mount trap system-call style... linux
checking style of mounting filesystems... linux
checking style of unmounting filesystems... default
checking autofs style... linux
checking the system call to unmount a filesystem... umount
checking unmount system-call arguments... mnt->mnt_dir
checking nfs address dereferencing style... linux
checking nfs hostname dereferencing style... linux
checking nfs file-handle address dereferencing style... linux
checking if to turn on/off noconn option... none
checking style of fixmount check_mount()... default
checking if system needs to restart signal handlers... no
```

Checking for certain characteristics of the current system: where it stores mount tables, how it calls the mount and unmount system calls, and more.

```
*** OUTPUT FILES:
creating ./config.status
creating aux_conf.h
creating Makefile
creating amd/Makefile
creating amq/Makefile
creating fixmount/Makefile
creating fsinfo/Makefile
creating hlfsd/Makefile
creating libamu/Makefile
creating mk-amd-map/Makefile
creating wire-test/Makefile
creating scripts/Makefile
creating doc/Makefile
```

```
creating scripts/am-eject

creating scripts/amd2ldif

creating scripts/amd2sun

creating scripts/automount2amd

creating scripts/ctl-amd

creating scripts/ctl-hlfsd

creating scripts/expn

creating scripts/fixrmtab

creating scripts/fix-amd-map

creating scripts/lostaltmail

creating scripts/wait4amd

creating scripts/wait4amd2die

creating config.h

linking ../conf/nfs_prot/nfs_prot_linux.h to amu_nfs_prot.h

linking ../conf/transp/transp_sockets.c to libamu/transputil.c

linking ../conf/mtab/mtab_file.c to libamu/mtabutil.c

linking ../conf/mount/mount_linux.c to libamu/mountutil.c

linking ../conf/umount/umount_default.c to libamu/umount_fs.c

linking ../conf/checkmount/checkmount_default.c to fixmount/check_
mount.c
```

Here, the configure script is almost done. It creates various Makefiles and automatically creates header files such as config.h, which record all the options configured during its run and various scripts that will be installed. Finally, configure creates symbolic links to a few files based on the characteristics of the running system.

*** END OF CONFIGURATION:

The configure script is done. Next we begin compilation:

gmake

This line of output comes from buildall. It prefers to execute GNU's make (gmake) whenever found, because gmake provides more functionality and is more stable than some vendors' own tools. Otherwise it will run make (which is not GNU's make on some systems).

```
gmake  all-recursive
```

```
gmake[1]: Entering directory `/usr/src/am-utils-6.1/A.i386-pc-linux-
rh7.0'
```

Making all in libamu

```
gmake[2]: Entering directory `/usr/src/am-utils-6.1/A.i386-pc-linux-
rh7.0/libamu'
```

```
/bin/sh ../libtool --mode=compile gcc -DHAVE_CONFIG_H -I. -I../../
libamu -I.. -I../../include   -Wall -Werror -g -O2  -Wall -Werror -c
../../libamu/misc_rpc.c
```

```
gcc -DHAVE_CONFIG_H -I. -I../../libamu -I.. -I../../include -Wall -
Werror -g -O2 -Wall -Werror -c ../../libamu/misc_rpc.c  -fPIC -DPIC -
o misc_rpc.lo
```

```
.

.

.
```

```
gcc -shared  misc_rpc.lo mount_fs.lo mtab.lo nfs_prot_xdr.lo util.lo
wire.lo xdr_func.lo xutil.lo transputil.lo mtabutil.lo mountutil.lo
umount_fs.lo   -Wl,-soname -Wl,libamu.so.2 -o .libs/libamu.so.2.2.0
```

The make process begins by building the libamu.so shared library.

```
gcc -DHAVE_CONFIG_H -I. -I../../amd -I.. -I../../include   -Wall -
Werror -g -O2  -Wall -Werror -c ../../amd/amd.c
```

```
.

.

.
```

```
/bin/sh ../libtool --mode=link gcc -Wall -Werror -g -O2  -Wall -
Werror  -o amd  am_ops.o amd.o amfs_auto.o amfs_direct.o amfs_error.o
amfs_host.o amfs_inherit.o amfs_link.o amfs_linkx.o amfs_nfsl.o amfs_
nfsx.o amfs_program.o amfs_root.o amfs_toplvl.o amfs_union.o amq_
subr.o amq_svc.o autil.o clock.o conf.o get_args.o map.o mapc.o
mntfs.o nfs_prot_svc.o nfs_start.o nfs_subr.o opts.o restart.o rpc_
fwd.o sched.o srvr_amfs_auto.o srvr_nfs.o ops_autofs.o ops_cdfs.o
ops_nfs.o ops_pcfs.o ops_ufs.o info_file.o info_ldap.o info_ndbm.o
info_nis.o info_nisplus.o info_passwd.o info_union.o conf_tok.o conf_
parse.o ../libamu/libamu.la -lgdbm -lldap -lber -lnsl -lrpcsvc  -lfl
```

mkdir .libs

libtool: link: warning: library `/usr/lib/libgdbm.la' was moved.

libtool: link: warning: library `/usr/lib/libgdbm.la' was moved.

```
gcc -Wall -Werror -g -O2 -Wall -Werror -o .libs/amd am_ops.o amd.o
amfs_auto.o amfs_direct.o amfs_error.o amfs_host.o amfs_inherit.o
amfs_link.o amfs_linkx.o amfs_nfsl.o amfs_nfsx.o amfs_program.o amfs_
root.o amfs_toplvl.o amfs_union.o amq_subr.o amq_svc.o autil.o
clock.o conf.o get_args.o map.o mapc.o mntfs.o nfs_prot_svc.o nfs_
start.o nfs_subr.o opts.o restart.o rpc_fwd.o sched.o srvr_amfs_
auto.o srvr_nfs.o ops_autofs.o ops_cdfs.o ops_nfs.o ops_pcfs.o ops_
ufs.o info_file.o info_ldap.o info_ndbm.o info_nis.o info_nisplus.o
info_passwd.o info_union.o conf_tok.o conf_parse.o  ../libamu/.libs/
libamu.so -L/usr/src/bs/BUILD/openldap-1.2.9/libraries /usr/lib/
libgdbm.so /usr/lib/libldap.so /usr/lib/liblber.so -lnsl -lrpcsvc
-lfl -Wl,--rpath -Wl,/usr/local/AMD/lib

creating amd

gmake[2]: Leaving directory `/usr/src/am-utils-6.1/A.i386-pc-linux-
rh7.0/amd'
```

The build process compiles the sources for Amd and then links it with the `libamu.so` shared library. After that, make goes on to building amq, scripts, and other programs.

```
gmake[1]: Leaving directory `/usr/src/am-utils-6.1/A.i386-pc-linux-
rh7.0'
```

The make process is done.

Preliminary Testing of am-utils before Installation

After a successful compile of am-utils, you should run amd -v on the version just built and verify that it indeed runs and that it includes the features you expected. This is seen in Listing 14.18.

Listing 14.18   Initial testing of an Amd binary built from sources

```
[ezk]$ ./amd/amd -v
Copyright (c) 1997-2000 Erez Zadok
Copyright (c) 1990 Jan-Simon Pendry
Copyright (c) 1990 Imperial College of Science, Technology & Medicine
Copyright (c) 1990 The Regents of the University of California.
am-utils version 6.1 (build 1).
Built by ezk@lorien.cs.columbia.edu on date Sat Sep  2 20:33:43 EDT 2000.
cpu=i686 (little-endian), arch=i386, karch=i686.
full_os=linux, os=linux, osver=2.2.16-22, vendor=pc.
Map support for: root, passwd, ldap, union, nisplus, nis, ndbm, file, error.
AMFS: nfs, link, nfsx, nfsl, host, linkx, program, union, inherit, ufs,
      cdfs, pcfs, auto, direct, toplvl, error.
FS: autofs, iso9660, nfs, vfat, ext2.
Network: wire="ezk-apt-net.cs.columbia.edu" (netnumber=128.59.8.24).
```

Note, for example, that we expected to have support for LDAP and Autofs but not for Hesiod or NFSv3 (the latter two were not detected during the configure phase).

You may now run ./amd/amd on any test amd.conf file you have to see if it performs as expected, as was described in Chapter 9. You can also try any of the other programs and scripts just built, as explained in Chapter 11, "Runtime Automounter Administration."

Common Build Problems

If am-utils did not configure or compile correctly, it usually stems from several possibilities:

Missing software   Make sure that all RPMs that your system needs are installed. If you suspect that your installation might be damaged, you can always reinstall those RPMs.

Mismatching system headers   Ensure that your running kernel is the same as the version of your system headers. If they are not the same, the configure script will warn you about it. To find the version of your running system, compare the output of uname -r to the contents of the system version files:

```
[ezk]$ uname -r
2.2.16-22
[ezk]$ grep UTS_RELEASE /usr/include/linux/version.h \
> /usr/include/linux/version-up.h
/usr/include/linux/version.h:#define UTS_RELEASE "2.2.16-22"
```

Misconfigured kernel   If the file /usr/include/linux/version.h cannot be found, your Linux system is not configured. In particular, this happens if you unpack a new version of the Linux kernel, but you do not configure it. If am-utils fails to find the version.h file, it will abort the configuration process until the problem is fixed. To find out how to configure your Linux kernel, see Chapter 7.

Using unstable kernels and libraries   If you are running a new version of the Linux kernel, especially from a development series (such as 2.3 or 2.5), it is possible that am-utils will not build correctly. This often happens because development Linux kernels change often and in incompatible ways. The same can happen if you use development versions of glibc. To solve this, try to use the latest official versions of that software, or see if a newer version of am-utils supports those development kernels and libraries.

Using an older version of am-utils   Am-utils is constantly under development. You can often find newer snapshots of upcoming releases, as well as alpha and beta cuts of am-utils available in ftp.am-utils.org. If you are facing a build problem with am-utils, and you have tried the other solutions mentioned here, you can then try the latest version of am-utils, even if it is not an official release.

If you tried all of these suggestions and nothing helped, you should contact your local administrator or post a message to one of the Amd mailing lists. To find more information about those lists, see Appendix B.

Installing Software Built from Sources

Once you have successfully built am-utils, you can install it using the make command as follows:

```
[root]# cd /usr/src/am-utils-6.1/A.i386-pc-linux-rh7.0
[root]# make install
long output suppressed
```

Recall that we configured am-utils to install into /usr/local/AMD; that is where make install installs the various files in. Note also that you will most likely have to install it while running as the superuser.

It is possible that your system had a Red Hat–installed am-utils RPM. In that case, you may check for and remove that installation:

```
[root]# rpm -q am-utils
am-utils-6.0.4s5-8
[root]# rpm -e am-utils
```

You can now start Amd—or restart it, if it is already running—using the ctl-amd script. When run without arguments, the script will show you what it does. Then you can give it the restart option to restart the new automounter just built and installed, as seen in Listing 14.19.

Listing 14.19   Restarting Amd using ctl-amd

```
[root]# /usr/local/AMD/sbin/ctl-amd
Usage: /usr/local/AMD/sbin/ctl-amd [ start | stop | restart | status]
[root]# /usr/local/AMD/sbin/ctl-amd restart
killing amd...
wait4amd2die: delay 5 sec (1 of 6)...
wait4amd2die: amd is down!
Restarting amd...
Sep  2 22:43:34 lorien amd[3728]/info:  using configuration file  /etc/
amd.conf
```

That procedure showed how to start Amd by hand. To make sure it starts at boot time, you have to turn off any previous start of Amd, copy the new startup script to the system initialization location, and then reconfigure Amd to start at boot time:

```
[root]# chkconfig amd off
[root]# cp /usr/local/AMD/sbin/ctl-amd /etc/rc.d/init.d/amd
[root]# chkconfig amd on
```

To be sure Amd starts at boot time, you also want to reboot your system. At this stage you have a fully rebuilt am-utils installed and configured to start at boot time.

In Sum

Using Amd is easy for many administrators: just get and install the precompiled binaries that come with your Linux distribution. Sometimes, however, the precompiled binaries are not sufficient. In this chapter we saw how to retrieve new sources for am-utils and related packages. We then described how to configure these packages and build them. You may need this to provide new functionality, run code that fixes bugs, or discover new system features.

Occasionally, you will have to rebuild your Linux kernel to turn on new operating systems features before Amd can use them. You may also have to retrieve user-level packages that support additional features for Amd to use. These procedures were described in Chapter 7.

Finally, while this chapter shows many aspects of building this software, most administrators will not have to rebuild am-utils often. If you do, we suggest using the simpler configure and build script, `buildall`, which comes with am-utils.

Appendices

Featuring:

- Appendix A: Sources in the am-utils Package
- Appendix B: Online Resources
- Appendix C: Amd Log and Debug Messages
- Appendix D: Amd Configuration File Parameters and Command-Line Flags

Sources in the am-utils Package

This appendix includes the complete list of all files in the am-utils package. Use this list to ensure that your source package is complete. The annotations explain what each file does. The latter is particularly helpful if you intend to modify any of the sources in the am-utils package. Note that the sources for the am-utils package are rarely changed by users. Experienced programmers who understand Amd and NFS well can make changes and submit them to the maintainers of the am-utils package for consideration. If you are interested in participating in this effort, see Appendix B, "Online Resources," for information about Amd-related mailing lists.

We annotate each subset of files together and explain their meaning and use before we list each subset of files. Note also that this set of sources is for am-utils version 6.1a3. Check the resources in Appendix B to ensure that you have the very latest version of am-utils.

Annotated List of Sources

The following directory contains auxiliary files that help in building am-utils:

```
am-utils-6.1a3/aux/
```

The macros directory contains many M4 tests specially written to help automate the building of am-utils. These macros are used in conjunction with GNU Autoconf:

am-utils-6.1a3/aux/macros/

am-utils-6.1a3/aux/macros/HEADER

am-utils-6.1a3/aux/macros/TRAILER

am-utils-6.1a3/aux/macros/c_void_p.m4

am-utils-6.1a3/aux/macros/cache_check_dynamic.m4

am-utils-6.1a3/aux/macros/check_amu_fs.m4

am-utils-6.1a3/aux/macros/check_checkmount_style.m4

am-utils-6.1a3/aux/macros/check_extern.m4

am-utils-6.1a3/aux/macros/check_fhandle.m4

am-utils-6.1a3/aux/macros/check_field.m4

am-utils-6.1a3/aux/macros/check_fs_headers.m4

am-utils-6.1a3/aux/macros/check_fs_mntent.m4

am-utils-6.1a3/aux/macros/check_hide_mount_type.m4

am-utils-6.1a3/aux/macros/check_lib2.m4

am-utils-6.1a3/aux/macros/check_map_funcs.m4

am-utils-6.1a3/aux/macros/check_mnt2_cdfs_opt.m4

am-utils-6.1a3/aux/macros/check_mnt2_gen_opt.m4

am-utils-6.1a3/aux/macros/check_mnt2_nfs_opt.m4

am-utils-6.1a3/aux/macros/check_mnttab_opt.m4

am-utils-6.1a3/aux/macros/check_mnttab_file_name.m4

am-utils-6.1a3/aux/macros/check_mnttab_location.m4

am-utils-6.1a3/aux/macros/check_mnttab_style.m4

am-utils-6.1a3/aux/macros/check_mnttab_type.m4

am-utils-6.1a3/aux/macros/check_mount_style.m4

am-utils-6.1a3/aux/macros/check_mount_trap.m4

am-utils-6.1a3/aux/macros/check_mount_type.m4

am-utils-6.1a3/aux/macros/check_mtype_printf_type.m4

am-utils-6.1a3/aux/macros/check_mtype_type.m4

am-utils-6.1a3/aux/macros/check_network_transport_type.m4

am-utils-6.1a3/aux/macros/check_nfs_fh_dref.m4

am-utils-6.1a3/aux/macros/check_nfs_hn_dref.m4

am-utils-6.1a3/aux/macros/check_nfs_prot_headers.m4

am-utils-6.1a3/aux/macros/check_nfs_sa_dref.m4

am-utils-6.1a3/aux/macros/check_nfs_socket_connection.m4

am-utils-6.1a3/aux/macros/check_os_libs.m4

am-utils-6.1a3/aux/macros/check_restartable_signal_handler.m4

am-utils-6.1a3/aux/macros/check_umount_style.m4

am-utils-6.1a3/aux/macros/check_unmount_args.m4

am-utils-6.1a3/aux/macros/check_unmount_call.m4

am-utils-6.1a3/aux/macros/expand_cpp_hex.m4

am-utils-6.1a3/aux/macros/expand_cpp_int.m4

am-utils-6.1a3/aux/macros/expand_cpp_string.m4

am-utils-6.1a3/aux/macros/expand_run_string.m4

am-utils-6.1a3/aux/macros/extern_optarg.m4

am-utils-6.1a3/aux/macros/extern_sys_errlist.m4

am-utils-6.1a3/aux/macros/field_mntent_t_mnt_time_string.m4

am-utils-6.1a3/aux/macros/func_bad_memcmp.m4

am-utils-6.1a3/aux/macros/func_bad_yp_all.m4

am-utils-6.1a3/aux/macros/host_macros.m4

am-utils-6.1a3/aux/macros/linux_headers.m4

am-utils-6.1a3/aux/macros/localconfig.m4

am-utils-6.1a3/aux/macros/mount_headers.m4

am-utils-6.1a3/aux/macros/msg.m4

am-utils-6.1a3/aux/macros/name_package.m4

am-utils-6.1a3/aux/macros/name_version.m4

am-utils-6.1a3/aux/macros/opt_amu_cflags.m4

am-utils-6.1a3/aux/macros/opt_cppflags.m4

am-utils-6.1a3/aux/macros/opt_debug.m4

am-utils-6.1a3/aux/macros/opt_ldflags.m4

am-utils-6.1a3/aux/macros/opt_libs.m4

Appendices

```
am-utils-6.1a3/aux/macros/os_cflags.m4
am-utils-6.1a3/aux/macros/os_cppflags.m4
am-utils-6.1a3/aux/macros/os_ldflags.m4
am-utils-6.1a3/aux/macros/save_state.m4
am-utils-6.1a3/aux/macros/struct_field_nfs_fh.m4
am-utils-6.1a3/aux/macros/struct_mntent.m4
am-utils-6.1a3/aux/macros/struct_mnttab.m4
am-utils-6.1a3/aux/macros/struct_nfs_args.m4
am-utils-6.1a3/aux/macros/struct_nfs_fh.m4
am-utils-6.1a3/aux/macros/struct_nfs_fh3.m4
am-utils-6.1a3/aux/macros/struct_nfs_gfs_mount.m4
am-utils-6.1a3/aux/macros/try_compile_anyfs.m4
am-utils-6.1a3/aux/macros/try_compile_nfs.m4
am-utils-6.1a3/aux/macros/try_compile_rpc.m4
am-utils-6.1a3/aux/macros/type_auth_create_gidlist.m4
am-utils-6.1a3/aux/macros/type_autofs_args.m4
am-utils-6.1a3/aux/macros/type_cachefs_args.m4
am-utils-6.1a3/aux/macros/type_cdfs_args.m4
am-utils-6.1a3/aux/macros/type_efs_args.m4
am-utils-6.1a3/aux/macros/type_lofs_args.m4
am-utils-6.1a3/aux/macros/type_mfs_args.m4
am-utils-6.1a3/aux/macros/type_pcfs_args.m4
am-utils-6.1a3/aux/macros/type_recvfrom_fromlen.m4
am-utils-6.1a3/aux/macros/type_rfs_args.m4
am-utils-6.1a3/aux/macros/type_svc_in_arg.m4
am-utils-6.1a3/aux/macros/type_time_t.m4
am-utils-6.1a3/aux/macros/type_tmpfs_args.m4
am-utils-6.1a3/aux/macros/type_ufs_args.m4
am-utils-6.1a3/aux/macros/type_xdrproc_t.m4
am-utils-6.1a3/aux/macros/type_xfs_args.m4
am-utils-6.1a3/aux/macros/type_yp_order_outorder.m4
```

These auxiliary files are part of GNU Autoconf, Automake, and Libtool. They perform various functions such as produce ready-to-use Makefiles and the large `configure` script at the top-level directory of the source tree. Note that most of these files reside in the top-level source directory:

```
am-utils-6.1a3/aux/GNUmakefile
am-utils-6.1a3/aux/amindent
am-utils-6.1a3/aux/autopat
am-utils-6.1a3/aux/chop-aclocal.pl
am-utils-6.1a3/aux/mk-aclocal
am-utils-6.1a3/aux/mkconf
am-utils-6.1a3/aux/rmtspc
am-utils-6.1a3/aux/update_build_version
am-utils-6.1a3/aux/copy-if-newbig
am-utils-6.1a3/aclocal.m4
am-utils-6.1a3/configure.in
am-utils-6.1a3/aux_conf.h.in
am-utils-6.1a3/config.guess
am-utils-6.1a3/config.h.in
am-utils-6.1a3/config.sub
am-utils-6.1a3/install-sh
am-utils-6.1a3/ltconfig
am-utils-6.1a3/ltmain.sh
am-utils-6.1a3/missing
am-utils-6.1a3/mkinstalldirs
am-utils-6.1a3/stamp-h.in
am-utils-6.1a3/acconfig.h
am-utils-6.1a3/acinclude.m4
am-utils-6.1a3/config.guess.long
am-utils-6.1a3/depcomp
```

This directory contains various source configuration files for different operating systems:

```
am-utils-6.1a3/conf/
```

Appendices

This directory contains helper code for the `fixmount` program:

```
am-utils-6.1a3/conf/checkmount/
am-utils-6.1a3/conf/checkmount/checkmount_aix.c
am-utils-6.1a3/conf/checkmount/checkmount_bsd44.c
am-utils-6.1a3/conf/checkmount/checkmount_default.c
am-utils-6.1a3/conf/checkmount/checkmount_osf.c
am-utils-6.1a3/conf/checkmount/checkmount_svr4.c
am-utils-6.1a3/conf/checkmount/checkmount_ultrix.c
```

This directory contains C code for dereferencing NFS file handles on different systems:

```
am-utils-6.1a3/conf/fh_dref/
am-utils-6.1a3/conf/fh_dref/fh_dref_aix3.h
am-utils-6.1a3/conf/fh_dref/fh_dref_aix42.h
am-utils-6.1a3/conf/fh_dref/fh_dref_bsd44.h
am-utils-6.1a3/conf/fh_dref/fh_dref_default.h
am-utils-6.1a3/conf/fh_dref/fh_dref_freebsd22.h
am-utils-6.1a3/conf/fh_dref/fh_dref_hpux.h
am-utils-6.1a3/conf/fh_dref/fh_dref_irix.h
am-utils-6.1a3/conf/fh_dref/fh_dref_isc3.h
am-utils-6.1a3/conf/fh_dref/fh_dref_linux.h
am-utils-6.1a3/conf/fh_dref/fh_dref_nextstep.h
am-utils-6.1a3/conf/fh_dref/fh_dref_osf2.h
am-utils-6.1a3/conf/fh_dref/fh_dref_osf4.h
am-utils-6.1a3/conf/fh_dref/fh_dref_sunos3.h
am-utils-6.1a3/conf/fh_dref/fh_dref_sunos4.h
am-utils-6.1a3/conf/fh_dref/fh_dref_svr4.h
```

This directory contains system-specific C code for dereferencing NFS hostnames:

```
am-utils-6.1a3/conf/hn_dref/
am-utils-6.1a3/conf/hn_dref/hn_dref_default.h
am-utils-6.1a3/conf/hn_dref/hn_dref_isc3.h
am-utils-6.1a3/conf/hn_dref/hn_dref_linux.h
```

This directory contains helper code for the mount(2) system call on different platforms:

```
am-utils-6.1a3/conf/mount/
am-utils-6.1a3/conf/mount/mount_aix.c
am-utils-6.1a3/conf/mount/mount_bsdi3.c
am-utils-6.1a3/conf/mount/mount_default.c
am-utils-6.1a3/conf/mount/mount_hpux.c
am-utils-6.1a3/conf/mount/mount_irix5.c
am-utils-6.1a3/conf/mount/mount_irix6.c
am-utils-6.1a3/conf/mount/mount_isc3.c
am-utils-6.1a3/conf/mount/mount_linux.c
am-utils-6.1a3/conf/mount/mount_mach3.c
am-utils-6.1a3/conf/mount/mount_stellix.c
am-utils-6.1a3/conf/mount/mount_svr4.c
```

This directory contains code for handling /etc/mtab on different systems:

```
am-utils-6.1a3/conf/mtab/
am-utils-6.1a3/conf/mtab/mtab_aix.c
am-utils-6.1a3/conf/mtab/mtab_bsd.c
am-utils-6.1a3/conf/mtab/mtab_file.c
am-utils-6.1a3/conf/mtab/mtab_isc3.c
am-utils-6.1a3/conf/mtab/mtab_mach3.c
am-utils-6.1a3/conf/mtab/mtab_osf.c
am-utils-6.1a3/conf/mtab/mtab_svr4.c
am-utils-6.1a3/conf/mtab/mtab_ultrix.c
```

This directory contains vital files that set the configuration and primary features for NFS, RPC, and other file systems on different systems. This is the first place to check and update when working on new ports of am-utils:

```
am-utils-6.1a3/conf/nfs_prot/
am-utils-6.1a3/conf/nfs_prot/nfs_prot_aix3.h
am-utils-6.1a3/conf/nfs_prot/nfs_prot_aix4.h
am-utils-6.1a3/conf/nfs_prot/nfs_prot_aix4_2.h
am-utils-6.1a3/conf/nfs_prot/nfs_prot_aix4_3.h
```

Appendices

```
am-utils-6.1a3/conf/nfs_prot/nfs_prot_bsdi2.h
am-utils-6.1a3/conf/nfs_prot/nfs_prot_bsdi3.h
am-utils-6.1a3/conf/nfs_prot/nfs_prot_default.h
am-utils-6.1a3/conf/nfs_prot/nfs_prot_freebsd2.h
am-utils-6.1a3/conf/nfs_prot/nfs_prot_freebsd3.h
am-utils-6.1a3/conf/nfs_prot/nfs_prot_hpux.h
am-utils-6.1a3/conf/nfs_prot/nfs_prot_hpux11.h
am-utils-6.1a3/conf/nfs_prot/nfs_prot_irix5.h
am-utils-6.1a3/conf/nfs_prot/nfs_prot_irix6.h
am-utils-6.1a3/conf/nfs_prot/nfs_prot_linux.h
am-utils-6.1a3/conf/nfs_prot/nfs_prot_ncr2.h
am-utils-6.1a3/conf/nfs_prot/nfs_prot_nextstep.h
am-utils-6.1a3/conf/nfs_prot/nfs_prot_netbsd.h
am-utils-6.1a3/conf/nfs_prot/nfs_prot_openbsd.h
am-utils-6.1a3/conf/nfs_prot/nfs_prot_netbsd1_3.h
am-utils-6.1a3/conf/nfs_prot/nfs_prot_netbsd1_4.h
am-utils-6.1a3/conf/nfs_prot/nfs_prot_osf2.h
am-utils-6.1a3/conf/nfs_prot/nfs_prot_osf4.h
am-utils-6.1a3/conf/nfs_prot/nfs_prot_osf5_1.h
am-utils-6.1a3/conf/nfs_prot/nfs_prot_sunos3.h
am-utils-6.1a3/conf/nfs_prot/nfs_prot_sunos4.h
am-utils-6.1a3/conf/nfs_prot/nfs_prot_sunos5_3.h
am-utils-6.1a3/conf/nfs_prot/nfs_prot_sunos5_4.h
am-utils-6.1a3/conf/nfs_prot/nfs_prot_sunos5_5.h
am-utils-6.1a3/conf/nfs_prot/nfs_prot_sunos5_6.h
am-utils-6.1a3/conf/nfs_prot/nfs_prot_sunos5_7.h
am-utils-6.1a3/conf/nfs_prot/nfs_prot_sunos5_8.h
am-utils-6.1a3/conf/nfs_prot/nfs_prot_svr4.h
am-utils-6.1a3/conf/nfs_prot/nfs_prot_ultrix.h
```

This directory contains code for dereferencing socket addresses on different systems:

```
am-utils-6.1a3/conf/sa_dref/

am-utils-6.1a3/conf/sa_dref/sa_dref_386bsd.h

am-utils-6.1a3/conf/sa_dref/sa_dref_aix3.h

am-utils-6.1a3/conf/sa_dref/sa_dref_aoi.h

am-utils-6.1a3/conf/sa_dref/sa_dref_bsd44.h

am-utils-6.1a3/conf/sa_dref/sa_dref_default.h

am-utils-6.1a3/conf/sa_dref/sa_dref_isc3.h

am-utils-6.1a3/conf/sa_dref/sa_dref_linux.h

am-utils-6.1a3/conf/sa_dref/sa_dref_svr4.h
```

This directory contains networking code that is specific to either socket-based or TLI-based (SVr4) systems:

```
am-utils-6.1a3/conf/transp/

am-utils-6.1a3/conf/transp/transp_sockets.c

am-utils-6.1a3/conf/transp/transp_tli.c
```

This directory describes actual calling conventions for the mount(2) system call on different platforms:

```
am-utils-6.1a3/conf/trap/

am-utils-6.1a3/conf/trap/trap_aix3.h

am-utils-6.1a3/conf/trap/trap_aux.h

am-utils-6.1a3/conf/trap/trap_default.h

am-utils-6.1a3/conf/trap/trap_dgux.h

am-utils-6.1a3/conf/trap/trap_hcx.h

am-utils-6.1a3/conf/trap/trap_hpux.h

am-utils-6.1a3/conf/trap/trap_hpux11.h

am-utils-6.1a3/conf/trap/trap_irix.h

am-utils-6.1a3/conf/trap/trap_isc3.h

am-utils-6.1a3/conf/trap/trap_linux.h

am-utils-6.1a3/conf/trap/trap_mach3.h

am-utils-6.1a3/conf/trap/trap_news4.h

am-utils-6.1a3/conf/trap/trap_rtu6.h
```

Appendices

```
am-utils-6.1a3/conf/trap/trap_stellix.h

am-utils-6.1a3/conf/trap/trap_svr4.h

am-utils-6.1a3/conf/trap/trap_ultrix.h
```

This directory contains helper code for the unmount(2) system call:

```
am-utils-6.1a3/conf/umount/

am-utils-6.1a3/conf/umount/umount_bsd44.c

am-utils-6.1a3/conf/umount/umount_default.c

am-utils-6.1a3/conf/umount/umount_osf.c
```

This directory contains support code and headers for Autofs for different operating systems and versions of the Autofs protocol:

```
am-utils-6.1a3/conf/autofs/

am-utils-6.1a2/conf/autofs/autofs_default.c

am-utils-6.1a2/conf/autofs/autofs_default.h

am-utils-6.1a2/conf/autofs/autofs_linux.c

am-utils-6.1a3/conf/autofs/autofs_linux.h

am-utils-6.1a2/conf/autofs/autofs_solaris_v1.c

am-utils-6.1a2/conf/autofs/autofs_solaris_v1.h

am-utils-6.1a2/conf/autofs/autofs_solaris_v2_v3.c

am-utils-6.1a2/conf/autofs/autofs_solaris_v2_v3.h
```

This directory contains header files that declare many common definitions for the rest of the C sources in the package. The main header file is am_utils.h:

```
am-utils-6.1a3/include/

am-utils-6.1a3/include/am_compat.h

am-utils-6.1a3/include/am_utils.h

am-utils-6.1a3/include/am_xdr_func.h

am-utils-6.1a3/include/am_defs.h

am-utils-6.1a3/include/amq_defs.h

am-utils-6.1a3/include/mount_headers1.h

am-utils-6.1a3/include/mount_headers2.h
```

This is the top-level directory in the am-utils source package. The first file is a general README file:

```
am-utils-6.1a3/README
```

This file lists the primary contributors to the am-utils package:

```
am-utils-6.1a3/AUTHORS
```

This file describes the license for using and copying am-utils:

```
am-utils-6.1a3/COPYING
```

This file lists all code changes that the package underwent:

```
am-utils-6.1a3/ChangeLog
```

This file briefly describes how to install am-utils:

```
am-utils-6.1a3/INSTALL
```

This file is the main Automake file:

```
am-utils-6.1a3/Makefile.am
```

This file is generated from Makefile.am by automake:

```
am-utils-6.1a3/Makefile.in
```

This file summarizes new features and changes in each release:

```
am-utils-6.1a3/NEWS
```

This large file is the main configuration script:

```
am-utils-6.1a3/configure
```

This file lists known system bugs that affect am-utils, not Amd bugs:

```
am-utils-6.1a3/BUGS
```

This file is a Linux Software Map file describing the am-utils package:

```
am-utils-6.1a3/LSM.am-utils
```

This file lists the official am-utils mirror sites:

```
am-utils-6.1a3/MIRRORS
```

This file provides information specific to the Autofs support in am-utils:

```
am-utils-6.1a3/README.autofs
```

This file describes Amd's compliance with Y2K:

```
am-utils-6.1a3/README.y2k
```

Appendices

This helper script configures and builds am-utils in a private subdirectory:

    am-utils-6.1a3/buildall

This file lists the various items that remain to do in the am-utils package:

    am-utils-6.1a3/tasks

These three files describe the status of LDAP support in am-utils, including a proposed LDAP schema:

    am-utils-6.1a3/README.ldap

    am-utils-6.1a3/ldap-id.ms

    am-utils-6.1a3/ldap-id.txt

This directory contains sources for the am-utils library libamu. These sources can be built as either a static or a shared library:

    am-utils-6.1a3/libamu/

    am-utils-6.1a3/libamu/amu.h

    am-utils-6.1a3/libamu/Makefile.am

    am-utils-6.1a3/libamu/Makefile.in

    am-utils-6.1a3/libamu/alloca.c

    am-utils-6.1a3/libamu/clnt_sperrno.c

    am-utils-6.1a3/libamu/hasmntopt.c

    am-utils-6.1a3/libamu/memcmp.c

    am-utils-6.1a3/libamu/strcasecmp.c

    am-utils-6.1a3/libamu/strdup.c

    am-utils-6.1a3/libamu/strstr.c

    am-utils-6.1a3/libamu/ualarm.c

    am-utils-6.1a3/libamu/misc_rpc.c

    am-utils-6.1a3/libamu/mount_fs.c

    am-utils-6.1a3/libamu/mtab.c

    am-utils-6.1a3/libamu/nfs_prot_xdr.c

    am-utils-6.1a3/libamu/util.c

    am-utils-6.1a3/libamu/wire.c

    am-utils-6.1a3/libamu/xdr_func.c

    am-utils-6.1a3/libamu/xutil.c

This directory contains the sources for Amd as well as its manual page:

```
am-utils-6.1a3/amd/
am-utils-6.1a3/amd/amd.h
am-utils-6.1a3/amd/Makefile.am
am-utils-6.1a3/amd/Makefile.in
am-utils-6.1a3/amd/am_ops.c
am-utils-6.1a3/amd/amd.c
am-utils-6.1a3/amd/amfs_auto.c
am-utils-6.1a3/amd/amfs_direct.c
am-utils-6.1a3/amd/amfs_error.c
am-utils-6.1a3/amd/amfs_host.c
am-utils-6.1a3/amd/amfs_inherit.c
am-utils-6.1a3/amd/amfs_link.c
am-utils-6.1a3/amd/amfs_linkx.c
am-utils-6.1a3/amd/amfs_nfsl.c
am-utils-6.1a3/amd/amfs_nfsx.c
am-utils-6.1a3/amd/amfs_program.c
am-utils-6.1a3/amd/amfs_root.c
am-utils-6.1a3/amd/amfs_toplvl.c
am-utils-6.1a3/amd/amfs_union.c
am-utils-6.1a3/amd/amq_subr.c
am-utils-6.1a3/amd/amq_svc.c
am-utils-6.1a3/amd/autil.c
am-utils-6.1a3/amd/clock.c
am-utils-6.1a3/amd/conf.c
am-utils-6.1a3/amd/get_args.c
am-utils-6.1a3/amd/map.c
am-utils-6.1a3/amd/mapc.c
am-utils-6.1a3/amd/mntfs.c
am-utils-6.1a3/amd/nfs_prot_svc.c
am-utils-6.1a3/amd/nfs_start.c
```

Appendices

am-utils-6.1a3/amd/nfs_subr.c

am-utils-6.1a3/amd/opts.c

am-utils-6.1a3/amd/restart.c

am-utils-6.1a3/amd/rpc_fwd.c

am-utils-6.1a3/amd/sched.c

am-utils-6.1a3/amd/srvr_amfs_auto.c

am-utils-6.1a3/amd/srvr_nfs.c

am-utils-6.1a3/amd/info_file.c

am-utils-6.1a3/amd/info_hesiod.c

am-utils-6.1a3/amd/info_ldap.c

am-utils-6.1a3/amd/info_ndbm.c

am-utils-6.1a3/amd/info_nis.c

am-utils-6.1a3/amd/info_nisplus.c

am-utils-6.1a3/amd/info_passwd.c

am-utils-6.1a3/amd/info_union.c

am-utils-6.1a3/amd/ops_cachefs.c

am-utils-6.1a3/amd/ops_cdfs.c

am-utils-6.1a3/amd/ops_efs.c

am-utils-6.1a3/amd/amd.8

am-utils-6.1a3/amd/ops_lofs.c

am-utils-6.1a3/amd/ops_mfs.c

am-utils-6.1a3/amd/ops_nfs.c

am-utils-6.1a3/amd/ops_nfs3.c

am-utils-6.1a3/amd/ops_nullfs.c

am-utils-6.1a3/amd/ops_pcfs.c

am-utils-6.1a3/amd/ops_tfs.c

am-utils-6.1a3/amd/ops_tmpfs.c

am-utils-6.1a3/amd/ops_ufs.c

am-utils-6.1a3/amd/ops_umapfs.c

am-utils-6.1a3/amd/ops_unionfs.c

am-utils-6.1a3/amd/ops_xfs.c

```
am-utils-6.1a3/amd/conf_tok.l
```

```
am-utils-6.1a3/amd/conf_parse.y
```

```
am-utils-6.1a3/amd/ops_TEMPLATE.c
```

This directory contains sources for Amq and pawd, as well as manual pages for both:

```
am-utils-6.1a3/amq/
```

```
am-utils-6.1a3/amq/amq.h
```

```
am-utils-6.1a3/amq/Makefile.am
```

```
am-utils-6.1a3/amq/Makefile.in
```

```
am-utils-6.1a3/amq/amq.c
```

```
am-utils-6.1a3/amq/amq_clnt.c
```

```
am-utils-6.1a3/amq/amq_xdr.c
```

```
am-utils-6.1a3/amq/pawd.c
```

```
am-utils-6.1a3/amq/amq.8
```

```
am-utils-6.1a3/amq/pawd.1
```

This directory contains the C sources and manual page for fixmount:

```
am-utils-6.1a3/fixmount/
```

```
am-utils-6.1a3/fixmount/Makefile.am
```

```
am-utils-6.1a3/fixmount/Makefile.in
```

```
am-utils-6.1a3/fixmount/fixmount.c
```

```
am-utils-6.1a3/fixmount/fixmount.8
```

This directory contains the C sources and manual page for fsinfo:

```
am-utils-6.1a3/fsinfo/
```

```
am-utils-6.1a3/fsinfo/fsi_data.h
```

```
am-utils-6.1a3/fsinfo/fsinfo.h
```

```
am-utils-6.1a3/fsinfo/Makefile.am
```

```
am-utils-6.1a3/fsinfo/Makefile.in
```

```
am-utils-6.1a3/fsinfo/fsi_analyze.c
```

```
am-utils-6.1a3/fsinfo/fsi_dict.c
```

```
am-utils-6.1a3/fsinfo/fsi_util.c
```

```
am-utils-6.1a3/fsinfo/fsinfo.c
```

```
am-utils-6.1a3/fsinfo/wr_atab.c
```

Appendices

```
am-utils-6.1a3/fsinfo/wr_bparam.c
am-utils-6.1a3/fsinfo/wr_dumpset.c
am-utils-6.1a3/fsinfo/wr_exportfs.c
am-utils-6.1a3/fsinfo/wr_fstab.c
am-utils-6.1a3/fsinfo/fsi_gram.y
am-utils-6.1a3/fsinfo/fsi_lex.l
am-utils-6.1a3/fsinfo/fsinfo.8
```

This directory contains sources and the manual page for hlfsd:

```
am-utils-6.1a3/hlfsd/
am-utils-6.1a3/hlfsd/hlfsd.h
am-utils-6.1a3/hlfsd/Makefile.am
am-utils-6.1a3/hlfsd/Makefile.in
am-utils-6.1a3/hlfsd/hlfsd.c
am-utils-6.1a3/hlfsd/homedir.c
am-utils-6.1a3/hlfsd/nfs_prot_svc.c
am-utils-6.1a3/hlfsd/stubs.c
am-utils-6.1a3/hlfsd/hlfsd.8
```

This directory contains sources and the manual page for mk-amd-map:

```
am-utils-6.1a3/mk-amd-map/
am-utils-6.1a3/mk-amd-map/Makefile.am
am-utils-6.1a3/mk-amd-map/Makefile.in
am-utils-6.1a3/mk-amd-map/mk-amd-map.c
am-utils-6.1a3/mk-amd-map/mk-amd-map.8
```

This directory contains sources and the manual page for wire-test:

```
am-utils-6.1a3/wire-test/
am-utils-6.1a3/wire-test/Makefile.am
am-utils-6.1a3/wire-test/Makefile.in
am-utils-6.1a3/wire-test/wire-test.c
am-utils-6.1a3/wire-test/wire-test.8
```

This directory contains various sources for Perl and shell scripts, as well as manual pages for them:

```
am-utils-6.1a3/scripts/
am-utils-6.1a3/scripts/Makefile.am
am-utils-6.1a3/scripts/Makefile.in
am-utils-6.1a3/scripts/am-eject.in
am-utils-6.1a3/scripts/amd2ldif.in
am-utils-6.1a3/scripts/amd2sun.in
am-utils-6.1a3/scripts/automount2amd.in
am-utils-6.1a3/scripts/ctl-amd.in
am-utils-6.1a3/scripts/ctl-hlfsd.in
am-utils-6.1a3/scripts/expn.in
am-utils-6.1a3/scripts/fix-amd-map.in
am-utils-6.1a3/scripts/fixrmtab.in
am-utils-6.1a3/scripts/lostaltmail.in
am-utils-6.1a3/scripts/wait4amd.in
am-utils-6.1a3/scripts/wait4amd2die.in
am-utils-6.1a3/scripts/amd.conf-sample
am-utils-6.1a3/scripts/lostaltmail.conf-sample
am-utils-6.1a3/scripts/amd.conf.5
am-utils-6.1a3/scripts/automount2amd.8
am-utils-6.1a3/scripts/expn.1
```

This directory contains the documentation for am-utils in Texinfo, Postscript, and DVI formats:

```
am-utils-6.1a3/doc/
am-utils-6.1a3/doc/Makefile.am
am-utils-6.1a3/doc/Makefile.in
am-utils-6.1a3/doc/stamp-vti
am-utils-6.1a3/doc/mdate-sh
am-utils-6.1a3/doc/version.texi
am-utils-6.1a3/doc/am-utils.texi
```

Appendices

```
am-utils-6.1a3/doc/hlfsd.ps
am-utils-6.1a3/doc/am-utils.info
am-utils-6.1a3/doc/am-utils.info-1
am-utils-6.1a3/doc/am-utils.info-2
am-utils-6.1a3/doc/am-utils.info-3
am-utils-6.1a3/doc/am-utils.info-4
am-utils-6.1a3/doc/am-utils.info-5
am-utils-6.1a3/doc/am-utils.info-6
am-utils-6.1a3/doc/am-utils.info-7
am-utils-6.1a3/doc/am-utils.dvi
am-utils-6.1a3/doc/am-utils.ps
am-utils-6.1a3/doc/texinfo.tex
```

B

Online Resources

This appendix lists the various online resources we referred to throughout this book. We provide URLs to these locations in a generic manner that is likely to remain valid for at least a couple of years. Nevertheless, the World Wide Web tends to change often, and some of these URLs may change, move, or cease to exist as time goes by. For that reason we provide the following general-purpose link that is unlikely to change:

> `www.am-utils.org/book`

At this site you will find any errata for this book, as well as updated URLs for anything listed in this appendix and the book.

We organize the links in this appendix into four groups:

- NFS links
- Amd links
- General Linux links
- Miscellaneous links

NFS Links

These links relate to the NFS system: protocols, mailing lists, sources, and binaries.

> `http://nfs.sourceforge.net`   The main site for most Linux-related NFS topics. It includes links to the `NFS-HOWTO` FAQ, downloadable sources, binaries and patches, updated procedures for applying and using newer versions of NFS, and more.

http://sourceforge.net/projects/nfs   The main project page for the Linux NFS project. It includes a link to the Linux-NFS mailing list nfs@nfs.sourceforge.net, its archives, and subscription information.

www.citi.umich.edu/projects/nfsv4   Download Linux NFSv4 sources and find information about the status of the NFSv4 Linux prototype.

http://playground.sun.com/pub/nfsv4/webpage   Download drafts of the NFSv4 RFC, information about the NFSv4 IETF working group (www.ietf.org), results from bake-offs and Connectathon (www.connectathon.org) prototype tests, information on how to subscribe to the NFSv4 WG mailing list nfsv4-wg@ sunroof.eng.sun.com, and more.

http://playground.sun.com/pub/nfsv4/nfsv4-wg-archive   The NFSv4 WG mailing list and archive.

ftp://ftp.isi.edu/in-notes/rfc3010.txt   The latest NFSv4 RFC. You can get a variety of other RFCs from ISI's FTP site ftp://ftp.isi.edu and from the IETF's FTP site ftp://ftp.ietf.org.

www.spec.org/osg/sfs97   The NFSv3 and NFSv2 File System testing benchmark—SFS 2.0—from the Standard Performance Evaluation Corporation. You can also get information about past SFS benchmarks for NFS.

ftp://wuarchive.wustl.edu/languages/c/unix-c/benchmarks/ nfsstone.tar.Z   The sources for the "nfsstone" NFS benchmark.

ftp://wuarchive.wustl.edu/languages/c/unix-c/benchmarks/ nhfsstone.tar.Z   The sources for the "nhfsstone" NFS benchmark.

Amd and Automounter Links

These links provide information for Amd: mailing lists, sources, binaries, and alternate packages that Amd can be built with.

www.am-utils.org   The main Amd automounter Web page. This URL includes links to related mailing lists, information on submitting bugs, and access to the am-utils online manual, with information about topics not covered in this book, such as FSinfo and HLFSD. This link also includes the latest versions of software downloads that are available from ftp://ftp.am-utils.org. The FTP link provides access to older am-utils software as well as the latest software.

www.openldap.org   Information about LDAP, including the latest sources. This is useful if you wish to rebuild Amd using the latest LDAP package.

`ftp://athena-dist.mit.edu/pub/ATHENA/hesiod`   Sources to Hesiod. This is useful for building Amd with Hesiod support.

`http://linux-xfs.sgi.com/projects/xfs`   Sources to the XFS file system for Linux, as well as information about this SGI-sponsored project.

`ftp://ftp.kernel.org/pub/linux/daemons/autofs`   Sources to the latest Autofs user-level utilities for Linux. The kernel Autofs file system is part of the Linux kernel.

`www.cs.columbia.edu/~ezk/research/fist`   Information about getting an LOFS file system for Linux.

Other Linux Links

These links provide general-purpose information about Linux: software, sources, mailing lists, and more.

`www.kernel.org`   General information about the Linux kernel including access to Linux kernel sources.

`www.tux.org/lkml`   The Linux-kernel mailing list FAQ. Contains a lot of useful information about the Linux operating system and the `linux-kernel` mailing list.

`www.redhat.com`   Red Hat's main Web site, with access to information about all versions of their Linux software, downloadable sources, and much more. For example, you can download RPM updates from `ftp://updates.redhat.com`.

`http://marc.theaimsgroup.com`   A collection of numerous mailing-list archives.

`www.freebsd.org/cgi/man.cgi`   Access to numerous manual pages for Linux and other systems.

`http://lxr.linux.no/source`   Cross-referenced searchable Linux sources.

`http://filewatcher.org`   A Linux-specific search engine for software.

`www.rpmfind.net`   A search engine for (mostly Linux) RPMs.

`www.rpm.org`   Information about the RPM tool itself.

`http://netfilter.filewatcher.org`   Information about configuring Linux filters using the IPTABLES system in the Linux 2.4 kernel.

`linux-fsdevel@vger.kernel.org`   The Linux File System Developers mailing list. To subscribe, send e-mail to `majordomo@vger.kernel.org` with the body `subscribe linux-fsdevel`.

Appendices

Miscellaneous Links

These miscellaneous links provide general-purpose information about software and security.

www.ftpsearchengines.com   If you are searching for software on the Web, this page provides links to many other FTP search engines. One particular advanced FTP search engine is `http://download.lycos.com/static/advanced_search.asp`.

www.cert.org   The CERT's Web site, with information about many security vulnerabilities.

www.securityfocus.com/forums/bugtraq/faq.html   Information about the popular BugTraq security mailing list.

Amd Log and Debug Messages

Amd is a large and complex program. In more than 60,000 lines of source code base, Amd contains more than 750 unique messages. During its run, Amd can print numerous messages, some repeatedly and others being slight variations on a basic message. Some of these messages are informational, some are tracing and debugging, some are genuine error messages, and more. To help administrators understand what Amd is doing, this appendix lists all the messages that Amd can display, with a brief explanation of each message. These messages are also useful for people who want to understand what Amd is doing internally, people such as developers or those who suspect an Amd bug and wish to fix it.

Each individual message is not intended to help fix or debug problems, but several messages together can help an Amd user determine what Amd is doing. Remember that Amd might print several messages all at once, and it is often important to look at several of them to understand what Amd is doing and what the problem might be. Refer to Chapters 9, "The Amd Configuration File," 10, "Automounter Maps," and 11, "Runtime Automounter Administration," for information about how to turn on specific levels of debugging.

The messages in this appendix are based on am-utils-6.1a3. We list the messages alphabetically and in a case-sensitive manner, by the message's text.

When you look at an individual message, say, one logged to /var/log/amd, you will see a full entry such as the following:

```
Jan 15 18:31:00 cricket amd[236]/info: ./u/zing/ezk mounted
fstype link on ./u/zing/ezk
```

The meaning of this message is as follows:

Jan 15 18:31:00   The date that the message was logged.

cricket   The hostname that produced the message.

amd[236]   The process name and PID (in square brackets) that produced the message.

/info: The type of message. In this case, an informational message.

./u/zing/ezk mounted fstype link on ./u/zing/ezk   The actual message.

In the rest of this appendix, we only list the actual messages, but we categorize them into different groups based on the type of the message.

Log Messages

As a reminder, the classes of logging messages are as follows:

debug   Minor debugging and tracing messages

error   Non-fatal system errors

fatal   Fatal errors

info   Information

map   Map errors

stats   Additional statistical information

user   Non-fatal user errors

warn   Warnings

Refer to the section "log_options" in Chapter 9 for the exact meaning of each of these log messages.

Minor Debugging and Tracing Messages

These messages include some debugging information, mostly for tracing NFS mount options used to mount and XDR functions being executed.

```
Allocated size S; block P
```

Amd allocated S more bytes into address P.

```
EOF is N
```

While processing a readdir request in a browsable directory, Amd got the EOF code *N*. A one indicates the end of the directory.

```
Environment gave "X" -> "V"
```

Amd has resolved the value of the map variable *X* from the calling environment, to the value *V*.

```
Expansion of "S"...
... is "V"
```

Amd has expanded the string *S* to the value *V*.

```
Free in F:L: block P
```

Amd is freeing the allocated address *P*. The freeing is called on line *L* of source file *F*.

```
Generic mount flags F
```

Amd is using the generic mount flags *F* while mounting a top-level mount.

```
Generic mount flags F used for NFS mount
```

Amd is mounting an NFS file system using the generic mount flags *F*.

```
Linux autofs_get_fh for P
```

While running a Linux Autofs mount, Amd is trying to retrieve a filehandle for the path name *P*.

```
NA->acdirmax = N
```

Printing the contents of an NFS mount structure. The maximum number of seconds to cache directories is *N*.

```
NA->acdirmin = N
```

Printing the contents of an NFS mount structure. The minimum number of seconds to cache directories is *N*.

```
NA->acregmax = N
```

Printing the contents of an NFS mount structure. The maximum number of seconds to cache regular files is *N*.

```
NA->acregmin = N
```

Printing the contents of an NFS mount structure. The minimum number of seconds to cache regular files is *N*.

```
NA->addr {netbuf} (maxlen=M, len=L) = "A"
```

Printing the contents of an NFS mount structure. The network address buffer is of length *L* and maximum length *M*. The network address is *A*.

```
NA->addr {sockaddr_in} (len=L) = "A"
```

Printing the contents of an NFS mount structure. The address of the mounted remote host is *A*, whose length is *L*.

```
NA->addr.sin_addr = "A"
```

Printing the contents of an NFS mount structure. The address of the mounted remote host is *A*.

```
NA->addr.sin_family = "F"
```

Printing the contents of an NFS mount structure. The transport family of the address of the mounted remote host is *F*.

```
NA->addr.sin_len = "L"
```

Printing the contents of an NFS mount structure. The length of the address of the mounted remote host is *L*.

```
NA->addr.sin_port = "P"
```

Printing the contents of an NFS mount structure. The port of the address of the mounted remote host is *P*.

```
NA->biods = N
```

Printing the contents of an NFS mount structure. The number of basic I/O threads to run is *N*.

```
NA->bsize = N
```

Printing the contents of an NFS mount structure. The value of the `bsize` parameter used is *N*. This parameter is not configurable in Amd.

```
NA->fh_len = N
```

Printing the contents of an NFS mount structure. The size of the NFS filehandle used is *N* bytes.

```
NA->fhsize = N
```

Printing the contents of an NFS mount structure. The size of the NFS filehandle used is *N* bytes.

```
NA->filehandle = "X"
```

Printing the contents of an NFS mount structure. The NFS filehandle used is *X*.

```
NA->flags = F
```

Printing the contents of an NFS mount structure. The NFS-specific mount flags used are *F*.

```
NA->fsname = "F"
```

Printing the contents of an NFS mount structure. The name of the mounted file system is *F*.

```
NA->hostname = "H"
```

Printing the contents of an NFS mount structure. The name of the mounted remote host is *H*.

```
NA->knconf->proto "P"
```

Printing the contents of an NFS mount structure. The kernel network configuration network protocol transport is *P*.

```
NA->knconf->protofmly "P"
```

Printing the contents of an NFS mount structure. The kernel network configuration protocol family is *P*.

```
NA->knconf->rdev R
```

Printing the contents of an NFS mount structure. The kernel network configuration raw device is *R*.

Appendices

```
NA->knconf->semantics N
```
Printing the contents of an NFS mount structure. The kernel network configuration semantics value is *N*.

```
NA->namlen = N
```
Printing the contents of an NFS mount structure. The length of the name of the mounted remote host is *N*.

```
NA->pg_thresh = N
```
Printing the contents of an NFS mount structure. The threshold of paging activity over NFS is set to *N* kilobytes.

```
NA->proto = T
```
Printing the contents of an NFS mount structure. The protocol type of socket used to mount the file system is *T*.

```
NA->retrans = N
```
Printing the contents of an NFS mount structure. The number of RPC retransmissions allowed for this mount is *N*.

```
NA->rsize = N
```
Printing the contents of an NFS mount structure. The value of the read size parameter used is *N*.

```
NA->sotype = T
```
Printing the contents of an NFS mount structure. The type of socket used to mount the file system is *T*.

```
NA->symttl = N
```
Printing the contents of an NFS mount structure. The symbolic TTL cache value for this mount is *N* seconds.

```
NA->syncaddr {netbuf} A
```
Printing the contents of an NFS mount structure. The synchronous address is *A*.

```
NA->timeo = N
```
Printing the contents of an NFS mount structure. The value of the timeout parameter used is *N*.

`NA->version = V`

Printing the contents of an NFS mount structure. The implementation version of the NFS mount data structure used is *V*. In some cases this is also used to determine the version of the NFS protocol used.

`NA->wsize = N`

Printing the contents of an NFS mount structure. The value of the write size parameter used is *N*.

`NULL nfs_args!`

Amd has been asked to print the contents of a NULL NFS mount structure.

`Reallocated size S; block P`

Amd reallocated address *P* with a new total of *S* bytes.

`Solaris autofs_get_fh for P`

While running a Solaris Autofs mount, Amd is trying to get a filehandle for the path name *P*.

`amfs_auto_readdir_browsable gen=G, count=I`

While processing a readdir request in a browsable directory, Amd has continued with generation cookie *G* and the offset index of *I*.

`dl_entries=X, te_next=Y, dl_eof=C`

While processing a readdir request in a browsable directory, Amd got the EOF code *N*. Amd is processing the next set of entries from address *X*, starting with address *Y*.

`end of readdir eof=TRUE, dl_entries=0`

Amd finished producing all of the entries for a readdir operation.

```
executing (un)mount command...
arg[0] = ARG
arg[1] = ARG
arg[2] = ARG

...
```

While using a `type:=program` file system, Amd is about to execute either a mount or an unmount command. The arguments (*ARG*) of the command follow one line at a time.

Appendices

gen1 key *I* "*N*"

While processing a readdir request in a browsable directory, Amd has produced a first generation entry named *N*, whose index is *I*.

gen1 key *I* "*N*" fi=*F* ck=*C*

Amd is producing first stage a readdir entry *N*, whose directory index is *I*, file ID *F*, and cookie *C*.

gen2 key *I* "*N*"

While processing a readdir request in a browsable directory, Amd has produced a second-generation entry named *N*, whose index is *I*.

gen2 key *I* "*N*" fi=*F* ck=*C*

Amd is producing a second stage readdir entry *N*, whose directory index is *I*, file ID *F*, and cookie *C*.

gen2+ key *I* "*N*" fi=*F* ck=*C*

Amd is producing an additional readdir entry *N*, whose directory index is *I*, file ID *F*, and cookie *C*.

gen3 key *I* "*N*"

While processing a readdir request in a browsable directory, Amd has produced a third generation entry named *N*, whose index is *I*.

getattr:

Amd's own NFS server is executing the getattr NFS procedure.

linux mount: Generic mount flags *F*

Amd was asked to mount a Linux file system using generic mount flags *F*.

linux mount: data *O*

Amd was asked to mount a file system using extra mount options on *O* on Linux.

linux mount: dir *D*

Amd was asked to mount a file system on mount directory *D* on Linux.

`linux mount: fd N`

Amd was asked to mount a file system using file descriptor *N* on Linux.

`linux mount: fsname N`

Amd was asked to mount the file system name *N* on Linux.

`linux mount: hostname H`

Amd was asked to mount a file system from hostname *H* on Linux.

`linux mount: opts O`

Amd was asked to mount a file system with mount options *O* on Linux.

`linux mount: port P`

Amd was asked to mount a file system from port number *P* on Linux.

`linux mount: type (mntent) T`

Amd was asked to mount the file system with mount entry type *T* on Linux.

`linux mount: type T`

Amd was asked to mount the file system with mount type *T* on Linux.

`linux mount: updated nfs_args...`

Amd is about to display the contents of an updated `nfs_args` structure on a Linux system.

`linux mount: version V`

Amd was asked to mount a file system with mount structure version *V* on Linux.

`lookup:`

Amd's own NFS server is executing the `lookup` NFS procedure.

`lookuppn(D, N)`

Amd's own NFS server is looking up the name *N* inside the directory *D*. This message is also used when Amd looks up a name inside an Autofs-mounted directory.

`make_entry_chain: mp is (NULL)`

Amd is not able to create a list of directory entries for a directory-reading NFS operation because the mount node is null.

Appendices

```
make_entry_chain: mp->am_mnt is (NULL)
```
Amd is not able to create a list of directory entries for a directory-reading NFS operation because the mount point is null.

```
make_entry_chain: mp->am_mnt->mf_private is (NULL)
```
Amd is not able to create a list of directory entries for a directory-reading NFS operation because the mount point is null.

```
make_entry_chain: no more space in chain
```
Amd ran out of memory while creating a list of directory entries for a directory-reading NFS operation.

```
readdir(D)
```
Amd's own NFS server is reading the contents of the directory *D*.

```
readdir:
```
Amd's own NFS server is executing the `readdir` NFS procedure.

```
readlink(P) = L
```
Amd's own NFS server has resolved the symbolic link *P* to point to *L*.

```
readlink:
```
Amd's own NFS server is executing the `readlink` NFS procedure.

```
remove(D, N)
```
Amd's own NFS server is deleting the name *N* in the directory *D*.

```
retry=N
```
Amd's own NFS server is reporting the value *N* for a retry attempt in a `getattr` function.

```
stat(P), size = B, mtime=T
```
Amd is tracing a `getattr` NFS operation for file *P*. The size of the file is *N* bytes and its last modification time is *T*.

```
stat_fs(D)
```
Amd's own NFS server is producing the file system statistics for the directory *D*.

`statfs:`

Amd's own NFS server is executing the `statfs` NFS procedure.

`strsplit saved "S"`

Amd split a full map entry to result in the string *S*.

`strsplit saved a total of N strings`

Amd parsed a full map entry and found that it contains *N* individual substrings (locations or default options).

`xdr_attrstat:`

Amd is invoking the RPC function `xdr_attrstat` as part of Amd's own NFS service.

`xdr_createargs:`

Amd is invoking the RPC function `xdr_createargs` as part of Amd's own NFS service.

`xdr_dirlist:`

Amd is invoking the RPC function `xdr_dirlist` as part of Amd's own NFS service.

`xdr_diropargs:`

Amd is invoking the RPC function `xdr_diropargs` as part of Amd's own NFS service.

`xdr_diropokres:`

Amd is invoking the RPC function `xdr_diropokres` as part of Amd's own NFS service.

`xdr_diropres:`

Amd is invoking the RPC function `xdr_diropres` as part of Amd's own NFS service.

`xdr_dirpath:`

Amd is invoking the RPC function `xdr_dirpath` as part of Amd's own NFS service.

`xdr_entry:`

Amd is invoking the RPC function `xdr_entry` as part of Amd's own NFS service.

`xdr_exportnode:`

Amd is invoking the RPC function `xdr_exportnode` as part of Amd's own NFS service.

`xdr_exports:`

Amd is invoking the RPC function `xdr_exports` as part of Amd's own NFS service.

`xdr_fattr:`

Amd is invoking the RPC function `xdr_fattr` as part of Amd's own NFS service.

`xdr_fhandle3:`

Amd is invoking the RPC function `xdr_fhandle3` as part of Amd's own NFS service.

`xdr_fhandle:`

Amd is invoking the RPC function `xdr_fhandle` as part of Amd's own NFS service.

`xdr_fhstatus:`

Amd is invoking the RPC function `xdr_fhstatus` as part of Amd's own NFS service.

`xdr_filename:`

Amd is invoking the RPC function `xdr_filename` as part of Amd's own NFS service.

`xdr_ftype:`

Amd is invoking the RPC function `xdr_ftype` as part of Amd's own NFS service.

`xdr_groupnode:`

Amd is invoking the RPC function `xdr_groupnode` as part of Amd's own NFS service.

`xdr_groups:`

Amd is invoking the RPC function `xdr_groups` as part of Amd's own NFS service.

`xdr_linkargs:`

Amd is invoking the RPC function `xdr_linkargs` as part of Amd's own NFS service.

`xdr_mntrequest:`

Amd is invoking the RPC function `xdr_mntrequest` while running a Solaris Autofs mount.

`xdr_mntres:`

Amd is invoking the RPC function `xdr_mntres` while running a Solaris Autofs mount.

xdr_mountbody:

Amd is invoking the RPC function xdr_mountbody as part of Amd's own NFS service.

xdr_mountlist:

Amd is invoking the RPC function xdr_mountlist as part of Amd's own NFS service.

xdr_mountres3:

Amd is invoking the RPC function xdr_mountres3 as part of Amd's own NFS service.

xdr_mountres3_ok:

Amd is invoking the RPC function xdr_mountres3_ok as part of Amd's own NFS service.

xdr_mountstat3:

Amd is invoking the RPC function xdr_mountstat3 as part of Amd's own NFS service.

xdr_name:

Amd is invoking the RPC function xdr_name as part of Amd's own NFS service.

xdr_nfs_fh:

Amd is invoking the RPC function xdr_nfs_fh as part of Amd's own NFS service.

xdr_nfscookie:

Amd is invoking the RPC function xdr_nfscookie as part of Amd's own NFS service.

xdr_nfspath:

Amd is invoking the RPC function xdr_nfspath as part of Amd's own NFS service.

xdr_nfsstat:

Amd is invoking the RPC function xdr_nfsstat as part of Amd's own NFS service.

xdr_nfstime:

Amd is invoking the RPC function xdr_nfstime as part of Amd's own NFS service.

xdr_pointer:

Amd is invoking the RPC function xdr_pointer as part of Amd's own NFS service.

`xdr_readargs:`

Amd is invoking the RPC function `xdr_readargs` as part of Amd's own NFS service.

`xdr_readdirargs:`

Amd is invoking the RPC function `xdr_readdirargs` as part of Amd's own NFS service.

`xdr_readdirres:`

Amd is invoking the RPC function `xdr_readdirres` as part of Amd's own NFS service.

`xdr_readlinkres:`

Amd is invoking the RPC function `xdr_readlinkres` as part of Amd's own NFS service.

`xdr_readokres:`

Amd is invoking the RPC function `xdr_readokres` as part of Amd's own NFS service.

`xdr_readres:`

Amd is invoking the RPC function `xdr_readres` as part of Amd's own NFS service.

`xdr_renameargs:`

Amd is invoking the RPC function `xdr_renameargs` as part of Amd's own NFS service.

`xdr_sattr:`

Amd is invoking the RPC function `xdr_sattr` as part of Amd's own NFS service.

`xdr_sattrargs:`

Amd is invoking the RPC function `xdr_sattrargs` as part of Amd's own NFS service.

`xdr_statfsokres:`

Amd is invoking the RPC function `xdr_statfsokres` as part of Amd's own NFS service.

`xdr_statfsres:`

Amd is invoking the RPC function `xdr_statfsres` as part of Amd's own NFS service.

`xdr_symlinkargs:`

Amd is invoking the RPC function `xdr_symlinkargs` as part of Amd's own NFS service.

```
xdr_umntrequest:
```
Amd is invoking the RPC function `xdr_umntrequest` while running a Solaris Autofs mount.

```
xdr_writeargs:
```
Amd is invoking the RPC function `xdr_writeargs` as part of Amd's own NFS service.

Non-fatal System Errors

These messages will log all non-fatal system errors such as a failure to contact a map service or mount an entry.

```
AUTOFS xdr decode failed for P V N
```
While running a Solaris Autofs mount, Amd failed to decode an XDR package for program number *P*, version *V*, and procedure number *N*.

```
AUTOFS_IOC_FAIL: E
```
While running a Linux Autofs mount, Amd failed to run the AUTOFS_IOC_FAIL `ioctl`, with the error message *E*.

```
AUTOFS_IOC_PROTOVER: E
```
While running a Linux Autofs mount, Amd failed to run the AUTOFS_IOC_PROTOVER `ioctl`, with the error message *E*.

```
AUTOFS_IOC_READY: E
```
While running a Linux Autofs mount, Amd failed to run the AUTOFS_IOC_READY `ioctl`, with the error message *E*.

```
Can't bind to reserved port
```
Amd could not bind a reserved socket on a Linux system.

```
Can't connect socket for kernel
```
Amd could not connect to a reserved socket on a Linux system.

```
Can't create privileged nfs port (TLI)
```
While using TLI networking, Amd failed to create a privileged port for the NFS service.

Appendices

`Can't create socket for kernel`

Amd could not create a UDP socket for communicating with the kernel while mounting a Linux file system.

`Can't create socket to connect to mountd: E`

While using socket-based networking, Amd failed to connect to a remote MOUNT daemon. The error message was *E*.

`Can't find root filehandle for D`

Amd could not find the root filehandle for the mount directory *D*.

`Can't open F: E`

Amd failed to open the mount table file name *F*. The error message was *E*.

`Can't read mount table`

Amd cannot read the mount table file on an OSF system.

`Can't set non-block on forwarding socket: E`

Amd was unable to set a non-blocking forwarding socket. The error message is *E*.

`Can't write entry to F`

Amd failed to write a mount table entry to a temporary file *F*.

`Cannot rewind netconfig: E`

While using TLI networking, Amd failed to run the `setnetconfig(3)` function. The error message is *E*.

`Could not mount D: E`

Amd could not mount the directory *D*. The error message is *E*.

`Couldn't close tmp file descriptor: E`

Amd failed to close a file descriptor for a temporary file. The error message was *E*.

`Couldn't create ping RPC message`

Amd was not able to create an RPC message for the NFS_NULL ping procedure.

`Couldn't find how to unmount M`

Amd is unable to determine how to unmount the mount point *M*.

`Couldn't flush F: E`

Amd failed to flush unwritten data to the mount table file name *F*. The error message was *E*.

`Couldn't lock F: E`

Amd failed to lock the mount table file name *F*. The error message was *E*.

`Couldn't write F: E`

Amd failed to write to the mount table file name *F*. The error message was *E*.

`Error accessing getnetconfig: E`

While using TLI networking, Amd failed to run the `getnetconfig(3)` function. The error message is *E*.

`Error reading RPC reply: E`

Amd failed to read a reply to a forwarded RPC message. The error message is *E*.

`Got a zero interval in timeout_mp()!`

Amd was asked to set an illegal timeout value of zero. Amd is forcing it to be at least 6 seconds.

`Missing filehandle for A`

While using a `type:=nfs` file system, Amd found that it is missing a filehandle for node *A*.

`NFS xdr decode failed for P V N`

Amd failed to decode the RPC XDR for program *P*, version *V*, and procedure number *N*.

`NISplus init <M>: E`

Amd failed to initialize the NIS+ map *M*. The error message is *E*.

`No mount point for D - skipping`

While using a `type:=host` file system, Amd detected that the *D* directory does not exist, and is skipping this mount.

No space to expand `"M"`

Amd ran out of memory for expanding the error message *M*.

Null map request for *K*

Amd was asked to search for the key *K* in an undefined map.

Process *P* exited with signal *N*

An Amd child process with PID *P* exited after receiving signal *N*.

Remount collision on *P*?

While using an inheritance file system mount, Amd suspected a collision of multiple remount attempts on the same file systems *P*.

Retrying memory allocation

Amd has failed to allocate memory, so it is retrying (up to 600 times, with a 1-second delay in between).

Tree unmount of *D* failed: *E*

While using a `type:=host` file system, Amd failed to unmount the directory tree *D*. The error message is *E*.

Unable to append *F*: *E*

Amd failed to append new data to the table file name *F*. The error message was *E*.

Unable to create index *I*: *E*

Amd failed to create an NIS+ index *I*. The error message is *E*.

Unable to create map_name *M*: *E*

While accessing an NIS+ information map service, Amd failed to create a map of name *M*. The error message is *E*.

Unable to open/creat *F*: *E*

Amd failed to open and/or create the mount table file name *F*. The error message was *E*.

Unknown autofs packet type *T*

While running a Linux Autofs mount, Amd detected an unknown packet of type *T*.

`D: 1SYS_vfsmount: E`

Amd failed to mount the file system *D* on a Mach 3 system. The error message was *E*.

`D: 2SYS_vfsmount: E`

Amd failed a second attempt to mount the file system *D* on a Mach 3 system. The error message was *E*.

`D: mkdirs: E`

Amd failed to create the full set of directories in *D*. The error message is *E*.

`D: mount (amfs_nfsx_cont): E`

While using a `type:=nfsx` file system, Amd failed to mount a directory *D*. The error message is *E*.

`D: mount: E`

Amd failed to mount the directory *D*. The error message is *E*.

`D: retry SYS_vfsmount T N`

Amd is retrying to mount *D* on a Mach 3 system, using the file system mount type *T* whose numeric type is *N*.

`D: type defaults to nfs...`

Amd determined that the file system *D* on a Mach 3 system is of type NFS.

`D: umount: E`

Amd failed to mount the directory in *D*. The error message is *E*.

`F: open: E`

Amd failed to open the mount table file name *F*. The error message was *E*.

`F: stat: M`

Amd failed to stat the mount table file name *F*. The error message was *E*.

`P: mount (amfs_auto_cont): E`

A continuation function for a mount of *P* determined that the mount failed. The error message is *E*.

P: unmount: *E*

Amd failed to unmount the path name *P*. The error message is *E*.

autofs: aborting the mount

While running a Linux Autofs mount, Amd decided to abort the mount.

autofs: assuming protocol version *V*

While running a Linux Autofs mount, Amd is assuming the use of Autofs protocol version *V*.

autofs: cannot restore pgrp: *E*

While running a Linux Autofs mount, Amd failed to restore the process group. The error message is *E*.

can't bind privileged port (rpc_fwd)

Amd cannot bind a socket to a privileged port as part of its RPC forwarder.

can't bind privileged port (socket)

While using socket-based networking, Amd failed to bind to a privileged port.

cannot create (tcp) tli service for amq

While using TLI networking, Amd failed to create a TCP RPC listener service for Amq.

cannot create (udp) tli service for amq

While using TLI networking, Amd failed to create a UDP RPC listener service for Amq.

cannot create autofs tli service for amd

While running a Solaris Autofs mount, Amd failed to create an Autofs service for Amd.

cannot create nfs tli service for amd

While using TLI networking, Amd failed to create a service listener for the automounter NFS service.

cannot get uid/gid from RPC credentials

Amd was not able to find the effective UID and GID from the NFS credentials passed to it by the client.

cannot getnetconfigent for *T*

While using TLI networking, Amd failed to run getnetconfigent(3) to get a configuration entry for type *T*.

clnt_control CLSET_RETRY_TIMEOUT for udp failed

While using TLI networking, Amd tried to set a timeout for a UDP connection and failed.

clnt_dg_create failed

While using TLI networking, Amd failed to create a datagram (UDP) RPC client to the MOUNT daemon.

clnt_vc_create failed

While using TLI networking, Amd failed to create a virtual-circuit (TCP) RPC client to the MOUNT daemon.

could not register amd AUTOFS service

While running a Solaris Autofs mount, Amd failed to create an Autofs service for Amd.

could not register amd NFS service

While using TLI networking, Amd failed to register the Amd NFS service with the portmapper.

could not stat() *D*: *E*

While using TLI networking, Amd failed to run stat(2) on the device *D*. The error message is *E*.

could not t_bind to any reserved port

While using TLI networking, Amd failed to bind to any port.

couldn't bind mountd socket to privileged port

While using TLI networking, Amd was unable to bind the MOUNTD socket using a privileged port.

couldn't get mountd address on udp: *E*

While using TLI networking, Amd was unable to get a UDP port to use with a remote MOUNT daemon. The error message was *E*.

Appendices

`create_autofs_service: cannot getnetconfigent for` *T*

While running a Solaris Autofs mount, Amd failed to run `getnetconfigent` to find a configuration entry of type *T*.

`create_autofs_service: get_autofs_address failed`

While running a Solaris Autofs mount, Amd failed to get the address for the Autofs service.

`create_autofs_service: t_alloca failed`

While running a Solaris Autofs mount, Amd failed to allocate a new transport socket object.

`create_autofs_service: t_open failed (`*E*`)`

While running a Solaris Autofs mount, Amd failed to start a new transport socket. The error message is *E*.

`discarding a retry mntfs for` *P*

Amd is discarding a retry attempt for mounting *P*.

`error grabbing nis map of` *M*: *E*

Amd failed to access the NIS map *M*. The error message is *E*.

`error grabbing nisplus map of` *M*: *E*

Amd failed to download an NIS+ map named *M*. The error message is *E*.

`exec failed:` *E*

While using a `type:=program` file system, Amd failed to execute the mount or unmount command. The error message is *E*.

`failed to initialize map` *M*

Amd failed to initialize map *M* with its respective map servers.

`file descriptor` *D* `already in the hash`

While running a Linux Autofs mount, Amd detected a duplicate file descriptor in use.

> `flush new mtab file: E`

Amd failed to flush a mount table file. The error message was *E*.

> `fwd_packet failed: t_errno=X, errno=C`

Amd failed to forward a packet on a TLI socket. The TLI error code is *X*. The system error code is *C*.

> `fwd_reply failed: t_errno=X, errno=C, flags=F`

Amd failed to reply to a forwarded packet on a TLI socket. The TLI error code is *X*. The system error code is *C*. The forwarding socket flags are *F*.

> `get_mount_client failed for H`

While using a `type:=host` file system, Amd failed to contact a remote mount daemon on host *H*.

> `get_mount_client failed for H: E`

While using a `type:=host` file system, Amd failed to contact a remote mount daemon on host *H*. The error message is *E*.

> `get_nfs_version: failed to contact portmapper on host "H": E`

While using socket-based networking, Amd failed to contact the portmapper on host *H*. The error message was *E*.

> `getdomainname: E`

Amd failed to get the NIS domain of the host. The error message is *E*.

> `getmountent: E`

Amd failed to run `getmountent(3)` on an Ultrix system. The error message was *E*.

> `getnetconfig for tcp failed: E`

While using TLI networking, Amd failed to run the `getnetconfig(3)` function over the TCP transport. The error message is *E*.

> `getnetconfig for udp failed: E`

While using TLI networking, Amd failed to run the `getnetconfig(3)` function over the UDP transport. The error message is *E*.

`getwire unable to get interface flags`

Amd was unable to find the status flags for a network interface, such as whether the NIC is up, running, supporting broadcasts, etc.

`hesiod_isup: error getting `/defaults' entry in map M: E`

While checking to see if a Hesiod map server is up, Amd failed to get the /defaults entry in map M. The error message is E.

`host_mount rpc failed: E`

While using a type:=host file system, Amd failed to mount a host partition. The error message is E.

`map P not found`

While running a Solaris Autofs mount, Amd could not find the mount map with path name P.

`mapc_sync: map M is down: not clearing map`

Amd has determined that the map server for map M is down, and therefore, Amd is keeping previously cached values.

`mntctl: E`

Amd failed to execute the mntctl system call on an AIX system. The error message was E.

`mount for D got signal N`

While using a type:=nfsx file system, Amd failed to mount the directory D and got a signal N.

`mount for P got signal N`

A top-level Amd mount for path name P failed with signal N.

`mount of P failed`

While running a Solaris Autofs mount, Amd failed to mount the path name P.

`mount point M: E`

Unmounting the mount point M produced the error message E.

`mount_aix3: vmount failed with errno C`

Amd failed to mount a file system on an AIX 3 system. The error code is C.

`mount_cachefs: E`

Amd failed to mount a CacheFS file system. The error message is E.

`mount_cachefs: options to no match: E`

While accessing a mount of `type:=cachefs`, Amd failed to process the mount options. The error message is E.

`mount_cdfs: E`

Amd failed to mount a CDFS file system. The error message is E.

`mount_efs: E`

Amd failed to mount an EFS file system. The error message is E.

`mount_lofs: E`

Amd failed to mount a loopback file system. The error message is E.

`mount_pcfs: E`

Amd failed to mount a PCFS file system. The error message is E.

`mount_ufs: E`

Amd failed to mount a native disk file system (EXT2, UFS, FFS, etc.). The error message is E.

`mount_xfs: E`

Amd failed to mount an XFS file system. The error message is E.

`mountd rpc failed: E`

While using a `type:=host` file system, Amd failed to contact a remote mount daemon. The error message is E.

`nis_isup: error getting the master of map M: E`

While checking to see if an NIS server is up, Amd failed to find the name of the NIS master for the map M. The error message is E.

Appendices

nis_isup: error getting the order of map *M*: *E*

While checking to see if an NIS server is up, Amd failed to retrieve the order number (a time stamp) for the map *M*. The error message is *E*.

nis_search: *M*: *E*

Amd failed to search for a map *M* in NIS. The error message is *E*.

nisplus_search: *M*: *E*

Amd failed to search for a map *M* in NIS+. The error message is *E*.

no port number specified for *D*

While using a top-level mount, Amd detected that no port was given for mounting directory *D*.

program: both mount and unmount must be specified

While using a type:=program file system, Amd detected that either the mount or the unmount parameters were not specified.

read error on *F*: *E* ´

Amd failed to read from a table file name *F*. The error message was *E*.

reload of map *M* failed - using old values

Amd failed to reload map *M* and is thus using the previously cached values.

rename *T* to *F*: *E*

Amd failed to rename a temporary mount table file name *T* to its permanent name *F*. The error message was *E*.

rmdir(*D*): *E*

Amd was unable to remove the directory *D*. The error message is *E*.

setmntent("*F*", "a"): *E*

Amd failed to run setmntent(3) on the mount table file name *F*, to open it for appending. The error message was *E*.

```
setmntent("F", "w"): E
```
Amd failed to run setmntent(3) on the mount table file name *F*, to open it for writing. The error message was *E*.

```
setmntent("F", M): E
```
Amd failed to run setmntent(3) on the mount table file name *F*, using mode *M*. The error message was *E*.

```
strdup returned null in mount_linux
```
Amd tried to duplicate a string in Linux but the duplication returned NULL.

```
t_alloc req
```
While using TLI networking, Amd detected an error to allocate a reserved transport request port.

```
t_alloc ret
```
While using TLI networking, Amd detected an error to allocate a reserved transport return port.

```
t_bind
```
While using TLI networking, Amd failed to bind to one port.

```
t_bind for port P: E
```
While using TLI networking, Amd failed to bind a transport socket on port *P*. The error message is *E*.

```
t_open D: E
```
While using TLI networking, Amd failed to open a transport socket on device *D*. The error message is *E*.

```
t_open failed: C: E
```
While using TLI networking, Amd failed to open a transport socket. The error code is *C* and the error message is *E*.

```
unable to create RPC forwarding TLI socket: E
```
Amd was not able to create a socket for forwarding RPC requests on TLI systems. The error message is *E*.

Appendices

unable to create RPC forwarding socket: *E*

Amd was not able to create a regular socket for forwarding RPC requests. The error message is *E*.

unable to release controlling tty

After several attempts, Amd failed to detach itself from its controlling terminal, and thus, Amd could not properly background itself.

unionfs: could not mount *D*: *E*

Amd failed to mount the union node *D*. The error message is *E*.

unmount all from *H* rpc failed: *E*

While using a type:=host file system, Amd failed to inform a remote mount daemon that it is unmounting some file systems. The error message is *E*.

unmount for *P* got signal *N*

Amd failed to unmount the path name *P* because it got the signal *N*.

use *O* instead of *X*

Amd is trying to get the file system mount options *O* from the asynchronous continuation. The address of the continuation (*X*) that Amd would have gotten the options from instead may be bad.

yp enumeration of *M*: *E*

Amd failed to enumerate the entries in an NIS map *M*. The error message is *E*.

yp enumeration of *M*: *E*, status=*S*, e=*C*

Amd failed to enumerate the entries in an NIS map *M*. The NIS server status code was *S*. The overall error message is *E* whose code is *C*.

yp_first() returned error: *E*

Amd failed to retrieve the first element in an NIS map. The error message is *E*.

Fatal Errors

These messages report fatal errors that prevent Amd from functioning normally.

Attempting to inherit not-a-filesystem

While using an inheritance file system mount, Amd detected that an attempt was made to inherit something that is not a mounted file system.

`Attempting to init not-a-filesystem`

While using an inheritance file system mount, Amd detected that an attempt was made to initialize something that is not a mounted file system.

`Can't bind to NIS domain "Y"`

Amd is unable to bind to the NIS domain named *Y*.

`Can't create privileged nfs port (socket)`

While using socket-based networking, Amd failed to create a privileged port.

`Can't find root file handle for D`

While using a top-level mount, Amd was unable to find the root filehandle for the directory *D*.

`Must be root to mount filesystems (euid = N)`

Amd is unable to mount a file system because it is not running as root. Instead, it is running with the effective UID *N*.

`No work to do - quitting`

Amd was not given any mount points to process.

`Out of memory`

Amd failed to allocate memory and even retry it many times.

`Out of memory in realloc`

Amd failed to reallocate memory.

`Unknown fattr type T - ignored`

Amd received an NFS node with unknown file attributes.

`Unknown op to amfs_auto_lookuppn: X`

Amd has detected an unknown lookup operation with code *X*.

`amfs_auto_mount: mount_amfs_toplvl failed: E`

An Amd top-level automount failed. The error message is *E*.

`amfs_host_mount: mf_info has no colon`

While using a `type:=host` file system, Amd detected that the mount information did not include a colon (which separates the hostname from the partition to mount).

`amfs_inherit_match called!`

While using an inheritance file system mount, Amd called a match function that should never have been called.

`amfs_toplvl_mount: mount_amfs_toplvl failed: E`

Amd failed to mount a top-level mount. The error message is *E*.

`cannot create rpc/udp service`

While using socket-based networking, Amd failed to create a UDP RPC service for its NFS server.

`cannot create tcp service for amq: soAMQp=S`

While using socket-based networking, Amd failed to create a TCP socket number *S* for use with its Amq RPC service listener.

`cannot create tcp socket for amq service: E`

While using socket-based networking, Amd failed to create a TCP socket for use with its Amq RPC service listener. The error message was *E*.

`cannot create udp service for amq: soAMQp=S`

While using socket-based networking, Amd failed to create a TCP socket number *S* for use with its Amq RPC service listener.

`cannot create udp socket for amq service: E`

While using socket-based networking, Amd failed to create a UDP socket for use with its Amq RPC service listener. The error message was *E*.

`cannot fill knetconfig structure for nfs_args`

Amd failed to find the kernel-level network configuration structure needed to mount NFS on TLI-based systems.

`cannot get local host address. using 127.0.0.1`

While using TLI networking, Amd was unable to find the address of the local host. Amd is defaulting to 127.0.0.1.

`first time load of map M failed!`

Amd failed to load map *M* for the first time.

`get_autofs_address: cannot get local host address: E`

While running a Solaris Autofs mount, Amd failed to get an address to local mount access. The error message is *E*.

`gethostname: E`

Amd failed to run the `gethostname` function to find the local host's name. The error message is *E*.

`host name is not set`

Amd found out that the local host does not have a name.

`linux mount: unknown fs-type: T`

Amd was asked to mount an unknown file system type *T* on Linux.

`run_rpc failed`

Amd failed to run its main RPC service loop.

`unable to free rpc arguments in amqprog_1`

Amd was unable to free the RPC object and arguments for the Amq service.

`unable to free rpc arguments in autofs_program_1`

While running a Solaris Autofs v1 mount, Amd failed to free allocated memory.

`unable to free rpc arguments in autofs_program_2`

While running a Solaris Autofs v2/v3 mount, Amd failed to free allocated memory.

`unable to free rpc arguments in nfs_program_2`

Amd was unable to free the RPC object and arguments used for its own NFS server.

Appendices

```
unable to register (AMQ_PROGRAM=N, V, tcp)
```
Amd is unable to register the Amq service program *N*, version *V*, using TCP.

```
unable to register (AMQ_PROGRAM=N, V, udp)
```
Amd is unable to register the Amq service program *N*, version *V*, using UDP.

```
unable to register (P, V, 0)
```
While using socket-based networking, Amd failed to register its NFS service for the NFS program *P* and version *V*.

Informational Messages

These messages represent informational "information" about major activities that Amd performs, such as reloading maps, contacting information servers, etc.

```
"A" discarded fstype T from D
```
Amd discarded node *A* of type *T*, which was mounted on directory *D*.

```
"A" mounted fstype T on D
```
Amd mounted node *A* of type *T*, which is on directory *D*.

```
"A" referenced fstype T on D
```
Amd noted a reference to node *A* of type *T*, which is mounted on directory *D*.

```
"A" unmounted fstype T from D
```
Amd unmounted node *A* of type *T*, which was mounted on directory *D*.

```
AM-UTILS VERSION INFORMATION:
```
Amd is about to log the version string that is seen by running amd -v.

```
Filehandle denied for "H:P"
```
Host *H* denied Amd a filehandle for path name *P*.

```
Filehandle error for "H:P": E
```
Amd failed to get a filehandle for path name *P* from host *H*. The error message is *E*.

```
Finishing with status C
```
The Amd process finished with status code *C*. A zero value indicates a successful termination.

`Flushed P; dependent on H`

Amd timed out the node *P* because it belongs to host *H*. (That host may be down.)

`Locked process text and data segment in memory`

Amd successfully locked (via `plock`) the process text and data segments into memory.

`Map M is out of date`

Amd has determined that the map *M* is not in sync with the map server.

`My ip addr is N`

Amd is using the IP address *N* to communicate with the local host.

`NIS map M reloading using am_yp_all`

Amd is reloading the map *M* using a special Amd function that does not leak file descriptors.

`Remounted host H`

While using a `type:=host` file system, Amd is trying to remount host *H*.

`Using MOUNT version: V`

Amd is contacting a remote mount daemon using the MOUNT protocol version *V*.

`Using NFS auth for FQHN "H"`

Amd is using Unix-style RPC authentication for the fully qualified hostname *H*.

`Using NFS version V, protocol T on host H`

Amd is using NFS version *V* and protocol transport *T* for host *H*.

`Using remopts="R"`

Amd is using the mount options *R* for the remote NFS mount.

`"P" forcibly timed out`

Amd got a request to force a timeout of the mount point *P*.

`"P" on D timed out`

Amd detected that the file system *P*, which is mounted on *D*, was not used in some time.

Appendices

A restarted fstype *T* on *D*

Amd restarted the mounted file system *A* of type *T* on local mount point directory *D*.

D: disabling nfs congestion window

Amd is turning off the "dumb timer" throughput-adjustment feature of certain systems so it does not interfere with Amd's own mount retries

N is on a remote network

Amd determined that the network given by the address *N* resides on a remote network—not one locally attached to any of this host's interfaces.

amfs_host_mount: NFS version *V*

While using a type:=host file system, Amd is performing an NFS-mount of version *V*.

amfs_host_umounted: NFS version *V*

While using a type:=host file system, Amd is performing an NFS unmount of version *V*.

amfs_nfsl: "*F*" does not exist, using type:=nfs

While using a type:=nfsl file system, Amd detected that the path name *F* does not exist and is thus using a normal NFS mount.

amfs_nfsl: "*F*" exists, using type:=link

While using a type:=nfsl file system, Amd detected that the path name *F* exists and is thus using a symbolic link mount.

amfs_nfsl: "*H*" is not local host, using type:=nfs

While using a type:=nfsl file system, Amd detected that the host *H* is not local and is thus using a normal NFS mount.

amq says flush cache

Amd received a request from Amq to flush its map caches.

autofs: bind-mounting *P* -> *L*

While running a Linux Autofs mount, Amd has decided to execute a bind mount for the path name *P* leading to the link *L*.

```
autofs: deleting symlink L
```
While running a Linux Autofs mount, Amd is deleting a symlink *L*.

```
autofs: lookup of N failed
```
While running a Linux Autofs mount, Amd failed to look up the name *N*.

```
autofs: mkdir mountpoint 'D'
```
While using a type:=auto file system, Amd is creating the directory mount point *D* for use with Autofs.

```
autofs: mounting D failed
```
While running a Solaris Autofs mount, Amd failed in mounting the path name *D*.

```
autofs: mounting D succeeded
```
While running a Solaris Autofs mount, Amd succeeded in mounting the path name *D*.

```
autofs: mounting P failed
```
While running a Linux Autofs mount, Amd succeeded in mounting path name *P*.

```
autofs: mounting P succeeded
```
While running a Linux Autofs mount, Amd succeeded in mounting path name *P*.

```
autofs: removing mountpoint directory D
```
While running a Linux Autofs mount, Amd is deleting a directory mount point *D*.

```
autofs: symlinking P -> L
```
While running a Linux Autofs mount, Amd decided to create a symbolic link from the path name *P* to the name *L*.

```
autofs: un-bind-mounting P
```
While running a Linux Autofs mount, Amd released a bind-type mount for path name *P*.

```
autofs: unmounting D failed
```
While running a Solaris Autofs mount, Amd failed in unmounting the path name *D*.

Appendices

```
autofs: unmounting D succeeded
```
While running a Solaris Autofs mount, Amd succeeded in unmounting the path name *D*.

```
autofs: using protocol version V
```
While running a Linux Autofs mount, Amd is using Autofs protocol version *V*.

```
autofs_mount_1_svc: M:N:O:P
```
Amd is executing a Solaris Autofs mount in map *M* for name *P*. The mount options are *O* and the full path name is *P*.

```
autofs_unmount_1_svc: F:D:R:X
```
Amd is running a Solaris Autofs unmount operation for device *D* and raw device *R*. The address of the next unmount request is *X*. If *F* is 1, then this was a direct mount.

```
call_mountd: NFS version N, mount version V
```
Amd is calling a remote mount daemon of version *V* to get a filehandle for NFS version *N*.

```
cannot chdir to /: E
```
Amd is not able to change its working directory to the root directory. The error message is *E*.

```
creating autofs service listener
```
Amd is creating an Autofs service for listening to RPC mount requests.

```
failed to create RPC client to "H"
```
While using TLI networking, Amd failed to create an RPC client to contact host *H*.

```
failed to create RPC client to "H" after S seconds
```
While using TLI networking, Amd failed to create an RPC client to contact host *H* and timed out after *S* seconds.

```
fetch_fhandle: NFS version V
```
While using a type:=host file system, Amd decided to retrieve an NFS filehandle of version *V*.

```
file server H, type T, state S
```
The file server on host *H*, of type *T*, changed status to *S*.

`find_nfs_srvr: force NFS protocol transport to T`

Amd was asked explicitly to use NFS protocol transport *T* (UDP or TCP).

`find_nfs_srvr: force NFS version to V`

Amd was asked explicitly to use NFS version *V*.

`first time load of map M succeeded`

Amd succeeded in loading map *M* for the first time.

`get_nfs_version NFS(V,P) failed for H`

While using socket-based networking, Amd failed to access host *H* using NFS version *V* and transport *P*.

`get_nfs_version NFS(X-Y,P) failed for H: E`

While using TLI networking, Amd failed to access host *H* using any NFS versions from *X* to *Y* and transport *P*. The error message is *E*.

`get_nfs_version trying a lower version`

While using socket-based networking, Amd failed to contact a remote NFS server using a given NFS version, so Amd is trying an older NFS version.

`get_nfs_version: returning (V,P) on host H`

While using socket-based networking, Amd was able to use NFS version *V* and transport *P* for host *H*.

`get_nfs_version[TLI] NFS(V,P) failed for H: E`

While using TLI networking, Amd failed to access host *H* using NFS version *V* and transport *P*. The error message is *E*.

`get_nfs_version[socket] NFS(V,P) failed for H: E`

While using socket-based networking, Amd failed to access host *H* using NFS version *V* and transport *P*. The error message is *E*.

`hesiod_isup: Hesiod came back up for map M`

Amd detected that a Hesiod server that was down for map *M* is now back up.

`initializing amd.conf map M of type T`

Amd has determined that the map *M* specified in your `amd.conf` file is using a map service type *T*.

`merge opts "X" add "Y" => "O"`

Amd merged the local mount options *X* and *Y* to produce *O*.

`merge rem/opts "X" add "Y" => "O"`

Amd merged the remote and local mount options *X* and *Y* to produce *O*.

`merge remopts "X" add "Y" => "O"`

Amd merged the remote mount options *X* and *Y* to produce *O*.

`mount of "P" has timed out`

Amd timed out trying to mount *P*.

`mount_nfs_fh: NFS version V`

Amd is mounting a remote partition of NFS version *V*.

`mount_nfs_fh: using NFS transport T`

Amd is mounting a remote partition of NFS using transport *T*.

`nis_isup: NIS came back up for map M`

Amd detected that an NIS server that was down for map *M* is up again. Hooray.

`on-exit attempt to unmount A`

Amd is trying to unmount the node *A* right before exiting. This is often used when you set `unmount_on_exit=yes` in your `amd.conf` file.

`prime_nfs_fhandle_cache: NFS version V`

Amd is trying to get an NFS filehandle for NFS version *V*.

`recompute_portmap: NFS version V`

Amd is contacting a remote mount daemon for a host whose NFS version is *V*.

`released controlling tty using ioctl(TIOCNOTTY)`

Amd successfully executed the `ioctl` to background itself, which is needed to properly run as a daemon.

`released controlling tty using setsid()`

Amd successfully detached from its controlling terminal, which is needed for it to properly run in the background (as many daemons do).

`reload #N of map M succeeded`

Amd succeeded in reloading map *M* for the *N*th time.

`reload of map M is not needed (in sync)`

Amd determined that a reload of map *M* is not necessary because the map is in sync with the map server.

`restarting A on D`

While using an inheritance file system mount, Amd is trying to restart the mount for node *A* on mount point directory *D*.

`running fsck on cache directory "D"`

Amd detected an error while processing a CacheFS file system. You must run `fsck` on the directory *D* first.

`start_ping: nfs_version: V`

Amd is starting to monitor a remote NFS server running NFS version *V*.

`switched to logfile "F"`

Amd switched to using the log file *F*. Whatever log file Amd was using before is closed.

`turning on AMF_AUTOFS for node P`

Amd detected that node *P* is using Autofs (Solaris) and is enabling it.

`turning on NFS option symttl and setting value to 0`

Amd has detected that the local system supports symbolic link caches in NFS. Amd is turning off this feature so it does not interfere with Amd and HLFSD.

```
using an overlay mount
```
Amd is using an overlay mount.

```
using configuration file F
```
Amd is using the Amd configuration file *F*.

Map Errors

These messages provide information about map errors such as parsing errors, as well as information about selectors being evaluated.

```
Map entry M for P did not match
```
Amd failed to match the path name *P* for the map entry *M*.

```
No map entry for P
```
Amd was unable to find a map entry for a looked up directory path name *P*.

```
Re-synchronizing cache for map M
```
Amd is revalidating the internal cache for map *M*.

```
Trying mount of A on D fstype T mount_type S
```
Amd is trying to mount *A* on directory *D*. The file system is of type *T*, and the mount type is of type *S*.

```
Waiting on map entry for P
```
Amd was unable to find a map entry for a looked up directory path name *P*.

```
did not match defaults for "K"
```
Amd could not find a default entry for map entry *K*.

```
invalid numeric option in "O": "V"
```
While parsing a mount option *O* (such as key=val), Amd expected a numeric value to be given but found that an illegal value *V* was used instead.

```
key K: map function F did not match O
```
While parsing the map entry for key *K*, Amd evaluated function *F* and found that it did not match the value *O*.

`key K: map function F did not mismatch O`

While parsing the map entry for key K, Amd evaluated function F and found that it did not mismatch the value O.

`key K: map selector S (=V) did not match O`

While parsing the map entry for key K, Amd evaluated the selector S against the value V and found that it did not match the current value O.

`key K: map selector S (=V) did not mismatch O`

While parsing the map entry for key K, Amd evaluated the selector S against the value V and found that it did not mismatch the current value O.

`matched default selectors "K"`

Amd matched a default entry for map entry K.

`numeric option to "O" missing`

While parsing a mount option O (such as key=val), Amd expected a numeric value to be given but found that no value was specified.

Additional Statistical Information

These messages provide a little additional statistical information: remote server uptimes and downtimes.

`"P" on D still active`

Amd cannot unmount the file system P, which is mounted on directory D, because it is still in use.

`file server H is down - timeout of "P" ignored`

Amd found that node P has not been used in some time and should expire, but the file server it is attached to appears to be down.

Non-fatal User Errors

These messages indicate non-fatal user errors such as map-parsing errors.

`-y: option ignored. No NIS support available.`

Amd is ignoring the command line option -y because Amd was not built with NIS support.

Appendices

`1st/2nd args missing to (un)mount program`

While using a `type:=program` file system, Amd detected that either the first or the second arguments were not specified to the unmount or mount parameters.

`Ambiguous map cache type "T"; using "inc"`

Amd was given an unknown map cache type *T* and is using the incremental cache mode.

`Cannot read directory D: E`

Amd failed to read the union-map directory *D*. The error message is *E*.

`Cannot switch logfile`

Amd is unable to begin using a new log file.

`Empty backslash escape`

While expanding an escaped sequence in a map, Amd could not find which character is being expanded.

`Empty timestamp value for map M`

Amd found an empty time stamp value for an LDAP map *M*.

`Empty value for K in map M`

Amd found an empty value for key *K* in an LDAP map *M*.

`LDAP panic: no map data`

Amd could not find any entries in an LDAP map.

`LDAP search failed: E`

Amd failed to find a key in an LDAP map. The error message is *E*.

`LDAP timestamp search failed: E`

Amd failed to get the time stamp on an LDAP map. The error message is *E*.

`Missing timestamp value for map M`

Amd failed to get the time stamp value for an LDAP map *M*.

`Missing value for K in map M`

Amd failed to find a value for key *K* in an LDAP map *M*.

`More than a single value for /defaults in M`

Amd found more than a single value for /defaults in the map *M* (and `selectors_on_default` was not used).

`Mount opts soft and spongy are incompatible - soft ignored`

Amd has detected the use of both the `soft` and `spongy` mount options. Amd is using the `spongy` option only.

`No closing '}' in "S"`

Amd detected a parenthesized expression *S* that does not include the closing braces.

`No fs type specified (key = "K, map = "M")`

While processing the key *K* in map *M*, Amd found out that the `fs` variable was not specified.

`No source data for map M`

Amd was not able to get any entries in map *M*. The map could be empty or its server malfunctioning.

`No timestamp entry for map M`

Amd failed to get the time stamp entry for an LDAP map *M*.

`Nonpositive timestamp T for map M`

Amd found a time stamp value *T* for an LDAP map *M* that is either zero or negative.

`Too large character constant N`

An escaped character sequence used a value that is greater than 255.

`Unable to (re)bind to any ldap hosts`

Amd failed to bind or rebind to any LDAP server.

`Unable to decode ldap timestamp T for map M`

Amd failed to decode the time stamp value *T* for an LDAP map *M*.

Appendices

`Unable to parse hostport P for ldap map M`

Amd failed to find the host port *P* of an LDAP server for map *M*.

`Unknown $ sequence in "S"`

Amd detected an unknown variable string *S* that could not be resolved at all.

`Unknown host: H`

Amd was unable to find the IP address for host *H*.

`Unknown sequence "${S}"`

Amd detected an unknown map variable that could not be resolved either by Amd's variables or by looking up the environment's variables.

`F: Can't open logfile: E`

Amd is unable to open the log file *F* for writing Amd's logging and debugging messages. The error message is *E*.

`M: line L has no value field`

Amd detected that a map entry on line *L* in a map file *M* is empty (only the key is specified, without a value).

`V is not on a local network`

While evaluating the `in_network` function, Amd has determined that the value *V* does not represent a hostname or address that is on any of the locally attached networks.

`V is on a local network`

While evaluating the `in_network` function, Amd has determined that the value *V* does not represent a hostname or address that is on one of the locally attached networks.

`amfs_nfsl: host $fs and $rhost must be specified`

While using a `type:=nfsl` file system, Amd detected that either the `fs` or the `rhost` parameters were not specified.

`amfs_nfsx: no remote filesystem specified`

While using a `type:=nfsx` file system, Amd detected that the `rfs` parameter was not specified.

```
amfs_nfsx: no remote host specified
```

While using a `type:=nfsx` file system, Amd detected that the `rhost` parameter was not specified.

```
amfs_nfsx: remount of D failed: E
```

While using a `type:=nfsx` file system, Amd failed to remount a directory *D*. The error message is *E*.

```
auto: no map named (fs:=)
```

While using a `type:=auto` file system, Amd detected that the `fs` parameter was not specified.

```
auto: no mount point named (rfs:=)
```

While using a `type:=auto` file system, Amd detected that the `rfs` parameter was not specified.

```
cachefs: must specify cachedir, rfs, and fs
```

While accessing a mount of `type:=cachefs`, Amd detected that one of these parameters was not defined: `cachedir`, `rfs`, and `fs`.

```
cdfs: no source device specified
```

While accessing a mount of `type:=cdfs`, Amd detected that the `dev` parameter was not defined.

```
efs: no device specified
```

While accessing a mount of `type:=efs`, Amd detected that the `dev` parameter was not defined.

```
error compiling RE "P": E
```

Amd failed to compile the regular expression pattern *P* into an internal form. The error message is *E*.

```
error matching RE "P" against "K": E
```

Amd failed to match the regular expression pattern *P* against the key *K*. The error message is *E*.

Appendices

`fs type "T" not recognized`

Amd does not recognize the file system type *T*.

`key K: Bad selector "S"`

While parsing the map entry for key *K*, Amd found an unknown selector *S*.

`key K: Can't assign to a selector (S)`

While parsing the map entry for key *K*, Amd found an unrecognized selector *S*.

`key K: Malformed function in "F"`

While parsing the map entry for key *K*, Amd found a function *F* that is syntactically incorrect.

`key K: No option or assignment in "S"`

While parsing the map entry for key *K*, Amd found that the string *S* did not include any options or assignments (possibly only selectors).

`key K: No value component in "S"`

While parsing the map entry for key *K*, Amd found a component with no value assigned to it.

`key K: Unrecognized key/option "O"`

While parsing the map entry for key *K*, Amd found an unrecognized key or option *O*.

`key K: unknown function "F"`

While parsing the map entry for key *K*, Amd found an unknown function *F*.

`link: no fs specified`

While using a `type:=link` file system, Amd detected that the `fs` parameter was not specified.

`lofs: no source filesystem specified`

While accessing a mount of `type:=lofs`, Amd detected that the `rfs` parameter was not defined.

`netgrp = `*`N`*` status = `*`C`*` host = `*`H`*`

While evaluating the `netgrp` function, Amd checked to see if the host *H* is a member of the netgroup *N*. The result of the match is *C* (a 1 indicates a successful match).

`netgrp = `*`N`*` status = `*`C`*` hostd = `*`H`*`

While evaluating the `netgrpd` function, Amd checked to see if the fully qualified host-name *H* is a member of the netgroup *N*. The result of the match is *C* (a 1 indicates a successful match).

`nfs: no remote filesystem specified`

While accessing a mount of `type:=nfs`, Amd detected that the parameter `rfs` was not specified.

`nfs: no remote host specified`

While accessing a mount of `type:=nfs`, Amd detected that the parameter `rhost` was not specified.

`option "`*`O`*`" not recognized`

Amd is unable to recognize the mount option *O*.

`pcfs: no source device specified`

While accessing a mount of `type:=pcfs`, Amd detected that the `dev` parameter was not defined.

`skipping selector to "`*`S`*`"`

While evaluating one selector in a location, Amd is skipping to the next component of the location (*S*), which could be another selector.

`ufs: no device specified`

While accessing a mount of `type:=ufs`, Amd detected that the `dev` parameter was not defined.

`xfs: no device specified`

While accessing a mount of `type:=xfs`, Amd detected that the `dev` parameter was not defined.

Appendices

Warnings

These are warning messages that are serious but not fatal enough to warrant shutting down Amd.

> `AIX: may need to lower stack size using ulimit(3) before calling plock`

Amd has detected the use of `plock=yes` on an AIX system, where use of this function can result in allocating all available memory. It is recommended first to run `ulimit` to force the maximum memory use of Amd to a smaller number than the default.

> `Could not disassociate tty (TIOCNOTTY): E`

Amd was unable to execute the `ioctl` to background itself, which is needed to properly run as a daemon. The error message is *E*.

> `Could not open controlling tty: E`

Amd was unable to open its controlling terminal, which is needed before it can execute the `ioctl` to background itself. The error message is *E*.

> `Could not release controlling tty using setsid(): E`

Amd was unable to detach from its controlling terminal, which is needed for it to properly run in the background (as many daemons do). The error message is *E*.

> `Couldn't lock process text and data segment in memory: E`

Amd failed to lock (via `plock`) the process text and data segments into memory. The error message is *E*.

> `Exhausted list of ldap servers, looping.`

Amd failed to access any LDAP server. It is thus trying again (up to 10 times).

> `Key "K" contains a disallowed character`

Amd detected that the key *K* contains illegal characters and is ignoring the entire key.

> `Long hostname H truncated to N characters`

Amd detected that the hostname *H* used is longer than the system allows for and is thus truncating the name to at most *N* characters.

`Map type "T" does not support cache type "all"; using "inc"`

Amd was asked to cache all entries for the map of type *T*, but this map service cannot be fully enumerated (perhaps because it is a hierarchical or recursive service). Amd is defaulting to the incremental cache mode.

`Map type "T" does not support cache type "re"`

Amd was asked to use regular expressions for the map of type *T*, but this map does not support regular expression (pattern) searches.

`NFS server entry assumed to be H:/`

Amd could not find a path name for an NFS mount, so it is assuming the path name to be the root (/) file system on server *H*.

`NIS domain name is not set. NIS ignored.`

The user did not set the NIS domain name for this run of Amd. NIS maps are not being processed.

`No '/' in mtab (F), using "." as tmp directory`

Amd was given a mount table file name *F* that is not an absolute path name; Amd is trying to access that file relative to the local directory.

`Possible mount table race - retrying D`

Amd detected a possible race condition while trying to lock a mount table file, so it is retrying the mount for the node *D*.

`Process memory locking not support by the OS`

Amd was asked to lock the process text and data segments, but the current host does not support a memory locking function.

`Unable to ldap_bind to H:P as I`

Amd failed to bind to an LDAP server on host *H* and port *P* with ID *I*.

`Unable to ldap_open to H:P`

Amd failed to open an LDAP map on host *H* and port *P*.

```
WARNING: automounter going down on signal N
```
Amd is terminating due to receiving signal N.

```
D is an existing automount point
```
Amd detected an attempt to reuse D as an automount point.

```
D is not a directory
```
While using a top-level mount, Amd detected that a mount was attempted on a non-directory D.

```
amfs_toplvl_unmount retrying D in 1s
```
Amd failed to unmount an entry D that expired, and is sleeping and retrying in one second.

```
children of "A" still exist - deleting anyway
```
Amd was asked to remove the automount node A, but that node still has subsidiary entries. Amd is removing this node nonetheless.

```
extra mkdirs required for D
```
Amd has determined that it needs to create several more directories for the mount point D.

```
extra umount required for D
```
Amd has determined that it needs to retry the unmount request of the directory D for the unmount to succeed.

```
file descriptor D not in the hash
```
While running a Linux Autofs mount, Amd could not find a file descriptor that was supposed to be in use.

```
find_nfs_srvr: NFS mount failed, trying again with NFSv2/UDP
```
Amd failed to contact a remote NFS host using the given version and transport and is thus trying again with just NFS version 2 and UDP.

```
found compatibility option "nfsv2": set options vers=2,proto=udp
for host H
```
Amd found a system that has a special NFS override mount option nfsv2 for host H. Amd is using NFS version 2 and the UDP protocol for this host.

`getnetbyaddr failed on N, succeeded on S`

Amd failed to find the name of the network given its full subnet number *N* but succeeded in doing so using the short form *S*.

`ignoring request from H:P, expected X`

Amd is ignoring an unexpected request from host *H* (port *P*) because Amd expected to get that request from host *X*.

`ignoring request from H:P, port not reserved`

Amd is ignoring a request from host *H* because port *P* is not reserved.

`ignoring timeout request for active node D`

Amd is ignoring a timeout request for mount node *D* because it is still in use.

`ignoring unknown protocol option for H:P`

Amd could not find what NFS transport to use for host *H* and file system *P*.

`job I rescheduled to run immediately`

Amd rescheduled the task with ID *I* to run right away.

`line L in "M" is too long`

Amd detected that a map entry on line *L* in a map file *M* is longer than 1500 characters.

`map= has a null map name. reset to amd.unknown`

While running a Solaris Autofs mount, Amd was given a map with no name.

`mtab nap failed: E`

Amd tried to sleep for a random number of microseconds before retrying to lock a mount table file name, but the sleep command failed with error *E*.

`noconn option not specified, and was just turned ON (OS override)!`
`(May cause NFS hangs on some systems...)`

Amd has determined that although the noconn NFS mount option was not specified, it is most likely needed. So Amd has turned it on. However, this could cause problems on some systems.

>   noconn option specified, and was just turned OFF (OS override)!
>
>   (May cause NFS hangs on some systems...)

Amd has determined that although the noconn NFS mount option was specified, it is most likely not needed. So Amd has turned it off. However, this could cause problems on some systems.

>   null syslog facility, using LOG_DAEMON"

The user specified the use of syslog to log Amd's messages, but the facility was specified; thus Amd will use the LOG_DAEMON facility.

>   realloc_mntfs: copy fallback ops "T" over "U"

Amd failed to mount a volume in a map entry, and this failure resulted in assigning the U type to the volume (most likely an error type). Amd is failing over to the next volume in the mount entry, which is of type T.

>   recompute_portmap: nfs_version = 0 fixed

Amd was asked to contact a remote mount daemon whose NFS version was unknown. Amd is assuming the default NFS version of the system.

>   start_ping: nfs_version = 0 fixed

Amd was asked to start monitoring (via NFS_NULL pings) a remote file server whose NFS version is unknown (0). Amd is assuming the default NFS version on the system.

>   syslog option not supported, logging unchanged

The user specified the use of syslog to log Amd's messages, but syslog is not supported on this system.

>   unknown syslog facility "F, using LOG_DAEMON"

The user specified an unknown syslog facility F to log Amd's messages. Amd thus defaults to the LOG_DAEMON facility.

>   unmount: D is not mounted

Amd was asked to unmount the directory D, but that directory is not mounted.

Debug Messages

The following are debugging messages that are printed when you compile Amd with debugging support and turn on debugging using the amd.conf parameter debug_options.

(skipping rewind)

Amd is resetting the location vector and has reset the default options, before processing the next || cut operator.

-D mtab option ignored

Amd is ignoring the mtab debugging option. To turn it on, this debug option must be specified explicitly (debug_options=all,mtab) in your /etc/amd.conf file.

.. in A gives P

Amd is inside the directory lookup function and has determined that the parent automounted node of A is P.

... gives S

Amd found the name S while performing a union mount.

/defaults chopped into L

Amd has split the value of a /defaults entry into a single location L, which is processed now. This is used when selectors_on_default is turned on.

/defaults gave V

Amd found the value V for a /defaults map entry.

Allocating a new xid...

Amd is allocating a new asynchronous RPC packet-forwarding handle.

Already running pings to H

Amd tried to start a pinging thread to server H but found that such a thread already exists.

Arranging to retry mount of A

Amd is preparing to retry the mount of node A.

Base is: B

Amd is using the LDAP base B.

Appendices

```
Blocked, trying to obtain exclusive mtab lock
```
Amd is trying to get an exclusive lock for an /etc/mtab file before writing to it.

```
Bound to H:P
```
Amd is connected to an LDAP server on host *H* and port *P*.

```
CACHEFS: using cache directory "D"
```
Amd is mounting a CacheFS file system using a cache directory *D*.

```
CDFS: mounting device "D" on "M"
```
Amd is mounting a CDFS file system from device *D* onto mount point *M*.

```
Calling wakeup on I
```
Amd is waking up a sleeping NFS mount thread with ID *I*.

```
Can't forward reply id I
```
Amd is unable to forward or process the RPC message with ID *I*.

```
Commencing retry for mount of A
```
Amd is retrying a mount of node *A*.

```
Cut: not trying any more locations for A
```
While processing the || map cut operator, Amd could not find any more locations for the automount node *A*.

```
Deleting file server H
```
Amd no longer has any active file systems that use the server *H*.

```
Discarding earlier rpc fwd handle
```
Amd is freeing an RPC forwarding handle that was in use, so it can be reused.

```
Discarding filehandle for H:P
```
Amd is removing an NFS filehandle for host *H* and path name *P*.

```
Discarding last mntfs reference to A fstype T
```
Amd has released the last user reference to an automounted node *A*, which mounted as a file system of type *T*.

```
Discarding remount hook for A
```
Amd is done with the automount node *A*, which was remounted.

```
Duplicate pending mount fstype T
```
Amd is ignoring a duplicate request to mount the same file system type *T*.

```
EFS: mounting device "D" on "M"
```
Amd is mounting an EFS file system from device *D* onto mount point *M*.

```
Error fetching port for mountd on H#error=E, port=P
```
Amd wasn't able to find the port number that `rpc.mountd` runs on for host *H*. The port that Amd tried was *P* and the error it got was error number *E*.

```
Fetching export list from H
```
Amd is retrieving the full list of exported file systems from host *H*.

```
Fetching fhandle for P
```
Amd is looking for a filehandle for remote file system *P*.

```
Filter is: F
```
Amd is using the LDAP filter *F*.

```
Finished unmount(D)
```
Amd finished unmounting the file system mounted on *D*.

```
Forced close on F in read_mtab
```
Amd forced a close on an open mtab file name *F*.

```
Getting timestamp for map M
```
Amd is retrieving the time stamps for an LDAP map *M*.

```
Got a hit with T
```
Amd matched a map entry to file system type *T*.

```
Got portmap for old port request
```
Amd was able to get the portmapper's port for a request that was pending.

Appendices

```
Got timestamp for map M: T
```
Amd got the time stamp *T* for an LDAP map *M*.

```
Hesiod base is: B
```
Amd is using the Hesiod base *B*.

```
Hostname S normalized to H
```
Amd normalized the host with a short name *S* to the FQHN name *H*.

```
Immediately discarding mntfs for A
```
Amd is done with the automount node *A* and is freeing its data structures.

```
LDAP panic: unable to find map data
```
Amd was unable to retrieve any data from an LDAP map.

```
LOFS: mounting fs "D" on "M"
```
Amd is mounting an LOFS file system from directory *D* onto mount point *M*.

```
LOOKUP REPLY: status=C
```
Amd got a reply from a Solaris Autofs lookup, whose status is *C* (0 means no error).

```
LOOKUP REQUEST: name=N[S] map=M opts=O path=P direct=F
```
Amd is using Solaris Autofs and is performing a lookup for the subdirectory *S* of mount point *N*. The map is *M* whose full automounted path is *P*, using mount options *O*. If this is a direct mount, then *F* is 1.

```
Last hard reference to file server H - will timeout in Ss
```
Amd has released the last file system from server *H*, and this file server structure will be removed in *S* seconds if it isn't used again.

```
Locating mntfs reference to A
```
Amd is looking for a reference to an automounted node *A*.

```
MOUNT REPLY: status=C, AUTOFS_ACTION
```
Amd got a reply from a Solaris Autofs mount request, whose status is *C* (0 means no error). Autofs is performing the mount.

`MOUNT REPLY: status=C, AUTOFS_DONE`

Amd got a reply from a Solaris Autofs mount request, whose status is C (0 means no error). Autofs is done mounting the volume.

`MOUNT REPLY: status=C, UNKNOWN`

Amd got a reply from a Solaris Autofs mount request, whose status is C (0 means no error). The type of action requested from Autofs was unknown.

`MOUNT REQUEST: name=N[S] map=M opts=O path=P direct=F`

Amd is using Solaris Autofs and is requesting a mount for the subdirectory S of mount point N. The map is M whose full automounted path is P, using mount options O. If this is a direct mount, then F is 1.

`Map M is ldap`

Map M comes from an LDAP server.

`Map M, K => V`

An LDAP search in map M for key K found the value V.

`Map for M coming from maptype T`

The type of map M is T.

`Mount backgrounded, not sending autofs reply yet`

Amd backgrounded a Linux Autofs mount request but is not sending a reply to the Autofs service just yet.

`Mount of A delayed by Ss`

Amd is delaying the mount of node A by S seconds.

`Mounting of P already pending`

Amd's mount of a Linux Autofs path name P is already in progress.

`NFS timeout in S seconds`

Amd will timeout all access to a file server in S seconds.

`NFS: mounting remote server "H", remote fs "P" on "D"`

Amd is mounting the remote path name P from host H onto the local directory D.

Appendices

```
NFSX: mounting remote server "H", remote fs "P" on "D"
```
Amd is mounting the remote NFS host *H*'s partition *P* on the local mount point *D*, as part of an NFSX mount.

```
NIS master for M@D has order O
```
The NIS master for map *M* for domain *D* has the NIS order (logical time stamp) of *O*.

```
NIS master for M@D is a NIS+ server
```
Amd detected that the NIS master for map *M* of domain *D* actually comes from an NIS+ server, which runs in NIS-compatibility mode.

```
NISplus callback for <K,V>
```
Amd sets up an NIS+ callback for key *K* and value *V*.

```
NISplus init <M>: E (C)
```
Amd could not initialize an NIS+ map *M* and got the error message *E* and error code *C*.

```
NISplus reload for M
```
Amd is reloading an NIS+ map *M*.

```
NISplus search callback for <K>
```
Amd is searching via callbacks for *K* in an NIS+ map.

```
NISplus search callback value <V>
```
Amd is searching via callbacks for value *V* in an NIS+ map.

```
NISplus search for K
```
Amd is searching an NIS+ map for key *K*.

```
NISplus search for K: E(C)
```
Amd searched for *K* in an NIS+ map, and the search failed with error message *E* and error code *C*.

```
NISplus search found <nothing>
```
Amd found an empty value when searching an NIS+ map for a key.

NISplus search found *V*

An Amd search in a NIS+ map found the value *V*.

NISplus search found nothing

Amd found no key when searching an NIS+ map.

NISplus search returned *C*

An Amd search in an NIS+ map failed and returned the status code *C*.

Next mount timeout in *S*s

Amd sets the next timeout to occur in *S* seconds.

No further timeouts

Amd could not find any more automount nodes that needed to be timed out.

No object

An LDAP search failed to find the object.

No-op unmount of error node *A*

Amd is performing "fake" unmount of an error type automounted node *A*.

PCFS: mounting device "*D*" on "*M*"

Amd is mounting a PCFS file system from device *D* onto mount point *M*.

POSTMOUNT REPLY: status=*C*

Amd got a reply from a Solaris Autofs post-mount request, whose status is *C* (0 means no error).

POSTMOUNT REQUEST: *M* dev=*D* special=*R O*

Amd requested a Solaris Autofs post-mount request for device *D* (raw device *R*) of mount point *M*. Mount options requested are *O*.

POSTUNMOUNT REPLY: status=*C*

Amd got a reply from a Solaris Autofs post-unmount request, whose status is *C* (0 means no error).

Appendices

`POSTUNMOUNT REQUEST: dev=D rdev=R`

Amd requested a Solaris Autofs post-unmount request for device *D* (raw device *R*).

`Process PID exited with status E`

Amd process *PID* exited with status *E* (0 means a successful termination of the Amd process).

`Quick reply sent for A`

Amd sent an immediate reply for the automounted node *A*.

`Quick reply sent for M`

Amd sent a quick RPC reply to a Solaris Autofs service for mount point *M*.

`Re-establishing ldap connection`

Amd is reconnecting to an LDAP server.

`Re-using packet forwarding slot - id I`

Amd is reusing a slot for a new packet forwarding task with ID *I*.

`Reading directory D...`

Amd is reading the directory *D* for performing a union mount.

`Receiving MOUNTD reply I`

Amd has received an asynchronous reply to a MOUNT RPC message with ID *I*.

`Receiving NFS ping I`

Amd has received an asynchronous reply to an NFS_PING RPC message with ID *I*.

`Receiving PORTMAP reply`

Amd has received an asynchronous reply to a PORTMAP RPC message.

`Restarting filesystem D`

Amd is restarting an already-mounted file system mounted on directory *D*.

`Returning error: E`

Amd detected error *E* while trying to mount a file system in the background.

SLEEP on *CHAN*

Amd has scheduled a task with ID *CHAN* to sleep until it is woken up.

Search found *N* entries

An LDAP search found *N* entries.

Search with filter: *F*

Amd is performing an LDAP search using the filter *F*.

Searching cache for *H:P*

Amd is looking in its cache for an NFS filehandle for host *H* and path name *P*.

Select waits for Godot

The select(2) system call is waiting forever for any activity.

Select waits for *S*s

The select(2) system call is waiting for *S* seconds for any activity.

Sending MOUNTD request *T*

Amd is sending an asynchronous PORTMAP RPC request of type *T*.

Sending NFS ping

Amd is sending an asynchronous NFS_NULL request.

Sending PORTMAP request

Amd is sending an asynchronous PORTMAP RPC request.

Sending packet id *I* to *H.P*

Amd is asynchronously sending the RPC packet with ID *I* to port *P* on host *H*.

Sent NFS ping to *H*

Amd sent an NFS ping to host *H*.

Setting def_opts to "*O*"

Amd is setting the default options to *O*.

```
Spurious ping packet
```
Amd received a response to an NFS_NULL request that Amd did not send.

```
TS value is:T:
```
The time stamp for an LDAP map is *T*.

```
The timestamp for M is T (err=C)
```
The LDAP map *M* time stamp is *T*, with a possible error code *C* (0 means no error).

```
Timestamp search timed out, trying again...
```
An Amd search for an LDAP map time stamp timed out. Amd is retrying.

```
Timing out automount points...
```
Amd has noticed that some automount nodes are no longer in use; thus it tries to time them out, so they can be discarded.

```
Trying for H:P
```
Amd is trying to contact an LDAP server on host *H* and port *P*.

```
Trying unmount in foreground
```
Amd is trying to unmount a file system in the foreground.

```
Trying unmount(D)
```
Amd is trying to unmount the file system mounted on *D*.

```
UFS: mounting device "D" on "M"
```
Amd is mounting a UFS file system from device *D* onto mount point *M*.

```
UNKNOWN RPC XID
```
Amd was asked to send an unknown RPC message asynchronously, or Amd has received a reply to an unknown RPC message.

```
UNMOUNT REPLY: status=C
```
Amd got a reply from a Solaris Autofs unmount request, whose status is *C* (0 means no error).

`UNMOUNT REQUEST: dev=D rdev=R F`

Amd requested a Solaris Autofs unmount request for device *D* (raw device *R*). *F* indicates if this was a direct or indirect mount.

`Unmounting D (A)`

Amd is trying to unmount the node *A*, mounted on directory *D*.

`Unmounting all from H`

Amd is unmounting all file systems that were mounted from host *H*.

`Waiting while N mount(s) in progress`

Amd is waiting while there are *N* backgrounded mounts in progress.

`Will background the unmount attempt`

Amd will try to run the unmount process in the background.

`XFS: mounting device "D" on "M"`

Amd is mounting an XFS file system from device *D* onto mount point *M*.

`"D" on A timed out`

Trying to unmount node *A* from directory *D* timed out.

`A mount ignored - going down`

Amd is ignoring a request to mount *A* because Amd has started to shut down.

`A: unmount: E`

Unmounting node *A* failed with error message *E*.

`B bytes of memory allocated; total is T`

Amd allocated *B* new bytes of memory, and the current total number of allocated bytes is *T*.

`B bytes of memory allocated; total is T (P pages)`

Amd allocated *B* new bytes of memory, and the current total number of allocated bytes is *T*, which consumes *P* pages.

Appendices

```
D fstype t (T) flags F (O)
```
Amd is mounting a file system of type *T* (numeric type *t*) on the directory *D*, using mount flags *F* and mount options *O*.

```
D: unmount: E
```
Amd failed to unmount *D* with the error message *E*.

```
F new fds allocated; total is T
```
Amd allocated *F* new file descriptors, and the current total number of allocated file descriptors is *T*.

```
F:X:D:O:B:P:T:S:
```
Amd is writing an /etc/mtab entry to file ID *F*, which includes the following: directory *D*, generic options *O*, backup frequency *B*, fsck pass number *P*, file system mount type *T*, and specific mount options *S*. If defined, *X* represents the special internal form of the mounted path name on this system.

```
K returns V
```
A file map search for key *K* returned the value *V*.

```
N pings to H failed - at most M allowed
```
Amd tried to ping a remote host *H*, but *N* (out of *M*) messages failed to be acknowledged.

```
P is already hung - giving up
```
A mounted node *P* is hung. Amd will no longer try to use it.

```
P/A mount ignored - going down
```
Amd is ignoring a request to mount remote path *P* for node *A* because Amd has started to shut down.

```
add_kv: K -> V
```
Amd parsed a map and found a key *K* with value *V*.

```
amfs_auto call to mount_node failed: E
```
Amd was not able to mount a node, and the error is *E*.

`amfs_auto_readdir: End of readdir in` *A*

Amd finished reading the directory of automount node *A*.

`amfs_auto_readdir: default search`

Amd is performing a normal directory-reading operation on an automount point.

`amfs_auto_readdir: real child`

While performing a readdir operation, Amd detected an entry other than the . (dot) and .. (dot-dot) Unix directories.

`amfs_auto_readdir_browsable: End of readdir in` *A*

Amd finished reading the directory of the browsable automount node *A*.

`amfs_auto_readdir_browsable: default search`

Amd is performing a directory-reading operation on a browsable automount point.

`amfs_auto_readdir_browsable: real child`

While performing a readdir operation on a browsable node, Amd detected an entry other than the . (dot) and .. (dot-dot) Unix directories.

`amfs_host: mounting fs` *P* `on` *D*

Amd is mounting the NFS file system *P* on the local mount point *D*.

`amfs_host: unmounts` *D*

Amd is unmounting the file system mounted on the local directory *D*.

`amfs_nfsx: init mount for` *H* `on` *D*

Amd is starting an NFS mount for server *H* on directory *D*.

`amu_hesiod_init(`*M*`)`

Amd is initializing a Hesiod map *M*.

`avoiding dup fhandle requested for` *P*

Amd is ignoring a duplicate request to retrieve a filehandle for partition *P* because an existing request is already being processed.

Appendices

`background process exiting with status` *E*

An Amd background process terminated with the exit status *E*. A zero indicates normal exiting.

`backgrounded`

The current Amd process backgrounded, forked, and daemonized itself.

`backgrounding mount of "`*A*`"`

Amd is backgrounding an NFS mount of node *A* as part of a regular NFS mount or an NFSX mount.

`calling map reload on` *M*

Amd will reload map *M*.

`calling mapc_search for wildcard`

Amd is trying to look up wildcard entries in a map.

`calling mountd for` *A*

Amd is informing a remote `rpc.mountd` on node *A* that it unmounted a file system from that host.

`calling underlying fumount on` *P*

As part of an NFSX mount, Amd is calling a low-level NFS unmount function for path name *P*.

`calling underlying mount on` *P*

Amd is performing a low-level NFS mount for path name *P* (as part of an NFSX mount).

`calling underlying umounted on` *P*

As part of an NFSX mount, Amd is calling a low-level auxiliary NFS unmount function for path name *P*.

`can't locate task block for pid` *PID*

Amd is trying to wake up a child process *PID* but is unable to find any scheduled tasks for this child process.

`create_autofs_service: returning C`

Amd is creating an initial Solaris Autofs service listener. If *C* is 0, this operation succeeded.

`duplicate mount of "A" ...`

Amd is ignoring a duplicate request to mount the node *A*.

`fh cache gives fp X, fs P`

Amd found an NFS filehandle in the cache, which has a pointer *X* and uses the path name *P*.

`fh cache search failed`

Amd failed to find a filehandle in the cache.

`fh_to_mp3: P (I) is hung:- call lookup`

Amd tried to convert an NFS filehandle to an automount node (a structure internal to Amd). The conversion failed for path name *P* from host/mount information *I*.

`fhandle fetch for mount version 1 failed: E`

Amd failed to get a MOUNT version 1 filehandle, and the error message is *E*.

`fhandle fetch for mount version 3 failed: E`

Amd failed to get a MOUNT version 3 filehandle, and the error message is *E*.

`file server H type nfs is still up`

Amd sent an NFS_NULL ping message to the NFS file server on host *H* and found that it is up and running.

`foreground mount of "A" ...`

Amd is running an NFS mount of path name *A* in the foreground, as part of an NFSX mount, or Amd is running any other mount in the foreground.

`found first assignment past selectors "S"`

Amd parsed a location and found the first assignment (*S*) after all of the selectors.

`freeing action list`

Amd is freeing the action list resources now that it is done with a Solaris Autofs mount.

`get_mount_client: using tcp, port P`

Amd is trying to make a TCP connection to a remote MOUNT daemon using port *P*.

`get_mount_client: using udp, port P`

Amd is trying to make a UDP connection to a remote MOUNT daemon using port *P*.

`get_nfs_version trying NFS(V,T) for H`

Amd is trying to contact an NFS server on host *H*, using NFS version *V* and protocol type *T* (UDP or TCP).

`get_nfs_version trying NFS(X-Y,T) for H`

Amd is trying to contact an NFS server on host *H*, using protocol type *T* (UDP or TCP) and a range of NFS versions from *X* to *Y*.

`get_root_nfs_fh substitutes pid PID`

During initialization of Amd's own mount points, the master Amd process provided an NFS root filehandle for an Amd process number *PID*.

`global split_opts ok`

Amd parsed the global options string (in /`defaults`) correctly.

`got filehandle for H:P`

Amd got an NFS filehandle for host *H* and path name *P*.

`got port (P) for mountd on H`

Amd will use port *P* for access to `rpc.mountd` running on host *H*.

`hesiod_isup(M): E`

Amd checked to see if the Hesiod server for map *M* was up, and it received the status message *E*.

`hesiod_search(m=A, map=M, key=K, pval=VP tp=TP)`

Amd is searching a Hesiod server's map *M* for key *K*. The automount node is *A*. The key's value (if found) will be stored in address *VP*, and the map's time stamp will be stored in address *TP*.

```
hesiod_search: Error: E
```
A Hesiod search failed with the error *E*.

```
hesiod_search: Returning: C
```
A Hesiod search function is terminating with the status code *C* (0 means no error).

```
hesiod_search: hes_resolve(K, B)
```
Amd is searching a Hesiod server for key *K* and base *B*.

```
ignoring mount of P in D -- flags (F) in progress
```
Amd is ignoring a request to mount remote path name *P* in directory *D* because of a conflicting or pending operation depicted by the flags *F*.

```
in amfs_auto_lookuppn
```
Amd is currently running inside the directory lookup function.

```
local eval_selectors ok
```
Amd evaluated the per-location selectors correctly.

```
local split_opts ok
```
Amd parsed the per-location options correctly.

```
lock F failed: E
```
Amd failed to lock the mount table lock file name *F* with the error message *E*.

```
lock failed: E
```
Amd failed to lock with the error message *E*.

```
lstat(A): E
```
Checking the existence of a top-level automount node *A* failed with error message *E*.

```
map M last load time is T1, last modify time is T2
```
Amd is not going to reload a map *M* because it has not changed. The last time that map was loaded was *T1*, and the last time it was modified was *T2*.

```
mapc recurses on K
```
Amd continues to recursively search for a wildcard entry named *K*.

```
matched S in P
```
Amd matched the file server name *S* for the mount path *P*.

```
mkdir(D)
```
Amd is creating a directory *D* to serve as a mount point.

```
mntfs reference for A still active
```
Amd cannot free the automounted node *A* because it is still active.

```
mount info is V
```
Amd found a mount map entry to have value *V*.

```
mount_aix3: fsname F, dir D, type T
```
Amd is trying to mount a file system on an IBM AIX 3 system. The mounted file system is *F*, the mount point is *D*, and the file system type is *T*.

```
mount_irix: fsname F, dir D, type T
```
Amd is trying to mount a file system on an SGI IRIX system. The mounted file system is *F*, the mount point is *D*, and the file system type is *T*.

```
mount_isc3: fsname F, dir D, type T
```
Amd is trying to mount a file system on an ISC3 Unix system (a variant of SVr3). The mounted file system is *F*, the mount point is *D*, and the file system type is *T*.

```
mount_nfs: M
```
Mounting an NFS file system failed with error message *M*.

```
not found - server going down anyway
```
Amd was not able to find a suitable server to mount and is ignoring this error because Amd is shutting down anyway.

```
passwd_search: map=M key=K -> V
```
Amd is parsing a password type map *M* and found key *K* whose value is *V*.

```
portmap request timed out
```
Amd waited too long trying to perform a portmapper operation.

`rescheduling job I back S seconds`

Amd detected a change in the system's clock and is adjusting future-scheduled job ID I accordingly by S seconds.

`rmdir(D)`

Amd is removing a directory D that served as a mount point.

`searching for /defaults entry`

Amd is searching for a /defaults entry in a map.

`select interrupted`

The `select(2)` system call was interrupted, possibly by a signal.

`server hung`

Amd detected a downed remote server.

`setting path to A`

Amd is creating an automount node for path name A.

`spurious call to sighup`

Amd got another signal while running a handle for the HUP signal. The other signal is ignored.

`stellix_mount: fsname F, dir D, type T`

Amd is trying to mount a file system on a Stellix Unix system. The mounted file system is F, the mount point is D, and the file system type is T.

`trying to initialize map M of type T ...`

Amd is initializing map M of type T.

`underlying fmount of H failed: E`

As part of an NFSX mount, Amd failed to mount the file server H; the error message is E.

`unmount attempt backgrounded`

Amd succeeded in backgrounding the unmount process in the background. Note that the unmount operation itself may not have succeeded yet.

> `unmount attempt done`

Amd's attempt to unmount a file system in the foreground succeeded. Note that the file system may not have gotten unmounted yet.

> `waiting for server H to become available`

Amd is waiting for remote host *H* to come back up.

> `will retry ...`

Amd is going to retry the backgrounded mount.

> `will search map info in M to find K`

Amd is searching map *M* for entry *K*.

> `yp_next() returned error: E`

Trying to enumerate the next entry in an NIS map failed with error *E*.

Console Messages

The following are console messages that are printed directly on the console, typically while Amd is initializing and before it is able to write to a log file.

> `ALLOC: N bytes, making X missing`

Amd has allocated *N* bytes of memory. This is part of memory debugging turned on by `debug_options = mem`. If *X* is greater than zero, then Amd is unable to account for that many bytes of data.

> `AMDCONF: syntax error on line N (section S)`

Amd detected a syntax error in an `amd.conf` file on line *N*. The section that Amd was parsing was *S* (`[global]` or any other map name).

> `FREE: N bytes, making X missing`

Amd has freed *N* bytes of memory. This is part of memory debugging turned on by `debug_options = mem`. If *X* is greater than zero, then Amd is unable to account for that many bytes of data.

> `P: -a option must begin with a '/'`

The Amd process named *P* detected that the argument given to the `-a` option does not start with a "/".

`P: not compiled with DEBUG option -- sorry.`

While parsing an `amd.conf` file or command-line options, the Amd process named *P* detected that debugging options were turned on, but Amd was not built with debugging support.

`cannot open P (errno=C)`

Amd is unable to open the PID file *P*. The error code is *C*.

`conf: bad LDAP cache (maxmem) option: V`

While parsing an `amd.conf` file, Amd detected an illegal value *V* passed to the `ldap_cache_maxmem` option.

`conf: bad LDAP cache (seconds) option: V`

While parsing an `amd.conf` file, Amd detected an illegal value *V* passed to the `ldap_cache_seconds` option.

`conf: hesiod_base option ignored. No Hesiod support available.`

While parsing an `amd.conf` file, Amd detected the use of the `hesiod_base` option, but Amd was not built with Hesiod support.

`conf: illegal amd program number "V"`

While parsing an `amd.conf` file, Amd detected an out-of-range value *V* passed to the `portmap_program` option.

`conf: illegal nfs_proto "V"`

While parsing an `amd.conf` file, Amd detected an illegal value *V* passed to the `nfs_proto` option.

`conf: illegal nfs_vers "V"`

While parsing an `amd.conf` file, Amd detected an illegal value *V* passed to the `nfs_proto` option.

`conf: ldap_base option ignored. No LDAP support available.`

While parsing an `amd.conf` file, Amd detected the use of the `ldap_base` option, but Amd was not built with LDAP support.

Appendices

conf: ldap_cache_maxmem option ignored. No LDAP support available.

While parsing an amd.conf file, Amd detected the use of the ldap_cache_maxmem option, but Amd was not built with LDAP support.

conf: ldap_cache_seconds option ignored. No LDAP support available.

While parsing an amd.conf file, Amd detected the use of the ldap_cache_seconds option, but Amd was not built with LDAP support.

conf: ldap_hostports option ignored. No LDAP support available.

While parsing an amd.conf file, Amd detected the use of the ldap_hostports option, but Amd was not built with LDAP support.

conf: map_name must be defined for map "V"

While parsing an amd.conf file, Amd detected that a map section V was defined without defining map_name for it.

conf: nis_domain option ignored. No NIS support available.

While parsing an amd.conf file, Amd detected the use of the nis_domain option, but Amd was not built with NIS support.

conf: no autofs support available

While parsing an amd.conf file, Amd detected an attempt to define an Autofs map, but Amd was not built with Autofs support.

conf: no such map type "T"

While parsing an amd.conf file, Amd detected a map of an unsupported or unknown type T.

conf: process_regular_option: null entries

While parsing an amd.conf file, Amd detected an empty mount map section.

conf: unknown global key: "K"

While parsing an amd.conf file, Amd detected a global key K that it does not recognize.

conf: unknown regular key "K" for section "S"

While parsing an amd.conf file, Amd detected an illegal key K in the section for the S automount point.

```
conf: unknown value to browsable_dirs "V"
```

While parsing an amd.conf file, Amd detected an illegal value V passed to the Boolean browsable_dirs option.

```
conf: unknown value to enable_default_selectors "V"
```

While parsing an amd.conf file, Amd detected an illegal value V passed to the Boolean enable_default_selectors option.

```
conf: unknown value to fully_qualified_hosts "V"
```

While parsing an amd.conf file, Amd detected an illegal value V passed to the fully_qualified_hosts option.

```
conf: unknown value to mount_type "V"
```

While parsing an amd.conf file, Amd detected an illegal value V passed to the mount_type option.

```
conf: unknown value to normalize_hostnames "V"
```

While parsing an amd.conf file, Amd detected an illegal value V passed to the Boolean normalize_hostnames option.

```
conf: unknown value to plock "V"
```

While parsing an amd.conf file, Amd detected an illegal value V passed to the Boolean plock option.

```
conf: unknown value to print_pid "V"
```

While parsing an amd.conf file, Amd detected an illegal value V passed to the Boolean print_pid option.

```
conf: unknown value to print_version "V"
```

While parsing an amd.conf file, Amd detected an illegal value V passed to the Boolean print_version option.

```
conf: unknown value to restart_mounts "V"
```

While parsing an amd.conf file, Amd detected an illegal value V passed to the Boolean restart_mounts option.

```
conf: unknown value to show_statfs_entries "V"
```

While parsing an amd.conf file, Amd detected an illegal value *V* passed to the Boolean show_statfs_entries option.

```
conf: unknown value to unmount_on_exit "V"
```

While parsing an amd.conf file, Amd detected an illegal value *V* passed to the Boolean unmount_on_exit option.

```
must specify both ldap_hostports and ldap_base
```

Amd detected that the user is using an LDAP map but did not specify both the ldap_hostports and ldap_base amd.conf configuration parameters.

```
processing regular map "M" before global one.
```

While parsing an amd.conf file, Amd detected that a regular map *M* was defined before the [global] one. This map will be processed without the global definitions.

```
skipping map M...
```

While parsing an amd.conf file, Amd detected a map *M* whose tag parameter did not match the tag name specified to the -T command-line option. Amd did not process this map.

Amd Configuration File Parameters and Command-Line Flags

This appendix consists of Table D.1, which summarizes Amd's configuration file options as well as any equivalent command-line startup flags. Note that all Boolean flags do not take arguments. All other flags take a single argument whose type is specified in the Type column. The Possible Values column contains two types of values: all possible values and some possible values. For example, the `browsable_dirs` parameter can take only one of these three values: `yes`, `no`, or `full`. On the other hand, the `auto_dir` parameter can take many possible values, and in the table, we show only two of those possible pathname values: `/tmp_mnt` and `/n`. To distinguish those parameters for which we show only a few of many possible values, we prefix the list in the Possible Values column with an "e.g."

Table D.1 Summary of All Amd Configuration Parameters and Their Command-Line Interface Equivalents

Amd.conf Parameter	CLI Equivalent	Type	Default Value	Possible Values
arch		String	Host architecture	E.g., i386, sparc, alpha
auto_dir	-a	Path name	/a	E.g., /tmp_mnt, /n
browsable_dirs		Tri-state	no	yes, no, full
cache_duration	-c	Numeric	300	Number of seconds
cluster	-C	String	Current cluster name	Any string
debug_options	-D	Comma-delimited list of strings	None	all, amq, daemon, fork, full, hrtime, info, mem, mtab, str, readdir, test, trace, xdrtrace
dismount_interval	-w	Numeric	120	Number of seconds
full_os		String	Full name of operating system with version	E.g., linux2.0.36, linux2.2.16, linux2.4.0
fully_qualified_hosts		String	no	yes, no
hesiod_base		String	automount	E.g., automount, amd, auto
karch	-k	String	Kernel architecture	E.g., i586, i686, sparc64

Table D.1   Summary of All Amd Configuration Parameters and Their Command-Line Interface Equivalents *(continued)*

Amd.conf Parameter	CLI Equivalent	Type	Default Value	Possible Values
ldap_base		String	None	E.g., "ou=Marketing, o=AMD Ltd, c=US"
ldap_cache_maxmem		Numeric	131072	Number of bytes
ldap_cache_seconds		Numeric	0	Number of seconds
ldap_hostports		String	None	E.g., ldap.example .com:389
local_domain	-d	String	Local DNS domain	E.g., example.com, cs.columbia.edu, am-utils.org
log_file	-l	Path name or log facility name	/dev/stderr	E.g., /dev/stderr, /var/log/amd, syslog, syslog:*facility*
log_options	-x	Comma-delimited list of options	None	all, fatal, error, user, warn, info, map, stats
map_name	Specify after all options	String or path name	Any string	E.g., amd.home, /usr/ share/maps/ amd.src
map_options	Specify after the map name on the command line	Semicolon delimited list of options (comma delimited)	None	E.g., cache:=inc,sync; browsable:=yes

Appendices

Table D.1   Summary of All Amd Configuration Parameters and Their Command-Line Interface Equivalents *(continued)*

Amd.conf Parameter	CLI Equivalent	Type	Default Value	Possible Values
map_type		String	Search all types in the order of Possible Values	passwd, hesiod, ldap, union, nisplus, nis, ndbm, file, error
mount_type		String	nfs	nfs, autofs
nfs_proto		String	All available transport protocols	tcp, udp
nfs_retransmit_ counter	-t *interval.counter*	Numeric	11	Number of retransmission attempts
nfs_retry_ interval	-t *interval.counter*	Numeric	8	Tenths of seconds
nfs_vers		Numeric	All available versions	2, 3
nis_domain	-y	String	Local NIS domain name	Any arbitrary string
normalize_ hostnames	-n	Boolean	no	yes, no
os	-O	String	Name of operating system	E.g., linux, solaris, freebsd
osver	-o	Numeric	Operating system (short) version	E.g., 2.2, 2.4, 5.7, 4.2

Table D.1 Summary of All Amd Configuration Parameters and Their Command-Line Interface Equivalents *(continued)*

Amd.conf Parameter	CLI Equivalent	Type	Default Value	Possible Values
pid_file		Path name	/dev/stdout	E.g., /dev/stdout, /var/run/amd.pid
plock	-S	Boolean	no	yes, no
portmap_program		Numeric	300019	Values from 300019 to 300029
print_pid	-p	Boolean	no	yes, no
print_version	-v	Boolean	no	yes, no
restart_mounts	-r	Boolean	no	yes, no
search_path		Colon-delimited pathname list	None	E.g., /local:/etc:/usr/share/amdmaps
selectors_on_default		Boolean	no	yes, no
show_statfs_entries		Boolean	no	yes, no
tag	-T	String	None	Any string
unmount_on_exit		Boolean	no	yes, no
vendor		String	Operating system vendor	E.g., redhat, sun, unknown
No equivalent	-H		Print help string	
No equivalent	-F	String	Amd configuration file name	E.g., /etc/amd.conf, /tmp/test.conf

Appendices

Index

Note to the Reader: Throughout this index **boldfaced** page numbers indicate primary discussions of a topic. *Italicized* page numbers indicate illustrations.

Index

Index

W

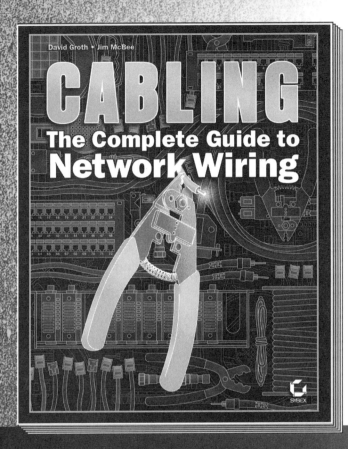

GET SYBEX'S®

CABLING:
The Complete
Guide to
Network Wiring

*Cabling: The Complete Guide
to Network Wiring*
David Groth and Jim McBee
ISBN 0-7821-2645-6
848pp • $49.99

The most comprehensive guide to network cabling available!

- Coverage spans cabling system design and installation, electrical and security issues, cabling components, and documenting and troubleshooting your system

- Provides all the information you need to know to work safely and effectively with cables in the workplace

- Includes a 32-page color insert for quick identification of connectors and cables, as well as vendor information and recommendations

SYBEX®

www.sybex.com

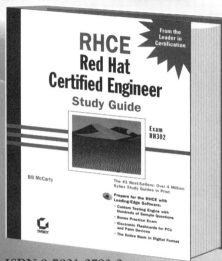

The Craig Hunt Linux Library

◆ Written under the direction of Craig Hunt, renowned Linux and TCP/IP guru

◆ Developed specifically for networking professionals working in Linux environments

◆ Offers the most advanced and focused coverage of key topics for Linux Administrators

by Craig Hunt
0-7821-2736-3
$39.99

by Charles Aulds
0-7821-2734-7
$39.99

by Rámon J. Hontañón
0-7821-2741-X
$39.99

by Vicki Stanfield and Roderick W. Smith
0-7821-2735-5
$39.99

by Craig Hunt
0-7821-2737-1
$39.99

by Erez Zadok
0-7821-2739-8
$39.99

by Roderick W. Smith
0-7821-2740-1
$39.99

SYBEX

25 YEARS
OF PUBLISHING
EXCELLENCE

WWW.SYBEX.COM

Craig Hunt is a noted TCP/IP and Linux expert who lectures regularly on the topics at the NetWorld+Interop, ComNet, and other networking trade shows. His other books include the best-selling *Linux Network Servers 24seven* from Sybex®.

Summary of Common NFS Export and Mount Options *(continued)*

Option	Export/Mount	Meaning
no_subtree_check	Export	Do not certify that a filehandle belongs to an exported subtree of a whole file system.
no_wdelay	Export	Do not delay synchronous writes.
noac	Mount	Disable all attribute caching.
noatime	Mount	Do not update file access times for each access.
noauto	Mount	This file system will not mount automatically on boot but can be mounted manually.
nocto	Mount	Do not check attributes of files that were closed and reopened.
nodev	Mount	Disallow access to devices.
noexec	Mount	Disallow execution of binaries.
nohide	Export	Expose subsidiary mounted file systems below this mount point.
nointr	Mount	Disallow users to interrupt hung processes.
nolock	Mount	Disable NFS locking.
nosuid	Mount	Run setuid or setgid binaries but with those set bits turned off.
nouser	Mount	Allow only the superuser to mount the file system.
port=N	Mount	Contact the NFS server on an alternate port N.
posix	Mount	Use POSIX semantics for this mount.
remount	Mount	Remount an already mounted file system.
retrans=N	Mount	Number of timeouts and retransmissions before failing an RPC request.